RHCSA & RHCE®
Red Hat® Enterprise Linux® 7

Training
and
Exam Preparation
Guide

Exams
EX200 and EX300
Third Edition

March 2015

Asghar Ghori

1246 Heil Quaker Blvd., La Vergne, TN USA 37086
Chapter House, Pitfield, Kiln Farm, Milton Keynes, UK MK11 3LW
Unit A1/A3, 7 Janine Street, Scoresby, Victoria 3179, Australia
www.lightningsource.com

Technical Reviewers: George Doumas and Mehmood Khan
Editors: Marlene and Allison with FirstEditing.com
Proof Reader for the RHCE Section: George Doumas
Cover Design: Wajahat Syed
Printers and Distributors: Lightning Source Inc.

Printed in the USA, UK, France, Germany, Italy, Spain, and Australia.

ISBN: 978-1-4951-4820-0
Library of Congress Control Number: 2015903831

Printed and Distributed by: Lightning Source Inc.

To order in bulk at special quantity discounts for sales promotions or for use in training programs, please contact the author at *asghar_ghori2002@yahoo.com*

Red Hat® is a registered trademark of Red Hat, Inc. in the U.S. and other countries.

RHCSA and RHCE® are registered trademarks of Red Hat, Inc. in the U.S. and other countries.

Linux® is a registered trademark of Linus Torvalds in the U.S. and other countries.

UNIX® is a registered trademark of The Open Group in the U.S. and other countries.

Microsoft® and Windows® are US registered trademarks of Microsoft Corporation.

Intel® is the trademark or registered trademark of Intel Corporation or its subsidiaries in the U.S. and other countries.

All other trademarks, registered trademarks, or logos are the property of their respective owners.

The author has made his best efforts to prepare this book. The contents are based on Red Hat® Enterprise Linux® version 7. The author makes no representation or warranties of any kind with regard to the completeness or accuracy of the contents herein and accepts no liability whatsoever including but not limited to merchantability, fitness for any particular purpose, or any losses or damages of any kind caused or allegedly caused directly or indirectly from this material.

This book is not a replacement for the official RHCSA/RHCE training courses offered by Red Hat, Inc. However, it may be used to prepare for the Red Hat Certified System Administrator (RHCSA) and the Red Hat Certified Engineer (RHCE) exams, EX200 and EX300, based on Red Hat® Enterprise Linux® version 7. Neither author nor publisher warrants that use of this publication will ensure passing the relevant exams or that the information contained herein is endorsed by Red Hat, Inc.

Preface

Red Hat® had revised their EX200 and EX300 exams for RHCSA and RHCE certifications soon after the release of Red Hat® Enterprise Linux® version 7 in June, 2014. These exams are performance-based and present scenarios that are to be accomplished on live systems within a stipulated time. This book is written to provide you with necessary coverage of theoretical and practical information to help you pass both exams. Furthermore, this book may be used for classroom training and as a deskside reference.

Keeping in view the hands-on nature of the exams, I have included a number of step-by-step procedures to implement tasks. I recommend that you get a 64-bit computer with a minimum of one dual-core processor and built-in support for hardware virtualization to practice the exercises and labs presented in this book. I have explained the hardware, virtualization, and networking requirements in detail in the first chapter for your convenience. I also advise you to either purchase a subscription for RHEL7 or download and use either CentOS or Scientific Linux, which are 100% compatible free non-commercial versions of RHEL.

I suggest you study the material presented in each chapter thoroughly before proceeding to the hands-on stuff. I have provided several review questions with answers at the end of each chapter. Take the quiz and then attempt the Do-It-Yourself (DIY) challenge labs offered thereafter. I have not furnished solutions to these labs intentionally, as I am confident that the knowledge and skills you would have gained by that time will be sufficient to accomplish the labs on your own. And in essence, this is what I want you to eventually get at. Once an entire section is finished— material read and understood, exercises performed, review questions completed, and DIY challenge labs accomplished—review the entire section quickly and then attempt the respective sample exams provided in the appendices.

While performing exercises and labs, if a command does not produce the published result, I ask that you check the message the command has generated and consult relevant log files. Minor issues, such as a wrong path, prevent commands from being executed correctly. Sometimes, there are syntax errors in the command construct. You might have to make appropriate modifications to your settings in order to make the command work. RHEL manual pages prove helpful and useful in comprehending commands and their syntaxes.

There are four areas I suggest you focus in order to develop expertise with RHEL (CentOS or Scientific Linux for that matter), as well as to prepare yourselves for the exams: 1) grasping concepts; 2) mastering implementation procedures, exercises, and labs; 3) learning commands, understanding configuration files, and knowing service daemons; and 4) being able to troubleshoot and resolve problems. An excellent understanding of which command involves which options and updates which files, which daemon provides what services, etc. should also be developed. This way you will have a better overall understanding of what exactly happens in the background when a command is executed. This book attempts to provide that knowledge too. Troubleshooting becomes easier when concepts are clear and working knowledge is solid.

I am maintaining *www.getitcertify.com* where I add errata, additional exam information, and links to useful resources. I encourage you to visit this website.

At the end, I would like to request for your feedback sent to my personal email *asghar_ghori2002@yahoo.com* about anything good or bad in the book, including any grammatical or technical errors or mistakes. Try to be as specific as possible in your description. Improvement is a continuous process and I am sure your feedback will help me write a better and improved next edition.

Good luck in your endeavors.   Asghar Ghori / March 2015 / Toronto, Canada

Acknowledgments

I am grateful to God who enabled me to write this book successfully.

I would like to acknowledge the valuable feedback my students and friends provided on the previous edition of this book. I am thankful to them for making this edition more error-free.

I recognize the constructive and positive feedback I had received from the readers of my previous books. I have used their comments toward the improvement of this edition.

I would like to express my special thanks to my wife, two daughters, and two sons, who tolerated my mental absence while sitting right in front of them working on this project. I could not have consummated this project without their support.

Lastly, I would like to offer my very special tributes to my mother and my deceased father.

Asghar Ghori

About the Author

Asghar Ghori is a seasoned UNIX/Linux consultant, trainer, and author. As a consultant, his experience ranges from deployment, support, and administration to solution architecture, design, and consulting; as a trainer, he has designed and delivered numerous training programs; and as a published author, he has five books on HP-UX and Red Hat Enterprise Linux to his credit.

Asghar holds a BS in Engineering. He is RHCE, RHCSA, HP CSA, HP CSE, SCSA, IBM Certified Specialist for AIX, and CNE, with ITIL and PMP certifications.

Asghar Ghori lives in a small town near Toronto, Ontario, Canada with his wife and four children, and can be reached via email asghar_ghori2002@yahoo.com or linkedin.

Other publications of Asghar are:

1. Red Hat Certified System Administrator & Engineer: Training Guide and a Quick Deskside Reference (ISBN: 978-1467549400) (RHEL version 6), published 2012

2. Red Hat Certified Technician & Engineer (RHCT and RHCE) Training Guide and Administrator's Reference (ISBN: 978-1615844302) (RHEL version 5), published 2009

3. HP-UX: HP Certified Systems Administrator, Exam HP0-A01, Training Guide and Administrator's Reference (ISBN: 978-1606436547) (HP-UX 11iv3), published 2008

4. HP Certified Systems Administrator, Exam HP0-095, Training Guide and Administrator's Reference (ISBN: 978-1424342310) (HP-UX 11iv2 and 11iv3), published 2007

5. Certified System Administrator for HP-UX: Study Guide and Administrator's Reference (ISBN: 978-1419645938) (HP-UX 11iv1), published 2006

Conventions Used in this Book

The following typographic and other conventions are used in this book:

Book Antiqua Italic 10 pt. is used in text paragraphs for new terms. For example:

> "Red Hat renamed the Red Hat Linux operating system series *Red Hat Enterprise Linux* (RHEL) in 2003."

Times Roman Italic 10 pt. is used in text paragraphs to highlight names of files, directories, commands, daemons, users, group, hosts, domains, and URLs. For example:

> "To go directly from */etc* to a sub-directory *dir1* under *user1*'s home directory, create *dir1*, as . . . ."

Times New Roman 9 pt. is used to segregate command output, shell script contents, and information expected to be entered in configuration files from the surrounding text. It is also used for text in tables.

Times Roman Bold 10 pt. is used to highlight commands and command line arguments that the user is expected to type at the command prompt. For example:

> **$ ls –lt**

Commands expected to be run by a normal user are preceded by the $ prompt and those that are expected to be run by the root user are preceded by the # prompt.

All headings and sub-headings are in California FB font, and are bolded.

Ctrl+x key sequence implies that you hold down the Ctrl key and then press the other key. Courier New font is used to highlight such combinations. This font is also used to identify keystrokes, such as Enter and Esc.

. . . . Dotted lines represent truncated command output.

About the RHCSA (EX200) and RHCE (EX300) Exams

The Red Hat Certified System Administrator (RHCSA) and the Red Hat Certified Engineer (RHCE) certification exams are performance-based hands-on exams designed for IT professionals. These exams are presented in electronic format on a live desktop computer running Red Hat Enterprise Linux 7. This desktop computer will have one RHEL7-based virtual machine for the RHCSA exam and two for the RHCE exam. During the exams, the candidates do not have access to the Internet, or printed or electronic documentation except for what comes standard with RHEL7. The official exam objectives are listed at *http://www.redhat.com/training/courses/ex200/examobjective* for RHCSA and that for RHCE at *http://www.redhat.com/training/courses/ex300/examobjective*. Visit the URLs for up-to-date and more in-depth information. The exam objectives are covered in sufficient detail in the chapters throughout this book. An enumerated list of exam objectives is presented below along with a chapter number where the objective is found.

RHCSA™ Specific Skills:

Understand and Use Essential Tools:

1. Access a shell prompt and issue commands with correct syntax (chapter 2)
2. Use input-output redirection (>, >>, |, 2>, etc) (chapter 4)
3. Use grep and regular expressions to analyze text (chapter 4)
4. Access remote systems using ssh (chapter 13)
5. Log in and switch users in multiuser targets (chapter 8)
6. Archive, compress, unpack, and uncompress files using tar, star, gzip, and bzip2 (chapter 2)
7. Create and edit text files (chapter 2)
8. Create, delete, copy, and move files and directories (chapter 3)
9. Create hard and soft links (chapter 3)
10. List, set, and change standard ugo/rwx permissions (chapter 3)
11. Locate, read, and use system documentation including man, info, and files in /usr/share/doc (chapter 2)

Operate Running Systems

12. Boot, reboot, and shut down a system normally (chapter 7)
13. Boot systems into different targets manually (chapter 7)
14. Interrupt the boot process in order to gain access to a system (chapter 7)
15. Identify CPU/memory intensive processes, adjust process priority with renice, and kill processes (chapter 4)
16. Locate and interpret system log files and journals (chapter 7)
17. Access a virtual machine's console (chapter 6)
18. Start and stop virtual machines (chapter 6)
19. Start, stop, and check the status of network services (chapter 7)
20. Securely transfer files between systems (chapter 13)

Configure Local Storage

21. List, create, and delete partitions on MBR and GPT disks (chapter 9)
22. Create and remove physical volumes, assign physical volumes to volume groups, and create and delete logical volumes (chapter 9)
23. Configure systems to mount file systems at boot by Universally Unique ID (UUID) or label (chapter 10)
24. Add new partitions and logical volumes, and swap to a system non-destructively (chapters 9 and 10)

Create and Configure File Systems

25. Create, mount, unmount, and use vfat, ext4, and xfs file systems (chapter 10)
26. Mount and unmount CIFS and NFS network file systems (chapters 10, 20, and 21)
27. Extend existing logical volumes (chapter 9)
28. Create and configure set-GID directories for collaboration (chapter 3)
29. Create and manage Access Control Lists (ACLs) (chapter 10)
30. Diagnose and correct file permission problems (chapter 3)

Deploy, Configure, and Maintain Systems

31. Configure networking and hostname resolution statically or dynamically (chapter 12 and 15)
32. Schedule tasks using at and cron (chapter 4)
33. Start and stop services and configure services to start automatically at boot (chapter 7)
34. Configure systems to boot into a specific target automatically (chapter 7)
35. Install Red Hat Enterprise Linux automatically using Kickstart (chapter 6)
36. Configure a physical machine to host virtual guests (chapter 6)
37. Install Red Hat Enterprise Linux systems as virtual guests (chapter 6)
38. Configure systems to launch virtual machines at boot (chapter 6)
39. Configure network services to start automatically at boot (chapter 7)
40. Configure a system to use time services (chapter 12 and 16)
41. Install and update software packages from Red Hat Network, a remote repository, or from the local file system (chapter 5)
42. Update the kernel package appropriately to ensure a bootable system (chapter 7)
43. Modify the system bootloader (chapter 7)

Manage Users and Groups

44. Create, delete, and modify local user accounts (chapter 8)
45. Change passwords and adjust password aging for local user accounts (chapter 8)
46. Create, delete, and modify local groups and group memberships (chapter 8)
47. Configure a system to use an existing authentication service for user and group information (chapter 12)

Manage Security

48. Configure firewall settings using firewall-config, firewall-cmd, or iptables (chapter 11)
49. Configure key-based authentication for SSH (chapter 13)
50. Set enforcing and permissive modes for SELinux (chapter 11)
51. List and identify SELinux file and process context (chapter 11)
52. Restore default file contexts (chapter 11)
53. Use boolean settings to modify system SELinux settings (chapter 11)
54. Diagnose and address routine SELinux policy violations (chapter 11)

RHCE™ Specific Skills:

System Configuration and Management
55. Use network teaming or bonding to configure aggregate network links between two Red Hat Enterprise Linux systems (chapter 15)
56. Configure IPv6 addresses and perform basic IPv6 troubleshooting (chapter 15)
57. Route IP traffic and create static routes (chapter 15)
58. Use firewallD and associated mechanisms such as rich rules, zones and custom rules, to implement packet filtering and configure network address translation (NAT) (chapter 17)
59. Use /proc/sys and sysctl to modify and set kernel runtime parameters (chapter 18)
60. Configure a system to authenticate using Kerberos (chapter 17)
61. Configure a system as either an iSCSI target or initiator that persistently mounts an iSCSI target (chapter 19)
62. Produce and deliver reports on system utilization (processor, memory, disk, and network) (chapter 18)
63. Use shell scripting to automate system maintenance tasks (chapter 14)
64. Configure a system to log to a remote system (chapter 18) [Recently removed from the objectives list]
65. Configure a system to accept logging from a remote system (chapter 18) [Recently removed from the objectives list]

Network Services
Network services are an important subset of the exam objectives. RHCE candidates should be capable of meeting the following objectives for each of the network services listed below:

- Install the packages needed to provide the service
- Configure SELinux to support the service
- Use SELinux port labelling to allow services to use non-standard ports
- Configure the service to start when the system is booted
- Configure the service for basic operation
- Configure host-based and user-based security for the service

HTTP/HTTPS (chapter 22)
66. Configure a virtual host
67. Configure private directories
68. Deploy a basic CGI application
69. Configure group-managed content
70. Configure TLS security

DNS (chapter 24)
71. Configure a caching-only name server
72. Troubleshoot DNS client issues

NFS (chapter 20)
73. Provide network shares to specific clients
74. Provide network shares suitable for group collaboration
75. Use Kerberos to control access to NFS network shares

SMB (chapter 21)
76. Provide network shares to specific clients
77. Provide network shares suitable for group collaboration
78. Use Kerberos to authenticate access to shared directories

SMTP (chapter 23)
79. Configure a system to forward all email to a central mail server

SSH (chapter 13) [This chapter is in the RHCSA section]
80. Configure key-based authentication
81. Configure additional options described in documentation

NTP (chapter 16)
82. Synchronize time using other NTP peers

Database Services (chapter 25)
83. Install and configure MariaDB
84. Backup and restore a database
85. Create a simple database schema
86. Perform simple SQL queries against a database

Taking the Exams

1. Save time wherever possible, as time is of the essence during the exams. Install X Window and GNOME if you prefer to use the graphical tools for completing your tasks (instructions are provided in chapter 01 on how to do it). Perform tasks using either text or graphical tools, whichever you feel more comfortable with. Install a graphical tool if you need it and if it is not already loaded.
2. Make certain that any changes you make must survive system reboots.
3. Use any text editor you feel comfortable with to modify text configuration files.
4. Inform the invigilator right away if you identify a hardware issue with your system.
5. Exams are administered with no access to the Internet, electronic devices, or paper material.
6. Read each exam task carefully and understand it thoroughly before attempting it.

Exam Fees and Registration Procedure

The fee for either the RHCSA (EX200) or RHCE (EX300) exam is US$400, or equivalent in local currencies. To register, visit *http://www.redhat.com/training/courses/ex200/examobjective* or *http://www.redhat.com/training/courses/ex300/examobjective* and click ENROLL. Choose a location and date, and click SEARCH for available choices. Click Enroll Now and submit your information and fee to register. The exams are administered on Fridays in a classroom setting. At many centers, individuals also have the convenience to schedule their exams on regular business days other than Fridays. The RHCSA exam lasts for 2.5 hours and the RHCE exam 4 hours.

About this Book

This book covers four major learning objectives: 1) a self-study guide for Red Hat exams RHCSA (EX200) and RHCE (EX300) for those who intend to take the two exams and pass them, 2) an in-class training guide for college students, 3) an on-the-job reference for administrators, programmers, and DBAs, and 4) an easy-to-understand guide for novice and non-RHEL administrators who plan to learn RHEL from scratch.

This book is divided into two sections—RHCSA and RHCE—based on exam and learning objectives. The RHCSA section covers tasks that are intended for a single system, while the RHCE section covers those that require two or more networked systems. The book has twenty-five chapters altogether that are organized logically, keeping in mind the four learning objectives mentioned above.

1. **The RHCSA Section** (chapters 1 to 13) covers the topics that will help the reader learn system administration tasks and prepare for the new RHCSA exam. Material presented includes local RHEL7 installation; general Linux concepts and basic commands; compression and archiving; text editor and online help; file and directory manipulation and security; processes, task scheduling, and bash shell features; package administration and yum repository; host virtualization, and network and automated installations; system boot, kernel management, systemd, and local logging; user and group administration; storage partitioning and file system build; AutoFS, swap, and ACLs; basic firewall and SELinux; network interface configuration and NTP/LDAP clients; and SSH and TCP Wrappers.

2. **The RHCE Section** (chapters 14 to 25) covers the topics that will help the reader learn network administration tasks and prepare for the new RHCE exam. Material presented includes automation with shell scripting; network interface bonding and teaming; IPv6 and routing setups; remote time synchronization, firewalld, and Kerberos authentication; kernel tuning, resource utilization reporting, and network logging; block storage sharing with iSCSI; file storage sharing with NFS and Samba; web servers and virtual hosting; mail transfer and DNS; and MariaDB configuration and query.

Each chapter in the book highlights the major topics and relevant exam objectives covered in that chapter and ends with a summary followed by review questions/answers and Do-It-Yourself challenge labs. Throughout the book, figures, tables, and screen shots have been furnished to support explanation. This book includes two sample exams for RHCSA and two for RHCE, and are expected to be done using the knowledge and skills gained from reading the material and practicing the exercises and challenge labs.

TABLE OF CONTENTS

RHCSA Section

06. Configuring Server Virtualization and Network Installing RHEL7 157

07. Booting RHEL7, Updating Kernel, and Logging Messages 191

RHCE Section

List of Figures

List of Tables

RHCSA
Section

RIGA
Section

Chapter 01

Installing RHEL7 on Physical Computer Using Local DVD

This chapter describes the following major topics:

➤ A brief history of Linux and Open Source
➤ Linux distributions from Red Hat
➤ Obtain Red Hat Enterprise Linux 7
➤ Plan for an installation
➤ Overview of virtual consoles and installation logs
➤ Recommended lab setup for exam preparation
➤ Install RHEL7 on a physical computer using local DVD medium
➤ Perform post-installation configuration

RHCSA Objectives:

None, but sets up the foundation for learning and practicing the exam objectives for both RHCSA and RHCE

Linux

Linux has been around for years. It is a free operating system with source code available to developers and amateurs for customization and other purposes. Red Hat Inc. tailored the source code and added many features, enhancements, and bug fixes to make their Linux distribution as stable, robust, and feature-rich as possible for enterprise use.

The Red Hat Enterprise Linux operating system is available to subscribers in ISO format for download and use. It has hardware requirements that should be met for a smooth and worry-free operation. In order to practice and pass the RHCSA and RHCE exams, a proper lab setup is mandatory. The install process requires prior planning to identify system configuration pieces related to locale, networking, disk partitioning, file system types and sizes, software components, and so on. Identification of these items before starting the installation makes for a smooth installation process.

Overview of Linux

Linux is a free computer operating system similar to the UNIX operating system in terms of concepts, features, and functionality. It is therefore referred to as a UNIX-like operating system.

In 1984, an initiative was undertaken by Richard Stallman with the goal to create a completely free, UNIX-compatible, open source operating system with global collaboration from software developers. The initiative was called the GNU (*GNU's Not Unix*) Project and by 1991, significant software had been developed. The only critical piece missing was a kernel to drive it. Around the same time, Linus Torvalds, who was working independently on the development of a kernel during his computer science studies, announced the availability of his kernel. The new kernel was given the name *Linux* and it was gradually integrated with the GNU software to form what is now referred to as *GNU/Linux, Linux operating system*, or simply *Linux*. Linux was released under the GNU *General Public License* (GPL). Initially written to run on Intel x86-based computers, the first version (0.01) of Linux was released in September 1991 with little more than 10,000 lines of code. In 1994, the first major release (1.0.0) debuted, followed by a number of versions until version 3.0 in 2011. Development and enhancements continued and version 3.0 was followed by stable versions 3.2 and 3.4 in 2012, and 3.10 in 2013. At the time of this writing, version 3.17, with many millions of lines of code, is the latest stable kernel. The Linux kernel, and the operating system in general, has been enhanced with contributions from tens of thousands of software programmers and amateurs around the world into a large and complex system under GNU GPL, which provides public access to its source code free of charge, and with full consent to amend and redistribute.

Today, Linux runs on an extensive range of computer hardware platforms, from laptop and desktop computers to massive mainframe and supercomputers. Linux also runs as the base operating system on a variety of other electronic devices such as routers, switches, storage arrays, tape libraries, video games, and mobile devices. Numerous vendors including Red Hat, HP, IBM, Oracle, Novell, and Dell offer commercial support to Linux users worldwide.

The functionality, adaptability, portability, and cost-effectiveness that Linux offers has made it the main alternative to proprietary UNIX and Windows operating systems. At present, over a hundred different flavors of Linux are circulating from various vendors, organizations, and individuals; though only a few of them are popular and are widely accepted.

Linux is largely used in government agencies, corporate businesses, academic institutions, and scientific organizations, as well as in home computers. Linux deployment and usage is constantly on the rise.

Linux Distributions from Red Hat

Red Hat, Inc., founded in 1993, assembled an operating system called *Red Hat Linux* (RHL) under the GNU GPL and released their first version as Red Hat Linux 1.0 in November 1994. Several versions followed until the last version in the series, called Red Hat Linux 9 (later also referred to as RHEL3), based on kernel 2.4.20 was released in March 2003. Red Hat renamed the Red Hat Linux operating system series *Red Hat Enterprise Linux* (RHEL) in 2003.

RHL was originally assembled and enhanced within the Red Hat company. In 2003, Red Hat began sponsoring a project called *Fedora* and invited the user community to participate in enhancing the source code. This project served as the test-bed for developing and testing new features for Red Hat and enabled the company to include the improved code in successive versions of RHEL. The Fedora distribution is completely free; RHEL is commercial. RHEL4 (based on kernel 2.6.9 and released in February 2005), RHEL5 (based on kernel 2.6.18 and released in March 2007), RHEL6 (based on kernel 2.6.32 and released in November 2010), and RHEL7 (based on kernel 3.10 and released in June 2014) have been built using Fedora distributions 3, 6, 12, 13, and 19, respectively. The following are RHEL7 variants available for commercial use:

- ✓ Red Hat Enterprise Linux for Desktop (targeting desktop and laptop computers)
- ✓ Red Hat Enterprise Linux for Workstation (targeting workstation-class computers)
- ✓ Red Hat Enterprise Linux for Server (targeting small to large deployments)
- ✓ Red Hat Enterprise Linux for High-Performance Computing (targeting scientific use)
- ✓ Red Hat Enterprise Linux for IBM Power (targeting IBM Power series computers)
- ✓ Red Hat Enterprise Linux for IBM System z (targeting IBM mainframe computers)
- ✓ Red Hat Enterprise Linux for SAP Business Applications (targeting SAP application deployments)
- ✓ Red Hat Enterprise Linux for SAP HANA (targeting SAP in-memory database management system)

There are two 100% rebuilds of Red Hat Enterprise Linux. These are referred to as CentOS (*Community Enterprise Operating System*) and Scientific Linux, and are available for Linux users and learners at no cost. These rebuilds are not sponsored or supported by Red Hat. CentOS may be downloaded from *www.centos.org* and Scientific Linux from *www.scientificlinux.org*. For practice and training purposes, you may like to download and use one of these instead of RHEL7.

Obtaining, Planning, and Installing RHEL7

Red Hat Enterprise Linux 7 may be downloaded from Red Hat's website as directed in the following sub-section. The downloaded image can then be burned to a DVD, used to create a bootable USB flash drive, placed on a hard drive to use the drive as an installation source, or located on a server to support network-based installations. Network-based installations are faster and can be done on numerous systems concurrently. Enough planning needs to be done to ensure installation meets desired needs. There are several options available for installing the operating system. We cover one of them in this chapter, another later in the book, and the rest are beyond the scope.

Downloading RHEL7 and Preparing Boot Media

You need to download the RHEL7 installation ISO image and burn it to a DVD (or use it to create a bootable USB flash drive). Follow the instructions below to download the full Server OS image for the x86_64 architecture, and burn it to a DVD:

1. Go to *www.redhat.com* and click "Customer Portal".
2. Click "Log In" in the upper right corner with account credentials, or click "Register" and fill out the form to open a new account.
3. Click "Downloads" to get to the "Product Downloads" page.
4. Click "Red Hat Enterprise Linux" from the list if you already have an active subscription, or click "Start Evaluation" to obtain a free 30-day trial. Follow the instructions and links to download the "RHEL 7.0 Binary DVD" Server variant for x86_64 architecture.

You can get technical support from Red Hat for your subscribed RHEL7 copy; the evaluation copy comes with 30-day limited support with no updates available after the expiry of that time period.

5. Use a DVD burner on Windows to burn the image to an empty physical DVD. To create a bootable USB stick, download "Fedora LiveUSB Creator" software from fedorahosted.org/liveusb-creator and use it. This procedure will destroy any data previously stored on the USB device.

Installation Media Options

There are multiple options available with respect to accessing the installation software. You can have the software located on a DVD, on a USB flash drive, on a hard drive, or on a network server accessible via the FTP, NFS, HTTP, or HTTPS protocol for network-based installations. In this chapter, we will perform an installation using the DVD that we have just created.

The RHEL7 installation program is called *Anaconda*. It provides three main interfaces for interaction: graphical, text-based, and kickstart. The graphical interface delivers an intuitive GUI to prepare a system for installation. It provides a central hub that lists groups of configuration options; you click the options that require modifications before beginning the installation process. One other major benefit of using the graphical installer is its ability to run some processor-intensive tasks such as storage layout detection in the background while allowing you to continue with the configuration.

The text-based interface is used on systems with no graphics card or to meet certain needs.

Kickstart is a fully-automated method for RHEL7 installation. It does not require user intervention during the installation. It may be used to load RHEL7 on a number of systems at the same time with identical configuration.

Hardware Requirements

The first thing that you need to do is understand the requirements for the installation. Critical items such as system and CPU types, amount of physical memory, and types and sizes of hard disks need to be determined. Installation may fail or the system may not function as expected if any of these requirements are not met. The following presents a discussion of these requirements.

System Requirements

There is a wide array of hardware platforms on which RHEL7 can be installed and run. The best place to check whether the hardware is certified to run RHEL7 without glitches is to refer to the Red Hat *Hardware Compatibility List* (HCL) available online at *https://hardware.redhat.com*. The HCL lists a number of computer system brands that Red Hat engineers have tested and certified to work with RHEL7; however, a large number of computers and laptops (both branded and unbranded) that are not on HCL may still work without issues. For laptop computers, visit *www.linux-laptop.net* where a wealth of information on thousands of different laptop models on which people have installed and run Linux is shared. If you have issues installing or running RHEL7 on your laptops, browse this website and search for the laptop model. It is likely that you will find a solution or a hint that helps fix the issue.

CPU Requirements

RHEL7 is supported on computer architectures with 64-bit Intel, AMD, IBM Power7, and IBM System zEnterprise processors. This hardware, along with integrated support for hardware virtualization, should be used for the purpose of RHCSA and RHCE exam preparation, general learning, or for hosting virtual machines.

RHEL7 has the capacity to support 5000+ logical CPUs on a single computer. It has integrated support for virtualization using *Kernel-based Virtual Machine* (KVM) hypervisor software, which allows the creation and execution of virtual machines to host RHEL or Microsoft Windows operating systems.

Memory Requirements

RHEL7 supports up to 3TiB of physical memory on a single computer. However, there are very few servers out there that require that much memory. For a typical RHEL7 server, enough physical memory should be available to support not only full RHEL but also the applications that the system is purposed to host. For a typical installation, reserve a minimum of 1GiB memory for RHEL; add more for better performance.

Planning the Installation

The installation program asks us for several configuration items during the installation. Some of the questions are compulsory and must be answered appropriately while others are optional, and may be skipped for post-installation setup if desired. The configuration can be done in any sequence that you prefer.

You should have the minimum mandatory configuration data handy and be ready to enter it when prompted. Some of the key configuration items are language, keyboard type, timezone, disk partitioning, hostname/IP, software selection, root password, user information, and kdump.

Virtual Console Screens

During the installation, there are six text-based virtual console screens available to you to monitor the installation process, view diagnostic messages, and discover and fix any issues encountered. You can switch between screens by pressing a combination of keys. The information displayed on the consoles is captured in installation log files.

Console 1 (Ctrl+Alt+F1): This is the main installer program console screen where you select a language to use during installation and which appears before Anaconda begins and switches the default console to the sixth screen.

Console 2 (Ctrl+Alt+F2): The bash shell interface for running commands as the *root* user.

Console 3 (Ctrl+Alt+F3): This screen displays installation messages and stores them in */tmp/anaconda.log* file. This file also captures information on detected hardware, in addition to other data.

Console 4 (Ctrl+Alt+F4): This screen shows storage messages and records them in */tmp/storage.log* file.

Console 5 (Ctrl+Alt+F5): This screen displays program messages and logs them to */tmp/program.log* file.

Console 6 (Ctrl+Alt+F6): This is the default graphical configuration and installation console screen.

Installation Logs

There are several log files created and updated as the installation progresses. These files record configuration and status information. We can view their contents after the installation has been completed to check how the installation proceeded. These files are described in Table 1-1.

File	Description
/root/anaconda-ks.cfg	Records the configuration entered.
/root/install.log	Lists the packages being installed.
/root/install.log.syslog	Stores general messages.
/var/log/anaconda.ifcfg.log	Captures messages related to network interfaces.
/var/log/anaconda.log	Contains informational, debug, and other general messages.
/var/log/anaconda.syslog	Records messages related to the kernel.
/var/log/anaconda.xlog	Stores X window information.
/var/log/anaconda.packaging.log	Records messages generated by the yum and rpm commands during software installation.
/var/log/anaconda.program.log	Captures messages generated by external programs.
/var/log/anaconda.storage.log	Records messages generated by storage modules.
/var/log/anaconda.yum.log	Contains messages related to yum packages.

Table 1-1 Installation Logs

Files in the */var/log* directory are actually created and updated in the */tmp* directory during the installation; however, they are moved to */var/log* once the installation is complete.

LAB Setup for Practicing RHCSA & RHCE Exam Objectives

Beginning in this chapter and throughout this book, several administration topics on system, network, and security will be presented, along with procedures on how to implement and administer them. A number of exercises will be performed and commands executed. The following minimum hardware and virtual machine configuration will be used to elucidate the procedures and perform the exercises and labs:

OS software: Download either RHEL7.0 or CentOS7.0 and burn it to a DVD.
PC/laptop architecture: 64-bit Intel dual-core (or equivalent AMD processor) with
                                          integrated hardware virtualization support.

Physical memory: 4GB
Physical disk space: 40GB
Physical network interfaces: 1
Physical host configuration: *host1* in *example.com* domain with IP 192.168.0.100 and 1x40GB
                                          disk (10GB for OS, 10GB each for two virtual machines, and
                                          10GB for storage exercises). This server will be installed locally
                                          using the RHEL7 installation DVD in this chapter. This server
                                          will provide the foundation to host two virtual machines *server1*
                                          and *server2*, and may be used to test configuration made on them.
                                          This system will also provide RHEL7 installation files via FTP to
                                          server1 and *server2*.

Number of VMs: 2
Memory in each VM: 1024MB
vCPUs in each VM: 1
OS in each VM: RHEL7 or CentOS7
VM1:   *server1* in *example.com* domain with IP 192.168.0.110, 1x10GB
                                          virtual disk for OS, 4x2GB virtual disks for various disk
                                          management exercises, and six virtual network interfaces. The
                                          first network interface will have the primary IPv4 address, the
                                          second interface will be used for an interface management
                                          exercise (192.168.0.111) in Chapter 12 and for IPv6 exercise in
                                          Chapter 15, and the last four (2 pairs) will be used for bonding
                                          (192.168.1.110) and teaming (192.168.2.110) exercises in the
                                          RHCE section. Most services will be configured on this VM and
                                          it will also be used as an iSCSI initiator. This VM will be created
                                          using the *virt-manager* GUI and the OS will be installed using the
                                          installation files located on the FTP server *host1*.
VM2:   *server2* in *example.com* domain with IP 192.168.0.120, 1x10GB
                                          virtual disk for OS, 1x2GB virtual disk for iSCSI exercises, and
                                          six virtual network interfaces. The first network interface will
                                          have the primary IPv4 address, the second interface will be used
                                          for an interface management exercise (192.168.0.121) in Chapter
                                          12 and for IPv6 exercise in Chapter 15, and the last four (2 pairs)
                                          will be used for bonding (192.168.1.120) and teaming
                                          (192.168.2.120) exercises in the RHCE section. This VM will be
                                          built using the *virt-install* command and the OS will be installed
                                          using a kickstart configuration file with installation files located
                                          on the FTP server *host1*. This server will be used as a client and
                                          test system for most services configured on *server1*, as an iSCSI
                                          target, and as a server for some services.

Though I highly recommend using a dedicated physical computer for the above, those who cannot
afford or want convenience may build and use two virtual machines in VirtualBox, VMware, or
some other virtualization software running on a Windows system. Do not forget that some of the
exam objectives do require virtualizing a physical host. Another option would be to get a physical

computer for a short period of time just to practice the exercises and the labs presented in the virtualization chapter, and use Windows-based virtual machines for the rest.

> **EXAM TIP:** The exam systems may not have the graphical support pre-installed. If you want to use the GUI environment during the exams, you will need to install X Window System and GNOME software groups using the **yum group install "X Window System" "GNOME" –y** command. After the installation is complete, run the **systemctl set-default graphical.target** and then reboot the system. Accept the license agreement and log on to the system. This entire process may take up to 15 minutes of your exam time. See Chapter 05 "Managing Software Packages" for details, and other chapters to gain access to additional graphical tools.

Exercise 1-1: Install RHEL7 Server Using DVD

This exercise should be done on the physical computer.

In this exercise, you will perform a RHEL7 Server installation using the graphical interface on a physical computer using the DVD. This procedure presumes that the physical computer meets the requirements presented in the previous sub-section. Name this system *host1.example.com* and use the IP and disk information provided in the previous sub-section. Additional configuration will be supplied as the installation advances. The interface configuration, partitioning, base environments, user creation, network authentication services, NTP, and other topics will not be explained as part of this exercise; however, we will study them in detail in their respective chapters later in this book.

Screenshots presented in the Configuring Installation Destination sub-section in this exercise are taken from an installation performed in a VirtualBox virtual machine. You may see different disk sizes while studying Chapter 09 "Partitioning and Managing Disk Storage". Ignore the discrepancies.

> **EXAM TIP:** RHEL7 installation is not an exam objective.

Initiating Installation

1. Power on the computer.
2. Insert the RHEL7 installation DVD in the drive.
3. Boot the computer from the DVD.
4. A graphical boot menu displaying three options on the main menu appears, as shown in Figure 1-1:

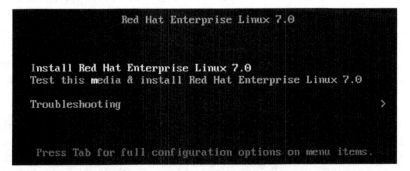

Figure 1-1 Boot Menu

The first option "Install Red Hat Enterprise Linux 7.0" is used for installing RHEL7 unless you want to use the second option, which is also the default option, to test the integrity of the installation media before continuing. The Anaconda installer program waits for 60 seconds for you to alter the selection, or it goes ahead and boots using the default option. You can also press the Enter key after highlighting the first or the second option to start the installation process right away. The installation begins in the graphical mode. The third option "Troubleshooting", as shown in Figure 1-2, encapsulates several choices to address boot-related issues.

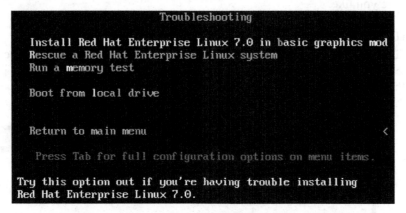

Figure 1-2 Boot Menu / Troubleshooting Sub Menu

These additional tasks allow you to perform an installation using a basic video driver (in case the installer cannot load a proper driver for the installed video card), interact with the system to recover an installed RHEL7 copy facing boot issues, run a memory test, or boot using a local disk drive.

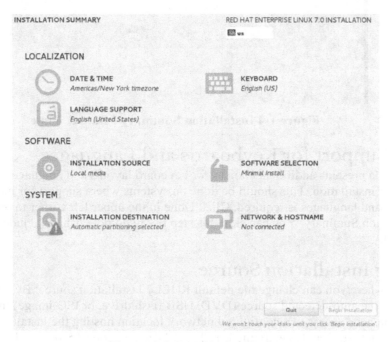

Figure 1-3 Installation Summary

5. The next screen allows you to choose a language for use during the installation. The default is English. Click Continue.
6. The "Installation Summary" screen appears next, as shown in Figure 1-3 (previous page). Here, you can make all necessary configuration changes prior to starting the installation. This screen presents a single interface to configure localization (date, time, timezone, keyboard, and language), software (installation source and selection), and system settings (disk selection & partitioning and network & hostname assignments). You can configure these items in any sequence you like.

Configuring Date & Time

7. Click Date & Time to set time zone (region and city), date, and time for the system. See Figure 1-4. Click Done in the upper left corner to save the changes and go back to the Installation Summary screen. If you do not wish to modify the default values shown, you can skip this step.

Figure 1-4 Installation Summary / Date & Time

Adding Support for Keyboards and Languages

8. Anaconda presents additional choices for keyboard layouts and languages for use during and after the installation. This should be done on systems where support for multiple keyboard layouts and languages is required. Click Done in the upper left corner to return to the Installation Summary. You can skip this step if you do not wish to include this additional support.

Choosing Installation Source

9. This is where you can change the default RHEL7 installation source. By default, Anaconda chooses the auto-detected source (DVD, USB flash drive, or ISO image) that is used to boot it. If you have access to a configured network location hosting the installation files, choose "On the network" and specify the HTTP, HTTPS, FTP, or NFS protocol, hostname or IP

address of the network server, and the path to the files. You can also specify the locations of additional software repositories; however, they are not required for a complete RHEL7 installation. Click Done to return to the Installation Summary page after making the changes on this screen.

Figure 1-5 Installation Summary / Installation Source

Selecting Software to be Installed

10. Here, you can choose the base operating environment that you want installed. Base environments are pre-defined groups of software packages designed for specific purposes. They are listed with a short description in Table 1-2.

Server Role	Description
Minimal Install	Installs basic RHEL OS.
Infrastructure Server	Minimal plus basic network services.
File and Print Server	Minimal plus file, print, and storage services.
Basic Web Server	Infrastructure plus Apache web service.
Virtualization Host	Infrastructure plus virtualization support to host virtual machines.
Server with GUI	Infrastructure with graphics support.

Table 1-2 Software Selection

Choosing a base environment in the left pane reveals additional components on the right that become available for selection to be installed as part of the selected base environment installation. See Figure 1-6.

Figure 1-6 Installation Summary / Software Selection

The installer program automatically selects and installs pre-requisite software components in order to fulfill dependency requirements for a successful installation of the selected environment. The default is the Minimal Install. For this installation, choose Server with GUI without selecting any additional components. Click Done to return to the Installation Summary page.

Configuring Installation Destination

11. The Installation Destination allows you to choose an available local disk for installation and partition it. See Figure 1-7. It also gives you the ability to add a remote disk and partition it. By default, Anaconda selects "Automatic partitioning selected" on the Installation Summary page. However, on the Installation Destination page, the installer lets you either retain the automatic partitioning or configure your own. The availability of a local disk represented as *sda* is also shown on this page. The "Encrypt my data" checkbox under the Encryption section permits the encryption of all partitions except for the */boot* partition. If you choose this option, you will be prompted to enter a passphrase to be used to access the partitions later. The "Full disk summary and bootloader" link at the bottom left corner on the Installation Destination page allows you to choose a disk to place the bootloader program on. On a single disk system, you do not need to modify it. The default, and the only, bootloader program available in RHEL7 is called GRUB2, and it is explained at length in Chapter 07 "Booting RHEL7, Updating Kernel, and Logging Messages".

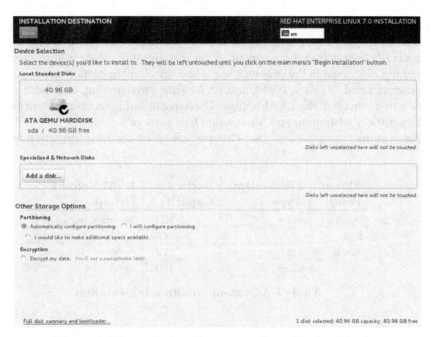

Figure 1-7 Installation Summary / Installation Destination

If you wish to choose automatic partitioning at this point, simply click the Done button to permit the installer to use automatic disk partitioning. This will create three partitions: */boot*, */*, and swap, and together they take up the full available capacity on the selected disk.

For this demonstration, choose "I will configure partitioning" under "Other Storage Options", and click Done to proceed to the Manual Partitioning sub-screen shown in Figure 1-8.

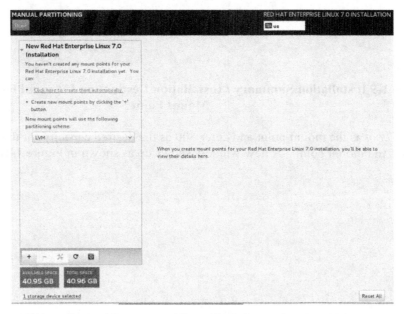

Figure 1-8 Installation Summary / Installation Destination / Manual Partitioning

12. The Manual Partitioning sub-screen lets you partition the selected disk. It shows the total and available disk space in the bottom left corner. The link "Click here to create them automatically" shows the three partitions the installer will create if you select the automatic partitioning discussed in the previous step. The installer supports four types of partitioning schemes: standard, BTRFS, LVM, and LVM Thin Provisioning, and these schemes are visible when you click the LVM option. These partitioning techniques are explained at length in Chapter 09 "Partitioning and Managing Disk Storage".

13. For this demonstration, partition the chosen disk based on the information provided in Table 1-3.

Mount Point	File System Type	Desired Capacity	LVM Volume Group
/boot	xfs	0.5GB	Standard partition
/	xfs	10GB	vg00
/home	xfs	1GB	vg00
	swap	1GB	vg00

Table 1-3 Custom Partition Information

 The installer program requires that three partitions: */boot*, */*, and swap must be created at a minimum.

Click the + sign in the bottom left to add custom partitions. The following window pops up.

Figure 1-9 Installation Summary / Installation Destination / Manual Partitioning / Add Mount Point

14. Select */boot* as the mount point and enter 500 as the desired capacity for the first partition. Click "Add mount point". A new window shows up as shown in Figure 1-10.

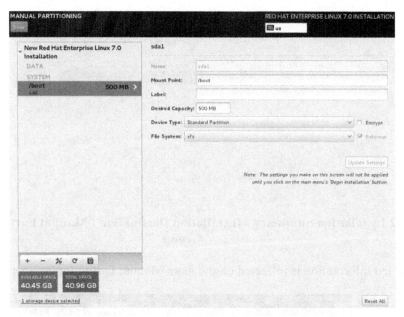

Figure 1-10 Installation Summary / Installation Destination / Manual Partitioning

The default device and file system types are automatically filled in for the */boot* file system.

 The */boot* partition must be created as a standard partition outside LVM boundaries.

Click the + sign again and enter the mount point and size for the / file system. Click "Add mount point" and the root file system properties become visible. Notice a new property called Volume Group appears with the default value "rhel". By default, LVM suggests "rhel" as the volume group name and placing the root file system in this volume group. See Figure 1-11.

Figure 1-11 Installation Summary / Installation Destination / Manual Partitioning

Click Modify beside Volume Group and enter *vg00* as the new volume group name. See Figure 1-12. Click Save to proceed.

Figure 1-12 Installation Summary / Installation Destination / Manual Partitioning / Volume Group

The updated information is reflected on the main Manual Partitioning screen.

Figure 1-13 Installation Summary / Installation Destination / Manual Partitioning

Repeat the above procedure for the */home* and swap partitions to ensure they are part of the *vg00* volume group as well. The final partitioning will look like Figure 1-14.

Figure 1-14 Installation Summary / Installation Destination / Manual Partitioning

You can highlight a partition on the left, and view or modify any of its properties. Several file system types are supported and these can be viewed by clicking on the down arrow beside File System. These include ext2, ext3, ext4, swap, BIOS Boot, xfs, and vfat, and are explained in Chapter 10 "Constructing and Using File Systems and Swap".

15. Click Done. The installer program asks for confirmation as indicated in Figure 1-15. Click Accept Changes to confirm the partitioning and return to the Installation Summary page.

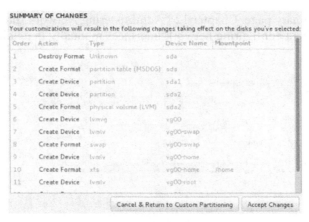

SUMMARY OF CHANGES

Your customizations will result in the following changes taking effect on the disks you've selected:

Order	Action	Type	Device Name	Mountpoint
1	Destroy Format	Unknown	sda	
2	Create Format	partition table (MSDOS)	sda	
3	Create Device	partition	sda1	
4	Create Device	partition	sda2	
5	Create Format	physical volume (LVM)	sda2	
6	Create Device	lvmvg	vg00	
7	Create Device	lvmlv	vg00-swap	
8	Create Format	swap	vg00-swap	
9	Create Device	lvmlv	vg00-home	
10	Create Format	xfs	vg00-home	/home
11	Create Device	lvmlv	vg00-root	

Cancel & Return to Custom Partitioning   Accept Changes

Figure 1-15 Installation Summary / Installation Destination / Manual Partitioning / Summary

Configuring Network & Hostname

16. Assigning appropriate IP information and a hostname is essential for system functionality in a network environment. Click Network & Hostname on the Installation Summary page and a window similar to the one shown in Figure 1-16 pops up. Anaconda detects all network interfaces available on the system; however, it does not automatically assign them IPs. Also the default hostname is set to localhost.localdomain. You need to modify these assignments so that your system is able to communicate with other systems on the network. Your system has one network interface, represented as *eth0*, and this is detected by the installer. You can obtain IP assignments automatically from an available DHCP server by simply moving the switch located in the top right-hand corner on this window. However, for this demonstration, click Configure in the bottom right corner and enter IP information manually for this interface.

Figure 1-16 Installation Summary / Network & Hostname

There are multiple tabs available on the interface configuration screen, as depicted in Figure 1-17. Go to IPv4 Settings and choose Manual from the drop-down list against Method. Click Add and enter IP information. Click Save to save the configuration and return to the previous window. Now enter *host1.example.com* in the Hostname field and click Done to return to the

Installation Summary page. Chapter 12 "Administering Network Interfaces and Network Clients" talks about configuring network interfaces manually in detail.

Figure 1-17 Installation Summary / Network & Hostname / Configure

Beginning Installation

17. The Installation Summary page now looks like Figure 1-18. Click Begin Installation in the bottom right to begin the installation based on the configuration entered in previous steps. Anaconda will now partition the disk and install the software in the partitions. Any data previously stored in the partitions will be overwritten and will not be recoverable. Before you click the Begin Installation button, you still have the opportunity to go back and configure or reconfigure any items you desire or have missed.

Figure 1-18 Installation Summary

The Begin Installation button is not visible unless all required configuration is entered.

Setting root Password and Creating a User Account

18. Once the installation has begun, a new screen appears that shows the installation progress. This screen also allows you to assign a password to the *root* user and create a user account.

Figure 1-19 Configuration

19. While the installer program continues with background configuration and software copy, click Root Password and set a password for the *root* user. Click Done to return to the installation progress screen.

20. Next, click User Creation and create a user account called *user1* and assign it a password of your choice. Click Done to return.

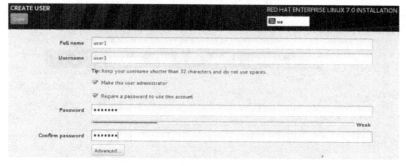

Figure 1-20 Configuration / Create User

Finishing Installation

21. When all software packages are installed, the Reboot button becomes active in the bottom right corner of the screen. Click this button to reboot the new system.

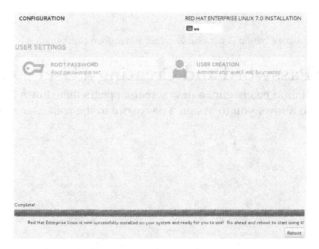

Figure 1-21 Configuration / Finishing Installation

Performing Post-Installation Tasks

22. Following the reboot, the system initiates the Initial Setup application so you can complete certain post-installation configuration tasks. Figure 1-22 shows the Initial Setup screen.

Figure 1-22 Initial Setup

23. On this screen you must accept the license agreement by clicking the License Information icon and then ticking the box beside "I accept the license agreement". Click Done and then Finish Configuration to continue.

Figure 1-23 Initial Setup / License Agreement

24. The next screen allows you to configure a kernel crash dump. The default shown here is 128MB, which should be sufficient for this system. The dump may prove helpful in

determining the root cause of a system crash. Accept the default value and click Forward to continue.

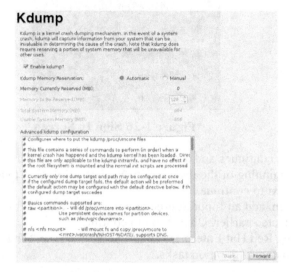

Figure 1-24 Initial Setup / Kernel Dump Configuration

25. If you have an active subscription, you should register this system with Red Hat to get benefits such as automatic software updates, etc. For this demonstration, tick "No, I prefer to register at a later time" and click Finish to continue.

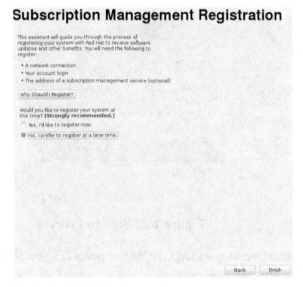

Figure 1-25 Initial Setup / Subscription Registration

26. Next is the login screen where the user account you created earlier is displayed. Click the user name and enter the password to sign in.

Figure 1-26 Sign In Screen

27. The login process continues and a Welcome screen pops up that shows the language that you selected at the beginning of the installation. You can change it to a different language if you wish to. Click Next to continue.
28. On the next screen, add an Input Source to be used. The default is the US English keyboard type that you selected earlier. Click Next to continue.
29. Click "Start using Red Hat Enterprise Linux Server" on the "Thank You" screen. This marks the end of the post-configuration tasks.

Figure 1-27 Sign In Process

30. The default graphical desktop called GNOME appears (Figure 1-28) and you should now be able to start using the system as *user1*.

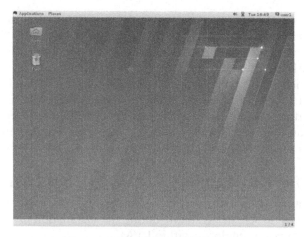

Figure 1-28 GNOME Desktop

31. After you are done navigating, click user1 at the top right corner and choose Log Out to log off the system.

Figure 1-29 Log Out

This completes the step-by-step procedure for installing RHEL7 using a local DVD medium.

Chapter Summary

In this chapter, we started by looking at Linux history and exploring available distributions from Red Hat. We looked at various pre-installation items to prepare for a smooth installation. We reviewed what was required to build the lab for practicing the exercises and labs presented in this book. We demonstrated downloading the OS ISO image, and performed a DVD-based installation on a physical computer. We completed several post-installation tasks to complete the installation. Finally, we logged in to the new system to verify the installation.

Chapter Review Questions

1. Can we install RHEL7 in text mode?
2. How many console screens do we have access to during the installation process?
3. We can use the */boot* partition within LVM to boot RHEL. True or False?
4. Which kernel version is the initial release of RHEL7 based on?
5. What are the two 100% rebuilds of Red Hat Enterprise Linux?

6. Several log files are created and updated in the */tmp* directory during the installation process. Where are these files moved to after the completion of installation?
7. Identify the two key hardware requirements for a computer to support KVM.
8. Name the RHEL installer program.
9. What server role would we choose during installation if we want KVM support added?
10. RHEL7 cannot be installed over the network. True or False?
11. RHEL7 supports both automatic and custom disk partitioning during installation. Would it use standard partitioning or LVM if we select automatic partitioning?
12. Minimal server installation provides X window as well. True or False?

Answers to Chapter Review Questions

1. Yes, RHEL7 can be installed in text mode.
2. There are six console screens available during the installation process.
3. False. */boot* must not be enclosed within LVM.
4. The initial release of RHEL7 is based on kernel version 3.10.
5. The two 100% rebuilds of Red Hat Enterprise Linux are CentOS and Scientific Linux.
6. These files are moved to the */var/log* directory.
7. A computer must be 64-bit and support hardware virtualization.
8. The name of the RHEL installer program is Anaconda.
9. We will choose Server with Virtualization during installation to ensure KVM support is added.
10. False. RHEL7 can be installed with installation files located on network servers.
11. It will select LVM if automatic partitioning is opted.
12. False. Minimal server installation does not include graphics support.

DIY Challenge Labs

The following labs are provided for those who wish to master the installation. I recommend that you practice these labs in a VMware, Oracle VirtualBox, or MS HyperV virtual machine and not overwrite the installation that we have done, unless you want to re-do it with the exact same configuration. Also, a step-by-step procedure is not included for these labs, as sufficient detail is already available in this chapter for your assistance. Use defaults or your own thinking for missing information.

Lab 1-1: Perform a Default Local Installation

Perform a local installation of RHEL7 on your physical computer or on a virtual machine. Use default partitioning. Add support for X Window and GNOME desktop. Create a local user account called *tricia* with all the defaults. Force the system to use the local clock for time updates. Use information at will for additional configuration.

Lab 1-2: Perform a Custom Local Installation

Perform a local installation of RHEL7 on your physical computer or on a virtual machine. Use a standard partition for */boot* and LVM for the rest. Create */boot* 400MB, */* 4GB, swap 1GB, */usr* 4GB, */var* 2GB, */tmp* 1GB, and */home* 1GB. Select necessary packages to support X Window, GNOME desktop, graphical administration tools, and CIFS, NFS, and Apache web services. Create a local user account called *joseph* with all default values and sync the system time with the default NTP servers. Use information at will for additional configuration.

Chapter 02

Using Basic Linux Tools

This chapter describes the following major topics:

- ➤ Access the system remotely using ssh
- ➤ Access the command prompt
- ➤ General Linux commands and how to execute them
- ➤ Search text within files and command outputs
- ➤ Use basic compression and archiving tools
- ➤ Introduction to the vi editor
- ➤ Obtain Linux online help

RHCSA Objectives:

01. Access a shell prompt and issue commands with correct syntax
06. Archive, compress, unpack, uncompress files using tar, star, gzip, and bzip2
07. Create and edit text files
11. Locate, read, and use system documentation including man, info, and files in /usr/share/doc

RHEL

RHEL systems can be accessed over the network using multiple ways. The most common of these methods is the use of the secure shell tool. This program is widely available and it is native on every UNIX and Linux system. It may be executed on Windows, UNIX, another RHEL, or systems with other Linux distributions running.

Linux offers a variety of commands for both privileged and non-privileged use. Privileged commands are for system management and intended solely for privileged users. Non-privileged commands do not require extra rights for execution and can be run with regular user rights. Knowledge of these commands is essential in order to work productively and administer the system efficiently. Normal and application users, and database and system administrators all need to edit text files on a regular basis as part of their job. This is normally done with a popular tool called vi. A sound working knowledge of this tool is essential for all these roles.

The availability of native help on the system makes life easier for both regular and privileged users. This assistance is available on commands and configuration files via locally installed searchable manual pages and documentation for installed packages.

Accessing a RHEL System Remotely

A user must log in to the Linux system in order to use it. The login process identifies the user to the system. Logging in and out at the console was demonstrated towards the end of Chapter 01 "Installing RHEL7 on Physical Computer Using Local DVD". For accessing a RHEL system remotely, the most common tool is the *ssh* (secure shell) command. Secure shell software (both client and server packages) is loaded by default during RHEL7 installation, and is covered in detail in Chapter 13 "Securing Access with SSH and TCP Wrappers". A graphical equivalent for the *ssh* client may be downloaded and run on MS Windows to access a RHEL system. The following sub-section provides basic information on how to use the *ssh* client from another Linux system, and from a Windows system to access *host1*.

Accessing from Another Linux System

The *ssh* command can be invoked on another Linux system with the hostname or IP address of the remote RHEL system specified. For example, if you are logged in as *user1* on a Linux system and wish to access *host1* as *user1*, run the command by specifying the IP address of *host1* as follows:

```
$ ssh 192.168.0.100
The authenticity of host '192.168.0.100' can't be established.
RSA key fingerprint is 12:78:84:2a:38:47:12:0a:4b:e0:ec:67:b1:00:f6:85.
Are you sure you want to continue connecting (yes/no)? yes
Warning: Permanently added '192.168.0.100' (RSA) to the list of known hosts.
user1@192.168.0.100's password:
[user1@host1 ~]$
```

Answer yes to the question and press Enter. This adds the system's IP address to a file in *user1*'s home directory on the client. This message will not re-appear for this user on subsequent login attempts to *host1* from this client. Enter *user1*'s valid password to be allowed in. After you are done, use either the *exit* or the *logout* command to log out. You may alternatively press Ctrl+d to log off.

If you wish to log on as a different user such as *user2* (assuming *user2* exists on *host1*), you may run *ssh* in either of the following ways:

 $ ssh –l user1 192.168.0.100
 $ ssh user1@192.168.0.100

In order to run graphical tools on *host1* and have the output redirected to the local Linux system where you are issuing the command from, run *ssh* with the –X option to connect to *host1* and execute a graphical application such as *gnome-calculator*.

 $ ssh –X 192.168.0.100

Accessing from Windows

On the Windows side, several ssh client programs, such as puTTY, are available. puTTY may be downloaded free of charge from the Internet. Figure 2-1 shows the puTTY interface.

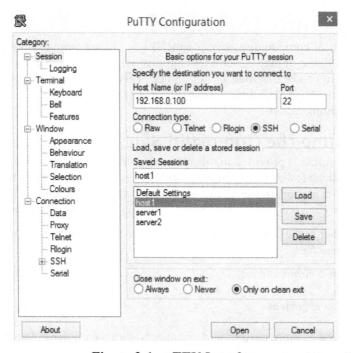

Figure 2-1 puTTY Interface

Enter the IP address of *host1* and select the radio button next to SSH under the Connection Type heading. The ssh protocol uses port 22, which is exhibited in the Port field. Assign a name to this session (typically a hostname) in the Saved Sessions field and click Save to store this information so as to avoid retyping in the future. Now click Open to attempt a connection.

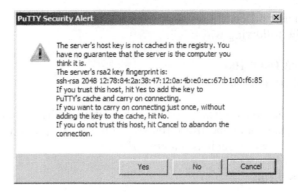

Figure 2-2 puTTY Security Alert

Click yes to the security alert question to get a login prompt. This alert will not re-appear on subsequent attempts. Enter a valid username and password to log in.

Common Linux Commands

There are hundreds of commands available in RHEL7. These commands range from simple to complicated ones. Some of them offer a few options, while others have as many as 70 or more, which we can use to produce outputs of our choice. This section provides an understanding of how commands are formed and then demonstrates the use of some of the commands commonly used in routine system administration.

Understanding the Command Syntax

To practice the commands provided in this chapter, you can log in as *user1*, run the commands, and observe their outputs. However, as you are learning system administration topics and have a desire to build your system administration skills, you need to feel comfortable working as *root* right from the beginning. *host1* is your test system anyway, and can be rebuilt if something breaks.

Sign in as *root* either at the console or using *ssh*. At the same time, you should also have another window open as *user1*.

The basic syntax of a command is:

command option argument

You can specify zero or more options and arguments with a command. Some commands have default options and arguments that they use when executed, and you do not have to specify them. Other commands do require at least one option or argument in order to work. An option, a.k.a. a *switch* or *flag*, modifies the behavior of the command, and an argument supplies a target on which to perform the command action. The following examples show some command structures with the text on the right state the number of options and arguments supplied:

$ **ls**	(no option, no argument; the default argument is the current directory name)
$ **ls –l**	(one option, no argument; the default argument is the current directory name)
$ **ls directory_name**	(no option, one argument)
$ **ls –l directory_name**	(one option, one argument)

Listing Files and Directories

The *ls* (*list*) command produces a list of files and directories and displays it on the screen. It supports several options, some of which are listed in Table 2-1 along with a short description.

Option	Description
–a	Lists hidden files also. If a file or directory name starts with a dot, it is considered hidden.
–lh	Displays long listing with file sizes in human readable format.
–l	Displays long listing with detailed file information including the file type, permissions, link count, owner, group, size, date and time of last modification, and name of the file.
–ld	Displays long listing of the specified directory, but hides its contents.
–R	Lists contents of the specified directory and all its sub-directories (recursive listing).
–lt	Lists all files sorted by date and time with the newest file first.
–ltr	Lists all files sorted by date and time with the oldest file first.

Table 2-1 ls Command Options

The following examples will help you understand the impact of options used with the *ls* command. Log in as *root* to run these examples.

To list files in the current directory with an assumption that you are in the / directory:

```
# ls
bin   dev home lib64   mnt proc run  srv tmp var
boot etc lib     media opt root sbin sys usr
```

To list files in the current directory with detailed information, use one of the following:

```
# ll
# ls –l
total 32
lrwxrwxrwx.   1 root root      7 Nov 16  19:12 bin -> usr/bin
dr-xr-xr-x.   3 root root 4096 Nov 16  20:53 boot
drwxr-xr-x.  20 root root 3120 Nov 17  19:11 dev
drwxr-xr-x. 132 root root 8192 Nov 20  08:12 etc
drwxr-xr-x.   3 root root     18 Nov 16  20:11 home
lrwxrwxrwx.   1 root root      7 Nov 16  19:12 lib -> usr/lib
lrwxrwxrwx.   1 root root      9 Nov 16  19:12 lib64 -> usr/lib64
drwxr-xr-x.   2 root root      6 Mar 13   2014 media
drwxr-xr-x.   2 root root      6 Mar 13   2014 mnt
 . . . . . . . .
```

To list all files in the current directory with detailed information and sorted by date and time with the newest file first:

```
# ls –lt
total 32
drwxrwxrwt.  14 root root  4096 Nov 25 03:31 tmp
drwxr-xr-x.  39 root root  1220 Nov 24 13:11 run
drwxr-xr-x. 132 root root  8192 Nov 20 08:12 etc
dr-xr-x---.   7 root root  4096 Nov 19 21:27 root
drwxr-xr-x.  20 root root  3120 Nov 17 19:11 dev
. . . . . . . .
```

To display all files in the current directory with their sizes in human readable format:

```
# ls –lh
total 32K
lrwxrwxrwx.   1 root root     7  Nov 16 19:12 bin -> usr/bin
dr-xr-xr-x.   3 root root  4.0K Nov 16 20:53 boot
drwxr-xr-x.  20 root root  3.1K Nov 17 19:11 dev
drwxr-xr-x. 132 root root  8.0K Nov 20 08:12 etc
drwxr-xr-x.   3 root root    18 Nov 16 20:11 home
. . . . . . . .
```

To list all files, including the hidden files, in the current directory with detailed information:

```
# ls –la
total 40
drwxr-xr-x.  17 root root  4096 Nov 17 15:09 .
drwxr-xr-x.  17 root root  4096 Nov 17 15:09 ..
lrwxrwxrwx.   1 root root     7 Nov 16 19:12 bin -> usr/bin
dr-xr-xr-x.   3 root root  4096 Nov 16 20:53 boot
drwxr-xr-x.  20  root root  3120 Nov 17 19:11 dev
. . . . . . . .
```

To list contents of the *etc* directory recursively:

```
# ls –R /etc
   < a very lengthy output will be generated >
```

Printing Working Directory

The *pwd (print working directory)* command displays a user's current location in the directory tree. The following example shows that *user1* is presently in the */home/user1* directory. Run it as *user1*.

```
$ pwd
/home/user1
```

Changing Directories

The *cd (change directory)* command is used to navigate the directory tree. Run the following commands as *user1*.

To change directory to */usr/bin*:

$ cd /usr/bin

To go back to the home directory, issue either of the following:

$ cd
$ cd ~

To go directly from */etc* to a sub-directory *dir1* under *user1 's* home directory, create *dir1*, as it does not currently exist:

$ mkdir –v dir1
mkdir: created directory 'dir1'
$ cd ~/dir1

tilde (~) is used as an abbreviation for the absolute pathname to a user's home directory. Refer to Chapter 03 "Working with Files and File Permissions" to understand what an absolute path is.

To go to the home directory of *user1* from anywhere in the directory structure, use the ~ character and specify the login name. Note that there is no space between ~ and *user1*. This command is only successful if *user1* has the execute permission bit set on their home directory at the public level. Refer to Chapter 03 "Working with Files and File Permissions" for details on file permissions.

$ cd ~user1

Usage of the ~ character as demonstrated, is called *tilde substitution*. Refer to Chapter 04 "Dealing with the Bash Shell, Processes, and Scheduling" for more information on tilde substitution.

To go to the root directory, use the forward slash character:

$ cd /

To switch between current and previous directories, issue the *cd* command with the dash character:

$ cd –

To go one directory up to the parent directory, use period twice:

$ cd ..

Showing the Terminal File

This command displays the terminal name we are currently logged on to:

$ tty
/dev/pts/0

Listing Currently Logged-In Users

The *who* command consults the */var/run/utmp* file and presents a list of users currently logged on to the system:

```
$ who
user1   :0         2014-11-17 19:11 (:0)
root    pts/0      2014-11-22 08:14 (192.168.0.13)
user1   pts/1      2014-11-17 22:05 (:0)
```

The first column displays the username, the second column shows the terminal session name, the third and fourth columns show the date and time the user logged in, and the fifth column indicates if the terminal session is graphical (:0) or remote (IP address).

The *who* command shows information only about the user running it if executed with the "am i" arguments:

```
$ who am i
root    pts/0      2014-11-22 08:14 (192.168.0.13)
```

The *w* (*what*) command displays information similar to the *who* command, but in more detail. It also tells the length of time the user has been idle for, along with CPU utilization and current activity. On the first line, it shows the current system time, the length of time the system has been up for, number of users currently logged in, and the current average load on the system over the past 1, 5, and 15 minutes.

```
$ w
09:40:20 up 7 days, 18:30,  3 users,  load average: 0.00, 0.01, 0.05
USER     TTY      LOGIN@   IDLE  JCPU  PCPU  WHAT
user1    :0       17Nov14  ?xdm? 42:18 1.00s  gdm-session-worker [pam/gdm-password]
root     pts/0    Sat08    4.00s 0.13s 0.11s -bash
user1    pts/1    17Nov14  5days 0.06s 0.90s /usr/libexec/gnome-terminal-server
```

Inspecting System's Uptime

The *uptime* command shows the system's current time, how long it has been up for, number of users currently logged in, and average number of processes over the past 1, 5, and 15 minutes:

```
# uptime
09:42:14 up 7 days, 18:32,  3 users,  load average: 0.00, 0.01, 0.05
```

The output above shows that the current system time is 9:42 am, the system has been up for 7 days, 18 hours, and 32 minutes, there are three users currently logged in, and the system load averages over the past 1, 5, and 15 minutes are 0.00, 0.01, and 0.05, respectively.

Viewing User Login Name

The *whoami* (*who am i*) command displays the effective username of the person executing this command:

```
$ whoami
user1
```

The *logname* (*login name*) command shows the name of the real user who originally logged in to the system. If that user uses the *su* command to switch identity, the *logname* command, unlike the *whoami* command, still shows the real username.

```
$ logname
root
```

Examining User and Group Information

The *id* (*identifier*) command displays a user's UID (*user identifier*), username, GID (*group identifier*), group name, all secondary groups the user is a member of, and SELinux security context:

```
$ id
uid=1000(user1) gid=1000(user1) groups=1000(user1),10(wheel)
context=unconfined_u:unconfined_r:unconfined_t:s0-s0:c0.c1023
```

Each user and group has a corresponding number (called UID and GID) for identification purposes. See Chapter 08 "Managing Users and Groups" for more information. For SELinux, see Chapter 11 "Controlling Access through Firewall and SELinux".

The *groups* command lists all groups a user is a member of:

```
$ groups
user1 wheel
```

The first group listed is the primary group for the user who executed this command; all others are secondary (or supplementary) groups. Consult Chapter 08 "Managing Users and Groups" for further details.

Viewing History of Successful User Login Attempts

The *last* command reports the history of successful user login attempts and system reboots by reading the */var/log/wtmp* file. This file keeps a record of all login and logout activities, including the login time, duration a user stayed logged in, and tty (where the user session took place). Consider the following examples.

To list all user login, logout, and system reboot occurrences, type the *last* command without any arguments:

```
$ last
user1   pts/2           192.168.0.13        Sat  Nov 22 09:25  - 09:25  (00:00)
user1   pts/2           192.168.0.13        Sat  Nov 22 09:12  - 09:12  (00:00)
root    pts/0           192.168.0.13        Sat  Nov 22 08:14    still logged in
root    pts/2           192.168.0.13        Fri  Nov 21 21:43  - 21:43  (00:00)
reboot  system boot 3.10.0-123.el7.x    Mon Nov 17 14:22  - 10:44 (7+20:21)

. . . . . . . .
```

To list only system reboot details:

$ last reboot

reboot   system boot 3.10.0-123.el7.x Mon Nov 17 14:22 - 10:44 (7+20:21)
reboot   system boot 3.10.0-123.el7.x Mon Nov 17 11:00 - 14:22 (03:21)
reboot   system boot 3.10.0-123.el7.x Sun Nov 16 20:52 - 11:00 (14:08)
wtmp begins Sun Nov 16 20:52:17 2014

Viewing History of Failed User Login Attempts

The *lastb* command reports the history of unsuccessful user login attempts by reading the */var/log/btmp* file. This file keeps a record of all unsuccessful login attempts, including the login name, time, and tty (where the attempt was made). Consider the following examples.

To list all unsuccessful login attempts, type the *lastb* command without any arguments. You must be *root* to run this command.

 # lastb

root   ssh:notty   192.168.0.13   Tue Nov 25 10:49 - 10:49 (00:00)
root   ssh:notty   192.168.0.13   Tue Nov 25 10:49 - 10:49 (00:00)
root   ssh:notty   192.168.0.13   Tue Nov 25 10:49 - 10:49 (00:00)
root   ssh:notty   192.168.0.13   Tue Nov 25 10:49 - 10:49 (00:00)
root   ssh:notty   192.168.0.13   Tue Nov 25 10:49 - 10:49 (00:00)
btmp begins Tue Nov 25 10:49:41 2014

Displaying Recent User Logins

The *lastlog* command displays the recent user logins by reading the */var/log/lastlog* file. This file keeps track of recent user login attempts. It also shows the users that have never logged in.

 # lastlog

Username	Port	From	Latest
root	pts/0	192.168.0.13	Sat Nov 22 08:14:24 -0500 2014
bin			**Never logged in**
daemon			**Never logged in**
. . . .			
gdm	:0		Mon Nov 17 15:10:15 -0500 2014
user1	pts/0		Tue Nov 25 10:24:48 -0500 2014

Viewing System Information

The *uname* command produces basic information about the system. Without any options, this command displays the operating system name only. You can use the –a option to get details.

 # uname
Linux
 # uname –a
Linux host1.example.com 3.10.0-123.el7.x86_64 #1 SMP Mon May 5 11:16:57 EDT 2014 x86_64 x86_64 x86_64 GNU/Linux

The information returned by the second command is:

Linux	Kernel name
host1.example.com	Hostname of this system
3.10.0-123.el7.x86_64	Kernel release
#1 SMP Mon May 5 11:16:57 EDT 2014	Date and time of this kernel built
x86_64	Machine hardware name
x86_64	Processor type
x86_64	Hardware platform
GNU/Linux	Operating system name

Try running the *uname* command with the –s (kernel name), –n (node name), –r (kernel release), –v (kernel build date), –m (hardware name), –p (processor type), –i (hardware platform), and –o (OS name) options separately to view specific information.

Displaying and Setting Hostname

The *hostnamectl* command can be used to view or set the system hostname. Run this command without any options to view the hostname as well as the hardware information of the system it is running on:

hostnamectl
    Static hostname: host1.example.com
        Icon name: computer-laptop
          Chassis: laptop
       Machine ID: 03858cff4a7b482e8b70a7cea28585b5
          Boot ID: d451b5a5f1494ac1a371d859593e3a90
 Operating System: Red Hat Enterprise Linux Server 7.0 (Maipo)
      CPE OS Name: cpe:/o:redhat:enterprise_linux:7.0:GA:server
           Kernel: Linux 3.10.0-123.el7.x86_64
     Architecture: x86_64

To change the hostname to *hostx.example.com*:

hostnamectl set-hostname hostx.example.com

To change the hostname back to *host1.example.com*:

hostnamectl set-hostname host1.example.com

You can also use the *hostname* command to display the system name:

hostname
host1.example.com

Clearing the Screen

The *clear* command clears the terminal screen and places the cursor at the beginning of the screen. We can alternatively use Ctrl+l for this purpose.

clear

Displaying and Setting System Date and Time

The *timedatectl* command can be used to display and set the system date and time. Without any options, this command shows the current date and time:

```
# timedatectl
        Local time:     Tue 2014-11-25 11:06:56 EST
    Universal time:     Tue 2014-11-25 16:06:56 UTC
          RTC time:     Tue 2014-11-25 16:06:56
          Timezone:     America/Toronto (EST, -0500)
       NTP enabled:     yes
  NTP synchronized:     yes
     RTC in local TZ:   no
        DST active:     no
   Last DST change:     DST ended at
                        Sun 2014-11-02 01:59:59 EDT
                        Sun 2014-11-02 01:00:00 EST
   Next DST change:     DST begins (the clock jumps one hour forward) at
                        Sun 2015-03-08 01:59:59 EST
                        Sun 2015-03-08 03:00:00 EDT
```

To modify the current date to August 12, 2015:

 # timedatectl set-time 2015-08-12

To change the time to 11am:

 # timedatectl set-time 11:00

Alternatively, we can use the *date* command to view or modify the system date and time. To view the date and time:

 # date
Wed Aug 12 11:00:03 EDT 2015

To modify the system date and time back to November 25, 2014 11:15, for instance, run the *date* command as follows:

 # date --set "2014-11-25 11:15:00"
Tue Nov 25 11:15:00 EST 2014

Listing and Modifying System Timezone

The *timedatectl* command can also be used to list and modify the system timezone setting. To list all available timezones, run the command with list-timezones option:

 # timedatectl list-timezones
Africa/Abidjan
Africa/Accra
Africa/Addis_Ababa

Africa/Algiers
Africa/Asmara
Africa/Bamako
. . . .

To change the time zone to America/Toronto, run the command as follows:

 # timedatectl set-timezone America/Toronto

Confirm the new timezone value with the *timedatectl* command.

Displaying Command Path

The *which* command shows the path to the command that will execute if it is run without using its absolute path:

 # which cat
/usr/bin/cat

The output means that the *cat* command will be executed from the */usr/bin* directory if you run it without specifying its full path.

Counting Words, Lines, and Characters

The *wc* (*word count*) command displays number of lines, words, and characters (or bytes) contained in a text file or input supplied. For example, when you run this command on the */etc/profile* file, you will see output similar to the following:

 # wc /etc/profile
76 252 1750 /etc/profile

The first column indicates the number of lines (76) followed by the number of words (252), number of characters (or bytes) (1750), and file name (*/etc/profile*) in subsequent columns.

We can use the options listed in Table 2-2 to obtain the desired output.

Option	Action
–l	Prints line count.
–w	Prints word count.
–c	Prints byte count.
–m	Prints character count.

Table 2-2 wc Command Options

The following example displays only the number of lines in */etc/profile*:

 # wc –l /etc/profile
76 /etc/profile

Try running *wc* with the other options and review the results.

Listing PCI, USB, and CPU Device Information

Information about PCI, USB, and CPU devices can be gathered and displayed using commands such as *lspci*, *lsusb*, and *lscpu*.

The *lspci* command displays information about PCI buses and the devices attached to them. Specify –v, –vv, or –vvv for detailed output. With the –m option, this command produces more legible output.

lspci –m
00:00.0 "Host bridge" "Intel Corporation" "2nd Generation Core Processor Family DRAM Controller" -r09 "Dell" "Device 0494"
00:01.0 "PCI bridge" "Intel Corporation" "Xeon E3-1200/2nd Generation Core Processor Family PCI Express Root Port" -r09 "" ""
00:02.0 "VGA compatible controller" "Intel Corporation" "2nd Generation Core Processor Family Integrated Graphics Controller" -r09 "Dell" "Device 0494"
. . . .

The *lsusb* command displays information about USB buses and the devices connected to them:

lsusb
Bus 001 Device 002: ID 8087:0024 Intel Corp. Integrated Rate Matching Hub
Bus 002 Device 002: ID 8087:0024 Intel Corp. Integrated Rate Matching Hub
Bus 001 Device 001: ID 1d6b:0002 Linux Foundation 2.0 root hub
Bus 002 Device 001: ID 1d6b:0002 Linux Foundation 2.0 root hub
Bus 001 Device 003: ID 1bcf:2802 Sunplus Innovation Technology Inc.
Bus 002 Device 003: ID 0a5c:5800 Broadcom Corp. BCM5880 Secure Applications Processor

The *lscpu* command shows information about the processor, including its architecture, operating modes, count, vendor, family, model, speed, and the presence of virtualization support:

lscpu
Architecture:	x86_64
CPU op-mode(s):	32-bit, 64-bit
Byte Order:	Little Endian
CPU(s):	8
On-line CPU(s) list:	0-7
Thread(s) per core:	2
Core(s) per socket:	4
Socket(s):	1
NUMA node(s):	1
Vendor ID:	GenuineIntel
CPU family:	6
Model:	42
Model name:	Intel(R) Core(TM) i7-2760QM CPU @ 2.40GHz
Stepping:	7
CPU MHz:	2901.187
BogoMIPS:	4789.14
Virtualization:	VT-x
L1d cache:	32K

L1i cache:	32K
L2 cache:	256K
L3 cache:	6144K
NUMA node0 CPU(s):	0-7

Compression Tools

Compression tools are used to compress one or more files or an archive to save space. Once a compressed archive is created, it can be copied to a remote system faster than a non-compressed archive. Compression tools may be used with archive commands, such as *tar*, to create a single compressed archive of hundreds of files and directories. RHEL provides a number of compression tools, such as *bzip2* (*bunzip2*) and *gzip* (*gunzip*), that can be used for this purpose.

Using gzip and gunzip

The *gzip* command creates a compressed file of each of the files specified at the command line and adds the *.gz* extension to each one of them.

To compress files *anaconda-ks.cfg* and *initial-setup-ks.cfg* in the */root* directory, issue the following *gzip* command, and then list them:

```
# gzip /root/anaconda-ks.cfg /root/initial-setup-ks.cfg
# ll /root | grep gz
-rw-------. 1 root root  979 Oct 28 23:04 anaconda-ks.cfg.gz
-rw-r--r--. 1 root root 1011 Oct 28 23:11 initial-setup-ks.cfg.gz
```

To uncompress the files, run either of the following commands on each file:

```
# gunzip /root/anaconda-ks.cfg.gz
# gzip –d /root/initial-setup-ks.cfg.gz
```

Check the files after the decompression using the *ll* command.

Using bzip2 and bunzip2

The *bzip2* command creates a compressed file of each of the files specified at the command line and adds the *.bz2* extension to each one of them.

To compress files *anaconda-ks.cfg* and *initial-setup-ks.cfg* in the */root* directory, issue the following *bzip2* command, and then list them:

```
# bzip2 /root/anaconda-ks.cfg /root/initial-setup-ks.cfg
# ll /root | grep bz2
-rw-------. 1 root root 1086 Oct 28 23:04 anaconda-ks.cfg.bz2
-rw-r--r--. 1 root root 1111 Oct 28 23:11 initial-setup-ks.cfg.bz2
```

To uncompress the files, run either of the following commands on each file:

```
# bunzip2 /root/anaconda-ks.cfg.bz2
# bzip2 –d /root/initial-setup-ks.bz2
```

Check the files after the decompression using the *ll* command.

Archiving Tools

RHEL offers many native tools that can be utilized to archive files for storage or distribution. These tools include *tar* and *star*, both of which have the ability to preserve general file attributes, such as ownership, group membership, and timestamp. The following sub-sections discuss these tools in detail.

Using tar

The *tar* (*tape archive*) command creates, appends, updates, lists, and extracts files to and from a single file, which is called a *tar* file (also a *tarball*). This command has the ability to archive SELinux file contexts as well as any extended attributes set on files. It can also be instructed to compress an archive while it is being created.

tar supports several options, some of which are summarized in Table 2-3.

Switch	Definition
–c	Creates a tarball.
–f	Specifies a tarball name.
–j	Compresses a tarball with bzip2 command.
–r	Appends files to the end of an existing tarball. Does not append to compressed tarballs.
–t	Lists contents of a tarball.
–u	Appends files to the end of an existing tarball if the specified files are newer. Does not append to compressed tarballs.
–v	Verbose mode.
–x	Extracts from a tarball.
–z	Compresses a tarball with gzip command.
--selinux --no-selinux	Includes (excludes) SELinux file contexts in archives.
--xattrs --no-xattrs	Includes (excludes) extended file attributes in archives.

Table 2-3 tar Command Options

A few examples have been provided below to elucidate the usage of *tar*. Note that the use of the – character is optional.

To create a tarball called */tmp/home.tar* of the entire */home* directory tree:

```
# tar cvf /tmp/home.tar /home
tar: Removing leading `/' from member names
/home/
/home/user1/
/home/user1/.mozilla/
/home/user1/.mozilla/extensions/
. . . . . . . .
```

To create a tarball called */tmp/files.tar* containing multiple files from the */etc* directory:

```
# tar cvf /tmp/files.tar /etc/host.conf /etc/shadow /etc/passwd /etc/yum.conf
```

To append files located in the /etc/yum.repos.d directory to home.tar:

tar rvf /tmp/home.tar /etc/yum.repos.d

To list the contents of home.tar:

tar tvf /tmp/home.tar
```
drwxr-xr-x root/root      0 2014-10-28 23:04 home/
drwx--x--- user1/user1    0 2014-11-25 10:42 home/user1/
drwxr-xr-x user1/user1    0 2014-10-29 19:19 home/user1/.mozilla/
. . . . . . . .
drwxrwxr-x user1/user1    0 2014-11-25 10:42 home/user1/dir1/
drwxr-xr-x root/root      0 2014-10-29 08:23 etc/yum.repos.d/
-rw-r--r-- root/root     83 2014-10-29 08:04 etc/yum.repos.d/ftp.repo
```

To list the contents of files.tar:

tar tvf /tmp/files.tar
```
-rw-r--r-- root/root       9 2013-06-07 10:31 etc/host.conf
---------- root/root    1177 2014-11-20 10:27 etc/shadow
-rw-r--r-- root/root    1999 2014-11-20 10:27 etc/passwd
-rw-r--r-- root/root     813 2014-04-15 09:54 etc/yum.conf
```

To restore /home from home.tar:

tar xvf /tmp/home.tar

To extract files from files.tar in the /tmp directory:

cd /tmp
tar xvf /tmp/files.tar

To create a tarball called /tmp/home.tar.gz of the /home directory and compress it with gzip:

tar cvzf /tmp/home.tar.gz /home

To create a tarball called /tmp/home.tar.bz2 of the /home directory and compress it with bzip2:

tar cvjf /tmp/home.tar.bz2 /home

> **EXAM TIP:** Archiving and compression are tasks done together to produce smaller archive files.

To list both compressed archives and check which of the two is smaller:

ll /tmp/home.tar*
```
-rw-r--r--. 1 root root 1481321 Nov 25 12:20 /tmp/home.tar.bz2
-rw-r--r--. 1 root root 1712239 Nov 25 12:20 /tmp/home.tar.gz
```

To create a tarball called */tmp/extattr.tar.bz2* of the files in */home* directory and include their extended attributes as well as SELinux contexts, and compress the archive with *bzip2*:

tar cvj --selinux --xattrs –f /tmp/extattr.tar.bz2 /home

Using star

The *star* (*standard tar*) command is an enhanced version of *tar*. It also supports SELinux security contexts and extended file attributes. Options for creating, listing, appending, updating, and extracting tarballs are the same as the *tar* command's. This utility is not installed by default; however, we can install the star package to install it.

To create a tarball */tmp/etc.tar* containing the entire */etc* directory with all extended file attributes and SELinux file contexts, run this command:

star cvf /tmp/etc.tar –xattr –H=exustar /etc

. . . .

a /etc/matchbox/kbdconfig 890 bytes, 2 tape blocks
a /etc/resolv.conf 114 bytes, 1 tape blocks
a /etc/nscd.conf 2384 bytes, 5 tape blocks
a /etc/nslcd.conf 4841 bytes, 10 tape blocks
star: 3210 blocks + 0 bytes (total of 32870400 bytes = 32100.00k).

To list and extract, run the following respectively:

star tvf /tmp/etc.tar

Release   star 1.5.2 (x86_64-redhat-linux-gnu)
Archtype   exustar
Dumpdate   1416959153.397205 (Tue Nov 25 18:45:53 2014)
Volno   1
Blocksize   20 records
     0 drwxr-xr-x@ root/root Nov 22 21:11 2014 /etc/
   541 -rw-r--r--@ root/root Oct 28 22:40 2014 /etc/fstab
     0 -rw-------@ root/root Oct 28 22:40 2014 /etc/crypttab
     0 lrwxrwxrwx@ root/root Oct 28 22:40 2014 /etc/mtab -> /proc/self/mounts

. . . .

star xvf /tmp/etc.tar

The vi (vim) Editor

The vi editor is an interactive, full-screen *visual* text editing tool that allows you to create and modify text files. This tool is available as a standard editor in all vendor UNIX versions and Linux distributions, and it does not require the graphical capability to run and be used. All text editing within vi takes place in a *buffer* (a small chunk of memory used to hold updates being done to the file). Changes can either be written to the disk or discarded. A graphical version of the vim editor, called *gvim*, is available on the RHEL7 installation DVD and can be installed.

It is essential for you as a system administrator to master the vi editor skills. The following sub-sections provide details on how to use and interact with this tool.

Modes of Operation

The vi editor essentially has three modes of operation: the Command mode, the Edit mode, and the Last Line mode.

The *command* mode is the default mode of vi. The vi editor places you into this mode when you start it. While in the command mode, you can carry out tasks such as copy, cut, paste, move, remove, replace, change, and search on text, in addition to performing navigational operations. This mode is also known as the *escape* mode because the Esc key is pressed to enter it.

In the *input* mode, anything you type at the keyboard is entered into the file as text. Commands cannot be run in this mode. The input mode is also called the *edit* mode or the *insert* mode. To return to the command mode, press the Esc key.

While in the command mode, you may carry out advanced editing tasks on text by pressing the colon (:) character, which places the cursor at the beginning of the last line of the screen, and hence it is referred to as the *last line* mode. This mode is considered a special type of command mode.

Starting vi

The vi editor may be started in one of the ways described in Table 2-4. Use the *vimtutor* command to view the man pages of vi.

Method	Description
vi	Starts vi and opens up an empty screen to enter text. We can save or discard the entered text at a later time.
vi existing_file	Starts vi and loads the specified file for editing or viewing.
vi new_file	Starts vi and creates the specified file when saved.

Table 2-4 Starting vi

Inserting text

To enter text, issue one of the commands described in Table 2-5 from the command mode to switch into the edit mode.

Command	Action
i	Inserts text before the current cursor position.
I	Inserts text at the beginning of the current line.
a	Appends text after the current cursor position.
A	Appends text at the end of the current line.
o	Opens up a new line below the current line.
O	Opens up a new line above the current line.

Table 2-5 Inserting Text

Press the Esc key when done to return to the command mode.

Navigating within vi

Table 2-6 elaborates key sequences that control the cursor movement while in vi.

Command	Action
h / left arrow / Ctrl+h	Moves left (backward) one character. We may type a number before this command to move that many characters. For example, 2h would move two characters to the left.
j / down arrow	Moves down one line. We may type a number before this command to move down that many lines. For example, 2j would move down two lines.
k / up arrow	Moves up one line. We may type a number before this command to move up that many lines. For example, 2k would move up two lines.
l / right arrow / Spacebar	Moves right (forward) one character. We may type a number before this command to move that many characters. For example, 2l would move two characters to the right.
w	Moves forward one word.
b	Moves backward one word.
e	Moves forward to the last character of the next word.
$	Moves to the end of the current line.
0	Moves to the beginning of the current line.
Enter	Moves down to the beginning of the next line.
Ctrl+f / Page Down	Moves forward (scrolls down) to the next page.
Ctrl+b / Page Up	Moves backward (scrolls up) to the previous page.
]]	Moves to the last line of the file.
[[	Moves to the first line of the file.

Table 2-6 Navigating within vi

Deleting Text

Commands listed in Table 2-7 carry out delete operations while in the command mode.

Command	Action
x	Deletes the character at the current cursor position. We may type a number before this command to delete that many characters. For example, 2x would remove two characters.
X	Deletes the character before the current cursor location. We may type a number before this command to delete that many characters. For example, 2X would remove two characters.
dw	Deletes the word or part of the word to the right of the current cursor location. We may type a number before this command to delete that many words. For example, 2dw would remove two words.
dd	Deletes the current line. We may type a number before this command to delete that many lines. For example, 2dd would remove two lines (current line plus next line).
D	Deletes at the current cursor position to the end of the current line.
:6,12d	Deletes lines 6 through 12.

Table 2-7 Deleting Text

Undoing and Repeating

Table 2-8 explicates the commands that undo the last change made and repeat the last command run.

Command	Action
u	Undoes the last command.
U	Undoes all the changes done on the current line.
:u	Undoes the previous last line mode command.
. (dot)	Repeats the last command run.
Ctrl+r	Repeats the last undone command.

Table 2-8 Undoing and Repeating

Searching and Replacing Text

Search and replace text functions are performed using the commands mentioned in Table 2-9.

Command	Action
/string	Searches forward for a string.
?string	Searches backward for a string.
n	Finds the next occurrence of a string. This would only work if we have run either a forward or a backward string search.
N	Finds the previous occurrence of a string. This would only work if we have run either a forward or a backward string search.
:%s/old/new	Searches and replaces the first occurrence of *old* with *new*. For example, to replace the first occurrence of profile with Profile, we would use *:%s/profile/Profile*.
:%s/old/new/g	Searches and replaces all occurrences of *old* with *new*. For example, to replace all the occurrences of profile with Profile in a file, we would use *:%s/profile/Profile/g*.

Table 2-9 Searching and Replacing Text

Copying, Moving, and Pasting Text

Table 2-10 describes the vi commands to perform copy, move, and paste functions.

Command	Action
yl	Yanks the current letter into the buffer. We may specify a number before this command to yank that many letters. For example, 2yl would yank two characters.
yw	Yanks the current word into the buffer. We may specify a number before this command to yank that many words. For example, 2yw would yank two words.
yy	Yanks the current line into the buffer. We may specify a number before this command to yank that many lines. For example, 2yy would yank two lines.
p	Pastes yanked data below the current line.
P	Pastes yanked data above the current line.
:1,3co5	Copies lines 1 through 3 and pastes them after line 5.

Command	Action
:4,6m8	Moves lines 4 through 6 after line 8.

Table 2-10 Copying, Moving, and Pasting Text

Changing Text

Use the commands given in Table 2-11 to change text. Some of these commands will switch you into the edit mode. To return to the command mode, press the Esc key.

Command	Action
cl	Changes the letter at the current cursor location.
cw	Changes the word (or part of the word) at the current cursor location to the end of the current word.
C	Changes text at the current cursor position to the end of the current line.
r	Replaces the character at the current cursor location with the character entered following this command.
R	Overwrites or replaces the text on the current line.
J	Joins the current line and the line below it.
xp	Switches the position of the character at the current cursor position with the character to the right of it.
~	Changes the letter case (uppercase to lowercase, and vice versa) at the current cursor location.

Table 2-11 Changing Text

Saving and Quitting vi

When you are done with modifications, you will want to save or discard them. Commands listed in Table 2-12 will help.

Command	Action
:w	Writes changes into the file without quitting vi.
:w file2	Writes changes into a new file called *file2* without quitting vi.
:w!	Writes changes to the file even if the file owner does not have write permission on the file.
:wq	Writes changes to the file and quits vi.
:wq!	Writes changes to the file and quits vi even if the file owner does not have write permission on the file.
:q	Quits vi if no modifications were made.
:q!	Quits vi if modifications were made, but we do not wish to save them.

Table 2-12 Saving and Quitting vi

Online Help

While working on the system, you may require help to obtain information about a command, its usage, and available options. RHEL offers online help via *man* (*manual*) pages. Manual pages are installed as part of the package installation, and provide detailed information on commands and configuration files including short and long description, usage, options, bugs, additional references, and the author. In addition to the man pages, *apropos*, *whatis*, and *info* commands, as well as documentation located in the */usr/share/doc* directory, are also available. These are also discussed in this section.

> **EXAM TIP:** If you need help with a command or configuration file, do not hesitate to use the man pages or refer to the documentation available in the /usr/share/doc directory.

Using man

Use the *man* command to view help for a command. The following example shows how to check man pages for the *passwd* command:

```
# man passwd
PASSWD(1)              User utilities              PASSWD(1)
NAME
     passwd - update user's authentication tokens
SYNOPSIS
     passwd [-k] [-l] [-u [-f]] [-d] [-e] [-n mindays] [-x maxdays]
     [-w warndays] [-i inactivedays] [-S] [--stdin] [username]
DESCRIPTION
     The passwd utility is used to update user's authentication
     token(s).
. . . . . . . .
     Manual page passwd(1) line 1 (press h for help or q to quit)
```

While we are in man pages, some common keys listed in Table 2-13 help us navigate efficiently.

Key	Action
Enter / Down arrow	Moves forward one line.
Up arrow	Moves backward one line.
f / Spacebar / Page down	Moves forward one page.
b / Page up	Moves backward one page.
d / u	Moves down / up half a page.
g / G	Moves to the beginning / end of the man pages.
:f	Displays line number and bytes being viewed.
q	Quits the man pages.
/pattern	Searches forward for the specified pattern.
?pattern	Searches backward for the specified pattern.
n / N	Finds the next / previous occurrence of a pattern.
H	Gives help on navigational keys.

Table 2-13 Navigating within man Pages

Open man pages for a command and navigate using the keys provided in Table 2-13 for practice.

man Sections

There are several sections within man pages. For example, section 1 refers to user commands, section 4 contains special files, section 5 describes system configuration files, section 8 includes system administration commands, and so on.

To search for help on file */etc/passwd*, issue the following:

```
# man 5 passwd
PASSWD(5)              Linux Programmer's Manual              PASSWD(5)
NAME
    passwd - password file
DESCRIPTION
    The /etc/passwd  file  is  a text file that describes user login
    accounts for the system.  It should have read permission  allowed
    for all users (many utilities, like ls(1) use it to map user IDs
    to usernames), but write access only for the superuser.
. . . . . . . .
Manual page passwd(5) line 1 (press h for help or q to quit)
```

Searching by Keyword

Sometimes we need to use a command but do not know its name. Linux allows a keyword search on installed manual pages using the *man* command with the *–k* option, or the *apropos* command. This command searches for the keyword in manual page names and descriptions. For instance, if we want to search the string "password", we run either of the following:

```
# man –k password
# apropos password
chage (1)             - change user password expiry information
chpasswd (8)          - update passwords in batch mode
cracklib-check (8)   - Check passwords using libcrack2
. . . . . . . .
```

Once we identify the command we were looking for, we can either check that command's man pages for usage or specify the --help or -? option with the command. For example, to get quick help on the *passwd* command, run either of the following:

```
# passwd --help
# passwd -?
Usage: passwd [OPTION...] <accountName>
 -k, --keep-tokens      keep non-expired authentication tokens
 -d, --delete           delete the password for the named account (root only)
 -l, --lock             lock the password for the named account (root only)
 -u, --unlock           unlock the password for the named account (root only)
. . . . . . . .
Help options:
 -?, --help             Show this help message
 --usage                Display brief usage message
```

The man database that stores all this information needs to be built with the *mandb* utility:

---

mandb

Purging old database entries in /usr/share/man...
mandb: warning: /usr/share/man/man8/fsck.fat.8.manpage-fix.gz: ignoring bogus filename
Processing manual pages under /usr/share/man...
Purging old database entries in /usr/share/man/hu...
. . . .
0 man subdirectories contained newer manual pages.
0 manual pages were added.
0 stray cats were added.
0 old database entries were purged.

You should run this command after adding packages to your system to ensure that the man database is updated with new information.

Displaying Short Description

The *whatis* command provides a quick method for searching the specified command or file in the man database for a short description. For instance, the following shows outputs of the command when run on *yum.conf* and *passwd* files:

whatis yum.conf
yum.conf (5)   - Configuration file for yum(8).
whatis passwd
passwd (1)   - update user's authentication tokens
sslpasswd (1ssl)   - compute password hashes
passwd (5)   - password file

The first output indicates that the specified file is a configuration file associated with the *yum* command, and the second output points to three entries for the *passwd* file (two commands and one password file).

We may alternatively run the *man* command with the –f option to get identical results:

man –f yum.conf
man –f passwd

The info Command

The *info* command is available as part of the info package to allow users to read command documentation as distributed by the GNU Project. It provides more detailed information than the *man* command. Documentation is divided into sections called *nodes*. The header is at the top of the screen and shows the name of the file being displayed, names of the current, next, and previous nodes, and the name of the node prior to the current node. The following example shows the first screen exhibited when this command is executed on the command *passwd*:

---

info passwd
```
File: *manpages*,  Node: passwd,  Up: (dir)
PASSWD(1)                   User utilities               PASSWD(1)
NAME
     passwd - update user's authentication tokens
SYNOPSIS
     passwd  [-k]  [-l]  [-u  [-f]]  [-d] [-e] [-n mindays] [-x maxdays] [-w
     warndays] [-i inactivedays] [-S] [--stdin] [username]
DESCRIPTION
     The passwd utility is used to update user's authentication token(s).
. . . . . . . .
-----Info: (*manpages*)passwd, 358 lines --Top--------------------------------------------
Welcome to Info version 5.1. Type h for help, m for menu item.
```

While viewing help with the *info* command, some common keys listed in Table 2-14 will help you navigate efficiently.

Key	Action
Down arrow	Moves forward one line.
Up arrow	Moves backward one line.
Spacebar	Moves forward one page.
Del	Moves backward one page.
q	Quits the info tutorial.
[	Goes to the previous node in the document.
]	Goes to the next node in the document.
t	Goes to the top node of this document.
s	Searches forward for the specified string.
{	Searches for the previous occurrence of the string.
}	Searches for the next occurrence of the string.

Table 2-14 Navigating within info Documentation

Open *info* for a command and navigate using the keys provided in Table 2-14 for practice.

Documentation in the /usr/share/doc Directory

The */usr/share/doc* directory stores documentation for all installed packages under sub-directories that match package names followed by their -<version>. For example, the entry for the gzip package looks like:

ll –d /usr/share/doc/gzip*
```
drwxr-xr-x.  2  root  root  84  Oct 28 22:47  /usr/share/doc/gzip-1.5
```

In this example, gzip is the name of the package followed by a dash and the package version 1.5. Now re-run the *ll* command but without –d to see what documentation is available for gzip:

ll /usr/share/doc/gzip-1.3.12
```
-rw-r--r--.  1  root  root      98  Aug 18 2009  AUTHORS
-rw-r--r--.  1  root  root  44706  Jun 17 2012  ChangeLog
-rw-r--r--.  1  root  root  18123  Jun 17 2012  NEWS
```

```
-rw-r--r--. 1 root root  6854 Jan  1 2012  README
-rw-r--r--. 1 root root 13262 Apr  6 2010  THANKS
-rw-r--r--. 1 root root  3684 Jan  1 2012  TODO
```

These files contain a huge amount of information about the gzip package.

Red Hat Enterprise Linux 7 Documentation

The Red Hat's documentation website at *docs.redhat.com* contains product documentation on RHEL7 in HTML, PDF, and EPUB formats. This set of documentation includes release and technical notes, and guides on installation, deployment, virtualization, Logical Volume Manager, storage administration, security, and SELinux. You can download any of these guides for reference at no charge.

Chapter Summary

We covered several topics in this chapter. We started by looking at the ssh command usage for accessing a remote RHEL system. We then looked at a variety of commands, most of which were intended for use by both privileged and non-privileged users. These commands included basic viewing tools, compression utilities, and archiving utilities. We learned about vi, one of the most common text editing tools used in the UNIX/Linux world, in sufficient detail.

We learned how to access online help on commands and configuration files. We saw how to search through the man pages for desired text. We know where to look for help when needed.

Chapter Review Questions

1. The *ssh* tool provides a non-secure tunnel over a network for accessing a RHEL system. True or False?
2. Name the file that the *who* command consults to display logged-in users.
3. A file compressed with *bzip2* can be uncompressed using *gunzip* command. True or False?
4. What is the use of the *apropos* command?
5. What does the *lastlog* command do?
6. What are the –R and –a options used for with the *ls* command?
7. Linux commands may be divided into privileged and non-privileged commands. True or False?
8. Which other command besides *uptime* can be used to display system load averages?
9. How can we display the line number and word count in a given file?
10. The *id* and *groups* commands are useful for listing a user identification. True or False.
11. Which file does the *last* command consult to display reports?
12. What type of information does section 5 in manual pages contain?
13. What information does the *lastb* command provide?
14. What is the function of the *pwd* command?
15. The *who* command may be used to view logged out users. True or False?
16. The *tar* command can be used to archive files with their SELinux contexts. True or False?
17. Which command can we use to display the tutorial of a command?
18. What are the three *ls** commands to view pci, usb, and cpu information?
19. The *star* command does not have the ability to include extended file attributes in archives. True or False?

Answers to Chapter Review Questions

1. False. The *ssh* command provides a secure tunnel over a network.
2. The *who* command consults the */var/run/utmp* file to list loggedin users.
3. False. The file will have to be uncompressed with either *bzip2* or *bunzip2*.
4. The *apropos* command can be used to perform a keyword search in the manual pages.
5. The *lastlog* command provides information about recent user logins.
6. The –R option is used for recursive directory listing and the –a option for listing hidden files.
7. True.
8. The *w* command may be used to display system load averages instead of the *uptime* command.
9. We can use the *wc* command to display line and word counts.
10. False. Only the *id* command is used for this purpose.
11. The *last* command consults the */var/log/wtmp* file to display reports.
12. Section 5 of the manual pages contain information on configuration files.
13. The *lastb* command reports the history of unsuccessful user login attempts.
14. The *pwd* command shows the absolute path of the current working directory.
15. False. The *who* command shows currently logged-in users only.
16. True. The *tar* command has the --selinux switch that provides this support.
17. We can use the *info* command to display the tutorial of a command.
18. The three commands are *lspci*, *lsusb*, and *lscpu*.
19. False. The *star* command does have the ability to include extended attributes in archives.

DIY Challenge Labs

The following labs are useful to strengthen most of the concepts and topics learned in this chapter. It is expected that you perform these labs without any additional help. A step-by-step guide is not provided, as the implementation of these labs requires the knowledge that has been presented in this chapter. Use defaults or your own thinking for missing information.

Lab 2-1: Navigate Linux Directory Tree

Log on to *host1* as *user1* and execute the *pwd* command to check your location in the directory tree. Run the *ls* command with appropriate switches to show files in the current directory along with all hidden files. Change directory into */etc* and run *pwd* again to confirm the directory change. Switch back to the directory where you were before and run *pwd* again to verify.

Lab 2-2: Verify User and Group Identity

Log on to *host1* as *user1* and execute the *logname*, *whoami*, *who*, and *w* commands one at a time. Verify the identity of *user1* by comparing the output of these commands. The output should show *user1* as the user logged on and running these commands. Execute the *id* and *groups* commands and verify the identity of *user1* by comparing the output of these commands. Identify the additional information that the *id* command provides but not the *groups* command. Record your results in a text file created with the *vi* editor in *user1*'s home directory.

Lab 2-3: Check User Login Attempts

Log on to *host1* as *root*, execute the *last* and *lastb* commands, and record in a file which users have recently logged in to and out of the system successfully and unsuccessfully. Also list the timestamp when the system was last rebooted. Use the *vi* editor to record your results.

Lab 2-4: Identify the System and Kernel

Log on to *host1* as *root* and execute the *hostname* and *uname* commands. Identify the system's name, kernel version, RHEL release, and the hardware architecture of this system. Record your results in a file using the *vi* editor.

Lab 2-5: Check and Modify System Date and Time

Log on to *host1* as *root* and execute the *date* and *timedatectl* commands to check the current system date and time. Identify the differences between the two outputs. Use *timedatectl* and change the system date to a date in January of the following year. Issue the *date* command and change the system time to one hour ahead of the current time. Observe the new date and time with both commands. Reset the date and time back to the current actual time using either the *date* or the *timedatectl* command.

Lab 2-6: Check System Uptime and Count Lines

Log on to *host1* as *root* and execute the *uptime* command. Identify the amount of time the system has been up for and the number of users currently logged on. Run the *wc* command and show how many lines, words, and bytes are in the */etc/profile* file.

Lab 2-7: Archive, List, and Restore Files

Log on to *host1* as *root* and execute the *tar* command to archive the contents of the entire */etc* directory tree. Run the *star* command and archive the */etc* directory contents again. Compare the file sizes of the two archives. Run the *gzip* and *bzip2* commands on these archives to produce compressed files, and compare their sizes. Run the commands to uncompress (*gunzip* and *bunzip2*) the files and then use the archiving tools to restore the contents of the */etc* directory.

Lab 2-8: Practice the vi Editor

Log on to *host1* as *user1* and create a file called *vipractice* in the home directory using the *vi* editor. Type (do not copy and paste) the first four sentences from Lab 2-2 in such a way that each sentence occupies one line (do not worry about line wrapping). Save the file and quit the editor. Open *vipractice* in the *vi* editor again and show line numbering. Copy the second and third lines to the end of the file to make the total number of lines in the file to six. Move the third line to make it the very first line. Go to the last line and append the contents of the *.bash_profile*. Substitute all occurrences of the string "Profile" with "Pro File" and all occurrences of the string "profile" with "pro file". Remove lines five to eight. Save the file and quit *vi*. Provide a count of lines, words, and characters in the *vipractice* file using the *wc* command.

## Chapter 03

Working with Files and File Permissions

This chapter describes the following major topics:

➤ The Red Hat Enterprise Linux directory structure
➤ Access files using absolute and relative pathnames
➤ Types of files
➤ Manage and manipulate files and directories including creating, listing, displaying, copying, moving, renaming, and removing them
➤ View and set control attributes on files and directories
➤ Search for files in the directory system
➤ Create file and directory links
➤ Permissions assigned to owners, owning group, and others
➤ Permission types – read, write, and execute
➤ Permission assignment modes – adding, revoking, and assigning
➤ Modify permissions using symbolic and octal notations
➤ Set default permissions on new files and directories
➤ Modify ownership and group membership
➤ Configure special permissions with setuid, setgid, and sticky bits
➤ Use setgid bit for group collaboration

RHCSA Objectives:

08. Create, delete, copy, and move files and directories
09. Create hard and soft links
10. List, set, and change standard ugo/rwx permissions
28. Create and configure set-GID directories for collaboration
30. Diagnose and correct file permission problems

Linux files are organized logically for ease of administration. This file organization is maintained in hundreds of directories located in larger containers called file systems. Red Hat Enterprise Linux follows the File system Hierarchy Standard (FHS) for file organization, which describes names, locations, and permissions for many file types and directories. File systems are primarily of two types: disk-based and memory-based, and they are used to store permanent and runtime data, respectively.

Files are static and dynamic, and are referenced using absolute and relative pathnames. Linux supports several different types of files and their type is based on the type of data they store. There are a number of management operations that can be performed on files and directories. Linux includes thousands of files and each file has certain default attributes that can be viewed or modified. There are tools available that prove to be very helpful in searching for files within a specified boundary and in linking them as desired.

Permissions are set on files and directories to restrict their access to authorized users only. Users are grouped into three distinct categories. Each user category is then assigned required permissions. Permissions can be modified using one of two available methods. The user mask may be defined for individual users so that the new files and directories they create always get preset permissions. Every file in Linux has an owner and a group associated with it. The OS offers three additional permission bits to control user access to certain executable files and shared directories. A directory with one of these permission bits set can be used for group collaboration.

File System Tree

Linux uses the conventional hierarchical directory structure where directories may contain both files and sub-directories. Sub-directories may further hold more files and sub-directories. A sub-directory, also referred to as a *child* directory, is a directory located under a *parent* directory. That parent directory is a sub-directory of some other higher-level directory. In other words, the Linux directory structure is similar to an inverted tree where the top of the tree is the root of the directory, and branches and leaves are sub-directories and files, respectively. The root of the directory is represented by the forward slash (/) character, and this is the point where the entire file system structure is ultimately connected. The forward slash character is also used as a directory separator in a path, such as */etc/rc.d/init.d/network*.

In this example, the *etc* sub-directory is located under /, making *root* the parent of *etc* (which is a child). *rc.d* (child) is located under *etc* (parent), *init.d* (child) is located under *rc.d* (parent), and at the very bottom, *network* (leave) is located under *init.d* (parent).

Each directory has a parent directory and a child directory, with the exception of the root and the lowest level directories. The root directory has no parent and the lowest level sub-directory has no child.

 The term sub-directory is used for a directory that has a parent directory.

The hierarchical directory structure keeps related information together in a logical fashion. Compare this concept with a file cabinet containing several drawers, with each drawer storing multiple file folders.

Two file systems, / and /boot, are created during a default RHEL7 installation. However, the custom installation procedure covered in Chapter 01 "Installing RHEL7 on Physical Computer Using Local DVD" allows us to create /var, /usr, /tmp, /opt, and /home file systems besides / and /boot. The main directories under the / and other file systems are shown in Figure 3-1. Some of these directories hold *static* data while others contain *dynamic* (or *variable*) information. Static data refers to file contents that are usually not modified, and dynamic or variable data refers to file contents that are modified and updated as required. Static directories normally contain commands, library routines, kernel files, device files, etc., and dynamic directories hold log files, status files, configuration files, temporary files, and so on.

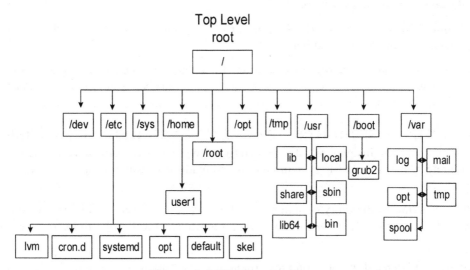

Figure 3-1 File System Tree

A brief description of disk-based and virtual file systems is provided in the following sub-sections.

The Root File System (/) – Disk-Based

The root file system is the top-level file system in the FHS and contains many higher-level directories holding specific information. Some of the key directories are:

/etc: The *etcetera* directory holds system configuration files. Some common sub-directories are— *systemd*, *default*, *lvm*, and *skel*—which contain configuration files for systemd, defaults for user accounts and some other services, the Logical Volume Manager, and per-user shell startup template files, respectively.

/root: This is the default home directory location for the *root* user.

/media: This directory is used by the system to automatically mount removable media, such as floppy, CD, DVD, USB, and Zip drives.

/mnt: This directory is used to mount a file system temporarily.

The Boot File System (/boot) – Disk-Based

The /boot file system contains the Linux kernel, boot support files, and boot configuration files. The default size of this file system is 500MB, and it may be expanded as part of the preparation to update the kernel.

The Variable File System (/var) – Disk-Based

/var contains data that frequently changes while the system is operational. Files holding log, status, spool, lock, and other dynamic data are located in this file system.

Some common sub-directories under */var* are:

/var/log: This is the storage for most system log files, such as system logs, boot logs, failed user logs, user logs, installation logs, cron logs, mail logs, etc.

/var/opt: For additional software installed in */opt*, this directory stores log, status, and other variable data files for that software.

/var/spool: Directories that hold print jobs, cron jobs, mail messages, and other queued items before being sent out are located here.

/var/tmp: Large temporary files or temporary files that need to exist for longer periods of time than what is allowed in */tmp* are stored here. These files survive system reboots and are not automatically deleted.

The UNIX System Resources File System (/usr) – Disk-Based

This file system contains general files related to the system, with some portions perhaps shared with other remote systems. This file system is mounted read-only. Some of the important sub-directories under */usr* are:

/usr/lib: The *library* directory contains shared library routines required by many commands and programs located in the */usr/bin* and */usr/sbin* directories, as well as by the kernel and other programs.

/usr/bin: The *binary* directory contains crucial user executable commands.

/usr/sbin: Most commands required at system boot are located in this *system binary* directory as well as most commands requiring root privileges to run. In other words, this directory contains crucial system administration commands that are not intended for execution by regular users (although they can still run a few of them). This directory is not included in the default search path for normal users because of the nature of data it contains.

/usr/local: This directory serves as a system administrator repository for storing commands and tools downloaded from the web, developed in-house, or obtained elsewhere. These commands and tools are not generally included with the original Linux distribution. In particular, */usr/local/bin* holds executables and */usr/local/etc* contains their configuration files.

/usr/include: This directory contains header files for *C* language.

/usr/src: This directory is used to store source code.

/usr/share: This is the directory location for man pages, documentation, sample templates, configuration files, etc. that may be shared on multi-vendor Linux platforms with heterogeneous hardware architectures.

The Optional File System (/opt) – Disk-Based

This file system holds additional software installed on the system. A sub-directory is created for each installed software.

The Home File System (/home) – Disk-Based

The */home* file system is designed to hold user *home* directories. Each user account is assigned a home directory in which to save personal files. Each home directory is owned by the user the directory is assigned to, with no access to other users.

The Devices File System (/dev) – Virtual

The */dev* file system contains device nodes for physical hardware and virtual devices. The Linux kernel communicates with these devices through corresponding device nodes located here. These device nodes are created and deleted by the *udevd* service as necessary.

There are two types of device files: *character* (or *raw*) device files and *block* device files. The kernel accesses devices using either or both types of device files.

Character devices are accessed serially, with streams of bits transferred during kernel and device communication. Examples of such devices are serial printers, mice, keyboards, terminals, tape drives, etc.

Block devices are accessed in a parallel fashion, with data exchanged in blocks (parallel) during kernel and device communication. Data on block devices is accessed randomly. Examples of block devices are hard disk drives, optical drives, parallel printers, etc.

The Process File System (/proc) – Virtual

The */proc* file system maintains information about the current state of the running kernel, including details on CPU, memory, disks, partitioning, file systems, networking, and running processes. This virtual file system contains a hierarchy of sub-directories containing thousands of zero-length files pointing to relevant data that is maintained by the kernel in the memory. This virtual directory structure simply provides an easy interface to interact with kernel-maintained information. The */proc* file system is automatically managed by the system.

The contents in */proc* are created in memory at boot time, updated during runtime, and destroyed at reboot time. Underneath this file system are stored current hardware configuration and status information. A directory listing of */proc* is provided below:

```
# ll /proc
dr-xr-xr-x.  8 root    root       0  Nov 17 14:22  1
dr-xr-xr-x.  8 root    root       0  Nov 17 14:22  10
dr-xr-xr-x.  8 root    root       0  Nov 17 14:23  1000
dr-xr-xr-x.  8 root    root       0  Nov 17 14:23  1009
. . . . . . . .
```

As mentioned, this file system contains thousands of files and sub-directories. Some sub-directory names are numerical and they point to information about specific processes, with process IDs matching the sub-directory names. Within each sub-directory, there are files and further sub-directories, which include information such as memory segment specific to that particular process. Other files and sub-directories point to configuration data for system components. If you wish to view configuration information for a specific item, such as the CPU or memory, you can *cat* the contents of *cpuinfo* and *meminfo* files as shown below:

```
# cat /proc/cpuinfo
processor     : 0
vendor_id     : GenuineIntel
cpu family    : 6
model         : 42
model name    : Intel(R) Core(TM) i7-2760QM CPU @ 2.40GHz
stepping      : 7
cpu MHz       : 2423.437
. . . . . . . .
# cat /proc/meminfo (also shows available memory)
MemTotal:      7889040 kB
MemFree:        757800 kB
MemAvailable:  1451248 kB
. . . . . . . .
```

The data located under */proc* is referenced by a number of system utilities, including *top*, *ps*, *uname*, and *vmstat*, for display purposes.

The System File System (/sys) – Virtual

Information about configured hotplug hardware devices is stored and maintained in the */sys* file system. This information is referenced for loading kernel modules, creating device nodes in the */dev* directory, and configuring each device. This file system is auto-maintained as well.

The Temporary File System (/tmp) – Virtual

This file system is a repository for temporary storage. Many programs create temporary files as they run or while they are being installed. The contents of this file system are automatically deleted at system reboots.

Absolute and Relative Pathnames

A *path* is like a road map showing how to get from one place in the directory tree to another. It uniquely identifies a particular file or directory by its absolute or relative location in the directory structure.

At any given time, the directory you are located in within the tree is referred to as your *present* (or *current*) working directory. When you log in to the system, you are placed in your home directory by default. Use the *pwd* command to determine your current location in the tree.

Absolute Path

An *absolute path* (a.k.a. a *full path* or a *fully qualified pathname*) points to a file or directory in relation to /. It always starts with the forward slash (/) character. The *pwd* command displays the current location in the tree.

```
# pwd
/root
```

The output indicates /root as the current location in the directory hierarchy. This path begins with /, which identifies it as a full path.

Relative Path

A *relative path* points to a file or directory in relation to your current location in the directory tree. A relative path never begins with a forward slash; rather it always begins in one of the following two ways:

With two periods: This represents a parent directory in relation to your current working directory. A parent directory is one level higher than the current working directory. For example, to go one level up to the parent directory, type:

cd ..

With a sub-directory name: Suppose you are in the / directory and want to go to the *sysconfig* sub-directory under */etc*, you would run the following:

cd etc/sysconfig

File Types

RHEL supports several different types of files. Some of the common file types are—regular files, directory files, executable files, symbolic link files, and device files—and are described in the following sub-sections.

Regular Files

Regular files may contain text or binary data. These files may be shell scripts or commands in the binary form. When you list a directory, all line entries for files in the output that begin with the – sign represent regular files:

ll /bin

```
. . . . . . . .
-rwxr-xr-x. 1  root  root      15392 Feb 12 2014  lastlog
-rwxr-xr-x. 1  root  root      19912 Jan 26 2014  lchfn
-rwxr-xr-x. 1  root  root      15776 Jan 26 2014  lchsh
. . . . . . . .
```

You can use a command called *file* to determine the type of a file. For example, the following shows that *.bash_profile* in the *root* user's home directory contains ascii text:

file .bash_profile
.bash_profile: ASCII text

Directory Files

Directories are logical containers that are used to hold files and sub-directories. Run *ll* on the */root* directory and you should see an output similar to:

ll /root

```
. . . . . . . .
drwxr-xr-x. 2  root  root    6 Oct 29 08:00  Desktop
drwxr-xr-x. 2  root  root    6 Oct 29 08:00  Documents
```

```
drwxr-xr-x. 2 root root   6 Oct 29 08:00  Downloads
. . . . . . . .
```

The letter d at the beginning of each line entry identifies the file as a directory. You can use the *file* command to see what it reports it as. For example, the following shows that */root* is a directory file:

file /root
/root: directory

Executable Files

Executable files could be commands in the binary format or shell scripts. In other words, any file that can be run is an executable file. A file that has an x in the fourth, seventh, or the tenth field in the output of the *ll* command is executable.

ll /usr/sbin

```
. . . . . . . .
-rwxr-xr-x. 1 root root    46456 Mar 17 2014  whatis
-rwxr-xr-x. 1 root root    20656 Mar 28 2014  whereis
-rwxr-xr-x. 1 root root    24336 Jan 27 2014  which
. . . . . . . .
```

The *file* command reports the type of an executable file as follows:

file /usr/bin/whoami
/usr/bin/whoami: ELF 64-bit LSB executable, x86-64, version 1 (SYSV), dynamically linked (uses shared libs), for GNU/Linux 2.6.32, BuildID[sha1]=0x130a11a3f5598dddb581134373700d6554fa6527, stripped

Symbolic Link Files

A *symbolic link* (a.k.a. a *soft link* or a *symlink*) may be considered a shortcut to another file or directory. When you issue *ll* on a symbolically linked file or directory, you will notice two things. One, the line entry begins with the letter l; and two, there is an arrow pointing to the linked file or directory. For example:

ll /usr/sbin/vigr
lrwxrwxrwx. 1 root root 4 Oct 28 22:47 /usr/sbin/vigr -> vipw

The *file* command can be used to confirm that the *vigr* file is a symlink:

file /usr/sbin/vigr
/usr/sbin/vigr: symbolic link to `vipw'

Device Files

Each piece of hardware in the system has an associated file used by the kernel to communicate with it. This type of file is called a *device file*. There are two types of device files: a *character* (or *raw*) device file and a *block* device file. The following example uses the *ll* command to display device files:

```
# ll /dev/sd*
brw-rw----. 1 root disk 8, 0 Nov 17 14:22 /dev/sda
brw-rw----. 1 root disk 8, 1 Nov 17 14:22 /dev/sda1
brw-rw----. 1 root disk 8, 2 Nov 17 14:22 /dev/sda2
# ll /dev/usb*
crw-------. 1 root root 251, 0 Nov 17 14:22 /dev/usbmon0
crw-------. 1 root root 251, 1 Nov 17 14:22 /dev/usbmon1
crw-------. 1 root root 251, 2 Nov 17 14:22 /dev/usbmon2
```

The first character in each line entry tells if the file type is block or character. A b denotes a block device file and a c represents a character device file. You can use the *file* command to determine their types:

```
# file /dev/sda
/dev/sda: block special
# file /dev/tty0
/dev/usbmon0: character special
```

File and Directory Operations

This section elaborates on various management operations that can be performed on files and directories. These operations include creating, listing, displaying contents of, copying, moving, renaming, and deleting files and directories. These are common operations that *root* and all normal users usually perform.

Creating Files and Directories

Files can be created in multiple ways; however, there is only one command to create directories.

Creating Files Using the touch Command

The *touch* command creates an empty file. If the file already exists, it updates the time stamp on it to the current system date and time. Execute the following as *user1* in their home directory to create *file1*, and then run the *ll* command to verify:

```
$ cd
$ touch file1
$ ll file1
-rw-rw-r--. 1 user1 user1 0 Nov 26 10:07 file1
```

As expected, the fifth field in the output is 0, meaning that *file1* is created with zero bytes. Now, if you re-run the command on *file1*, you will notice that it gets an updated time:

```
$ touch file1
$ ll file1
-rw-rw-r--. 1 user1 user1 0 Nov 26 10:14 file1
```

Creating Files Using the cat Command

The *cat* command allows you to create short text files:

```
$ cat > newfile
```

Nothing is displayed when you execute this command because the system is waiting on you to input something; it expects you to enter text that it will capture into *newfile*. Press Ctrl+d when done to save and return to the shell prompt.

Creating Files Using the vi (vim) Editor
You can use the vi editor to create and modify text files. Refer to Chapter 02 "Using Basic Linux Tools" on how to use this tool.

Creating Directories Using the mkdir Command
The *mkdir* command is used to create directories. This command shows an output if you run it with the –v option. The following example demonstrates the creation of a directory called *scripts.dir1* in *user1* user's home directory (*/home/user1*):

$ cd
$ pwd
/home/user1
$ mkdir scripts.dir1
mkdir: created directory 'scripts.dir1'

You must have appropriate permissions to create a directory; otherwise, an error message complaining of a lack of permissions is generated.

You can create a hierarchy of sub-directories by specifying the –p option with *mkdir*. In the following example, *mkdir* creates the hierarchy *scripts.dir2/perl/per5* in *user1*'s home:

$ mkdir –p scripts.dir2/perl/perl5 –v
mkdir: created directory 'scripts.dir2'
mkdir: created directory 'scripts.dir2/perl'
mkdir: created directory 'scripts.dir2/perl/perl5'

Listing Files and Directories
Use the *ll* command to list files and directories. This command shows the details for each listed file and directory in nine columns. For instance:

-rw-rw-r--.   1 user1 user1 0 Nov 26 10:14 file1
drwxrwxr-x. 2 user1 user1 6 Nov 26 10:48 scripts.dir

Each column in the above output furnishes a unique piece of information about the file or directory:

Column 1: The first character tells the file type and the next nine characters indicate permissions.
Column 2: Displays the number of links.
Column 3: Shows the owner name.
Column 4: Displays the owning group name.
Column 5: Identifies the file size in bytes. For directories, this number reflects the number of blocks being used by the directory to hold information about its contents.

Columns 6, 7, and 8: Display the month, day of the month, and time of creation or last modification.
Column 9: Indicates the name of the file or directory.

Displaying File Contents

Linux offers several tools for showing file contents. Directory contents are simply the files and sub-directories that it contains. Use the *ll* or the *ls* command as explained earlier to view directory contents.

For file viewing, you can use the *cat, more, less, head,* and *tail* commands. These tools are explained below.

Using the cat Command

cat displays the contents of a text file. In the example below, the *.bash_profile* file in *user1* 's home directory is displayed with the *cat* command:

$ cat /home/user1/.bash_profile
# Get the aliases and functions
if [-f ~/.bashrc]; then
    . ~/.bashrc
fi
# User specific environment and startup programs
PATH=$PATH:$HOME/.local/bin:$HOME/bin
export PATH

Using the more and less Commands

more can be used to view long text files one page at a time, starting at the beginning. In the example below, */etc/profile* is displayed with *more*. This command shows the percentage of the file being viewed in the last line.

$ more /etc/profile
. . . .
    USER="`id -un`"
--More--(43%)

Navigation keys listed in Table 3-1 are helpful while you are in a *more* session.

Key	Purpose
Spacebar / f	Scrolls forward one screen.
Enter	Scrolls forward one line.
b	Scrolls backward one screen.
d	Scrolls forward half a screen.
h	Displays help.
q	Quits and returns to the command prompt.
/string	Searches forward for a string.
?string	Searches backward for a string.
n / N	Finds the next / previous occurrence of a string.

Table 3-1 Navigating with more or less

less is similar to the *more* command but it offers some extended capabilities. It does not need to read the entire file before it starts to show it, thus making it faster than *more*. In the example below, */etc/profile* is shown with *less*:

$ less /etc/profile

. . . .
   USER="`id -un`"
/etc/profile

The same navigation keys listed in Table 3-1 are also helpful when viewing a large file with *less*.

Using the head and tail Commands

head displays the first few lines of a text file. By default, it shows the first ten lines. See the example below:

$ head /etc/profile
/etc/profile

System wide environment and startup programs, for login setup
Functions and aliases go in /etc/bashrc

It's NOT a good idea to change this file unless you know what you
are doing. It's much better to create a custom.sh shell script in
/etc/profile.d/ to make custom changes to your environment, as this
will prevent the need for merging in future updates.

There are three empty lines in the above output as well. You can specify a number with the command as an argument and it will show you that many lines only. For example, to view the first three lines from */etc/profile*:

$ head –3 /etc/profile
/etc/profile

System wide environment and startup programs, for login setup

tail, on the other hand, displays the last ten lines of a file by default unless a number is supplied to alter its behavior. The following example shows the last ten lines from */etc/profile*:

$ tail /etc/profile
    if ["${-#*i}" != "$-"]; then
     . "$i"
    else
     . "$i" >/dev/null
    fi
  fi
done
unset i
unset -f pathmunge

And the following example shows only the last three lines from the same file:

$ tail –3 /etc/profile
done
unset i
unset -f pathmunge

The *tail* command proves to be very useful when you wish to view a log file while it is being updated. The –f option enables this function. The following example shows how to view the system log file */var/log/messages* in real time:

 # tail –f /var/log/messages

Copying Files and Directories
The copy operation duplicates a file or directory. There is a single command called *cp* that is used for this purpose.

Copying Files
The *cp* command copies one or more files to either the current directory or another. If you want to duplicate a file in the same directory, you must give a different name to the target file. If you want to copy a file to a different directory, you can use the same file name or different. Consider the following examples.

To copy *file1* as *newfile1* in the same directory:

$ cp file1 newfile1

To copy *file1* by the same name to another existing directory called *scripts.dir1*:

$ cp file1 scripts.dir1

By default, the copy operation overwrites the destination (if it exists) without giving a warning. Use the –i option to instruct the *cp* command to prompt for confirmation before overwriting:

$ cp –i file1 scripts.dir1
cp: overwrite `scripts.dir1/file1'?

By default, you do not need to specify the –i option for yes/no confirmation if you are attempting to copy a file to overwrite the destination file as *root*. There is a pre-defined alias "alias cp='cp –i'" in the *root* user's ~/.*bashrc* file that takes care of that.

Copying Directories
The *cp* command with the –r (recursive) option copies an entire directory tree to another location. In the following example, *scripts.dir1* is copied to *scripts.dir2* and then the directory contents of *scripts.dir2* is displayed for validation:

$ cp –r scripts.dir1 scripts.dir2

$ ll scripts.dir2
drwxrwxr-x. 2 user1 user1 18 Nov 26 11:27 scripts.dir1

You may want to use the –i option for overwrite confirmation.

Moving and Renaming Files and Directories

A file or directory can be moved within the same file system or to another. Within the file system move, a corresponding entry is added to the target directory and the source entry is removed. In this case, the actual data remains intact. On the other hand, a move to a different file system physically moves the file or directory contents to the new location.

A rename simply changes the name of a file or directory; data is not touched.

Moving and Renaming Files

The *mv* command is used to move or rename files. The –i option can be specified for user confirmation if a file by that name already exists. The following example moves *file1* to *scripts.dir1* and prompts for confirmation:

$ mv –i file1 scripts.dir1
mv overwrite: scripts.dir1/file1? (y/n)

By default, you do not need to specify the –i option for yes/no confirmation if you are attempting to move a file to overwrite the destination file as *root*. There is a pre-defined alias "alias mv='mv –i'" in the *root* user's ~/.bashrc file that takes care of that.

To rename *newfile* as *newfile1*:

$ mv newfile newfile1

You can use the –i option with *mv*, if needed.

Moving and Renaming Directories

To move a directory along with its contents to somewhere else or simply change the name of the directory, use the *mv* command. For example, to move *scripts.dir1* into *scripts.dir2* (*scripts.dir2* must exist, otherwise it will simply rename it), issue the following:

$ mv scripts.dir1 scripts.dir2

To rename *scripts.dir2* as *scripts.dir20*:

$ mv scripts.dir2 scripts.dir20

Removing Files and Directories

The remove operation deletes a file entry from the directory structure and marks its data space as free. For a directory, it deletes corresponding entries from the file system structure.

Removing Files

You can remove a file using the *rm* command, which deletes one or more specified files at once. The following example deletes *newfile*:

$ rm newfile

The –i option can be used to prevent accidental removals. The option instructs the command to prompt for confirmation before proceeding with the removal. See the following example:

$ rm –i newfile
rm: remove regular empty file 'newfile'?

By default, you do not need to specify the –i option for yes/no confirmation if you are attempting to remove a file as *root*. There is a pre-defined alias "alias rm='rm –i'" in the *root* user's *~/.bashrc* file that takes care of that.

Removing Directories

There are two commands available to remove directories, which are demonstrated in the following examples.

Use the *rmdir* command to remove an empty directory:

$ rmdir scripts.dir20

Use the *rm* command with the –r switch to remove a non-empty directory:

$ rm –r scripts.dir10

You can provide the –i option with *rm* to instruct the command to prompt for confirmation for each file being deleted.

File and Directory Control Attributes

There are certain attributes that may be set on a file or directory in order to control what can or cannot be done to it. For example, you can enable attributes on a file or directory so that no users, including *root*, can delete, modify, rename, or compress it. These attributes can be set on files and directories located in an ext3, ext4, or xfs file system.

Table 3-2 lists common control attributes.

Attribute	Effect on File or Directory
a (append)	File can only be appended.
A	Prevents updating the access time.
c (compressed)	File is automatically compressed on the disk.
D	Changes on a directory are written synchronously to the disk.
e (extent format)	File uses extents for mapping the blocks on disk.
i (immutable)	File cannot be changed, renamed, or deleted.
S (synchronous)	Changes in a file are written synchronously to the disk.

Table 3-2 File and Directory Control Attributes

There are two commands—*lsattr* and *chattr*—that are used for attribute management. The first command displays the attributes and the second sets the specified attributes. The following examples demonstrate the usage of these commands with the assumption that you are in the */root* directory and *file1* exists.

To list current attributes for *file1*:

> # **lsattr file1**
> ---------------- file1

The output indicates the absence of control attributes on the file. To allow only append operation on this file, use the *chattr* command:

> # **chattr +a file1**
> # **lsattr file1**
> -----a---------- file1

Now, try copying the contents of */etc/fstab* file to it:

> # **cat /etc/fstab > file1**
> -bash: file1: Operation not permitted

However, if you attempt an append operation, it will work:

> # **cat /etc/fstab >> file1**

Now, add the immutable flag to this file to prevent it from being deleted or modified:

> # **chattr +i file1**
> # **lsattr file1**
> ----ia---------- file1

If you try to delete it now, this is what you will get:

> # **rm file1**
> rm: remove regular file `file1'? **y**
> rm: cannot remove 'file1': Operation not permitted

To unset both attributes:

> # **chattr –ia file1**

Finding Files

A typical running RHEL system has a few hundred thousand files distributed across various file systems. Sometimes it is imperative to look for one or more files based on certain criteria. One example would be to find all files owned by employees who left the company over a year ago. Another example would be to search for all the files that have been modified in the past 20 days by a specific user. For such situations RHEL offers a command called *find*. You supply your search criteria and this command gets you the result on the screen or redirect to a file. You can also instruct this utility to execute a command on the files as they are found. This command is expounded in the following sub-section.

Using the find Command

The *find* command recursively searches the directory tree, finds files that match the specified criteria, and optionally performs an action on the files as they are found. This powerful tool can be tailored to look for files in a number of ways. The search criteria may include tracking for files by name, ownership, owning group, permissions, inode number, last access or modification time, size, and file type. Figure 3-2 shows the command syntax.

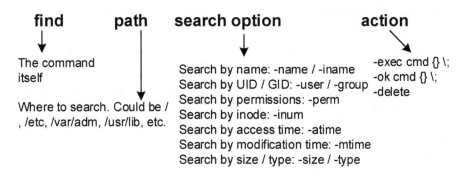

Figure 3-2 Find Command Syntax

With the *find* command, files that match the specified criteria are located and the full path to each file is displayed on the screen by default. Let's look at a few examples.

To search for a file called *newfile* by its name in *user1*'s home directory (assuming *newfile* exists):

$ **cd**
$ **find . –name newfile –print**

–print is optional. The *find* command, by default, displays the results on the screen. You do not have to specify this option.

To search for files and directories in */dev* that begin with vg00 followed by any characters. The –iname option directs the command to perform a case-insensitive search.

\# **find /dev –iname vg00***
/dev/vg00
/dev/mapper/vg00-home
/dev/mapper/vg00-root
/dev/mapper/vg00-swap

To find files smaller than 1MB in size in *root*'s home directory:

\# **find ~ –size –1M**
/root/.cache/abrt/applet_dirlist
/root/.local/share/gnome-settings-daemon/input-sources-converted

---

/root/.local/share/folks/relationships.ini
/root/.local/share/tracker/data/.meta.isrunning

. . . .

The tilde ~ character represents a user's home directory.

To find files larger than 40MB in size in */usr* directory:

find /usr –size +40M
/usr/lib/locale/locale-archive
/usr/lib/jvm/java-1.7.0-openjdk-1.7.0.51-2.4.5.5.el7.x86_64/jre/lib/rt.jar
/usr/lib64/firefox/libxul.so
/usr/share/icons/gnome/icon-theme.cache

To find files in the entire root file system with ownership set to *user1* and group membership set to any group other than *user1*:

find / –user user1 –not –group user1
/var/spool/mail/user1

To find files in the */etc* directory that were modified more than 2000 days ago:

find /etc –mtime +2000
/etc/xdg/menus/documentation.menu
/etc/xdg/menus/server-settings.menu
/etc/xdg/menus/settings.menu
/etc/xdg/menus/start-here.menu

To find files in the */var* directory that were modified exactly 12 days ago:

find /var –mtime 12
/var/log/sa/sa14
/var/log/sa/sar14

To search for character device files in the */dev* directory with permissions set to 666:

find /dev –type c –perm 666
/dev/kvm
/dev/net/tun
/dev/fuse
/dev/ptmx
/dev/tty
/dev/urandom
/dev/random
/dev/full
/dev/zero
/dev/null

To search for character device files in the *dev* directory that are world writeable:

 # find /dev –type c –perm –222
/dev/kvm
/dev/net/tun
/dev/fuse
/dev/ptmx
/dev/tty
/dev/urandom
/dev/random
/dev/full
/dev/zero
/dev/null

To search for *core* files in the entire directory tree and delete them as they are found without prompting for confirmation:

 # find / –name core –exec rm {} \;

 The pattern {} \; is part of the syntax and must be defined that way.

There are numerous other options available with the *find* command. Refer to the command's man pages and try some of them out.

Linking Files and Directories

Each file within a file system has several attributes assigned to it at the time of its creation. These attributes are collectively referred to as the file's *metadata*, and they change when the file is accessed or modified. A file's metadata includes several pieces of information, such as the file's type, size, permissions, owner's name, owner's group name, last access/modification time, ACL settings, link count, number of allocated blocks, and pointers to the location in the file system where the file data is actually stored. This metadata information takes 128-byte space in the file system for each file, and this tiny storage space is referred to- as the file's *inode* (index node). The inode is assigned a unique numeric identifier that is used by the kernel for accessing, tracking, and managing the file. The inode does not store the file's name in its metadata; the file name and corresponding inode number mapping is maintained in the directory's metadata.

Linking files or directories creates additional instances for them, but all point to the same physical data location in the directory tree. Linked files may or may not have identical inode numbers and metadata depending on how they are linked.

Linux has two ways of creating file and directory links, and they are referred to as soft and hard links.

Soft Link

A *soft* link (a.k.a. a *symbolic* link or a *symlink*) makes it possible to associate one file with another. It is similar to a shortcut in MS Windows where the actual file is resident somewhere in the directory structure but we may have multiple shortcuts (or pointers) with different names pointing to it. This allows accessing the file via the actual file name as well as any of the shortcuts. Each soft link has a unique inode number that stores the path to the file it is linked with.

A soft link can cross file system boundaries and can be used to link directories.

To create a soft link for *newfile* as *newfile10* in the same directory, use the *ln* command with the –s option:

```
$ cd
$ ln –s newfile newfile10
```

where:

> *newfile* is an existing file (create it if it does not exist)
> *newfile10* is soft-linked to *newfile*

After you have created the link, issue *ll* with –i and notice the letter l as the first character in the second column of the output. Also notice the arrow pointing from the linked file to the original file. Both of these signs indicate that *newfile10* is merely a pointer to *newfile*. The –i option displays associated inode numbers in the first column.

```
$ ll –i newfile*
1219 -rw-rw-r--.  1 user1 user1 0 Nov 27 16:13 newfile
1220 lrwxrwxrwx. 1 user1 user1 7 Nov 27 16:13 newfile10 -> newfile
```

If you remove the original file (*newfile* in this case), the link *newfile10* will stay but points to something that does not exist.

RHEL7 has four soft-linked directories in the / file system. You can list them with the *ll* command:

```
$ ll /
lrwxrwxrwx.  1  root  root   7  Oct 28 22:44  bin -> usr/bin
lrwxrwxrwx.  1  root  root   7  Oct 28 22:44  lib -> usr/lib
lrwxrwxrwx.  1  root  root   9  Oct 28 22:44  lib64 -> usr/lib64
lrwxrwxrwx.  1  root  root   8  Oct 28 22:44  sbin -> usr/sbin
```

The syntax for creating soft-linked directories is exactly the same as that for files.

Hard Link

A *hard* link associates one or more files with a single inode number, making all files indistinguishable from one another. This implies that the files will have identical permissions, ownership, time stamp, and file contents. Changes made to any of the files will be reflected in the other linked files as well. All hard-linked files share an identical data location.

A hard link cannot cross file system boundaries, and cannot be used to link directories because of restrictions within the operating system designed to avoid potential issues with some commands.

The following example uses the *ln* command and creates a hard link for *newfile2* located under */home/user1* to *newfile20* in the same directory (create *newfile20* as it currently does not exist):

```
$ cd
```

```
$ ln newfile2 newfile20
```

After creating the link, run *ll* with the –i option:

```
$ ll –i newfile2*
1221  -rw-rw-r--.  2  user1  user1  0  Nov 27 16:22  newfile2
1221  -rw-rw-r--.  2  user1  user1  0  Nov 27 16:22  newfile20
```

Look at the first and third columns. The first column indicates the common inode number and the third column tells you the number of hard links that each file has. *newfile2* points to *newfile20*, and vice versa. If you remove the original file (*newfile2* in this example), you will still have access to the data through the linked file *newfile20*.

File and Directory Permissions

As you know, Linux is a multi-user operating system that allows hundreds of users the ability to log in and work concurrently. Also, the operating system has hundreds of thousands of files and directories that it must maintain securely in order to warrant a successful system and application operation from a security standpoint. Given these features, it is imperative for us as system administrators to regulate user access to files and directories, and grant them appropriate rights to carry out their designated functions without jeopardizing system security. This control of permissions on files and directories for users may also be referred to as user *access rights*.

Determining Access Permissions

Access permissions on files and directories allow administrative control over which users (permission classes) can access them and to what level (permission types). File and directory permissions discussed in this section are referred to as standard ugo/rwx permissions.

Permission Classes

Users are categorized into three unique classes for maintaining file security through access rights. These classes are described in Table 3-3.

Permission Class	Description
User (u)	The owner of file or directory. Usually, the file creator is its owner.
Group (g)	A set of users that need identical access on files and directories that they share. Group information is maintained in the /etc/group file and users are assigned to groups according to shared file access needs.
Others (o)	All other users on the system except for the owner and group members. Also called public.

Table 3-3 Permission Classes

Permission Types

Permissions control what actions can be performed on a file or directory and by whom. There are three types of permissions, as defined in Table 3-4.

Perm Type	Symbol	File	Directory
Read	r	Lets us view file contents and copy them to another file.	Lets us view contents with the ll command.
Write	w	Allows us to modify file contents.	Allows us to create, remove, or rename files and sub-directories.
Execute	x	Lets us execute a file.	Allows us to cd into the directory.

Table 3-4 Permission Types

If a read, write, or execute permission is not desired, the – sign is used to represent its absence.

Permission Modes

A permission mode is used to add, revoke, or assign a permission type to a permission class. Table 3-5 shows various permission modes.

Permission Mode	Description
Add (+)	Allocates permissions.
Revoke (-)	Removes permissions.
Assign (=)	Allocates permissions to owner, group members, and public at once.

Table 3-5 Permission Modes

We can view permission settings on files and directories using the *ll* command. This information is enclosed in the first column of the command output. The first character indicates the type of file: d for directory, – for regular file, l for symbolic link, c for character device file, b for block device file, p for named pipe, s for socket, and so on. The next nine characters—three groups of three characters—show the read (r), write (w), and execute (x) permissions for the three user classes: user (owner), group, and others (public), respectively. The hyphen character represents a permission denial for that level.

Figure 3-3 illustrates the *ll* command output and its various components.

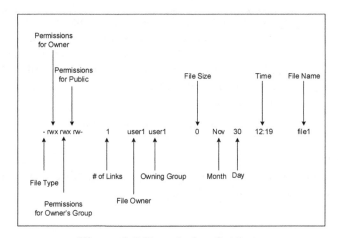

Figure 3-3 Permission Settings

The above figure depicts the file owner (*user1*) in the third column and the owning group (*user1*) in the fourth column.

Modifying Access Permissions

Linux provides the *chmod* command to modify access rights on files and directories. It works identically for both files and directories. *chmod* can be used by *root* or the file owner, and can modify permissions specified in one of two ways: *symbolic* or *octal*. Symbolic notation uses a combination of letters and symbols to add, revoke, or assign permissions to each class of users. The octal notation (a.k.a. the *absolute* notation), on the other hand, uses a three-digit numbering system ranging from 0 to 7 to express permissions for the three user classes. Octal values are given in Table 3-6.

Octal Value	Binary Notation	Symbolic Notation	Explanation
0	000	---	No permissions.
1	001	--x	Execute permission only.
2	010	-w-	Write permission only.
3	011	-wx	Write and execute permissions.
4	100	r--	Read permission only.
5	101	r-x	Read and execute permissions.
6	110	rw-	Read and write permissions.
7	111	rwx	Read, write, and execute permissions.

Table 3-6 Octal Permission Notation

From Table 3-6, it is obvious that each 1 corresponds to an r, w, or x, and each 0 corresponds to the – character for no permission at that level. Figure 3-4 shows weights associated with each digit position in the 3-digit octal numbering model.

Figure 3-4 Permission Weights

The right-most position has weight 1, the middle position carries weight 2, and the left-most position has 4. If we assign a permission of 6, for example, it would correspond to the two left-most digit positions. Similarly, a permission of 2 would point to the middle digit position only.

Exercise 3-1: Modify File Permissions Using Symbolic Notation

This exercise should be done on *host1*.

For this exercise, presume that *file1* with read permission for the owner (*user1*), owning group (*user1*), and others, exists, and that you are logged in as *user1*.

```
-r--r--r--. 1 user1 user1 0 Nov 30 12:30 file1
```

In this exercise, you will add the execute permission for the owner and the write permission for the group and public. You will then revoke the write permission from public and assign read, write, and execute permissions to the three user categories at the same time. The *chmod* command accepts the −v option to display what it has changed.

1. Add the execute permission for the owner and show the output of *ll* to verify:

    $ chmod u+x file1 −v
    mode of 'file1' changed from 0444 (r--r--r--) to 0544 (r-xr--r--)
    $ ll file1
    -r-xr--r--. 1 user1 user1 0 Nov 30 12:30 file1

2. Add the write permission for group members and public and verify:

    $ chmod go+w file1
    $ ll file1
    -r-xrw-rw-. 1 user1 user1 0 Nov 30 12:30 file1

3. Remove the write permission for the public and confirm:

    $ chmod o-w file1
    $ ll file1
    -r-xrw-r--. 1 user1 user1 0 Nov 30 12:30 file1

4. Assign read, write, and execute permissions to all three user categories and validate:

    $ chmod a=rwx file1
    $ ll file1
    -rwxrwxrwx. 1 user1 user1 0 Nov 30 12:30 file1

Exercise 3-2: Modify File Permissions Using Octal Notation

This exercise should be done on *host1*.

For this exercise, assume that *file2* with permissions 444 and ownership belongs to *user1* exists, and that you are logged in as *user1*.

    -r--r--r--. 1 user1 user1 0 Dec 1 08:27 file2

In this exercise, you will add the execute permission for the owner and the write permission for the group and public. You will then revoke the write permission from the public and assign read, write, and execute permissions to the three user categories at the same time.

1. Add the execute permission for the file owner and verify with the *ll* command:

    $ chmod 544 file2
    $ ll file2
    -r-xr--r--. 1 user1 user1 0 Dec 1 08:27 file2

2. Add the write permission for the owning group and others, and verify:

```
$ chmod 766 file2
$ ll file2
```
-rwxrw-rw-. 1 user1 user1 0 Dec 1 08:27 file2

3. Remove the write permission for the public and verify:

```
$ chmod 764 file2
$ ll file2
```
-rwxrw-r--. 1 user1 user1 0 Dec 1 08:27 file2

4. Assign read, write, and execute permissions to all three user categories and confirm:

```
$ chmod 777 file2
$ ll file2
```
-rwxrwxrwx. 1 user1 user1 0 Dec 1 08:27 file2

Default Permissions

Linux assigns *default permissions* to a file or directory at the time of its creation. Default permissions are calculated based on the *umask* (user mask) permission value subtracted from a preset value called *initial* permissions.

The umask is a three-digit value that refers to read/write/execute permissions for owner, group, and public. Its purpose is to set default permissions on new files and directories created without touching the existing files and directories. In RHEL, the default umask value is set to 0022 for the *root* and other system users and 0002 for all regular users with bash shell assigned. Note that the left-most 0 has no significance. Run the *umask* command without any options and it will display the current umask value:

```
$ umask
0002
```

Run the command again but with the –S option to display the umask in symbolic notation:

```
$ umask –S
u=rwx,g=rwx,o=rx
```

The pre-defined initial permission values are 666 (rw-rw-rw-) for files and 777 (rwxrwxrwx) for directories. Even if the umask is set to 000, the new files will always get a maximum of 666 permissions, and we use the *chmod* command to add executable bits explicitly if desired.

Calculating Default Permissions

Consider the following example to calculate the default permission values on files for regular users:

Initial Permissions	666
umask	– 002 (subtract)
==========================	
Default Permissions	664

This indicates that every new file will have read and write permissions assigned to the owner and the owning group, and a read-only permission to others.

To calculate default permission values on directories for regular users:

Initial Permissions	777	
umask	− 002	(subtract)
Default Permissions	775	

This indicates that every new directory will have read, write, and execute permissions assigned to the owner and the owning group, and read and execute permissions to everyone else.

Now, if you wish to have different default permissions set for new files and directories, you need to modify the umask. You first need to determine the desired default values. For instance, if you want all your new files and directories to get 640 and 750 permissions, respectively, you can set the value to 027 as follows:

   $ umask 027

The new value becomes effective right away, and it will only be applied to files and directories created thereafter. The existing files and directories will remain intact. Now create *file10* and *dir10* as *user1* under */home/user1* to test the effect of the new umask.

   $ touch file10
   $ ll file10
   -rw-r-----. 1 user1 user1 0 Dec 1 08:48 file10
   $ mkdir dir10
   $ ll –d dir10
   drwxr-x---. 2 user1 user1 6 Dec 1 08:48 dir10

The above examples show that the new file and directory were created with different permissions. The file got (666 − 027 = 640) and the directory (777 − 027 = 750) permissions.

The umask value set at the command line will be lost as soon as you log off. In order to retain the new setting, place it in an appropriate shell startup files discussed in Chapter 08 "Managing Users and Groups".

File Ownership and Group Membership

In Linux, every file and directory has an owner. By default, the creator assumes ownership but this may be altered and allocated to a different user if required.

Similarly, every user is a member of one or more groups. A group is a collection of users with common requirements. By default, the owner's group is assigned to a file or directory.

The following *ll* command output shows the owner and the owning group for file *file10*:

   $ ll file10
   -rw-r-----. 1 user1 user1 0 Dec 1 08:48 file10

The output indicates that the owner of *file10* is *user1* who belongs to group *user1*. If you wish to view the corresponding UID and GID instead, you can specify the –n option with *ll*:

$ ll –n file10
-rw-r-----. 1 1000 1000 0 Dec 1 08:48 file10

Linux provides the *chown* and *chgrp* commands that you can use to alter ownership and owning group for files and directories; however, you must be *root* to make these modifications.

Exercise 3-3: Modify File Ownership and Group Membership

This exercise should be done on *host1*.

For this exercise, presume that *file10* and *dir10* with ownership and owning group set to *user1* exist, and that you are logged in as *root*.

```
-rw-r-----.  1 user1  user1  0 Dec  1 08:48  file10
drwxr-x---. 2 user1  user1  6 Dec  1 08:48  dir10
```

In this exercise, you will first create user accounts *user100* and *user200*, and then change the ownership for *file10* to *user100* and the owning group to *user100*. You will apply both ownership and owning group on the file to *user200* at the same time. Finally, you will change both ownership and owning group on the directory to *user200* recursively.

1. Create user accounts *user100* and *user200*:

   # useradd user100
   # useradd user200

2. Change into the home directory of *user100* and modify the ownership on *file10*:

   # cd /home/user1
   # chown user100 file10
   changed ownership of 'file10' from user1 to user100
   # ll file10
   -rw-r-----. 1 user100 user1 0 Dec 1 08:48 file10

3. Change the owning group to *user100*:

   # chgrp user100 file10 –v
   changed group of 'file10' from user1 to user100
   # ll file10
   -rw-r-----. 1 user100 user100 0 Dec 1 08:48 file10

4. Assign both ownership and owning group to *user200* at the same time:

   # chown user200:user200 file10 –v
   changed ownership of 'file10' from user100:user100 to user200:user200
   # ll file10
   -rw-r-----. 1 user200 user200 0 Dec 1 08:48 file10

5. Change both ownership and group membership to *user200* recursively on *dir10*:

> # **chown –R user200:user200 dir10**
> # **ll –d dir10**
> drwxr-x---. 2 user200 user200 6 Dec 1 08:48 dir10

Use the –R option with *ll* to view file and directory information under *dir10*; however, it will not show anything as the directory is currently empty.

Special Permissions

Linux offers three types of special permission bits that may be set on executable files or directories to allow them to respond differently for certain operations. These permission bits are:

✓ *setuid* (set user identifier) bit
✓ *setgid* (set group identifier) bit
✓ *sticky* bit

The first two bits may be defined on executable files to provide non-owners and non-group members the ability to run executables with the privileges of the owner or the owning group, respectively. The setgid bit may also be set on shared directories for group collaboration. The last bit may be set on public directories for inhibiting file deletion by non-owners.

The use of the special bits should be regulated and monitored appropriately to avoid potential security issues to the system and applications.

The setuid Bit on Executable Files

The setuid flag is set on executable files at the file owner level. With this bit set, the file is executed by other regular users with the same privileges as that of the file owner. A common example is that of *su* command that is owned by the *root* user. This command has the setuid bit enabled on it by default. See the highlighted s in the owner's permission class below:

> $ **ll /usr/bin/su**
> -rwsr-xr-x. 1 root root 32032 Mar 28 2014 /usr/bin/su

When a normal user executes this command, it will run as if *root* (the owner) is running it and, therefore, the user is able to run it successfully and gets the desired result.

> The *su* (switch user) command allows a user to switch to some other user account provided the switching user knows the password of the user they are trying to switch to.

Now, remove the setuid bit from *su* and replace it with the underlying execute attribute. You must be *root* in order to make this change. List the file after this modification for verification.

> # **chmod u-s /usrbin/su**
> -rwxr-xr-x. 1 root root 32032 Mar 28 2014 /usr/bin/su

The file is still executable by non-owners as indicated by the execute flag; however, it will prevent regular non-owning users from switching accounts as they have lost that special privilege. Here is what will happen when *user1* tries to *su* into the *root* account with a valid password:

```
$ su –
Password:
su: Authentication failure
```

user1 gets an "authentication failure" message even though they entered the correct login credentials.

To reset the setuid bit on *su* (or on any other file), use the *chmod* command:

```
# chmod 4755 /usrbin/su
# ll /usr/bin/su
-rwsr-xr-x.  1  root  root  32032  Mar 28  2014  /usr/bin/su
```

When digit 4 is used with the *chmod* command in this manner, it enables setuid on the specified file. Alternatively, you can use the symbolic notation as follows:

```
# chmod u+s /usr/bin/su
```

You can search for all files in the system with this special bit defined using the *find* command:

```
# find / –perm –4000
/usr/bin/fusermount
/usr/bin/umount
/usr/bin/mount
/usr/bin/chage
/usr/bin/gpasswd
/usr/bin/newgrp
/usr/bin/chfn
/usr/bin/chsh
/usr/bin/su
/usr/bin/pkexec
/usr/bin/crontab
. . . . . . . .
```

The setgid Bit on Executable Files

The setgid attribute is set on executable files at the group level. With this bit set, the file is executed by non-owners with the exact same privileges that the group members have. For instance, the *wall* command is owned by *root* with group membership set to *tty* and setgid enabled. See the highlighted s in the group's permission class below:

```
# ll /usr/bin/wall
-r-xr-sr-x.  1  root  tty  15344  Jan 27  2014  /usr/bin/wall
```

The *wall* command allows users to broadcast a message to all logged-in users and print it on their terminal screens. By default, normal users are allowed this privilege because of the presence of the setgid flag on the file. To test, run the command and supply a message as an argument:

$ wall Hello, this is to test the setgid flag on the wall command
Broadcast message from user1@host1.example.com (pts/0) (Mon Dec 1 11:26:24 2014):
Hello, this is to test the setgid flag on the wall command

Now, remove the bit from */usr/bin/wall* and replace it with the underlying execute flag. You must be *root* in order to make this change. List the file after this modification for confirmation.

 # chmod g-s /usr/bin/wall
-r-xr-xr-x. 1 root tty 15344 Jan 27 2014 /usr/bin/wall

The file is still executable by non-owners; however, it will prevent regular non-owning users from sending out messages as they have lost that special privilege.

Now, put this bit back on */usr/bin/wall* and confirm:

 # chmod 2555 /usr/bin/wall
 # ll /usr/bin/wall
-r-xr-sr-x. 1 root tty 15344 Jan 27 2014 /usr/bin/wall

When digit 2 is used with the *chmod* command in this manner, it sets the setgid attribute on the specified file. Alternatively, you can use the symbolic notation as follows:

 # chmod g+s /usr/bin/wall

You can search for all files in the system with this special bit defined using the *find* command:

 # find / –perm –2000
/run/log/journal
/run/log/journal/03858cff4a7b482e8b70a7cea28585b5
/usr/bin/wall
/usr/bin/write
/usr/bin/ssh-agent
/usr/bin/locate
/usr/sbin/netreport
. . . .

The setgid Bit on Shared Directories
The setgid bit can also be set on group-shared directories to allow files and sub-directories created in that directory to automatically inherit the directory's owning group. This saves group members sharing the directory contents from changing the group on every new file and sub-directory that they add to that directory. The standard behavior for new files and sub-directories is to always receive the creator's group.

Exercise 3-4: Use setgid for Group Collaboration
This exercise should be done on *host1*.

In this exercise, you will create a group called *sdatagrp* with GID 9999, and add *user100* and *user200* to this group as members with shared data needs. You will create a directory called */sdata* with ownership and owning group belonging to *root* and *sdatagrp*, respectively, then set the setgid bit on */sdata* and test. For details on managing users and groups, consult Chapter 08 "Managing Users and Groups".

1. Add group *sdatagrp* with GID 9999 with the *groupadd* command:

   # **groupadd –g 9999 sdatagrp**

2. Add existing users *user100* and *user200* as members to *sdatagrp* using the *usermod* command:

   # **usermod –G sdatagrp user100**
   # **usermod –G sdatagrp user200**

3. Create the */sdata* directory:

   # **mkdir /sdata**

4. Set ownership and owning group on */sdata* to *root* and *sdatagrp*, respectively, using the *chown* command:

   # **chown root:sdatagrp /sdata –v**
   changed ownership of '/sdata' from root:root to root:sdatagrp

5. Set the setgid bit on */sdata* using the *chmod* command:

   # **chmod g+s /sdata –v**
   mode of '/sdata' changed from 0755 (rwxr-xr-x) to 2755 (rwxr-sr-x

6. Verify the attributes set in the above steps using the *ll* command on */sdata*:

   # **ll –d /sdata**
   drwxrwxs---. 2 root sdatagrp 18 Dec 1 14:06 /sdata

7. Switch or log in as *user100* and change to the */sdata* directory:

   # **su – user100 ; cd /sdata**

8. Create a file and list it to check the owning group on it:

   # **touch file1**
   # **ls –l file1**
   -rw-rw-r--. 1 user100 sdatagrp 0 Dec 1 14:06 file1

Both members of the group can now create files in */sdata* and modify them. They will own the files, but the owning group will be *sdatagrp* to which they both belong.

The Sticky Bit on Public Directories

The sticky bit is set on public writable directories (or other directories with rw permissions for everyone) to protect files and sub-directories owned by regular users from being deleted or moved by other regular users. This attribute is set on */tmp* and */var/tmp* directories by default as depicted below:

ll –d /tmp /var/tmp
drwxrwxrwt. 18 root root 4096 Dec 1 15:03 /tmp
drwxrwxrwt. 10 root root 4096 Nov 26 13:52 /var/tmp

Notice the bolded t in other's permissions, indicating the presence of this attribute on the two directories.

You can use the *chmod* command to set and unset the sticky bit. Add this flag to the */var* directory and then revoke it. Use the –v option for verbosity. The following lists the */var* directory, sets the bit on it, and then lists the directory again to confirm:

ll –d /var
drwxr-xr-x. 24 root root 4096 Nov 17 14:22 /var
chmod 1755 /var –v
mode of '/var' changed from 0755 (rwxr-xr-x) to 1755 (rwxr-xr-t)
ll –d /var
drwxr-xr-t. 24 root root 4096 Nov 17 14:22 /var

When digit 1 is used with the *chmod* command in this manner, it sets the sticky bit on the specified directory. Alternatively, you can use the symbolic notation to do exactly the same:

chmod o+t /var

To unset, use either of the following:

chmod 755 /var
mode of '/var' changed from 1755 (rwxr-xr-t) to 0755 (rwxr-xr-x)
chmod o-t /var

You can search for all files in the system with this special bit defined using the *find* command:

find / –type d –perm –1000
/dev/mqueue
/dev/shm
/tmp
/tmp/.X11-unix
/tmp/.ICE-unix
/tmp/.XIM-unix
/tmp/.font-unix
/tmp/.Test-unix
/tmp/systemd-private-vPX96e/tmp
. . . .

Chapter Summary

This chapter presented an overview of RHEL file system structure and significant higher-level sub-directories that consisted of static and variable files, and were grouped logically into lower level sub-directories. We looked at how files and sub-directories were accessed using a path relative to either the top-most directory of the file system structure or our current location in the tree.

We learned about different types of files, and looked at several file and directory manipulation tools for creating, listing, displaying, copying, moving, renaming, and removing them. We reviewed attributes set on files and directories, and used appropriate tools to set and unset them.

Searching for files within the directory structure using specified criteria provided us with an understanding and explanation of the tool required to perform such tasks. We discussed soft and hard links and their use.

We studied topics related to file and directory permissions. We covered permission classes, types, and modes, and saw how to modify permissions using symbolic and octal notations. We looked at default permissions, how to set them up for new files and directories, and the role of the umask value in determining the new default permissions.

The next topic explained how to modify ownership and owning group for files and directories.

Finally, we talked about special permission bits for executable files and directories to gain privileged access and prevent files and directories from being deleted by non-owners. We also looked at how to set up a shared directory for group collaboration.

Chapter Review Questions

1. Which command can be used to determine a file type?
2. The output generated by the umask command shows the current user mask in four digits. What is the significance of the left-most digit?
3. Default permissions are calculated by subtracting the initial permissions from the umask value. True or False?
4. The chgrp command may be used to modify both ownership and group membership on a file. True or False?
5. Name the permission classes, types, and modes.
6. The default umask for a regular user in bash shell is 0027. True or False?
7. What digit represents the setuid bit in the chmod command?
8. What would the command find /var -perm -1000 –type d do?
9. What would the command chmod g-s file1 do?
10. Sticky bit is recommended for every system directory. True or False?
11. The setgid bit enables group members to run a command at a higher priority. True or False?
12. The chown command may be used to modify both ownership and group membership on a file. True or False?
13. What is the equivalent symbolic value for permissions 751?
14. A file must have the .exe extension to be able to run. True or False?
15. /boot is a memory-based file system. True or False?
16. Name the two types of paths.
17. What are the two indications in the ll command output that tells us if the file is a symlink?
18. The rmdir command can be used to remove an entire directory structure. True or False?
19. The –A option with the chattr command makes a file immutable. True or False?
20. The ll command produces 9 columns in the output by default. True or False?

21. Soft linked directories cannot cross file system boundaries but hard linked directories can. True or False?
22. What permissions would the owner of the file get if the chmod command is executed with 555?
23. What would the find / -name core –ok rm {} \; command do?
24. Which special permission bit is set on a directory for team sharing?

Answers to Chapter Review Questions

1. The *file* command can be used to determine a file type.
2. The left-most digit has no significance in the *umask* value.
3. False. Default permissions are calculated by subtracting the umask value from the initial permission values.
4. False.
5. Permission classes are user, group, and public; permission types are read, write, and execute; and permission modes are add, revoke, and assign.
6. False. The default umask for bash shell users is 0002.
7. The digit 4 represents the setuid bit.
8. It would search the /var directory for directories with sticky bit set.
9. It would remove the setgid bit from file1.
10. False.
11. False.
12. True.
13. The equivalent for octal 751 is rwxr-x--x.
14. False.
15. False. /boot is a disk-based file system.
16. The two types of pathnames are absolute and relative.
17. A symlink file line entry in the ll command output begins with the letter l and has an arrow pointing to the source file.
18. False. The rmdir is used to remove empty directories.
19. False. The –i option is used with the chattr command to make a file immutable.
20. True.
21. False. Soft linked directories can and hard linked directories cannot cross file system boundaries.
22. The owner will get read and execute permissions.
23. The *find* command provided will display all files by the name core in the entire directory hierarchy and ask for removal confirmation as it finds them.
24. The setgid bit is set for team sharing.

DIY Challenge Labs

The following labs are useful to strengthen most of the concepts and topics learned in this chapter. It is expected that you perform these labs without any additional help. A step-by-step guide is not provided, as the implementation of these labs requires the knowledge that has been presented in this chapter. Use defaults or your own thinking for missing information.

Lab 3-1: Find Files and Determine File Types

Log on to *host1* as *root* and execute the *find* command to search for all files in the entire directory structure that have been modified in the past 10 days and display their type. Use the *find* command again and search for named pipe and socket files. Check the type of some of those files and directories with the *file* command.

Lab 3-2: File and Directory Operations

Log on to *host1* as *user1* and create one file and one directory in the home directory. List the file and directory and observe the permissions, ownership, and owning group. Try to move the file and directory to the */var/log* directory and observe the output. Try again to move them to the */tmp* directory. Duplicate the file with the *cp* command and then rename the duplicated file using any name. Finally, remove the file and directory created for this lab.

Lab 3-3: Find Files Using Different Criteria

Log on to *host1* as *root* and execute the *find* command to search for regular files in the entire directory structure that were accessed more than 10 days ago, are not bigger than 5MB in size, and are owned by the user *root*.

Lab 3-4: Manipulate File Permissions

Log on to *host1* as *user1* and create file *file11* and directory *dir11* in the user's home directory. Make a note of the permissions on them. Run the *umask* command to determine the current umask. Change the umask value to 0035 using the symbolic notation and then create *file22* and directory *dir22* in the user's home directory. Observe the permissions on *file22* and *dir22* and compare them with the permissions on *file11* and *dir11*. Using the *chmod* command, modify the permissions on *file11* to match that on *file22*. Using the *chmod* command, modify the permissions on *dir22* to match that on *dir11*. Do not remove *file11*, *file22*, *dir11*, and *dir22* yet.

Lab 3-5: Configure Group Collaboration

Log on to *host1* as *root* and create directory */shared_dir1*. Create a group called *shared_grp* and assign *user1000* and *user2000* to it (create these users if they do not already exist). Set up appropriate ownership, group membership, and permissions on the directory to support group collaboration.

Chapter 04

Dealing with the Bash Shell, Processes, and Scheduling

This chapter describes the following major topics:

➢ The bash shell and its features – local and environment variables; command and variable substitution; input, output, and error redirection; tab completion; command line editing; command history; tilde substitution; regular expressions; and metacharacters

➢ Understand and display system and user executed processes

➢ View process states and priorities

➢ Process niceness and reniceness

➢ Signals and their use

➢ Overview of job scheduling and access control

➢ Schedule and manage jobs using at and cron

RHCSA Objectives:

02. Use input-output redirection (>, >>, |, 2>, etc.)
03. Use grep and regular expressions to analyze text
15. Identify CPU/memory intensive processes, adjust process priority with renice, and kill processes
32. Schedule tasks using at and cron

S hells interface users with the kernel by enabling them to submit their requests for processing. RHEL supports several shells of which the bash shell is the most popular. It is also the default shell in RHEL7. The bash shell offers a variety of features that help administrators perform their job with great ease and flexibility.

A process is a program or command running on the system. Every process has a unique numeric identifier and it is managed by the kernel. It may be viewed, listed, niced, and reniced. A process is in one of several states at any given time during its lifecycle. There are several signals that may be passed to a process to kill or terminate it, among other actions. A program or command may be run in a way that precludes termination by a hangup signal (such as the disconnection of the terminal session in which the program or command is running).

Job scheduling allows a user to schedule a command for a one-time or recurring execution in future. A job may be submitted and managed by any authorized user. All executed jobs are logged.

Introducing the BASH Shell

The *shell* is referred to as the command interpreter, and it is an interface between a user and the kernel. The shell accepts instructions from users (or scripts), interprets them, and passes them on to the kernel for processing. The kernel utilizes all hardware and software components required for successfully processing the instructions. When finished, it returns the results to the shell and displays them on the screen. The shell also shows appropriate error messages, if generated.

A widely used shell by Linux users and administrators is the *bash* (*bourne again shell*) shell. bash is a replacement for the older *Bourne* shell, and has undergone a number of enhancements. It is the default shell in RHEL7 and offers several features such as variable manipulation, command substitution, variable substitution, input and output redirection, command history, command line editing, tab completion, tilde substitution, pattern matching, metacharacters, command aliasing, quoting, conditional execution, flow control, and shell scripting. Some of these features are discussed in this section.

The bash shell is identified by the $ sign for regular users and the # sign for the *root* user. This shell is resident in the */bin/bash* file.

Variables

A *variable* is a temporary storage of data in memory. It stores information that is used for customizing the shell environment and by many system and application processes to function properly. The shell allows us to store a value in a variable. This value may include a string of alphanumeric characters, white spaces, and some special characters. A variable value that contains one or more white space characters must be enclosed within quotes.

There are two types of variables: *local* and *environment*.

A local variable is private to the shell in which it is created and its value cannot be used by processes that are not started in that shell. This introduces the concept of *current* shell and *sub*-shell (or *child* shell). The current shell is where we execute a program, whereas a sub-shell is created by a running program. The value of a local variable is available only in the current shell, and not in the sub-shell.

The value of an environment variable, however, is passed from the current shell to the sub-shell during the execution of a script. In other words, the value stored in an environment variable is passed from the parent process to the child process. Any environment variable set in a sub-shell loses its value when the sub-shell terminates.

Some environment variables are defined automatically through system and user startup files at log in, and are described in Table 4-1.

Variable	Description
DISPLAY	Stores the hostname or IP address for X terminal sessions.
HISTFILE	Defines the file for storing the history of executed commands.
HISTSIZE	Defines the maximum size for the HISTFILE.
HOME	Sets the home directory path.
LOGNAME	Stores the login name.
MAIL	Contains the path to the user mail directory.
PATH	Defines a colon-separated list of directories to be searched when executing a command.
PS1	Defines the primary command prompt.
PS2	Defines the secondary command prompt.
PWD	Stores the current directory location.
SHELL	Holds the absolute path to the primary shell file.
TERM	Holds the terminal type value.

Table 4-1 Pre-Defined Environment Variables

We may also set custom environment variables at the command prompt or in scripts as required.

Setting and Unsetting Variables, and Viewing their Values

Local and environment variables may be set or unset at the command prompt or via programs, and their values may be viewed and used as necessary. It is recommended that you employ uppercase letters for naming variables so as to avoid any possible conflicts with existing command, program, file, or directory names. To understand how variables are defined, viewed, and undefined, a few examples are presented below. These examples are run as *user100* on *host1*.

To define a local variable called VR1:

    $ **VR1=rhel7**

To view the value stored in VR1:

    $ **echo $VR1**
    rhel7

To make this variable an environment variable, use the *export* command as follows:

    $ **export VR1**

To undefine this variable:

    $ **unset VR1**

You can define a local variable that contains a value with one or more white spaces as follows:

$ VR1="I love RHEL7"

The above may also be defined as an environment variable using the *export* command as follows:

$ export VR1="I love RHEL7"

In addition to the *echo* command to view variable values, the *set*, *env*, and *export* commands may also be used for this purpose. The *set* command lists current values for all shell variables, including local and environment variables, while the *env* and *export* commands list only the environment variables.

Command and Variable Substitution

The primary command prompt for the *root* user is the # sign and that for regular users is $. Customizing the primary command prompt to display useful information such as who you are, the system you are logged on to, and your current location in the directory tree is a good practice. The examples below illustrate how to modify the primary prompt for *user100* using either of the following:

$ export PS1="< $LOGNAME@`hostname`:\$PWD > "
$ export PS1="< $LOGNAME@$(hostname):\$PWD > "

The command prompt for *user100* will now look like:

< user100@host1.example.com:/home/user100 >

The value of the PWD variable will reflect the directory location in the prompt as *user100* navigates the tree. This is called *variable substitution*. For instance, if *user100* moves to */usr/bin*, the prompt will change to:

< user100@host1.example.com:/usr/bin >

Also, the value of LOGNAME will display the user's login name.

Running the command *hostname* and assigning its output to a variable is an example of a shell feature called *command substitution*. Note that the command whose output we want to assign to a variable must be enclosed within either single forward quotes or parentheses preceded by the $ sign.

Input, Output, and Error Redirection

Many programs read input from the keyboard and write output to the terminal window where they are initiated. Any errors, if encountered, are printed on the terminal window too. This is the default behavior. What if we do not want input to come from the keyboard or output to go to the terminal screen? The bash shell gives us the flexibility to redirect input, output, and error messages to allow programs and commands to read input from a non-default source and forward output and errors to a non-default destination.

The default (or the standard) locations for input, output, and error are referred to as *standard input* (or *stdin*), *standard output* (or *stdout*), and *standard error* (or *stderr*), respectively. These locations may also be epitomized using the < operator for stdin and > for both stdout and stderr, or using the file descriptors 0, 1, and 2 for stdin, stdout, and stderr, respectively.

Redirecting Standard Input

Input redirection instructs a command to read the required information from an alternative source, such as a file, instead of the keyboard. The < character is used for input redirection. For example, run the following to have the *cat* command read the */etc/cron.allow* file and display its contents on the standard output (terminal screen):

   $ cat < /etc/cron.allow

Redirecting Standard Output

Output redirection sends the output generated by a command to an alternative destination, such as a file, instead of to the terminal window. The > sign is used for this purpose. For instance, execute the following to direct the *ll* command to send the output to a file called *ll.out*. This will overwrite the existing *ll.out* file if there is one. If *ll.out* does not exist, it will be created.

   $ ll > ll.out

To direct the *ll* command to append the output to the *ll.out* file instead, use the >> characters:

   $ ll >> ll.out

Redirecting Standard Error

Error redirection forwards any error messages generated to an alternative destination such as a file, rather than to the terminal window. For example, the following directs the *find* command to search for all occurrences of files by the name core in the entire root directory tree and sends any error messages produced to */dev/null* (*/dev/null* is a special file that is used to discard data).

   $ find / –name core –print 2> /dev/null

Redirecting both Standard Output and Error

Both output and error can be redirected to alternative locations as well. For instance, issue the following to forward them both to a file called *outerr.out*:

   $ ls /usr /cdr &> outerr.out

This example will produce a listing of the */usr* directory and save the result in *outerr.out*. At the same time, it will generate an error message complaining about the non-existence of the */cdr* directory, and will send it to the same file as well. You may use >> signs in the above example to append to an existing file.

Command History

Command history keeps a log of all commands that you run at the command prompt. This feature is enabled by default. The bash shell stores command history in a file located in the user's home directory. You may retrieve these commands, modify them at the command line, and re-run them.

There are two variables that enable the command history feature, and their values may be viewed with the *echo* command:

```
$ echo $HISTFILE
/home/user100/.bash_history
$ echo $HISTSIZE
1000
```

The HISTFILE variable tells the bash shell to store all commands run by a user in the *.bash_history* file in that user's home directory. This file is created automatically if it does not already exist. Each command, along with options and arguments, is stored on a separate line.

The HISTSIZE variable controls the maximum number of command entries that can be stored in HISTFILE.

In addition to these variables, you also need to ensure that a text editor such as emacs or vi is set. This allows you the ability to use the command history feature, as well as some other features that are discussed in later sub-sections. The default editor is set to emacs. If not, you can issue the following to activate it:

```
$ set –o emacs        (or $ set –o vi)
```

The HISTSIZE variable is pre-defined in the */etc/profile* startup file and may be increased or decreased if desired. The *set* command above may be defined in the user or system startup file. Refer to Chapter 08 "Managing Users and Groups" on how to define variables and commands in startup files to customize the shell behavior.

RHEL provides the *history* command to display or use previously executed commands. It gets the information from the *~/.bash_history* file. By default, the last 500 entries are displayed if it is executed without any options.

```
$ history | more
  1  cd /sdata
  2  touch file1
  3  ll
  4  ll -d /sdata
. . . . . . . .
```

Let's use some of the *history* command options and observe the impact on the output.

To display this command and the ten entries preceding it:

```
$ history 11
```

To re-execute a command by its line number (line 38 for example) in the history file:

$ **!38**

To re-execute the most recent occurrence of a command that started with a particular letter or series of letters (ch for example):

$ **!ch**

To repeat the last command executed:

$ **!!**

Command Line Editing

Command line editing allows us to edit a line of text right at the command prompt. Depending on which editor is set, we can scroll backward (reverse chronological order) or forward (chronological order) through the command history. This feature is enabled by setting either the emacs or vi command line text editor (or some other editor of your choice). By default, emacs is set; however, we can also set vi as follows:

$ **set –o vi**

One of the differences between the two is the key combinations used for scrolling through the history file, *~/.bash_history*. Pressing the up arrow key (or Ctrl+k for vi) brings the last command we executed at the prompt, and pressing it (or the j key for vi) repeatedly scrolls backward through the command history. Pressing the down arrow key (or the j key for vi) repeatedly scrolls forward through the command history. When we get the desired command at the prompt, we may edit it right there using the emacs or vi editor commands. If we do not wish to edit the command or are done with editing, we can simply press Enter to execute it.

Tab Completion

Tab completion (a.k.a. *command line completion*) is a bash shell feature whereby typing one or more initial characters of a file, directory, or command name at the command line and then hitting the Tab key twice automatically completes the entire name. In case of multiple possibilities matching the entered characters, it completes up to the point they have in common and prints all the remaining possibilities on the screen. We can then type one or more following characters and press Enter again to further narrow down the possibilities. When the desired name appears on the command line, we press Enter to accept it and perform the action. One of the major benefits of using this feature is the time that we save on typing long file, directory, or command names.

Tab completion works if a text editor is set as explained in the previous two sub-sections.

Tilde Substitution

Tilde substitution (or *tilde expansion*) is performed on words that begin with the tilde ~ character. The rules to keep in mind when using the ~ sign are:

1. If ~ is used as a standalone character, the shell refers to the $HOME directory of the user running the command. The following example displays the $HOME directory of *user100*:

```
$ echo ~
/home/user100
```

2. If the plus sign follows the ~, the shell refers to the current directory. For example, if *user100* is in the */etc/systemd* directory and does ~+, the output displays the user's current directory location:

```
$ echo ~+
/etc/systemd
```

3. If the dash sign follows the ~, the shell refers to the previous working directory. For example, if *user100* switches into the */usr/share/man* directory from */etc/systemd* and does ~-, the output displays the user's last working directory location:

```
$ echo ~-
/etc/systemd
```

4. If a username has the ~ character prepended to it, the shell refers to the $HOME directory of that user:

```
$ echo ~user200
/home/user200
```

We can use tilde substitution with any commands such as *cd*, *ls*, and *echo* that refer to a location in the directory structure. Additional examples of tilde substitution were provided in Chapter 02 "Using Basic Linux Tools".

Regular Expression

A *regular expression*, also referred to as *pattern matching*, *regex*, or *regexp*, is a pattern that is matched against a string of characters in a file or supplied input. The pattern can be a single character, series of characters, word, or sentence. Any pattern with one or more white spaces must be enclosed within quotes.

Linux provides a powerful tool called *grep* (*global regular expression print*) for pattern matching. This tool searches the contents of one or more text files or supplied input for a regular expression. If the expression is matched, *grep* prints every line containing that expression on the screen without changing the source contents. Consider the following examples.

EXAM TIP: The grep command is a handy tool to extract needed information from a file or command output. The extracted information can then be redirected to a file. The sequence of the grepped data remains unchanged.

To search for the pattern user100 in the */etc/passwd* file:

```
$ grep user100 /etc/passwd
user100:x:1001:1001::/home/user100:/bin/bash
```

To search for the pattern nologin in */etc/passwd* and exclude the lines in the output that contain this pattern. Use –v for pattern exclusion and –n for line numbers associated with the lines that do not contain the pattern.

$ grep –nv nologin /etc/passwd
1:root:x:0:0:root:/root:/bin/bash
6:sync:x:5:0:sync:/sbin:/bin/sync
7:shutdown:x:6:0:shutdown:/sbin:/sbin/shutdown
8:halt:x:7:0:halt:/sbin:/sbin/halt
38:user1:x:1000:1000:user1:/home/user1:/bin/bash
41:user100:x:1001:1001::/home/user100:/bin/bash
42:user200:x:1002:1002::/home/user200:/bin/bash

To search for all lines in the */etc/passwd* file that begin with the pattern root. The bash shell treats the caret ^ sign as a special character which marks the beginning of a line or word. This is useful, for instance, if we wish to know whether there are more than one users with that name.

$ grep ^root /etc/passwd
root:x:0:0:root:/root:/bin/bash

To list all lines from the */etc/passwd* file that end with the pattern bash. The bash shell treats the $ sign as a special character which marks the end of a line or word. This is useful, for example, to determine which users have their shells set to the bash shell.

$ grep bash$ /etc/passwd
root:x:0:0:root:/root:/bin/bash
user1:x:1000:1000:user1:/home/user1:/bin/bash
user100:x:1001:1001::/home/user100:/bin/bash
user200:x:1002:1002::/home/user200:/bin/bash

To search for all empty lines in the */etc/passwd* file:

$ grep ^$ /etc/passwd

To search for all lines in the */etc/passwd* file that contain the pattern root. The –i option instructs the command to perform a case-insensitive search. This is useful to determine if there are any *root* user accounts with a combination of lowercase and uppercase letters.

$ grep –i root /etc/passwd
root:x:0:0:root:/root:/bin/bash
operator:x:11:0:operator:/root:/sbin/nologin

To print all lines from the output of the *ll* command that contain either the cron or qemu pattern. The pipe character is used as an OR operator in this example. This is referred to as *alternation*. We can have more than two alternative matches added to this set. The *grep* command with the –E option and the *egrep* command as demonstrated below function identically.

```
$ ll /etc | grep –E 'cron|qemu'
$ ll /etc | egrep 'cron|qemu'
-rw-------.  1 root root    541 Jan 27  2014 anacrontab
-rw-r--r--.  1 root root      8 Dec  4 19:24 cron.allow
drwxr-xr-x. 2 root root     72 Oct 28 22:58 cron.d
drwxr-xr-x. 2 root root     88 Oct 28 22:58 cron.daily
-rw-------.  1 root root      6 Dec  4 08:58 cron.deny
drwxr-xr-x. 2 root root     44 Oct 28 22:51 cron.hourly
drwxr-xr-x. 2 root root      6 Dec 27 2013 cron.monthly
-rw-r--r--.  1 root root    451 Dec 27 2013 crontab
drwxr-xr-x. 2 root root      6 Dec 27 2013 cron.weekly
drwxr-xr-x. 3 root root     48 Oct 28 22:58 qemu-ga
drwxr-xr-x. 2 root root     49 Oct 28 22:54 qemu-kvm
```

To print all lines from the output of the *ll* command that contain an exact match for a word (–w). We can use one or more period characters to match that many positions in the search string. The following example searches for any word in the */etc/lvm/lvm.conf* file that begin with letters "acce" followed by any two characters:

```
$ grep –w acce.. /etc/lvm/lvm.conf
    # prefixed with either an 'a' (for accept) or 'r' (for reject).
    # By default we accept every block device:
    # Whenever there are competing read-only and read-write  access requests for
    # serviced.  Without this setting, write access may be  stalled by a high
    # I/O errors on access.  You can instead use a device p ath, in which
```

In addition to the ^, $, and . signs, the asterisk and question mark symbols are also used for matching regular expressions. These two symbols are explained in the next sub-section.

Metacharacters

Metacharacters are special characters that possess special meaning to the shell. They include input and output redirection < >, caret ^, dollar $, period ., asterisk *, question mark ?, square brackets [], pipe |, curly brackets {}, parentheses (), plus +, and backslash \. Some of these characters are used in pattern matching, and as *wildcard* and *escape* characters. We covered < > ^ $. earlier. This sub-section discusses * ? [] and |.

The * Character

The * matches zero to an unlimited number of characters (except for the leading period in a hidden file). See the following examples for usage.

To list names of all files in the */etc* directory that begin with letters ali followed by any characters:

```
$ ls /etc/ali*
/etc/aliases /etc/aliases.db
```

To list names of all files in the */var/log* directory that end in .log:

```
$ ls /var/log/*.log
```
/var/log/boot.log   /var/log/Xorg.9.log
/var/log/pm-powersave.log   /var/log/yum.log
/var/log/Xorg.0.log

The ? Character

The ? character matches exactly one character, except for the leading period in a hidden file. See the following example to understand its usage.

To list all directories under */var/log* with exactly three characters in their names:

```
$ ls –d /var/log/???
```
/var/log/gdm   /var/log/ppp

The [] Characters

The [] can be used to match either a set of characters or a range of characters for a single character position.

For a set of characters specified in this enclosure, the order in which they are listed has no importance. This means [xyz], [yxz], [xzy], and [zyx] are treated alike. In the following example, two characters are enclosed within the square brackets. The output will include all files and directories that begin with either of the two characters followed by any number of characters.

```
$ ls /usr/sbin/[yw]*
```
/usr/sbin/weak-modules
/usr/sbin/wipefs
/usr/sbin/wpa_cli
/usr/sbin/wpa_passphrase
/usr/sbin/wpa_supplicant
/usr/sbin/yum-complete-transaction
/usr/sbin/yumdb

A range of characters must be specified in a proper sequence such as [a-z] or [0-9]. The following example matches all directory names that begin with any letter between m and p:

```
$ ls –d /etc/systemd/system/[m–p]*
```
/etc/systemd/system/multi-user.target.wants
/etc/systemd/system/nfs.target.wants
/etc/systemd/system/printer.target.wants

The | Character

The *pipe*, represented by the vertical bar | and residing with the \ on the keyboard, is a special character that is used to send the output of one command as input to the next. This character is also used to define alternations in regular expressions.

The following example runs the *ll* command on */etc* and sends the output to the *more* command for displaying the directory listing one screenful at a time:

```
$ ll /etc | more
total 1476
drwxr-xr-x.  3  root  root       97 Oct 28  22:51  abrt
-rw-r--r--.  1  root  root       16 Oct 28  23:04  adjtime
-rw-r--r--.  1  root  root     1518 Jun  7  2013  aliases
-rw-r--r--.  1  root  root    12288 Oct 28  23:08  aliases.db
. . . . . . . .
--More--
```

In another example, the *who* command is run and its output is piped to the *nl* command to number each line:

```
$ who | nl
     1  (unknown)      :0       2014-11-17  14:23  (:0)
     2  root           pts/0    2014-12-07  16:27  (192.168.0.13)
     3  root           pts/3    2014-11-24  22:25  (:2)
```

The following example forms a pipeline by piping the output of *ll* to *grep* for the lines that do not contain the pattern root. The new output is further piped for a case-insensitive selection of all lines that exclude the pattern dec. The filtered output is numbered and the final result is printed on the screen one screenful at a time.

```
$ ll /proc | grep –v root | grep –vi dec | nl | more
     1  total 0
     2  dr-xr-xr-x.  8  polkitd    polkitd   0  Nov  17  14:23  1073
     3  dr-xr-xr-x.  8  gdm        gdm       0  Nov  17  14:23  1649
. . . . . . . .
--More--
```

A construct like the above with multiple pipes is referred to as a *pipeline*.

Quoting Mechanisms

As we know, metacharacters have special meaning to the shell. In order to use them as regular characters, the bash shell offers three *quoting mechanisms* that disable their special meaning and allow the shell to treat them as regular characters. These mechanisms are provided by the backslash, single quote, and double quote characters, and work by prepending a special character to a backslash, or enclosing it within single or double quotation marks.

Prefixing with a Backslash

The backslash character, also referred to as the *escape* character in shell terminology, instructs the shell to mask the meaning of any special character that follows it. For example, if a file exists by the name * and we want to remove it with the *rm* command, we will have to escape the * so that it is treated as a regular character (and not as a wildcard character).

```
$ rm \*
```

In the above example, if we forget to escape the *, the *rm* command will remove all files in the directory.

Enclosing within Single Quotes

The single quote character instructs the shell to mask the meaning of all enclosed special characters. For example, LOGNAME is a variable and its value can be viewed with the *echo* command:

$ echo $LOGNAME
user100

If we enclose $LOGNAME within single quotes, the *echo* command will display what is enclosed instead of the value of the variable:

$ echo '$LOGNAME'
$LOGNAME

Similarly, the backslash character is echoed when it is enclosed within single quotes:

$ echo '\'
\

Enclosing within Double Quotes

The double quote character instructs the shell to mask the meaning of all but backslash, dollar sign, and single quote characters. These three special characters retain their special meaning when they are enclosed within double quotes. Look at the following examples to understand the usage of double quotes.

$ echo "$SHELL"
/bin/bash
$ echo "\$PWD"
$PWD
$ echo "'\'"
'\'

Understanding Processes

A *process* is a unit for provisioning system resources. It is any program, application, or command that runs on the system. A process is created in memory in its own address space when a program, application, or command is initiated. Processes are organized in a hierarchical fashion. Each process has a *parent process* (a.k.a. a *calling process*) that spawns it. A single parent process may have one or many *child processes* and passes many of its attributes to them at the time of their creation. Each process is assigned a unique identification number, known as the *process identifier* (PID), which is used by the kernel to manage and control the process through its lifecycle. When a process completes its lifecycle or is terminated, this event is reported back to its parent process, and all the resources provisioned to it are then freed and the PID is removed.

Several processes are spawned at system boot, many of which sit in the memory and wait for an event to trigger a request to use their services. These background system processes are called *daemons* and are critical to system operability.

Viewing and Monitoring Processes

An operational system may have hundreds or thousands of processes running concurrently, depending on the purpose of the system. These processes may be viewed and monitored using various native tools such as *ps* (process status) and *top*. The *ps* command offers several switches that influence its output, whereas *top* is used for real-time viewing and monitoring of processes and system resources.

The *ps* command, without any options or arguments, lists processes specific to the terminal where this command is run:

```
$ ps
  PID  TTY       TIME  CMD
18827  pts/4  00:00:00  bash
18864  pts/4  00:00:00  ps
```

The above output shows basic process information in four columns. It shows the PID in the first column, the terminal the process belongs to in the second column, the cumulative time the system CPU has given to this process in the third column, and the name of the actual command or program being executed in the last column.

Some common options that we may use with the *ps* command to generate desired reports include –a (all), –e (every), –f (full-format), –F (extra full-format), and –l (long format). A combination of eaFl options can produce a very detailed process report. However, it may or may not be useful in normal circumstances. There are a number of additional options available with this. Check the man pages for details and usage.

Here is what is produced when the command is executed with eaf options:

```
$ ps –eaf
UID         PID  PPID  C STIME TTY         TIME CMD
root          1     0  0 Nov17 ?       00:00:33 /usr/lib/system
d/systemd --switched-root --system --deserialize 23
root          2     0  0 Nov17 ?       00:00:00 [kthreadd]
root          3     2  0 Nov17 ?       00:00:02 [ksoftirqd/0]
root          5     2  0 Nov17 ?       00:00:00 [kworker/0:0H]
root          7     2  0 Nov17 ?       00:00:00 [migration/0]
root          8     2  0 Nov17 ?       00:00:00 [rcu_bh]
root          9     2  0 Nov17 ?       00:00:00 [rcuob/0]
root         10     2  0 Nov17 ?       00:00:00 [rcuob/1]
root         11     2  0 Nov17 ?       00:00:00 [rcuob/2]
root         12     2  0 Nov17 ?       00:00:00 [rcuob/3]
root         13     2  0 Nov17 ?       00:00:00 [rcuob/4]
root      25225 28998  0 Dec01 pts/0   00:00:00 su - user100
user100   25226 25225  0 Dec01 pts/0   00:00:00 -bash
root      26227     1  0 Nov18 ?       00:00:28 /usr/sbin/Netwo
root      28990  2067  0 Dec01 ?       00:00:00 sshd: root@pts/
root      28998 28990  0 Dec01 pts/0   00:00:00 -bash
```

This output is spread across eight columns that show details about every process running on the system. Table 4-2 describes the content type of each column.

Column	Description
UID	User ID or name of the process owner.
PID	Process ID of the process.
PPID	Process ID of the parent process.
C	Shows processor utilization for the process.
STIME	Process start date or time.
TTY	The terminal on which the process was started. Console represents the system console and ? represents a background process.
TIME	Aggregated execution time for the process, including time spent in both userland and kernel space.
CMD	The name of the command or the program.

Table 4-2 ps Command Output

The *ps* output above indicates the presence of several daemon processes running in the background. These processes have no association with any terminal devices and that is why they show a ? in the TTY column. Notice the PID and PPID numbers. The smaller the number, the earlier it is started. The process with PID 0 is started first at system boot, followed by the process with PID 1, and so on. Each PID has an associated PPID in the third column. The owner of each process is shown in the UID column, along with the name of the command or program under CMD.

Information for each running process is kept and maintained in the */proc* file system, which *ps* and other commands reference to obtain desired data for our viewing.

The other popular tool for viewing process information is the *top* command. This command displays the statistics in real-time and may be helpful in identifying possible performance issues on the system. A sample output from a running *top* session is shown below:

```
$ top
top - 10:13:34 up 14 days, 19:49,   4 users,   load average: 0.1
Tasks: 335 total,   1 running, 334 sleeping,   0 stopped,   0
%Cpu(s):  0.3 us,  2.5 sy,  0.0 ni, 97.2 id,  0.0 wa,  0.0 hi,
KiB Mem:   7889040 total,  7709744 used,   179296 free,
KiB Swap:  1023996 total,        4 used,  1023992 free.      4765

  PID USER      PR  NI    VIRT    RES    SHR S  %CPU %MEM
   93 root      25   5       0      0      0 S  20.6  0.0
 2038 root      20   0 1071912  22464   9296 S   2.0  0.3
 4863 root      20   0 5990008  4.037g 37488 S   1.3 53.7
29155 qemu      20   0 5760896 818528   8168 S   1.0 10.4
    1 root      20   0   53952   7924   2564 S   0.0  0.1
    2 root      20   0       0      0      0 S   0.0  0.0
    3 root      20   0       0      0      0 S   0.0  0.0
    5 root       0 -20       0      0      0 S   0.0  0.0
    7 root      rt   0       0      0      0 S   0.0  0.0
    8 root      20   0       0      0      0 S   0.0  0.0
    9 root      20   0       0      0      0 S   0.0  0.0
   10 root      20   0       0      0      0 S   0.0  0.0
```

Press q or Ctrl+c to quit *top*.

top also shows the CPU, memory, and swap utilization. In the top row, it displays the system uptime, the number of logged-in users, the system load average, and the total number of processes on the system along with their current operating state.

Viewing and Monitoring Processes Graphically

Another tool that is loaded as part of the gnome-system-monitor software package is called *system monitor*. This tool provides us the ability to view, monitor, and terminate processes in a graphical setting, as well as view CPU, memory, swap, network, and file system utilization. Execute the *gnome-system-monitor* command in an X terminal window or select Applications | System Tools | System Monitor in the GNOME desktop to start this tool. See Figure 4-1.

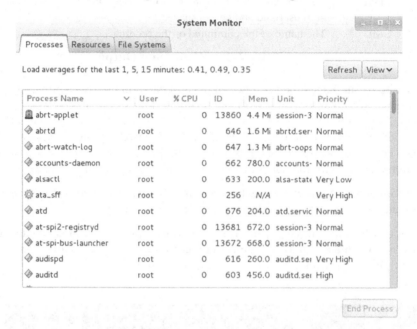

Figure 4-1 GNOME System Monitor – Process View

There are three tabs across the top that we can switch for viewing specific information. The Process tab shows details for all the processes running on the system. We can click the drop-down View button in the top right to list desired processes only. It also gives us the ability to highlight a process and terminate it by clicking the End Process button in the bottom right corner.

The Resources tab shows current and historic views of CPU, memory, swap, and network interface utilization. This data may be supportive when troubleshooting to determine the root cause of a potential bottleneck in the system. See Figure 4-2.

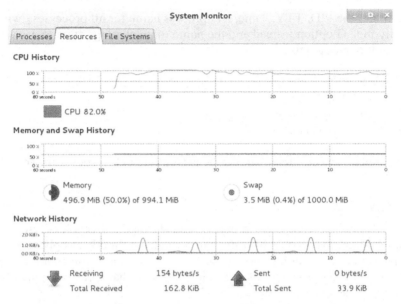

Figure 4-2 GNOME System Monitor – Resource Utilization View

The last tab, File Systems, lists all configured and mounted file systems, and shows their usage and other details.

Listing a Specific Process

Though the tools we have discussed in the previous sub-sections provide us with a lot of information about processes including their PIDs, RHEL offers the *pidof* and *pgrep* commands that only list the PID of a specific process. These commands have a few switches available to them; however, their simplest use is to pass a process name as an argument to view its PID. For instance, to list the PID of the *crond* daemon, use either of the following:

pidof crond
pgrep crond
998

Listing Processes by User and Group Ownership

A process can be listed by its ownership or owning group. We can use the *ps* command for this purpose. For example, to list all processes owned by *root*, specify the –U option with the command and then the username:

ps –U root
```
 PID TTY      TIME CMD
   1  ?    00:00:33 systemd
   2  ?    00:00:00 kthreadd
   3  ?    00:00:02 ksoftirqd/0
   5  ?    00:00:00 kworker/0:0H
   7  ?    00:00:00 migration/0
. . . . . . . .
```

The command lists the PID, TTY, Time, and process name for all processes owned by the *root* user. We can specify the –G option instead and the name of an owning group to print processes associated with that group only:

```
# ps –G qemu
  PID  TTY     TIME CMD
29124  ?    00:20:49 qemu-kvm
29155  ?    00:26:35 qemu-kvm
```

The graphical system monitor tool can also be used to view the process list sorted by a user or group name.

Process States

A process changes its operating state multiple times during its lifecycle. Factors such as processor load, memory availability, process priority, and response from other applications affect how often a process jumps from one operating state to another. It may be in a non-running condition for a while or waiting for some other process to feed it information so that it can continue to run. There are five basic process states, as illustrated in Figure 4-3.

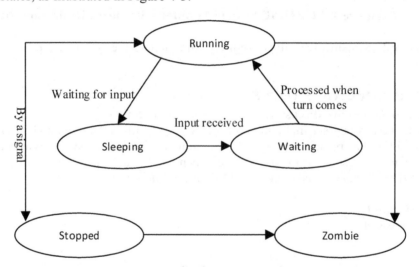

Figure 4-3 Process State Transition

Each process is in one state at any given time. These states are *running, sleeping, waiting, stopped,* and *zombie,* and are explained below:

Running: the process is being executed by the system CPU.

Sleeping: the process is waiting for input from a user or another process.

Waiting: the process has received the input it was waiting for and is now ready to run as soon as its turn arrives.

Stopped: the process is currently halted and will not run even when its turn comes, unless a signal is sent to it to change its behavior.

Zombie: the process is dead. A zombie process exists in the process table alongside other process entries, but it takes up no resources. Its entry is retained until the parent process permits it to die. A zombie process is also called a *defunct* process.

Understanding Process Niceness

A process is spawned at a certain priority, which is established at initiation based on a numeric value called *niceness* (or a *nice* value). There are 40 niceness values, with –20 being the highest and +19 the lowest. Most system-started processes use the default niceness of 0. A higher niceness lowers the execution priority of a process and a lower niceness increases it. In other words, a process running at a higher priority gets more CPU attention. A child process inherits the niceness of its calling process in calculating its priority. Though we normally run programs at the default niceness, we may choose to initiate them at a different niceness to adjust their priority based on urgency and system load.

Viewing and Changing Process Niceness

We can view current process priorities and niceness values with the *ps* command, the *top* command, and the system monitor GUI. With *ps*, specify the –l option and look for the priority (PRI, column seven) that is calculated based on the niceness value (NI, column eight):

```
# ps –efl
F S UID        PID  PPID  C PRI  NI ADDR SZ WCHAN  STIME TTY         TIME CMD
4 S root          1     0  0  80   0 - 13488 ep_pol Nov17 ?      00:00:36 /usr/lib/systemd/sys
temd --switched-root --system --deserialize 23
1 S root          2     0  0  80   0 -     0 kthrea Nov17 ?      00:00:00 [kthreadd]
1 S root          3     2  0  80   0 -     0 smpboo Nov17 ?      00:00:02 [ksoftirqd/0]
1 S root          5     2  0  60 -20 -     0 worker Nov17 ?      00:00:00 [kworker/0:0H]
```

The above output indicates the use of the default niceness for the first three processes and the highest niceness of –20 for the fourth one. These values are used by the process scheduler to adjust their execution time on the CPU.

We can check the default niceness using the *nice* command:

```
# nice
0
```

A different niceness may be assigned to a program or command at its startup. For example, to run the *top* command at a lower priority with a nice value of +2, we use the *nice* command as follows:

```
# nice –2 top
```

Open another terminal window and run the *ps* command to validate. Look for the priority and nice values in columns 7 and 8.

```
# ps –el | grep top
0 S  0 8845 29767  0 82   2 - 30945  poll_s pts/4   00:00:00   top
```

To run the same program at a higher priority with a niceness of –10, specify the value with a pair of dashes:

nice --10 top

Validate in the other window:

ps –el | grep top
```
4 S   0  9191 29767   0  70 -10  -  30945  poll_s pts/4   00:00:00  top
```

As we can see, the process is running at a higher priority (70) with a nice value of –10.

Renicing a Running Process

The niceness of a running process may be altered using the *renice* command. This adjustment will affect the priority at which the process is currently running. For example, to change the nice value of the running *top* session from –10 to +5, specify the PID (9191 from above) with the *renice* command:

renice 5 1919
1919 (process ID) old priority -10, new priority 5

We can validate the above change with *ps* or *top*, or using the GNOME system monitor.

The *renice* command also allows us to alter the nice values of all the processes owned by a specific user or members of a particular group by specifying the –u or –g option, respectively, with it.

Controlling Processes with Signals

As you know, a system may have hundreds or even thousands of processes running simultaneously on it. Sometimes it becomes necessary to alert a process of an event. We do that by sending a control signal to the process. Processes may use signals to alert each other as well. The receiving process halts its execution as soon as it gets the signal and takes an appropriate action as per instructions enclosed in the signal. The instructions may include terminating the process gracefully, killing it abruptly, or forcing it to re-read its configuration.

There are a number of signals available for use but we mostly deal with only a few of them. Each signal is associated with a unique numeric identifier, a name, and an action. A list of available signals can be displayed with the *kill* command using the –l option:

```
# kill –l
 1) SIGHUP       2) SIGINT       3) SIGQUIT      4) SIGILL       5) SIGTRAP
 6) SIGABRT      7) SIGBUS       8) SIGFPE       9) SIGKILL     10) SIGUSR1
11) SIGSEGV     12) SIGUSR2     13) SIGPIPE     14) SIGALRM     15) SIGTERM
16) SIGSTKFLT   17) SIGCHLD     18) SIGCONT     19) SIGSTOP     20) SIGTSTP
21) SIGTTIN     22) SIGTTOU     23) SIGURG      24) SIGXCPU     25) SIGXFSZ
26) SIGVTALRM   27) SIGPROF     28) SIGWINCH    29) SIGIO       30) SIGPWR
31) SIGSYS      34) SIGRTMIN    35) SIGRTMIN+1  36) SIGRTMIN+2  37) SIGRTMIN+3
38) SIGRTMIN+4  39) SIGRTMIN+5  40) SIGRTMIN+6  41) SIGRTMIN+7  42) SIGRTMIN+8
43) SIGRTMIN+9  44) SIGRTMIN+10 45) SIGRTMIN+11 46) SIGRTMIN+12 47) SIGRTMIN+13
48) SIGRTMIN+14 49) SIGRTMIN+15 50) SIGRTMAX-14 51) SIGRTMAX-13 52) SIGRTMAX-12
53) SIGRTMAX-11 54) SIGRTMAX-10 55) SIGRTMAX-9  56) SIGRTMAX-8  57) SIGRTMAX-7
58) SIGRTMAX-6  59) SIGRTMAX-5  60) SIGRTMAX-4  61) SIGRTMAX-3  62) SIGRTMAX-2
63) SIGRTMAX-1  64) SIGRTMAX
```

The output shows the availability of 64 signals for process-to-process and user-to-process communication. Table 4-3 describes the signals that are most often used.

Signal Number	Signal Name	Action
1	SIGHUP	Hang up signal causes a process to disconnect itself from a closed terminal that it was tied to. Also used to instruct a running daemon to re-read its configuration.
2	SIGINT	The ^c signal issued on the controlling terminal to interrupt the execution of a process.
9	SIGKILL	Kills a process abruptly.
15	SIGTERM	Sends a soft termination signal to stop a process in an orderly fashion. This signal may be ignored by a process. This is the default signal.

Table 4-3 Control Signals

The commands used to pass a signal to a process are *kill* and *pkill*. These commands are usually used to terminate a process. Ordinary users can kill processes that they own, while the *root* user can kill any process running on the system.

The *kill* command requires one or more PIDs and the *pkill* command requires one or more process names to send a signal to. We may specify a non-default single name or number with either utility.

Let's look at a few examples to understand the usage of these tools.

To pass the soft termination signal to the *crond* daemon, use either of the following:

 # pkill crond
 # kill `pidof crond`

The *pidof* command in the above example was used to determine the PID of the *crond* process and was enclosed with its argument in forward quotes (you may alternatively use the *pgrep* command to determine the PID of a process, as demonstrated in the next example). You may use the *ps* command to check whether the *crond* process has terminated.

Using the *pkill* or *kill* command without specifying a signal name or number sends the default signal of 15 to the process. This signal may or not terminate the process.

Some processes ignore signal 15 as they might be waiting for an input to continue processing. Such processes may be terminated forcefully using signal 9:

 # pkill –9 crond
 # kill –9 `pgrep crond`

You may wish to run the *killall* command to terminate all processes that match a specified criteria. Here is how you can use this command to kill all *crond* processes (assuming there are more than one running):

 # killall crond

Understanding Job Scheduling

Job scheduling is a feature that allows a user to submit a command or program for execution at a specified time in the future. The execution of the command or program could be one time or periodically based on a pre-determined time schedule. A one-time execution is normally scheduled for an activity that needs to be performed at times of low system usage. One example of such an activity would be the execution of a lengthy shell program. In contrast, recurring activities could include performing backups, trimming log files, monitoring the system, running custom scripts, and removing unwanted files from the system.

Job scheduling and execution is taken care of by two daemons: *atd* and *crond*. While *atd* manages the jobs scheduled to run one time in the future, *crond* is responsible for running jobs repetitively at pre-specified times. At startup, this daemon reads schedules in files located in the */var/spool/cron* and */etc/cron.d* directories, and loads them in the memory for later execution. It scans these files at short intervals and updates the in-memory schedules to reflect any modifications made. This daemon runs a job at its scheduled time only and does not entertain missed jobs. In contrast, the *atd* daemon retries a missed job at the same time next day. For any additions or changes, neither daemon needs a restart.

Controlling User Access

By default, all users are allowed to schedule jobs using the at and cron services. However, this access can be controlled and restricted to specific users only. This can be done by listing users in the allow or deny file located in the */etc* directory. For either service, a pair of allow/deny files can be used. For at, *at.allow* and *at.deny* files are used, and for cron, *cron.allow* and *cron.deny* files are used.

The syntax of all four files is identical. We only need to list usernames that require allow or deny access to these scheduling tools. Each file takes one username per line. The *root* user is always permitted; it is neither affected by the existence or non-existence of these files nor by the presence or absence of its entry in these files.

Table 4-4 shows various combinations and their impact on user access.

at.allow / cron.allow	at.deny / cron.deny	Impact
Exists, and contains user entries	Existence does not matter	All users listed in allow files are permitted.
Exists, but is empty	Existence does not matter	No users are permitted.
Does not exist	Exists, and contains user entries	All users, other than those listed in deny files, are permitted.
Does not exist	Exists, but is empty	All users are permitted.
Does not exist	Does not exist	No users are permitted.

Table 4-4 User Access Restrictions to Scheduling Tools

By default, the *deny* files exist and are empty, and the *allow* files do not exist. This opens up full access to using both tools for all users.

> **EXAM TIP:** A simple username is entered in an appropriate allow or deny file.

The following message appears if an unauthorized user attempts to execute *at*:

> You do not have permission to use at.

And the following message appears for unauthorized access attempt to the cron service:

> You (user1) are not allowed to use this program (crontab)
> See crontab(1) for more information

In both examples above, we have entries for *user1* in the *deny* files.

Scheduler Log File

All activities involving *atd* and *crond* are logged to the */var/log/cron* file. Information such as the time of activity, hostname, owner, PID, and a message for each invocation is captured. The file also keeps track of other activities for the *crond* service such as the service start time and any delays. A few sample entries from the log file are shown below:

cat /var/log/cron

```
. . . . . . . .
Dec 4 08:50:01 host1 CROND[21558]: (root) CMD   (/usr/lib64/sa/sa1 1 1)
Dec 4 08:59:20 host1 crontab[22331]: (user1) AUTH (crontab command not allowed)
Dec 4 09:00:01 host1 CROND[22388]: (root) CMD   (/usr/lib64/sa/sa1 1 1)
Dec 4 09:01:02 host1 CROND[22496]: (root) CMD   (run-parts /etc/cron.hourly)
Dec 4 09:01:02 host1 run-parts(/etc/cron.hourly)[22496]: starting 0anacron
. . . . . . . .
```

Using at

The *at* command is used to schedule a one-time execution of a program in the future. All submitted jobs are spooled in the */var/spool/at* directory and executed by the *atd* daemon at the specified time. Each submitted job will have a file created that contains all variable settings for establishing the user's shell environment to ensure a successful execution. This file also includes the name of the command or script to be run. There is no need to restart the *atd* daemon after a job submission.

There are multiple ways for expressing a time with the *at* command. Some examples are:

at 1:15am	(executes the task at the next 1:15am)
at noon	(executes the task at 12pm)
at 23:45	(executes the task at 11:45pm)
at midnight	(executes the task at 12am)
at 17:05 tomorrow	(executes the task at 5:05pm on the next day)
at now + 5 hours	(executes the task 5 hours from now. We can specify minutes, days, or weeks instead)
at 3:00 5/15/15	(executes the task at 3am on May 15, 2015)

 at assumes the current year if no year is mentioned. Similarly, it assumes today's date if no date is mentioned.

You may supply a filename with the *at* command using the –f option. The command will execute that file at the specified time. For instance, the following will run *script1.sh* (create this file, add the *ls* command to it, and ensure it is executable by the user) for *user100* from their home directory two hours from now:

> **$ at –f ~/script1.sh now + 2 hours**
> job 1 at Thu Dec 4 11:40:00 2014

By default, at is already installed on the system as part of the RHEL7 installation. You can confirm with the *yum* command as follows:

> **# yum list installed at**
> at.x86_64   3.1.13-17.el7   @anaconda/7.0

If this package does not exist, you can run the *yum* command to install it. See Chapter 05 "Managing Software Packages" for details on package management.

> **# yum –y install at**

Exercise 4-1: Submit, View, List, and Remove an at Job

This exercise should be done on *host1*.

In this exercise, you will submit an at job as the *root* user to run the *find* command at 11:30pm on June 30, 2015 to search for all core files in the entire directory structure and remove them as they are found. You will have the output and any error messages generated redirected to the */tmp/core.out* file. You will list the submitted job and show its contents for verification then finally you will remove the job.

1. Run the *at* command and specify the correct time and date for the job execution. Press Ctrl+d at the at> prompt when done.

    > **# at 11:30pm 6/30/15**
    > **at> find / –name core –exec rm {} \; & /tmp/core.out**
    > **at> <EOT>**
    > job 5 at Tue Jun 30 23:30:00 2015

    The system has assigned ID 5 to this at job.

2. List the job file created in the */var/spool/at* directory:

    > **# ll /var/spool/at**
    > -rwx------. 1 root root 2862 Dec 4 13:49 a00005016d1f72

3. Display the contents of this file with the *cat* or *at* command. Specify the job ID with *at*.

    > **# cat /var/spool/at/a00005016d1f72**
    > **# at –c 5**
    > #!/bin/sh
    > # atrun uid=0 gid=0
    > # mail root 0
    > umask 22

```
XDG_SESSION_ID=2383; export XDG_SESSION_ID
HOSTNAME=host1.example.com; export HOSTNAME
SELINUX_ROLE_REQUESTED=; export SELINUX_ROLE_REQUESTED
SHELL=/bin/bash; export SHELL
HISTSIZE=1000; export HISTSIZE
SSH_CLIENT=192.168.0.13\ 64816\ 22; export SSH_CLIENT
SELINUX_USE_CURRENT_RANGE=; export SELINUX_USE_CURRENT_RANGE
SSH_TTY=/dev/pts/4; export SSH_TTY
USER=root; export USER
. . . . . . . .
find / -name core -exec rm {} \; & /tmp/core.out
marcinDELIMITER0c40a7df
```

4. List the spooled job with the *at* or *atq* command:

    # **at –l**
    # **atq**
    5   Tue Jun 30 23:30:00 2015 a root

5. Finally, remove the spooled job with the *at* or *atrm* command:

    # **at –d 5**
    # **atrm 5**

This should remove the job file from the */var/spool/at* directory. You can confirm the deletion with the *atq* command as well.

Using crontab

Using the *crontab* command is the other method for scheduling tasks for execution in the future. Unlike *atd*, *crond* executes cron jobs on a regular basis if they comply with the format defined in the */etc/crontab* file. Crontables for users are located in the */var/spool/cron* directory. Each authorized user with a scheduled job has a file matching their login name in this directory. For example, the crontab file for *user100* would be */var/spool/cron/user100*. The other location where system crontables are stored is the */etc/cron.d* directory; however, only the *root* user is allowed to create, modify, or delete them. The *crond* daemon scans entries in the files at the two locations to determine a job execution schedule. The daemon runs the commands or scripts at the specified time and adds a log entry to the */var/log/cron* file. There is no need to restart the daemon after submitting or modifying a job.

By default, cron and crontable files are installed on the system as part of the RHEL7 installation. You can confirm that with the *yum* command as follows:

yum list installed | grep cron
cronie.x86_64   1.4.11-11.el7   @anaconda/7.0
cronie-anacron.x86_64   1.4.11-11.el7   @anaconda/7.0
crontabs.noarch   1.11-6.20121102git.el7 @anaconda/7.0

If these packages do not exist, you can run the *yum* command to install them. See Chapter 05 "Managing Software Packages" for details on package management.

yum –y install cronie crontabs

The *crontab* command is used to edit (–e), list (–l), and remove (–r) crontables. The –u option is available for users who wish to modify a different user's crontable, provided they are allowed to do so and that user is listed in the *cron.allow* file. The *root* user can also use the –u option to alter other users' crontables, even if the users are not listed in the *allow* file. By default, crontab files are opened in the vi editor when the *crontab* command is used to edit them.

Syntax of User Crontab Files

The */etc/crontab* file specifies the syntax that each user cron job must comply with in order for *crond* to interpret and execute it successfully. Each line in a user crontable with an entry for a scheduled job is comprised of six fields. See Figure 4-4 for the syntax.

Compared to user crontables, the system crontab files have seven fields. The first five and the last fields are identical; however, the sixth field specifies the user name of who will be executing the specified command or script.

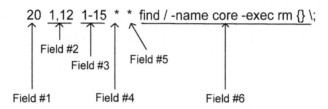

Figure 4-4 Syntax of Crontables

A description of each field is given in Table 4-5.

Field	Field Content	Description
1	Minute of hour	Valid values are 0 (the exact hour) to 59. This field can have one specific value (see #1), multiple comma-separated values (see #2), a range of values (see #3), a mix of #2 and #3 (1-5,6-19), or an * representing every minute of hour (see #4 and #5).
2	Hour of day	Valid values are 0 (midnight) to 23. Same usage applies as in the minute of hour field.
3	Day of month	Valid values are 1 to 31. Same usage applies as in the minute of hour field.
4	Month of year	Valid values are 1 to 12 or jan to dec. Same usage applies as in the minute of hour field.
5	Day of week	Valid values are 0 to 6 or sun to sat, with 0 representing Sunday, 1 representing Monday, and so on. Same usage applies as in the minute of hour field.
6	Command or script to execute	Specifies the full path name of the command or script to be executed, along with any arguments that it requires.

Table 4-5 Description of Crontable Syntax

Moreover, step values may be used with * and ranges in the crontab files using the forward slash (/) character. Step values allow the number of skips for a given value. For example, */2 in the minute field would mean every 2nd minute, */3 would mean every 3rd minute, 0-59/4 would mean every 4th minute, and so on. Step values are also supported in the same manner in the hour, day of month, month of year, and day of week fields.

EXAM TIP: Make sure you understand the order of the fields in user crontab files.

Exercise 4-2: Add, List, and Remove a Cron Job

This exercise should be done on *host1*.

For this exercise, assume that all users are currently denied access to cron.

In this exercise, you will submit a cron job for *user100* to run *script100.sh* (create this file, add "echo Hello, this is a test" to it, and ensure the script is executable by *user100*) located in this user's home directory. You will schedule this script to execute at every 5th minute past the hour from 1am to 5am on the 1st and the 15th of alternate months. You will have the output redirected to the */tmp/script100.out* file, list the cron entry, and then remove it.

1. As *user100*, open the crontable and append the following schedule to it. Save the file when done and exit out of the editor.

    $ crontab –e
    */5 1-5 1,15 */2 *   /home/user100/script100.sh &> /tmp/script100.out

2. As *root*, check for the presence of a new file by the name *user100* in the */var/spool/cron* directory:

    # ll /var/spool/cron/user100
    -rw-------. 1 user100 user100 68 Dec 4 19:26 user100

3. As *root*, edit the */etc/cron.allow* file and add *user100* to it:

    # vi /etc/cron.allow
    user100

4. As *user100*, list the contents of the crontable:

    $ crontab –l
    */5 1-5 1,15 */2 *   /home/user100/script100.sh &> /tmp/script100.out

5. As *user100*, remove the crontable and confirm the deletion:

    $ crontab –r
    $ crontab –l
    no crontab for user100

Chapter Summary

This chapter started with a discussion of the bash shell. The bash shell has numerous features but we touched upon only a few that are used more commonly. These features included variable settings, command prompt customization, redirection, command line editing, command history, tab completion, tilde substitution, regular expressions, and metacharacters.

We then studied processes. A good understanding of what user and system processes are running, what resources they are consuming, who is running them, what their execution priorities are, etc. is vital for overall system performance and health, as well as for you, the system administrator. We learned how to list processes in different ways. We looked at the five process states, niceness and reniceness for increasing and decreasing a process priority, and signals and how they are passed to running processes.

The last topic covered submitting and managing tasks to run in the future one time or on a recurring basis. We looked at the daemons that control the task execution and the control files where we list users who can or cannot submit jobs. We looked at the log file that stores information about all executed jobs. We reviewed the syntax of the crontab file and looked at a variety of date/time formats for use with both at and cron job submission. Finally, we performed two exercises to get a grasp on their usage.

Chapter Review Questions

1. Which is the default command line editor called?
2. When would the *cron* daemon execute a job that is submitted as */10 * 2-6 */6 * /home/user1/script1.sh
3. What is the other command besides *ps* to view processes running on the system?
4. Name two usages of the pipe symbol.
5. What are the two commands we learned to list the PID of a specific process?
6. What are the background processes normally referred to in Linux?
7. What is the default nice value?
8. The parent process gets the nice value of its child process. True or False?
9. What would the *nice* command display without any options or arguments?
10. Every process that runs on the system has a unique identifier called UID. True or False?
11. Why would we use the *renice* command?
12. Which user does not have to be explicitly defined in either *.allow* or *.deny* file to run the *at* and *cron* jobs?
13. When would the *at* command execute a job that is submitted as *at 01:00 12/12/15*?
14. What are the two commands that we can use to kill a process if the PID is known?
15. What is the directory location where user crontab files are stored?
16. By default the *.allow* files exist. True or False?
17. Name the three quoting mechanisms?
18. Where does the scheduling daemons store log information of executed jobs?
19. Which command can we use to edit a crontable?
20. The default location to send application error messages is the system log file. True or False?
21. We have to restart *crond* after modifying the */etc/crontab* file. True or False?
22. What are the five process states?
23. Signal 9 is used for a soft termination of a process. True or False?

Answers to Chapter Review Questions

1. The default command line editor is Emacs.
2. The *cron* daemon will run the script every tenth minute past the hour on the 2nd, 3rd, 4th, 5th, and 6th day of every 6th month.
3. The *top* command.
4. The pipe can be used as an OR operator and to send the output of one command as input to the next.
5. The *pidof* and *pgrep* commands.
6. The background processes are referred to as daemons.
7. The default nice value is zero.
8. False. The child process inherits its parent's niceness.
9. The *nice* command displays the default nice value when executed without any options.
10. False. It is called the PID.
11. The *renice* command is used to change the niceness of a running process.
12. The *root* user.
13. The *at* command will run it at 1am on December 12, 2015.
14. The *kill* and *pkill* commands.
15. The user crontab files are stored in the */var/spool/cron* directory.
16. False. By default, the *.deny* files exist.
17. The three quoting mechanisms are backslash, single quotes, and double quotes.
18. The scheduling daemons store log information of executed jobs in the */var/log/cron* file.
19. We can use the *crontab* command with the –e option to edit crontables.
20. False. The default location is the user screen where the program is initiated.
21. False. The *crond* daemon does not need a restart after a crontable is modified.
22. The five process states are running, sleeping, waiting, stopped, and zombie.
23. True. Singal 9 kills a process by force.

DIY Challenge Labs

The following labs are useful to strengthen most of the concepts and topics learned in this chapter. It is expected that you perform these labs without any additional help. A step-by-step guide is not provided, as the implementation of these labs requires the knowledge that has been presented in this chapter. Use defaults or your own thinking for missing information.

Lab 4-1: Customize the Shell Prompt

Log on to *host1* as *user1* and customize the primary shell prompt to display the information enclosed within the quotes "<username@hostname in directory_location >: ".

Lab 4-2: Redirect the Standard Input, Output, and Error

Log on to *host1* as *user1* and run the *ll* command on the */etc*, */dvd*, and the */var* dirctories. Have the output printed on the screen as well as redirected to the */tmp/ioutput* file and the errors forwarded to the */tmp/ioerror* file. Check both files after the execution of the command to validate.

Lab 4-3: Nice and Renice a Process

Open two terminal sessions on *host1* as *root*. Run the *system-config-users* command on one of the terminals. Run a command on the other terminal to determine the PID and the nice value of the *system-config-users* command. Stop *system-config-users* on the first terminal and re-run it at a lower priority of +8. Confirm the new nice value of the process by running the appropriate command on the second terminal. Execute the *renice* command on the second terminal and increase the priority of the *system-config-users* process to –10, and validate.

Lab 4-4: Configure a User Crontab File

Log on to *host1* as *user1* and create a cron entry to run the *find* command to search for the core files in the entire directory structure and delete them as they are found. Schedule this command in cron in such a way that it runs every other day of every other month at 15 minutes past 6am. As *root*, create an entry for *user1* if not already authorized to schedule cron jobs.

Chapter 05

Managing Software Packages

This chapter describes the following major topics:

➤ Overview of Red Hat packages, their naming, dependency, database
➤ Red Hat Subscription Management service, its components and benefits
➤ Register and unregister a system and attach and detach subscription
➤ List, install, upgrade, freshen, query, remove, extract, validate, and verify packages using the rpm command
➤ Overview of yum repository and how to create one
➤ List, install, update, search, remove, and check availability of packages as well as synchronize package header information using yum
➤ Add, view, update, and remove packages with graphical PackageKit

RHCSA Objectives:

41. Install and update software packages from Red Hat Network, a remote repository, or from the local file system

The Red Hat software management system was originally called Redhat Package Manager but is now known as RPM Package Manager (RPM). RPM also refers to one or more files that are packaged together in a special format and stored in files with the .rpm extension. These rpm files (also called rpms, rpm packages, or packages) are manipulated by the RPM package management system. Each package included in and available for RHEL and its derivatives is in this file format. Packages have meaningful names and contain necessary files, as well as metadata structures such as ownership, permissions, and directory location for each included file. Packages may be downloaded and saved locally or on a network share for quick access, and they may have dependencies over files or other packages. In other words, a package may require the presence of additional files, another package, or a group of packages in order to be installed successfully and operate properly. Once a package has been installed and its metadata information stored in a package database, each attempt to update the package updates its metadata information as well.

The Red Hat Subscription Management service is a web-based secure environment for Red Hat customers, with a valid subscription for system and subscription management and content updates. It requires customer registration for access and use. This service can also be accessed directly from a RHEL system to manage the subscription and content for that system only.

RHEL provides powerful tools for the installation and administration of RPM packages on the system. The rpm command is flexible and it offers a number of options though yum is superior to rpm in the sense that it resolves package dependencies automatically. PackageKit provides access to graphical tools for adding, updating, and removing packages.

Package Overview

RHEL is essentially a set of RPM packages grouped together to form an operating system. It is built around the Linux kernel and includes thousands of packages that are digitally signed, tested, and certified. There are several concepts associated with package management that are touched upon in the following sub-sections.

Packages and Packaging

A software *package* is a group of files organized in a directory structure and metadata that makes up a software application. Files contained in a package include installable scripts, configuration files, library files, commands, and related documentation. The documentation includes detailed instructions on how to install and uninstall the package, man pages for the configuration files and commands, and other necessary information pertaining to the installation and usage of the package.

All metadata related to packages is stored at a central location and includes information such as package versioning, the location it is installed at, checksum values, and a list of included files with their attributes. This allows package management tools to efficiently handle package administration tasks by referencing this metadata.

Package Naming

Red Hat software packages follow a standard naming convention. Typically, there are five parts to naming a package: the first part contains the package name, followed by the package version, the package release (revision or build), the Enterprise Linux the package is created for, and the processor architecture the package is built for. An installable package name always has the .rpm extension; however, this extension is removed from the installed package name.

For example, if the name of an installable package is openssl-1.0.1e-34.el7.x86_64.rpm, its installed name as reported by the *rpm* and *yum* commands would be openssl-1.0.1e-34.el7.x86_64. Here is a description of each part of the package:

- ✓ **openssl** – package name.
- ✓ **1.0.1e** – package version.
- ✓ **34** – package release.
- ✓ **el7** – stands for Enterprise Linux 7. Some packages have it, some do not.
- ✓ **x86_64** – processor architecture the package is created for. If we see "noarch" instead, the package will be platform-independent and can be installed on any hardware architecture. If we see "src", it will contain source code for the package.
- ✓ **.rpm** – the extension.

Package Dependency

An installable package may require the presence of certain packages in order to be installed successfully. Likewise, many software packages require other packages to be present in order to operate smoothly. This is referred to as *package dependency*, where one package depends on one or more other packages for installation or execution.

Package Database

Metadata information for the installed package files is stored in the */var/lib/rpm* directory. This directory location is referred to as the *package database*, and is referenced by package management tools to obtain information about ownerships, permissions, timestamps, and file sizes. The package database also contains information on package dependencies. All this information aids package management commands in verifying dependencies and file attributes, upgrading and uninstalling existing packages, and adding new packages.

Red Hat Subscription Management Service

The *Red Hat Subscription Management* (RHSM) service is provided by Red Hat for comprehensive subscription management and is the replacement for the older Red Hat Network Classic. Red Hat delivers software updates, technical support, and access to supported software versions in both binary and source forms by issuing subscriptions to its products. You purchase subscriptions based on your IT requirements and the Red Hat software you plan to use in the environment. You first register your systems with RHSM and then attach subscriptions to them based on the operating system and software they run.

Red Hat Customer Portal

RHSM offers Red Hat customers access to the web-based tool via the Customer Portal to add, organize, inventory, check status, track usage, and report on available subscriptions and any number of registered systems along with software products used by those systems. Software content for all supported software versions in both binary and source forms is delivered via geographically distributed Content Delivery Network (CDN). Figure 5-1 shows the overview section of Subscriptions Management after you have logged on to Customer Portal with your valid credentials. Using this dashboard, you can manage your subscriptions and registered systems.

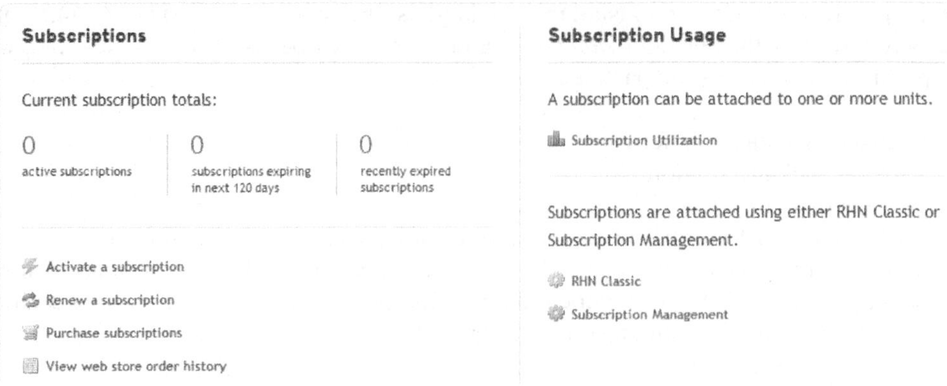

Figure 5-1 Red Hat Customer Portal Dashboard

Subscription Asset Manager

Local system administration and its subscriptions may be managed using the Subscription Asset Manager (SAM). SAM allows you to import entitlements via a manifest exported from the Customer Portal and gives you centralized control of the subscription assets. SAM can define groups and grant systems and users access to them. SAM controls the entitlements locally, but gets the contents from the Customer Delivery Network. In order to use SAM, you need to enable access to a Red Hat repository to install it. Configuring access to that repository and installing SAM is beyond the scope of this book.

Subscription-Manager

Subscriptions for a single system can also be managed using the Subscription Manager client application called *subscription-manager* that is installed locally on the system. This application has both graphical and command line interfaces, and it lets you manage the local system and its allocated subscriptions. Subscription Manager connects the local system with the Customer Portal or Subscription Asset Manager, and it gets contents from the Customer Delivery Network.

The *subscription-manager* command has several subcommands to perform various operations for local system subscriptions. Some of the subcommands are described in Table 5-1.

Subcommand	Description
attach	Attaches a subscription to a registered system.
auto-attach	Automatically attaches the closest-matched subscriptions.
clean	Removes all local system and subscription data.
list	Lists subscription and product information.
register / unregister	Registers (unregisters) a system to the Customer Portal.
remove	Removes subscription information.
repos	Lists available repositories.
status	Shows subscription and product status.

Table 5-1 subscription-manager Subcommands

Registering a System and Attaching Subscription

If you have an active subscription available, you can register your system with RHSM and attach it with the subscription that matches the system. You can do this from the command line by running the *subscription-manager* command, but you will need to supply valid user credentials in order to accomplish the tasks.

subscription-manager register --auto-attach

Username:
Password:
The system has been registered with ID: 2c9bc658-4cf8-4241-a388-ce50b8dce251
Installed Product Current Status:
Product Name: Red Hat Enterprise Linux Server
Status: Subscribed

After the system has been registered and a subscription has been attached to it, you can view the information by running the Subscription-Manager in the console by selecting Applications | System Tools | Red Hat Subscription Manager. A dashboard with three tabs will appear, as shown in Figure 5-2.

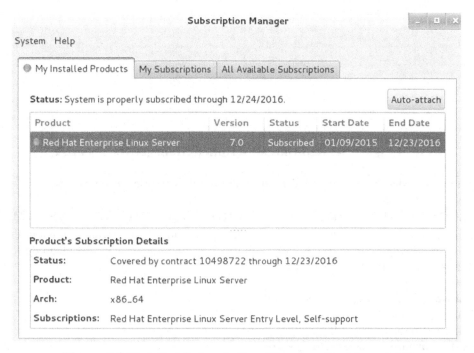

Figure 5-2 Red Hat Subscription-Manager Dashboard 1/2

The My Installed Products tab shows the product name and its version, subscription status, validity dates, and product subscription details.

The My Subscription tab, as depicted in Figure 5-3, shows the subscription and system information in more detail.

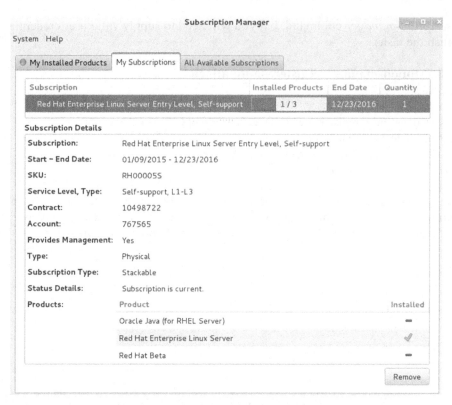

Figure 5-3 Red Hat Subscription-Manager Dashboard 2/2

The last tab, not shown here, lists information about all available subscriptions.

Detaching Subscription and Unregistering the System

You can remove the subscription assigned to the system and then unregister it using the *subscription-manager* command. Finally, run this command again with the clean option to remove any data stored locally for this system.

```
# subscription-manager remove --all
1 subscription removed at the server.
1 local certificate has been deleted.
# subscription-manager unregister
System has been unregistered.
# subscription-manager clean
All local data removed
```

The above can be achieved by using the graphical equivalent of the Subscription-Manager.

Managing Packages with rpm

This section discusses the package management tasks including installing, upgrading, freshening, overwriting, querying, removing, extracting, validating, and verifying packages using the *rpm* command. One caveat with this command is that it does not automatically satisfy package dependencies, which can become a big headache in the software installation and upgrade process.

Before getting into the details, let's take a look at Table 5-2 to see some common options that are used with the *rpm* command.

Query Options	Description
–q	Queries and displays packages.
–qa	Queries all installed packages.
–qc	Displays configuration files.
–qd	Displays documentation files.
–qf	Displays file information.
–qi	Shows package information.
–ql	Lists files in a package.
-q --whatprovides	Lists packages that provides the specified package or file.
-q --whatrequires	Lists packages that requires the specified package or file.
–qR	Lists dependencies.
Install Options	**Description**
–F	Upgrades an existing package.
–i	Installs a package.
–U	Upgrades an existing package or installs it if not already installed.
–h	Shows installation progress.
--force	Installs a package even if the same version already exists.
--replacepkgs	Overwrites existing packages.
Other Options	**Description**
–e	Removes a package.
--import	Imports a public key.
–K	Validates the signature and the package integrity.
–v or –vv	Displays detailed information.
–V	Verifies the integrity of package files.

Table 5-2 rpm Command Options

Before we look at various package management tasks, use the *mount* command to mount the RHEL7 DVD on the */mnt* mount point. Insert the DVD medium in the drive and run the following:

mount /dev/cdrom /mnt

If you have the RHEL7 ISO image copied to a directory on this system, you can mount it instead of the actual DVD. The following assumes that the ISO image is located in the */var/rhel7iso* directory and it is called *rhel-server-7.0-x86_64-dvd.iso*:

mount –o loop /var/rhel7iso/rhel-server-7.0-x86_64-dvd.iso /mnt

Here, the loop option tells the *mount* command that what is being mounted is not a block mountable device file but a mountable image file. This way the system treats the ISO image as if it is a real file system accessible via the */mnt* mount point. You can use the *df* command to determine the loop device file (*/dev/loop0* in this case) that was used by the above command:

df –h | grep mnt
/dev/loop0   3654720   3654720   0   100%   /mnt

Querying Packages

Querying one, more than one, or all packages searches for the required information and displays it on the screen. The following are some examples.

To query all installed packages:

```
# rpm –qa
libXxf86misc-1.0.3-7.1.el7.x86_64
perl-HTTP-Tiny-0.033-3.el7.noarch
baobab-3.8.2-4.el7.x86_64
. . . . . . . .
```

To query whether the specified package is installed:

```
# rpm –q perl
perl-5.16.3-283.el7.x86_64
```

To list all files in a package:

```
# rpm –ql iproute
/etc/iproute2
/etc/iproute2/ematch_map
/etc/iproute2/group
. . . . . . . .
```

To list only the documentation files in a package:

```
# rpm –qd audit
/usr/share/doc/audit-2.3.3/COPYING
/usr/share/doc/audit-2.3.3/ChangeLog
/usr/share/doc/audit-2.3.3/README
. . . . . . . .
```

To list only the configuration files in a package:

```
# rpm –qc coreutils
/etc/DIR_COLORS
/etc/DIR_COLORS.256color
/etc/DIR_COLORS.lightbgcolor
/etc/profile.d/colorls.csh
/etc/profile.d/colorls.sh
```

To identify which package the file is associated with:

```
# rpm –qf /etc/passwd
setup-2.8.71-4.el7.noarch
```

To display information about a package:

 # rpm –qi setup

Name	: setup
Version	: 2.8.71
Release	: 4.el7
Architecture	: noarch
Install Date	: Tue 08 Jul 2014 12:46:50 PM EDT
Group	: System Environment/Base
Size	: 696310
License	: Public Domain
Signature	: RSA/SHA256, Wed 02 Apr 2014 04:14:29 PM EDT, Key ID 199e2f91fd431d51
Source RPM	: setup-2.8.71-4.el7.src.rpm
Build Date	: Wed 12 Mar 2014 12:08:24 PM EDT
Build Host	: x86-024.build.eng.bos.redhat.com
Relocations	: (not relocatable)
Packager	: Red Hat, Inc. <http://bugzilla.redhat.com/bugzilla>
Vendor	: Red Hat, Inc.
URL	: https://fedorahosted.org/setup/
Summary	: A set of system configuration and setup files
Description	: The setup package contains a set of important system configuration and

setup files, such as passwd, group, and profile.

To list all dependencies for the specified package:

 # rpm –qR sox
/sbin/ldconfig
/sbin/ldconfig
libFLAC.so.8()(64bit)
. . . .

To query what the installable package is for:

 # rpm –qip /mnt/Packages/zsh*

Name	: zsh
Version	: 5.0.2
Release	: 7.el7
Architecture	: x86_64
Install Date	: (not installed)
Group	: System Environment/Shells
Size	: 5834433
License	: MIT
Signature	: RSA/SHA256, Wed 02 Apr 2014 06:53:21 PM EDT, Key ID 199e2f91fd431d51
Source RPM	: zsh-5.0.2-7.el7.src.rpm
Build Date	: Tue 28 Jan 2014 02:11:17 PM EST
Build Host	: x86-024.build.eng.bos.redhat.com
Relocations	: (not relocatable)
Packager	: Red Hat, Inc. <http://bugzilla.redhat.com/bugzilla>
Vendor	: Red Hat, Inc.

URL   : http://zsh.sourceforge.net/
Summary   : Powerful interactive shell
Description : The zsh shell is a command interpreter usable as an interactive login shell and as a shell script command processor. Zsh resembles the ksh shell (the Korn shell), but includes many enhancements. Zsh supports command line editing, built-in spelling correction, programmable command completion, shell functions (with autoloading), a history mechanism, and more.

To determine what packages require the specified package in order for them to operate properly:

rpm –q --whatrequires iproute
initscripts-9.49.17-1.el7.x86_64
dhclient-4.2.5-27.el7.x86_64
dracut-network-033-161.el7.x86_64
libreswan-3.8-5.el7.x86_64
libvirt-daemon-1.1.1-29.el7.x86_64
NetworkManager-0.9.9.1-13.git20140326.4dba720.el7.x86_64
fcoe-utils-1.0.29-6.el7.x86_64

Installing a Package

Installing a package creates the necessary directory structure for the package and installs the required files. The following command installs a package called zsh-5.0.2-7.el7.x86_64.rpm on the system:

rpm –ivh /mnt/Packages/zsh-5.0.2-7.el7.x86_64.rpm
Preparing...   ################################ [100%]
Updating / installing...
  1:zsh-5.0.2-7.el7   ################################ [100%]

If this package requires the presence of any missing packages, you will see an error message related to failed dependencies. You must first install the missing packages in order for this package to be loaded successfully.

Alternatively, you may specify the --force option to install the package in the absence of the dependent packages. Using this option is not recommended as it forcibly installs a package and overwrites the existing files if the same version of the package is already present.

If the zsh package is located on a remote ftp host *host1.example.com* in the repository at */pub/outgoing*, you need to specify the ftp server name and the package location with the *rpm* command:

rpm –ivh ftp://host1.example.com/pub/outgoing/zsh-5.0.2-7.el7.x86_64.rpm

The same syntax applies for the package residing on an http server; just change the protocol name and the location.

Upgrading a Package

Upgrading a package upgrades the specified package, provided an older version of the package is already there. In the absence of an older version, the upgrade simply installs the package.

To upgrade the package sushi-3.8.1-3.el7.x86_64.rpm, use the –U option:

> # **rpm –Uvh /mnt/Packages/sushi-3.8.1-3.el7.x86_64.rpm**

The command makes a backup of all the affected configuration files during the upgrade process and adds the extension *.rpmsave* to them. In the above example, the sushi package was installed as it was not already on the system.

Freshening a Package

Freshening a package requires that an older version of the package already exists.

To freshen the package sushi-3.8.1-3.el7.x86_64.rpm, use the –F option:

> # **rpm –Fvh /mnt/Packages/sushi-3.8.1-3.el7.x86_64.rpm**

To freshen all installed packages from the packages on the DVD, execute the following:

> # **rpm –Fvh /mnt/Packages/*.rpm**

Overwriting a Package

Overwriting a package replaces the existing files associated with the package with the same version.

To overwrite the package zsh-5.0.2-7.el7.x86_64.rpm, use the --replacepkgs option:

> # **rpm –ivh --replacepkgs /mnt/Packages/zsh-5.0.2-7.el7.x86_64.rpm**

Removing a Package

Removing a package uninstalls the package and all the associated files and the directory structure.

To remove the package zsh, use the –e option and also specify –v for verbosity:

> # **rpm –ev zsh**
> Preparing packages...
> zsh-5.0.2-7.el7.x86_64

This command performs a dependency check to see if there are any packages that require the existence of the package being removed, and fails if it determines that some other package has a dependency on it.

Extracting Files from an Installable Package

Files in an installable RPM package can be extracted using the *rpm2cpio* command. Each package contains several files placed in a directory structure, and may be retrieved to replace a corrupted or lost command or a critical configuration file. For example, to extract a lost */etc/ntp.conf* file, use the command below to determine what package contains it:

> # **rpm –qf /etc/ntp.conf**
> ntp-4.2.6p5-18.el7.x86_64

Assuming that the package is located in the *mnt/Packages/* directory, use the *rpm2cpio* command to extract (–i) all files from the ntp package and create (–d) directory structure as required:

 # cd /tmp
 # rpm2cpio /mnt/Packages/ntp-4.2.6p5-18.el7.x86_64.rpm | cpio –id
2795 blocks

Run the *ll* command to view the directory structure that is extracted:

 # ll *
etc:
total 4
drwxr-xr-x. 3 root root   60 Sep 19 11:29 dhcp
drwxr-xr-x. 3 root root   60 Sep 19 11:29 ntp
-rw-r--r--.   1 root root 1992 Sep 19 11:29 ntp.conf
drwxr-xr-x. 2 root root   60 Sep 19 11:29 sysconfig
usr:
total 0
drwxr-xr-x. 2 root root   60 Sep 19 11:29 bin
drwxr-xr-x. 3 root root   60 Sep 19 11:29 lib
drwxr-xr-x. 2 root root 160 Sep 19 11:29 sbin
drwxr-xr-x. 4 root root   80 Sep 19 11:29 share
var:
total 0
drwxr-xr-x. 3 root root 60 Sep 19 11:29 lib
drwxr-xr-x. 3 root root 60 Sep 19 11:29 log

The above output shows *etc*, *usr*, and *var* directories extracted that contain all NTP files. The *ntp.conf* file is under *etc/*. We can copy it to the */etc* directory now, and we're back in business.

Validating Package Integrity and Credibility

A package may be checked for integrity (completeness and error-free state) and credibility after it has been copied to another location, downloaded from the web, or obtained elsewhere, and before it is installed. We can use the MD5 checksum for verifying its integrity and the *GNU Privacy Guard* (GnuPG or GPG) public key signature for ensuring the credibility of its developer or publisher. This will ensure that we are using an uncorrupted and authentic piece of software.

To check the integrity of a package such as zsh-5.0.2-7.el7.x86_64.rpm located in */mnt/Packages/*, run the *rpm* command as follows:

 # rpm –K --nosignature /mnt/Packages/zsh-5.0.2-7.el7.x86_64.rpm
/mnt/Packages/zsh-5.0.2-7.el7.x86_64.rpm: sha1 md5 OK

The OK in the output confirms that the package is free of corruption.

Red Hat sign their products and updates with a GPG key, and include necessary public keys in the products for verification. For RHEL, the keys are located in files on the installation media, and are copied to the */etc/pki/rpm-gpg/* directory during the OS installation. Table 5-3 lists the files in that directory along with a short description of the kind of key they store.

GPG File	Description
RPM-GPG-KEY-redhat-release	Used for packages shipped after November 2009, and their updates.
RPM-GPG-KEY-redhat-beta	Used for beta test products shipped after November 2009.
RPM-GPG-KEY-redhat-legacy-release	Used for packages shipped after November 2006, and their updates.
RPM-GPG-KEY-redhat-legacy-former	Used for packages shipped prior to November 2006, and their updates.
RPM-GPG-KEY-redhat-legacy-rhx	Used for packages distributed by Red Hat Exchange.

Table 5-3 Red Hat GPG Key Files

To check the credibility of a package, we first need to import the relevant GPG key and then verify the package. From the above table, we know that the GPG file for the packages released recently is *RPM-GPG-KEY-redhat-release*. In the following example, we are going to run the *rpm* command to import the GPG key stored in this file and then verify the signature for the zsh-5.0.2-7.el7.x86_64.rpm package using the –K option with the command:

 # rpm --import /etc/pki/rpm-gpg/RPM-GPG-KEY-redhat-release
 # rpm –K /mnt/Packages/zsh-5.0.2-7.el7.x86_64.rpm
/mnt/Packages/zsh-5.0.2-7.el7.x86_64.rpm: rsa sha1 (md5) pgp md5 OK

The "pgp md5 OK" validates the package signature, and certifies the authenticity and integrity of the package.

Viewing GPG Keys

The key imported in the previous sub-section can be viewed with the *rpm* command. We can list the key and display its details as well. Run the command as follows to list the imported key:

 # rpm –q gpg-pubkey
gpg-pubkey-fd431d51-4ae0493b

The output indicates that there is one GPG public key currently imported on the system. We can view the details as follows:

 # rpm –qi gpg-pubkey-fd431d51-4ae0493b
Name   : gpg-pubkey
Version   : fd431d51
Release   : 4ae0493b
Architecture : (none)
Install Date : Thu 18 Sep 2014 06:58:59 PM EDT
Group   : Public Keys
Size   : 0
License   : pubkey
Signature   : (none)
Source RPM : (none)
Build Date   : Thu 22 Oct 2009 07:59:55 AM EDT
Build Host   : localhost
Relocations   : (not relocatable)

Packager   : Red Hat, Inc. (release key 2) <security@redhat.com>
Summary   : gpg(Red Hat, Inc. (release key 2) <security@redhat.com>)
Description :
-----BEGIN PGP PUBLIC KEY BLOCK-----
Version: rpm-4.11.1 (NSS-3)
mQINBErgSTsBEACh2A4b0O9t+vzC9VrVtL1AKvUWi9OPCjkvR7Xd8DtJxeeMZ5eF
0HtzIG58qDRybwUe89FZprB1ffuUKzdE+HcL3FbNWSSOXVjZIersdXyH3NvnLLLF
0DNRB2ix3bXG9Rh/RXpFsNxDp2CEMdUvbYCzE79K1EnUTVh1L0Of023FtPSZXX0c
u7Pb5DI5lX5YeoXO6RoodrIGYJsVBQWnrWw4xNTconUfNPk0EGZtEnzvH2zyPoJh
XGF+Ncu9XwbalnYde10OCvSWAZ5zTCpoLMTvQjWpbCdWXJzCm6G+/hx9upke546H
5IjtYm4dTIVTnc3wvDiODgBKRzOl9rEOCIgOuGtDxRxcQkjrC+xvg5Vkqn7vBUyW
9pHedOU+PoF3DGOM+dqv+eNKBvh9YF9ugFAQBkcG7viZgvGEMGGUpzNgN7XnS1gj
/DPo9mZESOYnKceve2tIC87p2hqjrxOHuI7fkZYeNIcAoa83rBltFXaBDYhWAKS1
PcXS1/7JzP0ky7d0L6Xbu/If5kqWQpKwUInXtySRkuraVfuK3Bpa+X1XecWi24JY
HVtlNX025xx1ewVzGNCTlWn1skQN2OOoQTV4C8/qFpTW6DTWYurd4+fE0OJFJZQF
. . . .
-----END PGP PUBLIC KEY BLOCK-----

Verifying Package Attributes

Verifying an installed package compares the attributes of files in the package with the original file attributes saved and stored in the package database at the time the package was installed. The verification process uses the *rpm* command with the −V option to compare the owner, group, permission mode, size, modification time, digest, and type among other attributes. The command returns to the prompt without displaying anything if no changes in the attributes are detected. We may use the −v or −vv option with the command for verbosity.

One of the files in the at package is */etc/sysconfig/atd*. Let's check the attributes for this file:

 # rpm −Vf /etc/sysconfig/atd

The command returned nothing, which implies that the file attributes are intact. Now let's change the owner, group, and permissions for this file to bin, bin, and 744, respectively, and then re-run the verification:

 # ll /etc/sysconfig/atd
-rw-r--r--. 1 root root 403 Jan 29 2014 /etc/sysconfig/atd
 # chown bin:bin /etc/sysconfig/atd ; chmod 744 /etc/sysconfig/atd
 # ll /etc/sysconfig/atd
-rwxr--r--. 1 bin bin 403 Jan 29 2014 atd
 # rpm −Vf /etc/sysconfig/atd
.M...UG.. c /etc/sysconfig/atd

The output now shows three columns: the first column contains nine fields, the second column shows the file type, and the third column indicates the name of the file. The command performs a total of nine checks, as illustrated by the codes in the first column of the output, and displays what, if any, changes have occurred since the package the file belongs to has been installed. Each of these codes has a meaning. Table 5-4 lists the codes as they appear from left to right, and describes them. The period appears for an attribute that is not in an altered state.

Code	Description
S	Appears if the file size is different.
M	Appears if the (mode) permission or file type is altered.
5	Appears if MD5 checksum does not match.
D	Appears if the file is a device file and its major or minor number has changed.
L	Appears if the file is a symlink and its path has altered.
U	Appears if the ownership has modified.
G	Appears if the group membership has modified.
T	Appears if timestamp has changed.
P	Appears if capabilities have altered.
.	Appears if no modifications have been detected.

Table 5-4 Package Verification Codes

The second column in the output above indicates a code that represents the type of file. Table 5-5 lists them.

File Type	Description
c	Configuration file.
d	Documentation file.
g	Ghost file.
l	License file.
r	Readme file.

Table 5-5 File Type Codes

Based on the information in the tables, the */etc/sysconfig/atd* is a configuration file with modified permission mode, user (owner), and group. Reset the file attributes to their original values and run the check again to ensure the file is back to its original state.

To verify the attributes for all the files included in a package with details:

 # rpm –Vv cronie-1.4.11-11.el7.x86_64
```
.........   /etc/cron.d
.........   /etc/cron.d/0hourly
.........  c /etc/cron.deny
.........  c /etc/pam.d/crond
.........  c /etc/sysconfig/crond
.........   /usr/bin/crontab
.........   /usr/lib/systemd/system/crond.service
.........   /usr/sbin/crond
.........   /usr/share/doc/cronie-1.4.11
.........  d /usr/share/doc/cronie-1.4.11/AUTHORS
.........  d /usr/share/doc/cronie-1.4.11/COPYING
.........  d /usr/share/doc/cronie-1.4.11/ChangeLog
.........  d /usr/share/doc/cronie-1.4.11/INSTALL
.........  d /usr/share/doc/cronie-1.4.11/README
. . . . . . . .
.........   /var/spool/cron
```

Exercise 5-1: Perform Package Management Tasks Using rpm

This exercise should be done on *host1*.

In this exercise, we will verify the integrity and authenticity of a package called dcraw located in the */mnt/Packages* directory on the RHEL installation DVD and then install it. We will display basic information about the package, show files it contains, list documentation files it has, verify the package attributes, and remove the package.

1. Make sure the RHEL7 installation media is in the DVD drive and is mounted on */mnt*. If not, run the following to mount it:

   # **mount /dev/cdrom /mnt**
   mount: /dev/sr0 is write-protected, mounting read-only

2. Run the *ll* command on the */mnt/Packages* directory to confirm that the dcraw package is available:

   # **ll /mnt/Packages/dcraw***
   -r--r--r--. 61 root root 232524 Apr 1 10:37 /mnt/Packages/dcraw-9.19-6.el7.x86_64.rpm

3. Run the *rpm* command and verify the integrity and credibility of the package:

   # **rpm –K /mnt/Packages/dcraw-9.19-6.el7.x86_64.rpm**
   /mnt/Packages/dcraw-9.19-6.el7.x86_64.rpm: rsa sha1 (md5) pgp md5 OK

4. Install the package:

   # **rpm –ivh /mnt/Packages/dcraw-9.19-6.el7.x86_64.rpm**
   Preparing...   ############################### [100%]
   Updating / installing...
     1:dcraw-9.19-6.el7   ############################### [100%]

5. Show basic information about the package:

   # **rpm –qi dcraw**
   Name   : dcraw
   Version   : 9.19
   Release   : 6.el7
   Architecture   : x86_64
   Install Date   : Fri 19 Sep 2014 09:33:36 AM EDT
   Group   : Applications/Multimedia
   . . . .

6. Show all the files the package contains:

   # **rpm –ql dcraw**
   /usr/bin/dcraw
   /usr/share/locale/ca/LC_MESSAGES/dcraw.mo
   . . . .

---

7. List the documentation files the package has:

   # **rpm –qd dcraw**
   /usr/share/man/ca/man1/dcraw.1.gz

   . . . .

8. Verify the attributes of the files in the package:

   # **rpm –V dcraw**

9. Remove the package:

   # **rpm –e dcraw**

Managing Packages with yum

The *yum* command (*yellowdog updater, modified*) is the front-end to the *rpm* command and is the preferred tool for package management. This utility requires that your system has access to a software repository, which may or may not require a valid user account to log in. The Red Hat Subscription Management service offers access to software repositories, but it is restricted to the subscribers only. There are several other web-based repositories that host packages that you may need on your system. CentOS repositories are one such example that do not require a subscription; they are accessible to everyone. Alternatively, you can set up a local repository on your system and add packages to it. You then create a definition file for this repository in the */etc/yum.repos.d/* directory. The primary benefit of using the *yum* command is that it automatically resolves dependencies by downloading and installing any additional required packages in order to successfully install the specified package. With multiple repositories set up, *yum* extracts the specified package from wherever it finds it. The default repositories for subscribers are the ones that are available through RHSM. The *yum* command is very versatile and provides multiple ways for doing certain tasks. Check the manual pages on how you can use this command with that flexibility.

Yum Configuration File

The key configuration file for *yum* is */etc/yum.conf*. The main section in the file sets directives that have a global effect on yum operations. You can define separate sections for each custom repository that you plan to set up on the system. However, a better approach is to store the repos in the */etc/yum.repos.d/* directory, which is the default location created for this purpose. The default contents of the *yum.conf* file are listed below:

   # **cat /etc/yum.conf**
   [main]
   cachedir=/var/cache/yum/$basearch/$releasever
   keepcache=0
   debuglevel=2
   logfile=/var/log/yum.log
   exactarch=1
   obsoletes=1
   gpgcheck=1
   plugins=1
   installonly_limit=3

Table 5-6 explains the above directives.

Directive	Description
cachedir	Specifies the location to store *yum* downloads. Default is */var/cache/yum/$basearch/$releasever*.
keepcache	Specifies whether to store the package and header cache following a successful installation. Default is 0 (disabled).
debuglevel	Specifies the level between 1 (minimum) and 10 (maximum) at which the debug is to be recorded in the logfile. Default is 2. A value of 0 disables this feature.
logfile	Specifies the name and location of the log file for *yum* activities. Default is */var/log/yum.log*.
exactarch	Specifies to update only those packages that match the CPU architecture of the installed packages. Default is 1 (enabled).
obsoletes	Checks and replaces any obsolete packages during updates. Default is 1 (enabled).
gpgcheck	Specifies whether to check the GPG signature for package authenticity. Default is 1 (enabled).
plugins	Specifies to include plug-ins with the packages to be downloaded. Default is 1 (enabled). Please check its description.
installonly_limit	Specifies the maximum number of versions of a single package, as defined by the installonlypkgs directive, to be kept installed simultaneously. Default is 3. Checks its desctiption.

Table 5-6 Directives in /etc/yum.conf

There are additional directives available that we may want to set in the main section or in custom repo sections of the file. These directives may be viewed with the *yum-config-manager* command:

```
# yum-config-manager
Loaded plugins: langpacks, product-id
============================== main ==============================
[main]
alwaysprompt = True
assumeno = False
assumeyes = False
autocheck_running_kernel = True
bandwidth = 0
bugtracker_url = https://bugzilla.redhat.com/enter_bug.cgi?product=Fedora&versio
n=rawhide&component=yum
cache = 0
cachedir = /var/cache/yum/x86_64/7Server
. . . . . . . .
======================= repo: rhel-7-server-rpms =======================
[rhel-7-server-rpms]
async = True
bandwidth = 0
base_persistdir = /var/lib/yum/repos/x86_64/7Server
. . . . . . . .
```

Yum Repository

A *yum repository* (or simply a *repo*) is a digital library for storing software packages. A repository is accessed for package retrieval, query, update, and installation, and it may either be for a subscription fee or free of charge. There are a number of repositories available on the Internet that are maintained by software publishers, such as Red Hat and CentOS. Additionally, you can have your own for internal IT use by configuring separate repositories for stocking different types of software and multiple versions of the same software. This is a good practice for an organization with a large number of RHEL systems as it takes care of dependencies automatically and aids in maintaining software consistency across the board. If you have developed a new package or built one, you can store it in one of those repositories as well. It is prudent to obtain packages from authentic and reliable sources such as the Red Hat Subscription Management service and CentOS to prevent potential damage to your system and to avoid possible software corruption.

A sample repository file is shown below with some key directives:

```
[rhel7.0_repo]
name= rhel7.0 repo
baseurl=file:///mnt
enabled=1
gpgcheck=0
```

EXAM TIP: Knowing how to configure a yum repository using a URL is very criticial for passing the exam. Use two forward slash characters to specify the FTP, HTTP, or NFS source.

The above example shows five lines in the sample repo file. It defines a unique ID within the square brackets, a brief description of the repo with the name directive, the location of the repodata directory with the baseurl directive, whether or not this repository is active, and if packages are to be GPG-checked for authenticity. Each repository file must have a name and a baseurl directive defined at a minimum, along with a repo ID; other directives are optional. The baseurl directive for a local directory path is defined as file:///local_path (three forward slash characters) and that for an FTP path as ftp://hostname/network_path, an HTTP path as http://hostname/network_path, or for an NFS path as file://hostname/network_path (two forward slash characters). The network path should include a resolvable hostname or an IP address.

The yum Command

Before getting into any further details, let's take a look at Table 5-7 and understand some common subcommands used with *yum*.

Subcommand	Description
check-update	Checks if updates are available for installed packages.
clean	Removes cached data.
group install	Installs or updates a package group.
group info	Displays package group details.
group list	Lists available package groups.
group remove	Removes a package group.
info	Displays package details.
install	Installs or updates a package.
list	Lists installed and available packages.

Subcommand	Description
localinstall	Installs or updates a local package.
provides (or whatprovides)	Searches for packages that contain the specified file.
remove / erase	Removes a package.
repolist	Lists enabled repositories.
repository-packages	Treats a repository as a collection of packages, allowing them to be installed or removed as a single entity.
search	Searches for packages that contain a string.
update	Updates installed package(s).
history	Allows to review previous yum activities as stored in the /var/lib/yum/history directory.

Table 5-7 yum Subcommands

Viewing Enabled Repositories

You can use the *yum* command with the repolist subcommand to list all enabled repositories accessible to your system. You can use the –v option for detailed information.

yum repolist
repo id   repo name   status
rhel-7-server-rpms/7Server/x86_64   Red Hat Enterprise Linux 7 Server (RPMs 4,759
repolist: 9,065

Exercise 5-2: Create a Local Yum Repository

This exercise should be done on *host1*.

In this exercise, you will create a local yum repository for your system. You will create a directory to store packages and then copy a single package from the mounted installation DVD in to that directory. You will install a package from the DVD that will allow you to set up the repository. Finally, you will create a definition file for the repository.

1. Create a directory */var/local* and *cd* into it:

    # **mkdir –p /var/local && cd /var/local**

2. Copy the package dcraw-9.19-6.el7.x86_64.rpm from */mnt/Packages* into this directory:

    # **cp /mnt/Packages/dcraw* .**

3. Install a package called createrepo on the system:

    # **yum –y install createrepo**
    . . . .
    Installed:
      createrepo.noarch 0:0.9.9-23.el7
    Complete!

4. Execute the *createrepo* command on the */var/local* directory to create the necessary file structure for the repo. A sub-directory called *repodata* is created containing the files.

    # **createrepo –v /var/local**
    Spawning worker 0 with 1 pkgs
    Worker 0: reading dcraw-9.19-6.el7.x86_64.rpm
    Workers Finished
    Saving Primary metadata
    Saving file lists metadata
    Saving other metadata
    Generating sqlite DBs
    Starting other db creation: Sat Sep 20 19:16:23 2014
    Ending other db creation: Sat Sep 20 19:16:23 2014
    Starting filelists db creation: Sat Sep 20 19:16:23 2014
    Ending filelists db creation: Sat Sep 20 19:16:23 2014
    Starting primary db creation: Sat Sep 20 19:16:23 2014
    Ending primary db creation: Sat Sep 20 19:16:23 2014
    Sqlite DBs complete
    # **ll /var/local/repodata**
    -rw-r--r--. 1 root root 405 Sep 20 20:12
    14a0de541849305bd40a7018b37fd84fdd0e01f3cdec84567fa120cd6a27300e-filelists.xml.gz
    -rw-r--r--. 1 root root 1266 Sep 20 20:12
    2dd56fc065d5cbaa0bc40d37fd8beda5201fee6ab841c03837dc46471f2b6e52-other.sqlite.bz2
    -rw-r--r--. 1 root root 1519 Sep 20 20:12
    4a9e531db6f1afd7fbd0a183b233fa7a67837b64be2081f3be9443b247a71da7-filelists.sqlite.bz2
    -rw-r--r--. 1 root root 857 Sep 20 20:12
    bd2e6608330c3a2fa47b617f5f6bbe13fcf6d3b9b0986a792182d4fb1ece433c-primary.xml.gz
    -rw-r--r--. 1 root root 2090 Sep 20 20:12
    d6eb83ee59b9e17930105f4f4e365e41dcd1e813eb7bd23e447b66068d33087f-primary.sqlite.bz2
    -rw-r--r--. 1 root root 646 Sep 20 20:12
    . . . .

5. Create a definition file */etc/yum.repos.d/local.repo* for the repository. Enter the information as shown:

    # **vi /etc/yum.repos.d/local.repo**
    [local]
    name=local repo
    baseurl=file:///var/local/
    enabled=1
    gpgcheck=0

6. Execute the following command to clean up the yum cache:

    # **yum clean all**
    Loaded plugins: langpacks, product-id, subscription-manager
    Cleaning repos: local rhel-7-server-rpms
    Cleaning up everything

7. Run the following to confirm that the repository has been created and is available for use:

yum –v repolist

. . . .
Repo-id   : local
Repo-name   : local repo
Repo-revision   : 1411258356
Repo-updated   : Sat Sep 20 20:12:37 2014
Repo-pkgs   : 1
Repo-size   : 227 k
Repo-baseurl   : file:///var/local
Repo-expire   : 21,600 second(s) (last: Sat Sep 20 20:17:19 2014)
Repo-filename   : ///etc/yum.repos.d/local.repo

Exercise 5-3: Create a DVD Yum Repository

This exercise should be done on *host1*.

In this exercise, you will create a DVD yum repository. You already have the RHEL7 installation DVD mounted on */mnt* so you will create a definition file for this repository.

1. Mount the RHEL7 installation DVD on */mnt*:

   # **mount –o ro /dev/cdrom /mnt**

2. Create a definition file */etc/yum.repos.d/dvd.repo* for the repository. Enter the information as shown:

   # **vi /etc/yum.repos.d/dvd.repo**
   [dvd]
   name=dvd repo
   baseurl=file:///mnt
   enabled=1
   gpgcheck=0

3. Confirm that the repository has been created and is available for use:

   # **yum –v repolist**

   . . . .
   Repo-id   : dvd
   Repo-name   : dvd repo
   Repo-revision   : 1399448732
   Repo-updated   : Wed May 7 03:45:34 2014
   Repo-pkgs   : 4,305
   Repo-size   : 3.1 G
   Repo-baseurl   : file:///mnt
   Repo-expire   : 21,600 second(s) (last: Sat Sep 20 20:25:28 2014)
   Repo-filename   : ///etc/yum.repos.d/dvd.repo

Listing Packages and Package Groups

Listing packages allows us to search for installed and available packages in a number of ways and display them on the screen.

To list all installed packages on the system:

```
# yum list installed
Installed Packages
GConf2.x86_64              3.2.6-8.el7                @anaconda/7.0
ModemManager.x86_64        1.1.0-6.git20130913.el7    @anaconda/7.0
. . . . . . . .
```

To list packages available for installation from all configured yum repositories:

```
# yum list available
Available Packages
389-ds-base.x86_64         1.3.1.6-26.el7_0  rhel-7-server-rpms
389-ds-base-libs.x86_64    1.3.1.6-26.el7_0  rhel-7-server-rpms
ElectricFence.i686         2.2.2-39.el7      dvd
. . . . . . . .
```

To list all packages available for installation from all enabled repositories as well as those that are already installed. This command basically shows what the previous two commands have displayed separately.

```
# yum list
```

To list all packages available from all enabled repositories that we should be able to update:

```
# yum list updates
```

To list whether a package (bc for instance) is installed or available for installation from any enabled repository:

```
# yum list bc
Installed Packages
bc.x86_64                  1.06.95-13.el7             @anaconda/7.0
```

To list all installed packages that begin with the string gnome:

```
# yum list installed gnome*
Installed Packages
gnome-abrt.x86_64          0.3.4-6.el7       @anaconda/7.0
gnome-backgrounds.noarch   3.8.1-3.el7       @anaconda/7.0
. . . . . . . .
```

To list recently added packages:

```
# yum list recent
```

To list a summary of installed and available groups:

yum groups summary

To list all environment and other groups that are available for installation:

yum group list
Available environment groups:
   Minimal Install
   Infrastructure Server
   File and Print Server
   Basic Web Server
   Virtualization Host
   Server with GUI
Available Groups:
   Compatibility Libraries
   Console Internet Tools
   Development Tools
   Graphical Administration Tools
   Legacy UNIX Compatibility
   Scientific Support
   Security Tools
   Smart Card Support
   System Administration Tools
   System Management
Done

To list all packages a specific group or environment group contains:

yum group info Base
. . . .
Group: Base
 Group-Id: base
 Description: The basic installation of Red Hat Enterprise Linux.
 Mandatory Packages:
   acl
   at
   attr
   authconfig
. . . .

Installing and Updating Packages and Package Groups
Installing a package creates the necessary directory tree for the package and installs the required files. It also installs the files that are part of any dependent packages. If the package being loaded is already present, the command updates it to the latest available version. By default, *yum* prompts for a yes or no confirmation unless we specify the –y option at the command line. It also allows us to download the package in the */var/cache/yum/$basearch/$releasever/packages* directory if we select d. The above is applicable on group installs and updates also.

The following attempts to install a package called ypbind, but proceeds with an update to the newest available version if the command detects the presence of an older version of the package. Use the − y option to proceed without confirmation:

 # yum −y install system-config-keyboard

. . . .
Installed:
  zsh.x86_64 0:5.0.2-7.el7
Complete!

To install or update the dcraw package located locally in the */var/local* directory, use the localinstall subcommand with *yum*:

 # yum −y localinstall /var/local/dcraw-9.19-6.el7.x86_64.rpm

To update an installed package to the latest available version, issue the following command. Note that *yum* will fail if the specified package is not already there.

 # yum −y update autofs

To update all installed packages to the latest version:

 # yum −y update

To install or update a group of packages such as Smart Card Support:

 # yum −y group install "Smart Card Support"

To update the Smart Card Support group to the latest version:

 # yum −y group update "Smart Card Support"

Displaying Package and Package Group Header Information

Packages and package groups have basic information that identify their names, version, release, size, description, architecture they are built for, license, and so on. This information is referred to as their header information. This information can be viewed with the yum command for individual packages as well as package groups.

To view header information for the autofs package:

 # yum info autofs

. . . .
Name   : autofs
Arch   : x86_64
Epoch   : 1
Version   : 5.0.7
Release   : 40.el7
Size   : 3.6 M
Repo   : installed

From repo   : dvd
Summary   : A tool for automatically mounting and unmounting filesystems
License   : GPLv2+
Description : autofs is a daemon which automatically mounts filesystems when you use them, and
unmounts them later when you are not using them. This can include network filesystems, CD-ROMs,
floppies, and so forth.
. . . .

To display header information associated with the System Administration Tools group:

yum group info "System Administration Tools"

. . . .
Group: System Administration Tools
 Group-Id: system-admin-tools
 Description: Utilities useful in system administration.
 Optional Packages:
  conman
  crypto-utils
  dump
  expect
  hardlink
  lsscsi
  mc
  mgetty
 . . . .

Searching Packages

To search for packages that contain a specific file such as */bin/bash*, use the provides subcommand
with *yum*:

yum provides /bin/bash

. . . .
Loaded plugins: langpacks, product-id, subscription-manager
bash-4.2.45-5.el7.x86_64 : The GNU Bourne Again shell
Repo   : dvd
Matched from:
Filename   : /bin/bash

bash-4.2.45-5.el7.x86_64 : The GNU Bourne Again shell
Repo   : rhel-7-server-rpms
Matched from:
Filename   : /bin/bash

bash-4.2.45-5.el7.x86_64 : The GNU Bourne Again shell
Repo   : @anaconda/7.0
Matched from:
Filename   : /bin/bash

The output indicates that the */bin/bash* file is part of the bash package, which is available from the DVD and rhel-7-server-rpms repositories. The output also shows that the bash package was installed during RHEL installation.

With the provides subcommand, we can also use the wildcard character to match all filenames:

yum provides /usr/bin/system-config-*

To search for all packages that match the specified string in their name, description, or summary:

yum search system-config
. . . .
==================== N/S matched: system-config ====================
system-config-firewall-base.noarch : system-config-firewall base components and
                      : command line tool
system-config-keyboard-base.noarch : system-config-keyboard base components
cups-pk-helper.x86_64 : A helper that makes system-config-printer use PolicyKit
system-config-date.noarch : A graphical interface for modifying system date and time
. . . .

Removing Packages and Package Groups

Removing packages and package groups automatically deletes dependent packages as part of the removal process. It prompts for confirmation to proceed unless we specify the –y option with the *yum* command.

To remove the dcraw package and any packages that depend on it:

yum –y remove dcraw
. . . .
Resolving Dependencies
--> Running transaction check
---> Package dcraw.x86_64 0:9.19-6.el7 will be erased
--> Finished Dependency Resolution
rhel-7-server-rpms/7Server/x86_64 | 3.7 kB   00:00
Dependencies Resolved

==
Package	Arch	Version	Repository	Size
==
Removing:				
dcraw	x86_64	9.19-6.el7	@dvd	468 k
Transaction Summary				
==

Remove 1 Package
Installed size: 468 k
Downloading packages:
Running transaction check
Running transaction test
Transaction test succeeded
Running transaction

```
Erasing   : dcraw-9.19-6.el7.x86_64                           1/1
Verifying : dcraw-9.19-6.el7.x86_64                           1/1
Removed:
 dcraw.x86_64 0:9.19-6.el7
Complete!
```

To remove a package group:

 # yum –y group remove "Scientific Support"

```
. . . . . . . .
Removed:
 atlas.x86_64 0:3.10.1-7.el7        lapack.x86_64 0:3.4.2-4.el7
 numpy.x86_64 1:1.7.1-10.el7
Dependency Removed:
 nfsometer.noarch 0:1.7-0.el7      python-matplotlib.x86_64 0:1.2.0-15.el7
Complete!
```

Checking for Package Updates

Sometimes we need to update one or more packages on the system to a newer or the newest version. This may be required to address a bug in the software or to leverage new features introduced in the new version. The *yum* command allows us to check whether updates are available for the installed packages and from which of the enabled repositories. Use the check-update subcommand with *yum* as follows:

 # yum check-update

```
. . . . . . . .
dhclient.x86_64                 12:4.2.5-27.el7_0.1  rhel-7-server-rpms
dhcp-common.x86_64              12:4.2.5-27.el7_0.1  rhel-7-server-rpms
dhcp-libs.x86_64                12:4.2.5-27.el7_0.1  rhel-7-server-rpms
. . . . . . . .
```

The above output indicates all newer versions available from all accessible repositories. Before you proceed with an update, ensure that you choose the version you need to update to.

Downloading Packages

Though *yum install* and *yum update* also allow you to download packages, you can use another tool called *yumdownloader* to download individual packages from an accessible repository.

To download a single package, specify the name of the package with *yumdownloader*, and ensure that you change into the directory, */var/local* for instance, where you want the package downloaded before issuing the command:

 # cd /var/local
 # yumdownloader –v dhclient

```
. . . . . . . .
dhclient-4.2.5-27.el7_0.1.x86_64.rpm            | 276 kB   00:00
```

Exercise 5-4: Perform Package Management Tasks Using yum

This exercise should be done on *host1*.

In this exercise, you will remove an installed package called ntp. After removing it, you will download it in the */var/local* directory, reinstall it, and display its header information. You will also install a package group called Smart Card Support. After the installation, you will display the package group's header information and then remove it.

1. Remove the ntp package:

    # **yum –y erase ntp**

    . . . .
    Running transaction
      Erasing   : ntp-4.2.6p5-18.el7.x86_64   1/1
      Verifying : ntp-4.2.6p5-18.el7.x86_64   1/1
    Removed:
      ntp.x86_64 0:4.2.6p5-18.el7
    Complete!

2. Change into the */var/local* directory and download the ntp package:

    # **cd /var/local ; yumdownloader ntp**
    ntp-4.2.6p5-18.el7.x86_64.rpm | 539 kB   00:00

3. Run the *ll* command on the ntp file to ensure the package has been downloaded:

    # **ll ntp***
    -rw-r--r--. 1 root root 552196 Apr 2 12:39 ntp-4.2.6p5-18.el7.x86_64.rpm

4. Install the package:

    # **yum –y localinstall /var/local/ntp-4.2.6p5-18.el7.x86_64.rpm**

    . . . .
    Running transaction
      Installing : ntp-4.2.6p5-18.el7.x86_64   1/1
      Verifying : ntp-4.2.6p5-18.el7.x86_64   1/1
    Installed:
      ntp.x86_64 0:4.2.6p5-18.el7
    Complete!

5. Display the package header information:

    # **yum info ntp**

    . . . .
    Installed Packages
    Name   : ntp
    Arch   : x86_64
    Version   : 4.2.6p5
    Release   : 18.el7
    Size   : 1.4 M
    Repo   : installed
    From repo   : /ntp-4.2.6p5-18.el7.x86_64

Summary   : The NTP daemon and utilities
URL   : http://www.ntp.org
License   : (MIT and BSD and BSD with advertising) and GPLv2
. . . .

6. Install the Smart Card Support package group:

yum –y group install "Smart Card Support"

. . . .
Installed:
  coolkey.x86_64 0:1.1.0-27.el7   esc.x86_64 0:1.1.0-27.el7
  pam_pkcs11.x86_64 0:0.6.2-17.el7   pcsc-lite-ccid.x86_64 0:1.4.10-5.el7
Dependency Installed:
  pcsc-lite.x86_64 0:1.8.8-4.el7   xulrunner.x86_64 0:24.8.0-1.el7_0
Complete!

7. Display the Smart Card Support package group information:

yum group info "Smart Card Support"

. . . .
Group: Smart Card Support
 Group-Id: smart-card
 Description: Support for using smart card authentication.
 Default Packages:
  =coolkey
  =esc
  =pam_pkcs11
  =pcsc-lite-ccid
 Optional Packages:
  opencryptoki

8. Remove the Smart Card Support package group:

yum –y group remove "Smart Card Support"

. . . .
Removed:
  coolkey.x86_64 0:1.1.0-27.el7   esc.x86_64 0:1.1.0-27.el7
  pam_pkcs11.x86_64 0:0.6.2-17.el7   pcsc-lite-ccid.x86_64 0:1.4.10-5.el7
Dependency Removed:
  pcsc-lite.x86_64 0:1.8.8-4.el7
Complete!

Viewing yum Transaction History

The *yum history* command can be used to view the history of yum transactions performed on packages and package groups. By default, *yum* stores this information in a database in the */var/lib/yum/history* directory. The history database contains a numeric ID assigned to each transaction, the user account that is used to run the transaction, date and time of the transaction, action taken, packages affected, completion status, and so on. In addition to viewing this information in a variety of different ways, we can also repeat or undo a transaction, or rollback to a certain point in the history. The following shows a few examples of pulling information from the history database.

To list the last 20 transactions:

yum history list

```
ID      | Command line         | Date and time       | Action(s)   | Altered
-------------------------------------------------------------------------------
    47  | group remove Smart Card | 2014-09-21 16:30 | Erase       | 5 EE
    46  | -y group install Smart C | 2014-09-21 16:29 | Install     | 6
    45  | -y localinstall /var/loc | 2014-09-21 16:24 | Install     | 1
    44  | -y erase ntp         | 2014-09-21 16:22    | Erase       | 1
    43  | -y install ntp       | 2014-09-21 16:21    | Install     | 2 <
    42  | group remove Scientific | 2014-09-20 23:08 | Erase       | 5 >
    41  | -y remove dcraw      | 2014-09-20 23:06    | Erase       | 1
    40  | -y install dcraw     | 2014-09-20 23:06    | Install     | 1
    39  | install zsh          | 2014-09-20 22:10    | Install     | 1
    38  | -y install ypbind    | 2014-09-20 21:00    | Install     | 2
    37  | -y install createrepo | 2014-09-20 19:12   | Install     | 1
    36  | -y erase createrepo  | 2014-09-20 19:12    | Erase       | 3 <
    35  | -y install *subscription | 2014-09-16 22:03 | Install    | 2 >
    34  | -y install zsh       | 2014-09-15 18:25    | Install     | 1
    33  | -y install ntp       | 2014-09-10 17:05    | Install     | 1
    32  | -y install openldap open | 2014-09-08 22:07 | Install     | 2
    31  | -y install mod_ssl   | 2014-09-07 12:59    | Install     | 1
    30  | -y install httpd     | 2014-09-07 12:36    | Install     | 1
    29  | -y erase httpd       | 2014-09-07 12:36    | Erase       | 1
    28  | install mariadb-server | 2014-09-02 22:44  | Install     | 6
history list
```

To list all previous transactions:

yum history list all

To view a summary of all previous transactions:

yum history summary

```
Login user        | Time          | Action(s)   | Altered
-------------------------------------------------------------------------------
root <root>       | Last day      | E, I        | 29
root <root>       | Last week     | Install     | 3
root <root>       | Last 2 weeks  | Install     | 3
 <david>          | Last 3 months | E, I        | 14
System <unset>    | Last 3 months | Install     | 1192
root <root>       | Last 3 months | E, I        | 131
history summary
```

To view transactions from 1 to 3 only:

yum history list 1..3

```
ID      | Login user       | Date and time       | Action(s)   | Altered
-------------------------------------------------------------------------------
     3  | <david>          | 2014-07-16 09:01    | Erase       | 2
     2  | <david>          | 2014-07-16 08:59    | Install     | 2
     1  | System <unset>   | 2014-07-08 12:46    | Install     | 1189
history list
```

Managing Packages with Graphical Toolset

RHEL provides a graphical package management toolset called PackageKit as a single rpm called gnome-packagekit for those who prefer to use the graphical interface. This package is for the GNOME desktop and is installed automatically during the RHEL7 installation when you choose the Server with GUI base environment in the Software Selection. If this rpm is missing from the system, run the following to install it:

yum –y install gnome-packagekit

PackageKit applications run the *yum* command in the background; however, these applications are not a replacement for *yum* nor a superset of it. PackageKit brings several graphical applications that make it easier to view, add, remove, and update packages. These applications are located in the */usr/bin* directory and are listed below for your reference:

rpm –ql gnome-packagekit | grep '/usr/bin'
/usr/bin/gpk-application
/usr/bin/gpk-dbus-service
/usr/bin/gpk-distro-upgrade
/usr/bin/gpk-install-catalog
/usr/bin/gpk-install-local-file
/usr/bin/gpk-install-mime-type
/usr/bin/gpk-install-package-name
/usr/bin/gpk-install-provide-file
/usr/bin/gpk-log
/usr/bin/gpk-prefs
/usr/bin/gpk-service-pack
/usr/bin/gpk-update-viewer

The following sub-sections discuss two of these tools: gpk-application, to add and remove packages, and gpk-update-viewer, to view and select updates to install.

Adding and Removing Packages

The Package Application tool allows us to add or remove one or more packages or package groups. It also allows us to view files included in each package, and the requirements and dependencies for each package.

To use this tool, execute *gpk-application* at the command prompt, or choose Applications | System Tools | Software to start it. An application interface similar to the one shown in Figure 5-8 will appear, which lists various Package Collections and available Software Sources (repositories) in the left pane. At the top left, we can enter a search string that may include the name, part of the name, description, or file name of a package. The tool searches in the installed package database and in enabled repositories, and produces a list of matching package names on the screen. The installed packages are highlighted and checkmarked while those available are grayed out and without a checkmark. You can choose one or more highlighted packages for removal. If you wish to install an uninstalled package, simply select it by clicking on the checkbox beside it and then click Apply Changes at the top right-hand corner to proceed with the installation. The installation progress shows at the bottom of the screen along with the name of the repository the package is being installed from. For both installed and available packages, you can view files included and list of required and dependent packages. A short description of what the package is about appears on the screen as well, along with its size and license information.

Figure 5-4 Add and Remove Packages

Viewing and Updating Packages

The Package Update Viewer tool allows us to view available updates for the installed packages and select them for installation.

To use this tool, execute *gpk-update-viewer* at the command prompt, or choose Applications | System Tools | Software Update to start it. An application interface similar to the one shown in Figure 5-5 will appear. This tool automatically runs the *yum* command in the backend with appropriate subcommands to search for all available updates and list them on the screen. By default, all available updates are checkmarked for installation. However, you only need to select the ones that you need unless your intention is to apply all of them.

Figure 5-5 The Package Update Viewer

Figure 5-5 shows that all software on the system is already up to date. However, if there were any updates available, they would be listed. In that case, you could highlight a specific update to view its details (by clicking Details at the bottom) or select one or more updates to install (by clicking Install Updates).

Chapter Summary

This chapter discussed software package management. We learned concepts around packages, packaging, naming convention, dependency, and patch database. We looked at the benefits of RHN and how to register a system to administer software. We studied and performed a number of package management tasks using the *rpm* command, looked at the concepts and benefits of having a yum repository, and then performed scores of package management tasks using the *yum* command.

Finally, we reviewed three graphical package administration tools that are part of the PackageKit package.

Chapter Review Questions

1. What would the *rpm –ql dcraw* command do?
2. What is the purpose of the *rpm2cpio* command?
3. What is the difference between freshing and upgrading a package?
4. What is the command that we would run to register your system with the RHN?
5. What are the names of the three graphical administration tools included in the PackageKit?
6. What would the *yum group info Base* command do?
7. What is the use of the –y option with the *yum install* and *yum remove* commands?
8. The Red Hat Network provides free access to package repositories. True or False?
9. What is the biggest advantage of using the *yum* command over the *rpm* command?
10. What is the difference between installing and upgrading a package?
11. Package database is located in the */var/lib/rpm* directory. True or False?
12. What subcommand would we use with the *yum* command to check for the availability of the updates for the installed packages?
13. What would the *rpm –qf /bin/bash* command do?
14. Which directory on an installed system does RHEL7 store GPG signatures in?
15. What should be the extension of a yum repository configuration file?
16. What would the *yum list dcraw* command do?
17. What is the name of the RHN daemon that must be running on the system in order for the system to be able to communicate with the RHN?
18. What would the options ivh cause the *rpm* command to do?
19. We can use the *downloadyum* command to download a package. True or False?
20. What would the *yum list installed *gnome** command do?
21. What would the *rpm –qa* command do?
22. How many package names can be specified at a time with the *yum install* command?
23. We can update all the packages within a package group using the groupupdate subcommand with *yum*. True or False?
24. What would the *yum info dcraw* command do?
25. Automatic software updates may be set up using the *gpk-prefs* command. True or False?
26. Which graphical tool may be used for adding and removing software packages?
27. Which package needs to be installed in order to set up a private yum repository on the system?
28. The Package Updater is the front-end to the *rpm* command. True or False?

Answers to Chapter Review Questions

1. The *rpm* command provided will list files in the dcraw package.
2. The purpose of the *rpm2cpio* command is to extract files from the specified package.
3. Both are used to upgrade an existing package, but freshing requires an older version of the package to exist.
4. The *rhn_register* command.
5. The three graphical administration tools included in the PackageKit are the Package Updater, the Software Updates Preferences, and the Add/Remove Software.
6. The *yum* command provided will list all packages in the Base package group.
7. The *yum* command will not prompt for user confirmation if the –y option is used with it.
8. False. RHN requires a subscription.
9. The *yum* command resolves and installs dependent packages automatically.
10. Installing will install a new package whereas upgrading will upgrade an exitsing package or install it if it does not already exist.
11. True.
12. The *check-update* subcommand.
13. The *rpm* command provided will display information about the */bin/bash* file.
14. The */etc/pki/rpm-gpg* directory.
15. The extension of a yum repository configuration file should be .repo.
16. The *yum* command provided will display if the dcraw package is already installed or available for installation.
17. The *rhnsd* daemon.
18. It will install the specified package and show installation details and hash signs for progress.
19. False. There is no such command.
20. The *yum* command provided will display all installed packages that contain gnome in their names.
21. The *rpm* command provided will display all installed packages.
22. There is no limit.
23. True.
24. The *yum* command provided will display the header information for the dcraw package.
25. True.
26. The Add/Remove Software program.
27. The createrepo package.
28. True.

DIY Challenge Labs

The following labs are useful to strengthen most of the concepts and topics learned in this chapter. It is expected that you perform these labs without any additional help. A step-by-step guide is not provided, as the implementation of these labs requires the knowledge that has been presented in this chapter. Use defaults or your own thinking for missing information.

Lab 5-1: Set up a Third Party Yum Repository

Set up a third party yum repository to access packages located at *atrpms.net* for RHEL7. Install a package called aalib from this repository. Consider using the --disablerepo option when installing the package to ensure that the *yum install* command does not search for this program in other enabled repositories.

Lab 5-2: Configure a Local Yum Repository

Configure a local yum repository to access packages located locally in a directory. Create a directory called */var/yum/repos.d/local* and copy all the contents of the RHEL7 installation DVD to it. Create a repo file for this repository and install packages policycoreutils* from this repository to validate it.

Lab 5-3: Install Package Groups

Install package groups Backup Server, Remote Desktop Clients, and Security Tools from the local yum repository configured in Lab 6-2. Review the *yum.log* file for confirmation after the installation is complete. Display the information for the three package groups.

## Chapter 06

Configuring Server Virtualization and Network Installing RHEL7

This chapter describes the following major topics:

- Understand server virtualization and its benefits
- Virtual network switches and interfaces
- Virtual storage pools and volumes
- Manage hypervisor with GUI and commands
- Create virtual networks with GUI and commands
- Create virtual storage with GUI and commands
- Configure FTP installation server
- Set up two-way communication between host and virtual machines
- Network install RHEL using GUI and remote installation server
- Benefits of using kickstart
- Create kickstart configuration file
- Network install RHEL using commands and kickstart configuration file
- Download files non-interactively from FTP and HTTP/HTTPS sources

RHCSA Objectives:

17. Access a virtual machine's console
18. Start and stop virtual machines
35. Install Red Hat Enterprise Linux automatically using Kickstart
36. Configure a physical machine to host virtual guests
37. Install Red Hat Enterprise Linux systems as virtual guests
38. Configure systems to launch virtual machines at boot

Server Virtualization Technology

Server virtualization is a feature that allows a physical computer to host several virtual machines, each of which acts as a standalone computer running a unique instance of RHEL, Solaris, Windows, or other Linux distribution. All virtual machines, and the operating systems they run, operate alongside one another in complete isolation.

RHEL may be installed over the network using a configured FTP, HTTP, or NFS server hosting the installation files. Installing over the network is much faster than a local DVD-based installation. A client system, where RHEL needs to be installed, can be booted locally and then redirected to one of these network installation servers for loading the operating system software. The client system can be configured during the installation or supplied with a file that contains all the configuration information, including disk partitioning. This way there is no need to go through the configuration process during installation, which makes the installation faster and fully unattended.

The wget utility is used to download files or entire directory trees non-interactively from FTP or HTTP/HTTPS sites. This tool can be scheduled to run during off-peak hours for large file retrievals.

Server Virtualization Technology

Server virtualization refers to the act of building and running multiple independent virtual computers on top of a single physical computer. In the process of virtualizing the physical computer, hardware components such as processors, memory, disk storage, optical storage, network interfaces, and ports, are shared among the virtual computers. An operating system such as RHEL, other Linux, Solaris, or Windows is deployed in each virtual computer, and run to support a database, web, DNS, or some other service or application. All virtual computers, along with the operating systems and services they host, run concurrently and in complete isolation from one another.

From a server virtualization standpoint, a physical computer that is configured to host virtual computers is referred to as a *host machine*; a virtual computer that is created to run on the host machine is referred to as a *virtual machine*; and an operating system instance that is deployed to run in a virtual machine is referred to as a *guest*.

For the purpose of virtualizing a host machine, there are many different software available. These software form a virtual layer on top of the physical hardware to create a virtualization infrastructure that enables the creation and hosting of virtual machines, giving the guest operating systems the notion that they are running on real, standalone, independent computers. Virtualization software deployed directly on bare-metal host machines is referred to as the *hypervisor* software. *Kernel-based Virtual Machine* (KVM) is an example of such software; it is part of the Linux kernel and comes as a native hypervisor software with RHEL7. It enables the mapping between physical CPUs on the host machine and virtual CPUs allotted to virtual machines, thereby providing hardware acceleration for virtual machines which results in performance increase. Once the virtualization infrastructure is set up with KVM, another software called *Quick Emulator* (QEMU) comes into action and plays an important role by making use of the physical-to-virtual CPU mappings provided by KVM. QEMU intercepts guest OS instructions destined for virtual CPUs and gets them executed on the physical CPUs using this mapping. It works with KVM to provide full virtualization capabilities on the host machine, and together they are able to attain the same level of performance for applications on virtual machines that the applications would normally get when they run on the physical hardware. See Figure 6-1.

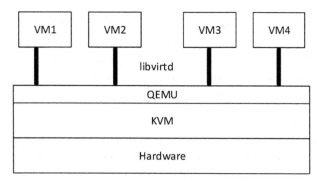

Figure 6-1 Virtualization Stack

With virtualization infrastructure in place, some software is needed to manage the hypervisor and virtual machines. The standard toolset available with RHEL7 is called *libvirt*. libvirt is a virtualization management library that includes necessary support and tools to manage the hypervisor and virtual machines. It consists of a daemon called *libvirtd*, a set of command line and graphical utilities, and an API library. Together, KVM, QEMU, and libvirt provide an end-to-end virtualization solution on RHEL7.

Virtualization Benefits

Virtualization technology brings a lot of benefits with it. Some of the key values that we may realize with its implementation are:

- ✓ Allows the creation of multiple virtual machines on a single host.
- ✓ Supports running instances of a variety of operating systems as guests.
- ✓ Each virtual machine and its guest is completely isolated and independent of other virtual machines and their guests.
- ✓ Provides the ability to consolidate older systems onto newer hardware platforms.
- ✓ Decreases the overall cost associated with computer hardware, and network and storage switches.
- ✓ Allows live migration of active virtual machines between physical hosts with a shared storage configuration.
- ✓ Supports the addition of virtual CPUs to active virtual machines.
- ✓ Supports overcommitting processor and memory, and thin provisioning of storage.
- ✓ Reduces the overall cost associated with power and cooling, floor and rack space, and network and fiber cabling.
- ✓ Supports quick virtual server deployments.
- ✓ Allows better utilization of computer hardware resources.
- ✓ Allows the addition of capacity to active virtual machines.

Verifying Host Virtualization Support

In order for the host machine to be able to support the virtualization infrastructure via KVM, its processors must have integrated support for hardware virtualization. This support is referred to as VT-x for Intel processors and AMD-V for AMD processors. We can run the *lscpu* command on the host machine to check whether the processors support this feature:

lscpu | grep Virtualization
Virtualization: VT-x

The above output indicates that the processors on this host support hardware virtualization.

Alternatively, we can *grep* for the vmx (for Intel processors) or svm (for AMD processors) attribute in the */proc/cpuinfo* file. The presence of this flag confirms that the processors on this host support hardware virtualization. The following command is issued on *host1* that has Intel i7 processor, and the output is from one of the processors:

grep vmx /proc/cpuinfo

flags   : fpu vme de pse tsc msr pae mce cx8 apic sep mtrr pge mca cmov pat pse36 clflush dts acpi mmx fxsr sse sse2 ss ht tm pbe syscall nx rdtscp lm constant_tsc arch_perfmon pebs bts rep_good nopl xtopology nonstop_tsc aperfmperf eagerfpu pni pclmulqdq dtes64 monitor ds_cpl **vmx** smx est tm2 ssse3 cx16 xtpr pdcm pcid sse4_1 sse4_2 x2apic popcnt tsc_deadline_timer aes xsave avx lahf_lm ida arat epb xsaveopt pln pts dtherm tpr_shadow vnmi flexpriority ept vpid

Virtualization Packages

In order for a physical computer to be able to host virtual machines, RHEL must be directly installed on it. During RHEL7 installation, we have the opportunity to select the virtualization environment group and the subgroups available within it. There are four virtualization subgroups, but not all of them are required on the host for full virtualization capabilities. Table 6-1 lists and describes them.

Package Group	Description
Virtualization Hypervisor	Provides the foundation to host virtual machines. Includes the libvirt and qemu-kvm packages.
Virtualization Client	Provides the support to install and manage virtual machines. Includes virsh, virt-install, virt-manager, virt-top, and virt-viewer packages.
Virtualization Tools	Provides tools for offline management of virtual machines. Includes the libguestfs package.
Virtualization Platform	Provides an interface to access and control virtual machines. Includes the libvirt, libvirt-client, and virt-who packages.

Table 6-1 Virtualization Package Groups

We can run the *yum group info* command on each of these groups to view details. For instance, the following shows the details when the command is executed on the virtualization hypervisor group:

yum group info "virtualization hypervisor"

. . . .
Group: Virtualization Hypervisor
Group-Id: virtualization-hypervisor
Description: Smallest possible virtualization host installation.
Mandatory Packages:
  libvirt
  qemu-kvm
Optional Packages:
 qemu-kvm-tools

If these package groups are not already installed, we can run the following to install all of them at once from an enabled repository:

 # yum –y group install "virtualization hypervisor" "virtualization client" "virtualization platform" "virtualization tools"

Virtual Network Switch and Virtual Network Interface

A *virtual network switch* is a libvirt-constructed software switch to allow the virtual machines to be able to communicate with the host and amongst one another. The host and the virtual machines see this switch as a virtual network interface. There is one virtual switch created on the host when the *libvirtd* daemon is first started, and it is represented as *virbr0*. The default IP assigned to this switch is 192.168.122.1. We can use the *ip* command to view its characteristics:

 # ip addr show virbr0
4: virbr0: <BROADCAST,MULTICAST,UP> mtu 1500 qdisc state UP
   link/ether f2:71:d7:37:6b:8b brd ff:ff:ff:ff:ff:ff
   inet 192.168.122.1/24 brd 192.168.122.255 scope global virbr0
    valid_lft forever preferred_lft forever

The default mode of operation for *virbr0* is NAT (*Network Address Translation*) with IP masquerading. NAT allows the network traffic of guest operating systems to access external networks via the IP address of the host machine, thereby hiding their own IP addresses from the outside world.

Furthermore, libvirt uses the dnsmasq program to enable DHCP and DNS on the virtual switch. It makes the IP range from 192.168.122.2 to .254 available for allocation to virtual machines. The DNS settings also become automatically available to virtual machines when the interface becomes active on them.

Libvirt supports two additional types of virtual network switch configurations; they are referred to as *isolated* and *routed*. Isolated switches restrict the ability of virtual machines to communicate to the outside world, whereas routed switches allow the virtual machines to talk to external networks directly.

Storage Pool and Storage Volume

A *storage pool* is a storage area that is used for the provision of storage to virtual machines. It is created and managed with libvirt tools and can be accessed by multiple virtual machines simultaneously as a shared storage space. A storage pool can be local to the host and configured as a file in a directory or as a file system in a partition, logical volume, or on an entire disk. Moreover, a storage pool can be set up on a remote system and accessed via iSCSI or NFS protocol.

Once a storage pool is set up, it can be carved up into one or more *storage volumes*, which can then be assigned to virtual machines as block storage devices.

Virtualization Management Tools

RHEL7 offers libvirt as the default hypervisor and virtual machine management software. This software is part of both virtualization hypervisor and virtualization platform package groups. Libvirt includes a powerful graphical administration tool called the *Virtual Machine Manager* or *virt-manager*, which is easy to understand and convenient to use. It also includes the *virt-install* command, which provides equivalent power at the command line. The *virt-install* command is used to create virtual machines and install RHEL in it. Libvirt includes a few additional tools also, but their coverage is beyond the scope of this book.

The Virtual Machine Manager (virt-manager)

The Virtual Machine Manager (*virt-manager*) is the graphical equivalent for both *virt-install* and *virsh* commands, and is used for the provision of virtual machines, installation of guest operating systems in both attended and unattended modes from a local or remote source, and management and monitoring of the hypervisor and virtual machines. It allows us to access the graphical console of the virtual machines, view performance statistics, and control their lifecycle. This desktop program includes wizards that make it easy for us to supply information as we set up a new virtual machine, virtual network, virtual network interface, storage pool, or storage volume. This tool gives us the ability to list, modify, and delete these objects as well.

To bring this tool up, run the *virt-manager* command in an X terminal or choose Applications | System Tools | Virtual Machine Manager. A screen similar to the one shown in Figure 6-2 appears.

Figure 6-2 Virtual Machine Manager Interface

To view the details of the hypervisor, right click it and select Details. You will see four tabs in the details window, as shown in Figure 6-3. These tabs are Overview, Virtual Networks, Storage, and Network Interfaces.

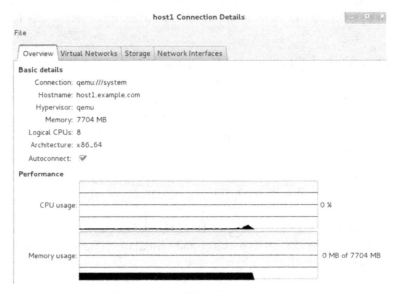

Figure 6-3 Hypervisor Basic Information

The Overview tab shows the basic information about the hypervisor, including its URI, hostname of the server it is running on, name of the hypervisor, memory and number of CPUs available, CPU architecture, and CPU/memory utilization information under Performance. There is also a checkmark whether to connect to the hypervisor each time the host machine is started.

The Virtual Networks tab displays the default virtual network configuration (see Figure 6-4).

Figure 6-4 Hypervisor Virtual Networks Tab

This tab provides basic details and displays IP configuration. It shows the virtual network name, the device associated with it, the state of the device, and whether to autostart it when a virtual machine using this virtual network is started. It does not show a DNS domain name, which implies that there is none currently set. IPv4 Forwarding indicates that NATting is enabled on the physical network interface. The IP configuration includes the subnet IP, the netmask, and a range of IP addresses that it may be able to supply to virtual machines if they are configured to use DHCP. The four little square buttons in the bottom left may be used to add, start, stop, or delete a virtual network.

The Storage tab displays the default virtual storage configuration (see Figure 6-5).

Figure 6-5 Hypervisor Storage Tab

This tab provides basic information about the configured storage. It indicates that the default location for storing virtual machine images is the */var/lib/libvirt/images* directory. It also tells us the current usage of the selected storage pool. Creation of a separate partition or logical volume large enough to hold the image files for all additional virtual machines that you plan on adding to this host is recommended. The New Volume button allows you to create volumes, which may be used to store virtual machine images. The Delete Volume button allows the removal of an existing volume. The State and Autostart buttons in the middle of the window as well as the four square buttons in the bottom left are self-explanatory.

The Network Interfaces tab displays the virtual network interfaces that are available for virtual machines to connect to (see Figure 6-6).

Figure 6-6 Hypervisor Network Interfaces Tab

This tab provides a list of all currently configured network interfaces. Highlighting one of them in the left window pane shows details on the right side of the window. By default, it shows only the loopback interface; however, you can add other network interfaces here too. Each interface shows the MAC address, state, autostart mode, and IP information, if available.

The virsh Command

The *virsh* command is used for the management and monitoring of the hypervisor and virtual machines. These management tasks include the ability of the tool to create, manage, and monitor virtual machines, virtual networks, virtual interfaces, storage pools, storage volumes, snapshots, and so on. There are a number of subcommands available. Table 6-2 lists and describes some of the more common ones.

Misc Subcommands	Description
cd	Changes into a different directory.
pwd	Displays the current directory location.
connect	Connects to the hypervisor in the form qemu:///system.
hostname	Displays the hypervisor name.
sysinfo	Prints the hypervisor information in XML format.
nodeinfo	Shows the host processor and memory information.
list	Lists domains and their state.

Misc Subcommands	Description
Domain Subcommands	
autostart	Sets a domain to autostart when the hypervisor is rebooted.
create	Creates a domain from an XML file.
define	Defines a domain from an XML file.
desc	Assigns a short description to a domain.
destroy	Terminates a running domain immediately. Emulates unplugging the power to a computer.
domdisplay	Shows the URI to be used to connect to the graphical display of the domain.
domhostname	Displays the hostname of a domain.
dominfo	Shows basic information of a domain.
domstate	Shows the current state of a domain.
dumpxml	Displays configuration of an existing domain.
edit	Edits the XML configuration file of a domain.
reboot / shutdown	Reboots a domain / shuts down a domain gracefully.
start	Starts up an inactive domain.
suspend / resume	Suspends a running domain / resumes a suspended domain.
vcpuinfo	Returns basic information about virtual processors assigned to a domain.
Device Subcommands	
attach-disk / detach-disk	Attaches / detaches a disk to / from a domain.
attach-interface / detach-interface	Attaches / detaches a network interface to / from a domain.
Virtual Network Subcommands	
net-autostart	Sets a virtual network to autostart at system reboot.
net-create	Creates a temporary virtual network.
net-define / net-undefine	Defines / removes a persistent virtual network.
net-destroy	Stops a temporary or persistent virtual network.
net-dumpxml	Displays configuration of an existing virtual network.
net-edit	Edits the XML configuration of a virtual network. Files located in the /etc/libvirt/qemu/networks directory.
net-info	Returns basic information about a virtual network.
net-list	Displays the list of active virtual networks.
net-start	Starts an inactive virtual network.
Virtual Network Interface Subcommands	
iface-bridge	Creates a bridge device and attaches an existing network interface to it.
iface-define	Defines a host interface from an XML file.
iface-destroy	Stops a host interface.
iface-dumpxml	Obtains configuration of an existing interface and dumps it to a file.
iface-edit	Edits the XML configuration of an interface. Files located in the /etc/libvirt/qemu/networks directory.
iface-list	Displays the list of active interfaces.
iface-start	Starts an inactive interface.
Storage Pool Subcommands	
pool-build	Builds a pool.

Misc Subcommands	Description
pool-create / pool-delete	Creates and starts a pool from an XML file / Deletes a pool.
pool-define	Creates a pool from an XML file. Files located in the /etc/libvirt/storage directory.
pool-destroy	Stops a pool.
pool-dumpxml	Displays configuration of an existing pool.
pool-edit	Edits the XML configuration of a pool.
pool-info	Returns basic information about a pool.
pool-list	Displays the list of active pools.
pool-start	Starts an inactive pool.
Storage Volume Subcommands	
vol-create / vol-delete	Creates a volume from an XML file / Deletes a volume.
vol-dumpxml	Displays configuration of an existing volume.
vol-info	Returns basic information about a volume.
vol-list	Displays the list of active volumes.
vol-pool	Shows the pool name of a volume.
vol-path	Returns the path of a volume.
vol-name	Shows the name of a volume.

Table 6-2 virsh Subcommands

The virt-install Command

The *virt-install* command is used for the provision of virtual machines. It supports both text and graphical installations of guest operating systems using an installation source located locally, or remotely via the NFS, HTTP, or FTP protocol. The *virt-install* command supports unattended kickstart installations also. There are a number of options available with this command. Table 6-3 lists and describes some common options.

Option	Description
--autostart	Sets the virtual machine to autostart when the host machine reboots.
--cdrom	Specifies the location of the installation image.
--connect	Specifies the non-default hypervisor in the form qemu:///system.
--description	A short description for the virtual machine.
--disk path/name	Specifies the path to store the virtual machine image. Also accepts a storage pool or storage volume name.
--graphics	Specifies the graphics type to be used, such as vnc or spice.
--location	Specifies the local or remote path for the installation image.
--name	Name of the virtual machine.
--network network --network bridge	Specifies the name of a virtual network or bridge.
--os-type	Specifies the type of OS desired. Valid values include Linux and Windows.
--os-variant	Specifies the OS variant for the OS type. Valid values include rhel7, rhel6, sles11, sles10, fedora19, win7, and win2k8.
--ram	Memory for the virtual machine.
--vcpus	Number of virtual CPUs for the virtual machine.
-v	Specifies to use full virtualization.

Option	Description
-x	Additional arguments to pass to Anaconda during a guest installation. For instance, specify the location of the kickstart file if kickstart installation is desired.

Table 6-3 virt-install Command Options

Managing Hypervisor

This section discusses adding a virtual network, storage pool, and storage volume using both *virt-manager* and *virsh*. The procedures outlined below using the *virsh* command are not the only ways to configure these objects; this command is versatile and can be used differently to achieve the same results. There are several other management tasks such as destroying, deleting, and undefining these objects that these tools can perform; however, I leave it up to you to try them out on your own.

Exercise 6-1: Create a NAT Virtual Network Using virt-manager

This exercise should be done on *host1*.

In this exercise, you will use the *virt-manager* GUI to define a persistent NAT virtual network called *rhnet_virt* with subnet 192.168.1.0/24, gateway 192.168.1.1, and DHCP range 192.168.1.128 to .254. This virtual network will activate and set to autostart automatically.

1. Run the *virt-manager* command or choose Applications | System Tools | Virtual Machine Manager to start it.
2. Highlight "localhost (QEMU)", right-click, and select Details.
3. Go to the Virtual Networks tab.
4. Click the + sign to start the "Creating a new virtual network" wizard. Click Forward.
5. Enter rhnet_virt as the virtual network name and click Forward.

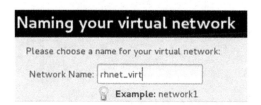

Figure 6-7 Create a Virtual Network – Select a name

6. Enter 192.168.1.0/24 as the IPv4 address space and select Enable DHCPv4. The default DHCP IP range for this network will be 192.168.1.128 to .254 and the range 192.168.1.2 to .127 will be available if you need to assign static addresses. Click Forward.

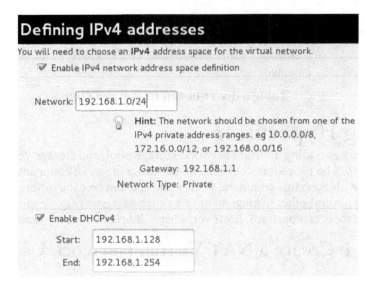

Figure 6-8 Create a Virtual Network – Choose Network IP and DHCP

7. Do not enable IPv6 addresses on the following screen. Click Forward to continue.
8. Next, select "Forwarding to physical network", destination "Any physical device", and mode "NAT". Do not assign a domain name. Click Forward.

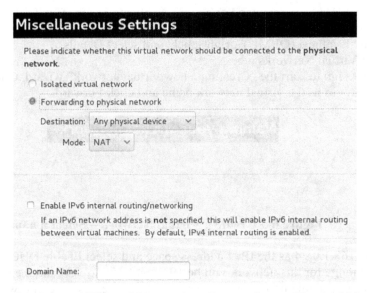

Figure 6-9 Create a Virtual Network – Connection to Physical Network

9. View the summary of your selections and click Finish to create the virtual network.

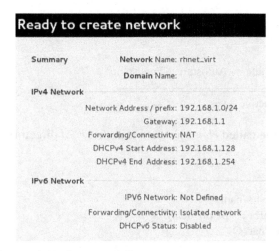

Figure 6-10 Create a Virtual Network – Summary

10. The Virtual Networks tab now shows the new virtual network.

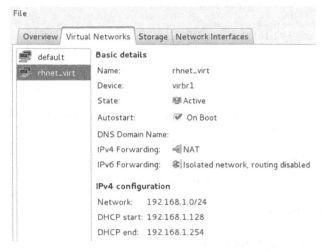

Figure 6-11 Create a Virtual Network – New Virtual Network Created

This virtual network is now ready. You can go to the Virtual Networks tab to view its details. You should now be able to attach this virtual network to virtual machines.

Exercise 6-2: Define a NAT Virtual Network Using virsh

This exercise should be done on *host1*.

In this exercise, you will use the *virsh* command to define a persistent NAT virtual network called *rhnet_virsh* with subnet 192.168.2.0/24, gateway 192.168.2.1, and DHCP range 192.168.2.2 to .254. You will use *virbr2* as the bridge name and a range of ports between 1024 and 65535. You will activate this virtual network and set it to autostart at each system reboot.

1. View available virtual networks:

   # **virsh net-list**

Name	State	Autostart	Persistent
default	active	yes	yes

2. Create an XML file called *rhnet_virsh.xml* in the */root* directory with the following information:

   ```
   <network>
    <name>rhnet_virsh</name>
    <bridge name='virbr2' stp='on' delay='0' />
    <forward mode='nat'>
     <nat>
      <port start='1024' end='65535'/>
     </nat>
    </forward>
    <ip address='192.168.2.1' netmask='255.255.255.0'>
     <dhcp>
      <range start='192.168.2.2' end='192.168.2.254' />
     </dhcp>
    </ip>
   </network>
   ```

3. Define *rhnet_virsh* as a persistent virtual network based on the configuration provided in the */root/rhnet_virsh.xml* file:

   # **virsh net-define /root/rhnet_virsh.xml**
   Network rhnet_virsh defined from /root/rhnet_virsh.xml

4. Set automatic start up of the new virtual network at system reboots:

   # **virsh net-autostart rhnet_virsh**
   Network rhnet_virsh marked as autostarted

5. Start the new virtual network:

   # **virsh net-start rhnet_virsh**
   Network rhnet_virsh started

6. List all virtual networks, including the new one:

   # **virsh net-list**

Name	State	Autostart	Persistent
default	active	yes	yes
rhnet_virsh	active	yes	yes

7. View details for the new virtual network:

 # virsh net-info rhnet_virsh

Name	rhnet_virsh
UUID	eed2e055-4817-4d04-bc84-6c2fe04732cf
Active:	yes
Persistent:	yes
Autostart:	yes
Bridge:	virbr2

This virtual network is now ready and you should be able to attach it to virtual machines.

Exercise 6-3: Create a Storage Pool and Volume Using virt-manager

This exercise should be done on *host1*.

In this exercise, you will use the *virt-manager* GUI to create a file-based storage pool called *rhpol_virt* and add a 10GB volume called *rhvol_virt* to it. You will use file system directory as the pool type and */var/lib/libvirt/rhpol_virt* as its location. You will ensure that the permissions on the pool directory are 0755 with ownership and group belonging to the *root* user. You will activate this storage pool and set it to autostart at each system reboot.

1. Run the *virt-manager* command or choose Applications | System Tools | Virtual Machine Manager to start it.
2. Highlight "localhost (QEMU)", right-click, and select Details.
3. Click Storage to go to the storage details tab. The information on this tab shows the existing pools, their sizes, location, current state, autostart setting, and list of volumes they have.

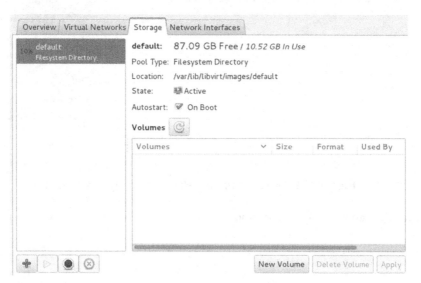

Figure 6-12 Add a Storage Pool – Existing Pools and Volumes

4. Click the + sign at the bottom of the screen to start the "Add Storage Pool" wizard.

5. Enter rhpol_virt as the name of the storage pool and filesystem directory as the type. Click Forward to continue.

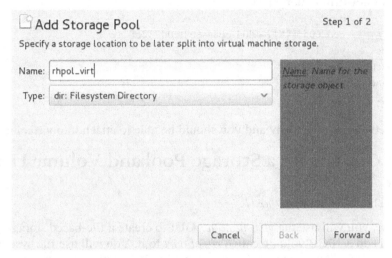

Figure 6-13 Add a Storage Pool – Assign a Name and Type

6. Specify */var/lib/libvirt/rhpol_virt* as the target path and click Finish to complete adding a storage pool and go back to the Storage tab.

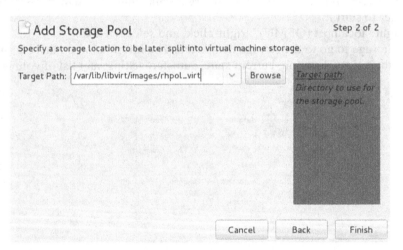

Figure 6-14 Add a Storage Pool – Specify a Target Path

7. The storage tab now shows the rhpol_virt pool in addition to the other two pools.

Figure 6-15 Add a Storage Pool – List of Storage Pools

8. Click New Volume to add rhvol_virt volume of size 10GB to rhpol_virt storage pool. Click Finish to create the volume and go back to the Storage tab.

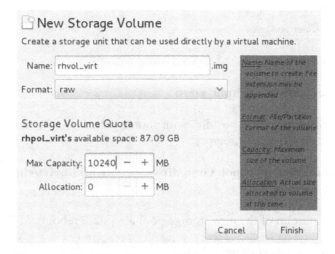

Figure 6-16 Add a Storage Volume – Add a Volume

9. The Storage tab now shows the new pool and the volume within it.

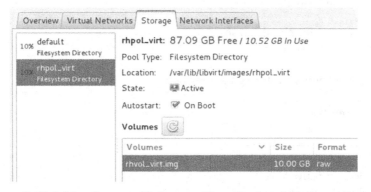

Figure 6-17 Add a Storage Volume – New Pool and Volume Created

This storage pool with a storage volume is now ready. You can go to the Storage tab to view their details. You should now be able to attach this volume to virtual machines.

Exercise 6-4: Create a Storage Pool and Volume Using virsh

This exercise should be done on *host1*.

In this exercise, you will use the *virsh* command to create a file-based storage pool called *rhpol_virsh* and add a 10GB volume called *rhvol_virsh* to it. You will use file system directory as the pool type and */var/lib/libvirt/rhpol_virsh* as its location. You will ensure that the permissions on the pool directory are 0755, with ownership and group belonging to the *root* user. You will activate this storage pool and set it to autostart at each system reboot.

1.   View available storage pools:

      # **virsh pool-list**

Name	State	Autostart
default	active	yes
rhpol_virt	active	yes

2.   Create the pool directory:

      # **mkdir /var/lib/libvirt/rhpol_virsh**

3.   Define the storage pool as type "dir" with source path "- - - -" and target */var/lib/libvirt/rhpol_virsh* directory:

      # **virsh pool-define-as rhpol_virsh dir - - - - /var/lib/libvirt/rhpol_virsh**
      Pool rhpol_virsh defined

4.   Set automatic start up of the new storage pool at system reboots:

      # **virsh pool-autostart rhpol_virsh**
      Pool rhpol_virsh marked as autostarted

5.   Start the new storage pool:

      # **virsh pool-start rhpol_virsh**
      Pool rhpol_virsh started

6.   List all storage pools including the new one:

      # **virsh pool-list**

Name	State	Autostart
default	active	yes
rhpol_virsh	active	yes
rhpol_virt	active	yes

7. View details of the new pool:

virsh pool-info rhpol_virsh
Name: rhpol_virsh
UUID: 94f2975f-7544-4ef0-b9c6-bf71e8dd07cf
State: running
Persistent: yes
Autostart: yes
Capacity: 49.98 GiB
Allocation: 6.69 GiB
Available: 43.29 GiB

8. Create volume rhvol_virsh of size 10GB in the rhpol_virsh pool:

virsh vol-create-as rhpol_virsh rhvol_virsh 10G
Vol rhvol_virsh created

9. List the available volumes in the rhpol_virsh pool:

virsh vol-list rhpol_virsh
Name   Path
----
rhvol_virsh   /var/lib/libvirt/rhpol_virsh/rhvol_virsh

This storage volume is now ready and you should be able to attach it to virtual machines.

Configuring FTP Installation Server

File Transfer Protocol (FTP) is the standard networking protocol for transferring files between systems, and has been used on Linux, UNIX, Windows, and other operating system platforms for decades. In RHEL, an enhanced implementation of FTP called *very secure File Transfer Protocol* (vsFTP) is available and is used as the default file transfer service. This enhanced version is faster, more stable, and more powerful than the standard FTP and at the same time allows us to enable, disable, and set security controls on incoming service requests. The vsFTP daemon called *vsftpd* communicates on port 21.

This section discusses setting up an FTP installation server in preparation for over-the-network RHEL7 installation in virtual machines that we are going to deploy in later exercises. The following exercise provides a step-by-step procedure on how to configure an FTP server to provide access to RHEL7 installation files.

Exercise 6-5: Configure an FTP Installation Server

This exercise should be done on *host1*.

In this exercise, you will configure an FTP installation server on *host1* using the *vsFTP* program. You will install the necessary packages associated with vsFTP from the DVD yum repository that was set up in Chapter 05 "Managing Software Packages", copy the files from the installation DVD to the */var/ftp/pub/rhel7* directory, set proper SELinux context, enable FTP traffic to pass through the firewall, and start the FTP service. Finally, you will open a browser window and test access to the files.

1. Install the vsftpd software:

   # **yum –y install vsftpd**

2. Create the directory */var/ftp/pub/rhel7* for storing the RHEL7 installation files. Ensure that there is at least 4GB of free space available in the */var* file system.

   # **mkdir /var/ftp/pub/rhel7**

3. Change the directory into */mnt* where the RHEL7 installation DVD is mounted and copy the entire directory structure from */mnt* to */var/ftp/pub/rhel7*:

   # **cd /mnt && find . | cpio –pmd /var/ftp/pub/rhel7**

4. Add a permanent rule to the firewall for the FTP traffic to pass through and reload it:

   # **firewall-cmd --permanent --add-service=ftp ; firewall-cmd --reload**

5. Start the vsFTP service and check the running status:

   # **systemctl start vsftpd**
   # **systemctl status vsftpd**
   vsftpd.service - Vsftpd ftp daemon
     Loaded: loaded (/usr/lib/systemd/system/vsftpd.service; disabled)
     Active: active (running) since Sat 2014-09-27 23:53:32 EDT; 4s ago
    Process: 23775 ExecStart=/usr/sbin/vsftpd /etc/vsftpd/vsftpd.conf (code=exited,
   status=0/SUCCESS)
    Main PID: 23776 (vsftpd)
     CGroup: /system.slice/vsftpd.service
           └─23776 /usr/sbin/vsftpd /etc/vsftpd/vsftpd.conf
   Sep 27 23:53:32 host1.example.com systemd[1]: Starting Vsftpd ftp daemon...
   Sep 27 23:53:32 host1.example.com systemd[1]: Started Vsftpd ftp daemon.

6. Set the vsFTP service to autostart at each system reboot:

   # **systemctl enable vsftpd**
   ln -s '/usr/lib/systemd/system/vsftpd.service' '/etc/systemd/system/multi-
   user.target.wants/vsftpd.service'

7. Open a browser window on *host1* and type the following URL to test access:

   ftp://192.168.0.100/pub/rhel7

Index of ftp://192.168.0.100/pub/rhel7/

⇧ Up to higher level directory

Name	Size	Last Modified	
EFI		05/07/2014	07:58:00 AM
EULA	9 KB	04/04/2014	12:00:00 AM
GPL	18 KB	03/06/2012	12:00:00 AM
LiveOS		05/07/2014	07:58:00 AM
Packages		05/07/2014	07:58:00 AM
RPM-GPG-KEY-redhat-beta	4 KB	04/01/2014	12:00:00 AM
RPM-GPG-KEY-redhat-release	4 KB	04/01/2014	12:00:00 AM
TRANS.TBL	2 KB	05/07/2014	07:58:00 AM
addons		05/07/2014	07:58:00 AM
images		05/07/2014	07:58:00 AM
isolinux		10/29/2014	08:32:00 PM
ks.cfg	2 KB	10/30/2014	02:33:00 PM
media.repo	1 KB	05/07/2014	07:53:00 AM
release-notes		05/07/2014	07:58:00 AM
repodata		05/07/2014	07:58:00 AM

Exercise 6-6: Replace DVD Yum Repository with FTP Yum Repository

This exercise should be done on *host1*.

In this exercise, you will unconfigure the DVD yum repository that was created in Chapter 05 and set up a new FTP yum repository pointing to the FTP location */var/ftp/pub/rhel7*. You will create a definition file for this new repository and test it to ensure it is available on the system.

1. Remove the *dvd.repo* file from the */etc/yum.repos.d* directory:

   # **rm /etc/yum.repos.d/dvd.repo**

2. Unmount and eject the RHEL7 installation DVD from the drive:

   # **eject /mnt**

3. Create a definition file */etc/yum.repos.d/ftp.repo* for the repository. Enter the information as shown:

   # **vi /etc/yum.repos.d/ftp.repo**
   [ftprepo]
   name=ftp repo
   baseurl=ftp://192.168.0.100/pub/rhel7
   enabled=1
   gpgcheck=0

4. Clean up the yum cache directory:

   # **yum clean all**

5. Confirm that the repository is created and is available for use:

```
# yum repolist

. . . . . . . .
repo id           repo name         status
ftprepo           ftp repo          4,305
repolist: 4,305
```

> **EXAM TIP:** Configuring a network yum repository is a critical task. You will not be able to load missing or required packages if you are unable to set up a repository successfully.

Exercise 6-7: Set Up Bi-directional Communication Between Host and Virtual Machines

This exercise should be done on *host1*.

In this exercise, you will create a virtual interface on *host1* that will allow this host and *server1* and *server2*, virtual guests that you will build in this chapter, to communicate directly with each other on the same 192.168.0 subnet using a bridge. This interface will also be used by *server1* and *server2* during their build to access the RHEL7 installation files on the FTP server that you configured in Exercise 6-5 on *host1*. This interface will be named *br0* and will use the IP assignments from *em1* physical interface. These assignments are 192.168.0.100 IP address, 255.255.255.0 subnet mask, and 192.168.0.1 gateway.

1. Change to */etc/sysconfig/network-scripts* directory and create a file called *ifcfg-br0* in *vi*. Add the directives as indicated below:

   ```
   # cd /etc/sysconfig/network-scripts; vi ifcfg-br0
   DEVICE=br0
   BOOTPROTO=static
   ONBOOT=yes
   IPADDR=192.168.0.100
   NETMASK=255.255.255.0
   GATEWAY=192.168.0.1
   TYPE=Bridge
   NM_CONTROLLED=no
   ```

2. Edit the *ifcfg-em1* file and set the following directives:

   ```
   # vi ifcfg-em1
   DEVICE=em1
   TYPE=Ethernet
   BRIDGE=br0
   ONBOOT=yes
   NM_CONTROLLED=no
   HWADDR=D4:BE:D9:2E:2E:D9
   ```

3. Confirm the setup of the new bridge using the *brctl* command:

brctl show br0

bridge name	bridge id	STP enabled	interfaces
br0	8000.d4bed92e2ed9	no	em1

4. Restart the network service:

systemctl restart network

5. Confirm that the new bridge interface has taken over the IP assignments from *em1*. Also ensure that these assignments are no longer assigned to *em1*.

ip addr show br0
4: br0: <BROADCAST,MULTICAST,UP,LOWER_UP> mtu 1500 qdisc noqueue state UP
    link/ether d4:be:d9:2e:2e:d9 brd ff:ff:ff:ff:ff:ff
    inet 192.168.0.100/24 brd 192.168.0.255 scope global br0
      valid_lft forever preferred_lft forever
    inet6 fe80::d6be:d9ff:fe2e:2ed9/64 scope link
      valid_lft forever preferred_lft forever
ip addr show em1
2: em1: <BROADCAST,MULTICAST,UP,LOWER_UP> mtu 1500 qdisc pfifo_fast master br0 state
UP qlen 1000
    link/ether d4:be:d9:2e:2e:d9 brd ff:ff:ff:ff:ff:ff
    inet6 fe80::d6be:d9ff:fe2e:2ed9/64 scope link
      valid_lft forever preferred_lft forever

The new virtual bridge *br0* is now ready for use. It will allow the virtual machines in the next section to be able to access the FTP services on *host1*.

Network Installing RHEL Using virt-manager

This section discusses creating a virtual machine using the *virt-manager* GUI and then installing RHEL7 in it using the installation files located on an FTP server.

Exercise 6-8: Network Install RHEL7 Using virt-manager

This exercise should be done on *host1*.

In this exercise, you will create a virtual machine on the hypervisor using the Virtual Machine Manager program. The name of the virtual machine will be *server1.example.com* and it will use the FTP server configured in the previous exercise as the installation source. It will have 1024MB of memory, one vcpu, and will use space in the *rhpol_virt/rhvol_virt* storage volume for the OS. You will use the OS type and variant as Linux / rhel7 and ensure that the installation runs in the graphical environment. You will create */boot* of size 500MB, swap 500MB, */home* 300MB, and the rest of the space for the root partition in the 10GB space provided by the *rhpol_virt/rhvol_virt* volume. You will ensure that root, home, and swap partitions are logical volumes in *vg00* volume group. You will assign source device "Host device em1 (Bridge 'br0')" as the network interface. During RHEL7 installation, You will assign IP 192.168.0.110, netmask 255.255.255.0, and gateway

192.168.0.1, use the default file system layout, and select "Server with GUI" software environment group.

1. Run the *virt-manager* command or choose Applications | System Tools | Virtual Machine Manager to start it.
2. Right click "localhost (QEMU)", and select New to start the Create a new virtual machine wizard.
3. Enter *server1.example.com* for the virtual machine name and select Network Install as the installation source. Click Forward to continue.

Figure 6-18 Create a Virtual Machine – Step 1 of 6

4. Specify the URL for the network install. Type ftp://192.168.0.100/pub/rhel7. Uncheck the "Automatically detect operating system based on install media" option and select OS type Linux and Version Red Hat Enterprise Linux 7. Click Forward to continue.

Figure 6-19 Create a Virtual Machine – Step 2 of 6

5. Enter 1024MB for memory and 1 for CPU. Click Forward to continue.

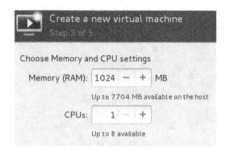

Figure 6-20 Create a Virtual Machine – Step 3 of 6

6. Check the "Enable storage for this virtual machine" box. Select "Select managed or other existing storage" and browse for available storage pools and volumes. Choose rhpol_virt storage pool and rhvol_virt volume, and click Choose Volume.

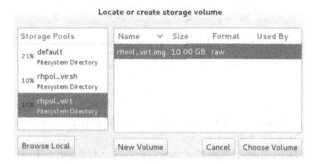

Figure 6-21 Create a Virtual Machine – Step 4 of 6

7. The storage volume is now selected. Click Forward to continue.

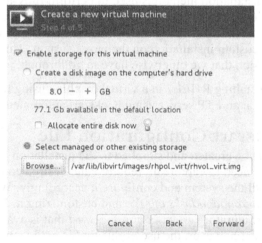

Figure 6-22 Create a Virtual Machine – Step 5 of 6

8. A summary of your selections is displayed. Expand "Advanced options" to view the settings, but do not alter them. Review all configuration items and click Finish to proceed with the installation.

Figure 6-23 Create a Virtual Machine – Step 6 of 6

9. Customize the OS as directed in the exercise objective and follow the procedure from Chapter 01 to finish the installation.

Kickstart Installation Method

The Red Hat Kickstart installation method is used to perform fully-automated, fully-customized, and unattended installation of RHEL on any number of servers concurrently. This method requires a single file supplied to the installation program, which uses the configuration defined in the file to accomplish an identical custom installation on the target system. This method eliminates the lengthy question and answer session that we otherwise have to go through.

This section discusses installing RHEL7 in a virtual machine using the *virt-install* command, with installation files located on an FTP server using Kickstart automated procedure.

Creating a Kickstart Configuration File

A configuration file must be created and supplied to the installation program in order to perform a kickstart installation. We need to capture all required and desired configuration for use by the kickstart process to install the system and configure it accordingly. We can create this file by making a copy of the */root/anaconda-ks.cfg* file and customizing it. Red Hat also offers a graphical tool called Kickstart Configurator *system-config-kickstart* that is available in RHEL7 to build a kickstart configuration file; however, the use of this tool is not recommended.

During the initial portion of RHEL installation, several pieces of configuration information are entered. The installation program creates a file called *anaconda-ks.cfg* in the */root* directory and stores this information in it. We can customize this file as per requirements and use it for new client deployments.

The following displays the modified contents of a copy of the *anaconda-ks.cfg* file called *ks.cfg*, located in the */var/ftp/pub/rhel7* directory. We will use this file for your automated installation on *server2*. Each directive in the file is on a separate line, which is numbered below with the *nl* command.

```
# cp /root/anaconda-ks.cfg /var/ftp/pub/rhel7/ks.cfg
# cd /var/ftp/pub/rhel7 ; nl ks.cfg
     1  url --url="ftp://192.168.0.100/pub/rhel7"
     2  lang en_US
     3  keyboard --vckeymap=us --xlayouts='us'
     4  network  --bootproto=static --device=eth0 --ip=192.168.0.120 --netmask=255.255.255.0
--gateway=192.168.0.1 --ipv6=auto --activate --hostname=server2.example.com
     5  rootpw --iscrypted
$6$ah1lE4adlnmNP7Bg$FwfTfXfDUyoN.QONQNU0gN8vukCCvdbSlX5Du3IzeZXhF7KDR7vXlRWX
sGwGOnE407V/2Aq7/7a78H.D601w..
     6  auth --enableshadow --passalgo=sha512
     7  reboot
     8  timezone America/Toronto --isUtc
     9  firstboot --disable
    10  eula --agreed
    11  ignoredisk --only-use=vda
    12  zerombr
    13  clearpart --all --initlabel --drives=vda
    14  bootloader --location=mbr --boot-drive=vda
    15  part /boot --fstype="xfs" --ondisk=vda --size=500
    16  part pv.16 --fstype="lvmpv" --ondisk=vda --size=9739
    17  volgroup vg00 --pesize=4096 pv.16
    18  logvol swap  --fstype="swap" --size=500 --name=swap --vgname=vg00
    19  logvol /home  --fstype="xfs" --size=300 --name=home --vgname=vg00
    20  logvol /  --fstype="xfs" --size=9230 --name=root --vgname=vg00
    21  user --groups=wheel --name=user1 --
password=$6$uHOiMAtuLcsyfCUB$R9vvAxTXYs3Vh0axmsVp/cEGdvylgBZc327kmmgV.JuLefz/BFn
E1ODiypG6d9SyHb9INRUUTZYhsVorfmhqC0 --iscrypted --gecos="user1"
    22  xconfig  --startxonboot
    23  %packages
    24  @base
    25  @core
    26  @desktop-debugging
    27  @dial-up
    28  @fonts
    29  @gnome-desktop
    30  @guest-agents
    31  @guest-desktop-agents
    32  @input-methods
    33  @internet-browser
    34  @multimedia
    35  @print-client
    36  @x11
    37  %end
```

Comments and empty lines have been omitted.

Line #1: uses the specified URL as the source for installation files.

Line #2: uses the US English language.

Line #3: uses the US keyboard layout.

Line #4: names the first network interface *eth0*, assigns it static IP address 192.168.0.120, netmask 255.255.255.0, gateway 192.168.0.1, sets it to auto-activate at system reboots, assigns this system hostname *server2.example.com*, and sets IPv6 support to automatic. If we wish to obtain networking information from a configured DHCP server, use "network --device eth0 --bootproto dhcp" instead.

Line #5: assigns the specified password to the *root* account. We can copy and paste the *root* password from the */etc/shadow* file on an existing RHEL system.

Line #6: enables password shadowing for user authentication and uses sha512 algorithm password encryption.

Line #7: reboots the system after the installation has finished.

Line #8: sets the time zone to America/Toronto based on the assumption that the hardware clock of the system is set to UTC time.

Line #9: disables the execution of the firstboot program after the first reboot following the installation.

Line #10: accepts the end-user license agreement.

Line #11: strictly uses the vda disk as the target disk for installation.

Line #12: wipes off all information from the MBR.

Line #13: removes all partitions from the target disk and initializes the disk label.

Line #14: installs the GRUB bootloader program in the MBR on the target disk.

Line #15: creates */boot* partition of size 500MB on the target disk and formats it to the xfs file system type.

Line #16: constructs an LVM physical volume called lvmpv on the target disk and allocates 9739MB to it.

Line #17: creates vg00 LVM volume group with PE size 4MB using the lvmpv physical volume.

Line #18: builds a swap logical volume of size 500MB in vg00 volume group.

Line #19: builds a home logical volume of size 300MB in vg00 volume group and formats it to the xfs file system type.

Line #20: creates a root partition of size 9230MB in vg00 volume group and formats it to the xfs file system type.

Line #21: creates a user account called user1 with membership to the administrative group called wheel, assigns the supplied encrypted password, and adds "user1" as the comments for this user.

Line #22: configures to start X Window on system reboots.

Line #23: marks the beginning of software selection.

Lines #24 to #36: installs these package groups during the installation process.

Line #37: marks the end of software selection.

There are several other directives and options available that you may want to use in the kickstart file, but not all of them are mandatory. If you do not define a compulsory directive, Anaconda prompts you to enter that particular piece of information during the installation process, which defeats the purpose of this automated process. Also make certain that the sequence of sections in the file remain unchanged; however, directives within a section can be in any order. As well, there are many settings such as selinux --enforcing and firewall --enabled that are defaults and need not be included in the file.

At the end of the configuration file, you may specify any pre-installation and/or post-installation commands or scripts that you wish Anaconda to execute.

Execute the *ksvalidator* command on the file after you are done with the editing to validate the directives, their values, and the file syntax. This tool is part of the pykickstart package and should be installed if you wish to use it.

ksvalidator /var/ftp/pub/rhel7/ks.cfg

If you see any errors in the output, you need to fix them before continuing.

You also need to set the appropriate SELinux context on the *ks.cfg* file with the *chcon* command, to ensure SELinux allows access to this file:

chcon –t public_content_t /var/ftp/pub/rhel7/ks.cfg

Exercise 6-9: Network Install RHEL7 Using virt-install with Kickstart Configuration

This exercise should be done on *host1*.

In this exercise, you will create a virtual machine on *host1* using the *virt-install* command. The name of the virtual machine will be *server2.example.com* and it will use the configuration stored in the *ks.cfg* file configured in the previous sub-section. It will have 1024MB of memory, one vcpu, and 10GB of disk space in volume *rhpol_virsh/rhvol_virsh.img*. You will use the OS type and variant as Linux / rhel7, assign *br0* as the network interface, and mark the virtual machine to start automatically upon *host1* reboot.

```
# virt-install --name=server2.example.com --ram=1024 --vcpus=1 --autostart \
--os-type=linux --os-variant=rhel7 --location=ftp://192.168.0.100/pub/rhel7 \
--network bridge=br0 --disk vol=rhpol_virsh/rhvol_virsh.img --extra-args \
ks=ftp://192.168.0.100/pub/rhel7/ks.cfg
Starting install...
Retrieving file .treeinfo...                        | 4.2  kB    00:00 !!!
Retrieving file vmlinuz...                          | 9.3 MB     00:00 !!!
Retrieving file initrd.img...                       |  68 MB     00:00 !!!
Creating domain...                                  |  0   B     00:00
Guest installation complete…  restarting guest .
```

The new server will be rebooted automatically after the installation is complete.

 The backslash character used in the *virt-install* command above marks the continuation of the line.

The wget Utility

wget is a non-interactive file download utility that allows you to retrieve a single file, multiple files, or an entire directory structure from an FTP, HTTP, or HTTPS source. This tool has the ability to retrieve files from both IPv4 and IPv6 addresses. There are several options available with *wget*;

however, some of them are used more often than the others. Table 6-4 lists a few common options in both short and long notations, and describes them. For additional options and details, refer to the command's man pages.

Option	Description
–d (--debug)	Turns the debug mode on.
–i (--input-file)	Downloads files from URLs listed in the specified file.
–N (--timestamping)	Retrieves files newer than the source files.
–nv (--no-verbose)	Hides the verbose output except for error messages and basic information.
–o (--output-file)	Redirects messages to the specified output file.
–P (--directory-prefix)	Specifies the directory location in which to download the files.
–q (--quiet)	Hides the output and any errors.
–r (--recursive)	Turns the recursive retrieval on.
–T (--timeout)	Specifies the number of seconds before the command times out.
–t (--tries)	Specifies the number of retries.
--ignore-case	Treats lowercase and uppercase letters alike.
--user	Specifies a username for FTP or HTTP access.
--password	Specifies a password for the --user option.

Table 6-4 wget Command Options

You can run the *wget* command with --help to list available options in both short and long forms, along with a short description of each:

wget --help
GNU Wget 1.14, a non-interactive network retriever.
Usage: wget [OPTION]... [URL]...
Mandatory arguments to long options are mandatory for short options too.
Startup:
  -V, --version   display the version of Wget and exit.
  -h, --help   print this help.
  -b, --background   go to background after startup.
  -e, --execute=COMMAND   execute a `.wgetrc'-style command.
Logging and input file:
  -o, --output-file=FILE   log messages to FILE.
  -a, --append-output=FILE   append messages to FILE.
  -d, --debug   print lots of debugging information.
  -q, --quiet   quiet (no output).
  -v, --verbose   be verbose (this is the default).
  -nv, --no-verbose   turn off verboseness, without being quiet.
      --report-speed=TYPE   Output bandwidth as TYPE. TYPE can be bits.
  -i, --input-file=FILE   download URLs found in local or external FILE.
  -F, --force-html   treat input file as HTML.
  -B, --base=URL   resolves HTML input-file links (-i -F) relative to URL.
      --config=FILE   Specify config file to use.
  . . . .

Let's look at a few examples to understand the usage of *wget*.

To download the kernel file *linux-3.9.9.tar.gz* in the current directory from *ftp.kernel.org*:

> # **wget ftp.kernel.org/pub/linux/kernel/v3.x/linux-3.9.9.tar.gz**
> --2015-02-10 14:35:46-- http://ftp.kernel.org/pub/linux/kernel/v3.x/linux-3.9.9.tar.gz
> Resolving ftp.kernel.org (ftp.kernel.org)... 199.204.44.194, 198.145.20.140, 149.20.4.69
> Connecting to ftp.kernel.org (ftp.kernel.org)|199.204.44.194|:80... connected.
> HTTP request sent, awaiting response... 200 OK
> Length: 108722589 (104M) [application/x-gzip]
> Saving to: 'linux-3.9.9.tar.gz'
> 100%[=================================>] 108,722,589 3.70MB/s   in 28s
> 2015-02-10 14:36:14 (3.69 MB/s) - 'linux-3.9.9.tar.gz' saved [108722589/108722589]

To download the kernel file *linux-3.9.8.tar.gz* in */var/tmp* directory and without displaying output:

> # **wget ftp.kernel.org/pub/linux/kernel/v3.x/linux-3.9.8.tar.gz –P /var/tmp –q**

To download the kernel file *linux-3.9.7.tar.gz* in the current directory with output redirected to */tmp/wget.out*:

> # **wget ftp.kernel.org/pub/linux/kernel/v3.x/linux-3.9.7.tar.gz –o /tmp/wget.out**

To download the *index.html* file from *www.redhat.com* with debug mode on:

> # **wget –d www.redhat.com**
> DEBUG output created by Wget 1.14 on linux-gnu.
> URI encoding = 'UTF-8'
> --2015-02-10 14:45:18-- http://www.redhat.com/
> Resolving www.redhat.com (www.redhat.com)... 96.7.207.214
> Caching www.redhat.com => 96.7.207.214
> Connecting to www.redhat.com (www.redhat.com)|96.7.207.214|:80... connected.
> Created socket 3.
> Releasing 0x0000000001dff930 (new refcount 1).
> ---request begin---
> GET / HTTP/1.1
> User-Agent: Wget/1.14 (linux-gnu)
> Accept: */*
> Host: www.redhat.com
> Connection: Keep-Alive
> ---request end---
> . . . .
> 2015-02-10 14:45:19 (1.22 MB/s) - 'index.html' saved [56072]

You can verify the download with the *ll* command:

> # **ll index.html**
> -rw-r--r--. 1 root root 56072 Feb 10 14:45 index.html

To download the *ks.cfg* file from the FTP site you set up in the previous exercise:

 # wget ftp://192.168.0.100/pub/rhel7/ks.cfg
--2015-02-10 14:46:10-- ftp://host1/pub/rhel7/ks.cfg
    => 'ks.cfg'
Resolving host1 (host1)... 192.168.0.100
Connecting to host1 (host1)|192.168.0.100|:21... connected.
Logging in as anonymous ... Logged in!
. . . .

EXAM TIP: Use the wget command to download files from an FTP or HTTP source as instructed in the exam.

Chapter Summary

In this chapter, we learned the concepts surrounding server virtualization, and learned the terms host machine, virtual machine, guest operating system, hypervisor, KVM, QEMU, and libvirt. We reviewed the benefits associated with using server virtualization. We looked at various package groups that support virtualization on bare-metal servers then moved on and learned additional concepts around virtual network switches, virtual network interfaces, virtual storage pools, and virtual storage volumes. We studied various virtualization management tools, including the GUI and commands. We reviewed the GUI Virtual Machine Manager program and saw how to interact with it to perform various management functions pertaining to virtual machines. We then performed several exercises and set up virtual networking and virtual storage using both GUI and commands.

We set up network installation services using the FTP protocol and configured bi-directional communication between the hypervisor and guests. We then performed a network installation using the GUI.

We studied the features and benefits associated with the kickstart method of hands-off installation. We customized a kickstart file and then used it to install RHEL7 in a virtual machine.

Finally, we learned about the wget utility and saw how to use this tool to download files from the specified network source.

Chapter Review Questions

1. What is the name of the package group that contains the qemu-kvm package?
2. What three protocols are supported for configuring over the network installation servers?
3. Which command can be used to start the virtual machine manager program?
4. What is the default location where the virtual machine files are stored?
5. The computer must be 64-bit and must have built-in support for hardware virtualization. True or False?
6. Kickstart supports fully unattended installations. True or False?
7. What is the name of the file that is created during the RHEL installation and it captures all configuration information entered?
8. The *wget* utility can be used to download an entire directory tree. True or False?
9. What is the name of the program that allows us to generate a kickstart file?
10. KVM is the default virtualization hypervisor software in RHEL7. True or False?
11. Which daemon must be running in order to connect to the hypervisor?
12. Which package group includes the graphical virtual machine manager program?

13. What is the command line tool to set up a virtual machine and optionally install an OS in it?
14. By default, SELinux is set to enforcing during installation. True or False?
15. What would happen if we set the onboot option to no in the *ks.cfg* file?
16. What are the three software components that are needed to provide full virtualization functionality on a RHEL7 server?
17. Which of these is not true about server virtualization: support for multiple guests, support for multiple virtual storage pools, availability of at least two fully functional physical servers, and support for multiple virtual networks.
18. Where do we create virtual volumes?

Answers to Chapter Review Questions

1. The Virtualization package group contains the qemu-kvm package.
2. The three protocols supported for accessing over the network installation server are FTP, HTTP, and NFS.
3. The *virt-manager* command.
4. The */var/lib/libvirt/images* directory.
5. True.
6. True.
7. The *anaconda-ks.cfg* file.
8. True.
9. The name of the program is Kickstart Configurator.
10. True.
11. The *libvirtd* daemon.
12. The Virtualization Client package group contains the graphical virtual machine manager program.
13. The virt-install tool.
14. True.
15. The network interface will not be activated automatically at system reboots.
16. The three software components are KVM, QEMU, and libvirt.
17. It requires only one physical system to operate.
18. We create virtual volumes in virtual pools.

DIY Challenge Labs

The following labs are useful to strengthen most of the concepts and topics learned in this chapter. It is expected that you perform these labs without any additional help. A step-by-step guide is not provided, as the implementation of these labs requires the knowledge that has been presented in this chapter. Use defaults or your own thinking for missing information.

Lab 6-1: Create a Virtual Network

Set up a virtual network called rhcsanet. Enable DHCP to provide IP addresses from 192.168.100.51 to 192.168.100.100 on subnet 255.255.255.0. Ensure that this virtual network uses NATting on all physical interfaces.

Lab 6-2: Create a Virtual Storage Pool

Set up a new storage pool called rhcsastr of 14GB in size. Use the directory filesystem as the storage type and store it in the */var/lib/libvirt/vstorage* directory. Create a virtual volume called rhcsavol that uses the entire pool space.

Lab 6-3: Perform a Network Installation of RHEL7

Create a virtual machine and install RHEL7 in it. Use IP 192.168.0.220, netmask 255.255.255.0, gateway 192.168.0.1, and hostname *server220.example.com*. Use standard partitioning to create */boot* 200MB, lvol1 for / 4GB, lvol2 for swap 1GB, lvol3 for */usr* 4GB, lvol4 for */var* 2GB, lvol5 for */opt* 1GB, lvol6 for */tmp* 500MB, and lvol7 for */home* 500MB in that order. You can use the virtual storage volume created in the previous lab. Select packages to support X Window, GNOME desktop, and graphical administration tools. Create a local user account called *user220* with all the defaults. Use configuration of your own for any missing information.

Lab 6-4: Perform a Kickstart Installation of RHEL7

Create a virtual machine and install RHEL7 in it, using kickstart as explained in this chapter. Use IP 192.168.0.230 and hostname *server230.example.com*. Select necessary packages to support X Window and a graphical desktop. Use partitioning and other missing configuration at will.

Lab 6-5: Add Virtual Disks to Virtual Machines

Set up a new storage volume and allocate one 2GB disk to *server3.example.com* and one 2GB disk to *server4.example.com* from this volume. Use storage settings as you wish.

## Chapter 07

Booting RHEL7, Updating Kernel, and Logging Messages

This chapter describes the following major topics:

➤ Linux boot process: firmware, GRUB, kernel, and systemd
➤ Understand and interact with GRUB to boot into different targets
➤ Linux kernel, its version and directory structure
➤ Install and update the kernel
➤ Manage kernel modules
➤ Init and Upstart
➤ Understand systemd, units, targets, and control groups
➤ Administer units and control groups
➤ Understand and interpret system log files
➤ Understand and manage systemd journal

RHCSA Objectives:

12. Boot, reboot, and shut down a system normally
13. Boot systems into different runlevels manually
14. Interrupt the boot process in order to gain access to a system
16. Locate and interpret system log files and journals
19. Start, stop, and check the status of network services
33. Start and stop services and configure services to start automatically at boot
34. Configure systems to boot into a specific target automatically
39. Configure network services to start automatically at boot
42. Update the kernel package appropriately to ensure a bootable system
43. Modify the system bootloader

RHEL goes through multiple phases during startup. It starts selective services during its transition from one phase into another, and provides the administrator with an opportunity to interact with the bootloader to boot the system into non-default targets. RHEL starts a number of services during its transition to the default or specified target.

The kernel controls everything on the Linux system. It controls the system hardware, enforces security and access controls, and runs, schedules, and manages processes and service daemons. The kernel is comprised of several modules. A new kernel must be installed or an existing kernel must be upgraded when the need arises from an application or functionality standpoint.

systemd is the new default system initialization scheme in RHEL7, replacing both init and Upstart. It has brought a number of enhancements, capabilities, and new tools to the operating system. It allows the system to boot into one of several pre-defined targets. The shutdown, halt, poweroff, and reboot commands are still around, and can be used for system power management.

RHEL7 logs all system activities by default in appropriate log files. These log files grow over a period of time and need to be rotated on a regular basis to ensure availability of enough space in the file system. systemd has introduced a new service for viewing and managing system logs in addition to the traditional syslog.

Linux Boot Process

RHEL goes through the *boot* process when the system is powered up or reset, with the boot process lasting until all enabled services are started and a login prompt appears on the screen. The boot process on an x86 computer may be split into four major phases: the firmware phase, the boot loader phase, the kernel phase, and the initialization phase. The system accomplishes these phases one after the other while performing and attempting to complete the tasks identified in each phase. The following sub-sections briefly explain each phase, and the subsequent sections provide more details on the last three phases.

The Firmware Phase

The firmware is the BIOS or the UEFI code that is stored in flash memory on the x86 system board. The first thing that it does is run the *power-on-self-test* (POST) to detect, test, and initialize the system hardware components. While doing this, it installs appropriate drivers for the video hardware and begins displaying system messages on the screen. The firmware scans the available storage devices in an effort to locate a boot device, starting with a 512-byte image containing 446 bytes of the boot loader program called GRUB2, 64 bytes for the partition table, and the last two bytes with the boot signature. As soon as it discovers a usable boot device, it loads GRUB2 into memory and passes control over to it.

The GRUB Phase

In RHEL7, a new, enhanced version of GRUB, called *GRUB2*, has been introduced, replacing the legacy GRUB. GRUB2 supports both BIOS/MBR and UEFI/GPT combinations.

After GRUB2 is loaded into memory and takes control, it searches for the kernel in the */boot* file system. It extracts the kernel code from */boot* into memory, decompresses it, and loads it based on the configuration defined in the */boot/grub2/grub.cfg* file. For UEFI-based systems, GRUB2 looks for the EFI system partition */boot/efi* instead, and runs the kernel based on the configuration defined in the */boot/efi/EFI/redhat/grub.efi* file. Once the kernel is loaded, GRUB2 transfers the control over to it for furthering the boot process.

The Kernel Phase

After getting control from GRUB2, the kernel loads the initial RAM disk (initrd) image from the */boot* file system into memory after decompressing and extracting it. The kernel then mounts this image as read-only to serve as a temporary root file system. This allows the kernel to bypass mounting the actual physical root file system in order to be fully functional. The kernel loads necessary modules from the initrd image to allow access to the physical disks and the partitions and file systems therein. It also loads any required drivers to support the boot process. Later, the kernel unmounts the initrd image and mounts the actual root file system in read/write mode. At this point, the necessary foundation is built for the boot process to carry on and start loading the enabled services.

The Initialization Phase

This is the last phase that takes over control from the kernel and continues the boot process. In RHEL7, systemd has replaced both SysVinit and Upstart as the default system initialization scheme. systemd starts all enabled userspace system and network services, and brings the system up to the preset boot target. The system boot process is considered complete when all enabled services are operational for the boot target and users are able to log in to the system.

Managing GRUB

After the firmware phase has finished, the boot loader presents a menu with a list of bootable kernels available on the system. The menu waits for a pre-defined amount of time before it times out and starts booting the default kernel. You may want to interact with GRUB at this time if you wish to boot with a non-default kernel, boot to a different target, or edit a kernel boot string before booting it.

Pressing a key before the timeout expires allows you to interrupt the autoboot process and interact with GRUB. If you wish to boot the system using the default boot device with all the configured default settings, do not press any key, as shown in Figure 7-1, and let the system go through the autoboot process.

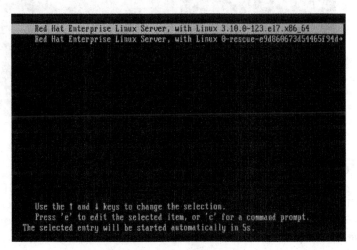

Figure 7-1 GRUB Menu

The line at the very bottom in Figure 7-1 above shows the autoboot countdown in seconds. The default setting is 5 seconds. If you press no keys within the 5 seconds, the highlighted kernel will be booted automatically.

Understanding the GRUB Menu

The GRUB menu shows a list of bootable kernels at the top. You can change the selection using the up or down arrow key. You can also edit a selected kernel menu entry by pressing *e* or go to the grub> command prompt by pressing *c*. In the edit mode, GRUB loads the selected entry from the */boot/grub2/grub.cfg* file in an editor, which you are allowed to modify before booting. You can press Ctrl+x to boot after making the change, Ctrl+c to switch into the grub> command prompt, or press ESC to discard the changes made and go back to the main menu. Figure 7-2 displays one of the entries and the action keys.

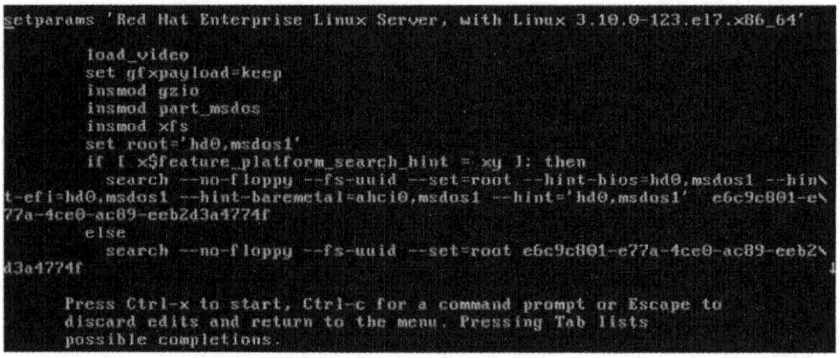

Figure 7-2 Edit Kernel String

The grub> prompt appears when you type *c*. While at the prompt, you can press the TAB key to view a list of all available commands that you can run to perform a desired action. See Figure 7-3.

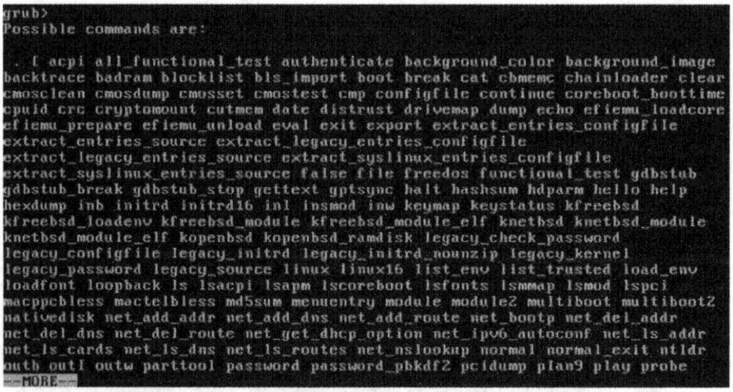

Figure 7-3 GRUB Command Prompt

The /etc/default/grub File

The */etc/default/grub* configuration file defines directives that govern how GRUB behaves at boot time. Values defined in this file are used to regenerate the */boot/grub2/grub.cfg* file, which controls the behavior of GRUB at boot time. Any changes made to the *grub* file will only take effect after the *grub2-mkconfig* utility has been executed.

Here are the default settings from the */etc/default/grub* file, with an explanation in Table 7-1:

```
GRUB_TIMEOUT=5
GRUB_DISTRIBUTOR="$(sed 's, release .*$,,g' /etc/system-release)"
GRUB_DEFAULT=saved
GRUB_DISABLE_SUBMENU=true
GRUB_TERMINAL_OUTPUT="console"
GRUB_CMDLINE_LINUX="rd.lvm.lv=vg00/swap vconsole.font=latarcyrheb-sun16 crashker
nel=auto vconsole.keymap=us rd.lvm.lv=vg00/root rhgb quiet"
GRUB_DISABLE_RECOVERY="true"
```

Directive	Description
GRUB_TIMEOUT	Sets the wait time, in seconds, before booting off the default kernel. Default value is 5.
GRUB_DISTRIBUTOR	Defines the name of the Linux distribution.
GRUB_DEFAULT	Boots the selected option from the previous system boot.
GRUB_DISABLE_SUBMENU	Enables/disables the appearance of GRUB submenu.
GRUB_TERMINAL_OUTPUT	Sets the default terminal.
GRUB_CMDLINE_LINUX	Specifies the command line options to pass to the kernel at boot time.
GRUB_DISABLE_RECOVERY	Disables showing system recovery entries in the GRUB menu.

Table 7-1 GRUB Default Configuration File

Generally, you do not need to make any changes to this file, as the default settings are good enough for normal system operation.

The /boot/grub2/grub.cfg File

This is the main configuration file that controls the behavior of GRUB at boot time. This file is located in the */boot/grub2* directory on BIOS-based systems and in the */boot/efi/EFI/redhat* directory on UEFI-based systems. This file can be regenerated manually with the *grub2-mkconfig* utility, or it is automatically regenerated when a new kernel is installed. During this process, any manual changes made to this file are lost.

Here is how you would run this utility to reproduce the *grub.cfg* file on BIOS and UEFI systems, respectively:

 # grub2-mkconfig –o /boot/grub2/grub.cfg
 # grub2-mkconfig –o /boot/efi/EFI/redhat/grub.cfg

When this utility runs, it uses the settings defined in the */etc/default/grub* file and in the helper scripts located in the */etc/grub.d/* directory to regenerate this file for kernels located in the */boot* directory. Here is the list of default helper scripts located in the */etc/grub.d/* directory:

 # ll /etc/grub.d
```
-rwxr-xr-x. 1 root root  8698 Mar 20 10:34 00_header
-rwxr-xr-x. 1 root root  9517 Mar 20 10:34 10_linux
-rwxr-xr-x. 1 root root 10275 Mar 20 10:34 20_linux_xen
```

```
-rwxr-xr-x.  1  root  root   2559  Mar 20 10:34  20_ppc_terminfo
-rwxr-xr-x.  1  root  root  11110  Mar 20 10:34  30_os-prober
-rwxr-xr-x.  1  root  root    214  Mar 20 10:34  40_custom
-rwxr-xr-x.  1  root  root    216  Mar 20 10:34  41_custom
-rw-r--r--.  1  root  root    483  Mar 20 10:34  README
```

The first script, *00_header*, sets the GRUB environment; the *10_linux* script searches for all installed kernels on the same disk partition; the *30_os-prober* searches for the presence of other operating systems; and the *40_custom* and *41_custom* scripts are for us to add any customization to the new GRUB configuration file. An example would be to add custom entries to the boot menu.

The *grub.cfg* file contains *menuentry* blocks for each installed kernel. Each block begins with a title and includes the names of the kernel and RAM disk image files, their location with respect to */boot*, and several options and modules to be loaded. These menu entry titles are displayed at the time of system boot and you can choose one of them to boot. A sample menuentry block is shown below for the kernel 3.10.0-123.el7.x86_64 installed on *server1*:

```
menuentry 'Red Hat Enterprise Linux Server, with Linux 3.10.0-123.el7.x86_64 ' --class red --class gnu-
linux --class gnu --class os --unrestricted $menuentry_id_option 'gnulinux-3.10.0-123.el7.x86_64-
advanced-964201bb-1e32-4794-a2f2-7a33e2fb591a' {
        load_video
        set gfxpayload=keep
        insmod gzio
        insmod part_msdos
        insmod xfs
        set root='hd0,msdos1'
        if [ x$feature_platform_search_hint = xy ]; then
          search --no-floppy --fs-uuid --set=root --hint-bios=hd0,msdos1 --hint-efi=hd0,msdos1 --hint-
baremetal=ahci0,msdos1 --hint='hd0,msdos1'  e6c9c801-e77a-4ce0-ac89-eeb2d3a4774f
        else
          search --no-floppy --fs-uuid --set=root e6c9c801-e77a-4ce0-ac89-eeb2d3a4774f
        fi
        linux16 /vmlinuz-3.10.0-123.el7.x86_64 root=UUID=964201bb-1e32-4794-a2f2-7a33e2fb591a ro
rd.lvm.lv=vg00/swap vconsole.font=latarcyrheb-sun16 crashkernel=auto  vconsole.keymap=us
rd.lvm.lv=vg00/root rhgb quiet LANG=en_US.UTF-8
        initrd16 /initramfs-3.10.0-123.el7.x86_64.img
}
```

If a new kernel is added to the system, existing kernel entries will remain in this file and can be chosen in the GRUB menu at startup to boot.

Booting into Specific Targets

RHEL is booted into graphical target state by default. It can also be booted into other non-default, but less capable, operating targets from the GRUB menu. Additionally, in situations when it becomes mandatory to boot the system into an administrative state for carrying out a function that cannot be otherwise performed in other target states or for system recovery, RHEL offers emergency and rescue targets. These special targets can be entered by interacting with the GRUB interface, selecting a boot menu entry, pressing *e* to enter the edit mode, and supplying the desired target with the systemd.unit directive.

For instance, to boot into the emergency target, append systemd.unit=emergency.target (or simply 'emergency') to the default linux kernel line entry, as shown below:

```
       linux16 /vmlinuz-3.10.0-123.el7.x86_64 root=UUID=964201bb-1e32-4794-a2\
r2-7a33e2fb591a ro rd.lvm.lv=vg00/swap vconsole.font=latarcyrheb-sun16 crashke\
rnel=auto  vconsole.keymap=us rd.lvm.lv=vg00/root rhgb quiet systemd.unit=emer\
gency.target_
```

Press Ctrl+x after making the modification to boot the system into the supplied target. You will be required to enter the *root* user password to log on. Run *systemctl reboot* after you are done to reboot the system.

```
Welcome to emergency mode! After logging in, type "journalctl -xb" to view
system logs, "systemctl reboot" to reboot, "systemctl default" to try again
to boot into default mode.
Give root password for maintenance
(or type Control-D to continue): _
```

The SysVinit parameters—s, S, single, 1, 2, 3, or 5—can still be supplied to the kernel to boot into one of these targets. systemd maps them to the associated runlevelX.target files.

Similarly, you can enter systemd.unit=rescue.target (or simply 1, s, or single) with the linux kernel line entry and press Ctrl+x to boot into the rescue target, which is also referred to as the single-user mode.

Exercise 7-1: Resetting the Root User Password

This exercise should be done on *server1*.

For this exercise, assume that the *root* user password has been lost or forgotten, and it needs to be reset.

In this exercise, you will boot the system into a special shell in order to reset the *root* password.

1.   Reboot or reset *server1*, and interact with GRUB by pressing a key before the autoboot timer runs out. Highlight the default kernel entry in the GRUB menu and press e to enter the edit mode. Scroll down and you will find a boot string similar to the following:

```
       linux16 /vmlinuz-3.10.0-123.el7.x86_64 root=UUID=d2b64070-287e-487a-98\
aa-4fb53c22bdc5 ro rd.lvm.lv=vg00/swap vconsole.font=latarcyrheb-sun16 crashke\
rnel=auto  vconsole.keymap=us rd.lvm.lv=vg00/root rhgb quiet LANG=en_CA.UTF-8
           initrd16 /initramfs-3.10.0-123.el7.x86_64.img
```

2. Modify this kernel string and append "init=/sysroot/bin/sh" to the end of the line to look like:

```
linux16 /vmlinuz-3.10.0-123.el7.x86_64 root=UUID=d2b64070-287e-487a-98\
aa-4fb53c22bdc5 ro rd.lvm.lv=vg00/swap vconsole.font=latarcyrheb-sun16 crashkc\
rnel=auto vconsole.keymap=us rd.lvm.lv=vg00/root rhgb quiet LANG=en_CA.UTF-8 \
init=/sysroot/bin/sh
           initrd16 /initramfs-3.10.0-123.el7.x86_64.img
```

3. Press Ctrl+x when done to boot to the special shell. The system mounts the root file system read-only on the */sysroot* directory. Make */sysroot* appear as mounted on / using the *chroot* command:

    # **chroot /sysroot**

4. Remount the root file system in read/write mode with the *mount* command:

    # **mount –o remount,rw /**

5. Enter a new password for *root* by invoking the *passwd* command:

    # **passwd**

6. Create an empty, hidden file called *.autorelabel* at the root of the directory tree to instruct the system to perform SELinux relabeling upon next reboot:

    # **touch /.autorelabel**

7. Exit out of the special shell:

    # **exit**

8. Reboot the system:

    # **reboot**

The system will perform SELinux relabeling during the first reboot, and it will reboot again to the default boot target after the relabeling is finished. This is how you can reset the password for *root*.

Modifying the Default Kernel to Boot

If you wish to change the default boot menuentry persistently to something other than the default, specify its number with the *grub2-set-default* command. For instance, the default *grub.cfg* file includes two menuentry blocks, with 0 representing the first kernel that boots RHEL normally and 1 identifying the second kernel that boots RHEL into the rescue target. For each additional menuentry block, a subsequent number is assigned. The default entry is set to the last successfully loaded kernel, as identified by the GRUB_DEFAULT=saved directive in the */etc/default/grub* file. Let's run the *grub2-set-default* command as follows and change the default to the second kernel entry:

    # **grub2-set-default 1**

Reboot the system after the above change and you will notice that it boots into the rescue target. To reinstate, run the command again with 0 as the argument followed by a system reboot.

The Linux Kernel

RHEL7.0 comes with Linux kernel 3.10 as the default. It provides a 64-bit operating environment and provides libraries to support both 32-bit and 64-bit applications. The Linux kernel is a set of software components called *modules* that work together as a single entity to allow programs, services, and applications to run smoothly and efficiently on the system. Modules are *device drivers* that are used for controlling hardware devices, such as controller cards and peripheral devices, as well as software components, such as LVM, file systems, networking, and RAID. Some of these modules are static to the kernel and are integral to system functionality, while others are loaded dynamically as needed.

A Linux kernel that comprises both static and dynamic modules is referred to as the *modular* kernel. It is made up of critical and vital components, and loads dynamic modules automatically on demand, making it faster and more efficient in terms of overall performance, and less vulnerable to crashes. Another benefit of a modular kernel is that software driver updates only require the associated dynamic module to be recompiled and reloaded; it does not need an entire kernel recompile or a system reboot.

RHEL7 is available with the kernel that is designed to support diverse processor architectures, such as 64-bit Intel/AMD/PowerPC in single, multicore, and multiprocessor configurations. RHEL7 is also available for IBM System z mainframes. On the x86 system, the *uname* command with the –m option lists the architecture of the system. In addition to the main kernel package, RHEL7 includes additional kernel packages that are described in Table 7-2. These kernel packages may be installed if necessary.

Kernel Package	Description
kernel	The main kernel package that contains the Linux kernel called vmlinuz. This package is installed as part of the OS installation.
kernel-devel	Includes support to build modules against the kernel package.
kernel-tools	Includes tools to manipulate the kernel.
kernel-tools-libs	Includes the libraries to support the kernel tools.
kernel-firmware	Includes firmware files that are required by various devices to operate.
kernel-headers	Includes C header files that specify the interface between the kernel and userspace libraries and programs.
kernel-debug	Includes debugging support.
kernel-debug-devel	Includes support to build modules against the debug kernel.

Table 7-2 Kernel Packages

Moreover, the source code for RHEL7 is also available for those who wish to customize and recompile the code for their precise needs.

Currently, the following kernel packages are installed on *server1*:

yum list installed kernel-*
Installed Packages
kernel.x86_64   3.10.0-123.el7   @anaconda/7.0
kernel-devel.x86_64   3.10.0-123.el7   @ftprepo

kernel-headers.x86_64	3.10.0-123.el7	@ftprepo
kernel-tools.x86_64	3.10.0-123.el7	@anaconda/7.0
kernel-tools-libs.x86_64	3.10.0-123.el7	@anaconda/7.0

The default kernel installed during the installation is usually adequate for most system needs; however, it requires a rebuild when a new functionality is added or removed. The new functionality may be introduced by installing a new kernel, upgrading the existing one, installing a new hardware device, or changing a critical system component. Likewise, an existing functionality that is no longer required may be removed to make the kernel smaller, resulting in improved performance and reduced memory utilization.

To control the behavior of the modules, and the kernel in general, several tunable parameters are set that define a baseline for kernel functionality. Some of these parameters must be tuned to allow certain applications and database software to be installed smoothly and operate properly.

RHEL allows us to generate and store several custom kernels with varied configuration and required modules, but only one of them is active at a time. Other kernels may be loaded via GRUB.

Determining Kernel Version

To determine the version of the running kernel on the system, run the *uname* command:

```
# uname –r
3.10.0-123.el7.x86_64
```

The output indicates the kernel version currently in use is 3.10.0-123.el7.x86_64. An anatomy of the version information is displayed in Figure 7-4 and explained below.

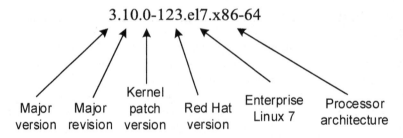

Figure 7-4 Anatomy of a Kernel Version

From left to right:

- ✓ (3) indicates the major version of the Linux kernel. The major number changes when significant alterations, enhancements, and updates to the previous major version are made.
- ✓ (10) indicates the major revision of the third major version.
- ✓ (0) indicates no patches were applied to this kernel. If we see a number n, it will represent the nth patched version of this kernel with minor bug and security hole fixes, minor enhancements, and so on.
- ✓ (123) indicates the custom kernel version from Red Hat.
- ✓ (el7) indicates the Enterprise Linux version this kernel is for.
- ✓ (x86_64) indicates the architecture for which this kernel is built.

A further analysis designates that 3.10.0 holds the general Linux kernel version information and the subsequent numbers and letters represent the Red Hat specific information.

Understanding Kernel Directory Structure

Kernel and its support files are stored at different locations in the directory hierarchy, of which three locations—*/boot*, */proc*, and */lib/modules*—are of significance and are explained below.

The /boot File System

The */boot* file system is created at system installation and its purpose is to store kernel and associated files. This file system also stores any updated or modified kernel data. An *ll* on */boot* produces the following information:

```
# ll /boot
-rw-r--r--. 1 root root   122059 May  5 11:21 config-3.10.0-123.el7.x86_64
drwxr-xr-x. 6 root root     4096 Oct  6 09:05
-rw-r--r--. 1 root root 40653201 Jul  8 13:02 initramfs-0-rescue-e9d860673d54465f94
db2961c6f10ba0.img
-rw-r--r--. 1 root root 17025688 Jul  8 13:04 initramfs-3.10.0-123.el7.x86_64.img
-rw-r--r--. 1 root root 16951233 Jul 11 09:03 initramfs-3.10.0-123.el7.x86_64kdump.
img
-rw-r--r--. 1 root root   866981 Jul  8 13:00 initrd-plymouth.img
-rw-r--r--. 1 root root   228562 May  5 11:23 symvers-3.10.0-123.el7.x86_64.gz
-rw-------. 1 root root  2840084 May  5 11:21 System.map-3.10.0-123.el7.x86_64
-rwxr-xr-x. 1 root root  4902000 Jul  8 13:02 vmlinuz-0-rescue-e9d860673d54465f94db
2961c6f10ba0
-rwxr-xr-x. 1 root root  4902000 May  5 11:21 vmlinuz-3.10.0-123.el7.x86_64
```

The output indicates that the current kernel is *vmlinuz-3.10.0-123.el7.x86_64*, its boot image is stored in the *initramfs-3.10.0-123.el7.x86_64.img* file, and configuration in the *config-3.10.0-123.el7.x86_64* file.

A sub-directory */boot/grub2* contains GRUB information as shown below:

```
# ll /boot/grub2
-rw-r--r--. 1 root root   84 Jul  8 13:04 device.map
drwxr-xr-x. 2 root root   24 Jul  8 13:04
-rw-r--r--. 1 root root 6015 Oct  3 11:39 grub.cfg
-rw-r--r--. 1 root root 1024 Oct  6 09:08 grubenv
drwxr-xr-x. 2 root root 8192 Jul  8 13:04
drwxr-xr-x. 2 root root 4096 Jul  8 13:04
drwxr-xr-x. 3 root root   19 Jul  8 12:51
```

The key file in */boot/grub2* is *grub.cfg*, which maintains a list of available kernels and defines the default kernel to boot, along with other information.

The /proc File System

/proc is a virtual file system and its contents are created in memory at system boot and destroyed when the system goes down. Underneath this file system lie current hardware configuration and status information. A directory listing of */proc* is provided below:

```
# ll /proc
dr-xr-xr-x.  8 root     root        0 Oct  6 09:08 1
dr-xr-xr-x.  8 root     root        0 Oct  6 09:08 10
dr-xr-xr-x.  8 gdm      gdm         0 Oct  6 09:09 1020
dr-xr-xr-x.  8 gdm      gdm         0 Oct  6 09:09 1054
dr-xr-xr-x.  8 root     root        0 Oct  6 09:08 11
dr-xr-xr-x.  8 gdm      gdm         0 Oct  6 09:09 1195
dr-xr-xr-x.  8 root     root        0 Oct  6 09:08 12
```

This file system contains several files and sub-directories. Some sub-directory names are numerical and contain information about a specific process, with process ID matching the sub-directory name. Within each sub-directory, there are files and further sub-directories that include information, such as memory segment specific to that particular process. Other files and sub-directories contain configuration data for system components. If you wish to view configuration for a particular item, such as the CPU or memory, *cat* the contents of *cpuinfo* and *meminfo* files as shown below:

```
# cat /proc/cpuinfo
processor       : 0
vendor_id       : GenuineIntel
cpu family      : 6
model           : 42
model name      : Intel(R) Core(TM) i7-2760QM CPU @ 2.40GHz
stepping        : 7
microcode       : 0x29
cpu MHz         : 881.906
cache size      : 6144 KB
. . . . . . . .
# cat /proc/meminfo
MemTotal:       7889040 kB
MemFree:        5550788 kB
MemAvailable:   6061284 kB
. . . . . . . .
```

The data stored under */proc* is referenced by a number of system utilities, including *top*, *ps*, *uname*, and *vmstat*, to display information.

The /lib/modules Directory

This directory holds information about kernel modules. Underneath it are located sub-directories specific to the kernels installed on the system. For example, the *ll* output on */lib/modules* below shows that there is only one kernel on this system:

```
# ll /lib/modules
drwxr-xr-x. 6 root root 4096 Sep 24 06:32 3.10.0-123.el7.x86_64
```

Now issue the *ll* command on the kernel sub-directory:

```
# ll /lib/modules/3.10.0-123.el7.x86_64
lrwxrwxrwx.  1 root root       38 Jul  8 12:52 build -> /usr/src/kernels
/3.10.0-123.el7.x86_64
drwxr-xr-x.  2 root root        6 May  5 11:23
drwxr-xr-x. 11 root root     4096 Jul  8 12:52
-rw-r--r--.  1 root root   656738 Jul  8 13:04 modules.alias
-rw-r--r--.  1 root root   637409 Jul  8 13:04 modules.alias.bin
-rw-r--r--.  1 root root     1296 May  5 11:23 modules.block
```

There are several files and a few sub-directories here. These files and sub-directories hold module-specific information.

One of the key sub-directories is *lib/modules/3.10.0-123.el7.x86_64/kernel/drivers*, which stores modules categorized in groups in various sub-directories as shown in the listing below:

```
# ll /lib/modules/2.6.32-220.el6.x86_64/kernel/drivers
drwxr-xr-x. 3 root root 4096 Jul  8 12:52 acpi
drwxr-xr-x. 2 root root 4096 Jul  8 12:52 ata
drwxr-xr-x. 2 root root   64 Jul  8 12:52 auxdisplay
drwxr-xr-x. 3 root root   19 Jul  8 12:52 base
. . . . . . . .
```

Several module categories exist, such as ata, bluetooth, cdrom, firewire, input, net, pci, scsi, usb, and video. These categories contain modules to control the hardware components associated with them.

Managing the Kernel

Managing the kernel involves performing several tasks, such as installing and updating the kernel, and listing, displaying, loading, unloading, and installing modules. It also includes the task of adding and removing modules to the initial ram disk; however, this is not usually done manually. This task is accomplished automatically when a new kernel is rebuilt. The tools that are used to install and update the kernel are the *yum* and *rpm* commands, while those for managing modules are *lsmod*, *modinfo*, *modprobe*, and *depmod*. The module management tools are part of the kmod package, and they automatically take into account any dependent modules during their execution.

Installing and Updating the Kernel

Unlike handling other package installs and upgrades, installing and updating kernel packages require extra care as you might end up leaving your system in an unbootable state. It is recommended that you have a bootable media handy prior to starting either process. With the *yum* command, the install and update function identically; they both add a new kernel to the system, leaving the existing kernel(s) intact. Neither of them replaces or overwrites the existing kernel files.

> **EXAM TIP:** Always install a higher version of the kernel instead of updating the existing one. This will add the new kernel to the system without affecting the current kernel. The existing kernel must still be intact and available for boot.

An upgraded kernel is typically required when deficiencies or bugs are identified in the existing kernel, hampering the kernel's smooth operation, or a new version of an application needs to be installed on the system that requires a different version of the kernel to operate. In either case, the new kernel addresses existing issues as well as adds bug fixes, security updates, new features, and support for additional hardware devices.

The process for installing and updating the kernel is the same. The *rpm* command may be used if you wish to perform these tasks manually, otherwise the *yum* command and the PackageKit graphical tools are available to carry out these tasks hassle-free.

When using the *rpm* command, always install (–i) the new kernel even though you want to upgrade (–U) the existing kernel. This will ensure that you can revert to the previous kernel if needed.

Exercise 7-2: Install a New Kernel

This exercise should be done on *server1*.

In this exercise, you will install the latest available kernel using the *yum* command with the assumption that your system is subscribed to the Red Hat Subscription Management service, and the service is accessible from your system. You will need to ensure that the existing kernel and its configuration remains intact.

1. Run the *uname* command and check the version of the running kernel:

   # **uname –r**
   3.10.0-123.el7.x86_64

2. Run the *yum* command to install the latest available kernel from the subscription management service using either the update or the install subcommand:

   # **yum –y update kernel**
   . . . .
   Resolving Dependencies
   --> Running transaction check
   ---> Package kernel.x86_64 0:3.10.0-123.8.1.el7 will be installed
   --> Finished Dependency Resolution
   Dependencies Resolved

   ==

Package	Arch	Version	Repository	Size

   ==

   Installing:
    kernel   x86_64   3.10.0-123.8.1.el7   rhel-7-server-rpms   29 M
   Transaction Summary

   ==

   Install 1 Package
   Total size: 29 M
   Installed size: 127 M
   Downloading packages:
   Running transaction check
   Running transaction test
   Transaction test succeeded
   Running transaction

```
Installing : kernel-3.10.0-123.8.1.el7.x86_64              1/1
Verifying  : kernel-3.10.0-123.8.1.el7.x86_64              1/1
Installed:
  kernel.x86_64 0:3.10.0-123.8.1.el7
Complete!
```

3. Confirm that the kernel package has been updated:

    # **yum list installed kernel**
    ```
    Installed Packages
    kernel.x86_64        3.10.0-123.el7          @anaconda/7.0
    kernel.x86_64        3.10.0-123.8.1.el7      @rhel-7-server-rpms
    ```

    The output indicates that a higher kernel version 3.10.0-123.8.1.el7 has been installed. It also shows the presence of the previous kernel.

4. The */boot/grub2/grub.cfg* file gets the newest kernel menuentry added to it as well:

    # **cat /boot/grub/grub.conf**
    ```
    ### BEGIN /etc/grub.d/10_linux ###
    menuentry 'Red Hat Enterprise Linux Server (3.10.0-123.8.1.el7.x86_64)
    7.0 (Maipo)' --class red --class gnu-linux --class gnu --class os –u nrestricted $menuentry_id_option
    'gnulinux-3.10.0-123.el7.x86_64-advanced-964201bb-1e32-4794-a2f2-7a33e2fb591a' {
            load_video
            set gfxpayload=keep
            insmod gzio
            insmod part_msdos
            insmod xfs
            set root='hd0,msdos1'
            if [ x$feature_platform_search_hint = xy ]; then
              search --no-floppy --fs-uuid --set=root --hint-bios=hd0,msdo
    s1 --hint-efi=hd0,msdos1 --hint-baremetal=ahci0,msdos1 --hint='hd0,msdos1' e6c9c801-e77a-4ce0-
    ac89-eeb2d3a4774f
            else
              search --no-floppy --fs-uuid --set=root e6c9c801-e77a-4ce0-ac89-eeb2d3a4774f
            fi
            linux16 /vmlinuz-3.10.0-123.8.1.el7.x86_64 root=/dev/mapper/vg00-root ro
    rd.lvm.lv=vg00/swap vconsole.font=latarcyrheb-sun16 crashkernel=auto  vconsole.keymap=us
    rd.lvm.lv=vg00/root rhgb quiet LANG=en_US.UTF-8
            initrd16 /initramfs-3.10.0-123.8.1.el7.x86_64.img
    }
    ```

5. Reboot the system and you will see the new kernel menu entry shows up in the GRUB boot list. The system will boot with this kernel as the install process has marked it as the default kernel.
6. Run the *uname* command again after the reboot to confirm the loading of the new kernel:

    # **uname –r**
    ```
    3.10.0-123.8.1.el7.x86_64
    ```

7. You can also view the contents of either of the following files to verify the new kernel:

    # **cat /proc/version**
    Linux version 3.10.0-123.8.1.el7.x86_64 (mockbuild@x86-025.build.eng.bos.redhat.com) (gcc
    version 4.8.2 20140120 (Red Hat 4.8.2-16) (GCC)) #1 SMP Mon Aug 11 13:37:49 EDT 2014
    # **cat /proc/cmdline**
    BOOT_IMAGE=/vmlinuz-3.10.0-123.8.1.el7.x86_64 root=/dev/mapper/vg00-root ro
    rd.lvm.lv=vg00/swap vconsole.font=latarcyrheb-sun16 crashkernel=auto vconsole.keymap=us
    rd.lvm.lv=vg00/root rhgb quiet LANG=en_US.UTF-8

    For those with CentOS or Scientific Linux, can access their repositories for kernel version update. Alternatively,
    you can download the required kernel version from *ftp.kernel.org* and install it. See Chapter 06 "Configuring Server
    Virtualization and Network Installing RHEL7" on how to do it with the *wget* command.

Listing Loaded Modules

RHEL provides the *lsmod* command to view currently loaded modules. Alternatively, you can view
them by displaying the contents of the */proc/modules* file. Both show module names, memory they
are consuming, the number of processes using this and any dependent modules, and a list of
dependent modules (if any).

    # **lsmod**

Module	Size	Used by	
ipt_MASQUERADE	12880	3	
xt_CHECKSUM	12549	1	
ip6t_rpfilter	12546	1	
ip6t_REJECT	12939	2	
ebtables	30913	3	ebtable_broute,ebtable_nat,ebtable_filter

    . . . .
    # **cat /proc/modules**
    ipt_MASQUERADE 12880 3 - Live 0xffffffffa0473000
    xt_CHECKSUM   12549 1 - Live 0xffffffffa046e000
    ip6t_rpfilter   12546 1 - Live 0xffffffffa0469000
    ip6t_REJECT   12939 2 - Live 0xffffffffa0464000
    . . . .

Displaying Module Information

The *modinfo* command can be used to display details about a module. For instance, the following
example shows information about a disk mirroring module called *dm_mirror*:

    # **modinfo dm_mirror**
    filename: /lib/modules/3.10.0-123.8.1.el7.x86_64/kernel/drivers/md/dm-mirror.ko
    license: GPL
    author: Joe Thornber
    description: device-mapper mirror target
    srcversion: 80B7705018D32620F6E86B0
    depends: dm-region-hash,dm-mod,dm-log
    intree: Y

vermagic:	3.10.0-123.8.1.el7.x86_64 SMP mod_unload modversions
signer:	Red Hat Enterprise Linux kernel signing key
sig_key:	D8:AC:C6:83:77:76:03:AC:49:21:21:97:4D:8A:77:F9:5D:F3:38:74
sig_hashalgo:	sha256
parm:	raid1_resync_throttle:A percentage of time allocated for raid resynchronization (uint)

The output shows the module file name, license type, author name, a short description, dependent module names, and other information.

Loading and Unloading Modules

Execute the *modprobe* command to load a module dynamically into memory. This command ensures that any dependent modules are also loaded prior to the specified module. The following example loads the *dm_mirror* module:

 # modprobe –v dm_mirror
insmod /lib/modules/3.10.0-123.8.1.el7.x86_64/kernel/drivers/md/dm-log.ko
insmod /lib/modules/3.10.0-123.8.1.el7.x86_64/kernel/drivers/md/dm-region-hash.ko
insmod /lib/modules/3.10.0-123.8.1.el7.x86_64/kernel/drivers/md/dm-mirror.ko

To unload the *dm_mirror* module along with all unused dependent modules, run the *modprobe* command with the –r option:

 # modprobe –vr dm_mirror
rmmod dm_mirror
rmmod dm_region_hash
rmmod dm_log

Installing New Modules

RHEL detects hardware devices and loads appropriate modules automatically; however, there may be instances when a device is left undetected or added online (as in the case of SAN disk allocation). In such a situation, execute the *depmod* command to force the system to scan the hardware, find appropriate modules for the new devices, create required module dependencies, and update the */lib/modules/3.10.0-123.8.1.el7.x86_64/modules.dep* file, in addition to creating and updating several corresponding map files in the */lib/modules/3.10.0-123.8.1.el7.x86_64* directory.

 # depmod –v
/lib/modules/3.10.0-123.8.1.el7.x86_64/kernel/arch/x86/crypto/ablk_helper.ko needs
"cryptd_alloc_ablkcipher": /lib/modules/3.10.0-123.8.1.el7.x86_64/kernel/crypto/cryptd.ko
/lib/modules/3.10.0-123.8.1.el7.x86_64/kernel/arch/x86/crypto/camellia-x86_64.ko needs
"glue_cbc_encrypt_128bit": /lib/modules/3.10.0123.8.1.el7.x86_64/kernel/arch/x86/crypto/glue_helper.ko
. . . .

Here is a listing of the module files in the */lib/modules/3.10.0-123.8.1.el7.x86_64* directory:

 # ll /lib/modules/3.10.0-123.8.1.el7.x86_64 | grep modules
-rw-r--r--. 1 root root 656738 Oct 7 23:17 modules.alias
-rw-r--r--. 1 root root 637409 Oct 7 23:17 modules.alias.bin
-rw-r--r--. 1 root root   1296 Aug 11 13:43 modules.block

```
-rw-r--r--. 1 root root   5912 Aug 11 13:41 modules.builtin
-rw-r--r--. 1 root root   7675 Oct  7 23:17 modules.builtin.bin
-rw-r--r--. 1 root root 213845 Oct  7 23:17 modules.dep
. . . . . . . .
```

init and Upstart

The *init* program (short for *initialization*) is the first process that spawns in the userland at system boot. It serves as the root process for all the processes that start on the system thereafter. It is a daemon process that is assigned PID 1. The init process debuted as a single main shell script in BSD UNIX that would call additional shell scripts one after the other in a pre-determined sequence to initialize the system. If a script had to wait for something during the execution, init had no other choice but to pause until what was required either became available to the script or the script timed out. The init process then continued to the next script in the sequence. This unexpected wait resulted in delays in the overall boot process. In order to support the system initialization, there was one configuration file listing names of enabled services and one optional script for handling miscellaneous tasks. During the initialization, the system had to start all enabled services.

init was enhanced in UNIX System V (SysVinit) with the introduction of numbered run levels. This enhanced approach modularized the entire initialization process by permitting the system to boot and run into one of several pre-configured operating states, such as system maintenance, and multi-user states with or without graphical support. Each operating state defined a set of services and numbered them to be started serially to get to that state of system operation. Though the services were numbered, it was the system administrator's responsibility to ensure that each script was sequenced in an appropriate order of dependency to lessen the chances of service failures and delays. This dependency adjustment was a manual process. Additionally, there was still the issue of slower processing of shell scripts. In SysVinit, the *inittab* file was referenced to determine the default run level to boot the system to. Based on this default run level, the *rc* script (part of the init program) called numbered start/stop scripts corresponding to the default run level and executed them. On a running system, these same scripts were used to transition from one operating state to another by only stopping or starting the services associated with the desired target run level. Red Hat had had this boot model in their Linux distribution for roughly a decade before they switched over to a more competent system boot model in RHEL6 called *Upstart*.

Upstart was introduced as a replacement for the SysVinit model. It offered three major benefits over its predecessor: asynchronous service startup; automatic restart of crashed services; and event-based service start and stop triggered by a process on the system, a change in hardware, or by the start or stop of another service. This enhanced boot model was presented in RHEL6 as the default initialization scheme. Upstart, like its predecessor, also referenced the *inittab* file, but only to determine the default run level to boot to. Upstart used a set of configuration files located in the */etc/init* directory and processed scripts from the */etc/rc.d* directory for bringing the system up to the default run level and for state transitioning. It used the *initctl* command for service control. Due to some shortcomings in the Upstart design, Red Hat decided not to continue with this init system in RHEL7 and they switched to an even better solution called *systemd*.

Overview of systemd

systemd (short for *system daemon*) is another alternative for the SysVinit model. It is a system and service management mechanism that has superseded its precursors in terms of rapidity and capability. It has fast-tracked system initialization and state transitioning by introducing parallel processing of startup scripts, improved handling of service dependencies, and an on-demand activation of service daemons using sockets and D-Bus. Moreover, it supports snapshotting of system states, tracks processes using control groups, and maintains automatic mount and automount points. systemd is the default system initialization mechanism in RHEL7, replacing both SysVinit and Upstart. It is backwards compatible with SysVinit scripts as described in the *Linux Standard Base* (LSB) specification. systemd is the first process that starts at boot and it is the last process that terminates at shutdown.

In order to benefit from parallelism, systemd initiates distinct services concurrently, taking advantage of multiple CPU cores and other computing resources. To achieve this, systemd creates sockets for all enabled services that support socket-based activation instantaneously at the very beginning of the initialization process, and passes them to daemon processes as they attempt to start in parallel. This approach lets systemd handle inter-service order dependencies and allows services to start without any delays. With systemd, dependent daemons need not be running, they only need the correct socket to be available. systemd creates all sockets first, all the daemons next, and any client requests to daemons not yet running are cached in the socket buffer and filled when the daemons come online. During the operational state, systemd maintains the sockets and uses them to reconnect other daemons and services that were interacting with an old daemon before it was terminated or restarted. Likewise, services that use activation based on D-Bus are started when a client application attempts to communicate with them the first time. Additional methods used by systemd for activation are device-based and path-based, with the former starting services when a specific hardware type such as USB is plugged in, and the latter starting services when a particular file or directory alters its state.

With the on-demand activation, systemd defers the startup of services such as Bluetooth and printing until they are actually needed during the boot process or during runtime. Together, parallelization and on-demand activation save time and computing resources, and contribute to speeding up the boot process considerably.

Socket is a communication method that allows a single process running on a system to talk to another process on the same or remote system.

D-Bus is another communication method that allows multiple services running in parallel on a system to talk to one another on the same or remote system.

Another major benefit of parallelism witnessed at system boot time is when systemd uses the autofs service to temporarily mount the file systems listed in the */etc/fstab* file. During the boot process, the file systems are checked that may result in unnecessary delays. With autofs, the file systems are temporarily mounted on their normal mount points and as soon as the checks on the file systems are finished, systemd remounts them using their standard devices. Parallelism in file system mounts does not affect the root and virtual file systems.

Some service shell scripts have been converted into the C programming language, resulting in their faster startup.

Parallelism in systemd also results in a flatter process tree, and this can be confirmed with the *pstree* command. With the –p and –u options, this command shows the PID and UID transitions.

```
# pstree –pu
systemd(1)───┬───ModemManager(642)───┬───{ModemManager}(715)
             │                        └───{ModemManager}(717)
             ├───NetworkManager(807)──┬───{NetworkManager}(866)
             │                        └───{NetworkManager}(874)
             ├───abrt-watch-log(637)
             ├───abrt-watch-log(641)
             ├───abrtd(636)
             ├───accounts-daemon(651)──┬───{accounts-daemon}(704)
             │                         └───{accounts-daemon}(708)
             ├───alsactl(623)
             ├───at-spi-bus-laun(2320,gdm)───┬───dbus-daemon(2324)─────{dbus-daemon}(2326)
             │                               ├───{at-spi-bus-laun}(2321)
             │                               ├───{at-spi-bus-laun}(2323)
             │                               └───{at-spi-bus-laun}(2325)
             ├───at-spi2-registr(2328,gdm)─────{at-spi2-registr}(2329)
             ├───atd(672)
```

Units

Units are systemd objects that are used for organizing boot and maintenance tasks, such as hardware initialization, socket creation, file system mounts, and service startups. Unit configuration is stored in their respective configuration files, which are auto-generated from other configurations, created dynamically from the system state, produced at runtime, or user-developed. Units are in one of several operational states, including active, inactive, in the process of being activated or deactivated, and failed. Units can be enabled or disabled. An enabled unit can be started to an active state; a disabled unit cannot be started.

Units have a name and a type, and they are encoded in files with names in the form unitname.type. Some examples are tmp.mount, sshd.service, syslog.socket, and umount.target. There are two types of unit configuration files: system unit files that are distributed with installed packages and located in the */usr/lib/systemd/system* directory, and user unit files that are generated by users and stored in the */etc/systemd/user* directory. This information can be vetted with the *pkg-config* command:

```
# pkg-config systemd --variable=systemdsystemunitdir
/usr/lib/systemd/system
# pkg-config systemd --variable=systemduserconfdir
/etc/systemd/user
```

Furthermore, there are additional system units that are created at runtime and destroyed when they are no longer needed. They are located in the */run/systemd/system* directory. These runtime unit files take precedence over the system unit files, and the user unit files take priority over the runtime files. The unit configuration files are a direct replacement of the initialization scripts found in the */etc/rc.d/init.d* directory in the older RHEL releases. systemd currently includes 12 unit types, which are described in Table 7-3.

Unit Type	Description
Automount	Offers automount capabilities for on-demand mounting of file systems.
Device	Exposes kernel devices in systemd and may be used to implement device-based activation.
Mount	Controls when and how to mount or unmount file systems.
Path	Starts a service when monitored files or directories are accessed.
Scope	Manages foreign processes instead of starting them.
Service	Starts, stops, restarts, or reloads service daemons and the processes they are made up of. Handles services controlled by scripts in the /etc/rc.d/init.d directory in previous RHEL releases.
Slice	May be used to group units, which manage system processes in a hierarchical tree for resource management.
Snapshot	Saves the current state of all units dynamically. This state may be restored later to go back to that state.
Socket	Encapsulates local IPC or network sockets for use by matching service units.
Swap	Encapsulates swap partitions.
Target	Defines logical grouping of units. Equivalent to run levels in SysV.
Timer	Useful for triggering activation of other units based on timers.

Table 7-3 systemd Unit Types

Unit files contain common and specific configuration elements. Common elements fall under the [Unit] and [Install] sections, and comprise description, documentation location, dependency information, conflict information, and other options that are independent of the type of unit. The unit specific configuration data is located under the unit type section: [Service] for the service unit type, [Socket] for the socket unit type, and so forth.

Units can have dependency relationship amongst themselves based on a sequence or a requirement. A sequence outlines one or more actions that need to be taken before or after the activation of a unit (options Before and After), and a requirement specifies what must already be running (option Requires) or not running (option Conflicts) in order for the successful launch of a unit. For instance, the *graphical.target* unit file tells us that the system must already be operating in the multi-user mode and must not be running in rescue mode in order for it to boot successfully into the graphical mode. Another option, Wants, may be used instead of Requires in the Unit or Install section so the unit is not forced to fail activation if a required unit fails to start.

There are a few other types of dependencies that you may see in unit configuration files. systemd generally sets and maintains inter-service dependencies automatically; however, this can be implemented manually as well.

You can use the *systemctl* command as follows to list all active units on the system:

systemctl

```
UNIT                             LOAD    ACTIVE  SUB        DESCRIPTION
proc-sys-...mt_misc.automount    loaded  active  waiting    Arbitrary Executable File For
sys-devic...-block-sr0.device    loaded  active  plugged    VBOX_CD-ROM
sys-devic...net-enp0s3.device    loaded  active  plugged    PRO/1000 MT Desktop Adapter
sys-devic...ound-card0.device    loaded  active  plugged    82801AA AC'97 Audio Controlle
sys-devic...k-sda-sda1.device    loaded  active  plugged    VBOX_HARDDISK
sys-devic...k-sda-sda2.device    loaded  active  plugged    LVM PV 96Pn91-CMum-1XGf-trAs-
sys-devic...-block-sda.device    loaded  active  plugged    VBOX_HARDDISK
sys-devic...-tty-ttyS0.device    loaded  active  plugged    /sys/devices/platform/serial8
sys-devic...-tty-ttyS1.device    loaded  active  plugged    /sys/devices/platform/serial8
sys-devic...-tty-ttyS2.device    loaded  active  plugged    /sys/devices/platform/serial8
sys-devic...-tty-ttyS3.device    loaded  active  plugged    /sys/devices/platform/serial8
sys-devic...ck-dm\x2d0.device    loaded  active  plugged    /sys/devices/virtual/block/dm
sys-devic...ck-dm\x2d1.device    loaded  active  plugged    /sys/devices/virtual/block/dm
sys-devic...ck-dm\x2d2.device    loaded  active  plugged    /sys/devices/virtual/block/dm
sys-module-configfs.device       loaded  active  plugged    /sys/module/configfs
sys-subsy...ces-enp0s3.device    loaded  active  plugged    PRO/1000 MT Desktop Adapter
-.mount                          loaded  active  mounted    /
boot.mount                       loaded  active  mounted    /boot
dev-hugepages.mount              loaded  active  mounted    Huge Pages File System
dev-mqueue.mount                 loaded  active  mounted    POSIX Message Queue File Syst
home.mount                       loaded  active  mounted    /home
mnt.mount                        loaded  active  mounted    /mnt
proc-fs-nfsd.mount               loaded  active  mounted    RPC Pipe File System
sys-kernel-config.mount          loaded  active  mounted    Configuration File System
sys-kernel-debug.mount           loaded  active  mounted    Debug File System
tmp.mount                        loaded  active  mounted    Temporary Directory
```

The UNIT column above shows the name of the unit and its location in the cgroup tree, LOAD reflects whether the unit configuration file was loaded properly, ACTIVE shows the high-level activation state, SUB depicts the low-level unit activation state, and DESCRIPTION illustrates the unit's content and functionality. By default, the *systemctl* command lists only the active units. You can use the --all option to see inactive units also. If you want to list a specific type of unit, use the –t switch and specify a type. For instance, the following shows the list of all active and inactive units of type socket:

systemctl –t mount --all

```
UNIT                  LOAD    ACTIVE    SUB        DESCRIPTION
avahi-daemon.socket   loaded  active    running    Avahi mDNS/DNS-SD
cups.socket           loaded  active    running    CUPS Printing Ser
dbus.socket           loaded  active    running    D-Bus System Mess
dm-event.socket       loaded  active    listening  Device-mapper eve
iscsid.socket         loaded  active    listening  Open-iSCSI iscsid
iscsiuio.socket       loaded  active    listening  Open-iSCSI iscsiu
lvm2-lvmetad.socket   loaded  active    running    LVM2 metadata dae
rpcbind.socket        loaded  active    running    RPCbind Server Ac
syslog.socket         loaded  inactive  dead       Syslog Socket
```

Targets

Targets are simply logical collections of units. They are a special systemd unit type with the *.target* file extension. Some targets are equivalent to SysVinit run levels; however, they are named rather than numbered. Targets are used to execute a series of units. This is typically true for booting the system to a specific operational level (similar to a numbered run level) with all the required services up and running at that level. Some targets inherit all services from other targets and add their own to them. systemd includes several pre-defined targets that are described in Table 7-4, along with the comparable run level associated with each one of them.

Target	SysVinit Run Level	Description
halt	0	Shuts down and halts the system.
poweroff or runlevel0	0	Shuts down and powers off the system.
shutdown	0	Shuts down the system.
rescue or runlevel1	1, s, or single	Single-user target for administrative and recovery functions. All local file systems are mounted. Some essential services are started, but networking remains disabled.
multi-user or runlevel2|3|4	3	Multi-user target with full network support, but without GUI.
graphical or runlevel5	5	Multi-user target with full network support and GUI.
reboot or runlevel6	6	Shuts down and reboots the system.
default	Typically set to 3 or 5	Default system boot target symlinked to either multi-user.target or graphical.target.
emergency	N/A	Runs an emergency shell. The root file system is mounted in read-only mode; other file systems are not mounted. Networking and all other services remain disabled.
hibernate	N/A	Puts the system into hibernation by saving the running state of the system on the hard disk and powering it off. When powered up, the system restores from its saved state rather than booting up.
suspend	N/A	Same as hibernation except that the system running state is saved in memory and the power to the memory and supporting modules is not turned off.
hybrid-sleep	N/A	Puts the system into hibernation and then suspend its operation.

Table 7-4 systemd Targets

Table 7-4 indicates one-to-one correspondence between most systemd targets and the old SysVinit run levels. The default target is graphical.target, which is executed to boot the system with full networking and graphical support.

You can use the *systemctl* command as follows to view a list of all loaded and active targets:

systemctl –t target

```
[root@host1 system]# systemctl list-units --type=target
UNIT                     LOAD    ACTIVE SUB     DESCRIPTION
basic.target             loaded  active active  Basic System
cryptsetup.target        loaded  active active  Encrypted Volumes
getty.target             loaded  active active  Login Prompts
graphical.target         loaded  active active  Graphical Interface
local-fs-pre.target loaded  active active  Local File Systems (Pre)
local-fs.target          loaded  active active  Local File Systems
multi-user.target        loaded  active active  Multi-User System
network.target           loaded  active active  Network
nfs.target               loaded  active active  Network File System Server
paths.target             loaded  active active  Paths
remote-fs.target         loaded  active active  Remote File Systems
slices.target            loaded  active active  Slices
sockets.target           loaded  active active  Sockets
sound.target             loaded  active active  Sound Card
swap.target              loaded  active active  Swap
sysinit.target           loaded  active active  System Initialization
timers.target            loaded  active active  Timers

LOAD   = Reflects whether the unit definition was properly loaded.
ACTIVE = The high-level unit activation state, i.e. generalization of SUB.
SUB    = The low-level unit activation state, values depend on unit type.

17 loaded units listed. Pass --all to see loaded but inactive units, too.
```

For each target unit, the above output shows the target unit's full name, load state, high-level and low-level activation states, and a short description. Add the --all option to the above command to see all loaded targets in either an active or inactive state.

Control Groups

systemd spawns several processes during a service startup. It places the processes in a private hierarchy composed of *control groups* (or *cgroups* for short), and uses them for monitoring and controlling system resources such as processor, memory, network bandwidth, and disk I/O. This includes limiting, isolating, and prioritizing their usage of resources. This way resources can be distributed among users, databases, and applications based on their needs and priorities, resulting in overall improved system performance. The *ps* command below can be used to view a PID-sorted list of processes within cgroups:

ps –eafxo pid,user,cgroup,args | sort –nk1

```
PID USER      CGROUP              COMMAND
  1 root      -                   /usr/lib/systemd/systemd --switched-root
--system --deserialize 23
  2 root      -                   [kthreadd]
  3 root      -                   \_ [ksoftirqd/0]
  5 root      -                   \_ [kworker/0:0H]
  6 root      -                   \_ [kworker/u2:0]
  7 root      -                   \_ [migration/0]
  8 root      -                   \_ [rcu_bh]
  9 root      -                   \_ [rcuob/0]
 10 root      -                   \_ [rcu_sched]
 11 root      -                   \_ [rcuos/0]
 12 root      -                   \_ [watchdog/0]
 13 root      -                   \_ [khelper]
 14 root      -                   \_ [kdevtmpfs]
 15 root      -                   \_ [netns]
 16 root      -                   \_ [writeback]
 17 root      -                   \_ [kintegrityd]
 18 root      -                   \_ [bioset]
 19 root      -                   \_ [kblockd]
 20 root      -                   \_ [khubd]
 21 root      -                   \_ [md]
 24 root      -                   \_ [kswapd0]
 25 root      -                   \_ [ksmd]
 26 root      -                   \_ [khugepaged]
 27 root      -                   \_ [fsnotify_mark]
 28 root      -                   \_ [crypto]
 37 root      -                   \_ [kthrotld]
 39 root      -                   \_ [kmpath_rdacd]
 40 root      -                   \_ [kpsmoused]
 59 root      -                   \_ [deferwq]
 82 root      -                   \_ [kauditd]
255 root      -                   \_ [ata_sff]
285 root      -                   \_ [scsi_eh_0]
286 root      -                   \_ [scsi_tmf_0]
287 root      -                   \_ [scsi_eh_1]
288 root      -                   \_ [scsi_tmf_1]
```

The output shows PIDs in the first column, owner name in the second column, and cgroup names and processes within them in the third and fourth columns.

Managing Units and Control Groups

systemd comes with a set of management tools for querying and controlling its operations. The primary tool in this command suite is *systemctl*, which supports a number of administrative functions. This command also includes the combined functionality that the *chkconfig* and *service* commands provided in RHEL6 to display service startup settings, set service start and stop at appropriate run levels, and start, stop, check the operational status of, and restart a service. Red Hat recommends avoiding the use of these two commands in RHEL7.

As we know, each systemd unit is named as unitname.type. When working with the *systemctl* command, we do not need to specify the unit type; the command automatically picks that information up.

This section covers general operations performed on units, specifically the service and target units, using the *systemctl* command. It also provides some instances of viewing cgroup contents with two new commands: *systemd-cgls* and *systemd-cgtop*.

The systemctl Command

systemctl is the primary command for interaction with systemd. It can be used to display unit information and manage it. This command is versatile and supports a variety of subcommands and flags. Table 7-5 lists and describes some common subcommands.

Subcommand/Option	Description
daemon-reload	Re-reads and reloads all unit configuration files and recreates the entire user dependency tree.
enable / disable	Activates (deactivates) a unit for autostart at system boot.
get-default (set-default)	Shows (sets) the default boot target unit.
get-property (set-property)	Returns (sets) the value of a property.
is-active	Checks whether a unit is running.
is-enabled	Displays whether a unit is set to autostart at system boot.
is-failed	Checks whether a unit is in the failed state.
isolate	Changes the running state of a system (similar to changing runlevels in SysVinit).
kill	Terminates all processes for a unit.
list-dependencies	Lists dependency tree for a unit.
list-sockets	Lists socket units.
list-unit-files	Lists installed unit files.
list-units	Lists known units. This is the default subcommand when systemctl is executed without any arguments.
mask / unmask	Prohibits (permits) auto and manual activation of a unit.
reload	Forces a running unit to re-read its configuration file. This action does not change the PID of the running unit.
restart	Stops a running unit and restarts it.

Subcommand/Option	Description
show	Shows unit properties.
start / stop	Starts (stops) a unit.
status	Presents the unit status information.

Table 7-5 systemctl Subcommands

We will use most of these options with the *systemctl* command in this book.

Managing Units

The *systemctl* command is used to view and manage all types of units. The following examples demonstrate some common operations related to viewing units and their information.

To list all known units and their status:

 # systemctl
```
UNIT                      LOAD    ACTIVE   SUB       JOB   DESCRIPTION
proc-sys...misc.automount loaded  active   running         Arbitrary Executable
sys-devi...ock-sr0.device loaded  active   plugged         VBOX_CD-ROM
sys-devi...-enp0s3.device loaded  active   plugged         PRO/1000 MT Desktop
sys-devi...d-card0.device loaded  active   plugged         82801AA AC'97 Audio
sys-devi...da-sda1.device loaded  active   plugged         VBOX_HARDDISK
sys-devi...da-sda2.device loaded  active   plugged         LVM PV 96Pn91-CMum-1
sys-devi...ock-sda.device loaded  active   plugged         VBOX_HARDDISK
```

To list all units of type socket sorted by the listening address:

 # systemctl list-sockets
```
LISTEN                            UNIT                            ACTIVATES
/dev/initctl                      systemd-initctl.socket          systemd-initctl.ser
/dev/log                          systemd-journald.socket         systemd-journald.se
/run/dmeventd-client              dm-event.socket                 dm-event.service
/run/dmeventd-server              dm-event.socket                 dm-event.service
/run/lvm/lvmetad.socket           lvm2-lvmetad.socket             lvm2-lvmetad.servic
/run/systemd/journal/socket       systemd-journald.socket         systemd-journald.se
/run/systemd/journal/stdout       systemd-journald.socket         systemd-journald.se
/run/systemd/shutdownd            systemd-shutdownd.socket         systemd-shutdownd.s
/run/udev/control                 systemd-udevd-control.socket    systemd-udevd.servi
/var/run/avahi-daemon/socket      avahi-daemon.socket             avahi-daemon.servic
/var/run/cups/cups.sock           cups.socket                     cups.service
/var/run/dbus/system_bus_socket   dbus.socket                     dbus.service
/var/run/rpcbind.sock             rpcbind.socket                  rpcbind.service
@ISCSIADM_ABSTRACT_NAMESPACE      iscsid.socket                   iscsid.service
@ISCSID_UIP_ABSTRACT_NAMESPACE    iscsiuio.socket                 iscsiuio.service
kobject-uevent_1                  systemd-udevd-kernel.socket     systemd-udevd.servi

16 sockets listed.
Pass --all to see loaded but inactive sockets, too.
```

To list all socket units and their status:

 # systemctl --type=socket

```
UNIT                        LOAD   ACTIVE SUB        DESCRIPTION
avahi-daemon.socket         loaded active running    Avahi mDNS/DNS-SD Stack Acti
cups.socket                 loaded active listening  CUPS Printing Service Socket
dbus.socket                 loaded active running    D-Bus System Message Bus Soc
dm-event.socket             loaded active listening  Device-mapper event daemon F
iscsid.socket               loaded active listening  Open-iSCSI iscsid Socket
iscsiuio.socket             loaded active listening  Open-iSCSI iscsiuio Socket
lvm2-lvmetad.socket         loaded active listening  LVM2 metadata daemon socket
rpcbind.socket              loaded active running    RPCbind Server Activation So
systemd-initctl.socket      loaded active listening  /dev/initctl Compatibility N
systemd-journald.socket     loaded active running    Journal Socket
systemd-shutdownd.socket    loaded active listening  Delayed Shutdown Socket
systemd-...d-control.socket loaded active running    udev Control Socket
systemd-udevd-kernel.socket loaded active running    udev Kernel Socket

LOAD   = Reflects whether the unit definition was properly loaded.
ACTIVE = The high-level unit activation state, i.e. generalization of SUB.
SUB    = The low-level unit activation state, values depend on unit type.

13 loaded units listed. Pass --all to see loaded but inactive units, too.
To show all installed unit files use 'systemctl list-unit-files'.
```

To list all unit files installed on the system and their state:

 # systemctl list-unit-files

```
UNIT FILE                           STATE
proc-sys-fs-binfmt_misc.automount   static
dev-hugepages.mount                 static
dev-mqueue.mount                    static
proc-fs-nfsd.mount                  static
proc-sys-fs-binfmt_misc.mount       static
sys-fs-fuse-connections.mount       static
sys-kernel-config.mount             static
sys-kernel-debug.mount              static
tmp.mount                           enabled
var-lib-nfs-rpc_pipefs.mount        static
```

To list all units that failed to start at the last system boot:

 # systemctl --failed

```
UNIT          LOAD   ACTIVE SUB    DESCRIPTION
kdump.service loaded failed failed Crash recovery kernel arming
rhnsd.service loaded failed failed LSB: Starts the Spacewalk Daemon
rngd.service  loaded failed failed Hardware RNG Entropy Gatherer Daemon

LOAD   = Reflects whether the unit definition was properly loaded.
ACTIVE = The high-level unit activation state, i.e. generalization of SUB.
SUB    = The low-level unit activation state, values depend on unit type.

3 loaded units listed. Pass --all to see loaded but inactive units, too.
To show all installed unit files use 'systemctl list-unit-files'.
```

Managing Service Units

The following examples demonstrate the use of the *systemctl* command on a service unit called *atd*.

To check the current operational status of the *atd* service and its location in the cgroup subtree:

 # systemctl status atd

atd.service - Job spooling tools
   Loaded: loaded (/usr/lib/systemd/system/atd.service; enabled)
   Active: active (running) since Fri 2014-08-08 11:48:05 EDT; 6 days ago
  Main PID: 672 (atd)
   CGroup: /system.slice/atd.service
       └─672 /usr/sbin/atd -f
Aug 08 11:48:05 server1.example.com systemd[1]: Started Job spooling tools.

To disable the *atd* service from autostarting at the next system reboot:

 # systemctl disable atd

rm '/etc/systemd/system/multi-user.target.wants/atd.service'

To enable the *atd* service to autostart at the next system reboot:

 # systemctl enable atd

ln -s '/usr/lib/systemd/system/atd.service' '/etc/systemd/system/multi-user.target.wants/atd.service'

To check whether the *atd* service is set to autostart at the next system reboot:

 # systemctl is-enabled atd

enabled

To check whether the *atd* service is running:

 # systemctl is-active atd

active

To stop and start the *atd* service:

 # systemctl stop atd
 # systemctl start atd

To list all dependencies for the *atd* service:

 # systemctl list-dependencies atd

atd.service
├─system.slice
└─basic.target
  ├─alsa-restore.service
  ├─alsa-state.service
  ├─firewalld.service
  ├─microcode.service
  ├─rhel-autorelabel-mark.service
  ├─rhel-autorelabel.service
  ├─rhel-configure.service
  ├─rhel-dmesg.service
  ├─rhel-loadmodules.service

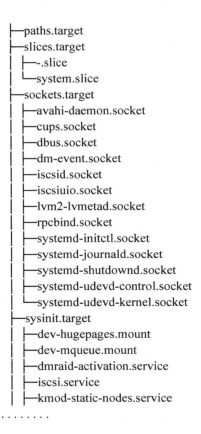
```
├──paths.target
├──slices.target
│   ├──-.slice
│   └──system.slice
├──sockets.target
│   ├──avahi-daemon.socket
│   ├──cups.socket
│   ├──dbus.socket
│   ├──dm-event.socket
│   ├──iscsid.socket
│   ├──iscsiuio.socket
│   ├──lvm2-lvmetad.socket
│   ├──rpcbind.socket
│   ├──systemd-initctl.socket
│   ├──systemd-journald.socket
│   ├──systemd-shutdownd.socket
│   ├──systemd-udevd-control.socket
│   └──systemd-udevd-kernel.socket
├──sysinit.target
│   ├──dev-hugepages.mount
│   ├──dev-mqueue.mount
│   ├──dmraid-activation.service
│   ├──iscsi.service
│   ├──kmod-static-nodes.service
. . . . . . . .
```

To show details for the *atd* service:

> **# systemctl show atd**
> Id=atd.service
> Names=atd.service
> Requires=basic.target
> Wants=system.slice
> WantedBy=multi-user.target
> Conflicts=shutdown.target
> Before=shutdown.target multi-user.target
> After=syslog.target systemd-user-sessions.service systemd-journald.socket basic.
> Description=Job spooling tools
> LoadState=loaded
> ActiveState=active
> SubState=running
> . . . .

Managing Target Units

The *systemctl* command is used to manage the target units as well. It can be used to switch from one running target into another at the command line. Examples of some common operations are provided below.

Viewing and Setting Default Boot Target

We can use the *systemctl* command to view and change the default boot target.

To check the current default boot target:

> # **systemctl get-default**
> graphical.target

EXAM TIP: You may have to modify the default boot target persistenly.

To change the current default boot target to multi-user.target:

> # **systemctl set-default multi-user.target**
> rm '/etc/systemd/system/default.target'
> ln -s '/usr/lib/systemd/system/multi-user.target' '/etc/systemd/system/default.target'

Switching into Specific Targets

The *systemctl* command can be used to transition the system from one target into another. There are a number of targets available to switch the system operating state into, and these are captured in Table 7-2. The following shows a few examples of switching targets from the command prompt.

To switch into the multi-user target (equivalent to legacy run level 3):

> # **systemctl isolate multi-user.target**

To transition into the graphical target (equivalent to legacy run level 5):

> # **systemctl isolate graphical.target**

To shut down the system to the halt state:

> # **systemctl halt**

To shut down the system to the poweroff state:

> # **systemctl poweroff**

To shut down the system and then reboot it:

> # **systemctl reboot**

To transition the system into hibernation and then suspend its activities:

> # **systemctl hybrid-sleep**

To switch into the legacy run level 3 target:

> # **systemctl isolate runlevel3.target**

Using the shutdown Command

The *shutdown* command is used to halt, power off, or reboot the system gracefully. This command broadcasts a warning message to all logged-in users, disables further user logins, waits for the specified amount of time for users to log off, and then goes ahead with stopping the services and shutting the system down to the specified target state.

The following examples show a few different ways for using this command:

shutdown –r now   (begins shutting down the system immediately, and reboots to the default target).

shutdown –h 5   (begins shutting down the system to the halt or power off state after a 5-minute wait).

shutdown –H 10   (begins shutting down the system to the halt state after a 10-minute wait).

shutdown –P 20   (begins shutting down the system to the power off state after a 20-minute wait).

Using the halt, poweroff, and reboot Commands

The *halt*, *poweroff*, and *reboot* commands are available in RHEL7 for compatibility reasons only. It is recommended to use the *systemctl* command instead when switching system states.

The three commands, without any arguments, perform the same action that the *shutdown* command would do with the "–H now", "–P now", and "–r now" arguments, respectively. We may specify the –f option with any of these commands to halt, power off, or reboot the system forcefully; however, this may introduce the risk of damaging application files and file system structures and, therefore, it is not advisable to use this option from any multi-user target.

Viewing System Boot Performance Statistics

systemd provides the *systemd-analyze* command that can be used to obtain and analyze statistics about system boot performance. This command produces reports that show the time the last system startup took in the kernel and user space programs. A couple of examples are provided below on the usage and the kind of data the command produces.

To view the total amount of time the last boot process took in kernel, initrd, and userspace:

systemd-analyze
Startup finished in 578ms (kernel) + 3.283s (initrd) + 38.091s (userspace) = 41.953s

To view the time spent by each task during the boot process:

systemd-analyze blame
    13.402s firewalld.service
    12.118s plymouth-quit-wait.service
    11.786s tuned.service
    6.803s accounts-daemon.service
    5.776s ModemManager.service
    5.513s postfix.service
    . . . .

Managing Control Groups

systemd uses control groups to organize processes for the purposes of monitoring and controlling system resources. It uses the service, scope, and slice unit types in this organization to achieve that. As we know, a service is a collection of processes that are treated as a single entity, a scope is a group of processes that are started and stopped by processes external to them, and a slice is essentially a structured assembly of service and scope units for managing processes encapsulated within them.

systemd offers the *systemd-cgls* and *systemd-cgtop* commands for the management of cgroups in addition to the *systemctl* command. The *systemd-cgls* command shows the cgroup hierarchy of actual processes and the *systemd-cgtop* command shows top cgroups by their CPU, memory, and disk I/O usage. The output of *systemd-cgtop* is refreshed every second. Some examples presented below use them.

To list the cgroup hierarchy:

```
# systemd-cgls
├─1 /usr/lib/systemd/systemd --switched-root --system --deserialize 23
├─user.slice
│ ├─user-0.slice
│ │ └─session-4.scope
│ │   ├─2724 sshd: root@pts/1
│ │   ├─2729 -bash
│ │   ├─4016 systemd-cgls
│ │   └─4017 systemd-cgls
│ └─user-42.slice
│   └─session-c1.scope
│     ├─ 843 gdm-session-worker [pam/gdm-launch-environment]
│     ├─1062 /usr/bin/gnome-session --autostart /usr/share/gdm/greeter/autostart
│     ├─1082 /usr/bin/dbus-launch --exit-with-session /usr/bin/gnome-session --a
│     ├─1226 /bin/dbus-daemon --fork --print-pid 4 --print-address 6 --session
│     ├─1356 /usr/libexec/at-spi-bus-launcher
│     ├─1363 /bin/dbus-daemon --config-file=/etc/at-spi2/accessibility.conf --no
│     ├─1371 /usr/libexec/at-spi2-registryd --use-gnome-session
│     ├─1960 /usr/libexec/gnome-settings-daemon
│     ├─2496 gnome-shell --mode=gdm
│     ├─2524 /usr/bin/pulseaudio --start --log-target=syslog
│     ├─2588 /usr/libexec/dconf-service
│     ├─2598 /usr/bin/ibus-daemon --replace --xim --panel disable
│     ├─2600 /usr/libexec/ibus-dconf
│     ├─2604 /usr/libexec/ibus-x11 --kill-daemon
│     ├─2608 /usr/libexec/ibus-engine-simple
│     ├─2872 /usr/libexec/mission-control-5
│     └─2883 /usr/libexec/goa-daemon
└─system.slice
  ├─colord.service
  │ └─2500 /usr/libexec/colord
  ├─upower.service
  │ └─2339 /usr/libexec/upowerd
```

```
├─polkit.service
│   └─744 /usr/lib/polkit-1/polkitd --no-debug
├─alsa-state.service
│   └─628 /usr/sbin/alsactl -s -n 19 -c -E ALSA_CONFIG_PATH=/etc/alsa/alsactl.co
├─auditd.service
│   ├─599 /sbin/auditd -n
│   ├─615 /sbin/audispd
│   └─617 /usr/sbin/sedispatch
. . . . . . . .
```

The highest level of cgroup tree is formed by slices (user.slice, system.slice, and so on) as depicted in the above output. These slices are shown containing service and scope units. The above output also indicates that PID 1 is located within a special slice called systemd.slice.

To limit the output to a specific resource such as CPU, issue the *systemd-cgls* command as follows:

systemd-cgls cpu
```
cpu:
├─1 /usr/lib/systemd/systemd --switched-root --system --deserialize 23
├─system.slice
│   ├─colord.service
│   │   └─2500 /usr/libexec/colord
│   ├─upower.service
│   │   └─2339 /usr/libexec/upowerd
│   ├─polkit.service
│   │   └─744 /usr/lib/polkit-1/polkitd --no-debug
│   ├─alsa-state.service
│   │   └─628 /usr/sbin/alsactl -s -n 19 -c -E ALSA_CONFIG_PATH=/etc/alsa/alsactl.co
│   ├─auditd.service
│   │   ├─599 /sbin/auditd -n
│   │   ├─615 /sbin/audispd
│   │   └─617 /usr/sbin/sedispatch
. . . . . . . .
```

To monitor cgroup resource consumption ordered by CPU, memory, and disk I/O:

systemd-cgtop
```
Path                                         Tasks   %CPU    Memory   Input/s  Output/s

/                                             130     2.0    495.1M       -        -
/system.slice/ModemManager.service             1       -        -         -        -
/system.slice/NetworkManager.service           1       -        -         -        -
/system.slice/abrt-oops.service                1       -        -         -        -
/system.slice/abrt-xorg.service                1       -        -         -        -
/system.slice/abrtd.service                    1       -        -         -        -
/system.slice/accounts-daemon.service          1       -        -         -        -
/system.slice/alsa-state.service               1       -        -         -        -
/system.slice/atd.service                      1       -        -         -        -
/system.slice/auditd.service                   3       -        -         -        -
/system.slice/avahi-daemon.service             2       -        -         -        -
/system.slice/chronyd.service                  1       -        -         -        -
/system.slice/crond.service                    1       -        -         -        -
/system.slice/dbus.service                     1       -        -         -        -
/system.slice/firewalld.service                1       -        -         -        -
/system.slice/gdm.service                      3       -        -         -        -
```

To view the current values of BlockIOWeight and CPUShares properties for a service such as atd, execute the *systemctl* command as follows:

 # systemctl show –p BlockIOWeight –p CPUShares atd
CPUShares=1024
BlockIOWeight=1000

To change the property values, use the set-property subcommand with *systemctl*. For instance, to set the BlockIOWeight value to 200 and that of CPUShares to 256, run the command as demonstrated below:

 # systemctl set-property atd BlockIOWeight=200 CPUShares=256

Run the *systemctl show* again to confirm the new values.

System Logging

System logging (*syslog* for short) is an essential and one of the most basic elements of an operating system. In RHEL, it is performed to capture messages generated by the kernel, daemons, commands, user activities, applications, and other events. These messages are forwarded to various log files, which store them for security auditing, service malfunctioning, system troubleshooting, or informational purposes.

The daemon that is responsible for system logging is called *rsyslogd*. This daemon is multi-threaded, with support for enhanced filtering, encryption protected message relaying, and a variety of configuration options. The *rsyslogd* daemon reads its configuration file */etc/rsyslog.conf* and the files located in the */etc/rsyslog.d* directory at startup. The default port this daemon uses is 514, which may be configured to use either UDP or TCP protocol. The default repository for most system log files is the */var/log* directory, as defined in */etc/rsyslog.conf*. Other services such as audit, libvirt, Samba, Apache, and GNOME desktop manager also have sub-directories under */var/log/* for storing their respective log files.

The syslog service is modular, allowing the modules listed in its configuration file to be dynamically loaded in the kernel as and when needed. Each module brings a new functionality to the system upon loading.

The *rsyslogd* daemon can be stopped or started manually with the *systemctl* command as follows:

 # systemctl stop rsyslog
 # systemctl start rsyslog

A PID is assigned to the daemon at startup and a file by the name *syslogd.pid* is created in the */var/run/* directory to store the PID. The reason for creating this file is to prevent the initiation of multiple instances of *rsyslog*.

The System Log Configuration File

The primary syslog configuration file is located in the */etc* directory and it is called *rsyslog.conf*. The default uncommented line entries from the file are shown below and explained subsequently. The section headings have been added to separate the directives in each section.

```
# grep –v ^# /etc/rsyslog.conf | grep –v ^$
#### MODULES ####
$ModLoad imuxsock # provides support for local system logging (e.g. via logger command)
$ModLoad imjournal # provides access to the systemd journal
#### GLOBAL DIRECTIVES ####
$WorkDirectory /var/lib/rsyslog
$ActionFileDefaultTemplate RSYSLOG_TraditionalFileFormat
$IncludeConfig /etc/rsyslog.d/*.conf
$OmitLocalLogging on
$IMJournalStateFile imjournal.state
#### RULES ####
*.info;mail.none;authpriv.none;cron.none          /var/log/messages
authpriv.*                                        /var/log/secure
mail.*                                            /var/log/maillog
cron.*                                            /var/log/cron
*.emerg                                           :omusrmsg:*
uucp,news.crit                                    /var/log/spooler
local7.*                                          /var/log/boot.log
```

As shown above, the syslog configuration file contains three sections: Modules, Global Directives, and Rules. The Modules section includes two modules: imuxsock and imjournal. These modules are specified with the ModLoad directive and are loaded on demand. The imuxsock module provides support for local system logging via the *logger* command, and the imjournal module allows access to the systemd journal.

The Global Directives section contains five active directives. The definitions in this section influence the *rsyslogd* daemon as a whole. The first of the five directives specifies the location for the storage of auxiliary files, the second directive instructs the daemon to save captured messages in the traditional way, the third directive directs the daemon to read additional configuration files from */etc/rsyslogd.d/* and loads them, the fourth directive orders the daemon to retrieve local messages via imjournal rather than the old local log socket, and the last directive defines the file name to store the position in the journal.

Under the Rules section, each line entry consists of two fields. The left field is called *selector* and the right field is referred to as *action*. The selector field is further divided into two dot-separated sub-fields called *facility* (left) and *priority* (right), with the former representing one or more system process categories that generate messages and the latter identifying the severity associated with the messages. The semicolon is used as a distinction if multiple facility.priority groups are present. The action field determines the destination to send the messages to.

The supported facilities are auth, authpriv, cron, daemon, kern, lpr, mail, news, syslog, user, uucp, and local0 through local7, while the asterisk character represents all of them.

Similarly, the supported priorities are emerg, alert, crit, error, warning, notice, info, debug, and none. This sequence is in the descending criticality order. The asterisk character represents all of them. If a lower priority is selected, the daemon logs all messages of the service at that and higher levels. We may use the = sign to capture messages at a specific priority or the ! sign to ignore messages at a particular priority.

The first line entry under the Rules section instructs the *rsyslogd* daemon to catch and store informational messages from all services to the */var/log/messages* file and ignore all messages generated by mail, authentication, and cron services.

The second, third, and fourth line entries command the daemon to collect and log all messages generated by authentication, mail, and cron to the *secure*, *maillog*, and *cron* files, respectively, located in */var/log*.

The fifth line orders the daemon to display emergency messages on the terminals of all logged-in users.

The sixth line shows two comma-separated facilities that are set at the same priority. These facilities tell the daemon to gather critical messages from uucp and news facilities, and log them to the */var/log/spooler* file.

And the last line entry is for logging the boot messages to the */var/log/boot.log* file.

If you have made any modifications to the *rsyslog.conf* file, run the *rsyslogd* command with the –N switch and specify a numeric verbosity level to check whether the file has any errors:

 # rsyslogd –N 1
rsyslogd: version 7.4.7, config validation run (level 1), master config /etc/rsyslog.conf
rsyslogd: End of config validation run. Bye.

Maintaining and Managing Log Files

In RHEL, the */var/log* directory is the central location for storing the log files. An *ll* on this directory reveals the log files it contains along with sub-directories that may have multiple service-specific logs:

 # ll /var/log
```
drwxr-xr-x. 2 root  root        4096 Jul  8 13:05 anaconda
drwxr-x---. 2 root  root          94 Oct  9 12:59 audit
-rw-r--r--. 1 root  root       10656 Oct 12 23:10 boot.log
-rw-------. 1 root  utmp           0 Oct  1 08:25 btmp
-rw-------. 1 root  utmp        1536 Sep 16 12:22 /var/log/btmp-20141001
-rw-r--r--. 1 root  root       19522 Oct 13 01:30 cron
drwxr-xr-x. 2 lp    sys         4096 Oct 12 03:42 cups
-rw-r--r--. 1 root  root       32211 Oct 12 23:10 dmesg
-rw-r--r--. 1 root  root       32164 Oct 12 22:53 dmesg.old
-rw-r--r--. 1 root  root       42838 Oct 10 09:49 firewalld
. . . . . . . .
```

The output indicates the presence of log files for different services. Depending on the usage and the number of messages generated and captured, log files may quickly fill up the file system they are located in. Also, if a log file grows to a very large size, it becomes troublesome to load and read it.

In RHEL, a script called *logrotate* in the */etc/cron.daily* directory invokes the *logrotate* command once every day to rotate log files by sourcing the */etc/logrotate.conf* file and the configuration files located in the */etc/logrotate.d* directory. These files may be modified to include additional tasks such as removing, compressing, and emailing identified log files.

Here is what the */etc/cron.daily/logrotate* script contains:

cat /etc/cron.daily/logrotate
#!/bin/sh
/usr/sbin/logrotate /etc/logrotate.conf
EXITVALUE=$?
if [$EXITVALUE != 0]; then
    /usr/bin/logger -t logrotate "ALERT exited abnormally with [$EXITVALUE]"
fi
exit 0

The following shows an excerpt from the *etc/logrotate.conf* file:

cat /etc/logrotate.conf
rotate log files weekly
weekly
keep 4 weeks worth of backlogs
rotate 4
create new (empty) log files after rotating old ones
create
use date as a suffix of the rotated file
dateext
uncomment this if you want your log files compressed
#compress
RPM packages drop log rotation information into this directory
include /etc/logrotate.d
# no packages own wtmp and btmp -- we'll rotate them here
/var/log/wtmp {
    monthly
    create 0664 root utmp
        minsize 1M
    rotate 1
}
/var/log/btmp {
    missingok
    monthly
    create 0600 root utmp
    rotate 1
}
# system-specific logs may be also be configured here.

The file content shows the default log rotation frequency (weekly). It indicates the period of time (4 weeks) to retain the rotated logs before deleting them. Each time a log file is rotated, a replacement file is created with the date as a suffix to its name, and the *rsyslogd* daemon is restarted. The script presents the option of compressing the rotated files using the *gzip* utility. During the script execution, the *logrotate* command checks for the presence of additional log configuration files in the */etc/logrotate.d* directory and includes them as necessary. For the *wtmp* and *btmp* files, separate rules are in place elaborating the frequency, permissions and ownership, the number of times to be rotated, etc. The directives defined in the *logrotate.conf* file have a global effect on all log files.

We may define custom settings for a specific log file in *logrotate.conf*, or create a separate file for it in the */etc/logrotate.d* directory. Any settings defined in user-defined files overrides the global settings. For instance, yum has a configuration file of its own in this directory that controls the rotation of the */var/log/yum.log* file:

```
/var/log/yum.log {
    missingok
    notifempty
    size 30k
    yearly
    create 0600 root root
}
```

The */etc/logrotate.d* directory includes additional configuration files for other service logs as well. Some of them are listed below:

ll /etc/logrotate.d

```
-rw-r--r--. 1 root root     194 Jul 17 09:58 httpd
-rw-r--r--. 1 root root     172 Mar 19 2014  iscsiuiolog
-rw-r--r--. 1 root root     165 Mar 24 2014  libvirtd
-rw-r--r--. 1 root root     162 Mar 24 2014  libvirtd.lxc
-rw-r--r--. 1 root root     163 Mar 24 2014  libvirtd.qemu
-rw-r--r--. 1 root root     893 May 27 04:32 mariadb
-rw-r-----. 1 root named    422 Jan  29 2014 named
. . . . . . . .
```

Here we see that logs for services—httpd, iscsi, libvirt, mariadb, and DNS—all have their rules in place in their own configuration files.

The Boot Log File

Logs generated during a system startup show the service startup sequence with a status stating whether the service was started successfully. This information may help in post-boot troubleshooting if required. Boot logs are stored in the *boot.log* file in */var/log*. Here is an excerpt from this file:

cat /var/log/boot.log

```
. . . . . . . .
[ OK ] Started Avahi mDNS/DNS-SD Stack.
[ OK ] Started Login Service.
[ OK ] Started GNOME Display Manager.
[ OK ] Started Modem Manager.
      Starting Authorization Manager...
```

The System Log File

The default location for storing most system activities is the */var/log/messages* file. This file saves log information in plain text and may be viewed with any file display utility, such as *cat*, *more*, *pg*, *less*, *head*, or *tail*. This file may be observed in real time using the *tail* command with the –f switch.

The *messages* file captures the date and time of the activity, hostname of the system, name of the service, PID of the service, and a short description of the activity being logged.

> **EXAM TIP:** It is a good practice to "tail" the contents of the messages file after starting or restarting a system service or during testing it to identify and address any issues encountered.

The following displays some sample entries from this file:

 # tail /var/log/messages
```
. . . . . . . .
Oct 12 23:10:53 server1 dbus-daemon: dbus[660]: [system] Successfully activated service
'org.freedesktop.locale1'
Oct 12 23:10:53 server1 dbus[660]: [system] Successfully activated service 'org.freedesktop.locale1'
Oct 12 23:10:53 server1 systemd: Started Locale Service.
Oct 12 23:10:55 server1 systemd: Started The Apache HTTP Server.
Oct 12 23:10:55 server1 NetworkManager[834]: <info> (virbr0): carrier is OFF (but ignored)
Oct 12 23:10:55 server1 NetworkManager[834]: <info> (virbr0): new Bridge device (driver: 'bridge'
ifindex: 3)
Oct 12 23:10:55 server1 NetworkManager[834]: <info> (virbr0): exported as
/org/freedesktop/NetworkManager/Devices/2
Oct 12 23:10:55 server1 NetworkManager[834]: ifcfg-rh:    read connection 'virbr0'
Oct 12 23:10:55 server1 NetworkManager[834]: <info> (virbr0): device state change: unmanaged ->
unavailable (reason 'connection-assumed') [10 20 41]
. . . . . . . .
```

Understanding the Journal

In addition to syslog, RHEL7 offers a new service for viewing and managing log files. This service is implemented via the *journald* daemon, which is an element of systemd. The function of *journald* is to collect and manage log messages from both kernel and daemon processes. It also captures syslog and initial RAM disk messages, and any alerts generated during the early boot stage. It stores these messages in the binary format in files called *journals* that are located in the */var/run/journal* directory. These files are structured and indexed for faster and easier searches, and may be viewed and managed using the *journalctl* command. As we know, */var/run* is a virtual file system that is created automatically in memory at system boot, and its contents are destroyed when the system is shut down. Therefore the log data stored therein is non-persistent; however, we can enable persistent storage for the logs.

RHEL7 allows the concurrent execution and use of both *rsyslogd* and *journald*. In fact, the data gathered by *journald* may be forwarded to *rsyslogd* for further processing and storage in text format.

Viewing the Journal

systemd offers the *journalctl* command to view the journals. For instance, if we wish to read all messages generated on the system since the last reboot, run the *journalctl* command without any options. The following output shows only the first two entries from the journal:

```
# journalctl
-- Logs begin at Thu 2014-09-04 20:49:36 EDT, end at Thu 2014-09-11 15:40:01 EDT. --
Sep 04 20:49:36 server1.example.com systemd-journal[81]: Runtime journal is using 6.2M (max 49.7M,
leaving 74.5M of free 490.9M, current limit 49.7M).
Sep 04 20:49:36 server1.example.com systemd-journal[81]: Runtime journal is using 6.2M (max 49.7M,
leaving 74.5M of free 490.9M, current limit 49.7M).
```

The above output is similar in format to that of the messages logged to the */var/log/messages* file. Each line begins with a timestamp followed by the hostname of the system and then the process name with its PID in square brackets, followed by the actual message.

With the –o option, we can specify the verbose option to view the output in a structured form:

```
# journalctl –o verbose
-- Logs begin at Fri 2014-10-10 10:03:40 EDT, end at Mon 2014-10-13 20:11:26 EDT. --
Fri 2014-10-10 10:03:40.935148 EDT
[s=dcff053888a44a66bce6e8ce208e54ed;i=2079;b=df4de941517e4d15b55242d06e39591d;m=
bea148b82;t=5051204298bec;x=5cb6d3b71626ab8f]
    _TRANSPORT=stdout
    PRIORITY=6
    SYSLOG_IDENTIFIER=gnome-session
. . . . . . . .
```

Run the *journalctl* command with the –b option to view all messages since the last system reboot:

```
# journalctl –b
-- Logs begin at Thu 2014-09-04 20:49:36 EDT, end at Thu 2014-09-11 15:40:01 EDT. --
Sep 04 20:49:36 server1.example.com systemd-journal[81]: Runtime journal is using 6.2M (max
Sep 04 20:49:36 server1.example.com systemd-journal[81]: Runtime journal is using 6.2M (max
Sep 04 20:49:36 server1.example.com kernel: Initializing cgroup subsys cpuset
```

We may specify –0, –1, –2, and so on to view messages from previous system reboots.

Run the *journalctl* command with the –k and –b options to view only kernel-generated messages since the last system reboot:

```
# journalctl –k –b –0
-- Logs begin at Thu 2014-09-04 20:49:36 EDT, end at Thu 2014-09-11 15:40:01 EDT. --
```

We can pass a number, such as 3, with the –n option to view that many previous entries only:

```
# journalctl –n 3
```

To show all messages generated by a specific executable, such as the *crond* daemon:

```
# journalctl /sbin/crond
```

To show all messages for a specific process, such as PID 1374:

journalctl _PID=1374
-- Logs begin at Thu 2014-09-04 20:49:36 EDT, end at Thu 2014-09-11 16:20:33 ED
Sep 04 20:50:28 server1.example.com kdumpctl[1374]: No memory reserved for crash
Sep 04 20:50:28 server1.example.com kdumpctl[1374]: Starting kdump: [FAILED]

To display all messages for a specific system unit, such as sshd:

journalctl _SYSTEM_UNIT=sshd

To view all error messages for a specific date range, such as all error messages logged on September 4 and 5:

journalctl --since 2014-09-04 --until 2014-09-05 –p err

To get all warning messages that have appeared today:

journalctl --since=today –p warning

We can specify a time range in hh:mm:ss format, or yesterday, today, or tomorrow instead.

To view the messages pertaining to a specific systemd unit, specify its name with the –u option:

journalctl -u httpd –b –0

Similar to the –f option that we use with the *tail* command for real-time viewing of a log file, we can use the same switch with *journalctl* as well:

journalctl –f

Storing Journal Information Persistently
By default, journals are stored temporarily in the */run/log/journal* directory, which is a memory-based virtual file system. The contents of this file system do not survive across reboots. The *journalctl* command examples demonstrated in the previous sub-section read journal information from that temporary location. The *rsyslogd* daemon, by default, reads the temporary journals and stores the messages in the */var/log* directory; however, if we enable persistent logging, journal files will be stored on disk in the */var/log/journal* directory, and will be available for future reference. Here is what we need to do in order to enable persistent logging:

mkdir –p /var/log/journal
systemctl restart systemd-journald
ll /var/log/journal
drwxr-sr-x. 2 root systemd-journal 49 Sep 11 20:12 e9d860673d54465f94db2961c6f10ba0

As soon as we restart the *journald* daemon, a directory matching the unique 128-bit machine ID created during the installation and stored in the */etc/machine-id* file is created in */var/log/journal/*. Here are the contents of the */etc/machine-id* file, which are exactly the same as the directory we have just created:

```
# cat /etc/machine-id
e9d860673d54465f94db2961c6f10ba0
```

Chapter Summary

This chapter started with a discussion of Linux boot process. We reviewed BIOS/firmware and looked at the pre-boot administration tasks, and kernel and system startup phases. Pre-boot administration included interacting with GRUB2, booting into specific targets, and an analysis of the bootloader configuration file; kernel initialization covered viewing messages generated during the system startup; and system startup included a detailed look at the new system initialization method called systemd. We examined how to enable services and configure them to autostart.

The next major topic talked about Linux kernel, its key components, and its management. We learned about modules that form the kernel. We performed an analysis on a kernel version and looked at key directories that hold kernel-specific information. We installed a new kernel using various common tools, and used commands to manage kernel modules.

We then discussed the new system initialization scheme called systemd. We compared it with the older sysVinit and Upstart initialization schemes. We looked at the key components of systemd, its key directories, and unit configuration files. We used various tools to view and manage units, targets, and control groups.

Finally, we studied system logging and systemd journaling, which are used to capture and store system alerts. We looked at key log files and saw how to rotate log files.

Chapter Review Questions

1. Both BIOS and UEFI are used in newer computers. True or False?
2. The *systemd* command may be used to rebuild a new kernel. True or False?
3. By default, GRUB is stored in the master boot record. True or False?
4. What is the location of the *grub.efi* file in the UEFI-based systems?
5. Which file stores the location information of the boot partition on the BIOS systems?
6. Which command is used to manage system services?
7. Name the two directory paths where systemd unit files are stored.
8. What is the name for the boot log file?
9. Which two files would we want to view to obtain processor and memory information?
10. What would the command *systemctl restart rsyslog* do?
11. In which target does the X window and the graphical desktop interface become available?
12. Which command can we use to determine the kernel release information?
13. The *lsmod* command is used to rebuild modules. True or False?
14. Which command can we use to unload a module?
15. We cannot use the *yum* command to upgrade a Linux kernel. True or False?
16. What is the difference between the –U and the –i options with the *rpm* command?
17. What is the new system initialization scheme introduced in RHEL7?

Answers to Chapter Review Questions

1. True.
2. False.
3. True.
4. The *grub.efi* file is located in the */boot/efi/EFI/redhat* directory.
5. The *grub.conf* file stores the location information of the boot partition.

6. The *systemctl* command.
7. The directory location are */etc/systemd/system* and */usr/lib/systemd/system*.
8. The */var/log/boot.log* file.
9. The *cpuinfo* and *meminfo* files in the */proc* file system.
10. The command provided will restart the *rsyslog* service.
11. The X window and the graphical desktop interface become available in the graphical target.
12. The *uname* command.
13. False.
14. The *modprobe* command.
15. False.
16. The –U option would instruct the *rpm* command to upgrade the specified package or install it if it does not already installed. The –i option, on the other hand, would instruct the command to install the package and fail if the package does not already exist.
17. It is called systemd.

DIY Challenge Labs

The following labs are useful to strengthen most of the concepts and topics learned in this chapter. It is expected that you perform these labs without any additional help. A step-by-step guide is not provided, as the implementation of these labs requires the knowledge that has been presented in this chapter. Use defaults or your own thinking for missing information.

Lab 7-1: Modify the Default Boot Target

Modify the default boot target from graphical to multi-user and reboot the system to test it. Run appropriate commands after the reboot to validate the change. Restore the default boot target back to graphical and reboot to test.

Lab 7-2: Install a New Kernel

Check the current version of the kernel on the system. Download a higher version and install it. Reboot the system and ensure it is booted with the new kernel. Configure the system to boot with the old kernel and reboot it to validate.

Chapter 08

Managing Users and Groups

This chapter describes the following major topics:

➢ Understand local user authentication files
➢ Maintain integrity of authentication files
➢ Prevent corruption in authentication files
➢ Activate and deactivate shadow password mechanism
➢ Create, modify, and delete local user accounts with default and custom values
➢ Set password aging on local user accounts
➢ Use su and sudo commands
➢ Create, modify, and delete local group accounts
➢ Overview of graphical User Manager tool
➢ Understand per-user and system-wide startup files

RHCSA Objectives:

05. Log in and switch users in multi-user targets
44. Create, delete, and modify local user accounts
45. Change passwords and adjust password aging for local user accounts
46. Create, delete, and modify local groups and group memberships

In order for an authorized person to gain access to the system, a unique username (a.k.a. login name) must be assigned and a user account must be created on the system. This user is apportioned membership to one or more groups. Members of the same group have the same access rights on files and directories. Other users and members of other groups may optionally be given access to those files. User and group account information is recorded in several files, which may be checked for inconsistencies, and edited manually if necessary, by one administrator at a time. Password aging may be set on user accounts for increased access control. Users may switch into other user accounts, including the root user, provided they know their passwords. Regular users on the system may be allowed access to privileged commands by defining them appropriately in the configuration file related to the sudo command. At user login, several user and system startup files are involved.

Understanding Local User Authentication Files

RHEL supports three fundamental user account types: *root*, *normal*, and *service*. The *root* user, the superuser or the administrator with full access to all services and administrative functions, possesses full powers on the system. This user is automatically created during RHEL installation. The normal users have user-level privileges. They cannot perform any administrative functions, but can run applications and programs that they are authorized to execute. The service accounts are responsible for taking care of the installed services. These accounts include apache, ftp, mail, ntp, postfix, and qemu.

User account information for local users is stored in four files in the */etc* directory. These files are *passwd, shadow, group*, and *gshadow*, and they are updated when a user account is created, modified, or deleted. The same files are referenced to check and validate the credentials for a user at the time of their login attempt into the system, and hence these files are referred to as user authentication files. These files are so critical to the operation of the system that, by default, the system maintains a backup of each of these files as *passwd-, shadow-, group-*, and *gshadow-* in the */etc* directory. The *shadow* and *gshadow* files, as well as the user administration commands that we will learn in this chapter, are part of the shadow-utils package that is installed on the system at the time of OS installation.

The passwd File

The */etc/passwd* file contains vital user login data. Each line entry in the file contains information about one user account. There are seven fields per line entry separated by the colon : character. A sample entry from the file is displayed in Figure 8-1.

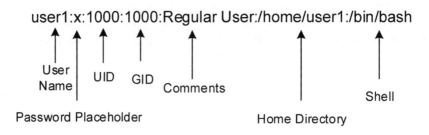

Figure 8-1 The /etc/passwd File

Here is what is stored in each field:

- ✓ The first field contains the login name that is used to log into the system. Usernames up to 255 characters, including underscore and hyphen characters, are supported; however, usernames should not use any special characters or uppercase letters.
- ✓ The second field can contain an "x" (points to the */etc/shadow* file for the actual password), an asterisk * character to identify a disabled account, or an encrypted password containing a combination of random letters, numbers, and special characters in the absence of *shadow* file.
- ✓ The third field comprises a unique number between 0 and approximately 2 billion. This number is known as the *User ID* (UID). User ID 0 is reserved for the *root* account; UIDs between 1 and 999 are reserved for system accounts; and UIDs 1000 and beyond are used for normal user and application accounts. By default, RHEL begins assigning UIDs to new users starting at 1000.
- ✓ The fourth field holds a number referred to as the *Group ID* (GID). This number corresponds with a group entry in the */etc/group* file. By default, RHEL creates a group for every new user matching their username and the same GID as their UID. The GID defined in this field represents a user's primary group.
- ✓ The fifth field (called GECOS – General Electric Comprehensive Operating System and later changed to GCOS) optionally stores general comments about the user that may include the user's name, phone number, location, or other useful information to help identify the person for whom, or the application for which, the account is set up. This data may be viewed and modified with the *finger* and *chfn* commands, respectively.
- ✓ The sixth field defines the absolute path to the user home directory. A *home* directory is the location where a user is placed after logging into the system, and it is typically used to store personal files for the user. The default location for user home directories is */home*.
- ✓ The last field consists of the absolute path of the shell file that the user will be using as their primary shell after logging in. Common shells are bash */bin/bash* and C */bin/csh*. The default shell assigned to users is the bash shell.

An excerpt from the *passwd* file is shown below:

```
# cat /etc/passwd
root:x:0:0:root:/root:/bin/bash
bin:x:1:1:bin:/bin:/sbin/nologin
daemon:x:2:2:daemon:/sbin:/sbin/nologin
. . . . . . . .
user1:x:1000:1000:user1:/home/user1:/bin/bash
```

Permissions on the */etc/passwd* file should be 644, and the file must be owned by *root.*

The shadow File

The implementation of the shadow password mechanism provides a more secure password security for local users. With this mechanism in place, not only are the user passwords encrypted and stored in a more secure */etc/shadow* file, but certain limits on user passwords in terms of expiration, warning period, etc., can also be applied on a per-user basis. These limits and other settings are defined in the */etc/login.defs* file, which the shadow password mechanism enforces on user accounts. This is referred to as *password aging*. Unlike the *passwd* file, which is world-readable, the *shadow* file is only readable by the *root* user. This is done to safeguard the file's contents.

With the shadow password mechanism active, a user is initially checked in the *passwd* file for existence and then in the *shadow* file for authenticity.

The *shadow* file contains extended user authentication information. Each row in the file corresponds to one entry in the *passwd* file. There are nine colon-separated fields per line entry. A sample entry from this file is exhibited in Figure 8-2.

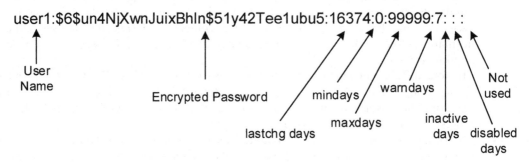

Figure 8-2 The /etc/shadow File

Here is what is stored in each field:

- ✓ The first field contains the login name as appears in the *passwd* file.
- ✓ The second field consists of an encrypted password. An exclamation mark ! at the beginning of this field implies that the user account is locked.
- ✓ The third field sets the number of days since the epoch time (January 01, 1970) when the password was last modified. An empty field represents the passiveness of password aging features, and a 0 in this field forces the user to change their password upon next login.
- ✓ The fourth field expresses the minimum number of days that must elapse before the user can change their password. This field can be altered using the *chage* command with the –m option or the *passwd* command with the –n option. A 0 or null in this field disables this feature.
- ✓ The fifth field defines the maximum number of days of password validity before the user starts getting warning messages to change it. This field may be altered using the *chage* command with the –M option or the *passwd* command with the –x option. A null value in this field disables this feature as well as the maximum password age, warning alerts, and the user inactivity period.
- ✓ The sixth field consists of the number of days for which the user gets warnings for changing their password. This field may be altered using the *chage* command with the –W option or the *passwd* command with the –w option. A 0 or null in this field disables this feature.
- ✓ The seventh field contains the maximum allowable number of days of user inactivity. This field may be altered using the *chage* command with the –I option or the *passwd* command with the –i option. A null value in this field disables this feature.
- ✓ The eighth field expresses the number of days since the epoch time (January 01, 1970) after which the account expires. This field may be altered using the *chage* command with the –E option.
- ✓ The last field is reserved for future use.

An excerpt from the *shadow* file is shown below:

cat /etc/shadow
root:$6$1KaOxxu2tfC2XSzH$uoH5Ajl.OEoK/Hpuy4iihSRloEF/6YPS6RewWQYNbgrUnFHFvIX02kk7
e9k0ILkjhYYuZvLCf/lIDQjzpiQoC1:16374:0:99999:7:::
bin:*:16141:0:99999:7:::
daemon:*:16141:0:99999:7:::

. . . .
user1:6un4NjXwnJuixBhln$51y42Tee1ubu5VkovOBMQgjoSMWX2eIlDStzpvTeGXsV1cFC3z4n8bn
wCsoh.Nq5x8KZqE7XjGpQ1kfINw19w1:16374:0:99999:7:::

 Permissions on the *shadow* file should be 000, and the file must be owned by *root*.

The group File

The */etc/group* file contains the group information. Each row in the file stores one group entry. Every user on the system must be a member of at least one group, which is referred to as the user's primary group. By default, a group name matches the user name it is associated with. This group is known as the *User Private Group* (UPG) and it safeguards a user's files from other users. Additional groups may be set up and users with common file access requirements can be added to them. There are four fields per line entry in the file, which are colon-separated. A sample entry from the file is exhibited in Figure 8-3.

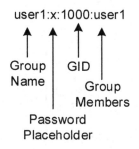

Figure 8-3 The /etc/group File

Here is what is stored in each field:

✓ The first field holds a unique group name, which must begin with a letter. By default, each user gets a unique group matching their name. Additional groups may be created as per need and users assigned to them. Group names up to 255 characters are supported.
✓ The second field is not typically used and is left blank. It may, however, contain an encrypted group-level password (copied and pasted from the *shadow* file or an x that points to the *gshadow* file for password). We may set a password on a group if we want non-members to be able to change their group identity to this group temporarily using the *newgrp* command. The non-members must enter the correct password in order to do so.
✓ The third field defines the group identifier (GID), which is also placed in the GID field of the *passwd* file. By default, groups are created with GIDs starting at 1000 with the same name as the user name that is assigned to them. The system allows several users to belong to a single group; it also allows a single user to be a member of several groups at the same time.

✓ The last field identifies the membership for the group. Note that a user's primary group is defined in the *passwd* file, and not in the *group* file.

An excerpt from the *group* file is shown below:

cat /etc/group
root:x:0:
bin:x:1:
daemon:x:2:
. . . .
user1:x:1000:user1

 Permissions on the *group* file should be 644, and the file must be owned by *root*.

The gshadow File

The shadow password implementation also provides an added layer of protection at the group level. With this mechanism active, the group passwords are encrypted and stored in a more secure */etc/gshadow* file, which is readable only by the *root* user. This is done to safeguard the file's contents.

The *gshadow* file stores encrypted group passwords. Each row in the file corresponds to one entry in the *group* file. There are four fields per line entry, which are colon-separated. A sample entry from this file is exhibited in Figure 8-4.

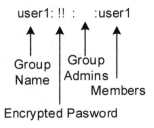

Figure 8-4 The /etc/gshadow File

Here is what is stored in each field:

✓ The first field consists of the group name as appears in the *group* file.
✓ The second field can contain an encrypted password, which may be set with the *gpasswd* command. A single exclamation point in this field disallows users from gaining access to this group with the *newgrp* command; a pair of exclamation marks places the same restriction as the single exclamation point, plus it also indicates that a group password has never been set; and a null value restricts the group members to change into this group with *newgrp*.
✓ The third field lists usernames of group administrators that are authorized to add or remove members to and from this group with the *gpasswd* command.
✓ The last field holds the usernames that belong to the group.

An excerpt from the *gshadow* file is shown below:

```
# cat /etc/gshadow
root:::
bin:::
daemon:::
. . . . . . . .
user1:!!:::user1
```

 Permissions on *gshadow* file should be 000, and the file must be owned by *root*.

Maintaining Integrity of Authentication Files

Over the period of time or, especially, after making a manual modification, inconsistencies may occur in any of the four authentication files and require administrative attention. The *passwd* and *shadow* files are particularly important, as they are the primary sources for validating local user existence and authenticating them. The shadow-utils package offers a tool called *pwck* that we can use to check the integrity and validity of data in these files. This command checks each line entry for the correct number of fields, uniqueness and validity of the login name, and validity of the UID, GID, primary group, login directory, and the shell file. For the *shadow* file, it checks for the existence of corresponding entries, the correct number of fields, duplicate entries, the presence of passwords, and some password aging attributes based on the directives defined in the */etc/login.defs* file. This command reports any inconsistencies as it finds.

```
# pwck
user 'ftp': directory '/var/ftp' does not exist
user 'avahi-autoipd': directory '/var/lib/avahi-autoipd' does not exist
user 'pulse': directory '/var/run/pulse' does not exist
user 'gnome-initial-setup': directory '/run/gnome-initial-setup/' does not exist
pwck: no changes
```

The shadow-utils package offers a cousin of *pwck* called *grpck* that is used to verify the information in the *group* and *gshadow* files for validity and consistency. This command performs checks on the validity of the number of fields in each line entry and whether a user belonging to a group is absent from the *passwd* or the *shadow* file. It reports inconsistencies as well.

Preventing Corruption in Authentication Files

Occasionally, it is imperative for the administrator to modify the *passwd* file manually using an editor such as *vi*. If another user attempts to change their password while the file is being edited, it results in a successful password update for the user. Unfortunately, this change is lost when the file is later saved by the administrator.

To prevent this from happening, and to prevent any corruption resulting from such a condition, the shadow-utils package offers two tools called *vipw* and *vigr* that allow a privileged user to edit the *passwd* and *group* files while disabling write access to them. The same commands are also used to edit the shadow versions of these files when they are executed with the –s option. Both commands make a copy of the respective file in the */etc* directory with the *.edit* extension and also a corresponding lock file with the *.lock* extension in the same directory. The *.edit* file stores the changes being made while the *.lock* file saves the PID of the process. During this time, if a user attempts to change their password, the *passwd* command accepts the new password and checks for the existence of a *.lock* file before attempting to update the original file. The presence of a *.lock* file is an indication for the *passwd* command that an edit session is in progress and that it has to wait for it to complete. As soon as the administrator finishes with the editing and quits the file, some automatic checks are performed on the file for data and syntax validity. The original file is backed up with the hyphen sign as a suffix to its name and the edited version replaces the original file. The *.edit* and *.lock* files are then removed. At this point, the *passwd* command that was waiting for the editing session to finish goes ahead and updates the user password successfully.

The same rule is applied to other commands that attempt to write to these files while they are being amended. Also, while an instance of either of these tools is running on any of the four files, invoking another session of either of these tools generates an error message similar to the following:

> # **vigr –s**
> vigr: Couldn't lock file: Interrupted system call
> vigr: /etc/gshadow is unchanged

At the end of an editing session for any of the four files, a message is displayed, reminding us of modifying the corresponding file also. For example, the following reminder is shown after the completion of *passwd* file modification with the *vipw* command:

> You have modified /etc/passwd.
> You may need to modify /etc/shadow for consistency.
> Please use the command 'vipw -s' to do so.

And after the execution of the *vigr* command on the *gshadow* file:

> You have modified /etc/gshadow.
> You may need to modify /etc/group for consistency.
> Please use the command 'vigr' to do so.

Activating and Deactivating Shadow Password Mechanism

The shadow password mechanism that enables the use of *shadow* and *gshadow* files for storing user and group passwords and password aging information may be deactivated if desired. However, this is an undesirable and unrecommended action unless there is a specific need to do so. The shadow-utils package offers four tools, two (*pwconv* and *grpconv*) to activate the mechanism and the other two (*pwunconv* and *grpunconv*) to deactivate it. These are described in Table 8-1.

Command	Description
pwconv	Creates and updates the shadow file and moves user passwords over from the passwd file.
pwunconv	Moves user passwords back to the passwd file and removes the shadow file.
grpconv	Creates and updates the gshadow file and moves group passwords over from the group file.
grpunconv	Moves group passwords back to the group file and removes the gshadow file.

Table 8-1 Password Shadowing Commands

The activation tools reference the *etc/login.defs* file for some password aging attributes while being executed. Here are a few examples that show the usage of these commands.

To activate password shadowing if it is not already active:

pwconv

This command works quietly and does not display any output unless there is a problem. It creates the *shadow* file with read-only permission for the *root* user:

ll /etc/shadow
-r--------. 1 root   root   1289   Nov   2   08:00   /etc/shadow

To activate password shadowing at the group level if it is not already active:

grpconv

This command works quietly and does not display any output unless there is a problem. It creates the *gshadow* file with read-only permission for the *root* user:

ll /etc/gshadow
-r--------. 1 root   root   671   Nov   2   08:02   /etc/gshadow

To deactivate password shadowing and remove the shadow files, execute the *pwunconv* and *grpunconv* commands, respectively.

Managing User Accounts and Password Aging with Commands

Managing user accounts involves creating, assigning passwords to, modifying, and deleting them. Managing password aging involves setting and modifying aging attributes on user accounts. RHEL provides a set of tools and a graphical tool called *User Manager* for performing these operations. The command toolset is part of the shadow-utils package and the User Manager tool becomes available when the system-config-users package is installed on the system.

Table 8-2 lists and describes the key commands used for user and password management.

Command	Description
useradd	Adds a user.
usermod	Modifies user attributes.
userdel	Deletes a user.
chage	Sets or modifies password aging attributes for a user.
passwd	Sets or modifies a user password, and some password aging attributes.

Table 8-2 User and Password Aging Commands

The useradd, usermod, and userdel Commands

This set of commands is used to add, modify, and delete a user account from the system. The *useradd* command adds entries to the *passwd*, *group*, *shadow*, and *gshadow* files for each user added to the system. This command creates a home directory for the user and copies the default user startup files from the skeleton directory */etc/skel* into the user's home directory. It can also be used to update the default settings that are used at the time of new user creation for unspecified settings. The *useradd* command has several options available with it. Table 8-3 lists most of them in both short and long versions, with an explanation.

Option	Description
−b (--base-dir)	Defines the absolute path to the base directory for placing user home directories.
−c (--comment)	Describes useful information about the user.
−d (--home-dir)	Defines the absolute path to the user home directory.
−D (--defaults)	Displays or modifies the default settings.
−e (--expiredate)	Specifies a date after which a user account is automatically disabled. The format for date specification is YYYY-MM-DD.
−f (--inactive)	Denotes maximum days of inactivity before a user account is declared invalid.
−g (--gid)	Specifies the primary group identifier. The base GID is 1000. If this option is not used, a group account matching the user name is created with the GID matching the UID. If you wish to assign a different GID, specify it with this option. Make sure that the group already exists.
−G (--groups)	Specifies the membership for up to 20 comma-separated supplementary groups. If this option is not specified, no supplementary groups are added.
−k (--skel)	Specifies the location of the skeleton directory (default is /etc/skel), which contains default user startup files. These files are copied to the user's home directory at the time of account creation. Three bash shell files − .bash_profile, .bashrc, and .bash_logout − are available in this directory by default.

You may customize these files or add more files to this directory to ensure new users get them. Existing user home directories are not affected by this change. |
−K (--key)	Overrides some of the default values specified in the /etc/login.defs file.
−M (--no-create-home)	Prevents the command from creating a home directory for the user.
−m (--create-home)	Creates a home directory if it does not already exist.
−N (--no-user-group)	Prevents the command from creating a private group for the user.
−o (--non-unique)	Creates a user account sharing the UID of an existing user. When two users share a common UID, both get identical rights on each other's files. This should only be done in specific situations.
−r (--system)	Creates a system account with a UID below 1000 and a never-expiring password.
−s (--shell)	Defines the absolute path to the shell file.

Option	Description
–u (--user-group)	Indicates a unique user identifier. The base UID is 1000. If this option is not specified, the next available UID from the /etc/passwd file is used.
login	Specifies a login name to be assigned to the new user account.

Table 8-3 useradd Command Options

We can modify the attributes of a user account with the *usermod* command. The syntax of this command is very similar to that of the *useradd*'s, with most options identical. Table 8-4 describes the options that are specific to *usermod* only, and shows them in both short and long versions.

Option	Description
-a (--append)	Adds a user to the supplementary group(s).
–l (--login)	Specifies a new login name.
–L (--lock)	Locks a user account by placing an exclamation mark at the beginning of the password field and before the encrypted password.
–m (--move-home)	Creates a new home directory and moves the contents from the old location to here.
–U (--unlock)	Unlocks a user's account by removing the exclamation sign from the beginning of the password field.

Table 8-4 usermod Command Options

The *userdel* command is straightforward. It removes entries for the specified user from all the authentication files. It also deletes the user's home directory if the –r option is specified. The –f flag may be used to force the removal even if the user is still logged in.

The chage Command

The *chage* command is used to set and alter password aging parameters on a user account. It supports a number of options in both short and long versions. Table 8-5 describes most of them.

Option	Description
–d (--lastday)	Specifies a date in the YYYY-MM-DD format, or number of days since the epoch time when the password was last modified. With –d 0, the user is forced to change the password at next login. It corresponds to the third field in the shadow file.
–E (--expiredate)	Sets a date in the YYYY-MM-DD format, or number of days since the epoch time on which the user account is deactivated. With -1, this feature can be disabled. It corresponds to the eighth field in the shadow file.
–I (--inactive)	Defines the number of days of inactivity after the password expiry and before the account is locked. With -1, this feature can be disabled. It corresponds to the seventh field in the shadow file.
–l	Lists password aging attributes set on a user account.
–m (--mindays)	Indicates the minimum number of days that must elapse before the password can be changed. A value of 0 in this field allows the user to change their password at any time. It corresponds to the fourth field in the shadow file.

Option	Description
−M (--maxdays)	Denotes the maximum days of validity of the password before the user starts getting warning messages to change the password. With -1, this feature can be disabled. It corresponds to the fifth field in the shadow file.
−W (--warndays)	Designates the number of days the user gets warning messages to change password before the password expiry. It corresponds to the sixth field in the shadow file.

Table 8-5 chage Command Options

We will use most of these options later in this chapter.

The passwd Command

The common use of the *passwd* command is to set or modify a user's password; however, we can also use this command to lock and unlock a user account and modify their password aging attributes. Table 8-6 lists some key options in both short and long versions, and describes them.

Option	Description
−d (--delete)	Deletes a user password without expiring the user account.
−e (--expire)	Forces a user to change their password upon next logon.
−i (--inactive)	Defines the number of days of inactivity after the password expiry and before the account is locked. It corresponds to the seventh field in the shadow file.
−k (--keep)	Re-activates an expired user account without changing the password.
−l (--lock)	Locks a user account.
−n (--minimum)	Specifies the number of days that must elapse before the password can be changed. It corresponds to the fourth field in the shadow file.
−u (--unlock)	Unlocks a user account.
−w (--warning)	Defines the number of days a user gets warning messages to change password. It corresponds to the sixth field in the shadow file.
−x (maximum)	Denotes the maximum days of validity of the password before a user starts getting warning messages to change password. It corresponds to the fifth field in the shadow file.

Table 8-6 passwd Command Options

We will use some of these options in this chapter.

The useradd and login.defs Files

The *useradd* command picks up the default values from the */etc/default/useradd* and */etc/login.defs* files for any options that are not specified at the command line. Moreover, the *login.defs* file is also consulted by the *usermod*, *userdel*, *chage*, and *passwd* commands as needed. We can view the *useradd* file contents with a command such as *cat* or *more*, or display the settings with the *useradd* command as follows:

# **useradd −D**
GROUP=100
HOME=/home

INACTIVE=-1
EXPIRE=
SHELL=/bin/bash
SKEL=/etc/skel
CREATE_MAIL_SPOOL=yes

We can modify these defaults and set them to our desired values. For instance, the following changes the default base directory to */usr/home* as the new location for placing home directories for new users:

useradd –D –b /usr/home

Confirm the new value by running *useradd –D* again.

The other file */etc/login.defs* comprises of additional directives that set several defaults. User and group management commands consult this file to obtain information that is not specified at the command line. A *grep* on the uncommented and non-empty lines is shown below:

grep –v ^# /etc/login.defs | grep –v ^$

MAIL_DIR	/var/spool/mail
PASS_MAX_DAYS	99999
PASS_MIN_DAYS	0
PASS_MIN_LEN	5
PASS_WARN_AGE	7
UID_MIN	1000
UID_MAX	60000
SYS_UID_MIN	201
SYS_UID_MAX	999
GID_MIN	1000
GID_MAX	60000
SYS_GID_MIN	201
SYS_GID_MAX	999
CREATE_HOME	yes
UMASK	077
USERGROUPS_ENAB	yes
ENCRYPT_METHOD	SHA512

These directives define the mail directory location for the user (MAIL_DIR), password aging attributes (PASS_MAX_DAYS, PASS_MIN_DAYS, PASS_MIN_LEN, and PASS_WARN_AGE), range of UIDs and GIDs to be allocated to new user and group accounts (UID_MIN, UID_MAX, GID_MIN and GID_MAX), range of UIDs and GIDs to be allocated to new system user and group accounts (SYS_UID_MIN, SYS_UID_MAX, SYS_GID_MIN and SYS_GID_MAX), and instructions for the *useradd* command to create a home directory (CREATE_HOME), set the default umask to 077 (UMASK), delete the user's group if it contains no more members (USERGROUPS_ENAB), and use the SHA512 algorithm for encrypting user passwords (ENCRYPT_METHOD).

Exercise 8-1: Create a User Account with Default Values

This exercise should be done on *server1*.

In this exercise, you will create a user account *user2* with all the defaults defined in the *useradd* and *login.defs* files. You will assign the user a password and show the line entries from the *passwd*, *shadow*, *group*, and *gshadow* files for this user.

1. Create *user2* with all the default values:

    # **useradd user2**

2. Create a password for this user:

    # **passwd user2**
    New password:
    Retype new password:
    passwd: all authentication tokens updated successfully.

3. *grep* for *user2* on the *passwd*, *shadow*, *group*, and *gshadow* files to check what the *useradd* command has added:

    # **cd /etc; grep user2 passwd shadow group gshadow**
    passwd:user2:x:1001:1001::/home/user2:/bin/bash
    shadow:user2:6GnGxfNMq$/WW79FsKs4dY2GuLPRfT31Q6/pBiavyjWilDabw7fF6z3Ek6Fainvu
    aZaGMc/Bk0EtWXuaUc1l3QQyyifFeSw0:16377:0:99999:7:::
    group:user2:x:1001:
    gshadow:user2:!::

4. Test this new account by logging in as *user2* and supplying the assigned password.

As we can see, the command used the next available UID and GID, and the default settings for the home directory, shell file, and password aging.

Exercise 8-2: Create a User Account with Custom Values

This exercise should be done on *server1*.

In this exercise, you will create an account *user3* with UID 1010, home directory */home/user3*, shell */bin/bash*, membership in group *user3* with GID 1010, and default startup files copied into this user's home directory. You will assign this user a password and *grep* the line entries from the *passwd*, *shadow*, *group*, and *gshadow* files.

1. Create *user3* with UID 1010 (–u), home directory */home/user3* (–m and –d) shell */bin/bash* (–s) membership in group 1001 (–g), and default startup files copied into this user's home directory (–k):

    # **useradd –u 1010 –g 1001 –m –d /home/user3 –k /etc/skel –s /bin/bash user3**

2. Assign user123 as password (passwords assigned this way is not recommended; however, it is okay in a lab environment):

echo user123 | passwd --stdin user3

3. *grep* for *user3* on the *passwd*, *shadow*, *group*, and *gshadow* files to see what was added for this user:

> # cd /etc ; grep user3 passwd shadow group gshadow
> passwd:user3:x:1010:1010::/home/user3:/bin/bash
> shadow:user3:6MA1lX3Qy$xhXx7oiEYDx1ELtGMxsovRnha7MHa5lRAhb8KUWJB2vh8zYFgD
> wR3TNExyluK0.Pz4rP2SzINXvMxr6P3yUky1:16377:0:99999:7:::
> group:user3:x:1010:
> gshadow:user3:!::

4. Test this account by logging in as *user3* and entering user123 as the password.

Exercise 8-3: Create a User Account with No Login Access

This exercise should be done on *server1*.

In this exercise, you will create an account *user4* with all the default values but without login access. You will assign this user a nologin shell to prevent it from logging into the system. You will *grep* the line entry from the *passwd* file and test the account.

1. Create *user4* with shell file */sbin/nologin*:

> # useradd –s /sbin/nologin user4

2. Assign user123 as password:

> # echo user123 | passwd --stdin user4

3. *grep* for *user4* on the *passwd* file and verify the shell field containing the nologin shell:

> # cd /etc ; grep user4 passwd
> passwd:user4:x:1011:1011::/home/user4:/sbin/nologin

4. Test this account by attempting to log in as *user4*:

> # su – user4
> This account is currently not available.

The message "This account is currently not available" is displayed when a user with a nologin shell attempts to log in. This shell is primarily used for application accounts that do not require login access to the system. It can also be assigned to a regular user to disable access temporarily using the *usermod* command.

Exercise 8-4: Set up Password Aging on User Accounts

This exercise should be done on *server1*.

In this exercise, you will configure password aging for *user2* using the *passwd* command. You will set mindays to 7, maxdays to 28, and warndays to 5. You will run the *chage* command to display the aging settings on this account.

Next, you will configure aging for *user3* using the *chage* command. You will set mindays to 10, maxdays to 30, warndays to 7, and expiry to December 31, 2015. You will run the *chage* command to display the updated settings.

1. Configure password aging for *user2* with mindays (–n) set to 7, maxdays (–x) to 28, and warndays (–w) to 5 using the *passwd* command:

   # **passwd –n 7 –x 28 –w 5 user2**
   Adjusting aging data for user user2.
   passwd: Success

2. Confirm the new settings with the *chage* command:

   # **chage –l user2**
   . . . .
   Minimum number of days between password change : 7
   Maximum number of days between password change : 28
   Number of days of warning before password expires   : 5

3. Configure password aging for *user3* with mindays (–m) set to 10, maxdays (–M) to 30, warndays (–W) to 7, and account expiry set to December 31, 2015:

   # **chage –m 10 –M 30 –W 7 –E 2015-12-31 user3**

4. Display the new settings for confirmation:

   # **chage –l user3**
   . . . .
   Account expires   : Dec 31, 2015
   Minimum number of days between password change : 10
   Maximum number of days between password change : 30
   Number of days of warning before password expires   : 7

Exercise 8-5: Modify and Delete a User Account

This exercise should be done on *server1*.

In this exercise, you will modify certain attributes for *user2* and *user3* using the *usermod* and *chage* commands, and then delete *user4* using the *userdel* command. You will change the login name for *user2* to *user2new*, UID to 2000, home directory to */home/user2new*, and login shell to */sbin/nologin*. You will *grep* the *passwd* file for *user2new* to validate the updates. You will set a new expiry on this user to February 29, 2016 and validate it with the *chage* command.

Next, you will modify *user3* to force this user to change password at next login, be unable to change password within five days following the last password change, and disable account expiry. You will validate the change with the *chage* command.

Finally, you will lock *user4*, delete it, and confirm the deletion.

1. Modify the login name for *user2* to *user2new* (–l), UID to 2000 (–u), home directory to */home/user2new* (–m and –d) and login shell to */sbin/nologin* (–s):

    # **usermod –u 2000 –m –d /home/user2new –s /sbin/nologin –l user2new user2**

2. Obtain the information for *user2new* from the *passwd* file to confirm the changes:

    # **grep user2new /etc/passwd**
    user2new:x:2000:1001::/home/user2new:/sbin/nologin

3. Set February 29, 2016 as the new expiry date for *user2new*:

    # **usermod –e 2016-02-29 user2new**

4. Confirm the new expiry for *user2new*:

    # **chage –l user2new**
    . . . .
    Account expires   : Feb 29, 2016
    . . . .

5. Modify *user3* to expire this user's password and prompt to change it at next login (–d), be unable to change password within five days following the last password change (–m), and disable account expiry (–E –1):

    # **chage –d 0 –m 5 –E -1 user3**

6. Confirm the aging updates for *user3*:

    # **chage –l user3**

Last password change	: password must be changed
Password expires	**: password must be changed**
Password inactive	: password must be changed
Account expires	**: never**
Minimum number of days between password change	**: 5**
Maximum number of days between password change	: 30
Number of days of warning before password expires	: 7

7. Lock *user4* using either of the following:

    # **usermod –L user4**   (or **passwd –l user4**)
    Locking password for user user4.
    passwd: Success

---

8. Remove *user4* along with home and mail spool directories (–r):

    # **userdel –r user4**

9. Confirm *user4* deletion:

    # **grep user4 /etc/passwd**

Switching Users

Even though we can log in to the system directly as *root*, it is not a recommended practice. The recommended practice is to log in with our own normal user account and then switch into the *root* account if necessary. This is safer and ensures system security and protection. In addition to becoming *root*, we can switch into another user account as well. In either case, we need to know the password for the target user account in order for a successful switch. The *su* command available in RHEL provides us with the ability to switch into other user accounts. The following presents a few examples to understand the usage.

To switch from *user1* to *root* without executing startup scripts for the target user:

    $ **su**
    Password:

To repeat the above while ensuring that startup scripts for the target user are also executed to provide an environment similar to a real login:

    $ **su –**
    Password:

To switch into a different user account, such as *user3*, specify the name of the target user with the command:

    $ **su – user1**
    Password:

To issue a command as a different user without switching into that user, the –c option is available with *su*. For example, the *firewall-cmd* command with the --list-services option requires superuser privileges. *user1* can use *su* as follows and execute this privileged command to obtain desired results:

    $ **su –c 'firewall-cmd --list-services'**
    Password:
    dhcpv6-client ssh

The *root* user can switch into any other user account on the system without being prompted for that user's password.

Doing as Superuser

RHEL offers a way for normal users to be able to run an assigned set of privileged commands without the knowledge of the *root* password. This allows the flexibility of assigning a specific command or a set of commands to an individual user or a group of users based on their needs. These users can then precede one of those commands with a utility called *sudo* (superuser do) at the time of executing that command. The users are prompted to enter their own password, and if correct, the command is executed successfully. The *sudo* utility is designed to provide protected access to administrative functions as defined in the */etc/sudoers* file. It can also be used to allow a user or a group of users to run scripts and applications owned by a different user.

Any normal user who requires access to one or more administrative commands is defined in the *sudoers* file. This file can be edited with the *visudo* command, which creates a copy of the file as *sudoers.tmp* and applies the changes there. After the *visudo* session is over, the updated file overwrites the original *sudoers* file, and *sudoers.tmp* is deleted. This is done to prevent multiple users editing the file simultaneously.

The syntax for user and group entries in the file is similar to the following example entries for user *user1* and group *dba*:

```
user1     ALL=(ALL)     ALL
%dba      ALL=(ALL)     ALL
```

These entries provide ALL privileges to ALL administrative commands on the system to both *user1* and members of the *dba* group (group is prefixed by the % sign).

Now, when *user1* or any *dba* group member executes a privileged command, they will be required to enter their own password. For instance:

$ sudo system-config-users
Password:

If we want *user1* and *dba* group members not to be prompted for a password, we can modify their entries in the *sudoers* file to look like:

```
user1     ALL=(ALL)     NOPASSWD:     ALL
%dba      ALL=(ALL)     NOPASSWD:     ALL
```

To restrict *user1* and *dba* group members to run only the *system-config-printer* and *system-config-users* commands, modify the directives as follows:

```
user1     ALL=/usr/bin/system-config-printer,/usr/bin/system-config-users
%dba      ALL=/usr/bin/system-config-printer,/usr/bin/system-config-users
```

Configuring sudo to work the way it has just been explained may result in a cluttered *sudoers* file containing too many entries. To avoid this and for better management of this file, sudo allows us to use aliases to define groups of users, commands, and hosts using the User_Alias, Cmnd_Alias, and Host_Alias directives available in the file. For instance, we can define a Cmnd_Alias called PKGCMD containing *yum* and *rpm* package management commands, and a User_Alias called PKGADM containing users *user1* to *user5*. These users may or may not belong to the same Linux group. We then give PKGADM access to PKGCMD. This way we set one rule that allows a group of users access to a group of commands. We can add or remove commands and users anytime as needed. Here is what needs to be added to the *sudoers* file to achieve this:

```
Cmnd_Alias        PKGCMD = /usr/bin/yum, /usr/bin/rpm
User_Alias        PKGADM = user1, user2, user3, user4, user5
%PKGADM           ALL = PKGCMD
```

The *sudo* command logs successful authentication and command data to the */var/log/secure* file. It uses the name of the actual user executing the command (and not *root*).

The *sudoers* file contains several examples with a brief explanation. It is a good idea to look at those examples for a better understanding.

Managing Group Accounts with Commands

Managing group accounts involves creating and modifying groups, adding and deleting group members and administrators, setting and revoking group-level password, and deleting groups. RHEL provides a set of tools and the graphical *User Manager* for performing these operations. The command toolset is part of the shadow-utils package and the User Manager GUI application becomes available when the system-config-users package is installed on the system.

Table 8-7 lists and describes group account management commands.

Command	Description
groupadd	Adds a group.
groupmod	Modifies group attributes.
groupdel	Deletes a group.
gpasswd	Adds group administrators, adds or deletes group members, assigns or revokes a group password, and disables newgrp command access to a group.

Table 8-7 Group Management Commands

We will use these commands for group management later in this chpater.

The groupadd, groupmod, and groupdel Commands

This set of commands is used to add, modify, and delete a group account from the system. The *groupadd* command adds entries to the *group* and *gshadow* files for each group added to the system. The *groupadd* command has a few options available with it. Table 8-8 lists them in both short and long versions, and explains them.

Option	Description
–g (--gid)	Specifies the GID to be assigned to the group.
–o (--non-unique)	Creates a group account sharing the GID of an existing group. When two groups share a common GID, members of each group get identical rights on each other's files. This should only be done in specific situations.
–r	Creates a system group account with a GID below 1000.
groupname	Specifies a group name.

Table 8-8 groupadd Command Options

The *groupadd* command picks up the default values from the *login.defs* file.

We can modify the attributes of a group account with the *groupmod* command. The syntax of this command is very similar to that of the *groupadd*'s, with most options identical. The only option that is additional with this command is −n, which allows us to change the name of an existing group.

The *groupdel* command is straightforward. It removes entries for the specified group from both *group* and *gshadow* files.

The gpasswd Command

The *gpasswd* command can be used to add group administrators, add or delete group members, assign or revoke a group password, and disable access to a group via the *newgrp* command. The *root* user can perform all of these tasks, while the group administrator can perform only the last three. This command prompts to change the group password if invoked by *root* or the group administrator. The *gpasswd* command updates the *group* and *gshadow* files. There are several options available with this command, and these are explained in Table 8-9.

Option	Description
−A (--administrators)	Adds one or more group administrators. Inserts an entry in the third field of the gshadow file.
−a (--add)	Adds a group member. Inserts an entry in the fourth field of both group and gshadow files.
−d (--delete)	Deletes a group member.
−M (--members)	Substitutes all existing group members.
−R (--restrict)	Disables access to a group for non-members. Members with a password can still join the group.
−r (--remove-password)	Revokes the password set on a group. Only group members can join the group.

Table 8-9 gpasswd Command Options

This command picks up the default values from the */etc/login.defs* file.

Exercise 8-6: Create, Modify, and Delete Group Accounts

This exercise should be done on *server1*.

In this exercise, you will create a group account called *linuxadm* with GID 5000 and another group account called *sales* sharing the GID 5000. You will change the group name from *sales* to *mgmt* and then change the GID for *linuxadm* from 5000 to 6000. You will add *user1* to *linuxadm* and verify this action with the *id* and *groups* commands. Finally, you will remove the *mgmt* group.

1. Create group account *linuxadm* with GID 5000:

   # **groupadd −g 5000 linuxadm**

2. Create group account *sales* sharing the GID of group *linuxadm*:

   # **groupadd −o −g 5000 sales**

3. Alter the name of group *sales* to group *mgmt*:

   # **groupmod −n mgmt sales**

4. Change the GID of *linuxadm* group to 6000:

   # groupmod –g 6000 linuxadm

5. Add user *user1* to group *linuxadm* while retaining the user's existing memberships:

   # usermod –a –G linuxadm user1

6. Verify group memberships for *user1*:

   # id user1
   uid=1000(user1) gid=1000(user1) groups=1000(user1),10(wheel),6000(linuxadm)
   # groups user1
   user1 : user1 wheel linuxadm

7. Delete the *mgmt* group:

   # groupdel mgmt

Exercise 8-7: Manage Groups with gpasswd Command
This exercise should be done on *server1*.

In this exercise, you will add *user1* and *user2new* as group administrators and *user2new* and *user3* as members of the *linuxadm* group. You will substitute both existing group members with *user4* (create this group if it does not exist) and assign a group password to the *linuxadm* group. You will log in as *user4* and list current primary group membership for *user4*. You will switch the primary group to *linuxadm* and validate.

1. Add *user1* and *user2new* as administrators to the *linuxadm* group:

   # gpasswd –A user1,user2new linuxadm

2. Add *user2new* and *user3* as members to the *linuxadm* group:

   # gpasswd –a user2new –a user3 linuxadm
   Adding user user3 to group linuxadm

3. Create *user4* with default values and assign password user123:

   # useradd user4 ; echo user123 | passwd --stdin user4
   Changing password for user user4.
   passwd: all authentication tokens updated successfully.

4. Substitute *user2new* and *user3* with *user4* as a member of the *linuxadm* group:

   # gpasswd –M user4 linuxadm

5. Set a password on the *linuxadm* group:

   # **gpasswd linuxadm**
   Changing the password for group linuxadm
   New Password:
   Re-enter new password:

6. Log in as *user4* and run the *groups* command to list group membership for *user4*. The primary group is listed first.

   $ **groups**
   user4 linuxadm

7. Temporarily change the primary group for *user4* to *linuxadm*:

   $ **newgrp linuxadm**

8. Verify the new primary group membership for *user4*. It should be listed first in the output.

   $ **groups**
   linuxadm user4

9. Return to the original primary group by issuing the *exit* command or pressing Ctrl+d, and verify:

   $ **exit**
   exit
   $ **groups**
   user4 linuxadm

Managing Users, Groups, and Password Aging with the User Manager Tool

The User Manager is a graphical equivalent for performing most user and group administrative functions. This application can be used to view, add, modify, and delete local user and group accounts, set and modify password aging attributes, lock and unlock user accounts, and so on. It can be invoked with the *system-config-users* command or by choosing Applications | Sundry | Users and Groups. The main window (similar to what is shown in Figure 8-5) will appear.

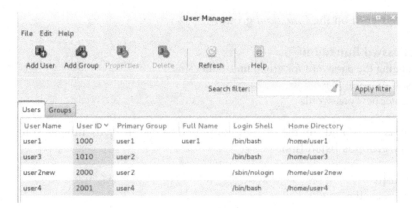

Figure 8-5 User Manager – Main Menu

There are two tabs: Users and Groups, as depicted in the main window above. The Users tab shows a list of all normal local users on the system that currently exist. Along with usernames, it also shows the corresponding UID, primary group, full name, login shell, and home directory. The Groups tab shows a list of all local groups on the system, along with their GIDs and membership.

Across the top are Add User and Add Group buttons that allow us to add new user and group accounts. Figures 8-6 and 8-7 show the interfaces that appear when we click on these buttons. The fields are self-explanatory.

Figure 8-6 User Manager – Add New User

Figure 8-7 User Manager – Add New Group

The Properties button at the top of the main window is activated when we highlight a user or group account. It allows us to display and modify the highlighted user or group. For User Properties, four tabs (User Data, Account Info, Password Info, and Groups) are available, as shown in Figure 8-8. Select User Data to modify general user information; select Account Info to enable and set account expiration or lock the user; choose Password Info to enable and set password aging; and choose Groups to modify the selected user's primary or secondary group membership.

Figure 8-8 User Manager – Display / Modify User Properties

Highlight a group account in the Groups tab and click Properties at the top to display and modify the highlighted group's name or membership. Here, two tabs (Group Data and Group Users) are available, as shown in Figure 8-9. Select Group Data to modify the group name and choose Group Users to modify group membership.

Figure 8-9 User Manager – Display / Modify Group Properties

The Delete button at the top of the main window is activated when we highlight a user or group account; this button is used to remove the highlighted user or group from the system.

Shell Startup Files

In Chapter 04 "Dealing with the Bash Shell, Processes, and Scheduling" we used local and environment variables, and modified the default command prompt to add useful information to it. In other words, we modified the default shell environment to customize it according to our needs. The changes we made were lost when we logged off. What if we wanted to make those changes permanent so that each time we logged in they were there for us?

Modifications to the default shell environment can be stored in *startup* (or *initialization*) files. These files are sourced by the shell following user authentication at the time of logging in and before the initial command prompt appears. In addition, aliases, functions, and scripts can be added to these files as well. There are two types of startup files: *system-wide* and *per-user*.

System-wide Shell Startup Files

System-wide startup files set the general environment for all users at the time of their login to the system. These files are located in the */etc* directory and are maintained by the system administrator. System-wide files can be modified to include or exclude general environment settings and customizations that are needed by every user on the system.

Table 8-10 lists and describes system-wide startup files for bash shell users.

File	Comments
/etc/bashrc	Defines functions and aliases, and sets the umask value, the command prompt, etc. It includes settings from the shell scripts located in the /etc/profile.d directory.
/etc/profile	Sets common environment variables such as PATH, USER, LOGNAME, MAIL, HOSTNAME, HISTSIZE, and HISTCONTROL for users and startup programs. It processes shell scripts located in the /etc/profile.d directory.
/etc/profile.d	Contains scripts for bash and C shell users that are executed by the /etc/profile file. Additional scripts may be created here for further customizing the environment.

Table 8-10 System-wide Startup Files

Excerpts from the *bashrc* and *profile* files, and a list of files in the *profile.d* directory are displayed below:

cat /etc/bashrc

```
. . . . . . . .
if [ "$PS1" ]; then
  if [ -z "$PROMPT_COMMAND" ]; then
    case $TERM in
    xterm*|vte*)
     if [ -e /etc/sysconfig/bash-prompt-xterm ]; then
        PROMPT_COMMAND=/etc/sysconfig/bash-prompt-xterm
     elif [ "${VTE_VERSION:-0}" -ge 3405 ]; then
        PROMPT_COMMAND="__vte_prompt_command"
     else
        PROMPT_COMMAND='printf "\033]0;%s@%s:%s\007" "${USER}" "${HOSTNAME%%.*}"
"${PWD/#$HOME/~}"'
     fi
     ;;
. . . . . . . .
```

cat /etc/profile

. . . .

```
if [ -x /usr/bin/id ]; then
    if [ -z "$EUID" ]; then
        # ksh workaround
        EUID=`id -u`
        UID=`id -ru`
    fi
    USER="`id -un`"
    LOGNAME=$USER
    MAIL="/var/spool/mail/$USER"
fi
```

. . . .

ll /etc/profile.d

```
-rw-r--r--. 1 root root  771 Apr  2 2014 256term.csh
-rw-r--r--. 1 root root  841 Apr  2 2014 256term.sh
-rw-r--r--. 1 root root  461 Mar  3 2014 abrt-console-notification.sh
-rw-r--r--. 1 root root  660 Nov 25 2013 bash_completion.sh
-rw-r--r--. 1 root root  337 Feb  4 2014 colorgrep.csh
-rw-r--r--. 1 root root  345 Feb  4 2014 colorgrep.sh
```

. . . .

Per-user Shell Startup Files

Per-user shell startup files override or modify system default definitions set by system-wide startup files. These files may be customized by individual users to suit their needs. By default, two such files (in addition to the *.bash_logout* file) located in the */etc/skel* directory are copied into user home directories at the time of their creation.

We may create additional files in our home directories to set more environment variables or shell properties.

Table 8-11 lists and describes per-user startup files for bash shell users.

File	Comments
~/.bashrc	Defines functions and aliases. This file sources global definitions from the /etc/bashrc file.
~/.bash_profile	Sets environment variables. This file sources the ~/.bashrc file to set functions and aliases.
~/.gnome2/	Directory that holds environment settings when GNOME desktop is started. Only available if GNOME is installed.

Table 8-11 Per-user Startup Files

Excerpts from the *.bashrc* and *.bash_profile* files for the *root* account are displayed below:

cat ~/.bashrc
```
# .bashrc
# User specific aliases and functions
alias rm='rm -i'
alias cp='cp -i'
```

```
alias mv='mv -i'
# Source global definitions
if [ -f /etc/bashrc ]; then
      . /etc/bashrc
fi
# cat ~/.bash_profile
# .bash_profile
# Get the aliases and functions
if [ -f ~/.bashrc ]; then
      . ~/.bashrc
fi
# User specific environment and startup programs
PATH=$PATH:$HOME/bin
export PATH
```

The order in which the system-wide and per-user startup files are executed is important. The system runs the */etc/profile* file first, followed by *~/.bash_profile*, *~/.bashrc*, and */etc/bashrc* files.

Chapter Summary

We started this chapter by building an understanding of local user authentication files: *passwd, shadow, group*, and *gshadow*. We looked at their contents and syntax, and saw how to verify their consistency. We looked at ways to lock these files while being edited to avoid losing changes made by other users during that time.

We discussed password shadowing and password aging. We learned about user management including creating, modifying, and deleting user accounts. We looked at setting and modifying password aging attributes on user accounts. We learned the tools to switch into other user accounts and to run privileged commands as a normal user.

We studied group management including creating, modifying, and deleting group accounts. We reviewed the graphical User Manager tool and saw how to manage user and group accounts, and password aging in a graphical setting.

Finally, we learned about the system-wide and per-user startup files, and understood their contents.

Chapter Review Questions

1. What are the two utilities for manually editing shadow password files exclusively?
2. What are the two tools for checking shadow password files consistency?
3. What does the "x" in the password field in the *passwd* file imply?
4. What would the command *useradd –D* do?
5. Name the four local user authentication files.
6. The *passwd* file contains secondary user group information. True or False?
7. What does the *gpasswd* command do?
8. What is the name and location of the *sudo* configuration file?
9. Which command would we use to add group administrators?
10. Name the two types of shell startup files?
11. What would the command *passwd –l user10* do?
12. What is the first UID assigned to a regular user?
13. Name the three fundamental user account categories in RHEL.

14. Every user in RHEL gets a private group by default. True or False?
15. What would the *userdel* command do if it is run with the –r option?
16. What is the first GID assigned to a group?
17. Write two command names for managing password aging.
18. What is the name of the default backup file for *shadow*?
19. What would the command *chage –E 2015-12-31 user10* do?
20. What would the command *chage –l user5* do?
21. What is the difference between running the *su* command with and without the dash sign?
22. What is the significance of the –o option with the *groupadd* and *groupmod* commands?
23. What would the command *passwd –n 7 –x 15 –w 3 user5* do?
24. What two commands are used to create and update the *shadow* and *gshadow* files?
25. What would the command *useradd user500* do?
26. Which command is used to change a user's primary group temporarily?
27. What would the command *chage –d 0 user60* do?
28. What four local files are updated when a user account is created?
29. UID 999 is reserved for normal users. True or False?
30. The */etc/bashrc* file contains shell scripts that are executed at user login. True or False?

Answers to Chapter Review Questions

1. The *vipw* and *vigr* utilities.
2. The *pwck* and *grpck* tools.
3. The "x" in the password field implies that the encrypted password is stored in the *shadow* file.
4. This command displays the defaults used at the time of user creation or modification.
5. The *passwd, shadow, group,* and *gshadow* files.
6. False. The *passwd* file contains primary user group information.
7. The *gpasswd* command is used to add group administrators, add or delete group members, assign and revoke a group password, and disable access to a group with the *newgrp* command.
8. The *sudo* configuration file is */etc/sudoers*.
9. The *gpasswd* command.
10. The two types of shell startup files are system-wide and per-user.
11. This command will lock *user10*.
12. The first UID assigned to a regular user is 1000.
13. The three fundamental user account categories are root, normal, and system.
14. True.
15. The command provided will delete the specified user and their home directory.
16. The first GID assigned to a regular user is 1000.
17. The *passwd* and *chage* commands.
18. The name of the default backup file for *shadow* is *shadow-*.
19. The command provided will set December 31, 2015 as the expiry date for *user10*.
20. The command provided will display password aging attributes for *user5*.
21. With the dash sign the *su* command will process the specified user's startup files, and it won't without this sign.
22. The –o option lets the commands set a duplicate GID on a group.
23. The command will set mindays to 7, maxdays to 15 and warndays to 3 for *user5*.
24. The *pwconv* and *grpconv* commands.
25. The command provided will add *user500* with all pre-defined default values.
26. The *newgrp* command.

27. The command provided will force *user60* to change their password at next login.
28. The *passwd*, *shadow*, *group*, and *gshadow* files are updated when a user account is created.
29. False.
30. False.

DIY Challenge Labs

The following labs are useful to strengthen most of the concepts and topics learned in this chapter. It is expected that you perform these labs without any additional help. A step-by-step guide is not provided, as the implementation of these labs requires the knowledge that has been presented in this chapter. Use defaults or your own thinking for missing information.

Lab 8-1: Create and Modify a User Account

Create a user account called *user4000* with UID 4000, GID 5000, and home directory located in */usr*. GID 5000 should be assigned to group *lnxgrp*. Assign this user a password and establish password aging attributes so that this user cannot change their password within 4 days after setting it, with a password validity of 30 days. This user should get warning messages for changing password for 7 days before their account is locked. This account needs to expire on the 20th of December, 2016.

Lab 8-2: Modify a Group Account

Modify the GID from 5000 to 6000 for the *lnxgrp* group. Add users *user1* and *user2new* as members, and *user3* as the group administrator. Assign a group password and use the *newgrp* command as *user4* to validate that the password is working. Change this group's name to *dbagrp* and verify.

Chapter 09

Partitioning and Managing Disk Storage

This chapter describes the following major topics:

➢ MBR vs GPT

➢ Add more storage for practice

➢ Create and delete partitions on MBR disks

➢ Create and delete partitions on GPT disks

➢ Overview of graphical Disk Utility

➢ Understand LVM concepts, components, and structure

➢ Use LVM to initialize and uninitialize a physical volume; create, display, extend, reduce, and remove a volume group; and create, display, extend, reduce, and remove a logical volume

RHCSA Objectives:

21. List, create, and delete partitions on MBR and GPT disks
22. Create and remove physical volumes, assign physical volumes to volume groups, and create and delete logical volumes
24. Add new partitions and logical volumes, and swap to a system non-destructively
27. Extend existing unencrypted logical volumes

Data is stored on disk drives that are logically divided into partitions. A partition can exist on a portion of a disk, on an entire disk, or it may span multiple disks. Each partition may contain a file system, a raw data space, a swap space, or a dump space.

A file system is used to hold files and directories, a raw data space may be used for databases and other applications for faster access, a swap space is defined to supplement the physical memory on the system, and a dump space is created to store memory and kernel images after a system crash has occurred.

RHEL offers several toolsets for partitioning and managing disk storage. These toolsets include the parted and gdisk utilities and the Logical Volume Manager (LVM). Additional tools, such as fdisk, sfdisk, and cfdisk, are also available for this purpose. Partitions created with a combination of most of these tools can co-exist on a single disk. This chapter provides detailed coverage for storage management using parted, gdisk, and LVM.

In this chapter, exercises will be performed on server1, which was built in Chapter 06 "Configuring Server Virtualization and Network Installing RHEL7".

MBR vs GPT

A disk in RHEL can be carved up into several partitions. This partition information is stored on the disk in a small region, which is read by the operating system at boot time. This region is referred to as the *Master Boot Record* (MBR) on the BIOS-based systems, and *GUID Partition Table* (GPT) on the UEFI-based systems. At system boot, the BIOS/UEFI scans all storage devices, detects the presence of MBR/GPT, identifies the boot disks, loads the boot loader program in memory from the default boot disk, executes the boot code to read the partition table and identify the */boot* partition, and continues with the boot process by loading the kernel in the memory and passing control over to it. Though MBR and GPT are designed for different PC firmware types, their job is the same: to store partition information and the boot code.

The MBR is resident on the first sector of the boot disk. It has limitations that led to the design, development, and use of GPT type. MBR allows the creation of only up to four primary partitions on a single disk, with the flexibility of using one of the four partitions as an extended partition to hold an arbitrary number of logical partitions in it. The other limitation is its lack of addressing space beyond 2TB. This is due to its 32-bit nature and the disk sector size of 512-byte that it uses. The MBR is non-redundant; the record it contains is not replicated, resulting in an unbootable system if it gets corrupted somehow.

With the increasing use of disks larger than 2TB on x86 computers, a new 64-bit partitioning standard called *Globally Unique IDentifiers* (GUID) *Partition Table* (GPT) was developed and integrated in to the UEFI firmware. This new standard introduced several enhancements, including allowing the construction of 128 partitions, use of disks much larger than 2TB, use of 4KB sector, and redundant location for the storage of partition information. Moreover, this standard allows a BIOS-based system to boot from a GPT disk, using the boot loader program stored in a protective MBR at the first disk sector.

RHEL offers several tools for disk storage management, which includes *parted*, *gdisk*, *fdisk*, and LVM. In this chapter, *parted*, *gdisk*, and LVM are presented. *parted* understands both MBR and GPT formats. *gdisk* (a.k.a. *GPT fdisk*) is designed to support the GPT format only and can be used instead of *parted*. The *fdisk* utility does not understand GPT and cannot address space exceeding 2TB, and hence it is not discussed.

Adding and Verifying Virtual Block Storage

This chapter and the next have several exercises that require block storage devices for practice. In Chapter 01 "Installing RHEL7 on Physical Computer Using Local DVD", we mentioned that *server1* will have access to five 2GB virtual disks created on *host1*; of these, four will be used for *parted* and LVM exercises and the last one will be utilized for iSCSI exercises later in the RHCE section of this book. Therefore, we will need to create four virtual disks now and make them available to *server1*. The fifth disk will be created in the iSCSI chapter.

Before we create any new disks, run the *lsblk* command on *server1* to determine what this server currently has in terms of disks and partitions:

```
# lsblk
```

NAME	MAJ:MIN	RM	SIZE	RO	TYPE	MOUNTPOINT
sr0	11:0	1	1024M	0	rom	
vda	252:0	0	10G	0	disk	
├─vda1	252:1	0	500M	0	part	/boot
└─vda2	252:2	0	9.5G	0	part	
├─vg00-swap	253:0	0	500M	0	lvm	[SWAP]
├─vg00-root	253:1	0	8.7G	0	lvm	/
└─vg00-home	253:2	0	300M	0	lvm	/home

The output indicates the presence of one virtual disk *vda* on *server1*. This disk is 10GB in size and it contains two partitions: *vda1* and *vda2*. The first partition holds */boot* and the second one is an LVM physical volume with *swap*, *root*, and *home* logical volumes residing in it. Both *vda1* and *vda2* partitions occupy the entire disk capacity. The *sr0* represents the CDROM device.

vd represents virtual disk, a represents the first disk, b represents the second disk, and so on. 1 identifies the first partition on the disk, 2 identifies the second partition on the disk, and so on. Therefore, *vda1* means the first partition on the first virtual disk and *vda2* is the second partition on the same disk.

Adding 3x2GB Virtual Block Disks Using virt-manager

Let's create on *host1* four 2GB virtual block disks and attach them to *server1* for use in *parted* and LVM exercises in this and the next chapter. For this purpose, we can either use the virt-manager GUI or the *virsh* command. The following procedure will demonstrate adding three virtual disk devices with the GUI tool.

Start virt-manager and open the console for *server1* by right-clicking on it. Click the "Show virtual hardware details" button right beside the console icon below the menu bar. See Figure 9-1.

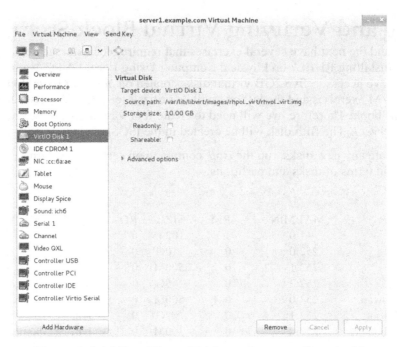

Figure 9-1 Adding Virtual Disks to Server – Step 1 of 2

Figure 9-1 shows the presence of the 10GB *vda* disk, which holds the operating system. Click Add Hardware in the bottom left and a window similar to the one shown in Figure 9-2 will appear. Assign 2GB size, select "Allocate entire disk now", and choose "Virtio disk" for the device type. Click Finish when done. Repeat the procedure and add two more disks.

Figure 9-2 Adding Virtual Disks to Server – Step 2 of 2

Adding 1x2GB Virtual Block Disk Using Command Line

Now create one virtual block disk on *host1* and attach it to *server1* using a combination of *qemu-img* and *virsh* commands. To that end, execute *qemu-img* while in the */var/lib/libvirt/images* directory and create a 2GB image file for the new disk using raw format:

 # cd /var/lib/libvirt/images
 # qemu-img create –f raw server1.example.com-virsh.img 2G
Formatting 'server1.example.com-virsh.img', fmt=raw size=2147483648

The next step is to attach this image file to *server1* using the *virsh* command so that the server sees it as a block virtual disk. Specify the image file name with the --source option and a disk name with the --target option. Ensure that this assignment is stored persistently.

**# virsh attach-disk server1.example.com --source \
/var/lib/libvirt/images/server1.example.com-virsh.img --target vde --persistent**
Disk attached successfully

Verifying the New Storage

Both the GUI and CLI tools used above for the creation and presentation of virtual disks store the virtual disk image files in the */var/lib/libvirt/images* directory on *host1*. Run the *ll* command on this directory to view the files:

 # ll /var/lib/libvirt/images
```
-rw-------. 1 qemu qemu 2147483648 Oct 21 16:25 server1.example.com-1.img
-rw-------. 1 qemu qemu 2147483648 Oct 21 16:25 server1.example.com-2.img
-rw-------. 1 qemu qemu 2147483648 Oct 21 16:25 server1.example.com.img
-rw-r--r--. 1 qemu qemu 2147483648 Oct 21 16:49 server1.example.com-virsh.img
```

The above output lists four image files, the top three are created by the GUI tool and the last one by the *qemu-img* command. We can also verify the new devices with the GUI, or using the *virsh* command on *host1* as follows:

 # virsh domblklist server1.example.com --details

Type	Device	Target	Source
file	disk	vda	/var/lib/libvirt/rhpol_virt/rhvol_virt.img
file	disk	vdb	/var/lib/libvirt/images/server1.example.com.img
file	disk	vdc	/var/lib/libvirt/images/server1.example.com-1.img
file	disk	vdd	/var/lib/libvirt/images/server1.example.com-2.img
file	disk	vde	/var/lib/libvirt/images/server1.example.com-virsh.img

Now, log on to *server1* and issue the *lsblk* command to confirm the presence of the new disks:

 # lsblk | grep vd
```
vda              252:0    0   10G    0   disk
├─vda1           252:1    0   500M   0   part   /boot
└─vda2           252:2    0   9.5G   0   part
  ├─vg00-swap    253:0    0   500M   0   lvm    [SWAP]
```

├─vg00-root	253:1	0	8.7G	0	lvm	/
└─vg00-home	253:2	0	300M	0	lvm	/home
vdb	252:16	0	2G	0	disk	
vdc	252:32	0	2G	0	disk	
vdd	252:48	0	2G	0	disk	
vde	252:64	0	2G	0	disk	

The above output confirms the presence of four new disks: *vdb*, *vdc*, *vdd*, and *vde*. It also indicates their sizes, along with other information.

Managing Storage with parted

The *parted* tool is used to carve up disks on RHEL systems. This text-based, menu-driven program allows us to view, add, check, modify, copy, resize, and delete partitions. *parted* understands and supports both MBR and GPT schemes. It can be used to create up to 128 partitions on a single GPT disk.

The main interface of the command looks similar to the following. It produces a list of subcommands when we run *help* at the parted prompt:

parted
GNU Parted 3.1
Using /dev/sda
Welcome to GNU Parted! Type 'help' to view a list of commands.
(parted) **help**
  align-check TYPE N   check partition N for TYPE(min|opt) alignment
  help [COMMAND]   print general help, or help on COMMAND
  mklabel,mktable LABEL-TYPE   create a new disklabel (partition table)
  mkpart PART-TYPE [FS-TYPE] START END make a partition
  name NUMBER NAME   name partition NUMBER as NAME
  print [devices|free|list,all|NUMBER] display the partition table, available devices, free space, all found
                                    partitions, or a particular partition
  quit   exit program
  rescue START END   rescue a lost partition near START and END
  rm NUMBER   delete partition NUMBER
  select DEVICE   choose the device to edit
  disk_set FLAG STATE   change the FLAG on selected device
  disk_toggle [FLAG]   toggle the state of FLAG on selected device
  set NUMBER FLAG STATE   change the FLAG on partition NUMBER
  toggle [NUMBER [FLAG]]   toggle the state of FLAG on partition NUMBER
  unit UNIT   set the default unit to UNIT
  version   display the version number and copyright information of GNU
                                    Parted

There are several subcommands in the main menu. Table 9-1 lists and describes them.

Subcommand	Description
align-check	Checks whether a partition satisfies the alignment constraints of the disk.
help	Displays available commands or help on the specified command.

Subcommand	Description
mklabel / mktable	Makes a new disk label for the partition table. Supported labels are aix, amiga, bsd, dvh, gpt, mac, msdos, pc98, sun, and loop.
mkpart	Makes a new partition.
name	Assigns a name to a partition.
print	Displays the partition table, a specific partition, or all devices. Information includes disk geometry and partition number, start and end, size, type, file system type, and associated flags.
quit	Quits parted.
rescue	Recovers a lost partition.
rm	Removes the specified partition.
select	Selects a device to edit.
disk_set	Sets a FLAG on the current disk.
disk_toggle	Toggles the state of FLAG on the current disk.
set	Sets a FLAG on the specified partition.
toggle	Toggles the state of FLAG on the specified partition number.
unit	Sets the default unit of measurement.
version	Displays version and copyright information for the parted utility.

Table 9-1 parted Subcommands

At the *parted* prompt, we can invoke help for a specific subcommand. For example, to obtain help on *mklabel*, issue the following:

(parted) **help mklabel**
    mklabel,mktable LABEL-TYPE   create a new disklabel (partition table)
        LABEL-TYPE is one of: aix, amiga, bsd, dvh, gpt, mac, msdos, pc98, sun, loop

Let's create and delete a partition with *parted* to understand its basic usage. As noted earlier, we have access to four disk drives—*/dev/vdb*, */dev/vdc*, */dev/vdd*, and */dev/vde*—on *server1*. After making a partition, use the *print* subcommand to ensure that what we have created is what we wanted. The */proc/partitions* file is also updated to reflect partition creation and deletion operations.

Exercise 9-1: Create an MBR Partition Table and a Partition Using parted

This exercise should be done on *server1*.

In this exercise, you will assign the partition type MSDOS to */dev/vdb*. You will create a 1GB primary partition on the disk for use as a file system using the *parted* utility, and confirm the creation.

1.   Execute the *parted* command on */dev/vdb*:

    # **parted /dev/vdb**
    GNU Parted 3.1
    Using /dev/vdb
    Welcome to GNU Parted! Type 'help' to view a list of commands.

2. Execute *print* to view the current partition information:

> (parted) **print**
> Error: /dev/vdb: unrecognised disk label
> Model: Virtio Block Device (virtblk)
> Disk /dev/vdb: 2147MB
> Sector size (logical/physical): 512B/512B
> Partition Table: unknown
> Disk Flags:

3. Assign disk label "msdos" to the disk with *mklabel*. This must be done on a new disk.

> (parted) **mklabel msdos**

 To use the GPT partition table type, run "mklabel gpt" instead.

4. Create a 1GB primary partition starting at 1MB using *mkpart*:

> (parted) **mkpart primary 1 1g**

5. Verify the new partition with *print* and quit *parted*.

> (parted) **print**
> . . . .
> Number   Start   End   Size   File system   Name   Flags
> 1   1049kB   1000MB   999MB   primary
> (parted) **quit**

 You may need to run the partprobe command after exiting the parted utility to inform the kernel of changes in the partition table if the disk previously had partitions. This is not required for new unpartitioned disks.

6. Confirm the partition information by running either of the following at the command prompt:

> # **parted /dev/vdb print**
> . . . .
> Number   Start   End   Size   File system   Name   Flags
> 1   1049kB   1000MB   999MB   primary
> # **grep vdb /proc/partitions**
> 252   16   2097152   vdb
> 252   17   975872   vdb1

Exercise 9-2: Delete an MBR Partition Using parted

This exercise should be done on *server1*.

In this exercise, you will delete the *vdb1* partition that you created in the previous exercise, and confirm the deletion.

1. Execute the *parted* command on the */dev/vdb* disk:

   # **parted /dev/vdb**

2. View the current partition table using the *print* subcommand:

   (parted) **print**

3. Execute *rm* and specify the partition number to delete:

   (parted) **rm 1**

4. Verify the new partition information with *print* and quit *parted*:

   (parted) **print**
   (parted) **quit**

5. Confirm the partition information using either of the following:

   # **parted /dev/vdb print**
   # **grep vdb /proc/partitions**

Managing Storage with gdisk

The *gdisk* utility is used to carve up disks using GPT format. This text-based, menu-driven program allows us to view, add, verify, modify, and delete partitions among other tasks. *gdisk* can be used to create up to 128 partitions on a single GPT disk on systems with UEFI firmware.

The main interface of the *gdisk* command looks similar to the following when we run it on an available disk device, such as */dev/vdc*. It produces a list of subcommands when we type *?* at the prompt and press the Enter key:

```
# gdisk /dev/vdc
GPT fdisk (gdisk) version 0.8.6
Partition table scan:
  MBR: not present
  BSD: not present
  APM: not present
  GPT: not present

Creating new GPT entries.

Command (? for help): ?
b    back up GPT data to a file
c    change a partition's name
d    delete a partition
i    show detailed information on a partition
l    list known partition types
n    add a new partition
o    create a new empty GUID partition table (GPT)
```

p   print the partition table
q   quit without saving changes
r   recovery and transformation options (experts only)
s   sort partitions
t   change a partition's type code
v   verify disk
w   write table to disk and exit
x   extra functionality (experts only)
?   print this menu

Command (? for help):

The output indicates that there is no partition table assigned to the disk. There are several subcommands in the main menu followed by a short description. Table 9-2 summarizes some key subcommands.

Subcommand	Description
c	Changes a partition's name.
d	Deletes a partition.
i	Displays a partition information.
l	Lists available partition types.
n	Creates a partition.
o	Labels the disk to use GPT scheme.
p	Prints the partition table.
q	Quits gdisk without saving modifications.
r	Provides subcommands for recovery and transformation purposes.
S	Displays a sorted partition list.
t	Changes the type code of a partition.
v	Verifies a disk.
w	Writes the changes and exits gdisk.
x	Provides subcommands for various expert-level disk operations.

Table 9-2 gdisk Subcommands

Let's label */dev/vdc* disk on *server1* to use GPT using *gdisk*, and then create and delete a partition to understand its basic usage. After making a partition, use appropriate subcommands for verification. The */proc/partitions* file is also updated to reflect partition creation and deletion operations.

Exercise 9-3: Create a GPT Partition Table and a Partition Using gdisk

This exercise should be done on *server1*.

In this exercise, you will assign tye partition type GPT to */dev/vdc*. You will create a 200MB partition on the disk for use as a file system using the *gdisk* utility, and confirm the creation.

1. Execute the *gdisk* command on */dev/vdc*:

```
# gdisk /dev/vdc
GPT fdisk (gdisk) version 0.8.6
Partition table scan:
  MBR: not present
  BSD: not present
  APM: not present
  GPT: not present
Creating new GPT entries.
Command (? for help):
```

2. Assign GPT as the partition table to the disk using the o subcommand. Enter y for confirmation to proceed.

```
Command (? for help): o
This option deletes all partitions and creates a new protective MBR.
Proceed? (Y/N): y
```

3. Run the *p* subcommand to view the disk label:

```
Command (? for help): p
Disk /dev/vdc: 4194304 sectors, 2.0 GiB
Logical sector size: 512 bytes
Disk identifier (GUID): AA668D3F-FEB4-4959-B949-7D15684F5254
Partition table holds up to 128 entries
First usable sector is 34, last usable sector is 4194270
Partitions will be aligned on 2048-sector boundaries
Total free space is 4194237 sectors (2.0 GiB)
Number  Start (sector)   End (sector) Size     Code  Name
```

The output shows the assigned GUID states that the partition table can hold up to 128 partition entries.

4. Create a 200MB partition using the *n* subcommand. Use all the defaults except for the size specification.

```
Command (? For help): n
Partition number (1-128, default 1):
First sector (34-4194270, default = 2048) or {+-}size{KMGTP}:
Last sector (2048-4194270, default = 4194270) or {+-}size{KMGTP}: +200M
Current type is 'Linux filesystem'
Hex code or GUID (L to show codes, Enter = 8300):
Changed type of partition to 'Linux filesystem'
```

5. Verify the new partition with *p*:

```
Command (? for help): p
. . . . . . . .
Number  Start (sector)   End (sector)   Size       Code   Name
   1       2048            411647      200.0 MiB   8300   Linux filesystem
```

---

6. Run the *w* subcommand to write the partition information to the partition table. Enter y to confirm.

> Command (? for help): **w**
> Final checks complete. About to write GPT data. THIS WILL OVERWRITE EXISTING
> PARTITIONS!!
> Do you want to proceed? (Y/N): **y**
> OK; writing new GUID partition table (GPT) to /dev/vdc.
> The operation has completed successfully.

> You may need to run the partprobe command after exiting the gdisk utility to inform the kernel of changes in the partition table if the disk previously had partitions. This is not required for new unpartitioned disks.

7. Confirm the partition information by running either of the following at the command prompt:

> # **gdisk –l /dev/vdc**
> GPT fdisk (gdisk) version 0.8.6
> Partition table scan:
>   MBR: protective
>   BSD: not present
>   APM: not present
>   GPT: present
> Found valid GPT with protective MBR; using GPT.
> Disk /dev/vdc: 4194304 sectors, 2.0 GiB
> Logical sector size: 512 bytes
> Disk identifier (GUID): AA668D3F-FEB4-4959-B949-7D15684F5254
> Partition table holds up to 128 entries
> First usable sector is 34, last usable sector is 4194270
> Partitions will be aligned on 2048-sector boundaries
> Total free space is 3784637 sectors (1.8 GiB)
> Number Start (sector) End (sector) Size   Code Name
>   1   2048   411647   200.0 MiB 8300 Linux filesystem
> # **grep vdc /proc/partitions**
> 252   32   2097152 vdc
> 252   33   204800 vdc1

Exercise 9-4: Delete a GPT Partition Using gdisk

This exercise should be done on *server1*.

In this exercise, you will delete the *vdc1* partition that you created in the previous exercise, and confirm the deletion.

1. Execute the *gdisk* command on the */dev/vdc* disk:

> # **gdisk /dev/vdc**

2. View the current partition table using the *p* subcommand:

Command (? for help): **p**

3. Execute the *d* subcommand and specify the partition number to delete:

    Command (? for help): **d1**

4. Verify the new partition information with *p* and quit *gdisk*:

    Command (? for help): **p**
    Command (? for help): **q**

5. Confirm the partition information using either of the following:

    # **gdisk –l /dev/vdc**
    # **grep vdc /proc/partitions**

Partitioning with the Graphical Disk Utility

Disk Utility is a graphical partition management tool that is available in the GNOME desktop, and it is used to accomplish basic functions on disks, partitions, and file systems. To check whether it is present on the system, use the *yum* command:

    # **yum list installed | grep gnome-disk-utility**
    gnome-disk-utility.x86_64   3.8.2-5.el7   @anaconda/7.0

Install the *gnome-disk-utility* package if this program is not present.

Disk Utility may be launched by running the *gnome-disks* utility at the shell prompt or choosing Applications | Utilities | Disks. Some of the key functions that this tool allows us to perform include creating, modifying, and deleting a partition; formatting, modifying, mounting, unmounting, measuring read/write performance of, and encrypting a file system; and creating and restoring a disk image. Figure 9-3 shows the main menu with *vdc* disk selected.

Figure 9-3 Graphical Disk Utility

The main window lists all block devices on the left-hand side along with their size and type. In Figure 9-3, it shows the main 11GB OS disk, 4x2.1GB disks, a CD/DVD device, and two LVM partitions that exist on the OS disk at the bottom. Upon clicking a device on the left, details associated with that device appear on the right side. For instance, the selected device in Figure 9-3 is an empty 2.1GB *vdc* virtual disk. This device can be partitioned by clicking the + sign and choosing a size, or manipulated by clicking the icon next to the + sign. See Figure 9-4 for options.

Figure 9-4 Graphical Disk Utility / Disk Manipulation Options

Once a partition is created and we highlight it, the grayed out options become visible as necessary, enabling us to perform additional tasks on the partition and file system.

Understanding Logical Volume Manager

The LVM solution is widely used for managing disk storage. It provides an abstraction layer between the physical storage and the file system, enabling the file system to be resized, to span across multiple physical disks, use random disk space, etc. LVM allows us to accumulate spaces taken from one or several partitions or disks (called *physical volumes*) to form a logical container (called *volume group*), which is then divided into logical partitions (called *logical volumes*). Primary benefits that LVM offers include, in addition to the three advantages mentioned above, the resizing of volume groups and logical volumes, online data migration between logical volumes and physical volumes, user-defined naming for volume groups and logical volumes, mirroring and striping across multiple physical disks, and snapshotting of logical volumes. RHEL7 includes version 2 of LVM called *LVM2*, which is the default when we use the LVM technique to carve up storage devices. Figure 9-5 depicts the LVM components.

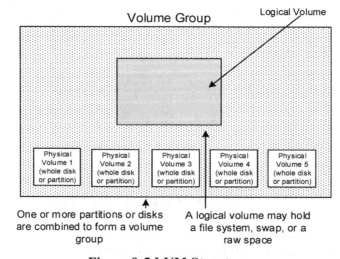

Figure 9-5 LVM Structure

As noted above, the LVM structure is made up of three key objects called physical volume, volume group, and logical volume. These objects are further carved up in *physical extents* (PEs) and *logical extents* (LEs). The LVM components are explained in the following sub-sections.

Physical Volume

A physical volume (PV) is created when a block storage device such as a partition or an entire disk is brought under LVM control after going through the initialization process. This process constructs LVM data structures on the device, including a label on the second sector and metadata information shortly thereafter. The label includes a UUID, device size, and pointers to the locations of data and metadata areas. Given the criticality of metadata, LVM stores a copy of it at the end of the physical volume as well. The rest of the device space is available for use.

Currently, there is one physical volume on *server1*, which was created during the installation. Run the *pvs* command to view it:

```
# pvs
  PV          VG      Fmt    Attr   PSize  PFree
  /dev/vda2   vg00    lvm2   a--    9.50g  4.00m
```

The output confirms the presence of one physical volume */dev/vda2* of size 9.5GB in *vg00* volume group. Additional information displays the metadata format (Fmt) used, status of the physical volume under the Attr column (a for allocatable), and the amount of free space available on the physical volume.

Run this command again with the −v option and it will show you more details.

Volume Group

A volume group (VG) is created when at least one physical volume is added to it. The space from all physical volumes in a volume group is aggregated to form one large pool of storage, which is then used to build one or more logical volumes. The physical volumes added to a volume group may be of varying sizes. LVM writes metadata information for the volume group on each physical volume that is added to it. The volume group metadata contains its name, a unique ID, date and time of creation, how it was created, the extent size used, a list of included physical volumes and their attributes, a list of logical volumes, a mapping of physical and logical extents, etc. A volume group can have any name assigned to it at the time of its creation. For example, it may be called *vg01*, *vgora*, or *vgweb* so as to identify the type of information it is constructed to store. The metadata includes volume group information, and a copy of it is maintained at two locations on each physical volume within the volume group.

Currently, there is one volume group on *server1*, which was created during the installation. Run the *vgs* command to view it:

```
# vgs
  VG       #PV    #LV    #SN    Attr      VSize   VFree
  vg00      1      3      0     wz--n-    9.50g   4.00m
```

The output confirms the existence of one volume group called *vg00* on the system containing one physical volume. Additional information displays the number of logical volumes (LV) and snapshots (SN) in the volume group, status of the volume group under the Attr column (w for writeable, z for resizable, and n for normal), size of the volume group, and the amount of free space available in the volume group.

Run this command again with the –v option and it will show you more details.

Physical Extent

A physical volume is divided into several smaller logical pieces when it is added to a volume group. These logical pieces are known as physical extents (PEs). An extent is the smallest allocatable unit of space in LVM. At the time we create a volume group, we can either define the size of the PE or leave it to the default size of 4MB. This means a 20GB disk would contain approximately 5,000 PEs. Any physical volumes added to this volume group thereafter will use the same PE size.

The following command displays the physical extent size used in the *vg00* volume group:

```
# vgdisplay vg00 | grep 'PE Size'
PE Size       4.00 MiB
```

Logical Volume

A volume group consists of a pool of storage taken from one or more physical volumes. This volume group space is divided into one or more logical partitions called logical volumes (LVs).

A logical volume can be expanded or shrunk, and can use space taken from one or several physical volumes inside the volume group.

The default naming convention for logical volumes is *lvol0, lvol1, lvol2*, and so on; however, we may assign any name that we wish. For example, a logical volume may be called *system, undo*, or *oraarch* so as to identify the type of information that it is constructed to store.

Currently, there are two logical volumes on *server1* that were created during the installation. Run the *lvs* command to view them:

```
# lvs
LV      VG     Attr         LSize    Pool Origin Data% Move Log Cpy%Sync Convert
home    vg00   -wi-ao----   300.00m
root    vg00   -wi-ao----     8.82g
swap    vg00   -wi-ao----   500.00m
```

The output indicates the presence of three logical volumes *home, root*, and *swap* in *vg00* volume group. Additional information displays the status of the logical volumes under the Attr column (w for writeable, i for inherited allocation policy, a for active, and o for open) and their sizes.

Run this command again with the –v option and it will show you more details.

Logical Extent

A logical volume is made up of extents called logical extents (LEs). Logical extents point to physical extents, and they may be random or contiguous. The larger a logical volume is, the more LEs it will have. Logical extents are a set of physical extents allocated to the logical volume.

The PE and LE sizes are usually kept the same within a volume group; however, a logical extent can be smaller or larger than a physical extent. The default LE size is 4MB, which corresponds to the default PE size. The following command displays the information about the *root* logical volume in the *vg00* volume group. The output does not indicate the LE size; however, we can convert the

LV size in MBs and then divide the result by the Current LE count to get the LE size (which comes to 4MB in the following example).

lvdisplay /dev/vg00/root
--- Logical volume ---

LV Path	/dev/vg00/root
LV Name	root
VG Name	vg00
LV UUID	3qq1S7-lXYk-s390-ZdQP-1la6-y7Ka-fcKZ9e
LV Write Access	read/write
LV Creation host, time	localhost.localdomain, 2014-10-21 06:49:04 -0400
LV Status	available
# open	1
LV Size	8.72 GiB
Current LE	2232
Segments	1
Allocation	inherit
Read ahead sectors	auto
- currently set to	256
Block device	253:1

Thin Provisioning

Thin provisioning technology allows for the economical allocation and utilization of storage space. With thin provisioning support in LVM, we can create a *thin pool* of storage space and assign logical volumes larger space than what the pool actually has available. Applications begin consuming the actual space when data writing occurs. We set a threshold (80%, for instance) on the actual consumption of the physical storage in the thin pool, and monitor it. As soon as the actual usage reaches the preset threshold, we expand the thin pool dynamically by adding more physical storage to it. The logical volumes will automatically begin taking advantage of the new space right away. Thin provisioning technique saves us from spending more money upfront.

Managing Storage with Logical Volume Manager

Managing storage with LVM involves several administrative tasks, such as creating a physical volume, creating and displaying a volume group, creating and displaying a logical volume, extending a volume group, extending a logical volume, reducing a logical volume, renaming a logical volume, removing a logical volume, reducing a volume group, removing a volume group, and uninitializing a physical volume. All of these tasks are covered in this chapter.

LVM Commands

There are several commands available to accomplish various LVM operations listed above. Table 9-3 describes the common tools.

Command	Description
Physical Volume Commands	
pvck	Checks the integrity of a physical volume.
pvcreate	Initializes a disk or partition for LVM use.
pvdisplay	Displays details of a physical volume.
pvresize	Resizes a physical volume.

Command	Description
pvmove	Moves data from one physical volume to another.
pvremove	Uninitializes a physical volume.
pvs	Lists physical volumes.
pvscan	Scans the entire system and lists all physical volumes found.
Volume Group Commands	
vgck	Checks the integrity of a volume group.
vgcreate	Creates a volume group.
vgdisplay	Displays the details of a volume group.
vgextend	Adds a physical volume to a volume group.
vgreduce	Removes physical volume from a volume group.
vgrename	Renames a volume group.
vgremove	Removes a volume group.
vgs	Lists volume groups.
vgscan	Scans the entire system and lists all volume groups found, and rebuilds the cache.
Logical Volume Commands	
lvcreate	Creates a logical volume.
lvdisplay	Displays the details of a logical volume.
lvextend	Extends the size of a logical volume.
lvreduce	Reduces the size of a logical volume.
lvremove	Removes a logical volume.
lvrename	Renames a logical volume.
lvresize	Resizes a logical volume. With the –r option, this command calls the resize2fs command and resizes the underlying file system as well.
lvs	Lists logical volumes.
lvscan	Scans the entire system and lists all logical volumes found.
Miscellaneous LVM Commands	
lvm	Interactive LVM management tool.
lvmdiskscan	Scans for existing LVM disks and partitions, and those that can be initialized for use in LVM.

Table 9-3 LVM Commands

All the commands listed in Table 9-3 support the –v option for verbosity. See the man pages of each command for additional options and usage.

As noted earlier in this chapter, you have *vdb*, *vdc*, *vdd*, and *vde* available on *server1* for practice. Issue the *lsblk* command to confirm this information:

```
# lsblk | grep vd
vda                252:0      0      10G   0   disk
├─vda1             252:1      0     500M   0   part   /boot
└─vda2             252:2      0     9.5G   0   part
  ├─vg00-swap      253:0      0     500M   0   lvm    [SWAP]
  ├─vg00-root      253:1      0     8.7G   0   lvm    /
  └─vg00-home      253:2      0     300M   0   lvm    /home
vdb                252:16     0       2G   0   disk
```

vdc	252:32	0	2G	0	disk
vdd	252:48	0	2G	0	disk
vde	252:64	0	2G	0	disk

Execute the *lvmdiskscan* command to identify the disks and partitions that you can use for LVM exercises:

```
# lvmdiskscan
/dev/vg00/swap    [    500.00 MiB]
/dev/vda1         [    500.00 MiB]
/dev/vg00/root    [      8.72 GiB]
/dev/vda2         [      9.51 GiB] LVM physical volume
/dev/vg00/home    [    300.00 MiB]
/dev/vdb          [      2.00 GiB]
/dev/vdc          [      2.00 GiB]
/dev/vdd          [      2.00 GiB]
/dev/vde          [      2.00 GiB]
6 disks
1 partition
0 LVM physical volume whole disks
1 LVM physical volume
```

The above output shows six disks/partitions of which *vda*'s are used for the operating system, and the rest are empty. We can use the four empty disks in the following exercises.

Exercise 9-5: Create a Physical Volume and a Volume Group

This exercise should be done on *server1*.

In this exercise, you will initialize one disk *vdb* (2GB) and one partition *vdc1* (200MB) for use as physical volumes. You will then create a volume group called *vg01* and add both physical volumes to it. You will use the PE size 16MB for the volume group and display the details of the volume group and the physical volumes.

1. Create *vdc1* of size 200MB using *parted* and confirm:

    ```
    # parted /dev/vdc mklabel msdos
    # parted /dev/vdc mkpart primary 1 201m
    # parted /dev/vdc print
    ```

Number	Start	End	Size	File system	Name	Flags
1	1049kB	201MB	200MB		primary	

2. Initialize *vdb* and *vdc1* using the *pvcreate* command:

---

pvcreate –v /dev/vdb /dev/vdc1
    Set up physical volume for "/dev/vdb" with 4194304 available sectors
    Zeroing start of device /dev/vdb
    Writing physical volume data to disk "/dev/vdb"
  Physical volume "/dev/vdb" successfully created
    Set up physical volume for "/dev/vdc1" with 391168 available sectors
    Zeroing start of device /dev/vdc1
    Writing physical volume data to disk "/dev/vdc1"
  Physical volume "/dev/vdc1" successfully created

EXAM TIP: Use lsblk to determine available disk space.

---

3. Create *vg01* volume group using the *vgcreate* command and add *vdb* and *vdc1* physical volumes to it. Use the –s option to specify the PE size in MBs.

    # vgcreate –s 16 vg01 /dev/vdb /dev/vdc1 –v
        Adding physical volume '/dev/vdb' to volume group 'vg01'
        Adding physical volume '/dev/vdc1' to volume group 'vg01'
        Archiving volume group "vg01" metadata (seqno 0).
        Creating volume group backup "/etc/lvm/backup/vg01" (seqno 1).
      Volume group "vg01" successfully created

4. Display basic information for *vg01* using the *vgs* and *vgscan* commands:

    # vgs vg01
      VG   #PV   #LV   #SN   Attr   VSize   VFree
      vg01   2   0   0   wz--n-   2.16g   2.16g
    # vgscan
      Reading all physical volumes. This may take a while...
      Found volume group "vg00" using metadata type lvm2
      Found volume group "vg01" using metadata type lvm2

We can also display the details for the volume group with the *vgdisplay* command. With the –v switch, this command also shows the physical volumes in it:

    # vgdisplay –v vg01
      --- Volume group ---
      VG Name   vg01
      System ID
      Format   lvm2
      Metadata Areas   2
      Metadata Sequence No   1
      VG Access   read/write
      VG Status   resizable
      MAX LV   0
      Cur LV   0
      Open LV   0
      Max PV   0

Cur PV	2
Act PV	2
VG Size	2.16 GiB
PE Size	16.00 MiB
Total PE	138
Alloc PE / Size	0 / 0
Free PE / Size	138 / 2.16 GiB
VG UUID	SXTjT1-xtrH-MtGg-U9Kl-aWgq-HEFc-55Hxdo

--- Physical volumes ---

PV Name	/dev/vdb
PV UUID	8cVKkL-VGQm-MW7Z-hnTZ-WS2m-M7LG-mKmw0F
PV Status	allocatable
Total PE / Free PE	127 / 127
PV Name	/dev/vdc1
PV UUID	qBtEPJ-Pb7p-AJf0-zDZX-RGeS-SmrH-IlHE6a
PV Status	allocatable
Total PE / Free PE	11 / 11

The *vgdisplay* command shows that there are two physical volumes in *vg01* volume group, with 127 PEs in the first physical volume and 11 in the second, totaling 138. The PE size is 16MB and total usable space is about 2.16GB.

5. Display basic information for *vdb* using the *pvs* and *pvscan* commands:

```
# pvs
PV          VG       Fmt      Attr     PSize      PFree
/dev/vda2   vg00     lvm2     a--      9.50g      4.00m
/dev/vdb    vg01     lvm2     a--      1.98g      1.98g
/dev/vdc1   vg01     lvm2     a--      176.00m    176.00m
# pvscan
PV  /dev/vda2  VG   vg00     lvm2     [9.50 GiB / 4.00 MiB free]
PV  /dev/vdb   VG   vg01     lvm2     [1.98 GiB / 1.98 GiB free]
PV  /dev/vdc1  VG   vg01     lvm2     [176.00 MiB / 176.00 MiB free]
Total:  3 [11.66 GiB]  /  in use: 3 [11.66 GiB]  /  in no VG: 0 [0  ]
```

We can also display the details for the physical volumes with the *pvdisplay* command:

```
# pvdisplay /dev/vdb
--- Physical volume ---
```

PV Name	/dev/vdb
VG Name	vg01
PV Size	2.00 GiB / not usable 16.00 MiB
Allocatable	yes
PE Size	16.00 MiB
Total PE	127
Free PE	127
Allocated PE	0
PV UUID	8cVKkL-VGQm-MW7Z-hnTZ-WS2m-M7LG-mKmw0F

pvdisplay /dev/vdc1

PV Name	/dev/vdc1
VG Name	vg01
PV Size	191.00 MiB / not usable 15.00 MiB
Allocatable	yes
PE Size	16.00 MiB
Total PE	11
Free PE	11
Allocated PE	0
PV UUID	qBtEPJ-Pb7p-AJf0-zDZX-RGeS-SmrH-IlHE6a

Once a disk or a partition is initialized and added to a volume group, both are treated identically. LVM does not differentiate between the two.

Exercise 9-6: Create a Logical Volume

This exercise should be done on *server1*.

In this exercise, you will create two logical volumes called *lvol0* and *oravol* in *vg01* volume group. You will use 600MB for *lvol0* and 1.3GB for *oravol* from the available pool of space. You will display the details of the volume group and the logical volumes.

1. Create *lvol0* of size 600MB using the *lvcreate* command. Use the –L option to specify the logical volume size. You may want to use the –v, –vv, or –vvv option with the command for verbosity.

   # **lvcreate –L 600 vg01 –v**
       Setting logging type to disk
       Finding volume group "vg01"
     Rounding up size to full physical extent 608.00 MiB
       Archiving volume group "vg01" metadata (seqno 7).
       Creating logical volume lvol0
       Creating volume group backup "/etc/lvm/backup/vg01" (seqno 8).
       Activating logical volume "lvol0".
       activation/volume_list configuration setting not defined: Checking only host tags for vg01/lvol0
       Creating vg01-lvol0
       Loading vg01-lvol0 table (253:4)
       Resuming vg01-lvol0 (253:4)
       Wiping known signatures on logical volume "vg01/lvol0"
       Initializing 4.00 KiB of logical volume "vg01/lvol0" with value 0.
       Creating volume group backup "/etc/lvm/backup/vg01" (seqno 8).
     Logical volume "lvol0" created

   The size may be specified in KBs (kilobytes), MBs (megabytes), GBs (gigabytes), TBs (terabytes), PBs (petabytes), EBs (exabytes), bytes, sectors, or a count of LEs; however, MB is the default if no unit is specified. The minimum size of a logical volume is the size of a PE set at the time of volume group creation, and it is always in multiples of the PE size. For instance, logical volumes that we can create in *vg01* with the PE size set at 16MB will be 16MB, 32MB, 48MB, 64MB, and so on; it cannot be any other size. Therefore, care must be taken when setting the PE size and creating logical volumes to avoid wasting space.

2. Create *oravol* of size 1.3GB using the *lvcreate* command. Use the –L option to specify the size and –n for the custom name. You may use –v for verbose information.

> # **lvcreate –L 1.3g –n oravol vg01**
>
> Rounding up size to full physical extent 1.31 GiB
> Logical volume "oravol" created

3. Display basic information for the two logical volumes using the *lvs* and *lvscan* commands:

> # **lvs**
>
> | LV | VG | Attr | LSize | Pool Origin Data% Move Log Cpy%Sync Convert |
> |----|----|------|-------|---|
> | home | vg00 | -wi-ao---- | 300.00m | |
> | root | vg00 | -wi-ao---- | 8.72g | |
> | swap | vg00 | -wi-ao---- | 500.00m | |
> | lvol0 | vg01 | -wi-a----- | 608.00m | |
> | oravol | vg01 | -wi-a----- | 1.31g | |
>
> # **lvscan**
>
> | | | | |
> |--|--|--|--|
> | ACTIVE | '/dev/vg00/swap' | [500.00 MiB] | inherit |
> | ACTIVE | '/dev/vg00/home' | [300.00 MiB] | inherit |
> | ACTIVE | '/dev/vg00/root' | [8.72 GiB] | inherit |
> | ACTIVE | '/dev/vg01/lvol0' | [608.00 MiB] | inherit |
> | ACTIVE | '/dev/vg01/oravol' | [1.31 GiB] | inherit |

Execute the *vgdisplay* command on *vg01* with the –v option to get details for the entire volume group including the logical volumes and the physical volumes it holds. You can also run the *lvdisplay* command on */dev/vg01/lvol0* and */dev/vg01/oravol* to obtain the details for the two logical volumes.

> # **lvdisplay /dev/vg01/lvol0**
>
> --- Logical volume ---
>
> | | |
> |--|--|
> | LV Path | /dev/vg01/lvol0 |
> | LV Name | lvol0 |
> | VG Name | vg01 |
> | LV UUID | e2c5W3-TLkU-0V6q-l8pg-dfFl-R0X8-Rd8UVT |
> | LV Write Access | read/write |
> | LV Creation host, time | server1.example.com, 2014-10-23 21:45:18 -0400 |
> | LV Status | available |
> | # open | 0 |
> | LV Size | 608.00 MiB |
> | Current LE | 38 |
> | Segments | 1 |
> | Allocation | inherit |
> | Read ahead sectors | auto |
> | - currently set to | 8192 |
> | Block device | 253:2 |

If you want to understand where the *vgdisplay* command gets volume group information from, go to the */etc/lvm/backup* directory and view the contents of the desired volume group file.

Exercise 9-7: Extend a Volume Group and a Logical Volume

This exercise should be done on *server1*.

In this exercise, you will add another disk *vdd* to *vg01* to increase the pool of allocatable space. You will run the *pvcreate* command to initialize the target disk prior to adding it to the volume group. You will increase the size of *lvol0* from 600MB to 1GB and that of *oravol* from 1.3GB to 2GB using the *lvextend* command. You will display basic and detailed information for the volume group and the logical volumes.

1. Prepare */dev/vdd* for use in LVM using the *pvcreate* command:

    # pvcreate /dev/vdd –v
        Set up physical volume for "/dev/vdd" with 4194304 available sectors
        Zeroing start of device /dev/vdd
        Writing physical volume data to disk "/dev/vdd"
    Physical volume "/dev/vdd" successfully created

2. Add */dev/vdd* to *vg01* using the *vgextend* command:

    # vgextend vg01 /dev/vdd –v
        Checking for volume group "vg01"
        Archiving volume group "vg01" metadata (seqno 1).
        Adding physical volume '/dev/vdd' to volume group 'vg01'
        Volume group "vg01" will be extended by 1 new physical volumes
        Creating volume group backup "/etc/lvm/backup/vg01" (seqno 2).
    Volume group "vg01" successfully extended

3. View basic information of *vg01*:

    # vgs vg01

VG	#PV	#LV	#SN	Attr	VSize	VFree
vg01	3	2	0	wz--n-	4.14g	2.23g

    The output reflects the addition of a third physical volume to *vg01*. The total capacity for the volume group has now increased to 4.14GB, with 2.23GB free.

4. Execute the *lvextend* command on *lvol0* and specify either the absolute desired size for the logical volume or the additional amount you wish to add to it:

    # lvextend –L 1g /dev/vg01/lvol0 (or lvextend –L +400m /dev/vg01/lvol0)
        Extending logical volume lvol0 to 1.00 GiB
        Logical volume lvol0 successfully resized

5. Execute the *lvresize* command on *oravol* and specify either the absolute desired size for the logical volume or the additional amount you wish to add to it:

 # lvresize –L 2g /dev/vg01/oravol (or lvresize –L +700m /dev/vg01/oravol)
Rounding size to boundary between physical extents: 704.00 MiB
Extending logical volume oravol to 2.00 GiB
Logical volume oravol successfully resized

EXAM TIP: Make sure the expansion of a logical volume does not affect the file system and the data it contains.

---

6. Issue *vgdisplay* on *vg01* with the –v switch for the updated details:

 # vgdisplay –v vg01
```
--- Volume group ---
VG Name                vg01
System ID
Format                 lvm2
Metadata Areas         3
Metadata Sequence No   55
VG Access              read/write
VG Status              resizable
MAX LV                 0
Cur LV                 2
Open LV                0
Max PV                 0
Cur PV                 3
Act PV                 3
VG Size                4.14 GiB
PE Size                16.00 MiB
Total PE               265
Alloc PE / Size        192 / 3.00 GiB
Free  PE / Size        73 / 1.14 GiB
VG UUID                SXTjT1-xtrH-MtGg-U9Kl-aWgq-HEFc-55Hxdo
--- Logical volume ---
LV Path                /dev/vg01/lvol0
LV Name                lvol0
VG Name                vg01
LV UUID                e2c5W3-TLkU-0V6q-l8pg-dfFl-R0X8-Rd8UVT
LV Write Access        read/write
LV Creation host, time server1.example.com, 2014-10-23 21:45:18 -0400
LV Status              available
# open                 0
LV Size                1.00 GiB
Current LE             64
Segments               3
Allocation             inherit
Read ahead sectors     auto
- currently set to     8192
Block device           253:2
```

```
--- Logical volume ---
LV Path                      /dev/vg01/oravol
LV Name                      oravol
VG Name                      vg01
LV UUID                      JeQF6O-ReLp-eg4z-wjZh-ufdf-aqAL-1efXgL
LV Write Access              read/write
LV Creation host, time       server1.example.com, 2014-10-24 07:45:35 -0400
LV Status                    available
# open                       0
LV Size                      2.00 GiB
Current LE                   128
Segments                     2
Allocation                   inherit
Read ahead sectors           auto
- currently set to           8192
Block device                 253:3
--- Physical volumes ---
PV Name                      /dev/vdb
PV UUID                      8cVKkL-VGQm-MW7Z-hnTZ-WS2m-M7LG-mKmw0F
PV Status                    allocatable
Total PE / Free PE           127 / 0
PV Name                      /dev/vdc1
PV UUID                      qBtEPJ-Pb7p-AJf0-zDZX-RGeS-SmrH-IlHE6a
PV Status                    allocatable
Total PE / Free PE           11 / 11
PV Name                      /dev/vdd
PV UUID                      2MWF1s-QGyj-Msb8-pi41-J226-Cfel-hC3cQ4
PV Status                    allocatable
Total PE / Free PE           127 / 62
```

The above output shows a lot of information about the volume group and the logical and physical volumes it contains. It reflects the updates made in this exercise. In fact, each time a volume group or a logical volume in it is resized, the *vgdisplay* command output reflects those updates. The above output shows three physical volumes with the combined allocatable space grown to 4.14GB. The number of PEs have increased to 265, with 192 allocated to logical volumes and 73 unused. The unused PEs amounts to 1.14GB of free space in the pool. The two Logical Volume sections display the updated information for the logical volumes. And at the very bottom, all three physical volumes are listed with their device names and total and available PEs in each.

Exercise 9-8: Rename, Reduce, and Remove a Logical Volume

This exercise should be done on *server1*.

In this exercise, you will rename *lvol0* to *lvolnew*. You will decrease the size of *lvolnew* to 800MB using the *lvreduce* command and then further reduce its size to 700MB with the *lvresize* command. You will then remove *oravol* and *lvolnew* logical volumes with the *lvremove* command. You will display the updated details for the volume group.

1. Rename *lvol0* to *lvolnew* using the *lvrename* command and confirm with *lvs*:

```
# lvrename vg01 lvol0 lvolnew
    Renamed "lvol0" to "lvolnew" in volume group "vg01"
# lvs | grep lvolnew
    lvolnew  vg01  -wi-a-----  1.00g
```

2. Reduce the size of *lvol0* logical volume to 800MB with the *lvreduce* command. Specify either the absolute desired size for the logical volume or the amount that you wish to subtract from it. Answer "Do you really want to reduce lvolnew?" in the affirmative.

```
# lvreduce –L 800m /dev/vg01/lvolnew (or lvreduce –L –200m /dev/vg01/lvolnew)
    WARNING: Reducing active logical volume to 800.00 MiB
    THIS MAY DESTROY YOUR DATA (filesystem etc.)
  Do you really want to reduce lvolnew? [y/n]: y
    Reducing logical volume lvolnew to 800.00 MiB
    Logical volume lvolnew successfully resized
```

3. Reduce the size of *lvolnew* logical volume to 700MB with the *lvresize* command. Specify either the absolute desired size for the logical volume or the amount that you wish to subtract from it. Answer "Do you really want to reduce lvolnew?" in the affirmative.

```
# lvresize –L 700m /dev/vg01/lvolnew (or lvresize –L –100m /dev/vg01/lvolnew)
    Rounding size to boundary between physical extents: 96.00 MiB
    WARNING: Reducing active logical volume to 704.00 MiB
    THIS MAY DESTROY YOUR DATA (filesystem etc.)
  Do you really want to reduce lvolnew? [y/n]: y
    Reducing logical volume lvolnew to 704.00 MiB
    Logical volume lvolnew successfully resized
```

There is risk involved when you reduce the size of a logical volume. You may end up losing data that is located on the logical extents being removed. To be on the safe side, perform a backup of the data in the logical volume before proceeding with size reduction.

4. Remove *lvolnew* and *oravol* logical volumes with the *lvremove* command. Use the –f option to suppress the "Do you really want to remove active logical volume <lvol_name>" message.

```
# lvremove –f /dev/vg01/lvolnew
    Logical volume "lvolnew" successfully removed
# lvremove –f /dev/vg01/oravol
    Logical volume "oravol" successfully removed
```

Removing a logical volume is a destructive task. You need to ensure that you perform a backup of any data in the target logical volume prior to deleting it. You will need to unmount the file system or disable swap in the logical volume. See Chapter 10 "Constructing and Using File Systems and Swap" on how to unmount a file system and disable swap.

5. Execute the *vgdisplay* command and *grep* for "Cur LV" to see the number of logical volumes currently available in *vg01*. It should show 0, as you have removed both logical volumes.

> **# vgdisplay vg01 | grep 'Cur LV'**
> Cur LV   0

Exercise 9-9: Reduce and Remove a Volume Group

This exercise should be done on *server1*.

In this exercise, you will reduce *vg01* by removing *vdb* and *vdc1* physical volumes from it using the *vgreduce* command, and then remove the volume group.

1. Remove *vdb* and *vdc1* physical volumes from *vg01* by issuing the *vgreduce* command:

> **# vgreduce vg01 /dev/vdb /dev/vdc1**
> Removed "/dev/vdb" from volume group "vg01"
> Removed "/dev/vdc1" from volume group "vg01"

2. Remove the volume group using the *vgremove* command. This will also remove the last physical volume from it.

> **# vgremove vg01**
> Volume group "vg01" successfully removed

 You can also use the –f option with the *vgremove* command to force the volume group removal even if it contains any number of logical and physical volumes.

 Remember to proceed with caution whenever you perform reduce and remove operations.

Exercise 9-10: Uninitialize a Physical Volume

This exercise should be done on *server1*.

In this exercise, you will uninitialize all three physical volumes *vdb*, *vdc1*, and *vdd* by deleting the LVM structural information from them using the *pvremove* command.

1. Issue the *pvremove* command on *vdb*, *vdc1*, and *vdd* physical volumes to uninitialize them:

> **# pvremove /dev/vdb /dev/vdc1 /dev/vdd**
> Labels on physical volume "/dev/vdb" successfully wiped
> Labels on physical volume "/dev/vdc1" successfully wiped
> Labels on physical volume "/dev/vdd" successfully wiped

The disks and the partition are now back to their raw state and can be repurposed or removed from *server1*.

Chapter Summary

This chapter started with an overview of disk management tools available in RHEL7 and features and benefits associated with them. Later, it presented several exercises for slicing and managing disks using these tools.

We performed functions such as creating, displaying, and deleting partitions using the parted and gdisk utilities. We looked at the graphical Disk Utility that may be used to perform several disk management tasks.

We learned the concepts, components, and structure of LVM at length. We learned how to perform LVM management tasks using commands, and strengthen our understanding by performing several exercises including converting disks and partitions into physical volumes; creating, displaying, extending, reducing, and removing volume groups; creating, displaying, extending, reducing, and removing logical volumes; and uninitializing physical volumes.

Chapter Review Questions

1. What are the two commands that we can use to reduce the number of logical extents from a logical volume?
2. Write the command to add physical volumes */dev/vdd1* and */dev/vdc* to *vg20* volume group.
3. Where is the partition table information stored by default on BIOS-based systems?
4. What would *vdd3* represent in a virtualized environment?
5. What are the two commands that we can use to add logical extents to a logical volume?
6. What is the maximum number of partitions that can be created on a GPT disk?
7. Write the command to create a volume group called *vg20* with physical extent size set to 64MB and include a physical volume */dev/vdd* to the volume group.
8. Write the command to remove *vg20* volume group along with any logical and physical volumes that it contains.
9. What is the default size of a physical extent in LVM?
10. The *gdisk* utility can be used to store partition information in MBR format. True or False?
11. Which file in the */proc* file system stores the in-memory partitioning information?
12. What is the default name of the first logical volume in a volume group?
13. What is one difference between the *pvs* and *pvdisplay* commands?
14. When can a disk or partition be referred to as a physical volume?
15. Write the command to remove *webvol* logical volume from *vg20* volume group.
16. It is necessary to create file system structures in a logical volume before it can be used to store files in it. True or False?
17. Physical and logical extents are typically of the same size. True or False?
18. What is the purpose of the *pvremove* command?
19. What would the command *pvcreate /dev/vdd* do?
20. A disk or partition can be added to a volume group without being initialized. True or False?
21. Write the command to create a logical volume called *webvol* of size equal to 100 logical extents in *vg20* volume group.
22. A volume group can be created without any physical volume in it. True or False?
23. Where does the LVM store volume group details?
24. A single disk can be used by both parted and LVM at the same time. True or False?
25. When should we run the *partprobe* command?
26. Write the command to remove */dev/vdd1* physical volume from *vg20* volume group.
27. A partition can be used as an LVM object. True or False?

---

28. Which command would we use to view the details of a volume group and logical and physical volumes within it?

Answers to Chapter Review Questions

1. The *lvreduce* and the *lvresize* commands.
2. *vgextend vg20 /dev/vdd1 /dev/vdc*
3. The partition table information is stored on the Master Boot Record.
4. *vdd3* points to the third partition on the fourth virtual disk.
5. The *lvextend* and the *lvresize* commands.
6. 128.
7. *vgcreate –s 64 vg20 /dev/vdd*
8. *vgremove –f vg20*
9. The default size of a PE in LVM is 4MB.
10. False. The *gdisk* tool is only for GPT type tables.
11. The *partitions* file.
12. *lvol0* is the default name for the first logical volume created in a volume group.
13. The *pvs* command lists the physical volumes, whereas the *pvdisplay* command displays the details.
14. After the *pvcreate* command has been executed on it successfully.
15. *lvremove /dev/vg20/webvol*
16. True, it is mandatory.
17. True.
18. The *pvremove* command is used to uninitialize a physical volume.
19. This command will initialize the */dev/vdd* disk for use in a volume group.
20. False, a disk or partition must be initialized before it can be added to a volume group.
21. *lvcreate –l 100 –n webvol vg20*
22. False.
23. In the */etc/lvm/backup* directory.
24. True, a single disk can be used by all three disk management solutions at a time.
25. The *partprobe* command should be run whenever partitioning is modified on a disk.
26. *vgreduce vg20 /dev/vdd1*
27. True.
28. The *vgdisplay* command with the –v option.

DIY Challenge Labs

The following labs are useful to strengthen most of the concepts and topics learned in this chapter. It is expected that you perform these labs without any additional help. A step-by-step guide is not provided, as the implementation of these labs requires the knowledge that has been presented in this chapter. Use defaults or your own thinking for missing information.

Lab 9-1: Manage Partitioning with parted

Create three 100MB primary partitions on */dev/vdd* using the *parted* utility and set appropriate flags to use them as a file system, a swap space, and an LVM partition, respectively.

Lab 9-2: Manage Partitioning with gdisk

Create three 50MB partitions on */dev/vdc* using the *gdisk* utility and set appropriate flags to use them as a file system, a swap space, and an LVM partition, respectively.

Lab 9-3: Manage Storage with LVM

Initialize *vdb* and *vdc* disks for use in LVM. Create a volume group called *vg10* and add both physical volumes to it. Ensure that *vg10* uses 32MB as the physical extent size. Add three logical volumes called *lvol0*, *swapvol*, and *oravol* to the volume group with sizes 1GB, 2.2GB, and 500MB, respectively. Create *vdd4* and *vdd5* partitions of size 1GB each and initialize them for use in LVM. Add both new physical volumes to *vg10*. Create an additional logical volume called *lvol1* using 30 LEs. Add 200MB to *oravol* logical volume and remove 150MB from *lvol0*.

## Chapter 10

Constructing and Using File Systems and Swap

This chapter describes the following major topics:

➢ Overview of file systems

➢ Types of file systems

➢ Manage extended and xfs file systems including creating, mounting, determining UUID, labeling, reporting usage, resizing, unmounting, and removing

➢ Create and mount vfat file system

➢ Check and repair extended and xfs file system structures

➢ Mount and unmount CIFS and NFS file systems

➢ Mount and unmount NFS file systems automatically

➢ Understand and manage swap spaces including creating, activating, deactivating, and removing them

➢ Set, view, and unset enhanced file permissions with Access Control Lists

RHCSA Objectives:

23. Configure systems to mount file systems at boot by UUID or label
24. Add new partitions and logical volumes, and swap to a system non-destructively
25. Create, mount, unmount, and use vfat, ext4, and xfs file systems
26. Mount and unmount CIFS and NFS network file systems
29. Create and manage Access Control Lists (ACLs)

A file system is a logical container that is used to store files and directories. Each file system must be connected to the root of the directory hierarchy in order to be accessible. This is typically done automatically when the system boots up; however, it can be done manually as well. Each file system can be mounted or unmounted by using the unique UUID associated with it or by using a label that can be assigned to it. The file system space may fill up quickly, depending on the usage; there are tools that help keep an eye on their utilization. A file system may become corrupted if it is not properly unmounted due to a system crash or other similar reasons. It is necessary to check and repair any issues arising out of such situations.

Remote file systems may be mounted (and unmounted) on a RHEL system and accessed in a similar fashion as a local file system. This can be done manually using the same tools that are used for mounting and unmounting local file systems. Alternatively, RHEL provides the AutoFS service that may be configured to mount entire remote file systems or individual directories located in remote file systems automatically without having to execute any commands explicitly.

Swapping and paging are used on every Linux system. In fact, a RHEL installation cannot proceed unless a swap space is defined. Swapping and paging provide a mechanism to move pages of data from the physical memory to the swap region and back as and when required.

ACLs allow the administrator to enforce extended security attributes on a file or directory. These attributes are in addition to the existing Linux access rights. A directory can have default ACL settings applied to it to allow multiple users to share its contents without having to change permissions on new files and sub-directories created within it.

Understanding File Systems

A *file system* is a logical container that is used to store files and directories. Each file system is created in a separate partition or logical volume. A typical RHEL system usually has numerous file systems. During OS installation, only two file systems are created by default: / and */boot*, though we can choose custom partitioning and construct separate containers to store dissimilar information. Typical additional file systems created during the installation are */home*, */opt*, */tmp*, */usr*, and */var*. / and */boot* are two mandatory file systems without which a system cannot be installed or booted.

Storing disparate data in separate file systems versus storing all data in a single file system offers the following advantages. We can:

- ✓ Make a specific file system accessible or inaccessible to users independent of other file systems on the system. This hides or reveals information contained in that file system.
- ✓ Perform file system repair activities on individual file systems.
- ✓ Keep dissimilar data in separate file systems.
- ✓ Optimize or tune each file system independently.
- ✓ Grow or shrink a file system independent of other file systems.

Moreover, some native backup tools such as *xfsdump* work only at the file system level.

Types of File System

There are several different types of file systems supported in RHEL that may be categorized in three basic groups: *disk-based*, *network-based*, and *memory-based*. Disk-based file systems are typically created on hard drives using SCSI, iSCSI, SAS, SATA, USB, Fibre Channel, and other technologies. Network-based file systems are basically disk-based file systems shared over the network for remote access. Memory-based file systems are virtual; they are created automatically at system startup and destroyed when the system goes down. The first two types of file systems store information persistently, while any data saved in virtual file systems is lost at system reboots. Table 10-1 lists and explains various common disk- and network-based file system types supported in RHEL7.

File System	Type	Description
ext2	Disk	The second generation of the extended file system. The first generation is no longer supported. ext2 is deprecated in RHEL7 and will be removed in a future RHEL release.
ext3	Disk	The third generation of the extended file system. It supports metadata journaling for faster recovery, offers superior reliability, supports file systems of sizes up to 16TiB, files of sizes up to 2TiB, and up to 32,000 sub-directories. ext3 writes each metadata update in its entirety to the journal after it has been completed. The system looks in the file system journal following a reboot after a system crash has occurred, and recovers the file system rapidly using the updated structural information stored in its journal.
ext4	Disk	The fourth generation of the extended file system developed as the successor to ext3. It supports all features of ext3 in addition to a larger file system size of up to 1EiB, a bigger file size of up to 16TiB, an unlimited number of sub-directories, metadata and quota journaling, and extended user attributes. ext4 uses a series of contiguous physical blocks on the hard disk called extents, resulting in improved read and write performance with reduced fragmentation.
xfs	Disk	XFS is a highly scalable and high-performance 64-bit file system. It supports metadata journaling for faster crash recovery, and online defragmentation, expansion, quota journaling, and extended user attributes. xfs is the default file system type in RHEL7. It supports file systems and files of sizes up to 8EiB.
btrfs	Disk	B-tree file system is introduced in RHEL7 as a technology preview. It supports a file system size of up to 50TiB. It is capable of addressing and managing more files, larger files, and larger volumes than ext4. It supports snapshotting and compression capabilities.
vfat	Disk	This is used for post-Windows 95 file system formats on hard disks, USB drives, and floppy disks.
iso9660	Disk	This is used for CD/DVD-based optical file systems.
BIOS Boot	Disk	A very small partition required for booting a device with a GUID partition table (GPT) on a BIOS system.
EFI System Partition	Disk	A small partition required for booting a device with a GUID partition table (GPT) on a UEFI system.
NFS	Network	Network File System. A directory or file system shared over the network for access by other Linux systems.
AutoFS	Network	Auto File System. An NFS file system set to mount and unmount automatically on a remote system.

File System	Type	Description
CIFS	Network	Common Internet File System (a.k.a. Samba). A directory or file system shared over the network for access by Windows and other Linux systems.

Table 10-1 File System Types

This chapter covers ext3, ext4, xfs, and vfat file systems at length. It also covers mounting and unmounting iso9660, CIFS, and NFS file systems. For a brief discussion on memory-based virtual file systems, see Chapter 03 "Working with Files and File Permissions". The rest of the file system types mentioned in Table 10-1 are beyond the scope of this book.

Extended File Systems

Extended file systems have been supported in RHEL for years. The first generation is obsolete and is no longer supported. The second generation is deprecated in RHEL7 and will be removed in a future release. The third generation has been part of RHEL for a long period of time. It was the first in the series that supported the *journaling* mechanism. The fourth generation is the latest in the series and is superior with respect to features and enhancements to the previous generations.

The structure of an extended file system is built on a partition or logical volume at the time of file system creation. This structure is divided into two sets. The first set holds the file system's metadata information and it is very tiny. The second set stores the actual data and it occupies almost the entire partition or the logical volume space.

The metadata includes the *superblock*, which keeps vital file system structural information, such as the type, size, and status of the file system, and the number of data blocks it contains. Since the superblock holds such critical information, it is automatically replicated and maintained at various locations throughout the file system. The superblock at the beginning of the file system is referred to as the *primary superblock*, and all its copies as *backup superblocks*. If, for any reason, the primary superblock is corrupted or lost, it renders the file system inaccessible. One of the backup superblocks is then used to replace the corrupted or lost primary superblock to bring the file system back to its normal state. The metadata also contains the *inode table*, which maintains a list of *index node* (inode) numbers. Each inode number is assigned to a file when the file is created, and holds the file attributes such as its type, permissions, ownership, group membership, size, and last access/modification time. The inode also holds and keeps track of the pointers to the actual data blocks where the file contents are located.

The ext3 and ext4 file systems support a journaling mechanism that provides them the ability to recover swiftly after a system crash. Both ext3 and ext4 file systems keep track of their structural (metadata) changes in a *journal* (or log). Each structural update is written in its entirety to the journal after completion. The system checks the journal of each extended file system following the reboot after a crash, and recovers the file system rapidly using the latest structural information stored in its journal.

In contrast with ext3, the ext4 file system supports very large file systems of sizes up to 1EiB (ExbiByte) and files of sizes up to 16TiB (TebiByte). Additionally, ext4 uses a series of contiguous physical blocks on the hard disk called *extents*. This technique improves the performance of very large files and reduces fragmentation. ext4 supports both extended user attributes and acl mount options, but neither of them is active by default.

XFS File System

The *X File System* (XFS) is a high-performance 64-bit extent-based journaling file system type that was originally developed by Silicon Graphics a little over two decades ago, and was used as the default file system in their version of UNIX. Later, it was ported to Linux. Today, it is supported on most Linux distributions, including RHEL7 that has it as the default file system type. XFS allows the creation of file systems and files of sizes up to 8EiB. It does not run file system checks at system boot; rather it relies on us to use the *xfs_repair* utility manually to fix any issues if found. XFS sets the extended user attributes and acl mount options by default on new file systems. It enables defragmentation on mounted and active file systems to keep as much data in contiguous blocks as possible for faster access. The only major caveat with using XFS is its inability to shrink.

Like ext3 and ext4, XFS also uses journaling for metadata operations, guaranteeing the consistency of the file system against abnormal or forced unmounting. The journal information is read and any pending metadata transactions are replayed when the XFS file system is remounted.

XFS uses some techniques in its architecture for speedy IO performance. These techniques include the use of allocation groups, direct IO, guaranteed rate IO, and delayed allocation. Allocation groups are fixed-sized virtual storage regions that allow concurrent read and write access to the file system especially for file systems that span multiple physical disks; direct IO sends file system data directly to the application memory space circumventing both processor and cache memory; guaranteed rate IO ensures dedicated bandwidth to and from the file system; and delayed allocation reserves file system blocks for data that is still in cache and allocates them when the operating system writes that data to disk.

The XFS file system can be snapshot while it is mounted and active. The snapshot thus produced can then be mounted for backup or other purposes.

VFAT File System

VFAT stands for *Virtual File Allocation Table*. It is an extension to the legacy FAT file system type that was introduced in 1981 with very early versions of MS-DOS. The support for FAT was later added to Microsoft Windows, Mac OS, and some UNIX versions, enabling them to read and write files written in that format. The FAT file system had limitations, however, it was designed to use not more than 11 characters, excluding the period, in filenames. Moreover, the names of files stored in FAT file systems must begin with a letter or number and were not allowed to contain spaces. The FAT file system treated lowercase and uppercase letters alike.

VFAT was introduced with Microsoft Windows 95 in 1995. It supported 255 characters in filenames including spaces and periods; however, it still did not differentiate between lowercase and uppercase letters. VFAT support was added to Linux and it is still supported. RHEL7 is able to read and write files written in this format. VFAT is used on systems running Windows operating systems, and on floppy and USB flash media.

Managing File Systems

Managing file systems involves such operations as creating (or formatting), manually mounting, labeling, viewing, growing, shrinking, unmounting, automatically mounting, modifying attributes of, and removing a file system. These management tasks are common to all three file system types discussed in the previous section. Some of these administrative functions are also applicable to network and optical file systems, and will be covered later in this chapter.

File System Administration Commands

There are several commands available to administer specific file systems such as Extended, XFS, and VFAT. Table 10-2 describes them. This table also lists commands that are common to these three file systems and are equally good for NFS and ISO9660.

Command	Description
Extended File System	
dumpe2fs	Displays metadata information.
e2fsck	Checks a file system for metadata consistency, and repairs it. Can also be invoked as fsck.ext3, fsck.ext4, fsck –t ext3, and fsck –t ext4.
e2label	Modifies the label of an extended file system.
mke2fs	Creates a file system. Can also be invoked as mkfs.ext3, mkfs.ext4, mkfs –t ext3, and mkfs –t ext4.
resize2fs	Resizes a file system. This command may also be invoked when the lvresize command is executed with the –r option.
tune2fs	Tunes file system attributes.
XFS	
mkfs.xfs	Creates an XFS file system.
xfs_admin	Tunes file system attributes.
xfs_growfs	Extends the size of a file system.
xfs_info	Displays information about a file system.
xfs_repair	Checks consistency of a file system and repairs it if necessary.
VFAT	
mkfs.vfat	Creates a vfat file system. It is equivalent to mkfs –t vfat.
Commands Common to All File Systems	
blkid	Displays block device attributes including their UUIDs.
df	Displays file system utilization in detail.
du	Calculates disk usage of directories and file systems.
findmnt	Lists all mounted file systems in tree form. Use –t to view specific file system type only.
fuser	Lists and terminates processes using a file system.
mount	Mounts a file system for user access, and also displays currently mounted file systems. Use –t to view specific file system type only.
umount	Unmounts a file system.

Table 10-2 File System Management Commands

Most of these commands will be used in this and subsequent chapters.

Mounting and Unmounting a File System

The *mount* command is used to attach a file system to a desired point in the directory hierarchy to make it accessible to users and applications. This desired point is referred to as the *mount point*, which is in essence an empty directory created solely for this purpose. The *mount* command requires the absolute pathname (or its UUID or label) to the block device containing the file system, and a mount point name in order to attach it to the directory tree. Options are available with this command to mount all or a specific type of file systems as listed in the */etc/fstab* file. The *mount* command is also used to mount other types of file systems such as optical and network file systems.

This command adds an entry to the */etc/mtab* file and instructs the kernel to add the entry to the */proc/mounts* file as well after a file system has been successfully mounted.

A mount point should be empty when an attempt is made to mount a file system on it, otherwise the contents of the mount point will hide. As well, the mount point must not be in use or the mount attempt will fail.

The *mount* command supports numerous options. Some of them are described in Table 10-3.

Option	Description
async (sync)	Allows file system I/O to occur asynchronously (synchronously). This option does not have an effect on XFS file systems.
acl (noacl)	Enables (disables) the support for ACLs.
atime (noatime)	Updates (does not update) the inode access time for each access.
auto (noauto)	Mounts (does not mount) the file system when the –a option is specified.
defaults	Accepts all default values (async, auto, dev, exec, nouser, rw, and suid).
dev (nodev)	Interprets (does not interpret) the device files on the file system.
exec (noexec)	Permits (does not permit) the execution of a binary file.
loop	Mounts an ISO image as a loop device.
owner	Allows the file system owner to mount the file system.
_netdev	Used for a file system that requires network connectivity in place before it can be mounted. Examples are iSCSI, NFS, and CIFS.
remount	Remounts an already mounted file system to enable or disable an option.
ro (rw)	Mounts a file system read-only (read/write).
suid (nosuid)	Enables (disables) running setuid and setgid programs.
user (nouser)	Allows (disallows) a normal user to mount a file system.
users	Allows all users to mount and unmount a file system.

Table 10-3 mount Command Options

The opposite of the *mount* command is *umount*, which is used to detach a file system from the directory hierarchy and make it inaccessible to users and applications. This command expects the absolute pathname to the block device containing the file system or its mount point name in order to detach it. Options are available with the *umount* command to unmount all or a specific type of file systems. This command removes the corresponding entry from the */etc/mtab* file and instructs the kernel to remove it from the */proc/mounts* file as well.

Examples on the usage of the *mount* and *umount* commands are provided in exercises later in this chapter.

Determining the UUID of a File System

A file system created in a standard partition or a logical volume has a UUID (*Universally Unique IDentifier*) assigned to it at the time of creation. Assigning a UUID makes the file system unique amongst many file systems that potentially exist on the system. The primary benefit of using a UUID is the fact that it always stays persistent across system reboots. A UUID is used by default in RHEL7 in the */etc/fstab* file for any file system that is created by the system in a standard partition.

The system attempts to mount all file systems listed in the */etc/fstab* file at reboots. Each file system has an associated device file and UUID, but may or may not have a corresponding label. The system checks for the presence of each file system's device file, UUID, or label, and then attempts to mount it.

The */boot* file system, for instance, is located in a partition and the device file associated with it on *server1* is */dev/vda1*. The *xfs_admin* command with the –u option can be used to determine the UUID of */boot* as it is created by default as an XFS file system at install time. Alternatively, we can use the *blkid* command or *grep* for boot in the */etc/fstab* file.

> # **xfs_admin -u /dev/vda1**
> UUID = 362e0c12-a644-4611-b4ce-656c72750483
> # **blkid /dev/vda1**
> /dev/vda1: UUID="362e0c12-a644-4611-b4ce-656c72750483" TYPE="xfs"
> # **grep boot /etc/fstab**
> UUID=362e0c12-a644-4611-b4ce-656c72750483 /boot   xfs   defaults 1 2

This indicates the use of a UUID for mounting the */boot* file system rather than its partition name (*/dev/vda1*), and this was automatically set at install time. A discussion on the */etc/fstab* file is provided in a later sub-section.

For an extended file system, we can use the *tune2fs* command with the –l option to find its UUID.

> **EXAM TIP:** Knowing how to determine the UUID of a file system created in a standard partition is important.

A UUID is also assigned to a file system that is created in a logical volume; however, it need not be used in the *fstab* file as the device files associated with physical and logical volumes always stay unique amongst any number of logical volumes that exist on the system. They remain persistent across system reboots as well.

Labeling a File System
A label may be used instead of a UUID to keep the file system association with its device file unique and persistent across system reboots. The */boot* file system, for instance, is located in a partition and the device file associated with it on *server1* is */dev/vda1*. The *xfs_admin* command with the –l option can be issued to determine the label set on */dev/vda1*:

> # **xfs_admin –l /dev/vda1**
> label = ""

The output indicates that there is currently no label assigned to the */boot* file system. A label is not needed for a file system if we are using its UUID or logical volume name; however, we can still apply one using the *xfs_admin* command with the –L option. We must unmount an XFS file system before we are able to change its label. The following example unmounts */boot*, sets the label "bootfs" on the corresponding device file, and then remounts it:

```
# umount /boot
# xfs_admin –L bootfs /dev/vda1
writing all SBs
new label = "bootfs"
# mount /boot
```

Confirm the label by reissuing the *xfs_admin* command. We can also use the *blkid* command for verification.

 For an extended file system, we can use the *e2label* command to apply a label and *tune2fs* with –l to verify.

Now we can replace the UUID for */boot* in the *fstab* file with LABEL=bootfs, and unmount and remount */boot* as demonstrated above for confirmation. A discussion on the */etc/fstab* file is provided in the next sub-section.

A label may also be applied to a file system created in a logical volume; however, it is not recommended for use in the *fstab* file as the device files for physical volumes and logical volumes are always unique and remain persistent across reboots.

Automatically Mounting a File System at Reboots

File systems defined in the *fstab* file are mounted automatically at reboots. This file must contain proper and complete information for each listed file system. An incomplete or inaccurate entry might leave the system in an undesirable state. Another benefit to adding entries to this file is that we need to specify only one of the attributes—block device name, UUID, label, or mount point—of the file system that we wish to mount manually with the *mount* command. The *mount* command will obtain the rest of the information from this file by itself. Similarly, we only need to specify one of these attributes with the *umount* command to detach it from the directory hierarchy.

The default *fstab* file contains entries for file systems that are created at the time of installation. On *server1*, for instance, this file currently has the following three entries:

```
# cat /etc/fstab
/dev/mapper/vg00-root                              /      xfs      defaults 1 1
UUID=362e0c12-a644-4611-b4ce-656c72750483          /boot  xfs      defaults 1 2
/dev/mapper/vg00-swap                              swap   swap     defaults 0 0
```

EXAM TIP: Any missing or invalid information in this file may render the system unbootable. You will have to boot to single-user mode to fix this file. Ensure that you understand each field in this file properly for both file system and swap entries.

The format of this file is such that each row is broken out into six columns to identify the required attributes for each file system to successfully mount it. Here is what each column contains:

✓ The first column defines the physical or virtual device where the file system is resident, or its associated UUID or label. We may see entries for network file systems here as well.
✓ The second column identifies the mount point for the file system. For swap partitions, use either "none" or "swap".

✓ The third column specifies the type of file system such as ext3, ext4, xfs, vfat, or iso9660. For swap, type "swap" is used.

✓ The fourth column identifies one or more comma-separated options to be used when mounting the file system. Some options that we may want to use were described in Table 10-3 earlier.

✓ The fifth column is used by the *dump* utility to ascertain the file systems that need to be dumped. A value of 0 (or the absence of this column) disables this check.

✓ The last column indicates the sequence number in which to run the *e2fsck* (file system check) utility on the file system at system reboots. By default, 0 is used for memory-based, remote, and removable file systems, 1 for /, and 2 for /boot and other physical file systems. 0 can also be used for /, /boot, and other physical file systems if we do not want to use this feature.

Reporting File System Usage

On a live system, we often need to check file system usage to determine if a file system needs to be expanded for growth or cleaned up to generate free space. This involves checking the used and available space for a file system. The *df* (*disk free*) command is used for this purpose. It reports details of file system blocks and lists each file system along with its device file; total, used, and available blocks; percentage of used blocks; and its mount point. By default, the *df* command reports the usage in KBs if no options are specified. However, we can specify the –m option to view the output in MBs or the –h option to view the information in human readable format.

Run the *df* command with the –h option:

```
# df –h
Filesystem              Size    Used    Avail   Use%    Mounted on
/dev/mapper/vg00-root   8.8G    3.0G    5.8G    34%     /
devtmpfs                488M    0       488M    0%      /dev
tmpfs                   498M    0       498M    0%      /dev/shm
tmpfs                   498M    6.9M    491M    2%      /run
tmpfs                   498M    0       498M    0%      /sys/fs/cgroup
/dev/mapper/vg00-home   297M    20M     278M    7%      /home
/dev/vda1               497M    119M    379M    24%     /boot
```

With the –h option, the command shows the usage in KBs, MBs, GBs, or TBs as appropriate. Try running *df* with –T, "–t xfs", and "–t ext4" options, and observe the outputs.

Exercise 10-1: Create and Mount Extended File Systems

This exercise should be done on *server1*.

In this exercise, you will label *vdb* disk as msdos. You will create a 200MB *vdb1* partition and format it as an ext3 file system. You will initialize *vdd* disk for use in LVM, create *vg10* volume group, create *lvolext4* logical volume of size 1.5GB in it, and format it as an ext4 file system. You will create /mntext3 and /mntext4 mount points and manually mount both file systems. You will run appropriate commands to confirm their mount status and sizes. You will append entries to the *fstab* file for *vdb1* using its UUID and the *lvolext* file system. You will unmount both file systems manually using their mount points. You will then reboot the system and run appropriate commands to confirm that they have been automatically mounted.

1. Label the *vdb* disk as msdos using the *parted* command:

   # **parted /dev/vdb mklabel msdos**
   # **parted /dev/vdb print | grep msdos**
   Partition Table: msdos

2. Create a 200MB primary partition on *vdb* disk with the *parted* command, and confirm:

   # **parted /dev/vdb mkpart primary ext3 1 201m**
   # **parted /dev/vdb print**
     1   1049kB 201MB 200MB ext3   primary

3. Format the partition with ext3 file system type using the *mke2fs* command:

   # **mke2fs –t ext3 /dev/vdb1**
   mke2fs 1.42.9 (28-Dec-2013)
   Filesystem label=
   OS type: Linux
   Block size=1024 (log=0)
   Fragment size=1024 (log=0)
   Stride=0 blocks, Stripe width=0 blocks
   48960 inodes, 195584 blocks
   9779 blocks (5.00%) reserved for the super user
   First data block=1
   Maximum filesystem blocks=67371008
   24 block groups
   8192 blocks per group, 8192 fragments per group
   2040 inodes per group
   Superblock backups stored on blocks:
        8193, 24577, 40961, 57345, 73729
   Allocating group tables: done
   Writing inode tables: done
   Creating journal (4096 blocks): done
   Writing superblocks and filesystem accounting information: done

4. Initialize *vdd* disk for use in LVM using the *pvcreate* command:

   # **pvcreate /dev/vdd –v**
     Set up physical volume for "/dev/vdd" with 4194304 available sectors
     Zeroing start of device /dev/vdd
     Writing physical volume data to disk "/dev/vdd"
    Physical volume "/dev/vdd" successfully created

5. Create *vg10* volume group using the *vgcreate* command and add physical volume *vdd* to it:

   # **vgcreate –v vg10 /dev/vdd**
     Adding physical volume '/dev/vdd' to volume group 'vg10'
     Archiving volume group "vg10" metadata (seqno 0).
     Creating volume group backup "/etc/lvm/backup/vg10" (seqno 1).

Volume group "vg10" successfully created

6. Create *lvolext4* logical volume of size 1.5GB in *vg10* volume group using the *lvcreate* command:

 # lvcreate –L 1.5g –n lvolext4 vg10 –v
   Setting logging type to disk
   Finding volume group "vg10"
   Archiving volume group "vg10" metadata (seqno 3).
   Creating logical volume lvolext4
   Creating volume group backup "/etc/lvm/backup/vg10" (seqno 4).
   Activating logical volume "lvolext4".
   activation/volume_list configuration setting not defined: Checking only host tags for vg10/lvolext4
   Creating vg10-lvolext4
   Loading vg10-lvolext4 table (253:3)
   Resuming vg10-lvolext4 (253:3)
   Wiping known signatures on logical volume "vg10/lvolext4"
   Initializing 4.00 KiB of logical volume "vg10/lvolext4" with value 0.
   Creating volume group backup "/etc/lvm/backup/vg10" (seqno 4).
  Logical volume "lvolext4" created

7. Format *lvolext4* logical volume with ext4 file system type using the *mke2fs* command:

 # mke2fs –t ext4 /dev/vg10/lvolext4
mke2fs 1.42.9 (28-Dec-2013)
Filesystem label=
OS type: Linux
Block size=4096 (log=2)
Fragment size=4096 (log=2)
Stride=0 blocks, Stripe width=0 blocks
98304 inodes, 393216 blocks
19660 blocks (5.00%) reserved for the super user
First data block=0
Maximum filesystem blocks=402653184
12 block groups
32768 blocks per group, 32768 fragments per group
8192 inodes per group
Superblock backups stored on blocks:
     32768, 98304, 163840, 229376, 294912
Allocating group tables: done
Writing inode tables: done
Creating journal (8192 blocks): done
Writing superblocks and filesystem accounting information: done

8. Create */mntext3* and */mntext4* mount points:

 # mkdir –v /mntext3 /mntext4
mkdir: created directory '/mntext3'
mkdir: created directory '/mntext4'

9. Mount */dev/vdb1* on */mntext3* and */dev/vg10/lvolext4* on */mntext4* using the *mount* command:

   # mount /dev/vdb1 /mntext3
   # mount /dev/vg10/lvolext4 /mntext4

10. Confirm the mount status and sizes with the *df* command:

    # df –h | grep mntext

/dev/vdb1	181M	1.6M	167M	1%	/mntext3
/dev/mapper/vg10-lvolext4	1.5G	4.5M	1.4G	1%	/mntext4

11. Determine the UUID for */dev/vdb1* using the *tune2fs* command:

    # tune2fs –l /dev/vdb1 | grep UUID
    Filesystem UUID: c8dd716e-b9ba-465d-859b-d7115a1ea289

12. Open the */etc/fstab* file and append entries for both file systems:

    # vi /etc/fstab
    . . . .
    UUID=c8dd716e-b9ba-465d-859b-d7115a1ea289   /mntext3   ext3   defaults 1 2
    /dev/vg10/lvolext4   /mntext4   ext4   defaults 1 2

13. Unmount both file systems using their mount points:

    # umount /mntext3 /mntext4

14. Reboot the system using the *reboot* command:

    # reboot

15. Check the mount status of both file systems using the *mount* and *df* commands after the system has returned to its normal operating state:

    # mount | grep mntext
    /dev/vdb1 on /mntext3 type ext3 (rw,relatime,seclabel,data=ordered)
    /dev/mapper/vg10-lvolext4 on /mntext4 type ext4 (rw,relatime,seclabel,data=ordered)
    # df –h | grep mntext

/dev/vdb1	181M	1.6M	167M	1%	/mntext3
/dev/mapper/vg10-lvolext4	1.5G	4.5M	1.4G	1%	/mntext4

Exercise 10-2: Resize an Extended File System

This exercise should be done on *server1*.

In this exercise, you will create a 500MB *vdb2* partition, initialize it for use in LVM, extend *vg10* volume group to include this physical volume, and grow the size of *lvolext4* online by 500MB ensuring that the underlying file system is also grown to take advantage of the new space. You will then shrink the file system size by 900MB, ensuring that *lvolext4* is also reduced. You will confirm the new size of the logical volume and the file system.

1. Create a 500MB primary partition on *vdb* disk with the *parted* command, and confirm:

   # **parted /dev/vdb mkpart primary 202m 703m**
   # **parted /dev/vdb print | grep 703**
      2   202MB 703MB 500MB   primary

EXAM TIP: Extend the size of the logical volume before attempting to increase the file system in it.

---

2. Initialize *vdb2* partition for use in LVM using the *pvcreate* command. Use the –v option if you want to view details.

   # **pvcreate /dev/vdb2**
   Physical volume "/dev/vdb2" successfully created

3. Extend *vg10* volume group using the *vgextend* command and add the new physical volume to it. Use the –v option if you want to view details.

   # **vgextend vg10 /dev/vdb2**
   Volume group "vg10" successfully extended

4. Extend *lvolext4* logical volume from 1.5GB in *vg10* volume group to 2GB using the *lvresize* command, ensuring that the underlying file system is also extended (–r option):

   # **lvresize –r –L 2g /dev/vg10/lvolext4**
   Extending logical volume lvolext4 to 2.00 GiB
   Logical volume lvolext4 successfully resized
   resize2fs 1.42.9 (28-Dec-2013)
   Filesystem at /dev/mapper/vg10-lvolext4 is mounted on /mntext4; on-line resizing required
   old_desc_blocks = 1, new_desc_blocks = 1
   The filesystem on /dev/mapper/vg10-lvolext4 is now 524288 blocks long.

5. Confirm the mount status, and the sizes of both the logical volume and the file system:

   # **lvs | grep lvolext4**
     lvolext4   vg10   -wi-ao----   2.00g
   # **df –h | grep mntext4**
   /dev/mapper/vg10-lvolext4   2.0G   4.5M   1.9G   1%   /mntext4

6. Shrink the file system size by 900MB using the *lvresize* command. This operation will prompt us to unmount the file system for shrinking it. Respond with y to proceeed.

   # **lvresize –r –L 1.1g /dev/vg10/lvolext4**
   Rounding size to boundary between physical extents: 1.10 GiB
   Do you want to unmount "/mntext4"? [Y|n] **y**
   fsck from util-linux 2.23.2
   /dev/mapper/vg10-lvolext4: 11/131072 files (9.1% non-contiguous), 17580/524288 blocks
   resize2fs 1.42.9 (28-Dec-2013)
   Resizing the filesystem on /dev/mapper/vg10-lvolext4 to 288768 (4k) blocks.

The filesystem on /dev/mapper/vg10-lvolext4 is now 288768 blocks long.

Reducing logical volume lvolext4 to 1.10 GiB

Logical volume lvolext4 successfully resized

7. Confirm the new size of the logical volume and the file system:

 # lvs | grep lvolext4

   lvolext4   vg10   -wi-ao----   1.10g

 # df –h | grep mntext4

/dev/mapper/vg10-lvolext4   1.1G   3.8M   1009M 1%   /mntext4

Exercise 10-3: Create, Mount, and Extend an XFS File System

This exercise should be done on *server1*.

In this exercise, you will use an existing 188MB *vdc1* partition created in the previous chapter. You will initialize it for use in LVM, add it to *vg10* volume group, create *lvolxfs* logical volume to occupy the entire *vdc1* physical volume only, and format it as an xfs file system. You will create */mntxfs* mount point and manually mount this file system using its device name. You will run appropriate commands to confirm its mount status and size. You will append an entry for it to the *fstab* file. You will grow it online by 112MB on the space that is available in the volume group, ensuring that the underlying file system is also expanded. You will then reboot the system and run appropriate commands to confirm the automatic mount of the new file system, along with all other file systems defined in the file.

1. Initialize the partition for use in LVM and add it to the *vg10* volume group. Use the –v option if you want to view details.

 # pvcreate /dev/vdc1

Physical volume "/dev/vdc1" successfully created

 # vgextend vg10 /dev/vdc1

Volume group "vg10" successfully extended

2. Create *lvolxfs* logical volume of size 188MB in *vg10* volume group using the *lvcreate* command. Make sure that the command uses only *vdc1* partition and no other physical volume space. Use the –v option if you want to view details.

 # lvcreate –L 188m –n lvolxfs vg10 /dev/vdc1

Logical volume "lvolxfs" created

3. Format *lvolxfs* logical volume with xfs file system type using the *mkfs.xfs* command:

 # mkfs.xfs /dev/vg10/lvolxfs

meta-data=/dev/vg10/lvolxfs	isize=256	agcount=4, agsize=42496 blks
=	sectsz=512	attr=2, projid32bit=1
=	crc=0	
data =	bsize=4096	blocks=169984, imaxpct=25
=	sunit=0	swidth=0 blks
naming =version 2	bsize=4096	ascii-ci=0 ftype=0
log =internal log	bsize=4096	blocks=853, version=2

=	sectsz=512	sunit=0 blks, lazy-count=1
realtime =none	extsz=4096	blocks=0, rtextents=0

4. Create */mntxfs* mount point:

    # mkdir /mntxfs

5. Mount */dev/vg10/lvolxfs* on */mntxfs* using the *mount* command:

    # mount /dev/vg10/lvolxfs /mntxfs

6. Confirm the mount status and sizes with the *df* command:

    # df –h | grep mntext
    /dev/mapper/vg10-lvolxfs   661M   33M   629M   5%   /mntxfs

7. Open the */etc/fstab* file and append an entry for this file system:

    # vi /etc/fstab
    . . . .
    /dev/vg10/lvolxfs   /mntxfs   xfs   defaults 1 2

8. Grow the new file system online by 112MB, using the available space in *vg10* volume group. Make sure that the underlying xfs file system also grows with the logical volume.

    # lvresize –r –L 300m /dev/vg10/lvolxfs
    Extending logical volume lvolxfs to 300.00 MiB
    Logical volume lvolxfs successfully resized
    . . . .

9. Check the logical volume size with the *lvs* command. You can also issue the *lvdisplay /dev/vg10/lvolxfs* command to view details about the logical volume.

    # lvs | grep lvolxfs
    lvolxfs vg10   -wi-ao----   300.00m

10. Reboot the system using the *reboot* command:

    # reboot

11. Check the mount status of the XFS file system using the *mount* command after the system has returned to its normal operating system. Ensure with the *df* command that all file systems previously created are also mounted.

    # mount | grep mntxfs
    /dev/mapper/vg10-lvolxfs on /mntxfs type xfs (rw,relatime,seclabel,attr2,inode64,noquota)
    # df –h | grep mntxfs
    /dev/mapper/vg10-lvolxfs   297M   9.7M   288M   4%   /mntxfs

12. Display information about the XFS file system using the *xfs_info* command:

 # xfs_info /mntxfs

meta-data=/dev/vg10/lvolxfs		isize=256		agcount=7, agsize=12032 blks
=		sectsz=512		attr=2, projid32bit=1
=		crc=0		
data	=	bsize=4096		blocks=76800, imaxpct=25
	=	sunit=0		swidth=0 blks
naming	=version 2	bsize=4096		ascii-ci=0 ftype=0
log	=internal log	bsize=4096		blocks=853, version=2
	=	sectsz=512		sunit=0 blks, lazy-count=1
realtime	=none	extsz=4096		blocks=0, rtextents=0

Exercise 10-4: Create and Mount a VFAT File System

This exercise should be done on *server1*.

In this exercise, you will label *vde* disk as msdos. You will create a 400MGB *vde1* partition and format it as a VFAT file system. You will create */mntvfat* mount point and manually mount this file system using its device name. You will run appropriate commands to confirm its mount status and size. You will append an entry to the *fstab* file for this file system. You will reboot the system and run appropriate commands to confirm that the new file system has been automatically mounted without affecting the previously configured file systems.

1. Label *vde* disk as msdos with the *parted* command, and confirm:

    # parted /dev/vde mklabel msdos
    # parted /dev/vde print | grep –i partition
    Partition Table: msdos

2. Create a 400MB primary partition on *vde* disk with the *parted* command, and confirm:

    # parted /dev/vde mkpart primary fat32 1 401m
    # parted /dev/vde print
    Model: Virtio Block Device (virtblk)
    Disk /dev/vde: 2147MB
    Sector size (logical/physical): 512B/512B
    Partition Table: msdos
    Disk Flags:

Number	Start	End	Size	Type	File system	Flags
1	1049kB	401MB	400MB	primary		lba

3. Format the partition with vfat file system type using the *mkfs.vfat* command:

    # mkfs.vfat /dev/vde1
    mkfs.fat 3.0.20 (12 Jun 2013)

4. Create */mntvfat* mount point:

 # mkdir /mntvfat

5. Mount */dev/vde1* on */mntvfat* using the *mount* command:

   # mount /dev/vde1 /mntvfat

6. Confirm the mount status and sizes with the *df* command:

   # df –h | grep mntext
   /dev/vde1   381M   0M   1381M 0%   /mntvfat

7. Determine the UUID for */dev/vde1* using the *blkid* command:

   # blkid /dev/vde1
   /dev/vde1: SEC_TYPE="msdos" UUID="4741-2068" TYPE="vfat"

8. Open the */etc/fstab* file and append an entry for this file system:

   # vi /etc/fstab
   . . . .
   UUID=4741-2068   /mntvfat   vfat   defaults 1 2

9. Reboot the system using the *reboot* command:

   # reboot

10. Check the mount status of all the file systems after the system has come up using the *df* command:

    # df –h

Filesystem	Size	Used	Avail	Use%	Mounted on
/dev/mapper/vg00-root	8.8G	3.0G	5.8G	34%	/
devtmpfs	488M	0	488M	0%	/dev
tmpfs	498M	80K	497M	1%	/dev/shm
tmpfs	498M	7.0M	491M	2%	/run
tmpfs	498M	0	498M	0%	/sys/fs/cgroup
/dev/vdb1	181M	1.6M	167M	1%	/mntext3
/dev/mapper/vg10-lvolxfs	297M	9.7M	288M	4%	/mntxfs
/dev/mapper/vg10-lvolext4	1.1G	3.8M	1005M	1%	/mntext4
/dev/vda1	497M	119M	379M	24%	/boot
/dev/vde1	381M	0	381M	0%	/mntvfat

Exercise 10-5: Create, Mount, Unmount, and Remove File Systems

This exercise should be done on *server1*.

In this exercise, you will create a 100MB *vdc2* partition and format it as xfs. You will create another partition *vde2* of size 100MB and initialize it for use in LVM. You will create *vg20* volume group, create *lvolext4rem* logical volume using the *vde2* partition, and format it as ext4. You will create

/mntxfsrem and */mntext4rem* mount points. You will apply label *mntxfsrem* to the xfs file system. You will append entries to the *fstab* file for *vdc2* using its label and for *lvolext4rem*. You will reboot the system and run appropriate commands to confirm that these two and all other file systems added to the *fstab* file in previous exercises have been mounted successfully and automatically.

Next, you will *cd* into the */mntxfsrem* mount point and try to unmount the xfs file system. You will take appropriate measures to unmount it if you get a "device busy" or a similar message. You will destroy both file systems and delete their mount points. You will remove their entries from the *fstab* file. You will then reboot the system and confirm that the system has been booted up without any issues. You will run appropriate commands after the system is up to verify the deletion of both file systems. Use the –v option with the LVM commands if you want to view details.

1. Create one 100MB second primary partition on *vdc* disk and one 100MB second primary partition on *vde* disk. Make sure these partitions begin right after the previous existing partition.

   # parted /dev/vdc mkpart primary 202 303m
   # parted /dev/vde mkpart primary 402 503m

2. Format the *vdc2* partition with xfs file system type using the *mkfs.xfs* command:

   # mkfs.xfs /dev/vdc2

3. Initialize the *vde2* partition for use in LVM using the *pvcreate* command:

   # pvcreate /dev/vde2

4. Create *vg20* volume group and add physical volume *vde2* to it using the *vgcreate* command:

   # vgcreate vg20 /dev/vde2

5. Create *lvolext4rem* logical volume in *vg20* volume group using the *lvcreate* command:

   # lvcreate –L 96m –n lvolext4rem vg20

6. Format *lvolext4rem* logical volume with ext4 file system type using the *mkfs.ext4* command:

   # mkfs.ext4 /dev/vg20/lvolext4rem

7. Create */mntxfsrem* and */mntext4rem* mount points:

   # mkdir /mntxfsrem /mntext4rem

8. Apply label *mntxfsrem* to the xfs file system using the *xfs_admin* command:

   # xfs_admin –L mntxfsrem /dev/vdc2

9. Mount */dev/vdc2* on */mntxfsrem* using its label and */dev/vg20/lvolext4rem* on */mntext4rem*:

mount LABEL=mntxfsrem /mntxfsrem
mount /dev/vg20/lvolext4rem /mntext4rem

10. Confirm the mount status with the *df* command:

    # df –h | grep rem

11. Open the */etc/fstab* file and append entries for both file systems:

    # vi /etc/fstab
    . . . .
    LABEL=mntxfsrem   /mntxfsrem   xfs   defaults 1 2
    /dev/vg20/lvolext4rem   /mntext4rem   ext4   defaults 1 2

12. Reboot the system:

    # reboot

13. Check the mount status of all file systems that you have added previously after the system reboot:

    # df –h

14. Change the directory into the */mntxfsrem* mount point and try to unmount it:

    # cd /mntxfsrem
    # umount /mntxfsrem
    umount: /mntxfsrem: target is busy.

15. Determine which user(s) and process(es) are using this mount point by issuing the *fuser* command with the –cu options (c for the PID and u for the user owning the PID):

    # fuser –cu /mntxfsrem
    /mntxfsrem: 2599c(root)

16. *cd* out of the mount point and run the previous command again:

    # cd
    # fuser –cu /mntxfsrem

17. Now you should be able to umount this file system. Also, unmount */mntext4rem* file system.

    # umount /mntxfsrem /mntext4rem

18. Remove the *vdc2* partition using the *parted* command:

    # parted /dev/vdc rm 2

---

19. Remove the *lvolext4rem* logical volume and the *vg20* volume group using the *lvremove* and *vgremove* commands:

    # **lvremove –f /dev/vg20/lvolext4rem**
    # **vgremove vg20**

20. Remove both mount points:

    # **rmdir /mntxfsrem /mntext4rem**

21. Remove their corresponding entries from the */etc/fstab* file.
22. Reboot the system with the *reboot* command:

    # **reboot**

23. Verify that the two file systems are not there anymore using the *findmnt* command:

    # **findmnt | egrep 'xfsrem|ext4rem'**

At this point or during this exercise, you can use several other commands listed in Table 8-2 and Table 9-2 to view LVM and file system information.

Checking and Repairing Extended File Systems

The structure of an extended file system could be damaged when an abnormal system shutdown or crash occurs, potentially leaving the mounted and active file systems in an inconsistent state. To maintain integrity, a utility called *e2fsck* is used. This utility is hardlinked to *fsck.ext3* and *fsck.ext4* commands that may be used instead on the specific file system type. The behavior of this command is based on whether the file system has a journal or not. *e2fsck* is invoked automatically during the reboot following a system crash. It runs a full check and repair on the entire file system that is without a journal, reports any inconsistencies as it finds them, and attempts to fix them automatically. It prompts for user intervention if it is unable to resolve an inconsistency. Conversely, if it determines that the file system has a journal, it simply replays the journal and brings the file system back to its previous consistent state.

The *e2fsck* utility can also be executed manually on an unmounted extended file system from the command line. During the check, it expects a yes or no response while attempting to correct discovered discrepancies, unless the –p (preen) option is specified, which gives the command a go ahead to fix problems automatically.

During the check, if *e2fsck* encounters a corruption in the primary superblock, it exits out to the command prompt, as it requires us to take a corrective measure. The system does not allow a file system to be mounted if its primary superblock is lost or corrupt. In this situation, we need to determine the backup superblock locations with the *dumpe2fs* command for that file system, and then re-invoke *e2fsck* by specifying with it one of these locations to overwrite the primary superblock. We should be able to mount the file system back after the primary superblock has been fixed.

While checking a file system, *e2fsck* may come across a file with a missing name. It moves the file to the *lost+found* directory located in that file system. This file is known as an *orphan* file and it is renamed to match its inode number. You need to figure out the actual name of the file and its

---

original location. You can use the *file* command to identify the file type. If it is a text file, use *cat* or *more* to view its contents; otherwise, use the *strings* command to extract its legible contents for review. You may likely get enough information on the name and location of the file to rename it and move it back to its place.

Exercise 10-6: Repair a Damaged Extended File System

This exercise should be done on *server1*.

In this exercise, you will unmount the */mntext4* file system and run the file system check and repair utility on it. You will replace its primary superblock assuming that it is corrupt, and then mount the file system back.

1. Unmount the */mntext4* file system using the *umount* command:

   # **umount /mntext4**

2. Execute the *e2fsck* command on its logical volume device file */dev/vg10/lvolext4*:

   # **e2fsck /dev/vg10/lvolext4**
   /dev/vg10/lvolext4: clean, 11/73728 files, 13789/288768 blocks

3. Obtain the list of backup superblock locations for this file system using the *dumpe2fs* command:

   # **dumpe2fs /dev/vg10/lvolext4 | grep superblock**
   Primary superblock at 0, Group descriptors at 1-1
   Backup superblock at 32768, Group descriptors at 32769-32769
   Backup superblock at 98304, Group descriptors at 98305-98305
   Backup superblock at 163840, Group descriptors at 163841-163841
   Backup superblock at 229376, Group descriptors at 229377-229377

4. Run the *e2fsck* command and specify the location of the first backup superblock (32768) to repair the primary superblock:

   # **fsck –b 32768 /dev/vg10/lvolext4**
   e2fsck 1.42.9 (28-Dec-2013)
   /dev/vg10/lvolext4 was not cleanly unmounted, check forced.
   Pass 1: Checking inodes, blocks, and sizes
   Pass 2: Checking directory structure
   Pass 3: Checking directory connectivity
   Pass 4: Checking reference counts
   Pass 5: Checking group summary information
   /dev/vg10/lvolext4: ***** FILE SYSTEM WAS MODIFIED *****
   /dev/vg10/lvolext4: 11/73728 files (9.1% non-contiguous), 13789/288768 blocks

5. Mount the file system back:

   # **mount /mntext4**

Checking and Repairing an XFS File System

An XFS file system may be checked and repaired if a corruption in its metadata is suspected. The *xfs_repair* utility is available for this purpose. This tool requires that the file system be unmounted and in a clean state. When invoked, it replays the journal while performing all operations automatically without prompting for user input. The *xfs_repair* program goes through seven phases during its execution lifecycle on a file system. It runs checks elements such as inodes, directories, pathnames, link counts, and superblocks. The following is an example of running this tool on the */mntxfs* file system that resides in *lvolxfs* logical volume in *vg10* volume group. Remember, we have to unmount the file system before running this command on it.

```
# umount /mntxfs
# xfs_repair /dev/vg10/lvolxfs
Phase 1      - find and verify superblock...
Phase 2      - using internal log
             - zero log...
             - scan filesystem freespace and inode maps...
             - found root inode chunk
Phase 3      - for each AG...
             - scan and clear agi unlinked lists...
             - process known inodes and perform inode discovery...
             - agno = 0
             - agno = 1
             - process newly discovered inodes...
Phase 4      - check for duplicate blocks...
             - setting up duplicate extent list...
             - check for inodes claiming duplicate blocks...
             - agno = 0
             - agno = 1
Phase 5      - rebuild AG headers and trees...
             - reset superblock...
Phase 6      - check inode connectivity...
             - resetting contents of realtime bitmap and summary inodes
             - traversing filesystem ...
             - traversal finished ...
             - moving disconnected inodes to lost+found ...
Phase 7      - verify and correct link counts...
done
# mount /mntxfs
```

The *xfs_repair* command does not run at boot even if an xfs file system is not cleanly unmounted. In the event of an unclean unmount, this command simply replays the log at mount time, ensuring a consistent file system.

Mounting and Unmounting Remote File Systems

Remote file systems, such as NFS and CIFS, are treated as any other local file systems after they are mounted and attached to the directory tree on a client system. They can also be added to the file system table, just like local file systems, so that they are automatically mounted during a reboot. In the same manner, they can be detached from the directory tree and made inaccessible to users and applications. This section presents exercises to demonstrate how to mount and unmount NFS and CIFS file systems.

Exercise 10-7: Mount and Unmount an NFS File System

This exercise should be done on *server2*.

For this exercise, an NFS server is set up in Chapter 20 "Sharing File Storage with NFS" on *server1*, sharing */nfsrhcsa* directory in read-only mode with appropriate firewall rules and SELinux settings in place.

In this exercise, you will mount this NFS file system on */nfsrhcsamnt*, check its status, and unmount it. You will add an entry for it to the *fstab* file and reboot the system to confirm the file system's automatic remount.

1. Install the NFS client package nfs-utils:

    # **yum –y install nfs-utils**
    Package 1:nfs-utils-1.3.0-0.el7.x86_64 already installed and latest version
    Nothing to do

2. Create a mount point called */nfsrhcsamnt*:

    # **mkdir /nfsrhcsamnt**

3. Add the following entry to the */etc/fstab* file to ensure an automatic file system remount after system reboots:

    192.168.0.110:/nfsrhcsa   /nfsrhcsamnt   nfs   _netdev   0   0

    The _netdev option will instruct the system to wait for networking to establish before attempting to mount this file system.

    > **EXAM TIP:** If you miss adding an entry to the fstab file for a remote file system, you will lose the marks.

4. Execute either of the following to mount the file system:

    # **mount –t nfs 192.168.0.110:/nfsrhcsa /nfsrhcsamnt**
    # **mount /nfsrhcsamnt**

5. Check the status of the remote file system using the *mount* command:

    # **mount | grep nfsrhcsa**
    192.168.0.110:/nfsrhcsa on /nfsrhcsamnt type nfs4
    (ro,relatime,vers=4.0,rsize=131072,wsize=131072,namlen=255,hard,proto=tcp,port=0,timeo=600,retr
    ans=2,sec=sys,clientaddr=192.168.0.120,local_lock=none,addr=192.168.0.110)

6. Unmount the file system using the *umount* command:

   # **umount /nfsrhcsamnt**

7. Reboot the system:

   # **shutdown –ry now**

8. Issue the *mount* command again and check if the file system has been automatically remounted after the reboot:

   # **mount | grep nfsrhcsa**
   192.168.0.110:/nfsrhcsa on /nfsrhcsamnt type nfs4
   (ro,relatime,vers=4.0,rsize=131072,wsize=131072,namlen=255,hard,proto=tcp,port=0,timeo=600,retr
   ans=2,sec=sys,clientaddr=192.168.0.120,local_lock=none,addr=192.168.0.110)

This completes the setup and testing of mounting, unmounting, and remounting of an NFS file system on the client.

Exercise 10-8: Mount and Unmount a CIFS File System

This exercise should be done on *server2*.

For this exercise, a Samba server is set up in Chapter 21 "Sharing File Storage with Samba" on *server1*, sharing */smbrhcsa* directory in browsable mode with login and write access allocated to *user1* and read-only to *user3*. The server has appropriate firewall rules and SELinux settings in place. For more details on CIFS client configuration, review Chapter 21.

In this exercise, you will access and mount this share on */smbrhcsamnt*, and add an entry to the */etc/fstab* file so that it is automatically mounted at system reboots. You will confirm the share access and mount, and test access by creating a file in the mount point. You will store the username and password for *user1* in a file owned by *root* with 0400 permissions to allow this user to be able to mount this share. Lastly, you will reboot the system and validate the automatic remount after the system is back up.

1. Install the Samba client packages samba-client and cifs-utils:

   # **yum –y install samba-client cifs-utils**
   . . . .
   Installed:
     cifs-utils.x86_64 0:6.2-6.el7
     samba-client.x86_64 0:4.1.1-31.el7
   Complete!

2. Log on to the */smbrhcsa* share as *user1* using the *smbclient* command:

   # **smbclient //192.168.0.110/smbrhcsa –U user1**
   Enter user1's password:
   Domain=[EXAMPLE] OS=[Unix] Server=[Samba 4.1.1]
   smb: \\>

The connection is successfully made to the *smbrhcsa* share. You can run the *help* subcommand to list available subcommands, use *ls* to list files in the share, use *get/mget* and *put/mput* to transfer one or more files, and so on. Issue *exit* when done to disconnect.

3. Create */smbrhcsamnt* mount point:

   # **mkdir /smbrhcsamnt**

4. Mount */smbrhcsa* on to the */smbrhcsamnt* mount point as *user1*:

   # **mount //192.168.0.110/smbrhcsa /smbrhcsamnt –o username=user1**
   Password for user1@//192.168.0.110/smbrhcsa: *******

5. Check the mount status of the share using the *df* and *mount* commands:

   # **df –h | grep smbrhcsa**
   //192.168.0.110/smbrhcsa   8.8G 3.4G 5.4G 39% /smbrhcsamnt
   # **mount | grep smbrhcsa**
   //192.168.0.110/smbrhcsa on /smbrhcsamnt type cifs
   (rw,relatime,vers=1.0,cache=strict,username=user1,domain=SERVER1,uid=0,noforceuid,gid=0,nofor
   cegid,addr=192.168.0.110,unix,posixpaths,serverino,acl,rsize=1048576,wsize=65536,actimeo=1)

6. Create */etc/samba/smbrhcsacred* file and add the credentials for *user1* to it:

   # **vi /etc/samba/smbrhcsacred**
   username=user1
   password=user123

7. Set ownership on the file to *root* and permissions to 0400:

   # **chown root /etc/samba/smbrhcsacred && chmod 0400 /etc/samba/smbrhcsacred**

8. Open the */etc/fstab* file and add the following entry to automatically mount the share at system reboots:

   //192.168.0.110/smbrhcsa /smbrhcsamnt cifs rw,credentials=/etc/samba/smbrhcsacred 0   0

   You can add the _netdev option to instruct the system to wait for networking to establish before attempting to mount this file system.

9. Create a file called *smbrhcsatest* as *user1* under */smbrhcsamnt* and confirm its creation by running *ll* on */smbrchsa* on the Samba server:

   [server2] $ **touch /smbrhcsamnt/smbrhcsatest**
   [server1] # **ll /smbrhcsa**
   -rw-r--r--. 1 root   root   0 Jan 27 14:22 nfsrhcsatest
   -rw-r--r--. 1 user1   user1   0 Jan 29 21:21 smbrhcsatest

---

10. Unmount the file system using the *umount* command:

    # **umount /smbrhcsamnt**

11. Reboot the system:

    # **shutdown –ry now**

12. Issue the *mount* command again and check if the file system has been automatically remounted after the reboot:

    # **mount | grep smbrhcsa**
    //192.168.0.110/smbrhcsa on /smbrhcsamnt type cifs
    (rw,relatime,vers=1.0,cache=strict,username=user1,domain=SERVER1,uid=0,noforceuid,gid=0,nofor
    cegid,addr=192.168.0.110,unix,posixpaths,serverino,acl,rsize=1048576,wsize=65536,actimeo=1)

The remote share is successfully mounted and remounted on *server2*, and it can be accessed as any other local file system. Access to it is also tested by creating a file on the Samba client and validating its presence on the Samba server. *user3*, and all other users on the system, should be able to access this share in read-only mode. This ability is enabled by adding the "public = yes" directive on the Samba server.

AutoFS

In the previous section, we learned how to attach (mount) an NFS file system to the Linux directory tree manually for access by users and applications. Once attached, the NFS file system was treated just like any other local file system. We also learned how to detach (unmount) an NFS file system manually from the directory tree and make it inaccessible to users and applications. We placed an entry for the NFS file system in the */etc/fstab* file to guarantee its mount during system reboots.

RHEL offers an alternative way of mounting and unmounting an NFS file system during runtime and system reboots, and it is referred to as the AutoFS (*Auto File System*) service. AutoFS is a client-side service, which is used to mount an NFS file system on-demand. With a proper entry placed in AutoFS configuration files, the AutoFS service automatically mounts an NFS file system upon detecting an activity in its mount point with a command such as *ls* or *cd*. In the same manner, the AutoFS service unmounts the NFS file system automatically if the file system has not been accessed for a pre-defined period of time.

The AutoFS service also supports the automounting and autounmounting of CIFS and removable file systems via the */etc/auto.smb* and */etc/auto.misc* configuration files, respectively.

The use of the AutoFS service saves the Linux kernel from dedicating system resources to maintain unused NFS file systems, ultimately contributing to the overall system performance. Imagine a system with many NFS mounts!

In order to avoid inconsistencies, mounts managed with AutoFS should not be mounted or unmounted manually or via the /etc/fstab file.

Benefits of Using AutoFS

There are several benefits associated with using the AutoFS service over placing entries in the */etc/fstab* file. Some of the key benefits are described below:

- ✓ AutoFS requires that NFS file systems be defined in text configuration files called *maps*, which are located in the */etc* directory. AutoFS does not use the */etc/fstab* file.
- ✓ AutoFS does not require *root* privileges to mount an NFS file system; manual mounting and mounting via *fstab* do require that privilege.
- ✓ AutoFS prevents an NFS client from hanging if an NFS server is down or inaccessible. With the other method, the unavailability of the NFS server may cause the NFS client to hang.
- ✓ With AutoFS, an NFS file system is unmounted automatically if it is not accessed for five minutes by default. With the *fstab* method, the NFS file system stays mounted until it is either manually unmounted or the client shuts down.
- ✓ AutoFS supports wildcard characters and environment variables, which the other method does not support.
- ✓ A special map is available with AutoFS that mounts all available NFS file systems from a reachable NFS server automatically without explicitly defining them in the AutoFS configuration. The *fstab* method does not offer any such feature.

How AutoFS Works

The AutoFS service consists of a daemon called *automount* in the userland that mounts configured NFS file systems automatically upon access. This daemon is invoked at system boot. It reads the AutoFS master map and creates initial mount point entries in the */etc/mtab* file; however, it does not mount any corresponding file systems yet. During runtime when the daemon detects a user activity under a mount point, it goes ahead and actually mounts the requested file system at that time. If an NFS file system remains idle for a certain time period, *automount* unmounts it by itself.

AutoFS Configuration File

The configuration file for AutoFS is */etc/sysconfig/autofs*, which AutoFS consults at service startup. Some key directives from this file are shown below along with preset values:

```
MASTER_MAP_NAME="auto.master"
TIMEOUT=300
NEGATIVE_TIMEOUT=60
BROWSE_MODE="no"
MOUNT_NFS_DEFAULT_PROTOCOL=4
APPEND_OPTIONS="yes"
LOGGING="none"
OPTIONS=""
```

There are additional directives available in this file and more can be added to modify the default behavior of the AutoFS service. Table 10-4 describes the above directives.

Directive	Description
MASTER_MAP_NAME	Defines the name of the master map. The default is auto.master, which is located in the /etc directory.
TIMEOUT	Specifies, in seconds, the maximum idle time after which a file system is automatically unmounted. The default is five minutes.
NEGATIVE_TIMEOUT	Specifies, in seconds, a timeout value for failed mount attempts. The default is one minute.
BROWSE_MODE	Defines whether maps are to be made browsable.
MOUNT_NFS_DEFAULT_PROTOCOL	Sets the default NFS version to be used to mount NFS file systems.
APPEND_OPTIONS	Identifies additional options to the OPTIONS directive.
LOGGING	Specifies a logging level. Other options are verbose and debug.
OPTIONS	Defines global options.

Table 10-4 AutoFS Directives

These directives are usually kept to their default values; however, you can alter them if required.

AutoFS Maps

The AutoFS service needs to know the NFS file systems to be mounted and their locations. It also needs to know any specific options to use for mounting. This information is defined in AutoFS maps. There are four types of AutoFS maps: *master*, *special*, *direct*, and *indirect*.

The Master Map

The */etc/auto.master* file is the default master map, as defined in the */etc/sysconfig/autofs* configuration file with the MASTER_MAP_NAME directive. This map maintains entries for indirect, special, and direct maps. Three sample entries are provided below and explained subsequently:

```
/net        –hosts
/–          /etc/auto.direct
/misc       /etc/auto.misc
```

The first entry is for a special map, which directs AutoFS to mount all shares available from the NFS server listed as */net/<NFS_server>* when an activity occurs under this mount point.

The second entry defines a direct map and points to the */etc/auto.direct* file for mount details.

The third entry is for an indirect map, notifying AutoFS to refer to the */etc/auto.misc* file for mount details. The umbrella mount point */misc* will precede all mount point entries listed in the */etc/auto.misc* file. This indirect map entry is used to automount removable file systems, such as CD, DVD, floppy, JAZ, external USB disks, and so on.

You may append an option to any of the entries in the *auto.master* file; however, that option will apply globally to all sub-entries in the specified map file.

The Special Map

The –hosts special map allows all NFS shares from all accessible NFS servers to be mounted under the */net<NFS_server>* mount point without explicitly mounting each one of them. The */etc/auto.net* file is executed to obtain a list of NFS servers and shares available from them. Accessing */net/<NFS_server>* will instruct AutoFS to mount all available resources from that NFS server. By default, the entry "/net –hosts" exists in the */etc/auto.master* file, and is enabled. This map is not recommended in an environment with many NFS servers and many shares, as AutoFS will attempt to mount all of them whether or not they are needed.

The Direct Map

The direct map is used to mount NFS shares automatically on any number of unrelated mount points. Each direct map entry places a separate share entry to the */etc/mtab* file, which maintains a list of all mounted file systems whether they are local or remote. Some key points to note when working with direct maps are:

- ✓ Direct mounted shares are always visible to users.
- ✓ Local and direct mounted shares can co-exist under one parent directory.
- ✓ Accessing a directory containing many direct mount points mounts all shares.

Exercise 10-9: Access an NFS Share with a Direct Map

This exercise should be done on *server2*.

For this exercise, an NFS server is set up in Chapter 20 "Sharing File Storage with NFS" on *server1*, sharing */nfsrhcsa* directory in read-only mode with appropriate firewall rules and SELinux settings in place.

In this exercise, you will configure a direct map for this NFS share to mount it automatically on */autodir* with AutoFS.

1. Install the autofs package called autofs:

    # **yum –y install autofs**
    . . . .
    Package 1:autofs-5.0.7-40.el7.x86_64 already installed and latest version
    Nothing to do

2. Create a mount point called */autodir* if it does not already exist. This mount point will be used to mount the NFS share.

    # **mkdir /autoind**

3. Edit the */etc/auto.master* file and add the following entry if it does not already exist. This entry will instruct the AutoFS service to consult the *auto.direct* file for direct map entries.

    /–   /etc/auto.direct

4. Create */etc/auto.direct* file and add the mount point and the NFS server and share information:

    /autodir   server1.example.com:/nfsrhcsa

5. Set the AutoFS service to autostart at system reboots:

 # systemctl enable autofs
ln -s '/usr/lib/systemd/system/autofs.service' '/etc/systemd/system/multi-user.target.wants/autofs.service'

6. Start the AutoFS service and verify its operational state:

 # systemctl start autofs
 # systemctl status autofs
autofs.service - Automounts filesystems on demand
   Loaded: loaded (/usr/lib/systemd/system/autofs.service; enabled)
   Active: active (running) since Mon 2015-03-16 23:35:47 MIST; 1h 1min ago
 Main PID: 8219 (automount)
  CGroup: /system.slice/autofs.service
        └─8219 /usr/sbin/automount --pid-file /run/aut...

7. Run the *ll* command on the mount point */autodir* and then execute the *mount* command to verify that the share is automounted and accessible for use:

 # ll /autodir
 # mount | grep autodir
/etc/auto.direct on /autodir type autofs
(ro,relatime,fd=18,pgrp=9129,timeout=300,minproto=5,maxproto=5,direct)
server1.example.com:/nfsrhcsa on /autodir type nfs4
(ro,relatime,vers=4.0,rsize=131072,wsize=131072,namlen=255,hard,proto=tcp,port=0,timeo=600,retrans=2,sec=sys,clientaddr=192.168.0.120,local_lock=none,addr=192.168.0.110)

This completes the AutoFS setup for an NFS file system on the client using a direct map. You can wait for five minutes and then run the *mount* command again to observe the disappearance of the file system. A *cd* or *ll* on the mount point will bring the file system back.

The Indirect Map

The indirect map is used to automatically mount shares under one common parent directory. Some key points to note when working with indirect maps are:

✓ Indirect mounted shares become visible only after they have been accessed.
✓ Local and indirect mounted shares cannot co-exist under the same parent directory.
✓ Each indirect map puts only one entry in the */etc/mtab* file.
✓ Accessing a directory containing many indirect mount points shows only the shares that are already mounted.

All three maps have their own advantages and disadvantages. However, by comparing their features, it seems more prudent to use indirect maps for automounting NFS shares. This statement may not be true for every environment, as there are specifics that dictate which option or combination to go with.

Exercise 10-10: Access an NFS Share with an Indirect Map

This exercise should be done on *server2*.

For this exercise, an NFS server is set up in Chapter 20 "Sharing File Storage with NFS" on *server1*, sharing */nfsrhcsa* directory in read-only mode with appropriate firewall rules and SELinux settings in place.

In this exercise, you will configure an indirect map for this NFS share to mount it automatically under */misc* with AutoFS. You will observe that the specified mount point "autoind" will be automatically created by AutoFS under */misc*.

1. Install the autofs package called autofs:

    # **yum –y install autofs**

2. Edit */etc/auto.master* and ensure that the following indirect map entry is defined. This entry will instruct the AutoFS service to consult the *auto.misc* file for indirect map entries.

    /misc   /etc/auto.misc

3. Edit */etc/auto.misc* file and add the mount point and the NFS server and share information to the bottom of the file:

    autoind   server1.example.com:/nfsrhcsa

4. Set the AutoFS service to autostart at system reboots:

    # **systemctl enable autofs**

5. Start the AutoFS service and verify its operational state:

    # **systemctl start autofs**
    # **systemctl status autofs**

6. Run the *ll* command on the mount point */misc/autoind* and then execute the *mount* command to verify that the share is automounted and accessible for use. Observe the creation of *autoind* under */misc* by AutoFS.

    # **ll /misc/autoind**
    # **mount | grep autoind**
    server1.example.com:/nfsrhcsa on /misc/autoind type nfs4
    (ro,relatime,vers=4.0,rsize=131072,wsize=131072,namlen=255,hard,proto=tcp,port=0,timeo=600,retr
    ans=2,sec=sys,clientaddr=192.168.0.120,local_lock=none,addr=192.168.0.110)

This completes the AutoFS setup for an NFS file system on the client using an indirect map. You can wait for five minutes and then run the *mount* command again to observe the disappearance of the file system. A *cd* or *ll* on the mount point will bring the file system back.

Automounting User Home Directories Using Wildcard Substitution

AutoFS allows us to use two special characters in indirect maps. These special characters are asterisk (*) and ampersand (&), and are used to replace the references to specific mount points, and

NFS servers and share subdirectories, respectively. With user home directories located under */home*, for instance, and shared by one or more NFS servers, the *automount* daemon will contact all of them simultaneously when a user attempts to log on to the client. The daemon will only mount that specific user's home directory rather than the entire */home*. The indirect map entry for this type of substitution is defined in an indirect map, such as */etc/auto.home*, and will look like:

```
*    –nfs4,rw   &:/home/&
```

With this entry in place, there is no need to update any AutoFS configuration files if NFS servers with */home* shared are added or removed. Similarly, if user home directories are added or deleted, there will be no impact on the functionality of AutoFS either. If there is only one NFS server sharing the home directories, you can simply specify its name in place of the first & sign in the above entry.

You will also need to update the */etc/auto.master* map to reflect the addition of this indirect map:

```
/home        /etc/auto.home
```

Reload the AutoFS maps or restart the AutoFS service after the above changes have been made, and then try to log in with a valid user account. You should be able to log in with your home directory automounted.

To test the above configuration, set up a system to share /home using NFS. Create a few user accounts on both the server and client. Do not create user home directories on the client, just have /home available. Refer to Chapter 20 "Sharing File Storage with NFS" to get assistance on the NFS server setup.

EXAM TIP: You may need to configure AutoFS for mounting user home directories for one or more users. A successful implementation of this setup will also allow OpenLDAP users to be able to log in and be placed in their automounted home directories.

Understanding and Managing Swap

Physical memory in the system is a finite temporary storage resource used for loading kernel and data structures, and running user programs and applications. *Swap space* is a region on the physical disk used for holding idle data temporarily until it is needed. The system divides the physical memory into smaller chunks called *pages* and maps their physical locations to virtual locations on the swap to facilitate access by system processors. This physical-to-virtual mapping of pages is stored in a *page table* and is maintained by the kernel.

When a program or process is spawned, it requires space in the physical memory to run and be processed. Although many programs can run concurrently, the physical memory cannot hold all of them at the same time. The kernel monitors the memory usage. As long as the free memory remains below a high threshold, nothing happens. However, when the free memory falls below that threshold, the system starts moving selected idle pages of data from physical memory to the swap space in an effort to make room to accommodate other programs. This piece in the process is referred to as *page out*. Since the system CPU performs the process execution in a round-robin fashion, when the system needs this paged-out data for execution, the CPU looks for that data in the physical memory and a *page fault* occurs, resulting in moving the pages back to the physical memory from the swap. The return of this data to the physical memory is referred to as *page in,* and the entire process of paging data out and in is known as *demand paging.*

RHEL systems with less physical memory but high memory requirements can become so busy with paging out and in that they do not have enough cycles to carry out other useful tasks, resulting in degraded system performance. In this situation the system appears to be frozen. The excessive amount of paging that affects the system performance is called *thrashing.*

When thrashing begins, or when the free physical memory falls below a low threshold, the system deactivates idle processes and prevents new processes from being initiated. The idle processes only get reactivated and new processes are only allowed to be started when the system discovers that the available physical memory has climbed above the threshold level and thrashing has ceased.

Determining Swap Usage

The size of a swap should not be less than the amount of physical memory; however, depending on application requirements, it may be twice the size, or even larger. It is also not uncommon to see systems with less swap than the actual amount of physical memory. This is especially witnessed on systems with a very large physical memory size.

We can issue the *free* command to view how much physical memory is installed, used, and free on the system. The –h flag may be used to list the values in human readable format.

free –h

	total	used	free	shared	buffers	cached
Mem:	994M	441M	552M	6.9M	3.0M	226M
-/+ buffers/cache:	212M	782M				
Swap:	499M	0M	499M			

Alternatively, we can also view the contents of the */proc/meminfo* file to determine memory information:

cat /proc/meminfo

MemTotal:	1017992 kB
MemFree:	566216 kB
MemAvailable:	710144 kB
. . . .	
SwapTotal:	511996 kB
SwapFree:	511996 kB
. . . .	

There is about 1GB (MemTotal) of total memory on this system. For better performance, the kernel uses as much memory as it can for caching data. As reads and writes occur constantly, the kernel struggles to keep the data in cache as pertinent as possible. The caching information is reported as the sum of the number of buffers and cached pages. The portion of the cache memory used by a certain process is released when the process is terminated, and is allocated to a new process as needed. The above output indicates that about 184MB (Inactive) of the total memory is available for use by new processes. The output also displays the total configured swap (SwapTotal) and how much of it is currently available (SwapFree).

Exercise 10-11: Create and Activate Swap Spaces

This exercise should be done on *server1*.

In this exercise, you will create swap structures in *vdb2* using the *mkswap* command. You will create *swapvol* logical volume in *vg10* of size 300MB. You will enable swap in both using the *swapon* command. You will add entries to the */etc/fstab* file so that both swap regions are activated at reboots. Finally, you will reboot the system and confirm by using appropriate commands that the new swap regions have been successfully activated.

> **EXAM TIP:** Use lsblk to determine available disk space.

1. Create swap structures in the *vdb2* partition using the *mkswap* command:

   # mkswap /dev/vdb2
   mkswap: /dev/vdb2: warning: wiping old LVM2_member signature.
   Setting up swapspace version 1, size = 488444 KiB
   no label, UUID=40809164-d5a3-40f7-9862-cce2a6e532ce

2. Create logical volume *swapvol* in *vg10* of size 300MB using the *lvcreate* command:

   # lvcreate –L 300m –n swapvol vg10
   Logical volume "swapvol" created

3. Create swap structures in *swapvol* using the *mkswap* command:

   # mkswap /dev/vg10/swapvol
   Setting up swapspace version 1, size = 307196 KiB
   no label, UUID=5ccdcb52-fd4b-4409-a5e9-38fa390c20f6

4. Enable swapping in the partition and the logical volume using the *swapon* command:

   # swapon /dev/vdb2
   # swapon –v /dev/vg10/swapvol
   swapon /dev/vg10/swapvol
   swapon: /dev/mapper/vg10-swapvol: found swap signature: version 1, page-size 4, same byte order
   swapon: /dev/mapper/vg10-swapvol: pagesize=4096, swapsize=314572800, devsize=314572800

5. Confirm the activation of swap in the new areas by running either the *swapon* command with the –s switch or viewing the contents of the */proc/swaps* file:

   # swapon –s
   # cat /proc/swaps

Filename	Type	Size	Used	Priority
/dev/dm-0	partition	511996	0	-1
/dev/vdb2	partition	488444	0	-2
/dev/dm-5	partition	307196	0	-3

6. Display virtual memory statistics using the *vmstat* command:

```
# vmstat
procs -------------memory------------- --swap-- -----io---- ---system-- --------cpu----------
 r  b   swpd    free     buff    cache   si  so   bi   bo    in   cs   us sy  id   wa st
 2  0    0     564316   4084   231616   0   0    3    2    11   14    0  0  100   0  0
```

The command produced the output in six categories: procs, memory, swap, io, system, and cpu. The r and b under procs show the number of processes waiting to run and in uninterruptible sleep; the swpd, free, buff, and cache under memory indicate the amount of used virtual memory, idle memory, memory used as buffers, and cache memory; the si and so under swap determine the amount of memory swapped in and out; the bi and bo under io display the number of input and output blocks; the in and cs under system indicate the number of interrupts and context switches per second; and us, sy, id, wa, and st identify the percentage of total CPU time spent in running the non-kernel code, kernel code, idle state, waiting for I/O, and stolen from a virtual machine.

We can run the *vmstat* command with the –s switch to display the output in a different format:

```
# vmstat –s
     1017992 K total memory
      454584 K used memory
. . . . . . . .
     1307636 K total swap
           0 K used swap
     1307636 K free swap
. . . . . . . .
      365467 pages paged in
      210291 pages paged out
. . . . . . . .
```

7. Finally, edit the *fstab* file and add entries for both swap areas for auto-activation during reboots:

```
UUID=40809164-d5a3-40f7-9862-cce2a6e532ce      swap    swap    defaults  0      0
/dev/vg10/swapvol                              swap    swap    defaults  0      0
```

> **EXAM TIP:** You will not be given any credit for this work if you forget to add an entry to the /etc/fstab file.

8. Reboot the system now and issue commands used earlier in this exercise after the system comes back up to validate the activation of the new swap regions.

Exercise 10-12: Deactivate and Remove Swap Spaces

This exercise should be done on *server1*.

In this exercise, you will deactivate both swap regions that you added in the previous exercise with the *swapoff* command. You will remove their entries from the *fstab* file and reboot the system to confirm.

1. Deactivate swap in *vdb2* and *swapvol* using the *swapoff* command:

```
# swapoff –v /dev/vdb2
swapoff /dev/vdb2
# swapoff /dev/vg10/swapvol
swapoff /dev/vg10/swapvol
```

2. Remove the partition and the logical volume using appropriate tools:

```
# parted /dev/vdb rm 2
# lvremove –f /dev/vg10/swapvol
Logical volume "swapvol" successfully removed
```

3. Edit the *fstab* file and remove their entries.
4. Reboot the system to confirm a smooth startup following the removals. Use appropriate commands to validate the removal.

Access Control Lists (ACLs)

The *Access Control Lists* (ACLs) provide an extended group of permissions that may be set on files and directories. These permissions are in addition to the standard Linux file and directory permissions, and the special setuid, setgid, and sticky bit permissions that we discussed earlier in Chapter 03 "Working with Files and File Permissions". The ACLs allow us to define permissions for specific users and groups using either the octal or symbolic notation of permission allocation. The specific users may or may not be part of the same group. ACLs are configured and treated the same way on both files and directories. Before any ACLs are applied to a file or directory, the file system it is located in has to be mounted or remounted with ACL support enabled. This support is turned on for XFS file systems by default; however, it needs to be activated for extended file systems. ACLs can also be used on both NFS and CIFS file systems.

ACLs are categorized into two groups based on their types, and are referred to as *access ACLs* and *default ACLs*. Access ACLs are set on individual files and directories whereas default ACLs can only be applied at the directory level. Files and sub-directories under a parent directory with default ACLs set inherit the default ACL settings.

ACL Management Commands

ACL support is loaded on the system at the time of OS installation via the *acl* software package. This package includes three management commands—*chacl*, *getfacl*, and *setfacl*—and are described in Table 10-5.

Command	Description
chacl	Changes ACL settings on a file or directory. Available for users who are familiar with its use from IRIX UNIX.
getfacl	Displays ACL settings for a file or directory.
setfacl	Sets, modifies, substitutes, and deletes ACL settings on a file or directory.

Table 10-5 ACL Management Commands

Here we are going to use the *getfacl* and *setfacl* commands only as they are more common than *chacl*. The *getfacl* command has several options that we may specify to see the output as desired;

however, it displays all necessary information without furnishing any options with it. The example below creates an empty file *file1* in */root* and then displays the ACLs on it:

```
# pwd
/root
# touch file1
# getfacl file1
# file: file1
# owner: root
# group: root
user::rw-
group::r--
other::r--
```

The output shows the names of the file, the owner, and the owning group as comments and then it displays the present permissions placed on the file: read and write for the owner and read-only for everyone else. Notice the two colon characters in the permission rows. They currently contain nothing between them but this is where a specific user, a specific group, or their corresponding UID or GID is inserted when extended permissions are set on the file with the *setfacl* command. For instance, ACLs user:1000:r-- on a file would imply that a user with UID 1000, who is not the owner of the file or a member of the owning group, is allowed only read access to this file. Similarly, the ACL setting group:dba:rw- would give a non-owning group (dba in this case) read and write access to the file.

In addition to using the *getfacl* command for viewing ACL settings, the *ll* command also indicates the presence of ACLs by showing the + sign right beside the permissions column in the output. An example permissions column from the *ll* command would be -rw-rw-r--+.

The *setfacl* command is used to apply or modify ACL settings on a file or directory. The way it accepts specific permissions at the command line is explained in Table 10-6.

ACL Rule	Description
u[ser]:UID:perms	Permissions assigned to a specific user (user name or UID). The user must exist in the /etc/passwd file.
g[roup]:GID:perms	Permissions assigned to a specific group (group name or GID). The group must exist in the /etc/group file.
m[ask]:perms	Maximum permissions a specific user or a specific group can have on a file or directory. If this is set to rw-, for example, then no specific user or group will have more permissions than read and write.
o[ther]:perms	Permissions assigned to users not in the owning group.

Table 10-6 ACL Rules

The *setfacl* command provides several switches to use depending on what we want to achieve. Table 10-7 describes some of them.

Switch	Description
-b	Removes all ACL settings.
-d	Applies to the default ACLs.
-k	Removes all default ACL settings.

Switch	Description
-m	Sets or modifies ACL settings.
-R	Applies recursively to all files and sub-directories.
-x	Removes an ACL setting.

Table 10-7 setfacl Command Switches

We will use some of these switches shortly.

The Role of the mask Value

The value of mask determines the maximum allowable permissions placed for a specific user or group on a file or directory. If it is set to rw, for instance, no specific user or group will exceed those permissions. The mask value is displayed on a separate line in the *getfacl* command output. Each time ACLs are modified for a file or directory, the mask is recalculated automatically and applied unless we supply our own desired mask value with the command. On *file1*, there are no ACLs currently set as shown below. The –c option instructs the command not to display the header information.

```
# getfacl –c file1
user::rw-
group::r--
other::r--
```

If we give read and write permissions to *user1* and change the mask to read-only at the same time, the command will allocate the permissions as mentioned; however, the effective permissions for the user will only be read-only.

```
# setfacl –m u:user1:rw,m:r file1
# getfacl –c file1
user::rw-
user:user1:rw-              #effective:r--
group::r--
mask::r--
other::r--
```

This means that *user1* will not be able to modify this file even though they appear to have the write permission. The actual permissions for *user1* include both read and write, but only the read bit is in effect. Now, let's promote the mask value to include the write bit as well, and observe the result:

```
# setfacl –m m:rw file1
# getfacl –c file1
user::rw-
user:user1:rw-
group::r--
mask::rw-
other::r--
```

The actual permissions for *user1* are now promoted to include the write bit to reflect the new higher mask value.

Exercise 10-13: Determine, Set, and Delete Access ACLs

This exercise should be done on *server1*.

In this exercise, you will create *file1* as *user1* in */home/user1* and will check to see if there are any ACL settings on the file. You will check to ensure that the */home* file system is mounted with acl support turned on. You will apply ACL settings on the file for *user3* and allow them full access. You will observe the change in the mask value. You will add *user4* to the ACL settings on the file. You will delete the settings for *user3* and then delete all other ACL settings from the file.

1. Log in as *user1* and create *file1*. Run the *ll* and *getfacl* commands on the file and see if there are any ACL entries placed on it.

   $ **pwd**
   /home/user1
   $ **touch file1**
   $ **ll file1**
   -rw-rw-r--. 1 user1 user1 0 Nov 4 21:12 file1
   $ **getfacl file1**
   # file: file1
   # owner: user1
   # group: user1
   user::rw-
   group::rw-
   other::r--

   The output indicates an absence of ACL settings on the file. It also shows the owner and owning group names. The owner and group members have read and write permissions and everyone else has the read-only permission.

2. Now, log in as *root* on a different terminal (or switch into *root* with the *su* command) and check the file system type for */home*. If it is an extended file system, run *mount | grep home* to determine if acl support is turned on. If not, issue the following to remount the file system with that support:

   # **mount −o remount,acl /home**

   > **EXAM TIP:** Modify the /etc/fstab file and replace 'defaults' with 'acl' (or add 'acl' if other options are listed) in the mount options field for the extended file system where you want ACLs set up.

   There is no need to check this for an XFS file system as the acl support is an integral part of it.

3. Allocate read/write/execute permissions to *user3* with the *setfacl* command using the octal notation for permission representation. Run this command as *user1*.

   $ **setfacl −m u:user3:7 file1**

4. Run the *ll* command to check if the + sign has appeared by the permission settings and the *getfacl* command to check the new ACL settings:

```
$ ll
-rw-rwxr--+ 1 user1 user1 0 Nov 4 21:12 file1
$ getfacl –c file1
user::rw-
user:user3:rwx
group::rw-
mask::rwx
other::r--
```

A row is added for *user3* showing rwx (7) permissions. Another row showing the mask is also added and is set to rwx (7) as well. The mask value determines the maximum permissions assigned to a specific user or group. In this case, the maximum permissions allocated to *user3* are rwx and the mask reflects it.

5. Add *user4* with read/write permissions to *file1* using the symbolic notation for permission representation:

```
$ setfacl –m u:user4:rw file1
$ getfacl file1
user::rw-
user:user3:rwx
user:user4:rw-
group::rw-
mask::rwx
other::r--
```

6. Delete the ACL entries set for *user3* and confirm:

```
$ setfacl –x u:user3 file1
$ getfacl file1
user::rw-
user:user4:rw-
group::rw-
mask::rw-
other::r--
```

Notice that the mask value has reduced to read/write, which reflects the current maximum permissions placed on the specific user *user4*.

7. Delete all the ACL entries set on *file1*:

```
$ setfacl –b file1
```

Confirm after the deletion using the *getfacl* command.

Default ACLs
Sometimes it is imperative for several users that belong to different groups to be able to share the contents of a common directory. They want permissions set up on this directory in such a way that the files and sub-directories created underneath inherit its permissions. This way the users do not

have to adjust permissions on each file and sub-directory they create under the parent directory. Setting default ACLs on a directory fulfills this requirement.

The default ACLs can be described as the maximum discretionary permissions that can be allocated on a directory. Table 10-8 describes the syntax for applying default entries with the *setfacl* command.

ACL Entry	Description
d[efault]:u:perms	Default standard Linux permissions for the owner.
d[efault]:u:UID:perms	Default permissions for a specific user (user name or UID).
d[efault]:g:perms	Default standard Linux permissions for the owning group.
d[efault]:g:GID:perms	Default permissions for a specific group (group name or GID).
d[efault]:o:perms	Default permissions for public.
d[efault]:m:perms	Default maximum permissions a user or group can have when they create a file in a directory with default ACLs in place.

Table 10-8 Format for Using Default ACLs

Let's apply the concept in the following exercise for a better understanding.

Exercise 10-14: Set, Confirm, and Delete Default ACLs

This exercise should be done on *server1*.

In this exercise, you will create a directory */home/user4/projects* as *user4* and set default ACL entries for *user1* and *user3* to allow them read and write permissions on this directory. You will create a sub-directory *prj1* and a file *file1* under *projects* and observe the effect of default ACLs on them. You will delete all the default entries at the end of the exercise.

1. Log in as *user4* and create *projects*. Run the *getfacl* command and see what the default permissions are on the directory.

    $ pwd
    /home/user4
    $ mkdir projects
    $ getfacl projects
    # file: project
    # owner: user4
    # group: user4
    user::rwx
    group::rwx
    other::r-x

2. Allocate default read and write permissions to *user1* and *user3* with the *setfacl* command. Run this command as *user4* and use octal notation.

    $ setfacl –m d:u:user1:6,d:u:user3:6 projects
    $ getfacl –c projects
    user::rwx
    group::rwx
    other::r-x

```
default:user::rwx
default:user:user1:rw-
default:user:user3:rw-
default:group::rwx
default:mask::rwx
default:other::r-x
```

3. Create a sub-directory *prj1* under *projects* and observe that it has inherited the ACL settings from its parent directory:

   $ cd projects ; mkdir prj1
   $ getfacl –c prj1
   ```
   user::rwx
   user:user1:rw-
   user:user3:rw-
   group::rwx
   mask::rwx
   other::r-x
   default:user::rwx
   default:user:user1:rw-
   default:user:user3:rw-
   default:group::rwx
   default:mask::rwx
   default:other::r-x
   ```

4. Create a file *file1* under *projects* and observe the inheritance of ACLs from the parent directory:

   $ touch file1
   $ getfacl –c file1
   ```
   user::rw-
   user:user1:rw-
   user:user3:rw-
   group::rwx          #effective:rw-
   mask::rw-
   other::r--
   ```

   The output indicates that the maximum permissions the group members have on the file are read and write, and the execute permission for them is ineffective due to the mask setting.

5. Delete all the default ACL settings from the directory and confirm:

   $ setfacl –k project
   $ getfacl –c project
   ```
   user::rwx
   group::rwx
   other::r-x
   ```

Confirm the deletion with the *getfacl* command.

Chapter Summary

This chapter discussed local and remote file systems, AutoFS, swap, and ACLs. We reviewed file system concepts and types, and learned about extended and xfs file systems. We looked at various file system administration utilities. We studied the concepts around mounting and unmounting file systems. We examined the UUID associated with file systems and applied labels to file systems. We analyzed the file system table and added entries to it to automatically activate file systems at system reboots. We looked at a tool for reporting file system usage. We learned about file system check utilities for determining and fixing issues related to unhealthy file systems. We performed a number of exercises on file system administration and repair to reinforce the concepts learned.

We looked at mounting and unmounting remote file systems on the client manually, via the fstab file, and using the AutoFS service. We discussed the concepts, benefits, and components associated with AutoFS. We performed exercises to fortify our understanding of mounting remote file systems using the three mount methods.

We studied the concepts around swapping and paging, and looked at how they worked. We performed exercises on creating, activating, viewing, deactivating, and removing swap spaces, as well as configuring them for auto-activation at system reboots.

Finally, we covered ACLs at length. We learned concepts and the purpose of applying extended security attributes on files and directories. We performed exercises to strengthen our understanding.

Chapter Review Questions

1. xfs is the default file system type in RHEL7. True or False?
2. What would the entry " *   server10:/home/& " in an AutoFS indirect map imply?
3. What type of information does the *blkid* command display?
4. What is the process of paging out and paging in known as?
5. What would the command *mkswap /dev/vdc2* do?
6. Where does AutoFS automount a DVD?
7. Which two files contain entries for mounted file systems?
8. What would happen if we mount a file system on a directory that already contains files in it?
9. What type of AutoFS map would have the "/- /etc/auto.media" entry in the *auto.master* file?
10. A UUID is always assigned to a file system at its creation time. True or False?
11. What would the command *mount –t cifs –o ro //192.168.0.120/cifs1 /cifs1* do?
12. The difference between the primary and backup superblocks is that the primary superblock includes pointers to the data blocks where the actual file contents are stored whereas the backup superblocks don't. True or False?
13. What would the command *setfacl –m d:u:user1:7,d:u:user4:6,d:o:4 dir* do?
14. AutoFS requires root privileges to automatically mount a network file system. True or False?
15. What would the command *mkfs.ext4 /dev/vgtest/lvoltest* do?
16. Arrange the tasks in correct sequence: umount file system, mount file system, create file system, remove file system.
17. The *parted* utility may be used to create LVM logical volumes. True or False?
18. Which command can we use to create a label for an xfs file system?
19. What is the default timeout value for a file system before AutoFS unmounts it automatically?
20. What would the *mount* command do with the –a switch?
21. Name the four types of maps that AutoFS support.
22. What would the command *df –t xfs* do?

23. What would happen if we try to apply ACL settings to a file that resides in an ACL-deactivated file system?
24. What would the command *setfacl –m u::7,g::4,o:4,u:user3:7 file* do?
25. What is the difference between the *mkfs.ext4* and *mke2fs* commands?
26. What two commands can be used to determine the total and used physical memory and swap in the system?
27. Which virtual file contains information about the current swap?
28. The */etc/fstab* file can be used to activate swap spaces automatically at system reboots. True or False?
29. The *xfs_repair* command must be run on a mounted file system. True or False?
30. What is the name of the AutoFS configuration file and where is it located?
31. Name of the AutoFS daemon is *automountd*. True or False?
32. What are the commands to activate and deactivate swap spaces manually? Write two commands.

Answers to Chapter Review Questions

1. True.
2. This indirect map entry would mount individual user home directories from server10.
3. The *blkid* command displays block device file attributes.
4. The process of paging out and in is known as demand paging.
5. The command provided will create swap structures in the */dev/vdc2* partition.
6. AutoFS mounts a DVD under */misc*.
7. The */etc/mtab* and the */proc/mounts* files.
8. The files in the directory will hide.
9. A direct map.
10. True.
11. The command provided will mount the CIFS file system *cifs1* in read-only mode on the */cifs1* mount point from Samba server with IP address 192.168.0.120.
12. False.
13. The command provided will set default ACLs of rwx for *user1*, rw for *user4*, and r-only for everyone else on the *dir* directory.
14. False.
15. The command provided will format */dev/vgtest/lvoltest* logical volume with ext4 file system type.
16. Create, mount, unmount, and remove.
17. False.
18. The *xfs_admin* command can be used to create a label for an xfs file system.
19. Five minutes.
20. The command provided will mount all file systems listed in the */etc/fstab* file but are currently not mounted.
21. The AutoFS service supports master, special, direct, and indirect maps.
22. The command provided will display all mounted file systems of type xfs.
23. The attempt to apply ACLs to a file located in an ACL-deactivated file system is not allowed.
24. The command provided will assign rwx permissions to file owner and user3, and read-only permission to everyone else.
25. No difference.
26. The *free* and *vmstat* commands.
27. The */proc/swaps* file contains information about the current swap.

28. True.
29. False.
30. The name of the AutoFS configuration file is autofs and it is located in the */etc/sysconfig* directory.
31. False.
32. The *swapon* and *swapoff* commands.

DIY Challenge Labs

The following labs are useful to strengthen most of the concepts and topics learned in this chapter. It is expected that you perform these labs without any additional help. A step-by-step guide is not provided, as the implementation of these labs requires the knowledge that has been presented in this chapter. Use defaults or your own thinking for missing information.

Lab 10-1: Create and Mount an Extended File System

Destroy all partitions and volume groups created on *vdb*, *vdc*, *vdd*, and *vde* drives in previous labs and exercises.

Create a partition in *vdb* of size 1GB and initialize it with ext4 file system structures. Initialize the *vdc* disk for use in LVM, create a volume group called *vgtest* and include the *vdc* disk in it. Create *oravol* logical volume of size 1GB in the volume group and initialize it with ext4 file system structures. Create mount points of your choice, and mount both file systems manually. Apply any label to the file system created in *vdb1* and add both file systems to the *fstab* file using the label of *vdb1* and the LV name of *oravol*. Reboot the system and test if it boots up successfully and mounts both new file systems.

Lab 10-2: Automount a Network File System

In Exercise 20-1, a directory called */common* is shared in read/write mode via the NFS protocol. In order to perform this lab, complete that exercise, and then set AutoFS maps appropriately on the client to automount */common* on */mntauto* using a direct map. Set the idle time period to 60 seconds. Reboot the system and test to ensure the automount works as expected. Remove the direct map configuration and replace it with an indirect map to automount */common* on */mnt/automnt*. Test the configuration.

Lab 10-3: Create and Enable Swap

Create *vdb2* of size 1.2GB and *lvswap2* in *vgtest* of size 1.8GB. Initialize both for use as swap. Create swap structures in them and add entries to the file system table so that they are automatically activated at each system reboot. Use defaults or your own ideas for missing information.

Lab 10-4: Apply ACL Settings

Create a file called *testfile* in *user1*'s home directory. Create a directory in *user2*'s home directory and call it *dir1*. Ensure that the */home* file system is mounted with acl option activated. Apply settings on *testfile* so that *user2* gets 7, *user3* gets 6, and *user4* gets 4 permissions. Apply default settings on *dir1* so that *user4* gets 7 and *user2* gets 5 permissions on it.

## Chapter 11

Controlling Access through Firewall and SELinux

This chapter describes the following major topics:

➤ Comprehend iptables firewall for host-based security control
➤ Control iptables and firewalld services
➤ Use iptables command to manage firewall rules
➤ Understand firewalld configuration files and command
➤ Use firewall-cmd command to manage firewall rules
➤ Overview of Firewall Configuration tool
➤ Describe Security Enhanced Linux and its terminology
➤ Understand SELinux contexts for users, processes, files, and ports
➤ What is domain transitioning?
➤ Copy, move, and archive files with SELinux contexts
➤ Overview of SELinux booleans
➤ Manage SELinux via commands
➤ Modify SELinux contexts for users, files, and ports
➤ Overview of SELinux administration tool
➤ View and analyze SELinux alerts

RHCSA Objectives:

48. Configure firewall settings using firewall-config, firewall-cmd, or iptables
50. Set enforcing and permissive modes for SELinux
51. List and identify SELinux file and process context
52. Restore default file contexts
53. Use boolean settings to modify system SELinux settings
54. Diagnose and address routine SELinux policy violations

R unning a system in a networked or an Internet-facing environment requires that some measures be taken to tighten access to the system by identifying the type and level of security needed, and implementing it. Security features such as file and directory permissions, user and group-level permissions, shadow password and password aging mechanisms, and ACLs have been discussed in the previous chapters. This chapter covers firewall and SELinux in fair detail. In the RHCE section of this book, we will be using the knowledge gained in this chapter at an advanced level to modify firewall rules and SELinux settings to allow network services to work with these security services without issues.

Understanding and Managing Firewall

A *firewall* is a protective layer that is configured between a private and a public network to segregate traffic. There are several types of firewalls, one of which performs data packet filtering. A data packet is formed as a result of a process called *encapsulation* whereby the header information is attached to a message during the formation of the packet. The header includes information such as source and destination IP addresses, port, and type of data. Based on pre-defined *rules*, a firewall intercepts each inbound and outbound data packet, inspects its header, and decides whether to allow the packet to pass through. A port is defined in the */etc/services* file for each network service available on the system, and is typically standardized across all network operating systems, including RHEL. Some common services and the ports they listen on are: *ftp* on port 21, *ssh* on 22, *telnet* on 23, *postfix* on 25, *http* on 80, and *ntp* on port 123.

RHEL comes standard with a host-based packet-filtering firewall software called *iptables* that communicates with the netfilter module in the kernel for policing the flow of data packets. Other major usages of iptables are to provide support for Network Address Translation (NAT) and port forwarding, which are explained in detail in Chapter 17 "Working with Firewalld and Kerberos".

iptables with and without firewalld

Beginning with RHEL7, the *iptables* service and firewall rulesets may be configured and managed through a new dynamic firewall service daemon called *firewalld*. The major advantage is the daemon's ability to immediately apply the updates without causing a disruption to current network connections, and this can be done anytime. It has eliminated the need to save or apply the changes, reload the rules, restart the service, or reboot the system. These benefits provide us with the flexibility to add and modify firewall rules and activate them on operational systems as and when desired. This service daemon lets us perform management operations at the command line using the *firewall-cmd* command, graphically using the *firewall-config* tool, or manually by editing necessary files. See Figure 11-1 for a comparison between how the netfilter module is accessed with and without firewalld.

Knowing that *firewalld* is a better way of managing iptables on RHEL7, if we still do not want to use it for one or the other reason, we can simply disable it and continue to use the *iptables* command to manage iptables rules the way we did on previous RHEL versions.

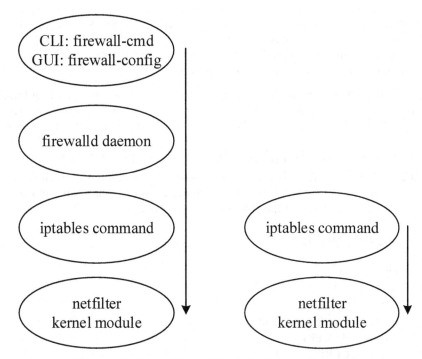

Figure 11-1 iptables with and without firewalld

While iptables without *firewalld* stores all rules in the */etc/sysconfig/iptables* file, iptables with *firewalld* saves firewall policy rules in the */etc/firewalld/* directory and provides several templates for various services in the */usr/lib/firewalld/* directory. These templates may be copied and modified for new services. In addition, *firewalld* presents the concept of zones that allow us to define policies based on the trust level for network connections, interfaces, and source IP addresses that are bound to the zone. A zone may include configuration items comprising services, ports, protocols, masquerading, port forwarding, ICMP filters, and rich language rules. The firewalld software package provides several pre-defined zone files in the XML format in the */usr/lib/firewalld/zones/* directory. These zone files include templates for traffic that must be blocked or dropped, and for traffic that is intended for public-facing, internal, external, home, public, trusted, and work-related network traffic. Of these, the public zone is the default and it is activated by default when the *firewalld* service is started. We may create custom zones to meet our specific requirements.

In the presence of both iptables and firewalld software, only one of the two can be used at a time; they cannot be used simultaneously.

To check whether iptables and firewalld packages are installed on the system, issue the *yum* command as follows:

```
# yum list installed | egrep 'iptables|firewalld'
iptables.x86_64              1.4.21-13.el7      @anaconda/7.0
iptables-services.x86_64     1.4.21-13.el7      @anaconda/7.0
firewall-config.noarch       0.3.9-7.el7        @anaconda/7.0
firewalld.noarch             0.3.9-7.el7        @anaconda/7.0
```

The above output indicates the presence of required support on the system for both iptables and firewalld. In case of a missing package for the service that we intend to employ on our system, we need to use the *yum* command to install it along with any dependent packages that are required for a successful installation and subsequent service operation.

In this chapter, our focus will be on learning the basics of both services, and on familiarizing ourselves with respective administration tools. We will see how these tools are used to add, modify, and delete rules. In the RHCE section of this book, we will discuss firewalld in more detail.

Understanding the iptables Configuration File

The configuration file for iptables is called *iptables* and it is located in the */etc/sysconfig* directory. This file stores all necessary rulesets that are needed to control the inbound and outbound traffic on the system. The default contents of the file are shown below:

```
# cat /etc/sysconfig/iptables
*filter
:INPUT ACCEPT [0:0]
:FORWARD ACCEPT [0:0]
:OUTPUT ACCEPT [9:1624]
-A INPUT -m state --state RELATED,ESTABLISHED -j ACCEPT
-A INPUT -p icmp -j ACCEPT
-A INPUT -i lo -j ACCEPT
-A INPUT -p tcp -m state --state NEW -m tcp --dport 22 -j ACCEPT
-A INPUT -j REJECT --reject-with icmp-host-prohibited
-A FORWARD -j REJECT --reject-with icmp-host-prohibited
COMMIT
```

iptables allows us to define tables containing groups of rules called *chains*, with each table related to a different type of packet processing. In the output above, one default table called *filter* is defined (marked with *), which includes three pre-defined chains (INPUT, FORWARD, and OUTPUT), with the INPUT chain containing several rules. Each inbound and outbound packet goes through at least one of these configured chains. Packets destined for the local system use the INPUT chain, packets originating from the local system use the OUTPUT chain, and packets that need to be routed to a different network use the FORWARD chain. Each chain has a policy called *target*, which can have a value such as ACCEPT, REJECT, DROP, or LOG. The ACCEPT policy allows a packet to pass through, the REJECT policy throws a packet away and sends a notification back, the DROP policy throws a packet away without returning a notification, and the LOG policy sends packet information to the *rsyslogd* daemon for logging.

We also notice a connection "state" in the file contents above. It determines the state of the incoming connection that is inspected and based on which the firewall restricts the access. Some of the common connection states are NEW, ESTABLISHED, RELATED, and INVALID. The NEW state identifies a packet that is not part of an existing communication, the ESTABLISHED state indicates that the packet is part of an existing communication, the RELATED state signifies a packet that is generated in relation with some other existing communication, and the INVALID state identifies a packet that does not match other states.

The first rule in the configuration file above will continue to accept all inbound connection requests, the second rule will accept incoming ICMP requests, the third rule will accept all inbound connection requests on the loopback interface, the fourth rule will accept all new TCP requests received on port 22, and the last two entries will reject any network packets originating from any source with the icmp-host-prohibited rejection reason sent back to the source system.

It is imperative that we modify the default iptables rules to match our requirements for packet filtering associated with application accessibility.

This file may be customized using a text editor, the *iptables* command, or the *lokkit* command (part of the system-config-firewall-base package). The use of the *iptables* command for rule additions and modifications is more common. RHEL7 does not include the *system-config-firewall* graphical tool anymore.

Controlling iptables and firewalld Services

The iptables and firewalld services can be started, restarted, and stopped manually. They can also be configured to remain disabled or start automatically at system boot. As noted earlier, either of them can be used at a time. Let's use the *systemctl* command to control their actions on *server1*.

To mark the *firewalld* service for autostart:

systemctl enable firewalld
ln -s '/usr/lib/systemd/system/firewalld.service' '/etc/systemd/system/dbus-
org.fedoraproject.FirewallD1.service'
ln -s '/usr/lib/systemd/system/firewalld.service' '/etc/systemd/system/basic.target.wants/firewalld.service'

To start the *firewalld* service:

systemctl start firewalld

To check the status of this service:

systemctl status firewalld –l
firewalld.service - firewalld - dynamic firewall daemon
   Loaded: loaded (/usr/lib/systemd/system/firewalld.service; enabled)
   Active: active (running) since Sat 2014-11-08 08:10:31 EST; 1min 27s ago
 Main PID: 18228 (firewalld)
   CGroup: /system.slice/firewalld.service
        └─18228 /usr/bin/python -Es /usr/sbin/firewalld --nofork --nopid
Nov 08 08:10:30 server1.example.com systemd[1]: Starting firewalld - dynamic firewall daemon...
Nov 08 08:10:31 server1.example.com systemd[1]: Started firewalld - dynamic firewall daemon.

To stop this service:

systemctl stop firewalld

To deactivate this service:

systemctl disable firewalld
rm '/etc/systemd/system/basic.target.wants/firewalld.service'
rm '/etc/systemd/system/dbus-org.fedoraproject.FirewallD1.service'

To mark the *iptables* service for autostart:

 # systemctl enable iptables

ln -s '/usr/lib/systemd/system/iptables.service' '/etc/systemd/system/basic.target.wants/iptables.service'

To start the *iptables* service:

 # systemctl start iptables

To check the status of this service:

 # systemctl status firewalld –l

iptables.service - IPv4 firewall with iptables
  Loaded: loaded (/usr/lib/systemd/system/iptables.service; enabled)
  Active: active (exited) since Sat 2014-11-08 08:16:59 EST; 23s ago
 Process: 18784 ExecStart=/usr/libexec/iptables/iptables.init start (code=exited, status=0/SUCCESS)
 Main PID: 18784 (code=exited, status=0/SUCCESS)
Nov 08 08:16:59 server1.example.com iptables.init[18784]: iptables: Applying firewall rules: [OK]
Nov 08 08:16:59 server1.example.com systemd[1]: Started IPv4 firewall with iptables.

Now that you have iptables active and firewalld disabled, you will learn and use the iptables service in the next few sub-sections. Following that, you will disable iptables and restart firewalld to work with it.

The iptables Command

The *iptables* command is used to modify the firewall rules on the system in the absence of the *firewalld* service. This command supports several options, some of which are listed and described in Table 11-1.

Option	Description
–A (--append)	Appends one or more rules to a chain.
–D (--delete)	Deletes one or more rules from a chain.
–F (--flush)	Flushes a chain or a table.
–I (--insert)	Inserts one or more rules in a chain.
–L (--list)	Displays currently loaded rules.
–N (--new-chain)	Adds a new chain.
–R (--replace)	Replaces a rule in a chain.
–X (--delete-chain)	Deletes a chain.
–d (--destination)	Specifies a destination address.
--dport	Specifies the destination port number.
–i (--in-interface)	Specifies a network interface to be used for inbound packets.
–j (--jump)	Specifies where a packet will jump if it matches a rule.
–m (--match)	Specifies a matching name.
–o (--out-interface)	Specifies a network interface to be used for outbound packets.
–p (--protocol)	Defines a protocol as listed in the /etc/protocols file.
–s (--source)	Specifies the source address.
–t (--table)	Specifies the type of table. Default is the filter table.
–v (--verbose)	Prints verbose output.

Table 11-1 iptables Command Options

We run the *iptables* command with the –L flag to list the rules currently in place on the system:

```
# iptables –L
Chain INPUT (policy ACCEPT)
target     prot opt source          destination
ACCEPT     all  --  anywhere        anywhere             state RELATED,ESTABLISHED
ACCEPT     icmp --  anywhere        anywhere
ACCEPT     all  --  anywhere        anywhere
ACCEPT     tcp  --  anywhere        anywhere             state NEW tcp dpt:ssh
REJECT     all  --  anywhere        anywhere             reject-with icmp-host-prohibited

Chain FORWARD (policy ACCEPT)
target     prot opt source          destination
REJECT     all  --  anywhere        anywhere             reject-with icmp-host-prohibited

Chain OUTPUT (policy ACCEPT)
target     prot opt source          destination
```

The above output indicates that the INPUT, FORWARD, and OUTPUT chains are currently set to ACCEPT all traffic.

Exercise 11-1: Add and Activate iptables Rules

This exercise should be done on *server1*.

In this exercise, you will first delete all existing rules and then append rules to the filter table to allow inbound HTTP traffic on port 80, reject outbound ICMP traffic with no return notification, and forward all inbound traffic to the 192.168.0.0/24 network. You will insert a rule to allow the first and subsequent incoming FTP connection requests on port 21 and append a rule to disallow all outgoing connection requests on port 25. You will save these rules in the *iptables* file and make necessary settings so that these rules are loaded each time we reboot the system. You will restart the *iptables* service and run the appropriate command to ensure the new rules have taken place.

1. Run the *iptables* command with the –F option to remove all existing rules:

   # **iptables –F**

2. Append a rule to the filter table to allow inbound HTTP traffic on port 80:

   # **iptables –t filter –A INPUT –p tcp --dport 80 –j ACCEPT**

3. Append a rule to reject outbound ICMP traffic without sending a notification back:

   # **iptables –A OUTPUT –p icmp –j DROP**

4. Append a rule to forward all inbound traffic to the 192.168.0.0/24 network:

   # **iptables –A FORWARD –d 192.168.0.0/24 –j ACCEPT**

5. Insert a rule to allow the first and subsequent incoming FTP connection requests on port 21:

iptables –I INPUT –m state --state NEW –p tcp --dport 21 –j ACCEPT

6. Append a rule to disallow all existing and new outgoing connection requests on port 25:

    # iptables –A OUTPUT –m state --state NEW,ESTABLISHED –p tcp --dport 25 \
    –j DROP

7. Save the rules in the */etc/sysconfig/iptables* file:

    # service iptables save
    iptables: Saving firewall rules to /etc/sysconfig/iptables: [OK]

8. Set the iptables firewall service to autostart at each system reboot and validate:

    # systemctl enable iptables

9. Issue the *iptables* command and check whether the new rules have taken effect:

    # iptables –L
    Chain INPUT (policy ACCEPT)
    target   prot opt source   destination
    ACCEPT   tcp   -- anywhere   anywhere   state NEW tcp dpt:ftp
    ACCEPT   tcp   -- anywhere   anywhere   tcp dpt:http

    Chain FORWARD (policy ACCEPT)
    target   prot opt source   destination
    ACCEPT   all   --   anywhere   192.168.0.0/24

    Chain OUTPUT (policy ACCEPT)
    target   prot opt source   destination
    DROP   icmp --   anywhere   anywhere
    DROP   tcp   --   anywhere   anywhere   state NEW,ESTABLISHED tcp dpt:smtp

The output highlights in bold the presence of the five new rules you have applied in this exercise. You can also view the contents of the *iptables* file to check the rules.

Exercise 11-2: Add and Remove iptables Rules

This exercise should be done on *server1*.

In this exercise, you will insert/append rules to the default table to allow inbound traffic on port 90 from 192.168.1.0/24, reject all inbound traffic from 192.168.3.0/24 on *eth1* interface, reject outbound ICMP traffic to all systems on 192.168.3.0/24 except for the system with IP 192.168.3.3, forward all inbound traffic from 192.168.1.0/24 to 192.168.2.0/24, and delete the last rule added. You will save these rules in the *iptables* file and make necessary adjustments to have these rules loaded each time you reboot the system. You will reload the rules and ensure their presence.

1. Insert a rule to allow inbound traffic on port 90 from 192.168.1.0/24 only:

    # iptables –I INPUT –s 192.168.1.0/24 –p tcp --dport 90 –j ACCEPT

2. Append a rule to reject all inbound traffic from 192.168.3.0/24 on *eth1* interface:

    # **iptables –A INPUT –s 192.168.3.0/24 –i eth1 –j DROP**

3. Insert a rule to reject all outbound ICMP traffic to all systems on 192.168.3.0/24, except for the system with IP 192.168.3.3/24:

    # **iptables –I INPUT ! –d 192.168.3.3/24 –p icmp –j DROP**

4. Append a rule to forward all inbound traffic from 192.168.1.0/24 to 192.168.2.0/24:

    # **iptables –A FORWARD –s 192.168.1.0/24 –d 192.168.2.0/24 –j ACCEPT**

5. Delete the above rule:

    # **iptables –D FORWARD –s 192.168.1.0/24 –d 192.168.2.0/24 –j ACCEPT**

6. Save all the rules just added to the *iptables* file:

    # **service iptables save**

7. Check the presence of rules:

    # **iptables –L**
    Chain INPUT (policy ACCEPT)

target	prot	opt	source	destination	
DROP	**icmp**	**--**	**anywhere**	**!192.168.3.0/24**	
ACCEPT	**tcp**	**--**	**192.168.1.0/24**	**anywhere**	**tcp dpt:dnsix**
ACCEPT	tcp	--	anywhere	anywhere	state NEW tcp dpt:ftp
ACCEPT	tcp	--	anywhere	anywhere	tcp dpt:http
DROP	**all**	**--**	**192.168.3.0/24**	**anywhere**	

Chain FORWARD (policy ACCEPT)

target	prot	opt	source	destination
ACCEPT	all	--	anywhere	192.168.0.0/24

Chain OUTPUT (policy ACCEPT)

target	prot	opt	source	destination	
DROP	icmp	--	anywhere	anywhere	
DROP	tcp	--	anywhere	anywhere	state NEW,ESTABLISHED tcp dpt:smtp

The output highlights in bold the presence of the three new rules you have applied in this exercise. You can also view the contents of the *iptables* file to check the rules.

Understanding firewalld Configuration Files

The *firewalld* service stores firewall rules in XML file format at two different locations: the system-defined rules in the */usr/lib/firewalld* directory and the user-defined in */etc/firewalld*. The files at the former location can be used as templates for adding or modifying new rules. We simply need to

---

copy the required file to the */etc/firewalld/services* directory and make necessary updates. The *firewalld* service reads the files located in */etc/firewalld* and applies the rules defined in them. A listing of both directories is shown below:

 # ll /usr/lib/firewalld

```
drwxr-x---. 2 root  root 4096 Oct 31 13:07  icmptypes
drwxr-x---. 2 root  root 4096 Oct 31 13:07  services
drwxr-x---. 2 root  root 4096 Oct 31 13:07  zones
```

 # ll /etc/firewalld

```
-rw-r-----. 1 root root 1026 Feb 28 2014  firewalld.conf
drwxr-x---. 2 root root    6 Feb 28 2014  icmptypes
-rw-r-----. 1 root root  267 Feb 28 2014  lockdown-whitelist.xml
drwxr-x---. 2 root root    6 Feb 28 2014  services
drwxr-x---. 2 root root   23 Nov 8 09:48  zones
```

A sample rule template for the ssh service is displayed below:

 # cat /usr/lib/systemd/services/ssh.xml

```
<?xml version="1.0" encoding="utf-8"?>
<service>
 <short>SSH</short>
 <description>Secure Shell (SSH) is a protocol for logging into and executing commands on remote
machines. It provides secure encrypted communications. If you plan on accessing your machine remotely
via SSH over a firewalled interface, enable this option. You need the openssh-server package installed for
this option to be useful.</description>
 <port protocol="tcp" port="22"/>
</service>
```

As we can see, the file has a short and long description for the service, and it also tells us the protocol and port number that it uses.

The firewall-cmd Command

The *firewall-cmd* command is a powerful command line tool that is used to create, modify, manage, and remove rules for the *firewalld* service. This tool can be used to make runtime and permanent changes. It supports several options, some of which are described in Table 11-2.

Option	Description
--state	Displays the running status of firewalld.
--reload	Reloads firewall rules. All runtime changes will be lost.
--permanent	Stores a change persistently. The change becomes active after a reboot or service restart/reload.
--get-default-zone	Displays the name of the default zone.
--get-services	Prints pre-defined services.
--list-all	Lists all information.
--list-services	Lists services.
--add-service	Adds a service.
--remove-service	Removes a service.
--query-service	Queries for the presence of a service.

Option	Description
--list-ports	Lists network ports.
--add-port	Adds a port (or a range).
--remove-port	Removes a port.
--query-port	Queries for the presence of a port.
--list-forward-ports	Lists forwarded ports.
--add-forward-port	Adds an IPv4 forward port (or a range).
--remove-forward-port	Removes an IPv4 forward port.
--query-forward-port	Queries for the presence of a forward port.
--list-interfaces	Lists network interfaces.
--add-interfaces	Binds a network interface.
--remove-interfaces	Unbinds a network interface.
--query-interfaces	Queries for the presence of a network interface.

Table 11-2 firewall-cmd Command Options

With all the --add and --remove options mentioned in Table 11-2, the --permanent switch may be specified to ensure the rule is stored permanently in the */etc/firewalld* directory. There are many other options available with *firewall-cmd*. Some of these options are used in examples in the following sub-sections and more will be introduced in Chapter 17 "Working with Firewalld and Kerberos" in the RHCE section of this book.

In order to practice *firewalld* operations, you need to stop and deactivate the *iptables* service on *server1* by issuing the following pair of commands:

systemctl stop iptables
systemctl disable iptables
rm '/etc/systemd/system/basic.target.wants/iptables.service'

Now activate (enable) and start the *firewalld* service:

systemctl enable firewalld
ln -s '/usr/lib/systemd/system/firewalld.service' '/etc/systemd/system/dbus-
org.fedoraproject.FirewallD1.service'
ln -s '/usr/lib/systemd/system/firewalld.service' '/etc/systemd/system/basic.target.wants/firewalld.service'
systemctl start firewalld

Check the running status using either the *systemctl* or the *firewall-cmd* command:

systemctl status firewalld
firewalld.service - firewalld - dynamic firewall daemon
   Loaded: loaded (/usr/lib/systemd/system/firewalld.service; enabled)
   Active: active (running) since Sat 2014-11-08 21:11:47 EST; 29s ago
 Main PID: 8689 (firewalld)
   CGroup: /system.slice/firewalld.service
       └─8689 /usr/bin/python -Es /usr/sbin/firewalld --nofork...
Nov 08 21:11:47 server1.example.com systemd[1]: Started firewalld ...
Hint: Some lines were ellipsized, use -l to show in full.

```
# firewall-cmd --state
```
running

Now we are ready to perform the exercises presented below.

Exercise 11-3: Add and Manage Firewall Rules

This exercise should be done on *server1*.

In this exercise, you will display the name of the default zone and then add three rules to it. You will first add and activate a permanent rule to allow HTTP traffic on port 80, and then add a runtime rule for traffic intended for TCP port 443 (the HTTPS service). You will add another permanent rule to allow VNC traffic on any TCP port between 5901 and 5910. You will run appropriate commands to confirm your changes, and also display the contents of the default zone file to see the addition of the permanent rule.

1. Determine the name of the current default zone:

    ```
    # firewall-cmd --get-default-zone
    ```
    public

2. Add a permanent rule to allow HTTP traffic on its default port:

    ```
    # firewall-cmd --permanent --add-service=http
    ```
    success

    This command has added the http service name to the default zone file *public.xml* located in the */etc/firewalld/zones/* directory. When this new rule is activated, it will use the port and protocol defined in the template file */usr/lib/firewalld/services/http.xml*.

3. Activate the new rule:

    ```
    # firewall-cmd --reload
    ```
    success

4. Add a runtime rule to allow traffic on TCP port 443:

    ```
    # firewall-cmd --add-port=443/tcp
    ```

5. Add a permanent rule for VNC traffic on TCP port range 5901 to 5910, and activate it immediately:

    ```
    # firewall-cmd --permanent --add-port=5901-5910/tcp ; firewall-cmd --reload
    ```

6. List the services and ports to confirm the success of all three changes:

    ```
    # firewall-cmd --list-services
    ```
    dhcpv6-client http ssh
    ```
    # firewall-cmd --list-ports
    ```
    443/tcp 5901-5910/tcp

---

7. Issue the *iptables* command for an additional validation by listing (–L) the current rules in place for the public zone in numeric format (–n):

iptables –L –n
. . . .
Chain IN_public_allow (1 references)

target	prot	opt	source	destination	
ACCEPT	tcp	--	0.0.0.0/0	0.0.0.0/0	tcp dpt:80 ctstate NEW
ACCEPT	tcp	--	0.0.0.0/0	0.0.0.0/0	tcp dpt:22 ctstate NEW
ACCEPT	tcp	--	0.0.0.0/0	0.0.0.0/0	tcp dpt:443 ctstate NEW
ACCEPT	tcp	--	0.0.0.0/0	0.0.0.0/0	tcp dpts:5901:5910 ctstate NEW

. . . .

The above output shows all three allow rules that you have just added. They are all listed under the INPUT chain of the public zone.

8. Display the contents of the default zone file to confirm the addition of both permanent rules:

cat /etc/firewalld/zones/public.xml
. . . .
  <service name="dhcpv6-client"/>
  <service name="http"/>
  <service name="ssh"/>
  <port protocol="tcp" port="5901-5910"/>
</zone>

The *firewall-cmd* command makes a copy of the affected zone file with *.old* extension whenever an update is made to the zone.

Exercise 11-4: Modify and Remove Firewall Rules

This exercise should be done on *server1*.

In this exercise, you will modify the three rules that you added in the previous exercise and then delete two of them. You will remove the permanent rules for both HTTP (port 80) and HTTPS (port 443), and restrict the port range for VNC service to 5901 and 5902. You will run appropriate commands to confirm the changes, and also display the contents of the default zone file to validate the modifications.

1. Remove the permanent rule for HTTP:

    # **firewall-cmd --permanent --remove-service=http**

2. Remove the runtime rule for port 443, and confirm the immediate deletion:

    # **firewall-cmd --remove-port=443/tcp**
    # **firewall-cmd –list-ports**
    5901-5910/tcp

    Since it was a runtime rule, running the first command above deleted it right away.

3. Remove the permanent rule for ports 5901 to 5910, and add a new permanent rule to restrict VNC to listen only on 5901 and 5902 ports:

   # firewall-cmd --permanent --remove-port=5901-5910/tcp
   # firewall-cmd --permanent --add-port=5901-5902/tcp

4. Activate the new permanent changes:

   # firewall-cmd --reload

5. List the services and ports to confirm the success of all three changes:

   # firewall-cmd --list-services
   dhcpv6-client ssh
   # firewall-cmd --list-ports
   5901-5902/tcp

   Both outputs reflect the updates.

6. Issue the *iptables* command for an additional verification:

   # iptables –L

   . . . .
   Chain IN_public_allow (1 references)
   target   prot opt source   destination
   ACCEPT   tcp -- anywhere   anywhere   tcp dpt:ssh ctstate NEW
   ACCEPT   tcp -- anywhere   anywhere   tcp dpts:5901:5902 ctstate NEW
   . . . .

   The above output reflects the updates under the INPUT chain of the public zone.

7. Display the contents of the public zone file to validate the removal, and update to both permanent rules:

   # cat /etc/firewalld/zones/public.xml

   . . . .
     \<service name="dhcpv6-client"/>
     \<service name="ssh"/>
     \<port protocol="tcp" port="5901-5902"/>
   \</zone>

Overview of the Firewall Configuration Tool

The Firewall Configuration tool allows us to manage the iptables firewall in a graphical setting. This tool interacts with the *firewalld* daemon to make changes and updates. The main interface is opened when we execute the *firewall-config* command in an X terminal window or we select Applications | Sundry | Firewall in the GNOME desktop. See Figure 11-2 for the main screen.

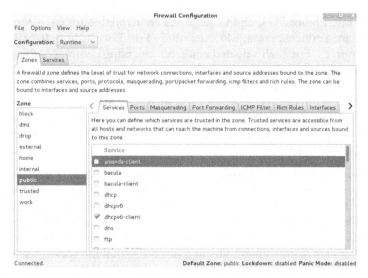

Figure 11-2 Firewall Configuration Tool – Zones Tab

There are two main tabs across the top labeled Zones and Services that allow us to view and manage configuration for zones and services. Both list available zones and services on the left hand side. We can highlight a zone or service to bring up associated details on the right side for viewing or modification.

By default, this tool starts with the runtime mode pre-selected. We can switch the mode to permanent by clicking the drop-down menu and selecting it. A group of icons will appear in the bottom left for us to be able to add a new zone or service, and modify or delete a highlighted zone or service. Note that these functions are only available in the permanent mode. See Figure 11-3 for the icons.

Figure 11-3 Firewall Configuration Tool – Permanent Mode Icons

Under the Zones tab, Figure 11-3, eight categories are available for each zone listed in the left pane. These categories are Services, Ports, Masquerading, Port Forwarding, ICMP Filter, Rich Rules, Interfaces, and Sources. For each selected zone, we can adjust corresponding attributes as desired. The Services category permits or blocks traffic for a service; the Ports category allows us to open a port or a range of ports; Masquerading provides us with the ability to conceal internal IP addresses from the Internet; Port Forwarding enables us to forward traffic destined for one port to another port on the same or remote system; ICMP Filter disallows certain ICMP types from passing through the firewall; Rich Rules enables us to set rich language rules; Interfaces lets us bind interfaces; and the Sources category allows us to bind source addresses.

Under the Services tab, Figure 11-4, three categories are available for each service listed in the left pane; however, we can only modify them if the permanent configuration mode is in effect. These categories are Ports and Protocols, Modules, and Destination. For each selected service, we can adjust corresponding attributes as desired. The Ports and Protocols categories allow us to add a port or a range of ports for TCP, UDP, or some other protocol; Modules lets us add or modify a netfilter helper module; and Destination enables us to place a limit on the service to the specified destination address and type.

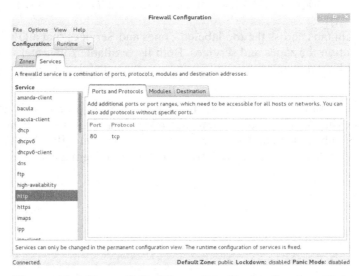

Figure 11-4 Firewall Configuration Tool – Services Tab

The Options menu item at the top of the Firewall Configuration window gives us access to additional functions. It allows us to reload any permanent changes made to the firewall rules, choose a different connection zone, change the default zone, begin dropping every inbound and outbound packet, and disallow unwanted configuration changes by applications and services.

Overview of Security Enhanced Linux

Security Enhanced Linux (SELinux) is an implementation of the *Mandatory Access Control* (MAC) architecture developed by the U.S. *National Security Agency* (NSA) in collaboration with other organizations and the Linux community for flexible, enriched, and granular security controls in Linux. MAC is integrated into the Linux kernel as a set of patches using the *Linux Security Modules* (LSM) framework that allows the kernel to support various security implementations, including SELinux. MAC provides an added layer of protection above and beyond the standard

Linux *Discretionary Access Control* (DAC) security architecture, which includes the traditional file and directory permissions, ACL settings, setuid/setgid bit settings, su/sudo privileges, and so on. MAC limits the ability of a *subject* (user or process) to access an *object* (file, directory, file system, device, network interface, port, pipe, socket, etc.) in order to reduce or eliminate the potential damage the subject may be able to cause to the system if compromised due to the exploitation of vulnerabilities in service processes, programs, or applications. MAC controls are fine-grained; they protect other services in the event one of the services is negotiated. For instance, if the FTP server process is compromised, the attacker can only damage the files the hacked process has access to, and not the other processes running on the system or the objects the other processes have access to. To ensure this coarse-grained control, MAC uses a set of defined authorization rules called *policy* to examine security attributes associated with subjects and objects when a subject tries to access an object, and decides whether or not to permit this access attempt. These attributes are stored in *contexts* (a.k.a. *labels*) and are applicable to both subjects and objects.

SELinux decisions are stored in a special cache area referred to as *Access Vector Cache* (AVC). This cache area is checked each time a process attempts an access to determine whether this access attempt was previously allowed. With this mechanism in place, SELinux does not have to check the policy ruleset repeatedly, thus improving performance.

By default, SELinux controls are enabled at the time of RHEL installation, with the default configuration confining the processes to the minimum privileges that they need to function.

Key Terms

In order to comprehend SELinux, an understanding of some key terms is essential. These terms are used to explain the concepts and SELinux functionality in the remainder of this chapter.

Subject: A *subject* is any user or process that accesses an object. Some examples include system_u for the SELinux system user and unconfined_u for subjects that are not bound by the SELinux policy. The subject is stored in the first field of the context.

Object: An *object* is a resource such as a file, directory, hardware device, network interface, port, pipe, or socket that a subject accesses. Some examples include object_r for general objects, system_r for system-owned objects, and unconfined_r for objects that are not bound by the SELinux policy.

Access: An *access* is an action performed by the subject on an object. Some examples include creating, reading, or updating a file, creating or navigating a directory, and accessing a network port or socket.

Policy: A *policy* is a defined ruleset that is enforced system-wide and is used to analyze security attributes assigned to subjects and objects. This ruleset is referenced to decide whether to permit a subject's access attempt for an object or a subject's attempt to interact with another subject. The default behavior of SELinux in the absence of a rule is to deny the access. Two standard pre-configured policies are available in RHEL and they are referred to as *targeted* and *strict*, with targeted being the default policy. This policy dictates that any processes that are targeted run in confined domains and any processes that are not targeted run in unconfined domains. For instance, SELinux runs logged-in users in the unconfined domain and the httpd process in a confined domain by default. Any subject running unconfined is more vulnerable than the one running confined.

Context: A *context* is a tag that SELinux uses to store security attributes for subjects and objects. The term context may be used interchangeably with the term *label*. In SELinux, every subject and object has a context assigned to it, which consists of a SELinux user, role, type (or domain), and optional sensitivity level. SELinux uses this information to make access control decisions.

Labeling: *Labeling* is the mapping between files in a file system with their file contexts.

SELinux User: There are several pre-defined SELinux user identities that exist in the SELinux policy. These user identities are authorized for a particular set of roles. SELinux maps Linux users to SELinux user identities in the policy to allow the Linux users to inherit the restrictions placed on SELinux users. These SELinux users are used in the SELinux context for processes in that session to define what roles and levels they can enter. A Linux user, for instance, will not be able to run the *su* and *sudo* commands or the programs located in their home directories if they are mapped to the SELinux user user_u.

Role: A *role* is an attribute of the *Role-Based Access Control* (RBAC) security model that is part of SELinux. It defines which subject is allowed to access which domains or types. SELinux users are authorized for roles, and roles are authorized for domains and types. Each subject has an associated role to ensure that the system and user processes are separated. A subject can transition into a new role in order to gain access to other domains and types. Some role examples include user_r for ordinary system users, sysadm_r for system administrators, and system_r for processes that initiate under the system_r role. The role is stored in the second field of the context.

Type and Domain: A *type* is an attribute of *Type Enforcement* (TE). It is a group of objects based on uniformity in their security requirements. Objects such as files and directories with common security requirements are grouped within a specific type. Similarly, processes with common security requirements have their own unique types, which are referred to as domains. In other words, a type defines a type for files and a domain for processes. SELinux policy rules outline how types can access each other (whether it be a domain accessing a type, or a domain accessing another domain). Some examples of available SELinux types include user_home_dir_t for objects located in user home directories and usr_t for most objects stored in the */usr* directory. The type is stored in the third field of the context.

A *domain* determines the type of access that a process has. Each process runs confined within a domain. Some examples of the SELinux domain include init_t for the systemd process, firewalld_t for the firewalld process, and unconfined_t for all processes that are not bound by the SELinux policy. The domain type is also stored in the third field of the context.

Type Enforcement: *Type enforcement* identifies and limits a subject's ability to access domains for processes and types for files. It references the contexts of the subjects and objects for this enforcement.

Level: A *level* is an attribute of *Multi-Level Security* (MLS) and *Multi-Category Security* (MCS). It is a pair of sensitivity:category values that defines the level of security in the context. A category may be defined as a single value or a range of values such as c0.c4 to represent c0 through c4. In RHEL7, the targeted policy is used as the default, which enforces MCS (MCS only supports s0 sensitivity level; however, it supports a range of 0 to 1023 different categories).

SELinux Contexts for Users

SELinux contexts define security attributes placed on individual subjects and objects. Each context contains a type (or domain) and a security level along with subject and object information. For user accounts, we use the *id* command with the –Z option to view the context set on our Linux users. The following example shows the command executed for the *root* account:

```
# id –Z
unconfined_u:unconfined_r:unconfined_t:s0-s0:c0.c1023
```

The output indicates that there are no restrictions placed on this user from a SELinux perspective. We get the exact same output if we run this command for user accounts other than *root*. This entails that all Linux users, including *root*, run unconfined by default, which gives the users full access to the system with no restrictions placed on them by SELinux. The above output also tells us that *root* is mapped to the SELinux unconfined_u user and is running as unconfined_r role in the unconfined_t domain with security level 0 in all 1024 categories.

In addition to the unconfined user with unlimited privileges, SELinux includes seven confined user accounts with restricted access to objects. These accounts are mapped to Linux users via SELinux policy to provide them with controlled access by inheriting the restrictions placed on the SELinux users that they are mapped to. This regulated access helps safeguard the system from potential damage that Linux users might inflict on the system.

We can use the *seinfo* query command to list the available SELinux users; however, we must install the setools-console software package before doing so.

```
# seinfo –u
Users: 8
  sysadm_u
  system_u
  xguest_u
  root
  guest_u
  staff_u
  user_u
  unconfined_u
```

The output shows the eight pre-defined SELinux users. We can now use the *semanage* command to view the mapping currently in place:

```
# semanage login –l
```

Login Name	SELinux User	MLS/MCS Range	Service
__default__	unconfined_u	s0-s0:c0.c1023	*
root	unconfined_u	s0-s0:c0.c1023	*
system_u	system_u	s0-s0:c0.c1023	*

The above output displays Linux users in the first column and the SELinux users they are mapped to in the second column. The next two columns show the associated security level and the SELinux context for the Linux user (the * represents any service). By default, all non-*root* Linux users are represented as __default__, which is mapped to the unconfined_u user in the policy.

SELinux Contexts for Processes

Similarly, we can also determine the context on processes. We use the *ps* command for this purpose and we supply the –Z option with it. The following example shows the first two lines from the *ps* command output:

```
# ps –eZ
LABEL                             PID    TTY    TIME     CMD
system_u:system_r:init_t:s0        1      ?    00:00:02   systemd
```

In the above output, the subject (system_u) provides a SELinux username mapped to the Linux user *root*; the object is system_r; the domain (init_t) indicates the type of protection applied to the process; and the last field determines the level of security. Any process that is unprotected will run in the unconfined_t domain.

SELinux Contexts for Files

In the same manner, we can spot the context information for files and directories. To this end, we use the *ll* command with the –Z switch. The following shows the four attributes set on the */etc/passwd* file:

```
# ll –Z /etc/passwd
-rw-r--r--.  root root system_u:object_r:passwd_file_t:s0 /etc/passwd
```

The output indicates the subject (system_u), the object (object_r), the type (passwd_file_t), and the security level (s0) for the *passwd* file. Here the subject is a SELinux user (system_u) mapped to the Linux user *root*; the object is a SELinux role (object_r); the type is a SELinux type (passwd_file_t); and the security level (s0) is the level of security as defined in the */etc/selinux/targeted/setrans.conf* file. Default contexts for many files are stored in the */etc/selinux/targeted/contexts/files/file_contexts* file, which also saves the contexts updated via the *semanage fcontext* command. This command is part of the policycoreutils-python software package, which must be installed on the system to use it. Contexts for newly created files and directories that are not found in *file_contexts* are placed in another file named *file_contexts.local*, which is located in the same directory. Notice the dot next to the public execute permission bit in the first column of the above output. This dot indicates the presence of SELinux context. By default, files created in a directory inherit the context placed on the directory. If a file is moved to another directory, it takes its context with it, which may differ from the destination directory's context.

SELinux Contexts for Ports

SELinux contexts also define security attributes for individual network ports. We use the *semanage* command to view the context information. The following shows only a few example entries from the long output of this command:

```
# semanage port –l
SELinux Port Type             Proto    Port Number
http_port_t                   tcp      80, 81, 443, 488, 8008, 8009, 8443, 9000
kerberos_admin_port_t         tcp      749
kerberos_password_port_t      tcp      464
kerberos_password_port_t      udp      464
kerberos_port_t               tcp      88, 750, 4444
```

By default, SELinux allows services to listen on a restricted set of network ports only. This is evident from the above output that shows the ports HTTP and Kerberos services use.

Domain Transitioning

SELinux allows a process running in one domain to enter another domain to execute an application authorized to run in that domain only, provided a proper rule exists in the policy to support such transition. SELinux defines a permission setting called *entrypoint* in its policy to control applications that can be used to enter a new domain. In order to understand how transitioning into a new domain works, a basic example is provided below that shows how it works when a Linux user attempts to change their password using the */usr/bin/passwd* command.

The *passwd* command is labeled with the passwd_exec_t type, which we can confirm as follows:

ll –Z /usr/bin/passwd
-rwsr-xr-x. root root system_u:object_r:**passwd_exec_t**:s0 /usr/bin/passwd

The *passwd* command requires access to the */etc/shadow* file to modify a user password. The shadow file has a different type shadow_t set on it:

ll –Z /etc/shadow
----------. root root system_u:object_r:**shadow_t**:s0   /etc/shadow

The SELinux policy has rules that specifically allow processes running in the passwd_t domain to be able to read and modify the files with the shadow_t type and allow them entrypoint permission into the passwd_exec_t domain. This rule enables the user's shell process executing the *passwd* command to switch into the passwd_t domain and update the *shadow* file.

Let's open two terminal windows and demonstrate this. In one window, issue the *passwd* command as *user1* and wait at the prompt:

$ passwd
Changing password for user user1.
Changing password for user1.
(current) UNIX password:

In the second window, run the *ps* command as follows:

ps –eZ | grep passwd
unconfined_u:unconfined_r:**passwd_t**:s0-s0:c0.c1023 26103 pts/0 00:00:00 passwd

As we can see, the *passwd* command process has transitioned into the passwd_t domain in order to change the user password successfully.

Copying, Moving, and Archiving Files with SELinux Contexts

We copy, move, and archive files on a regular basis as part of our day-to-day job responsibilities. With SELinux running, we need to keep certain rules in mind to ensure we maintain proper contexts on files and directories during copy, move, and archive operations using the *cp*, *mv*, and *tar* commands. These rules are:

---

1. If a file is copied over on an existing file in the same or different directory, the context of the source file receives that of the destination file's.
2. If a file is copied to a different directory as a new file, the context of the source file is replaced with the default context of the destination directory's context, unless we specify the --preserve=context option with the *cp* command to preserve the file's original context.
3. If a file is moved to the same or different directory, the SELinux type on the source file remains intact; however, the user attribute changes to unconfined_u.
4. If a file is archived with the *tar* command, use the --selinux option to preserve the context.

SELinux Booleans

Booleans are on/off switches that are used by SELinux to determine whether to permit an action. Booleans allow us to immediately activate or deactivate a particular rule in the SELinux policy without the need to recompile or reload it. For instance, the ftpd_anon_write boolean can be turned on to allow anonymous users to be able to upload files. This privilege can be revoked by turning this boolean off. Boolean values are stored in corresponding boolean files located in the */sys/fs/selinux/booleans* directory. A sample listing for this directory is provided below:

ll /sys/fs/selinux/booleans
-rw-r--r--. 1 root root 0 Nov 11 19:47 abrt_anon_write
-rw-r--r--. 1 root root 0 Nov 11 19:47 abrt_handle_event
-rw-r--r--. 1 root root 0 Nov 11 19:47 abrt_upload_watch_anon_write
. . . .

Each file here represents a boolean. We can view their values using the *getsebool*, *sestatus*, or *semanage* command. The *getsebool* command with the –a option lists all booleans along with their current values:

getsebool –a
abrt_anon_write --> off
abrt_handle_event --> off
abrt_upload_watch_anon_write --> on

To check the setting of a single boolean, we specify the boolean's name with the command. For instance, the following shows the current state of the abrt_anon_write boolean:

getsebool abrt_anon_write
abrt_anon_write --> off

Alternatively, the *sestatus* command can be run with the –b switch:

sestatus –b
. . . .
Policy booleans:
abrt_anon_write   off
abrt_handle_event   off
abrt_upload_watch_anon_write   on
. . . .

And the *semanage* command may be used to list all the Booleans, along with a short description for each and their current settings:

```
# semanage boolean –l
SELinux boolean     State    Default  Description
ftp_home_dir        (off   ,  off)    Determine whether ftpd can read and write files in user home
directories.
smartmon_3ware      (off   ,  off)    Determine whether smartmon can support devices on 3ware
controllers.
. . . . . . . .
```

A boolean value may be flipped either temporarily or permanently using the *setsebool* command. The following first enables the abrt_anon_write boolean and then turns it off by simply furnishing "on" or "1" to enable it, or "off" or "0" to disable it:

```
# setsebool abrt_anon_write 1
# setsebool abrt_anon_write off
```

The above changes take effect right away without the need to reboot the system, and store a 1 or 0 in the corresponding boolean file in the */sys/fs/selinux/boolean* directory; however, they are temporary and the new value will not survive the next reboot.

In order to apply the new value immediately as well as ensure that it is available after the subsequent system reboot, we specify the –P option with the *setsebool* command. We can also use the *semanage* command (–m to modify and --1 to enable) for this purpose. The following demonstrates how to turn the abrt_anon_write boolean on using both commands:

```
# setsebool –P abrt_anon_write on
# semanage boolean –m --1 abrt_anon_write
```

We can now use the *getsebool*, *sestatus*, or *semanage* command for validation:

```
# getsebool –a | grep abrt_anon_write
abrt_anon_write --> on
# sestatus –b | grep abrt_anon_write
abrt_anon_write      on
# semanage boolean –l | grep abrt_anon_write
abrt_anon_write   (on , on) Allow ABRT to modify public files used for public file transfer services.
```

Managing SELinux

Managing SELinux involves a number of tasks, including controlling the activation mode, checking status, setting security contexts on subjects and objects, and toggling boolean values. Booleans are covered later in this chapter. RHEL provides a set of commands and a graphical tool called *SELinux Manager* for performing these operations. The command toolset is spread over multiple packages, such as libselinux-utils, which includes the *getenforce*, *setenforce*, *getsebool*, and *matchpathcon* commands; policycoreutils, which contains the *sestatus*, *setsebool*, and *restorecon* commands; policycoreutils-python, which consists of the *semanage* command; and setools-console, which offers commands such as *seinfo* and *sesearch*. The graphical tool is part of the policycoreutils-gui package. For viewing SELinux alerts and troubleshooting, RHEL7 provides a graphical tool SELinux Alert Browser, which is part of the setroubleshoot-server package. In order to fully manage SELinux on our system, we need to ensure that all these packages are installed on the system along with their dependencies.

Besides the toolset mentioned above, there are additional commands and graphical tools available for performing specific SELinux administration tasks; however, their use is not as frequent.

Management Commands

SELinux brings with it a number of management commands and two graphical administration tools. Table 11-3 lists and explains some common administration commands.

Command	Description
Context Management	
chcon	Changes context on files. Changes do not survive file system relabeling.
matchpathcon	Compares a file context to that of the defaults, and reports it.
restorecon	Restores default contexts on files by referencing the files in the /etc/selinux/targeted/contexts/files directory.
semanage	Modifies context on files and manages policies. Changes survive file system relabeling.
Mode Management	
getenforce	Displays the current mode of operation.
sestatus	Shows SELinux status.
setenforce	Sets the operating mode to enforcing or permissive.
Policy Management	
seinfo	Provides information on policy components.
sesearch	Searches rules in the policy.
Boolean Management	
getsebool	Displays booleans and their current settings.
setsebool	Modifies boolean values.
Troubleshooting	
sealert	The graphical troubleshooting tool.
Graphical Management	
system-config-selinux	The graphical administration tool.

Table 11-3 SELinux Administration Command

We will use most of these commands in this and subsequent chapters.

Controlling Activation Mode

One of the key configuration files that controls the SELinux activation mode and sets its default type is called *config* and it is located in the */etc/selinux* directory. The default contents of this file are displayed below, followed by an explanation:

```
# cat /etc/selinux/config
# This file controls the state of SELinux on the system.
# SELINUX= can take one of these three values:
#    enforcing - SELinux security policy is enforced.
#    permissive - SELinux prints warnings instead of enforcing.
#    disabled - No SELinux policy is loaded.
SELINUX=enforcing
# SELINUXTYPE= can take one of these two values:
#    targeted - Targeted processes are protected,
#    minimum - Modification of targeted policy. Only selected processes are protected.
#    mls - Multi Level Security protection.
SELINUXTYPE=targeted
```

The SELINUX directive in the file sets the activation mode for SELinux. Enforcing activates it and allows or denies actions based on policy rules. Permissive activates SELinux, but permits all actions. It records all security violations; however, it does not hinder actions being taken. This mode is useful for troubleshooting, and in developing or tuning the policy. The third option is to completely disable it. When activated in the enforcing mode, the SELINUXTYPE directive dictates the type of policy to be enforced. SELinux supports three policies: *targeted*, *minimum*, and *mls* (*multi-level security*). The targeted policy allows us to modify SELinux restrictions placed on subjects and objects, the minimum policy is a light version of the targeted policy, and the mls policy lets us tighten security at more granular levels. The default policy in RHEL7 is targeted.

At the command prompt, we can issue the *getenforce* command to determine the current operating mode:

```
# getenforce
Enforcing
```

We may alter the SELinux operating state immediately from enforcing to permissive using the *setenforce* command as follows:

 # setenforce permissive   (or # setenforce 0)

This change, however, will be lost if the system is rebooted.

To make the mode change persistent across reboots, we edit */etc/selinux/config* and set the value of SELINUX to permissive. We can then reboot the system to validate the change.

Switching between enforcing and permissive is easy and can be achieved on the fly. However, disabling SELinux completely requires SELINUX to be set to disabled in the *config* file and the system must be rebooted.

EXAM TIP: You may switch SELinux to permissive for troubleshooting a non-functioning service. Change it back to enforcing when the issue is resolved.

In the future, if we wish to reactivate SELinux in either the enforcing or the permissive mode, we just need to change the SELINUX directive appropriately in the *config* file and reboot the system. The reboot will take longer than normal as SELinux will go through the process of relabeling the files.

Querying Status

We can query the running state of SELinux using the *sestatus* command. This command also displays the location of key directories, effective policy, and activation mode in addition to other information.

```
# sestatus
SELinux status:                 enabled
SELinuxfs mount:                /sys/fs/selinux
SELinux root directory:         /etc/selinux
Loaded policy name:             targeted
Current mode:                   enforcing
Mode from config file:          enforcing
Policy MLS status:              enabled
Policy deny_unknown status:     allowed
Max kernel policy version:      28
```

The above output indicates that SELinux is running in enforcing mode and the targeted policy is in effect.

We can invoke the *sestatus* command with the –v switch to report on security contexts set on files and processes that are listed in the */etc/sestatus.conf* file. The default contents of this file are shown below:

```
# cat /etc/sestatus.conf
[files]
/etc/passwd
/etc/shadow
/bin/bash
/bin/login
/bin/sh
/sbin/agetty
/sbin/init
/sbin/mingetty
/usr/sbin/sshd
/lib/libc.so.6
/lib/ld-linux.so.2
/lib/ld.so.1
[process]
/sbin/mingetty
/sbin/agetty
/usr/sbin/sshd
```

Let's run the *sestatus* command with –v:

```
# sestatus –v
. . . . . . . .
Process contexts:
Current context:        unconfined_u:unconfined_r:unconfined_t:s0-s0:c0.c1023
Init context:           system_u:system_r:init_t:s0
```

/usr/sbin/sshd	system_u:system_r:sshd_t:s0-s0:c0.c1023
File contexts:	
Controlling terminal:	unconfined_u:object_r:user_devpts_t:s0
/etc/passwd	system_u:object_r:passwd_file_t:s0
/etc/shadow	system_u:object_r:shadow_t:s0
/bin/bash	system_u:object_r:shell_exec_t:s0
/bin/login	system_u:object_r:login_exec_t:s0
/bin/sh	system_u:object_r:bin_t:s0 -> system_u:object_r:shell_exec_t:s0
/sbin/agetty	system_u:object_r:getty_exec_t:s0
/sbin/init	system_u:object_r:bin_t:s0 -> system_u:object_r:init_exec_t:s0
/usr/sbin/sshd	system_u:object_r:sshd_exec_t:s0

Exercise 11-5: Modify SELinux Contexts for Users

This exercise should be done on *server1*.

In this exercise, you will create a Linux user account called *user5* with all default settings and ensure that this user is mapped to SELinux user *staff_u* at the time of its creation. You will verify the mapping for *user5*. You will map an existing Linux user *user4* to SELinux user *user_u*, and confirm. You will modify the SELinux policy to ensure all future new Linux users automatically receive *staff_u* mapping at the time of their creation.

1. Create a Linux user account called *user5* with default settings and mapping to SELinux user *staff_u*. Assign this user password user123 (passwords assigned this way is not recommended; however, it is okay in a lab environment).

   # useradd –Z staff_u user5
   # echo user123 | passwd --stdin user5
   Changing password for user user5.
   passwd: all authentication tokens updated successfully.

2. Verify the mapping between *user5* and *staff_u* using the *semanage* command:

   # semanage login –l | grep user5
   user5   staff_u   s0-s0:c0.c1023   *

3. Log on to *server1* as *user5* and confirm the mapping with the *id* command:

   $ id –Z
   staff_u:staff_r:staff_t:s0-s0:c0.c1023

4. Map an existing user *user4* to SELinux user *user_u* using the *semanage* command and confirm:

   # semanage login –a –s user_u user4
   # semanage login –l | grep user4
   user4   user_u   s0   *

5. Modify the SELinux policy so that all new Linux user accounts are automatically mapped to *staff_u* at the time of their creation, and confirm:

```
# semanage login –m –S targeted –s staff_u –r s0 __default__
# semanage login –l | grep default
 __default__      staff_u      s0      *
```

Exercise 11-6: Modify SELinux Contexts for Files

This exercise should be done on *server1*.

In this exercise, you will change the user and type on the */root/file1* file to user_u and public_content_t, respectively, and verify. You will add this context to the SELinux policy persistently to ensure the file survives file system relabeling in case SELinux support is disabled and then re-enabled. You will modify the user and type for the */root* directory to user_u and var_run_t, and then restore the default context back to it.

1. Determine the current context for */root/file1* using the *ll* command with –Z:

    ```
    # ll –Z /root/file1
    -rw-rw-r--+ root  root  unconfined_u:object_r:admin_home_t:s0 /root/file1
    ```

    The output shows the SELinux user (unconfined_u) and type (admin_home_t) for *file1*.

2. Modify the context on the file to user_u (–u) and public_content_t (–t) using the *chcon* command in verbose mode:

    ```
    # chcon –vu user_u –t public_content_t /root/file1
    changing security context of `/root/file1'
    ```

3. Add the new context to the SELinux policy to ensure that it survives file system relabeling (if SELinux is disabled and then re-enabled). Use the *semanage* command to add (–a) the file context (fcontext) with the specified user (–s) and type (–t).

    ```
    # semanage fcontext –a –s user_u –t public_content_t /root/file1
    ```

    This custom context is stored in the */etc/selinux/targeted/contexts/files/file_contexts.local* file.

4. Validate the new context:

    ```
    # ll –Z /root/file1
    -rw-rw-r--+ root  root  user_u:object_r:public_content_t:s0 /root/file1
    ```

5. Modify the user (–u) and type (–t) to staff_u and var_run_t on */root/*, and validate:

    ```
    # chcon –vu staff_u –t var_run_t /root
    changing security context of `/root'
    # ll –dZ /root
    drwxrwx---. root  root  staff_u:object_r:var_run_t:s0  /root
    ```

6. Restore the original context back to the */root* directory using the *restorecon* command, and confirm:

restorecon –vF /root
restorecon reset /root context user_u:object_r:var_run_t:s0->system_u:object_r:admin_home_t:s0
ll –dZ /root
drwxrwx---. root root system_u:object_r:admin_home_t:s0 /root

> **EXAM TIP:** Use the combination of semanage and restorecon commands to add a file context to the SELinux policy and then apply it. This will prevent the context on file to reset to the original value should SELinux relabeling has to occur.

Exercise 11-7: Add a Non-Standard Port to SELinux Policy

In this exercise, you will add a non-standard port to the SELinux policy for the *httpd* service. For this purpose, you will make appropriate changes in the policy and confirm.

1. List (–l) the ports the *httpd* service is currently listening on using the *semanage* command:

    # semanage port –l | grep http_port
    http_port_t   tcp   80, 81, 443, 488, 8008, 8009, 8443, 9000

    The output shows that the *httpd* service is currently listening on eight network ports.

2. Add (–a) port 8010 with type http_port_t (–t) and protocol (–p) tcp to the policy:

    # semanage port –a –t http_port_t –p tcp 8010

3. Confirm the addition of the ports:

    # semanage port -l | grep http_port
    http_port_t   tcp   8010, 80, 81, 443, 488, 8008, 8009, 8443, 9000

4. Delete (–d) port 8010 from the policy, and confirm:

    # semanage port –d –t http_port_t –p tcp 8010
    # semanage port –l | grep http_port
    http_port_t   tcp   80, 81, 443, 488, 8008, 8009, 8443, 9000

Now, you can configure the Apache web server to use this port for service rather than its default port.

> **EXAM TIP:** Any non-standard port you want to use for any service, make certain to add it to the SELinux policy with a correct type.

Exercise 11-8: Copy Files with and without SELinux Context

In this exercise, you will check the SELinux context on */root/file1*. You will copy this file to the */etc* directory and observe the change in the context. You will remove *file1* from */etc* and re-copy it, ensuring that the destination file takes the source file's context with it.

1. Check the context on */root/file1*:

   # **ll –Z /root/file1**
   -rw-rw-r--+ root root user_u:object_r:public_content_t:s0 /root/file1

2. Copy *file1* to the */etc* directory and check the context:

   # **cp /root/file1 /etc**
   # **ll –Z /etc/file1**
   -rw-r--r--. root root unconfined_u:object_r:etc_t:s0 /etc/file1

As we can see, the context has changed to the default context of the destination directory.

3. Remove */etc/file1* and copy */root/file1* again to */etc* with the --preserve=context option:

   # **rm –f /etc/file1**
   # **cp --preserve=context /root/file1 /etc**
   # **ll –Z /etc/file1**
   -rw-r--r--. root root user_u:object_r:public_content_t:s0 /etc/file1

The original context is preserved on the new file after the copy operation has finished.

Overview of the SELinux Administration Tool

The SELinux Administration tool is a graphical tool that enables us to perform a number of configuration and management operations, including setting the default activation mode and disabling it. The main window, as shown in Figure 11-5, appears when we start this tool by running the *system-config-selinux* command in an X terminal window or we select Applications | Other | SELinux Management in the GNOME desktop.

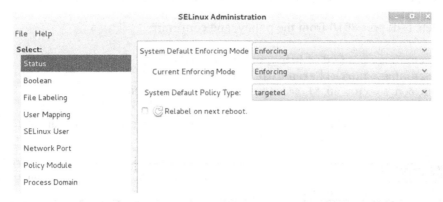

Figure 11-5 SELinux Administration Tool – Main Window

The SELinux GUI separates the information in eight distinct categories for ease of administration. These categories are listed on the left hand side and they are Status, Boolean, File Labeling, User Mapping, SELinux User, Network Port, Policy Module, and Process Domain. We can click a category to view or modify the specifics. The Status category shows the default and current enforcing modes, and allows us to modify them. It also displays the default policy type. The option "Relabel on next reboot" can be ticked to relabel the files at the following reboot. This is automatically done when SELinux is enabled from the disabled state. The rest of the categories are explained below.

Boolean: Displays whether booleans are active, the modules they are associated with, a short description, and their names. It also allows us to turn a boolean on or off.

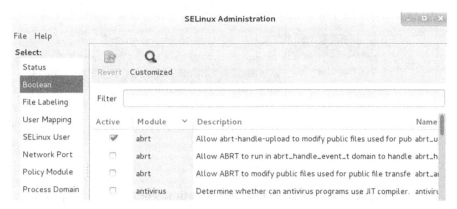

Figure 11-6 SELinux Administration Tool – Boolean

File Labeling: Displays file labels, and allows us to add, modify, and delete them.

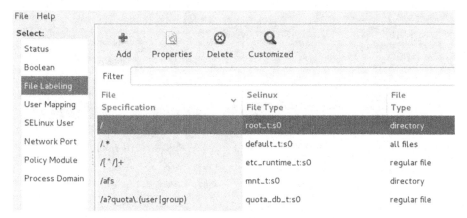

Figure 11-7 SELinux Administration Tool – File Labeling

User Mapping: Displays Linux user to SELinux user mappings, and allows us to add, modify, and delete them.

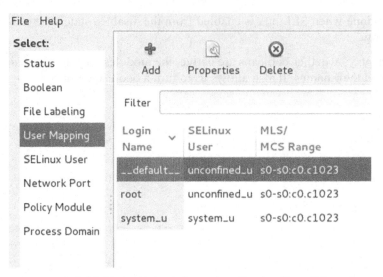

Figure 11-8 SELinux Administration Tool – User Mapping

SELinux User: Displays SELinux users, and allows us to add, modify, and delete them.

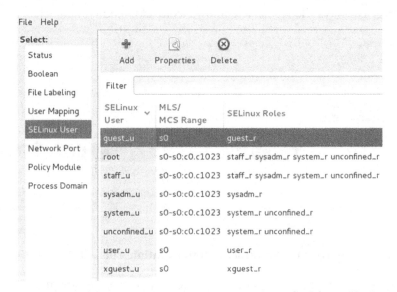

Figure 11-9 SELinux Administration Tool – SELinux User

Network Port: Shows SELinux ports and associated protocols, security level, and port numbers, and allows us to add, modify, and delete them.

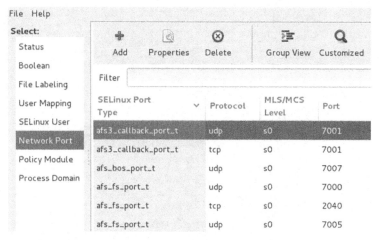

Figure 11-10 SELinux Administration Tool – Network Port

Policy Module: Displays module names and their versions, and allows us to add or remove modules, and enable module auditing.

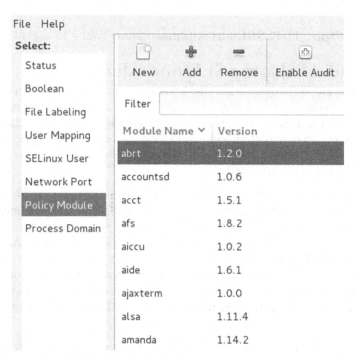

Figure 11-11 SELinux Administration Tool – Policy Module

Process Domain: Displays SELinux status, and allows us to switch between permissive and enforcing modes.

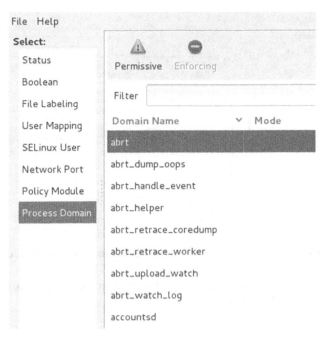

Figure 11-12 SELinux Administration Tool – Process Domain

Viewing and Analyzing SELinux Alerts

SELinux generates alerts for system activities when it runs in either enforcing or permissive mode. It writes the alerts to the */var/log/audit/audit.log* file if the *auditd* daemon is running, or to the */var/log/messages* file via the *rsyslog* daemon in the absence of *auditd*. SELinux also logs the alerts that are generated due to denial of an action and identifies them with a type tag such as AVC (*Access Vector Cache*) in the *audit.log* file. It also writes the rejection in the *messages* file with a message ID and how to view its details.

SELinux denial messages are analyzed and the audit data is examined to identify the potential cause of the rejection. The results of the analysis are recorded, along with recommendations on how to fix it. These results can be reviewed to aid in troubleshooting and recommended actions taken to address the issue. SELinux runs a service daemon called *setroubleshootd* that performs this analysis and examination in the background. This service also has a client interface called *SELinux Troubleshooter* (the *sealert* command) that reads that data and displays it for our assessment. The client tool has both text and graphical interfaces. The server and client components are part of the setroubleshoot-server software package that must be installed on the system prior to using this service.

The following shows a sample allowed record from the */var/log/audit/audit.log* file:

> type=USER_CHAUTHTOK msg=audit(1415936606.469:2614): pid=22402 uid=0 auid=0 ses=252 subj=unconfined_u:unconfined_r:passwd_t:s0-s0:c0.c1023 msg='op=PAM:chauthtok acct="user3" exe="/usr/bin/passwd" hostname=? addr=? terminal=pts/1 res=success'type=USER_CHAUTHTOK msg=audit(1415936606.469:2615): pid=22402 uid=0 auid=0 ses=252 subj=unconfined_u:unconfined_r:passwd_t:s0-s0:c0.c1023 msg='op=change password id=1010 exe="/usr/bin/passwd" hostname=? addr=? terminal=pts/1 res=success'

And below is a sample denial record from the same file:

type=AVC msg=audit(1415936299.844:2602): avc: denied { create } for pid=22320 comm="passwd" name="nshadow" scontext=unconfined_u:unconfined_r:passwd_t:s0-s0:c0.c1023 tcontext=system_u:object_r:etc_t:s0 tclass=file

A corresponding denial message from the */var/log/messages* file:

messages:Nov 13 22:38:21 server1 setroubleshoot: SELinux is preventing /usr/bin/passwd from create access on the file. For complete SELinux messages. run sealert -l 7720f534-79c4-488f-9e8a-56645f070ca1

We get the idea after evaluating the above two messages that the *passwd* command was prevented from updating the */etc/shadow* file in its attempt to change user password. The alert in the *messages* file also suggests using the *sealert* command to lookup (–l) the specified ID for details. Let's run the command as suggested:

sealert –l 7720f534-79c4-488f-9e8a-56645f070ca1
SELinux is preventing /usr/bin/passwd from create access on the file.
***** Plugin catchall_labels (83.8 confidence) suggests *******************
If you want to allow passwd to have create access on the file, then you need to change the label on $FIX_TARGET_PATH
Do
semanage fcontext -a -t FILE_TYPE '$FIX_TARGET_PATH'
where FILE_TYPE is one of the following: faillog_t, krb5_host_rcache_t, lastlog_t, passwd_file_t, shadow_t.
Then execute:
restorecon -v '$FIX_TARGET_PATH'
***** Plugin catchall (17.1 confidence) suggests **************************
If you believe that passwd should be allowed create access on the file by default. Then you should report this as a bug. You can generate a local policy module to allow this access. Do allow this access for now by executing:
grep passwd /var/log/audit/audit.log | audit2allow -M mypol
semodule -i mypol.pp
Additional Information:
Source Context   unconfined_u:unconfined_r:passwd_t:s0-s0:c0.c1023
Target Context   system_u:object_r:etc_t:s0
Target Objects   [file]
Source   passwd
Source Path   /usr/bin/passwd
Port   <Unknown>
Host   <Unknown>
Source RPM Packages   passwd-0.79-4.el7.x86_64
Target RPM Packages
Policy RPM   selinux-policy-3.12.1-153.el7.noarch
Selinux Enabled   True
Policy Type   targeted
Enforcing Mode   Enforcing
Host Name   server1.example.com

Platform	Linux server1.example.com 3.10.0-123.el7.x86_64 #1
	SMP Mon May 5 11:16:57 EDT 2014 x86_64 x86_64
Alert Count	1
First Seen	2014-11-13 22:38:19 EST
Last Seen	2014-11-13 22:38:19 EST
Local ID	11d166d9-85c2-468d-8060-2355bf5a0020
Raw Audit Messages	

type=AVC msg=audit(1415936299.844:2602): avc: denied { create } for pid=22320 comm="passwd"
name="nshadow" scontext=unconfined_u:unconfined_r:passwd_t:s0-s0:c0.c102
tcontext=system_u:object_r:etc_t:s0 tclass=file

type=SYSCALL msg=audit(1415936299.844:2602): arch=x86_64 syscall=open success=no
exit=EACCES a0=7fd138db82ea a1=241 a2=1b6 a3=0 items=0 ppid=21897 pid=22320 auid=0 uid=0
gid=0 euid=0 suid=0 fsuid=0 egid=0 sgid=0 fsgid=0 tty=pts1 ses=252 comm=passwd exe=/usr/bin/passwd
subj=unconfined_u:unconfined_r:passwd_t:s0-s0:c0.c1023 key=(null)
Hash: passwd,passwd_t,etc_t,file,create

The above SELinux denial was due to the fact that I created that scenario by changing the SELinux type on the *shadow* file to something random. I then ran the *passwd* command as *root* to modify the password for *user3*. As expected, SELinux denied *root* write access to the *shadow* file, and logged the password rejection attempt to both log files. I then restored the type on the *shadow* file with the *restorecon* command. I retried changing the password and it worked.

Now, let's run the client in the GUI mode by either issuing the *sealert* command with the –b switch in an X window terminal or selecting Applications | Sundry | SELinux Troubleshooter in the GNOME desktop. An interface similar to the one depicted in Figure 11-13 will appear.

Figure 11-13 SELinux Troubleshooter Client

The figure indicates the presence of four denials and shows the most recent one first. We can list all the alerts by clicking List All Alerts in the bottom right. For each alert, the tool allows us to view troubleshooting suggestions, forward to the administrator, see the complete details, ignore it, or delete it.

Chapter Summary

In this chapter, we discussed two advanced methods for enhanced system protection: firewall and SELinux. We reviewed the concepts of firewall. We looked at both iptables and firewalld services and understood their configuration files. We studied available commands and options for listing and modifying firewall rules and starting and stopping the firewall. We also learned the graphical tool for firewall management.

We studied the concept and features of SELinux at length. We looked at how security contexts were associated with users, processes, and files, and we viewed and modified the contexts for them. We analyzed the SELinux configuration file that controls its state and defines the policy to be used. We learned several SELinux administrative commands and performed actions such as checking and modifying the activation mode and checking its operating status. We studied SELinux booleans and saw how to modify certain parts of the SELinux policy temporarily and persistently. We looked at the graphical SELinux configuration tool and reviewed each category briefly. Finally, we reviewed the SELinux Troubleshooter program and saw how SELinux related messages were logged.

Chapter Review Questions

1. What is the name of the command to start the graphical SELinux administration tool?
2. What would the command *iptables –A OUTPUT –p tcp --dport 25 –j DROP* do?
3. What are the two commands to display and modify the SELinux mode?
4. Iptables is a packet-filtering firewall. True or False?
5. SELinux is an implementation of discretionary access control. True or False?
6. Where do SELinux denial messages are logged in the absence of the *auditd* daemon?
7. What is the name of the graphical tool for firewalld administration?
8. What is the name of the SELinux configuration file and where is it located in the system?
9. A firewall cannot be configured between two networks. True or False?
10. Which command can be used to ensure modified SELinux contexts survive file system relabeling, *chcon* or *semanage*?
11. Which option is used with the *ps* command to view the security contexts on processes?
12. What would the command *restorecon –F /etc* do?
13. What is the name of the default SELinux policy used in RHEL7?
14. What is the name of the iptables configuration file and where is it located in the system?
15. What would the rule "-I INPUT -m state --state NEW -p tcp --dport 23 -j ACCEPT" do?
16. What is the purpose of the command *sestatus*?
17. What is the name of the directory that stores SELinux boolean files?
18. What one task must be done to change the SELinux mode from enforcing to disabled?
19. What is the process of data packet formation called?
20. Which option with the *cp* command must be specified to preserve the SELinux contexts?
21. What would the command *semanage login –a –s user_u user10* do?
22. Name the two commands that can be used to modify a boolean value.
23. If one service on the system running SELinux is compromised, all other services will be affected as well. True or False?
24. What would the command *iptables –L* do?
25. Name the command to start the SELinux Troubleshooter program.

Answers to Chapter Review Questions

1. The name of the command to start the graphical SELinux administration tool is *system-config-selinux*.
2. This command will append a rule to the output chain to prevent TCP packets from leaving the system via port 25.
3. The *getenforce* and *setenforce* commands.
4. True.

---

5. False.
6. The SELinux denial messages are logged to the */var/log/messages* file.
7. The graphical tool for firewalld administration is called *firewall-config*.
8. The configuration file name is selinux and it is located in the */etc/sysconfig* directory.
9. False.
10. The *semanage* command.
11. The –Z option.
12. This command will restore the default SELinux contexts on the */etc* directory.
13. The default policy used in RHEL7 for SELinux is the targeted policy.
14. The configuration file name is iptables and it is located in the */etc/sysconfig* directory.
15. The specified string will insert a rule in the iptables firewall to allow new traffic on port 23 to pass through without affecting any of the existing connections on this port.
16. The *sestatus* command displays the SELinux status.
17. The */sys/fs/selinux/booleans* directory.
18. The system has to be rebooted.
19. The process of data packet formation is called encapsulation.
20. The --preserve=context option.
21. This command will map Linux user user10 with SELinux user user_u.
22. The *semanage* and *setsebool* commands.
23. False.
24. This command will display all loaded firewall rules on the system.
25. The command name is *sealert*.

DIY Challenge Labs

The following labs are useful to strengthen most of the concepts and topics learned in this chapter. It is expected that you perform these labs without any additional help. A step-by-step guide is not provided, as the implementation of these labs requires the knowledge that has been presented in this chapter. Use defaults or your own thinking for missing information.

Lab 11-1: Add Firewall Rules

Insert a rule in the OUTPUT chain to allow UDP traffic to network 192.168.4.0/24 via port 100. Append a rule to the INPUT chain to disallow TCP traffic from network 192.168.3.0/24 via port 101 without sending a notification back to the requester, but allow from 192.168.3.33/24. Insert a rule in the INPUT chain to permit the established ssh communication channels to continue to function and allow for subsequent ssh requests to pass through the firewall as well.

Lab 11-2: Disable and Enable the SELinux Operating Mode

Check and make a note of the current SELinux operating mode. Modify the configuration file and set the mode to disabled. Reboot the system and validate the change. Restore the system to the original SELinux mode and reboot to validate. Measure the time it takes for either reboot.

## Chapter 12

Administering Network Interfaces and Network Clients

This chapter describes the following major topics:

➢ Basic networking including hostname, IPv4, IPv6, network classes, subnet, subnet mask, protocol, TCP/UDP, Ethernet addresses, and ARP

➢ Understand network interfaces and consistent interface naming

➢ Comprehend interface configuration files, hosts table, and management commands

➢ Overview of NetworkManager

➢ Configure a network interface manually and with NetworkManager

➢ Use ping to test connectivity

➢ Manage network interfaces via Graphical Network Administration tool

➢ Configure a system to get time from NTP servers

➢ OpenLDAP concepts, terminology, roles, and client packages

➢ Understand OpenLDAP client configuration files

➢ Configure OpenLDAP client with authconfig tool

➢ Overview of Graphical Authentication Configuration tool

RHCSA Objectives:

31. Configure networking and hostname resolution statically or dynamically
40. Configure a system to use time services
47. Configure a system to use an existing authentication service for user and group information

Acomputer network is a group of two or more physical or virtual computers connected together to share their resources and data. The computers may be interlinked via wired or wireless means, and a device such as a switch is required to interconnect several computers so that they can communicate with one another on the network.

To comprehend how networks work and how network services are configured properly, some basic networking terminology needs to be understood first. For a system to be able to talk to other networked systems, one of its network interfaces must be configured with a unique IP address, hostname, and other essential network parameters. Several files are involved for the interface configuration, which may be modified by hand or by using commands and graphical tools. After networking has been configured, testing is done to confirm the system's ability to communicate with other systems on the network.

NTP is a networking protocol that allows a system to synchronize its clock with a more reliable source of time in order for time-sensitive applications running on the system to function accurately.

OpenLDAP is an open source implementation of LDAP. In order for a system to have its users authenticated by a remote OpenLDAP server and to obtain other directory information, the OpenLDAP client functionality needs to be configured on the system. There are certain configuration files that are modified for this purpose, and they may be edited manually, or via commands and graphical tools.

Basic Networking

There are many basic concepts and terms that you need to grasp before being able to configure network interfaces and perform advanced network client and server setups. Likewise, there are also many configuration files and commands related to various network services that you need to thoroughly understand. Some of the concepts, terms, configuration files, and commands are explained in this chapter, and many more will be introduced in the RHCE section of this book.

Hostname

A *hostname* is a unique alphanumeric label (the dash, underscore, and dot characters are also allowed) that is assigned to a system to identify it on the network. It can consists of up to 64 characters. It is normally allotted based on the purpose and primary use of the system. In RHEL7, the hostname is stored in the */etc/hostname* file.

The hostname of a system can be viewed with the use of several different commands, such as *hostname*, *hostnamectl*, and *uname*. We can also display the contents of the */etc/hostname* file where the hostname is stored. Moreover, the NetworkManager service is also available to show us the hostname at the command prompt, in text mode, and in graphical mode.

```
# hostname
server1.example.com
# hostnamectl | grep hostname
    Static hostname: server1.example.com
# uname –n
server1
# cat /etc/hostname
server1.example.com
# nmcli general hostname
server1.example.com
```

Similarly, the hostname can be changed using any of the methods mentioned above, except for the *uname* command. The *hostname* command allows you to rename the hostname temporarily. For instance, to rename *server1.example.com* to *server10.example.com*, run this command as follows:

 # hostname server10.example.com

The *hostnamectl* command changes the hostname on a permanent basis. The following renames *server10.example.com* to *server100.example.com*:

 # hostnamectl set-hostname server100.example.com

Alternatively, you can simply edit the */etc/hostname* file and make the desired change in it. After saving the file and exiting the editor, restart the systemd-hostnamed service for this permanent change to take effect right away. The following changes the hostname back to *server1.example.com*:

 # vi /etc/hostname
server1.example.com
 # systemctl restart systemd-hostnamed

Do not forget to update the */etc/hosts* file to reflect the new hostname.

The NetworkManager can also be used to change the hostname via its command line interface (*nmcli*) or text interface (*nmtui*).

IPv4 Address

IPv4 stands for *Internet Protocol version 4* and it represents a unique 32-bit software address that every single system on the network must have in order to communicate with other systems. It was the first version of IP that was released for public use. IPv4 addresses can be assigned on a temporary or permanent basis. Temporary addresses are referred to as *dynamic* addresses and are typically leased from a DHCP server for a specific period of time. Permanent addresses, on the other hand, are called *static* addresses and are set either manually or using the NetworkManager service. Permanent addresses are typically not changed unless there is a need.

We use the *ip* command with the addr argument to view current IP assignments on our system:

 # ip addr
1: lo: <LOOPBACK,UP,LOWER_UP> mtu 65536 qdisc noqueue state UNKNOWN
    link/loopback 00:00:00:00:00:00 brd 00:00:00:00:00:00
    inet 127.0.0.1/8 scope host lo
      valid_lft forever preferred_lft forever
    inet6 ::1/128 scope host
      valid_lft forever preferred_lft forever
2: eth0: <BROADCAST,MULTICAST,UP,LOWER_UP> mtu 1500 qdisc pfifo_fast state UP qlen 1000
    link/ether 52:54:00:17:91:8d brd ff:ff:ff:ff:ff:ff
    inet 192.168.0.110/24 brd 192.168.0.255 scope global eth0
    valid_lft forever preferred_lft forever
    inet6 fe80::5054:ff:fe17:918d/64 scope link
      valid_lft forever preferred_lft forever

We can also use the *ifconfig* command to obtain this information, but this command is deprecated in RHEL7 and will be removed from a future RHEL release.

The above output indicates the presence of one configured network interface called *eth0* on the system with IPv4 address 192.168.0.110 assigned to it. The other interface, called *lo*, is a special purpose software interface reserved for use on every UNIX and Linux system. Its IPv4 address is always 127.0.0.1 and it is referred to as the system's *loopback* (or *localhost*) address. This hostname is used by network applications to access the networking resources on the local system.

Network Classes

An IP address is comprised of four dot-separated octets that are divided into a *network* portion and a *node* portion. The network portion identifies the correct destination network and the node portion identifies the correct destination node on that network. Network addresses are classified into three classes, referred to as class A, class B, and class C. Classes D and E are also defined and in use; however, their use is limited to special areas such as scientific and engineering.

A node is any device on the network with an IP address. Examples include computers, storage devices, routers, switches, hand-held devices, printers, and so on.

Class A addresses are used for large networks with up to 16 million nodes. The network address range for class A networks is between 1 and 126. This class uses the first octet as the network portion and the rest of the octets as the node portion.

Class B addresses are used for mid-sized networks with up to 65 thousand nodes. The network address range for class B networks is between 128 and 191. This class uses the first two octets as the network portion and the other two octets as the node portion.

Class C addresses are used for small networks with up to 254 nodes. The network address range for class C networks is between 192 and 223. This class uses the first three octets as the network portion and the last octet as the node portion.

Subnetting and Subnet Mask

Subnetting is a method by which a large network address space can be divided into several smaller and more manageable logical sub-networks, commonly referred to as *subnets*. Subnetting usually results in reduced network traffic, improved network performance, and de-centralized and easier administration, among other benefits.

The following should be kept in mind when dealing with subnetting:

- ✓ Subnetting does not increase the number of IP addresses in a network. In fact, it reduces the number of usable IP addresses.
- ✓ All nodes in a given subnet have the same subnet mask.
- ✓ Each subnet acts as an isolated network and requires a router to talk to other subnets.
- ✓ The first and the last IP address in a subnet are reserved. The first address points to the subnet itself and the last address is the broadcast address.

After a given address has been subnetted, we determine something called *subnet mask* or *netmask*. The subnet mask is the network portion plus the subnet bits. In other words, the subnet mask segregates the network bits from the node bits. It is used by routers to identify the start and end of the network/subnet portion and the start and end of the node portion for a given IP address.

The default subnet masks for class A, B, and C networks are 255.0.0.0, 255.255.0.0, and 255.255.255.0, respectively.

Protocol

A *protocol* is a set of rules governing the exchange of data between two networked entities. These rules include how data is formatted, coded, and controlled. The rules also provide error handling, speed matching, and data packet sequencing. In other words, a protocol is a common language that all nodes on the network speak and understand. Some common protocols are TCP, UDP, IP, and ICMP. Protocols are defined in the */etc/protocols* file. An excerpt from this file is provided below:

```
# cat /etc/protocols
ip         0    IP        # internet protocol, pseudo protocol number
hopopt     0    HOPOPT    # hop-by-hop options for ipv6
icmp       1    ICMP      # internet control message protocol
igmp       2    IGMP      # internet group management protocol
ggp        3    GGP       # gateway-gateway protocol
ipv4       4    IPv4      # IPv4 encapsulation
st         5    ST        # ST datagram mode
tcp        6    TCP       # transmission control protocol
. . . . . . . .
```

TCP and UDP Protocols

Two key protocols besides IP are TCP and UDP. TCP is reliable, connection-oriented, and point-to-point. When a stream of packets is sent to the destination node using the TCP protocol, the destination node checks for errors and packet sequencing upon its arrival. Each packet contains information such as the IP addresses for the source and destination systems, port numbers, data, a sequence number, and checksum fields. The TCP protocol at the source node establishes a point-to-point connection with the peer TCP protocol at the destination. When the packet is received by the receiving TCP, an acknowledgment is returned. If the packet contains an error or is lost in transit, the destination node requests the source node to resend the packet. This ensures guaranteed data delivery and makes TCP reliable.

UDP, on the other hand, is unreliable, connectionless, and multi-point. If a packet is lost or contains errors upon arrival at the destination, the source node is unaware of it. The destination node does not send an acknowledgment back to the source node. UDP is normally used for broadcast purposes.

Both TCP and UDP protocols use ports for data transmission between a client and its associated server program. Ports are defined in the */etc/services* file. Some common services and the ports they listen on are: ftp 21, ssh 22, postfix 25, http 80, and ntp 123. An excerpt from the */etc/services* file is shown below:

```
# cat /etc/services
# service-name      port/protocol    [aliases ...]        [# comment]
ftp                 21/tcp
ftp                 21/udp           fsp fspd
ssh                 22/tcp                                # The Secure Shell (SSH) Protocol
. . . . . . . .
```

Ethernet Address and Address Resolution Protocol

An *Ethernet* address represents a unique 48-bit address that is used to identify the correct destination node for data packets transmitted from the source node. The data packets include Ethernet addresses for both the source and the destination node. A network protocol called ARP, maps the Ethernet address to the destination node's IP address. The Ethernet address is also referred to as the *hardware, physical, link layer,* or *MAC* address.

We can use the *ip* command to list all network interfaces available on the system along with their hardware addresses:

```
# ip addr | grep ether
    link/ether 52:54:00:17:91:8d brd ff:ff:ff:ff:ff:ff
```

IP and Ethernet addresses work hand in hand, and a combination of both is critical to identifying the correct destination node on the network. A protocol called *Address Resolution Protocol* (ARP) is used to enable IP and hardware addresses to work together. ARP determines the hardware address of the destination node when its IP address is already known.

ARP broadcasts messages over the network requesting each alive neighbor to reply with its link layer and IP addresses. The addresses received are cached locally on the node, and can be viewed using the *ip* command with the neighbor argument:

```
# ip neighbor
192.168.0.13   dev eth0  lladdr dc:85:de:02:71:ef  STALE
192.168.0.100 dev eth0  lladdr d4:be:d9:2e:2e:d9  STALE
192.168.0.1    dev eth0  lladdr 18:59:33:f7:6a:14  STALE
192.168.0.120 dev eth0  lladdr 52:54:00:5d:ba:f9  REACHABLE
```

 We can also use the *arp* command to obtain this information, but this command is now obsolete.

The above output shows IP addresses of the neighbors in the first column followed by the interface devices that they are using, their link layer addresses, and their NUD (*Nieghbor Unreachability Detection*) states. A neighbor can be in one of four states: permanent, noarp, reachable, and stale. The permanent state indicates a valid entry that can only be deleted manually, the noarp state designates a valid entry that expires at the end of its lifetime, the reachable state shows a valid entry that expires when its reachability timeout expires, and the stale state specifies a valid but suspicious entry.

Network Interfaces

Network Interface Cards are the hardware adapters that provide one or more Ethernet ports for network connectivity, and they are abbreviated as NICs. NICs may also be referred to as network adapters and individual ports as network interfaces or simply interfaces. NICs may be built-in to the system board or are add-on adapters. They are available in one to four port configuration on a single adapter. Two or more interfaces can be configured to provide bonding and teaming for redundancy and faster throughput. Individual interfaces as well as bonding and teaming can be configured with IPv4 and IPv6 assignments by editing files, or using either commands or the NetworkManager toolset. Additional tasks such as activating and deactivating them manually and auto-activating them at system reboots can also be performed with these tools. We discuss interface configuration and their administration in this chapter; bonding and teaming are RHCE topics and are covered in Chapter 15 "Configuring Bonding, Teaming, IPv6, and Routing".

Consistent Interface Naming

In earlier RHEL versions, network interfaces were named eth (Ethernet), em (embedded), and wlan (wireless lan) and were numbered beginning at 0 as the interfaces were discovered during a system boot. This was the default interface naming scheme that had been in place for years. Given a large number of interfaces located onboard and on add-on NIC adapters, these number assignments could possibly change on the next boot, resulting in all kinds of connectivity and system operational issues. As of RHEL7, the default naming scheme is now based on several rules governed by systemd and udevd, which assign names based on BIOS/topology/location information. The key rules are presented below for Ethernet interfaces and are applied in the order in which they are listed. These rules are applicable to wireless adapters as well.

1. Onboard interfaces at firmware/BIOS-supplied index numbers (e.g. eno1).
2. Interfaces at PCI Express hotplug slot numbers (e.g. ens3).
3. Adapters in the specified PCI slot, with slot index number on the adapter (e.g. enp3s0).
4. If the above rules are disabled or the information furnished by firmware/BIOS is invalid, the system reverts to the traditional ethX convention.

This advanced ruleset has resulted in consistent naming, eliminating the odds of re-enumeration during a hardware rescan. Moreover, the assigned names are not affected by the addition or removal of interface cards. This naming scheme helps in identifying, configuring, troubleshooting, and replacing the right adapter without hassle.

In order to apply the above naming, we need to ensure that the biosdevname software package is removed from the system and no custom udev rules are in place for interface naming.

Understanding Interface Configuration File

Each network interface has a configuration file that stores IP assignments and other relevant parameters for the interface. The system reads this file and applies the settings at the time the interface is activated. Configuration files for all interfaces are stored at a central location, which is the */etc/sysconfig/network-scripts* directory. The interface file names begin with *ifcfg-* and is followed by the name of the interface by which the system recognizes it. Some instances of interface file names are *ifcfg-eth0, ifcfg-enp0s3, ifcfg-br0,* and *ifcfg-em1*.

On *server1* and *server2*, we used *eth0* for the interface that we had configured at the time of installation as we picked up the virtual bridge *br0* for the default interface. If we had chosen 'default NAT', the interface name would have been ens3 as the default.

The current contents of the *ifcfg-eth0* file from *server1* are presented below:

```
# cat /etc/sysconfig/network-scripts/ifcfg-eth0
DEVICE="eth0"
ONBOOT=yes
NETBOOT=yes
UUID="0764d665-dd86-4001-bdc5-3b280d32a11d"
IPV6INIT=yes
BOOTPROTO=none
TYPE=Ethernet
NAME="eth0"
HWADDR=52:54:00:17:91:8D
IPADDR0=192.168.0.110
PREFIX0=24
GATEWAY0=192.168.0.1
DEFROUTE=yes
IPV4_FAILURE_FATAL=no
IPV6_AUTOCONF=yes
IPV6_DEFROUTE=yes
IPV6_FAILURE_FATAL=no
IPV6_PEERDNS=yes
IPV6_PEERROUTES=yes
```

These and a few other directives that can be defined in this file are described in Table 12-1.

Directive	Description
BOOTPROTO	Defines the boot protocol to be used. Values include "dhcp" to obtain IP from a DHCP server, "bootp" to boot off of a network boot server and get IP, and "none" or "static" to use a static IP set with the IPADDR directive.
BRIDGE	Specifies the name of the network bridge to be used. On host1, we created br0 in Chapter 06 "Configuring Server Virtualization and Network Installing RHEL7".
BROADCAST0	Sets the broadcast IP address for the first IP on this interface.
DEFROUTE	Whether to use this interface as the default route.
DEVICE	Specifies the device name for the network interface.
DNS1	Places an entry for the first DNS server in the /etc/resolv.conf file if PEERDNS directive is set to "yes" in this file.
GATEWAY0	Specifies the gateway address for the first IP on this interface.
HWADDR	Describes the hardware address for this interface.
IPADDR0	Specifies the IP for this interface.
IPV6INIT	Whether to enable IPv6 support for this interface.
NAME	Any description given to this interface.
NETMASK0	Sets the netmask address for the first IP on this interface.
NM_CONTROLLED	Whether the NetworkManager service is allowed to modify the configuration in this file. Default is yes.
ONBOOT	Whether to activate this interface at system boot.
PEERDNS	Whether to modify the DNS client resolver file /etc/resolv.conf. Default is "yes" if BOOTPROTO=dhcp is set.
USERCTL	Whether to allow non-root users to activate this interface.

Directive	Description
UUID	The UUID associated with this interface.
TYPE	Specifies the type of this interface.

Table 12-1 Network Interface Configuration File

Understanding the Hosts Table

Each IP configured on an interface has a hostname assigned to it. In an environment with multiple networked systems, it is prudent to have some kind of hostname to IP resolution in place to avoid typing the destination system IP over and over when we need to access it. DNS is one such method. It is designed for large networks such as corporate networks and the Internet. For small, internal networks, the use of a local host table (the */etc/hosts* file) is more common. This table is used to maintain hostname to IP mapping for all systems on the local network, allowing us access to a system by simply typing its hostname. From the standpoint of this book, we have three systems in place: *host1.example.com* with IP 192.168.0.100 and alias *host1*; *server1.example.com* with IP 192.168.0.110 and alias *server1*; and *server2.example.com* with IP 192.168.0.120 and alias *server2*. We can append this IP and hostname information to the */etc/hosts* file as shown below:

```
192.168.0.100        host1.example.com        host1
192.168.0.110        server1.example.com      server1
192.168.0.120        server2.example.com      server2
```

Each row in the file contains an IP address in the first column followed by the *official* (or *canonical*) hostname in the second column, and one or more aliases subsequently. The official hostname and one or more aliases give us the flexibility of accessing a system using any of these names.

EXAM TIP: In the presence of an active DNS with all hostnames resolvable, there is no need to worry about updating the hosts file.

As indicated above, the *hosts* file is normally used on small networks only, and therefore must be updated on each individual system to reflect changes.

Interface Administration Commands

There are several commands available to administer network interfaces. The NetworkManager service includes a toolset for this purpose as well, which provides us with access to a command line interface and a text interface. Table 12-2 lists and describes the commands and the NetworkManager tools.

Command	Description
ifdown / ifup	Deactivates / activates an interface.
ip	A powerful tool for administering interfaces, routing, etc. It is a replacement for ifconfig and netstat obsoleted commands.
nm-connection-editor	A graphical tool for interface administration.
Network Settings	A graphical connection status and network administration tool.
NetworkManager Tools	
nmcli	A command line tool for interface administration.
nmtui	A text-based tool for interface administration.

Table 12-2 Network Interface Administration Tools

What is NetworkManager?

NetworkManager is the default interface configuration and monitoring service available in RHEL7. It has a daemon program called *NetworkManager* that dynamically keeps configured interfaces up and active. It has a set of client programs for managing network interfaces and controlling the service itself from the command line (*nmcli*) or via the text tool (*nmtui*). The availability of these tools is dependent on the presence of NetworkManager and NetworkManager-tui software packages on the system. By default, the NetworkManager service is enabled and active.

The *nmcli* utility is powerful and has many options available for effective interface administration. Its text equivalent is *nmtui*, which also allows us to add, modify, and delete an interface connection, activate and deactivate an interface, and change the hostname of the system. The main window, as depicted in Figure 12-1, appears when we issue *nmtui* at the command prompt:

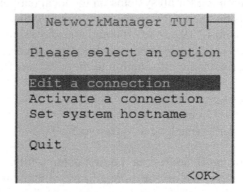

Figure 12-1 NetworkManager TUI

This tool updates appropriate files on the system for any operations that we perform.

Exercise 12-1: Present, Configure, and Activate a Network Interface Manually

This exercise should be done on *host1* and *server1*.

In this exercise, you will add a new network interface to the virtual machine hosting *server1*, with the source device "Host device em1 (Bridge 'br0')", default MAC address, and device model virtio. On *server1*, you will call this interface *eth1* and manually assign the IP 192.168.0.111/24 for temporary use. You will copy the *ifcfg-eth0* file in the */etc/sysconfig/network-scripts* directory as *ifcfg-eth1* and modify it. You will set this interface to autoactivate at system reboots. You will deactivate and reactivate this interface at the command prompt. You will reboot *server1* and verify the persistence of IP assignments for this new interface. You will assign it hostname *server1ipv4.example.com* and alias *server1ipv4* and update the *hosts* file accordingly.

1. Open the virtual console for *server1* on *host1*. Click "Show virtual hardware details" | Add Hardware | Network. Select host device "Host device em1 (Bridge 'br0')" from the drop-down list and device model virtio. Leave the MAC address to the default. Click Finish to complete the new interface assignment.
2. Log on to *server1* as *root* and run the *ip* command to look for the new interface:

ip addr

. . . .

3: eth1: <BROADCAST,MULTICAST,UP,LOWER_UP> mtu 1500 qdisc pfifo_fast state UP qlen 1000
    link/ether 52:54:00:39:16:9a brd ff:ff:ff:ff:ff:ff

The output indicates the presence of a new interface by the name *eth1*.

3. Assign IP 192.168.0.111/24 to *eth1*:

 # ip addr add 192.168.0.111/24 broadcast 192.168.0.255 dev eth1

4. Verify the new IP assignments on *eth1*:

 # ip addr
3: eth1: <BROADCAST,MULTICAST,UP,LOWER_UP> mtu 1500 qdisc pfifo_fast state UP qlen 1000
    link/ether 52:54:00:39:16:9a brd ff:ff:ff:ff:ff:ff
    inet 192.168.0.111/24 brd 192.168.0.255 scope global eth1
    valid_lft forever preferred_lft forever

At this point, if you reboot *server1*, this IP information will be lost. You need to configure the settings in a file for persistence.

5. Copy the *ifcfg-eth0* file as *ifcfg-eth1* in the */etc/sysconfig/network-scripts* directory:

 # cd /etc/sysconfig/network-scripts
 # cp ifcfg-eth0 ifcfg-eth1

6. Open *ifcfg-eth1* in a text editor and modify the contents accordingly. On my *server1*, it will look as shown below:

 # vi ifcfg-eth1
DEVICE="eth1"
ONBOOT=yes
NETBOOT=yes
IPV6INIT=yes
BOOTPROTO=none
TYPE=Ethernet
NAME="eth1"
IPADDR0=192.168.0.111
PREFIX0=24
GATEWAY0=192.168.0.1
DEFROUTE=yes
IPV4_FAILURE_FATAL=no
IPV6_AUTOCONF=yes
IPV6_DEFROUTE=yes
IPV6_FAILURE_FATAL=no
HWADDR=52:54:00:39:16:9A
IPV6_PEERDNS=yes

IPV6_PEERROUTES=yes

7. Deactivate this interface and then reactivate using the *ifdown* and *ifup* commands:

   # **ifdown eth1**
   # **ifup eth1**
   Connection successfully activated (D-Bus active path:
   /org/freedesktop/NetworkManager/ActiveConnection/2)

8. Reboot the system:

   # **reboot**

9. Verify the presence of *eth1* assignments:

   # **ip addr**
   3: eth1: <BROADCAST,MULTICAST,UP,LOWER_UP> mtu 1500 qdisc pfifo_fast state UP qlen
   1000
       link/ether 52:54:00:39:16:9a brd ff:ff:ff:ff:ff:ff
       inet 192.168.0.111/24 brd 192.168.0.255 scope global eth1
       valid_lft forever preferred_lft forever

10. Open the *hosts* file and append the following entry to it:

    # **vi /etc/hosts**
    192.168.0.111   server1ipv4.example.com   server1ipv4

You can use puTTY in Windows and attempt to access the server using this new IP.

The nmcli Command

The *nmcli* command is a NetworkManager service tool, which allows us to create, view, modify, remove, activate, and deactivate network interfaces, and control and report their status. This tool operates on one of five objects at a time, with each object supporting several options to form a complete command. The five objects are general, networking, radio, connection, and device. For our purposes, the objects connection and device are important, and are described in Table 12-3.

Object	Description
Connection: activates, deactivates, and administers network connections.	
show	Lists connection profiles.
up / down	Activates/deactivates a connection.
add	Adds a connection.
edit	Edits an existing connection or adds a new one.
modify	Modifies one or more properties in the connection profile.
delete	Deletes a connection.
reload	Instructs NetworkManager to re-read all interface configuration files.
load	Instructs NetworkManager to re-read the specified interface configuration file.
Device: displays and administers network interfaces.	

Object	Description
status	Displays device status.
show	Displays detailed information about all or the specified interface.

Table 12-3 Network Interface Administration Tools

Objects may be abbreviated. For instance, the connection object may be specified as a 'c' or 'con'. Similarly, the device object can be abbreviated as a 'd' or 'dev'.

Exercise 12-2: Present, Configure, and Activate a Network Interface Using NetworkManager CLI

This exercise should be done on *host1* and *server2*.

In this exercise, you will add a new network interface to the virtual machine hosting *server2*, with the source device "Host device em1 (Bridge 'br0')", default MAC address, and device model virtio. On *server2*, you will call this interface *eth1* and assign IP 192.168.0.121/24 using the NetworkManager CLI. You will deactivate and reactivate this interface at the command prompt. You will reboot *server2* and verify the persistence of IP assignments for this new interface. You will assign it hostname *server2-eth1.example.com* and alias *server2-eth1* and update the *hosts* file accordingly.

1. Open the virtual console for *server2* on *host1*. Click "Show virtual hardware details" | Add Hardware | Network. Select host device "Host device em1 (Bridge 'br0')" from the drop-down list and device model virtio. Leave the MAC address to the default. Click Finish to complete the new interface assignment.

2. Log on to *server2* and check the running status of NetworkManager service:

    # **systemctl status NetworkManager**
    NetworkManager.service - Network Manager
      Loaded: loaded (/usr/lib/systemd/system/NetworkManager.service; enabled)
      Active: active (running) since Mon 2014-11-17 11:00:52 EST; 28min ago
    . . . .

3. Look for the new interface with the *ip* command:

    # **ip addr**
    . . . .
    3: eth1: <BROADCAST,MULTICAST,UP,LOWER_UP> mtu 1500 qdisc pfifo_fast state UP qlen 1000
      link/ether 52:54:00:96:13:58 brd ff:ff:ff:ff:ff:ff

    The output indicates the presence of a new interface by the name *eth1*.

4. List all configured interfaces on the server:

    # **nmcli con show**
    NAME   UUID   TYPE   DEVICE
    eth0   b76b735d-74c5-4d55-91f0-b81181f858b5   802-3-ethernet eth0

5. Show the status of all available interfaces on the server:

nmcli dev status

DEVICE	TYPE	STATE	CONNECTION
eth0	ethernet	connected	eth0
eth1	ethernet	disconnected	--
lo	loopback	unmanaged	--

6. Add a connection of type Ethernet, interface name *eth1*, connection name *eth1*, IP 192.168.0.121/24, and gateway 192.168.0.1:

nmcli con add type Ethernet ifname eth1 con-name eth1 ip4 192.168.0.121/24 \\ gw4 192.168.0.1
Connection 'eth1' (7f365451-fd33-44f0-bffb-45de70d06fe0) successfully added.

The *nmcli* command has added the new interface and has activated it. In addition, it has created the *ifcfg-eth1* file in the */etc/sysconfig/network-scripts* directory with all necessary directives.

7. Check the new connection and IP assignments:

ip addr
. . . .
3: eth1: <BROADCAST,MULTICAST,UP,LOWER_UP> mtu 1500 qdisc pfifo_fast state UP qlen 1000
    link/ether 52:54:00:96:13:58 brd ff:ff:ff:ff:ff:ff
    inet 192.168.0.121/24 brd 192.168.0.255 scope global eth1
      valid_lft forever preferred_lft forever
    inet6 fe80::5054:ff:fe96:1358/64 scope link
      valid_lft forever preferred_lft forever

8. Check the contents of the *ifcfg-eth1* file:

# **cat /etc/sysconfig/network-scripts/ifcfg-eth1**
TYPE=Ethernet
BOOTPROTO=none
IPADDR0=192.168.0.121
PREFIX0=24
GATEWAY0=192.168.0.1
DEFROUTE=yes
IPV4_FAILURE_FATAL=no
IPV6INIT=yes
IPV6_AUTOCONF=yes
IPV6_DEFROUTE=yes
IPV6_PEERDNS=yes
IPV6_PEERROUTES=yes
IPV6_FAILURE_FATAL=no
NAME=eth1
UUID=7f365451-fd33-44f0-bffb-45de70d06fe0
DEVICE=eth1

ONBOOT=yes

9. Show the connection information for *eth1*:

    # **nmcli con show | grep eth1**
    eth1 7f365451-fd33-44f0-bffb-45de70d06fe0 802-3-ethernet eth1

10. Show the connection status of *eth1*:

    # **nmcli dev status | grep eth1**
    eth1   ethernet connected eth1

11. Deactivate this interface and then reactivate:

    # **nmcli con down id eth1**
    # **nmcli con up id eth1**
    Connection successfully activated (D-Bus active path:
    /org/freedesktop/NetworkManager/ActiveConnection/3)

12. Reboot the system:

    # **reboot**

13. Verify the presence of *eth1* assignments:

    # **ip addr**
    . . . .
    3: eth1: <BROADCAST,MULTICAST,UP,LOWER_UP> mtu 1500 qdisc pfifo_fast state UP qlen
    1000
        link/ether 52:54:00:96:13:58 brd ff:ff:ff:ff:ff:ff
        inet 192.168.0.121/24 brd 192.168.0.255 scope global eth1
          valid_lft forever preferred_lft forever
        inet6 fe80::5054:ff:fe96:1358/64 scope link
          valid_lft forever preferred_lft forever

14. Open the *hosts* file and append the following entry to it:

    # **vi /etc/hosts**
    192.168.0.121   server2-eth1.example.com server2-eth1

You can use puTTY in Windows and attempt to access the server using this new IP.

Testing Network Connectivity with ping

After the new connections have been established on *server1* and *server2*, we need to test whether
the IP addresses are pingable and accessible from other systems. Log on to *host1* or another RHEL
system and run the *ping* (packet internet gropper) command. The *ping* command is used to check
the network connectivity at the IP level when the physical connectivity is ok and proper IP address
and network assignments are in place. This command sends out a series of 64-byte *Internet Control*

Message Protocol (ICMP) test packets to the destination IP and waits for a response. With the –c option, we can specify the number of packets that we want to send.

The following will send two packets from *host1* to 192.168.0.111 and two packets to 192.168.0.121:

ping –c2 192.168.0.111
PING 192.168.0.111 (192.168.0.111) 56(84) bytes of data.
64 bytes from 192.168.0.111: icmp_seq=1 ttl=64 time=0.240 ms
64 bytes from 192.168.0.111: icmp_seq=2 ttl=64 time=0.269 ms
--- 192.168.0.111 ping statistics ---
2 packets transmitted, 2 received, 0% packet loss, time 999ms
rtt min/avg/max/mdev = 0.240/0.254/0.269/0.021 ms
ping –c2 192.168.0.121
PING 192.168.0.121 (192.168.0.121) 56(84) bytes of data.
64 bytes from 192.168.0.121: icmp_seq=1 ttl=64 time=0.237 ms
64 bytes from 192.168.0.121: icmp_seq=2 ttl=64 time=0.234 ms
--- 192.168.0.121 ping statistics ---
2 packets transmitted, 2 received, 0% packet loss, time 999ms
rtt min/avg/max/mdev = 0.234/0.235/0.237/0.015 ms

Under the ping statistics, the outputs show the number of packets transmitted, received, and lost. The packet loss should be 0% and the round trip time should not be too high for a healthy connection. In general, we can use this command to test connectivity with a system's own IP, the loopback IP, the default route, other systems on the local network, systems on a different network, and systems beyond the local network.

If *ping* fails in any of the situations, we need to check if the network adapter is seated properly, its driver installed, network cable secured appropriately, IP and subnet mask values set correctly, the default route configured right, and proper rules are defined in the firewall. We also need to verify entries in the *hosts* file and files in the */etc/sysconfig/network-scripts* directory.

Overview of Graphical Network Administration Tools

RHEL7 offers Network Settings and Network Connections tools for graphical management of network interfaces. The Network Settings (or Control Network) is located in the Control Center and it may be accessed by clicking the network icon at the top right-hand corner in the GNOME desktop as shown in Figure 12-2 or by clicking Applications | System Tools | Settings | Network.

Figure 12-2 Network Icon

The Network Settings graphical tool allows us to view the status of available network interfaces, activating and deactivating them by sliding the bar to ON or OFF, add a new interface by clicking the + sign in the bottom left, delete an existing interface by highlighting an existing connection on the left and clicking the – sign in the bottom left, and modify an existing connection by selecting an existing connection on the left and clicking the gear wheel icon in the bottom right. See Figure 12-3.

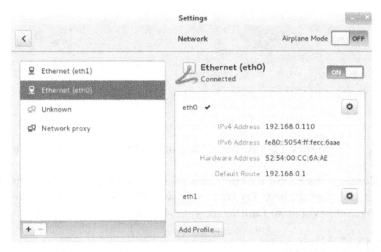

Figure 12-3 Network Settings

There are five types of network connections that we can add with this tool. These are VPN, Bond, Team, Bridge, and VLAN. Choosing any one of them brings up a new window with four tabs available in it. Figure 12-4 shows the window when we choose to add a Bridge. One of the three tabs is specific to the type of connection chosen; the rest are common for all interface types. Each tab allows us to enter necessary configuration information, including user-defined connection and interface names, static or dynamic IPv4 or IPv6 settings, DNS client and routing information, name of the firewall zone, and so on.

Figure 12-4 Network Settings / Add Connection

If we choose to modify a connection, the tabs will appear vertically on the left side, as shown in Figure 12-5. We can see the details for the interface; modify its IP, DNS, and routing information; reset all current assignments; and so on.

Figure 12-5 Network Settings / Modify a Connection

The Network Connections Editor tool provides pretty much the same functionality as the Network Settings tool we have just studied. Try running it with the *nm-connection-editor* command in an X terminal window and navigate to familiarize yourself with it.

The NTP Client

Network Time Protocol (NTP) is a networking protocol for synchronizing the system clock with more reliable remote providers of time. Using this protocol, a system can be configured as a server, peer, or client. The configuration changes to implement any of these roles are straightforward. In fact, the NTP client functionality comes pre-configured with the installation of NTP software. You simply need to enable and start the service, and your system will begin synchronizing its clock with one of the pre-defined timeservers.

The NTP client service can be modified by hand-editing a configuration file and restarting the service. This can alternatively be done using a graphical tool called *System-Config-Date*. You need to install the software packages for the base NTP software and, optionally, the GUI tool to configure your system to obtain time from a remote timeserver and maintain it. The software packages are referred to as ntp and system-config-date, respectively.

Activate the NTP Client

In order to establish the binding with a remote timeserver for time synchronization, install the ntp software on the system, along with the GUI tool:

> **# yum –y install ntp system-config-date**
>
> . . . .
> Installed:
>   ntp.x86_64 0:4.2.6p5-18.el7
>   system-config-date.noarch 0:1.10.6-2.el7
> Dependency Installed:
>   ntpdate.x86_64 0:4.2.6p5-18.el7
>   system-config-date-docs.noarch 0:1.0.11-4.el7
> Complete!

By default, the NTP client functionality is pre-configured in the */etc/ntp.conf* file, which is the primary configuration file for NTP in RHEL7. You simply need to enable and start the service.

There are four default remote timeservers listed in the *etc/ntp.conf* file, and they can be viewed as follows:

 # grep ^server /etc/ntp.conf
server 0.rhel.pool.ntp.org iburst
server 1.rhel.pool.ntp.org iburst
server 2.rhel.pool.ntp.org iburst
server 3.rhel.pool.ntp.org iburst

EXAM TIP: As you will not have access to the outside network during the exam, you will need to point your system to an NTP server available on the local network. Simply comment the four server directives and add a single directive "server <hostname>" to the file. Replace <hostname> with an NTP server name or its IP address.

After the installation of the software is complete, run the following pair of commands to enable and start the service:

 # systemctl enable ntpd
ln -s '/usr/lib/systemd/system/ntpd.service' '/etc/systemd/system/multi-user.target.wants/ntpd.service'
 # systemctl start ntpd

The NTP daemon is now started. Execute the *ntpq* command with the –p switch to determine the association of your system with a timeserver:

 # ntpq –p

remote	refid	st t	when	poll	reach	delay	offset	jitter
+ks4001083.ip-19	140.203.204.77	2 u	2	64	1	27.733	2.818	0.731
*penguin.hopcoun	209.51.161.238	2 u	9	64	1	20.781	1.706	0.807
+ntp-1.asininete	128.4.1.1	2 u	8	64	1	51.061	2.306	1.158
-69.28.83.155	209.87.233.53	3 u	14	64	3	15.507	1.696	1.454

The output displays several timeservers. Your system has time association with the second server on the list prefixed with the * character.

Overview of the System-Config-Date GUI

The NTP client functionality may also be configured using the System-Config-Date graphical tool. This tool reads the definitions from the *etc/ntp.conf* file and shows them graphically. In order to bring this tool up, execute *system-config-date* in an X terminal window or choose Applications | Sundry | System-Config-Date in the GNOME desktop. The System-Config-Date tool will open up as shown in Figure 12-6.

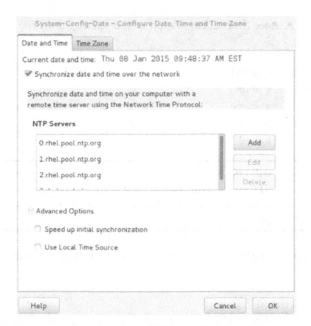

Figure 12-6 System-Config-Date GUI for NTP Client Configuration

Select the option "Synchronize date and time over the network" to enable the service, and click Add to add hostnames or IP addresses for remote timeservers that you wish your system clock to synchronize with. You may leave the default server entries there. Expand Advanced Options to view two additional choices. Select "Speed up initial synchronization" to instruct the tool to run the *ntpdate* command and immediately bring the local system clock close to that of the first NTP server listed. Choose "Use Local Time Source" if you wish to use the local system clock as the provider of time. Click OK when done.

Chapter 16 "Synchronizing Time with NTP" discusses NTP in more detail.

The OpenLDAP Client

Lightweight Directory Access Protocol (LDAP) is a trivial, simplified networking protocol for obtaining centrally-stored information over the network. LDAP is designed to retrieve information that may include user account data (username, location, address, phone number, job title, etc.), group information (group names, members, etc.), calendar services, and other system and network configuration data. It can be configured and used to authenticate users over the network rather than storing and managing users locally on individual systems. Most of this information is static and does not change frequently, making OpenLDAP a suitable solution for write-once-read-many-times applications. All this data, configuration items, and other similar information can be stored on the central server running an LDAP-supported database.

LDAP was derived from *Directory Access Protocol* (DAP), which is one of the protocols within X.500 specifications developed jointly by the *International Telecommunication Union* (ITU) and the *International Organization for Standardization* (ISO). One of the major disadvantages of DAP was its heavy requirement for computer hardware resources to work efficiently. LDAP (also referred to as *X.500 Lite*), on the other hand, is thinner and requires less client-side compute power. LDAP is platform-independent, which has contributed in its wide availability on a variety of vendor hardware platforms running heterogeneous operating system software.

LDAP is hierarchical; its structure is similar to the Linux/UNIX directory tree and DNS. It can be based on logical boundaries defined by geography or organizational arrangements. A typical LDAP directory structure for a company called ABC with domain *abc.com* and offices located in Canada, USA, UK, and Australia, may look analogous to what is shown in Figure 12-7.

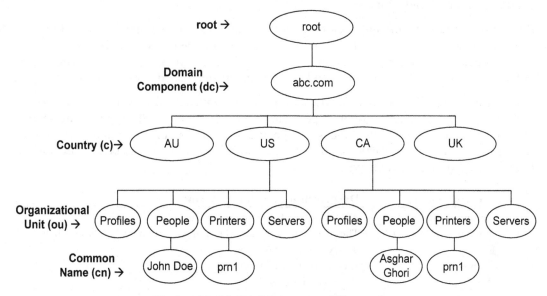

Figure 12-7 LDAP Directory Hierarchy

The top of the company is referred to as the *root* of the LDAP directory hierarchy. Underneath it, *domain component* (dc) is located, which is usually the name of the company; *country* (c) falls under the domain component; and *organizational units* (ou) separate categories of directory information and may or may not be country-specific. The actual information resides at the lowest level of the hierarchy, which may include resources, such as users, profiles, people, printers, servers, photos, text, URLs, pointers to information, binary data, and public key certificates.

Benefits of Using OpenLDAP

There are many benefits associated with implementing and using OpenLDAP solution in an enterprise. In addition to its wide availability and its flexible design to suit an organizational structure, OpenLDAP offers the following key benefits:

- ✓ Has a hierarchical directory structure that provides organizations with information and resources in a logical fashion.
- ✓ Allows the consolidation of common data and storing it in separate organizational units.
- ✓ Provides users and applications with a unified, standard interface to a single, extensible directory service, allowing rapid development and deployment of directory-enabled applications.
- ✓ Enables fast searches and cost-effective management of users and security.
- ✓ Maintains directory-wide consistent and non-redundant information.

OpenLDAP Terminology

Before we go any further on this topic, let's review and comprehend the following key terms.

Directory: A *directory* is a kind of a specialized database that stores information about objects such as people, profiles, printers, and servers. This information is trivial and is intended for write-once, read-many operations. A directory organizes the information in a hierarchical fashion, making it easier for users to look up and retrieve needed data, and at the same time making it simpler from an administration standpoint.

Entry: An *entry* is a building block for a directory and represents a specific record in it. In other words, an entry is a collection of information consisting of one or more attributes for an object. An LDAP directory, for instance, might include entries for employees, contractors, printers, servers, and buildings. Each entry is recognized by its unique distinguished name in the LDAP hierarchy.

Attribute: An *attribute* is associated with one or more entries and is made up of an *attribute type* and an *attribute value*. The attribute type such as jobTitle represents the type of information the attribute contains. An attribute value is the specific information contained in that entry. For instance, a value for the jobTitle attribute type could be "director" or "associate director". Table 12-4 lists some common attribute types.

Attribute Type	Description / Attribute Value
CommonName (cn)	A common or full name of an entry, such as cn=John Doe.
DomainComponent (dc)	The distinguished name (DN) of a component in DNS such as dc=example and dc=com.
Country (c)	A country abbreviation such as c=ca.
Mail (mail)	An email address.
Organization (o)	The name of an organization such as o=redhat.
OrganizationalUnit (ou)	The name of a unit within an organization such as ou=Printers.
Owner (owner)	The owner of an entry such as cn=John Doe, ou=Printers, dc=example, and c=ca.
Surname (sn)	A person's last name (or surname), such as Doe.
TelephoneNumber (telephoneNumber)	A telephone number, such as (123) 456-7890 or 1234567890.
User ID (uid)	A user's login name.

Table 12-4 Common LDAP Attribute Types

An attribute type can use long names or corresponding abbreviations as identified in the above table.

Matching Rule: A *matching rule* matches the attribute value sought against the attribute value stored in the directory in a search and compare task. For example, matching rules associated with the telephoneNumber attribute could cause "(123) 456-7890" to match with either "(123) 456-7890" or "1234567890", or both.

Object Class: Each entry belongs to one or more *object classes*. An object class is a group of required and optional attributes that define the structure of an entry. For instance, an organizationalUser object class may include commonName and Surname as required attributes and telephoneNumber, UID, streetAddress, and userPassword as optional attributes.

Schema: A *schema* is a collection of attributes and object classes along with matching rules and syntax, and other related information, that defines rules surrounding them. A properly configured schema ensures data consistency and helps keep the data organized.

LDAP Data Interchange Format (LDIF): *LDAP Data Interchange Format* (LDIF) is a special format used for importing and exporting LDAP records among LDAP servers. The data is in the text format and consists of entries or alterations to entries, or a combination.

Each record is represented as a group of attributes, with each attribute listed on a separate line comprising "name:value" pair. The following is a sample directory entry, with attributes representing a record in LDIF:

```
dn: cn=John Doe,ou=People, c=ca,dc=abc
objectClass: inetLocalMailRecipient
sn: Doe
mail: john.doe@abc.com
cn: John Doe
givenName: John
uid: jdoe
telephoneNumber: (416) 123-4567
```

Distinguished Name: A *Distinguished Name* (DN) uniquely identifies an entry in the entire directory tree. It is similar in concept to the absolute pathname of a file in the Linux directory hierarchy. For instance, cn=prn1,ou=Printers,c=ca,dc=abc is the distinguished name for prn1 printer. A DN is thus a sequence of RDNs separated by commas.

Relative Distinguished Name: A *Relative Distinguished Name* (RDN), in contrast, represents individual components of a DN. It is similar in concept to the relative pathname of a file in the Linux directory hierarchy. As an example, the RDN for the printer prn1 under Printers located in Canada (See Figure 12-6) is cn=prn1. Similarly, the RDN for Printers is ou=Printers, the RDN for ca is c=ca, and that for abc is dc=abc.

OpenLDAP Roles

There are four roles – server, replica, client, and referral – that systems within an LDAP environment may perform. One system can be configured to execute more than one role.

Server: A *server* is the central system that holds the LDAP directory information. It may be referred to as the *master* server. There must be at least one such server in the environment.

Replica: A *replica* is the system that receives a copy of the information that the LDAP server maintains. It may be referred to as a *slave* server. It is recommended to have at least one replica available on the network for enhanced availability and load sharing.

Client: A *client* is the system that binds itself with a server or replica to establish a communication session to perform queries on directory entries and carry out necessary modifications.

Referral: A *referral* is an entity on an LDAP server that redirects a client request to some other LDAP server or replica if it is unable to fulfill the request. It contains names and locations of other LDAP servers that might store the requested information.

OpenLDAP Client Packages

In order to implement and use OpenLDAP client functionality, software packages openldap, openldap-clients, and nss-pam-ldapd are required on the system. Furthermore, we have the option of choosing between one of two types of authentication services that are available in RHEL7. These services are *System Security Services Daemon* (SSD) and *Name Service Local Caching Daemon*

(NSLCD), and their purpose is to facilitate user authentication against a directory server. We can use either of them; however, the use of SSSD is preferred. Therefore, in addition to the three OpenLDAP packages, we will also need the sssd package and all the packages that it relies on. Together, these software bring with them necessary configuration files, library routines, and tools to support the implementation. The openldap package includes library and configuration files, the openldap-clients package contains client utilities such as *ldapadd*, *ldapmodify*, *ldapcompare*, *ldapsearch*, and *ldapdelete* to perform add, modify, compare, search, and delete operations on the directory, the nss-pam-ldapd package comprises of a library routine that must be installed for LDAP support to work properly, and the sssd package installs the *sssd* service on the client to support identity lookups and user authentication, authorization, and password modifications. We will need either TLS or LDAPs to establish an encrypted channel between the client and the server.

RHEL7 provides two more packages that are used to set up user identity and authentication on the client using LDAP, NIS, Kerberos, and a few other services. These packages are authconfig and authconfig-gtk, and they contain the *authconfig* command and its graphical equivalent *system-config-authentication*, a.k.a. *authconfig-gtk*, (the Authentication Configuration tool), respectively. The authconfig package also includes the *authconfig-tui* text tool that is equivalent to the graphical tool.

OpenLDAP Client Configuration Files

With the installation of the OpenLDAP client packages, configuration file */etc/openldap/ldap.conf* becomes available on the system. This file sets system-wide default settings for LDAP client operations. Another file */etc/sssd/sssd.conf* is created at the time of client configuration to store control data for the *sssd* daemon.

Table 12-5 lists and describes some key directives that are used in the *ldap.conf* file.

Directive	Description
BASE	Sets the base DN to be used for LDAP operations.
URI	Specifies the URI for the LDAP server.
TLS_CACERTDIR	Specifies the location where TLS certificates are stored. The default location is in /etc/openldap/cacerts directory.

Table 12-5 /etc/openldap/ldap.conf File

The authconfig Command

The LDAP client configuration can be done using the *authconfig* command. This command offers several options; Table 12-6 lists and describes the ones that affect LDAP client setup only.

Option	Description
--enableldap / --disableldap	Enables/disables LDAP for user information.
--enableldapauth / --disableldapauth	Enables/disables LDAP for user authentication.
--enableldaptls / --disableldaptls	Enables/disables the use of TLS with LDAP.
--enablesssd / --disablesssd	Enables/disables the use of SSSD for user information.
--ldapserver	Specifies the LDAP server hostname or IP.

--ldapbasedn	Sets the default LDAP base distinguished name.
--test	Displays new settings without updating the configuration.
--update	Updates the configuration with the supplied information. This option should be specified each time a change is desired in the configuration.

Table 12-6 The authconfig Command

We are going to use this command to configure an LDAP client in our next exercise.

Exercise 12-3: Configure LDAP Client to Obtain User and Group Information

This exercise should be done on *server1*.

It is assumed that *server2* has the OpenLDAP service, such as FreeIPA or Red Hat Directory Server, configured and running, and it has a user account *ldapuser1* and group account *dba* available to test authentication.

In this exercise, you will configure the LDAP client with the *authconfig* command. You will ensure that the client is autostarted at each system reboot. You will run appropriate commands to test it.

1. Install the necessary LDAP client software packages:

   # **yum –y install openldap openldap-clients nss-pam-ldapd sssd authconfig**

2. Set up the client and update the configuration files. Enable the use of LDAP, LDAP authentication, and SSSD. Specify the hostname for the LDAP server and the base DN.

   # **authconfig --enableldap --enableldapauth --ldapserver=ldap://server2.example.com \
   --enablesssd --ldapbasedn="dc=example,dc=com" --update**

3. Show the contents of the */etc/sssd/sssd.conf* and */etc/openldap/ldap.conf* files:

   # **cat /etc/sssd/sssd.conf**
   [domain/default]
   autofs_provider = ldap
   cache_credentials = True
   krb5_realm = #
   ldap_search_base = dc=example,dc=com
   id_provider = ldap
   auth_provider = ldap
   chpass_provider = ldap
   ldap_uri = ldap://server2.example.com/
   ldap_id_use_start_tls = True
   ldap_tls_cacertdir = /etc/openldap/cacerts
   [sssd]
   services = nss, pam, autofs
   config_file_version = 2
   domains = default
   [nss]

```
[pam]
[sudo]
[autofs]
[ssh]
[pac]
# grep –v ^# /etc/openldap/ldap.conf
TLS_CACERTDIR /etc/openldap/cacerts
URI ldap://server2.example.com/
BASE dc=example,dc=com
```

4. Edit the */etc/nsswitch.conf* file and ensure the passwd, shadow, and group entries look like the following (for details on this file, see Chapter 24 "Configuring DNS"):

```
passwd: files  sss
shadow: files  sss
group:   files  sss
```

5. Enable the *sssd* service to autostart at system reboots:

    # **systemctl enable sssd**

6. Start the *sssd* service, which will also start the OpenLDAP client on the system:

    # **systemctl start sssd**

7. Test group data by pulling *dba* group information from the server with the *getent* command (the *getent* command displays entries from the databases listed in the */etc/nsswitch.conf* file):

    # **getent group dba**

8. Test authentication by logging in as *ldapuser1* from *server1* to *server2*, using the *ssh* command:

    # **ssh ldapuser1@server2**

If you want the client to use TLS for secure communication with the server, add --enableldaptls and --ldaploadcacert options with the *authconfig* command in step 2. You will need to ensure that a valid certificate is stored on *server2* at an appropriate location.

Moreover, you may want to use Kerberos for authentication in place of LDAP's password authentication method. For this, supply options specific to Kerberos with the *authconfig* command and do not specify the --ldapauth option. See Chapter 17 "Working with Firewalld and Kerberos" for details on Kerberos client setup.

EXAM TIP: Use either the graphical (authconfig-gtk or system-config-authentication) or the text (authconfig-tui) Authentication Configuration tool for LDAP client setup with or without Kerberos.

Overview of Graphical Authentication Configuration Tool

The Authentication Configuration tool is used for convenience if we do not feel comfortable with using the *authconfig* command. This graphical tool is easier to use provided we have the data handy that we want entered. This tool may be invoked by running the *authconfig-gtk* or the *system-config-authentication* command in an X terminal window or choosing Applications | Sundry | Authentication in the GNOME desktop. It will open up as shown in Figure 12-8.

Figure 12-8 Authentication Configuration Tool

There are three tabs across the top for configuring identity & authentication, advanced options, and password options. As we know, this tool allows us to access user information stored on various types of databases and to configure the service to be used for user authentication purpose. For any user account database that we select from the drop-down list under Identification & Authentication, we see the window size changes providing room to enter data specific to the selected database. Figure 12-9 depicts the window for LDAP.

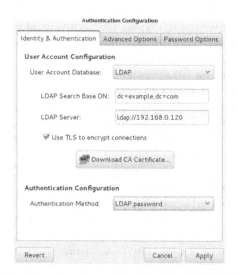

Figure 12-9 Authentication Configuration Tool – LDAP Client Configuration

Similarly, we can use a method for authentication. For instance, LDAP can use either the LDAP password or Kerberos password. If the latter is chosen, we will need to enter Kerberos server details.

The Advanced Options provide additional configuration selections for authentication, and the Password Options tab allows us to set password rules.

Chapter Summary

This chapter discussed networking and OpenLDAP client configuration. It started by providing an understanding of various essential networking terms to build the foundation for networking topics going forward. Topics such as the hostname, IPv4, IPv6, network classes, subnetting, subnet mask, protocol, and Ethernet address were covered.

We configured one network interface on server1 and another one on server2 using commands. We had an overview of the graphical tool. We reviewed various files involved in the configuration. We performed activation and deactivation of interfaces manually and defined the IP and hostname mappings in the *hosts* databases on both servers. We used tools to test network connectivity.

We covered the configuration of an NTP client on our system to synchronize the clock with a more accurate provider of time. We looked at how to enable the service using commands and the graphical setup tool.

Finally, we studied OpenLDAP: concepts, benefits, terminology, and roles. We performed an exercise to configure the LDAP client service on our system, and then tested it. We looked at the graphical authentication tool and saw how to use it to configure the OpenLDAP client.

Chapter Review Questions

1. What is a relative distinguished name?
2. What is meant by the object Entry in LDAP terminology?
3. The NTP client is pre-configured when the ntp software is installed on the system. We just need to start the service to begin synchronizing the clock. True or False?
4. Which class of IP addresses has the least number of node addresses?
5. What is the use of *ifup* and *ifdown* commands?
6. Which command may we use to display the hardware address of a network interface?
7. Which directory does the Network Manager store the interface configuration files?
8. Which file defines the protocols in the system?
9. List three benefits of using LDAP as a directory server.
10. What is the purpose of the ONBOOT directive in the interface configuration file?
11. The */etc/hosts* file maintains the hostname to hardware address mappings. True or False?
12. Which file contains service, port, and protocol mappings?
13. What is the name of the graphical NTP client configuration tool?
14. What would the *ip addr* command produce?
15. Which command can be run at the command prompt in an X terminal window to bring up the graphical Network Connections tool?
16. List any two benefits of subnetting.
17. The *ip neighbor* command uses the RARP protocol to provide MAC to IP address mappings. True or False?
18. What would the command *system-config-authentication* do?

Answers to Chapter Review Questions

1. The relative distinguished name represents individual components of a DN.
2. The object Entry represents a specific record in the LDAP directory.
3. True.
4. The C class has the least number of node addresses.
5. The purpose of these two commands is to activate and deactivate an interface.
6. The *ip* command.
7. The */etc/sysconfig/network-scripts* directory.
8. The */etc/protocols* file.
9. Three benefits are access to uniform information, centralized storage for information, and user authentication.
10. The purpose of this directive is to tell the boot scripts whether to activate this interface.
11. False. This file maintains hostname to IP address mappings.
12. The */etc/services* file.
13. The name of the graphical NTP client configuration tool is System-Config-Date.
14. This command will display information about interfaces including IP and hardware address information.
15. The command to bring up the graphical Network Connections tool is *nm-connection-editor*.
16. Better manageability and less traffic.
17. False. It uses ARP protocol.
18. This command will bring up the graphical Authentication Configuration tool.

DIY Challenge Labs

The following labs are useful to strengthen most of the concepts and topics learned in this chapter. It is expected that you perform these labs without any additional help. A step-by-step guide is not provided, as the implementation of these labs requires the knowledge that has been presented in this chapter. Use defaults or your own thinking for missing information.

Lab 12-1: Assign a New IP to the System

Remove the current IP assignments for *eth0* on *server1.example.com* and replace them with something different but on the same subnet. Apply the new IP information using appropriate tools and test it using the *ip* and *ping* commands, then edit appropriate files to make this modification persistent across reboots. Activate and deactivate the interface manually. Reboot the system and verify the new IP using appropriate commands.

## Chapter 13

Securing Access with SSH and TCP Wrappers

This chapter describes the following major topics:

➢ Understand the OpenSSH service, versions, and algorithms

➢ Overview of encryption techniques and authentication methods

➢ Overview of OpenSSH administration commands and configuration files

➢ Configure private/public key-based authentication

➢ Use OpenSSH client commands: ssh, scp, and sftp

➢ Access OpenSSH server from Windows

➢ Understand the use and syntax of TCP Wrappers

RHCSA/RHCE Objectives:

04. Access remote systems using ssh
20. Securely transfer files between systems
49. Configure key-based authentication for SSH
80. Configure key-based authentication (an RHCE objective)
81. Configure additional options described in documentation (an RHCE objective)

Secure Shell is a network protocol that delivers a secure mechanism for data transmission between source and destination systems over insecure network channels. The secure shell includes a set of utilities that provides remote users the ability to log in, transfer files, and execute commands securely using encryption and authentication. These tools have widely replaced their insecure counterparts in the corporate world.

TCP Wrappers is a host-based service that is used to control access to network services running on the system. It may be configured to permit (or prevent) specific users, hosts, networks, and domains to access one or more network services on the system.

The OpenSSH Service

Secure Shell (SSH) provides a secure mechanism for data transmission between source and destination systems over IP networks. It was designed to replace the old remote login programs that transmitted user passwords in clear text and data unencrypted. SSH uses encryption techniques to secure a communication channel and employs digital signatures for user authentication, making it extremely hard for people to gain unauthorized access to passwords or the data in transit. It also performs checks on the data being transferred throughout a session to ensure integrity. SSH includes a set of utilities, providing remote users with the ability to log in, transfer files, and execute commands securely using strong encryption and authentication mechanisms. Due to their powerful security features, SSH utilities have widely replaced their conventional unsecured login and file transfer counterparts in computing environments.

OpenSSH is a free, open source implementation of proprietary SSH. Once applied successfully on the system, the *telnetd, rlogind, rshd, rexec,* and *ftpd* services can be disabled after a careful examination to eliminate potential impact. The secure command that has replaced *telnetd, rlogin, rsh,* and *rexec* is called *ssh* and those that have replaced *rcp* and *ftp* are referred to as *scp* and *sftp,* respectively.

OpenSSH supports additional features such as tunneling, arbitrary TCP port forwarding, and X11 forwarding. A discussion of these topics is beyond the scope of this book.

OpenSSH uses TCP Wrappers for access control.

OpenSSH Versions and Algorithms

OpenSSH has evolved over the years. It currently supports two versions: v1 and v2, and both are available in RHEL7. However, we should be using the newer version as it integrates many enhancements and improvements over the older version, and includes numerous advanced configuration options. The default in RHEL7 is v2 as defined in the */etc/ssh/sshd_config* file. Both versions support various algorithms for data encryption and user authentication (digital signatures). OpenSSH v1 supports the RSA algorithm only whereas the other version supports three algorithms: RSA, DSA, and ECDSA (a new variant of DSA). RSA includes the support for both encryption and authentication. In contrast, the use of DSA and ECDSA is restricted to providing digital signatures only.

RSA stands for *Rivest-Shamir-Adleman,* who first published this algorithm, DSA for *Digital Signature Algorithm,* and ECDSA is an acronym for *Elliptic Curve Digital Signature Algorithm.* RSA is more common and is widely used in the industry partly because it supports both encryption and digital signatures.

Encryption Techniques

Encryption is a way of transforming information into a scrambled form to conceal the real information from unauthorized access. Encryption is done at the client end and the reverse process, called *de-encryption*, happens on the server. OpenSSH employs various encryption techniques during an end-to-end communication session. These techniques include symmetric and asymmetric encryption.

Symmetric Encryption Technique: This type of encryption uses a single secret key (or a pair of keys) to protect authentication traffic as well as the entire subsequent communication session. This key is generated as a result of a negotiation process between the client and server.

Asymmetric Encryption Technique: This technique uses a private/public key combination for encryption. These keys are randomly-generated lengthy strings of alphanumeric characters attached to messages during a communication session. The client transmutes the information using a *public* key and the server decrypts it using the paired *private* key. The private key must be kept secure since it is private to that one system only. The public key is distributed to clients. This technique is used for channel encryption as well as for user authentication.

Authentication Methods

Once an encrypted channel is established between the client and server, additional negotiations take place between the two to authenticate the user trying to gain access to the server. OpenSSH offers several methods for this purpose, and they are listed below in the order in which they are attempted during the authentication process:

- GSSAPI-based (*Generic Security Service Application Program Interface*) authentication
- Host-based authentication
- Public key-based authentication
- Challenge-response authentication
- Password-based authentication

GSSAPI-Based Authentication: GSSAPI provides a standard interface that allows security mechanisms such as Kerberos to be plugged in. OpenSSH uses this interface and the underlying Kerberos for authentication. With this method, an exchange of tokens take place between the client and server to validate user identity. This authentication method is only supported in OpenSSH version 2.

Host-Based Authentication: This type of authentication allows a single user, a group of users, or all users on the client to be authenticated on the server. A user may be configured to log in with a matching username on the server or as a different user that exists on the server. For each user that requires an automatic entry on the server, a *.shosts* file is set up in that user's home directory on the server containing the client name or IP, and, optionally, a different username (this user must exist on the server). The same rule applies to a group of users or all users on the client; however, the setup is done in the */etc/ssh/shosts.equiv* file.

Private/Public Key-Based Authentication: This method uses a private/public key combination for user authentication. The user on the client has a public key and the server stores the corresponding private key. At the login attempt, the server prompts the user to enter the key and logs the user in if the key is validated.

Challenge-Response Authentication: This method is based on the response(s) to one or more arbitrary challenge questions that the user has to answer correctly in order to gain login access to the server.

Password-Based Authentication: This is the last fall back option. The server prompts the user to enter their password. It checks the password against the stored entry in the *shadow* (or *passwd*) file and allows the user in if the password is confirmed.

Of the five authentication methods described above, the password-based method is common and requires no further explanation. The first two and the challenge-response methods are beyond the scope of this book. We will be using public/private authentication and encryption methods in our exercises to follow.

OpenSSH Packages

OpenSSH has three packages that are of interest. These are openssh, openssh-clients, and openssh-server. The openssh package provides the ssh-keygen command and some supported library routines; the openssh-clients package includes commands, such as *scp*, *sftp*, *slogin*, *ssh*, and *ssh-copy-id*, and a client configuration file */etc/ssh/ssh_config*; and the openssh-server package contains the *sshd* daemon, a server configuration file */etc/ssh/sshd_config*, and library routines. By default, the openssh-server package is installed during OS installation, allowing users to log in to the system using the *ssh* command.

Commands and Daemon

As indicated, OpenSSH packages install several commands on the system. Moreover, the server package also loads the *sshd* daemon that must run on the system to allow users to be able to connect to the system over the ssh channel. This daemon listens on the well-known TCP port 22 by default. Table 13-1 lists and explains some of the key commands.

Command	Description
scp	Secure alternative to the rcp command.
sftp	Secure alternative to the ftp command.
slogin	Secure alternative to the rlogin command.
ssh	Secure alternative to the telnet and rlogin commands.
ssh-add	Adds RSA/DSA/ECDSA characteristics to ssh-agent.
ssh-agent	Authentication Agent. Holds private keys used for the RSA/DSA/ECDSA authentication.
ssh-copy-id	Copies RSA/DSA/ECDSA keys to remote systems.
ssh-keygen	Generates private and public keys.

Table 13-1 OpenSSH Commands

We will be using most of these commands later in this chapter.

System-Wide Server and Client Configuration Files

OpenSSH has configuration files that define default global settings for both server and client to control how they should operate. These files are located in the */etc/ssh* directory, and are called *sshd_config* and *ssh_config*, respectively. The server has an additional configuration file called *sshd* and it is located in the */etc/sysconfig* directory. In addition, the */var/log/secure* log file is used to capture authentication messages.

A few directives from the *sshd_config* file are displayed below:

```
# cat /etc/ssh/sshd_config
#Port                            22
#Protocol                        2
HostKey                          /etc/ssh/ssh_host_rsa_key
HostKey                          /etc/ssh/ssh_host_ecdsa_key
SyslogFacility                   AUTHPRIV
AuthorizedKeysFile               .ssh/authorized_keys
PasswordAuthentication           yes
ChallengeResponseAuthentication  no
GSSAPIAuthentication             yes
UsePAM                           yes
X11Forwarding                    yes
```

The above shows just a few directives from the file; there are many more that we may change if required. Some of these are explained in Table 13-2.

Directive	Description
Port	Default is 22. Specifies the port to listen on.
ListenAddress	Specifies the IP to be used for incoming ssh requests.
Protocol	Default is 2. Specifies the ssh protocol version to be used.
SyslogFacility	Default is AUTHPRIV. Defines the facility code to be used when logging messages to the /var/log/secure file. This is based on the configuration in the /etc/rsyslog.conf file.
LogLevel	Default is INFO. Defines the level of criticality for the messages to be logged.
LoginGraceTime	Default is 2 minutes. Defines the period after which the server disconnects the user if the user did not successfully log in.
PermitRootLogin	Default is yes. Allows the root user to be able to log in directly on the system.
MaxAuthTries	Default is 6. Specifies the number of authentication attempts per connection.
MaxSessions	Default is 10. Allows to open up to this many ssh sessions.
RSAAuthentication	Default is yes. Specifies whether to allow the RSA authentication.
PubKeyAuthentication	Default is yes. Specifies whether to enable public key-based authentication.
AuthorizedKeysFile	Default is ~/.ssh/authorized_keys. Specifies the name and location of the file containing the authorized keys for a user.
PasswordAuthentication	Default is yes. Specifies whether to enable local password authentication.
PermitEmptyPasswords	Default is no. Specifies whether to allow null passwords.
ChallengeResponseAuthentication	Default is yes. Specifies whether to allow challenge-response authentication.
UsePAM	Default is yes. Enables or disables user authentication via PAM. If enabled, only root will be able to run the daemon.

Directive	Description
AllowAgentForwarding	Default is yes. Enables or disables the ssh-agent command to forward private keys to remote systems.
AllowTCPForwarding	Default is yes. Specifies whether to allow forwarding TCP communication over an ssh channel.
X11Forwarding	Default is yes. Allows or disallows remote access to GUI applications.
TCPKeepAlive	Default is yes. Specifies whether to send TCP keepalive signals to the ssh server to check its accessibility.
UseLogin	Default is no. Allows or disallows the use of the login command for interactive login sessions.
Compression	Default is delayed. Specifies whether to allow or delay compression until the user has authenticated successfully.
ClientAliveInterval	Default is 0. Defines a timeout interval in seconds for the server to send a message to the client seeking a response.
ClientAliveCountMax	Default is 3. If the ClientAliveInterval directive is set to a non-zero value, this directive specifies the maximum number of messages to be sent to the client.
AllowUsers	Allows only the listed users access to the server. Syntax is: AllowUsers user1 user2 AllowUsers user3@server2.example.com AllowUsers user4@192.168.0.110 user5@192.168.0.120
AllowGroups	Allows only the listed group members access to the server. Syntax is: AllowGroups dba unixadmins AllowGroups dba@server2.example.com
DenyUsers	Do not allow the listed users access to the system. Syntax is: DenyUsers user1 user2 DenyUsers user3@server2.example.com DenyUsers user4@192.168.0.110 user5@192.168.0.120
DenyGroups	Do not allow the listed group members access to the system. Syntax is: DenyGroups dba unixadmins DenyGroups dba@server2.example.com

Table 13-2 OpenSSH Server Configuration File

Besides using the AllowUsers, DenyUsers, AllowGroups, and DenyGroups directives in the *sshd_config* file for setting user-based security, we can instead define these restrictions in the TCP Wrappers files *hosts.allow* and *hosts.deny* as appropriate. Furthermore, we can restrict system access from specific systems, domains, or networks via port 22 using the iptables firewall.

Now, let's look at a few directives from the beginning of the system-wide client configuration file *ssh_config*:

```
# cat /etc/ssh/ssh_config
. . . . . . . .
# Host *
#   ForwardAgent no
#   ForwardX11 no
#   RhostsRSAAuthentication no
#   RSAAuthentication yes
#   PasswordAuthentication yes
#   HostbasedAuthentication no
#   GSSAPIAuthentication no

. . . . . . . .
```

We can define client-specific configuration in this file. For each client or a group of clients, we can add a separate section beginning with the keyword Host and listing the directives specific to that client or group only. Many of the directives are the same as for the server. See Table 13-2 earlier for details.

Per-User Client Files

OpenSSH allows us to store default values for our ssh communication sessions in a separate file. These per-user settings override the system-wide defaults and they are saved in a file called *config* in the *~/.ssh* directory. The format of this file is the same as that of the *ssh_config* file. *~/.ssh* does not exist by default; it is created when we attempt to connect to the server the first time and it accepts the presented key.

The *~/.ssh* directory has a file called *known_hosts*. This file stores the hostname, IP address, and a copy of the public key of the remote system that we have accessed. A sample entry from this file on *server1* is shown below:

```
server2,192.168.0.120 ecdsa-sha2-nistp256
AAAAE2VjZHNhLXNoYTItbmlzdHAyNTYAAAAIbmlzdHAyNTYAAABBBCP4LK2GHWIDv+a/QX
/gp0ggl8Q1H85SLExeyeS4ph6o8Nl/ArWWeBUWSl1PLDUIczGGsLjeUBtUgXdVDhwO/CQ=
```

There are three additional files in *~/.ssh* that we may be interested in looking at. These files do not exist by default. Two of them hold private (*id_rsa*, *id_dsa*, or *id_ecdsa*) and public (*id_rsa.pub*, *id_dsa.pub*, or *id_ecdsa.pub*) keys, and the third one (*authorized_keys*) is used when we set up a trust relationship between two systems. I will show the contents of these files in one of the exercises below to give you an idea of how they look like.

Exercise 13-1: Configure Private/Public Key-Based Authentication

This exercise should be done on *server1* and *server2*.

For this exercise, assume that *user1* exists on both *server1* and *server2*.

In this exercise, you will generate RSA private/public key combination for *user1* on *server1* and use it to allow this user access to *server2* using the *ssh* command. You will show the private and public file contents and the log file messages related to the login attempt.

1. Log on to *server1* as *user1*.

---

2. Generate RSA keys and save them in *~/.ssh* in default files. Enter passphrase redhat123 when prompted.

$ ssh–keygen
Generating public/private rsa key pair.
Enter file in which to save the key (/home/user1/.ssh/id_rsa):
Created directory '/home/user1/.ssh'.
Enter passphrase (empty for no passphrase):
Enter same passphrase again:
Your identification has been saved in /home/user1/.ssh/id_rsa.
Your public key has been saved in /home/user1/.ssh/id_rsa.pub.
The key fingerprint is:
9c:09:ec:b9:ab:67:f7:77:aa:9a:c6:38:ca:3d:e8:af user1@server1.example.com
The key's randomart image is:
+--[RSA 2048]----+
. . . .

The contents of *id_rsa* (private key) and *id_rsa.pub* (public key) files are shown below:

$ cat ~/.ssh/id_rsa
-----BEGIN RSA PRIVATE KEY-----
Proc-Type: 4,ENCRYPTED
DEK-Info: AES-128-CBC,1B940AE24240F15CBF5CB82B756655AF
YoeDYpyExsC7YFNvfNXB8zDmw3A6xvaXyum5DhN3Qr1Hvn5g6uz8dG+MbM1AGDi4
uymHfLPuXd/KP4ju1p3MxcEXcX6a0YynwUgtPGkURcF9MywF/sGYoueVDev2VP00
ViAJPJyn9vet14p0Lp16skGgU0Eiwx+cvixEaemOfFA9vYDxqJKoGYpd8cAUissK
ZXPVH0Zf0XuYTNAI038fMxkcANdKlXg1CrAp+3hp69+A7cqrAZH4oYlQY3Q5wMsY
YAB2OsGj52cZsMBPcGKL4JYcFmQbhq/NJPRJOhUXxOxLpyojkMIvm7KDqD7X6oW7
8CTXLWeeR2wTxmY0niHcbzMEA/ByIxcXwJvu/yDksYEboxAYmqjzRv3tXHkrCAQ2
RXsedTjBFeRAqZ1TAg1CfccrZK/cz0JRLvG04aIZ+10eUs/cEnrwTtYGzJZ9gLjg
mPQdQngdKJvZdFSTjXO8CXEQ5JdVhb+CgIRy+D2mMsJgGtmy8nUWVZupgU479wbm
Eld4PNTiBsw8DoLYdj6gzJM66/D0q+6S3uA73+AatEJcWx2j7fHLW1ZwbUd3eWMW
FMXqljFm0pma9mFtqi+i5033YG3uikV5lpsMOd+Vn66sNpEN/bvwdVwTlX0uFYhD
KFK1dT4VQt7/NYYNFp1A61rykwxD9GyOB7yAo012lBCsjD80uaiauo7Ut9U3Kdf9
8nZHrsOt98N5Fdt5aef1htLs2xaGmKp5SPrdHwLLmFt8IKklLaPXkG+5+fxFLclO
t/G0nEYjLFapdKAtut6r+NAFGVF1zko7FOG5Nce2H0TYHyQgToOw1oNsd7qCuaec
LF4oQKL5esqOJxx7g0exGuhgVV7x1Y0+Dg1rSKBLouLt2fwPxvDubURfD3lc3WRX
OMYgL9GFMGw6mDn8J0Lqm1Rmq8rG08/XRJS+UsezNDDibBqFGvqebdUGhh0qdSWM
LmLWRr262AgBAxtRtDGevTZ+8i2PP30T9Cgd6ZZaDgLf9R5DQeAp2o+2/qZUtjzA
B/sTV3EJm9H+nZVseoJYU5Eiat6kgeiZqTXJMoBiv8czGY3u2sPLLtYv/xGnKizn
Uos+qOwt2XRlGhnkI4EsTB6p/sHpGW3U9D86LsbZa+aAMYfMXRBd+3uKknOnLPR/
72wUAyVhmHfAssPayeHz0XbupVKQzc6+xNCOmTJhL639xQqLGav1fCrp0EFLL0SZ
jZlpW7nuuDakKRisLbEErkLJ2XgKMZcWDTJ8Oc26gl1ofrJnAVZOAq0TBbGEbuC0
w+zxmEwVcUQ7RBet/4+l+zJQo3tlXZFgl8qYDVKK7X7M8QLC3gvSy35PNYYbv9JI
7WkjSUEl+cCWfk4jTzhPETqRKYg7cCPM8Vu29vq1u3LrmIT58WeqQclu5J8XMrX+
SdIrz2Ppy1GqFtN9JnldkIns+zoeieEYZuKXjQei7BEi6rFUjaD1609zenBVjqr8
AlmnaZFbhoeeuIJDNvYANmO0R9poWmoZfylCWRS9TlLwuKz7rQPm4wx2kNQSAGnL
Fi8DNzg/VV0Pjhp5xkwnLR8rHirdLrUB+Eveqb9qNoX2Vw/Cps86UchAUu8CYPeU
-----END RSA PRIVATE KEY-----

```
$ cat ~/.ssh/id_rsa.pub
```
ssh-rsa
AAAAB3NzaC1yc2EAAAADAQABAAABAQDTypuZx+D+soDxXgi8aAy/+Kg30xO2AtQF0HDP
Ct+xwTH7QYHyTM9CXS7NL0wvZsuCN6It1aVXnNnOk3D0nOQZonOxTGlJpdrpBYXp09nuAdC
MfO+78toXEDJQTL/FoZG+efsoi1dIlCsKP2wKv4LUmz+JQwrttag0FjHE4m7H7hlZftTclfeZyHg33
9VkDu7ue+tqA2AuxfrEkFcImPwxW0f0goLWWwY20ToDv94Adl9JWADr1cOs8UWgXiO4gfUIRI
bwr/wnKKQwJLP2bsp8ONp844W9VHL29imysRTboSI5eiuIVta1sZYyWhDbLJEmZ2bD8MAlI7q7
99ARJisz user1@server1.example.com

3. Copy the public key file to *server2* under */home/user1/.ssh*. Accept the fingerprints for *server2* when prompted. Then enter the password for *user1* set on *server2* to continue with the file copy. This file will be copied as *authorized_keys*.

```
$ ssh-copy-id –i ~/.ssh/id_rsa.pub server2
```
The authenticity of host 'server2 (192.168.0.120)' can't be established.
ECDSA key fingerprint is e8:b1:ce:8b:71:92:b2:8a:50:ed:d4:15:a3:e3:63:ec.
Are you sure you want to continue connecting (yes/no)? **yes**
/bin/ssh-copy-id: INFO: attempting to log in with the new key(s), to filter out any that are already installed
/bin/ssh-copy-id: INFO: 1 key(s) remain to be installed -- if you are prompted now it is to install the new keys
user1@server2's password:
Number of key(s) added: 1
Now try logging into the machine, with: "ssh 'server2'"
and check to make sure that only the key(s) you wanted were added.

At the same time, this command also creates or updates the *known_hosts* file on *server1* and stores the fingerprints for *server2* in it:

```
$ cat ~/.ssh/known_hosts
```
server2,192.168.0.120 ecdsa-sha2-nistp256
AAAAE2VjZHNhLXNoYTItbmlzdHAyNTYAAAAIbmlzdHAyNTYAAABBBCP4LK2GHWIDv+a
/QX/gp0ggl8Q1H85SLExeyeS4ph6o8Nl/ArWWeBUWSl1PLDUIczGGsLjeUBtUgXdVDhwO/CQ=

4. On *server1*, run the *ssh* command as *user1* to connect to *server2*. Answer yes when prompted to accept the server's fingerprints. Supply the passphrase for *user1*.

```
$ ssh server2
```
Enter passphrase for key '/home/user1/.ssh/id_rsa':
Last login: Sat Nov 22 08:54:33 2014 from server1.example.com

We can view this login attempt in the */var/log/secure* file on *server2*. You need to be *root* to view this log file.

```
# tail /var/log/secure
```
Nov 22 09:02:07 server2 sshd[27133]: Accepted publickey for user1 from 192.168.0.110 port 46996
ssh2: RSA 9c:09:ec:b9:ab:67:f7:77:aa:9a:c6:38:ca:3d:e8:af
Nov 22 09:02:07 server2 sshd[27133]: pam_unix(sshd:session): session opened for user user1 by
(uid=0)

Executing a Command Remotely Using ssh

The *ssh* command is a secure replacement for *telnet*, *rlogin*, and *rsh*. It allows us to securely sign in to a remote system or execute a command without actually logging on to it. The previous exercise demonstrated how a user can log in using this command. The following shows how to use this command to execute the specified command on a remote system.

Issue *ssh* on *server1* to view the listing of *user1*'s home directory on *server2*. Enter the passphrase when prompted.

```
$ ssh server2 /bin/ls –l
Enter passphrase for key '/home/user1/.ssh/id_rsa':
total 0
drwxr-xr-x. 2 user1 user1 6 Nov 17 09:57 Desktop
drwxr-xr-x. 2 user1 user1 6 Nov 17 09:57 Documents
drwxr-xr-x. 2 user1 user1 6 Nov 17 09:57 Downloads
drwxr-xr-x. 2 user1 user1 6 Nov 17 09:57 Music
drwxr-xr-x. 2 user1 user1 6 Nov 17 09:57 Pictures
drwxr-xr-x. 2 user1 user1 6 Nov 17 09:57 Public
drwxr-xr-x. 2 user1 user1 6 Nov 17 09:57 Templates
drwxr-xr-x. 2 user1 user1 6 Nov 17 09:57 Videos
```

Copying Files Using scp

Similarly, *user1* can execute the *scp* command to transfer files from *server1* to *server2*, and vice versa. To copy *server1:/home/user1/file1* to *server2:/home/user2*, use the *scp* command as follows. Enter the passphrase for *user1* when prompted.

```
$ cd
$ scp file1 server2:
Enter passphrase for key '/home/user1/.ssh/id_rsa':
file1           100%    0      0.0KB/s  00:00
```

Now let's copy the *server2:/usr/bin/zip* file to *server1:/home/user1*:

```
$ scp server2:/usr/bin/zip .
Enter passphrase for key '/home/user1/.ssh/id_rsa':
zip             100%  211KB   210.7KB/s  00:00
```

As long as *user1* has the required read and write permissions, they can transfer any file between source and destination systems into any directory.

Transferring Files Using sftp

In the same manner, we can execute the *sftp* command on *server1* to connect to *server2* and download or upload files between the two systems:

```
$ sftp server2
Enter passphrase for key '/home/user1/.ssh/id_rsa':
Connected to server2.
sftp>
```

Type ? at the prompt to view available commands. A short description of what each command does is also displayed.

```
sftp> ?
Available commands:
bye                          Quit sftp
cd path                      Change remote directory to 'path'
chgrp grp path               Change group of file 'path' to 'grp'
chmod mode path              Change permissions of file 'path' to 'mode'
chown own path               Change owner of file 'path' to 'own'
df [-hi] [path]              Display statistics for current directory or filesystem containing 'path'
exit                         Quit sftp
get [-Ppr] remote [local]    Download file
reget remote [local]         Resume download file
help                         Display this help text
lcd path                     Change local directory to 'path'
lls [ls-options [path]]      Display local directory listing
lmkdir path                  Create local directory
ln [-s] oldpath newpath      Link remote file (-s for symlink)
lpwd                         Print local working directory
ls [-1afhlnrSt] [path]       Display remote directory listing
lumask umask                 Set local umask to 'umask'
mkdir path                   Create remote directory
progress                     Toggle display of progress meter
put [-Ppr] local [remote]    Upload file
pwd                          Display remote working directory
quit                         Quit sftp
rename oldpath newpath       Rename remote file
rm path                      Delete remote file
rmdir path                   Remove remote directory
symlink oldpath newpath      Symlink remote file
version                      Show SFTP version
!command                     Execute 'command' in local shell
!                            Escape to local shell
?                            Synonym for help
```

Some of the common commands at the sftp> prompt are *cd/lcd*, *get/put*, *ls/lls*, *pwd/lpwd*, *mkdir/rmdir*, *quit/exit*, *rename*, and *rm*.

Accessing OpenSSH Server from Windows

On the Windows side, several freeware ssh client programs are available. One such program is puTTY, which can be downloaded free of cost from the Internet. Figure 13-1 shows its interface.

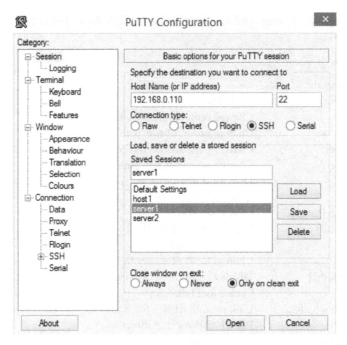

Figure 13-1 puTTY Interface

puTTY is a straightforward program to use. We simply enter the hostname or IP address of the remote system and click Open to establish a connection. We need to ensure that port 22 is entered and SSH protocol is selected. We can assign a name for this connection and click Save to save it for future use.

TCP Wrappers

TCP Wrappers is a host-based mechanism that is used to limit access to wrappers-aware TCP services on the system by inbound clients. The access can be controlled by specifying which services are allowed or denied access by which users and from which sources (host, network, or domain). The services that wrappers can control include ftp, ssh, telnet, tftp, finger, rsh, and talk. The software package associated with the wrappers is loaded by default as part of the OS installation, and it is called tcp_wrappers. We can produce details for this package using the *yum* command:

```
# yum info tcp_wrappers
Name         : tcp_wrappers
Arch         : x86_64
Version      : 7.6
Release      : 77.el7
Size         : 202888
Repo         : installed
From repo    : anaconda
Summary      : A security tool which acts as a wrapper for TCP daemons
URL          : ftp://ftp.porcupine.org/pub/security/index.html
License      : BSD
Description  : The tcp_wrappers package provides small daemon programs which can
```

: monitor and filter incoming requests for systat, finger, FTP,
: telnet, rlogin, rsh, exec, tftp, talk and other network services.
: Install the tcp_wrappers program if you need a security tool for
: filtering incoming network services requests.
: This version also supports IPv6.

Two files – *hosts.allow* and *hosts.deny* – located in the */etc* directory are critical to the functionality of TCP Wrappers. The default files contain no access restrictions. The *.allow* file is referenced before the *.deny* file is. If these files do not contain an entry for the requesting user or the source, wrappers grants access to the inbound request.

Here is how it works: when a TCP client request comes in, the wrappers daemon *tcpd* scans the *.allow* file and requests the start of the respective service process for the client if it finds a match in that file. If *.allow* does not have a match, wrappers consults the *.deny* file and denies access to the service if it discovers a match there. If no match is detected in the *.deny* file either, *tcpd* requests the start of the respective server daemon to establish a link with the client. Wrappers entertains only the first matching entry as it scans the files and it discontinues the search as soon as it finds the first match. Any changes made to either file take effect right away.

The format of both files is identical and it is based on "service : user@source" as shown below:

<name of service process> : <user@source>

The first column lists the name of a service daemon such as *telnetd*, *sshd*, and *ftpd*, and the second column specifies who (username) from where (hostname, network address, or a domain name) is or is not permitted. If a username is missing, the rule applies to all users. Similarly, a missing source represents all sources.

Wrappers supports some wildcards to match sets of services or sources. These include ALL, LOCAL, KNOWN, and UNKNOWN. The ALL wildcard may be used in either field to represent "open to all"; the LOCAL wildcard matches any hostnames that do not contain a leading dot; the KNOWN wildcard matches resolveable hostnames; and the UNKNOWN wildcard is the opposite of KNOWN. In addition, wrappers allows us to use an operator called EXCEPT to define an exception within a rule.

EXAM TIP: A thorough understanding of the syntax of entries placed in these files is important.

Several service:user@source combinations can be defined in the wrappers access control files. Table 13-3 provides some examples.

service : user@source	/etc/hosts.allow	/etc/hosts.deny
ALL:ALL	Allows all services from all sources.	Denies all services from all sources.
ALL:user1	Allows all services to user1.	Denies all services to user1.
ALL:user1@server1	Allows all services to user1@server1.	Denies all services to user1@server1.
ALL:.example.com	Allows all services from example.com domain.	Denies all services from example.com domain.

service : user@source	/etc/hosts.allow	/etc/hosts.deny
ALL:192.168.0.	Allows all services from 192.168.0 network.	Denies all services from 192.168.0 network.
sshd:ALL	Allows ssh access from all sources.	Denies ssh access from all sources.
sshd:LOCAL	Allows ssh access from local network.	Denies ssh access from local network.
vsftpd:192.168.0.	Allows ftp access from 192.168.0 network.	Denies ftp access from 192.168.0 network.
vsftpd:192.168.0.0/24	Allows ftp access from 192.168.0.0/24 network.	Denies ftp access from 192.168.0.0/24 network.
vsftpd:192.168.0. EXCEPT 192.168.0.25	Allows ftp access from 192.168.0 network except for system with IP 192.168.0.25.	Denies ftp access from 192.168.0 network, except for system with IP 192.168.0.25.
vsftpd:192.168.0. EXCEPT 192.168.0.25, 192.168.0.26	Allows ftp access from 192.168.0 network except for systems with IPs 192.168.0.25 and .26.	Denies ftp access from 192.168.0 network, except for systems with IPs 192.168.0.25 and .26.
vsftpd,sshd:user1@192.168.0.	Allows ftp and ssh access to user1 from 192.168.0 network.	Denies ftp and ssh access to user1 from 192.168.0 network.
vsftpd,sshd@192.168.0.110: 192.168.1.	Allows ftp and ssh access from 192.168.1 network via interface configured with IP 192.168.0.110.	Denies ftp and ssh access from 192.168.1 network via interface configured with IP 192.168.0.110.
ALL EXCEPT sshd:192.168.0.	Allows all services except for ssh from 192.168.0 network.	Denies all services, except for ssh from 192.168.0 network.

Table 13-3 TCP Wrappers Access Control Files

We need to keep these rules in mind when dealing with TCP Wrappers. All messages related to TCP Wrappers are logged to the */var/log/secure* file.

Chapter Summary

This chapter discussed the secure shell server and TCP Wrappers. It started with an introduction of the secure shell service: what it is, how it works, available versions, and algorithms used. It continued with describing encryption techniques and authentication methods. It described software packages to support the service, commands, daemon, and configuration files. It demonstrated the setup for user authentication using private/public keys, and the use of this service for remote logging and transferring files. It also shows how to access the ssh service from a Window system.

The next and the last topic discussed TCP Wrappers in detail. TCP Wrappers is a simple service that controls access to various system services through entries placed in access control files.

Chapter Review Questions

1. What is the secure equivalent for the *rcp* command?
2. Name the two files for TCP wrapper through which it controls access to system services.
3. The secure shell may be defined to use TCP Wrappers for access control. True or False?
4. The primary secure shell server configuration file is *ssh_config*. True or False?
5. What are the encryption and/or authentication algorithms used in ssh version 2?

6. What is the secure shell equivalent for the *telnet* command?
7. Provide the names of four directives that may be used to set user-level access control for the secure shell server.
8. List any five network services that can be access-controlled by TCP Wrappers.
9. Where are the user ssh keys stored?
10. What would the command *ssh-copy-id* do?
11. What is the use of the *ssh-keygen* command?
12. List the two encryption techniques described in this chapter.
13. What is the default port used by the secure shell service?
14. Which log file stores the authentication messages?
15. What would the entry ALL EXCEPT telnetd:user100@192.168.0. in */etc/hosts.deny* file do?

Answers to Chapter Review Questions

1. The *scp* command is the secure equivalent for the *rcp* command.
2. TCP wrappers uses the *hosts.allow* and *hosts.deny* files located in the */etc* directory to control access to system services.
3. True.
4. False. The primary secure shell configuration file is *sshd_config*.
5. The ssh version 2 uses RSA, DSA, and ECDSA algorithms.
6. The secure equivalent for *telnet* is the *ssh* command.
7. The four directives that can be used to set user-level access control for the ssh server are AllowUsers, DenyUsers, AllowGroups, and DenyGroups.
8. Some of the services that may be controlled via TCP wrappers include ssh, telnet, ftp, and rsh.
9. In the *.ssh* sub-directory under the user's home directory.
10. The *ssh-copy-id* command is used to install public keys on remote systems.
11. The *ssh-keygen* command is used to generate authentication keys for the ssh use.
12. The two encryption techniques are symmetric and asymmetric.
13. The default port used by the secure shell service is 22.
14. The */var/log/secure* file stores authentication messages.
15. This entry would allow *user100* from 192.168.0 network access to the telnet service.

DIY Challenge Labs

The following labs are useful to strengthen most of the concepts and topics learned in this chapter. It is expected that you perform these labs without any additional help. A step-by-step guide is not provided, as the implementation of these labs requires the knowledge that has been presented in this chapter. Use defaults or your own thinking for missing information.

Lab 13-1: Establish Key-Based Authentication

Establish a private/public key combination for *user3* on *server1* so that this user is prompted for a passphrase (and not password) upon login to *host1*.

Lab 13-2: Configure TCP Wrappers to Secure Services

Edit TCP Wrappers access control files as appropriate and allow *user1* and *user3* from 192.168.1 and *example.net* to access *sshd* and *vsftpd* services, but disallow their access for *user2new* and *user4* from 192.168.2.120 and *example.org*. Log in as *user1* and *user3* from RHEL systems (one with IP 192.168.1.120 and the other with IP 192.168.2.120) and test access. Observe messages as they are logged to the */var/log/messages* and */var/log/secure* files.

RHCE
Section

Chapter 14

Writing Shell Scripts

This chapter describes the following major topics:

➢ Overview of shell scripts
➢ Write scripts to display basic system information, use local and environment variables, parse command output to a variable, understand the use of command line arguments, and the role of the shift command
➢ Execute and debug scripts
➢ Write interactive scripts
➢ Exit codes and test conditions
➢ Logical constructs: if-then-fi, if-then-else-fi, if-then-elif-fi, and case
➢ Write scripts using logical statements
➢ Arithmetic test conditions
➢ Looping constructs: for-do-done and while-do-done
➢ Write scripts using looping statements

RHCE Objectives:

63. Use shell scripting to automate system maintenance tasks

S hell scripts are text files that contain Linux commands, control structures, and comments, and they are written to automate long and repetitive tasks. Scripts can accept any simple to complex command and can be executed directly at the command prompt. Shell scripts do not need to be compiled, because they are interpreted by the shell line by line. This chapter presents many example scripts that are examined in detail to solidify understanding. These scripts begin with simple programs and advance to more complicated ones. As with any other programming language, the scripting skill develops over time as more and more scripts are read, written, and analyzed. This chapter also discusses a debug technique that can be used to troubleshoot issues in the code.

Shell Scripts

Shell scripts (a.k.a. *shell programs* or simply *scripts*) are text files that contain Linux commands and control structures for the automation of lengthy, complex, or repetitive tasks such as managing packages and users, administering LVM and file systems, monitoring file system utilization, trimming log files, archiving and compressing files, removing unnecessary files, starting and stopping database services and applications, and producing reports. Commands in the script are interpreted and run by the shell one at a time in the order in which they are listed in the script. Each line is executed as if it is typed and run at the command prompt. Control structures are utilized for creating and managing logical and looping constructs. Comments are also usually included to add general information about the script such as the author name, creation date, previous modification dates, purpose of the script, and its usage. If the script encounters an error during execution, the error message is displayed on the screen.

Scripts presented in this chapter are written in the bash shell and may be used in other shells with some modifications.

You can use any available text editor to write scripts; however, it is suggested to use the *vi* editor so you can practice. To quickly identify where things are in your scripts, use the *nl* command to enumerate their lines in the output. We will store our shell scripts in the */usr/local/bin* directory and add it to the PATH variable.

Displaying System Information

Let's create the first script called *sys_info.sh* on *server1* and examine it line by line. Change the directory into */usr/local/bin* and use the *vi* editor to write the script. Type what you see below excluding the line numbering:

```
# nl sys_info.sh
   1    #!/bin/bash
   2    # This script is called sys_info.sh and it was written by Asghar Ghori on December 11, 2014.
   3    # This script should be located in the /usr/local/bin directory.
   4    # The script was written to show basic RHEL and system information.
   5    echo "Display Basic System Information"
   6    echo "============================="
   7    echo
   8    echo "The hostname, hardware, and operating system information for this system is:"
   9    /usr/bin/hostnamectl
  10    echo
  11    echo "The following users are currently logged on to this system:"
```

Within vi, press the ESC key and then type :set nu to view line numbers associated with each line entry.

In this script, comments and commands are used as follows:

The first line indicates the shell in which the script will run. This line must start with the "#!" character combination followed by the full pathname to the shell file.

The next three lines contain comments: the script name, author name, creation time, default location for storage, and its purpose. The # sign implies that anything written to the right of it is for informational purposes only and will be ignored during script execution. Note that the first line also uses the number character (#), but it is followed by the exclamation mark (!); this combination has a special meaning to the shell, which is used to specify the location of the shell file. Do not get confused between the two usages of the # sign.

The fifth line has the first command of the script. The echo command prints on the screen whatever follows it. In our case, we will see "Display Basic System Information" printed.

The sixth line will underline the text "Display Basic System Information".

The seventh line has the *echo* command followed by nothing. This will insert an empty line in the output.

The eighth line will print "The hostname, hardware, and operating system information for this system is:".

The ninth line will execute the *hostnamectl* command to display basic information about the system.

The tenth line will insert an empty line.

The eleventh line will print "The following users are currently logged on to this system:" on the screen.

The twelfth line will execute the *who* command to list logged-in users.

Here is the *sys_info.sh* file created in the */usr/local/bin* directory:

```
-rw-r--r--. 1 root root 512 Dec 11 08:39 /usr/local/bin/sys_info.sh
```

Executing a Script
The script created above does not have the execute permission since the default umask value for the *root* user is set to 0022, which allows read/write permissions to the owner, and read-only permission to the rest. You will need to run the *chmod* command on the file and add the execute bit for everyone:

 # chmod +x /usr/local/bin/sys_info.sh

Any user on the system can now run this script using either its relative path or the fully qualified pathname:

 # sys_info.sh
 # /usr/local/bin/sys_info.sh

By default, the *usr/local/bin* directory is included in the PATH of all users. However, if it is not the case, you will need to define it in the */etc/profile* file so that whoever logs on to the system gets this path set. Alternatively, individual users may add the path to their *~/.bash_profile* file. The following shows how to add the new path to the existing PATH setting at the command prompt:

 # export PATH=$PATH:/usr/local/bin

Let's now run *sys_info.sh* and see what the output will look like:

 # sys_info.sh
Display Basic System Information
========================

The hostname, hardware, and operating system information for this system is:
   Static hostname: server1.example.com
      Icon name: computer
         Chassis: n/a
      Machine ID: 718b8d4164d341cb8cc9d38f90683d3e
        Boot ID: 9bb78e5077ba4c76a41b4dc9ca637210
   Virtualization: kvm
Operating System: Red Hat Enterprise Linux Server 7.0 (Maipo)
   CPE OS Name: cpe:/o:redhat:enterprise_linux:7.0:GA:server
        Kernel: Linux 3.10.0-123.el7.x86_64
    Architecture: x86_64

The following users are currently logged on to this system:
(unknown)   :0   2014-11-17 14:23 (:0)
root   pts/0   2014-12-10 09:47 (192.168.0.13)
root   pts/3   2014-11-24 22:25 (:2)

Debugging a Shell Script

Before you have a perfectly working script in place, you may have to run and modify it repeatedly. You can use a debugging technique that will help identify where the script might have failed or did not function as expected. You can either add the –x option to the "#!/bin/bash" at the beginning of the script to look like "#!/bin/bash –x", or you can execute the script as follows:

 # bash –x /usr/local/bin/sys_info.sh
+ echo 'Display Basic System Information'
Display Basic System Information
+ echo ================================
================================
+ echo

+ echo 'The hostname, hardware, and operating system information for this system is:'
The hostname, hardware, and operating system information for this system is:
+ /usr/bin/hostnamectl
   Static hostname: server1.example.com
      Icon name: computer

```
        Chassis: n/a
     Machine ID: 718b8d4164d341cb8cc9d38f90683d3e
        Boot ID: 9bb78e5077ba4c76a41b4dc9ca637210
  Virtualization: kvm
Operating System: Red Hat Enterprise Linux Server 7.0 (Maipo)
    CPE OS Name: cpe:/o:redhat:enterprise_linux:7.0:GA:server
         Kernel: Linux 3.10.0-123.el7.x86_64
   Architecture: x86_64
+ echo


+ echo 'The following users are currently logged on to this system:'
The following users are currently logged on to this system:
+ /usr/bin/who
(unknown)  :0        2014-11-17  14:23  (:0)
root       pts/0     2014-12-10  09:47  (192.168.0.13)
root       pts/3     2014-11-24  22:25  (:2)
```

The above output now also includes the actual lines from the script prefixed by the + sign and followed by the command execution result. It also shows the line number of the problem line in the output. This way you can identify any issues pertaining to the path, command name, use of special characters, etc., and address it quickly. Try changing any of the *echo* commands in the script to "iecho" and re-run the script in the debug mode to confirm what has just been said.

Using Local Variables

We have dealt with variables previously and have seen their usage. To recap, there are two types of variables: *local* (or *private*) and *environment*. Both can be defined and used in scripts and at the command line.

Script *use_var.sh* will define a local variable and print its value on the screen. We will re-check the value of this local variable after the script execution has been completed. The comments have been excluded for brevity.

```
# nl use_var.sh
1    #!/bin/bash
2    echo "Setting a Local Variable".
3    echo "==================="
4    SYSNAME=server1.example.com
5    echo "The hostname of this system is $SYSNAME".
```

Add the execute bit to this script. The following output will be generated when you run this script:

```
# use_var.sh
Setting a Local Variable.
===================
The hostname of this system is server1.example.com.
```

If you run the *echo* command to see what is stored in the SYSNAME variable, you will get nothing:

```
# echo $SYSNAME
```

Using Pre-Defined Environment Variables

The following script called *pre_env.sh* will display the values of two pre-defined environment variables SHELL and LOGNAME:

 # nl pre_env.sh

```
1    #!/bin/bash
2    echo "The location of my shell command is:"
3    echo $SHELL
4    echo "We are logged in as $LOGNAME".
```

Add the execute bit to this script, and run to view the result:

 # pre_env.sh
```
The location of my shell command is:
/bin/bash
We are logged in as root.
```

Parsing Command Output

During the execution of a script, you can use the command substitution feature of the bash shell and store the output generated by the command into a variable. For example, the following script called *cmd_out.sh* will run the *hostname* and *uname* commands and store their output in variables. This script shows two different ways to use command substitution.

 # nl cmd_out.sh

```
1    #!/bin/bash
2    SYSNAME=$(hostname)
3    KERNVER=`uname –r`
4    echo "The hostname of this system is $SYSNAME".
5    echo "This system is running kernel version: $KERNVER".
```

Add the execute bit and run the script:

 # cmd_out.sh
```
The hostname of this system is server1.example.com.
This system is running kernel version: 3.10.0-123.el7.x86_64..
```

Understanding and Using Command Line Arguments

Command line arguments (also called *positional parameters*) are the arguments supplied to a command or script to produce desired results in the output. The location of the arguments, as well as the location of the command or script itself, is stored in corresponding variables. These variables are special shell variables. Figure 14-1 gives a pictorial view of the location of each command line argument.

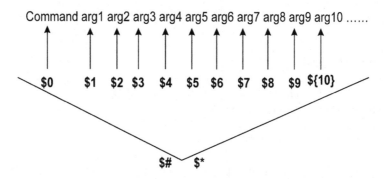

Figure 14-1 Command Line Arguments

The variables representing various positions and meanings are explained in Table 14-1.

Variable	Description
$0	Represents the command or script.
$1 to $9	Represents arguments 1 through 9.
${10} and above	Represents arguments 10 and beyond.
$#	Represents the count of all arguments.
$*	Represents all arguments.
$$	Represents the PID of the command or script.

Table 14-1 Command Line Arguments

The script *com_line_arg.sh* below will show furnished command line arguments, their total count, the value of the first argument, and the process ID of the script:

 # nl com_line_arg.sh

```
1   #!/bin/bash
2   echo "There are $# arguments specified at the command line".
3   echo "The arguments supplied are: $*"
4   echo "The first argument is: $1"
5   echo "The Process ID of the script is: $$"
```

The result will be as follows when this script is executed with four arguments. Do not forget to add the execute bit.

 # com_line_arg.sh baku timbuktu xingyang quito
There are 4 arguments specified at the command line.
The arguments supplied are: baku timbuktu xingyang quito
The first argument is: baku
The Process ID of the script is: 17149

Shifting Command Line Arguments

The *shift* command is used to move command line arguments one position to the left. During this move, the value of the first argument is lost. The *comlineargshift.sh* script below is an extension to the *com_line_arg.sh* script. It uses the *shift* command to demonstrate what happens when arguments are moved.

nl com_line_arg_shift.sh

```
1   #!/bin/bash
2   echo "There are $# arguments specified at the command line".
3   echo "The arguments supplied are: $*"
4   echo "The first argument is: $1"
5   echo "The Process ID of the script is: $$"
6   shift
7   echo "The new first argument after the first shift is: $1"
8   shift
9   echo "The new first argument after the second shift is: $1"
```

Let's execute the script with four arguments. Notice that a new value is assigned to $1 after each shift.

com_line_arg_shift.sh baku timbuktu xingyang quito

```
There are 4 arguments specified at the command line.
The arguments supplied are: baku timbuktu xingyang quito
The first argument is: baku
The Process ID of the script is: 17151
The new first argument after the first shift is: timbuktu
The new first argument after the second shift is: xingyang
```

Multiple shifts in a single attempt may be performed by furnishing the number of shifts desired to the *shift* command as an argument. For example, "*shift 2*" will carry out two shifts, "*shift 3*" will make three shifts, and so on.

Writing an Interactive Script

Interactive scripts prompt for an input and continue their execution based on the input received. The entered input is stored in a variable. The *read* command is used for receiving the input and storing it in a variable (FILE in the following example). This command is normally preceded by a message telling the user what is expected as an input.

The *inter_read.sh* script below will list files and prompt to enter the file name to be removed. Notice the \c in the fifth line. This is an example of *escape sequence*. It will tell the *echo* command to wait for user input right after printing the message, "Enter the name of file you want to remove:". Try running this script with and without the \c and observe the difference. In addition, the PWD environment variable is used in the script to display our location in the directory tree.

nl inter_read.sh

```
1   #! /bin/bash
2   echo  "Here is a list of all files in the $PWD directory:"
3   /bin/ls –l
4   echo –e "Enter the name of file to be removed: \c".
5   read FILE
6   echo "Type 'y' to remove, 'n' if you do not want to:"
7   /bin/rm –i $FILE
```

Assuming you are logged in as *user1* and in the home directory, here is what the *inter_read.sh* script will do:

$ inter_read.sh
Here is a list of all files in the /home/user1 directory:
total 0
```
drwxr-xr-x.  2 user1  user1   6 Oct 28 23:12  Desktop
drwxrwxr-x.  2 user1  user1   6 Nov 27 08:02  dir1
drwxr-xr-x.  2 user1  user1   6 Oct 28 23:12  Documents
drwxr-xr-x.  2 user1  user1   6 Oct 28 23:12  Downloads
-rw-rw-r--.  1 user1  user1   0 Nov 27 09:09  file1
-rwxrwxrwx.  1 user1  user1   0 Dec  1 08:27  file2
drwxr-xr-x.  2 user1  user1   6 Oct 28 23:12  Music
-rw-rw-r--.  1 user1  user1   0 Nov 27 16:21  newfile
lrwxrwxrwx.  1 user1  user1   7 Nov 27 16:21  newfile10 -> n ewfile
-rw-rw-r--.  2 user1  user1   0 Nov 27 16:22  newfile2
-rw-rw-r--.  2 user1  user1   0 Nov 27 16:22  newfile20
drwxr-xr-x.  2 user1  user1   6 Oct 28 23:12  Pictures
drwxr-xr-x.  2 user1  user1   6 Oct 28 23:12  Public
drwxrwxr-x.  3 user1  user1  26 Nov 26 23:02  scripts30
drwxrwxr-x.  2 user1  user1  18 Nov 26 23:07  scripts.dir20
drwxr-xr-x.  2 user1  user1   6 Oct 28 23:12  Templates
drwxr-xr-x.  2 user1  user1   6 Oct 28 23:12  Videos
```
Enter the name of file to be removed: **file1**
Type 'y' to remove, 'n' if you do not want to:
/bin/rm: remove regular empty file 'file1'? **y**

There are several files in *user1*'s home directory. We entered "file1" when prompted and then 'y' for confirmation to delete it. You can run the *ll* command afterwards to verify the removal.

We used the \c escape sequence in this script. The bash shell provides additional escape sequences for use in scripts to improve readability. These additional sequences include the \t for tab, \n for new line, \a for beep, \f for form feed, \r for carriage return, and \b for backspace. Try using them in the *inter_read.sh* script and observe the change in output.

Additional escape sequences such as \h, \u, and \w may be used to display the hostname, username, and current working directory. For instance, the following will change the primary command prompt to display the username, hostname, and current working directory location:

 # PS1="\u@\h:\w :> $ "
root@server1:/usr/local/bin :> $

Logical Statements
So far, we have talked about simple scripts that run the code line by line and produce the results. The shell lets us employ logical constructs to control the flow of scripts. It does this by allowing us to use test conditions, which decides what to do next based on the true or false status of the condition.

The shell offers two logical constructs: the *if-then-fi* construct and the *case* construct. The if-then-fi construct has a few variations, which will also be covered in this chapter.

Before starting to look at the example scripts and see how logical constructs are used, let's discuss exit codes and various test conditions. We will use them later in our example scripts.

Exit Codes

Exit codes refer to the value returned by a program or script when it finishes execution. This value is based on the outcome of the program. If the program runs successfully, we get a zero exit code, otherwise, a non-zero value is returned. This code or value is also referred to as a *return code,* and is stored in a special shell variable called ?. Let's look at the following two examples to understand their usage:

```
# ls
anaconda-ks.cfg  initial-setup-ks.cfg
# echo $?
0
# man
What manual page do you want?
# echo  $?
1
```

In the first example, the *ls* command ran successfully and it produced the desired result, hence a zero exit code was returned and stored in the variable ?. In the second example, the *man* command did not run successfully because of a missing argument, therefore a non-zero exit code was returned and stored in the variable ?. In either case, we echoed the ? variable value.

We can define exit codes within a script at different locations in order to help debug the script by knowing exactly where the script quit.

Test Conditions

Test conditions can be set on numeric values, string values, or files using the *test* command. You can enclose a test condition within square brackets [] without using the *test* command explicitly. This is exhibited in later examples.

Table 14-2 shows various test condition operations that can be performed.

Operation on Numeric Value	Description
integer1 –eq integer2	Integer1 is equal to integer2.
integer1 –ne integer2	Integer1 is not equal to integer2.
integer1 –lt integer2	Integer1 is less than integer2.
integer1 –gt integer2	Integer1 is greater than integer2.
integer1 –le integer2	Integer1 is less than or equal to integer2.
integer1 –ge integer2	Integer1 is greater than or equal to integer2.
Operation on String Value	**Description**
string1–string2	Tests whether the two strings are identical.
string1! –string2	Tests whether the two strings are not identical.
–l string or –z string	Tests whether the string length is zero.
–n string	Tests whether the string length is non-zero.
string	Same as "–n string".

Operation on File	Description
−b file	Tests whether the file exists and is a block device file.
−c file	Tests whether the file exists and is a character device file.
−d file	Tests whether the file is a directory.
−e file	Tests whether the file exists.
−f file	Tests whether the file exists and is a normal file.
−g file	Tests whether the file exists and has the setgid bit.
−L file	Tests whether the file exists and is a symlink.
−r file	Tests whether the file exists and is readable.
−s file	Tests whether the file exists and is non-zero in length.
−u file	Tests whether the file exists and has the setuid bit.
−w file	Tests whether the file exists and is writable.
−x file	Tests whether the file exists and is executable.
file1 −nt file2	Tests whether the file1 is newer than file2.
file1 −ot file2	Tests whether the file1 is older than file2.
Logic Operator	**Description**
!	The logical NOT operator.
−a	The logical AND operator.
−o	The logical OR operator.

Table 14-2 Test Conditions

Having described the exit codes and various test conditions, let's look at a few example scripts and observe some of their applications.

The if-then-fi Statement

The if-then-fi statement evaluates the condition for true or false. It executes the specified action if the condition is true; otherwise, it will take you out of this construct. The if-then-fi statement begins with an if and ends in a fi, as depicted in the syntax below:

```
if    condition
then
      action
fi
```

It was demonstrated earlier how to check the number of arguments supplied at the command line. The following example script called *if_then_fi.sh* determines the number of arguments and prints an error message if there are none provided:

```
# nl if_then_fi.sh
1    #!/bin/bash
2    if       [ $# −ne 2 ]
3    then
4             echo "Error: Invalid number of arguments supplied."
5             echo "Usage: $0 source_file destination_file."
6    exit 2
7    fi
8    echo "Script terminated."
```

This script will display the following messages on the screen if it is executed without specifying exactly two arguments at the command line:

Error: Invalid number of arguments supplied.
Usage: if_then_fi.sh source_file destination_file

A value of 2 will appear upon checking the return code. This value reflects the exit code that we defined in the script on line number 6.

echo $?
2

Conversely, if we supply exactly two arguments, the return code will be 0 and the message will be:

Script terminated.
echo $?
0

The if-then-else-fi Statement

The if-then-fi statement has a limitation and it can execute an action only if the specified condition is true. It quits the statement if the condition is not true. The if-then-else-fi statement, on the other hand, is more advanced in the sense that it can execute an action if the condition is true and another action if the condition is false. The general syntax of this structure is:

```
if   condition
then
        action1
else
        action2
fi
```

action1 or action2 is performed for a true or false evaluation of the condition, respectively. The following script called *if_then_else_fi.sh* will accept an integer value as an argument and tell if the value is positive or negative. If no argument is provided, it will display the usage of the script.

nl if_then_else_fi.sh
```
1    #!/bin/bash
2    if       [ $1 –gt 0 ]
3    then
4            echo  "$1 is a positive integer value".
5    else
6            echo  "$1 is a negative integer value".
7    fi
```

Run this script one time with a positive integer value and the next time with a negative value:

if_then_else_fi.sh 10
10 is a positive integer value.
if_then_else_fi.sh −10
-10 is a negative integer value.

The if-then-elif-fi Statement

This is a more advanced construct than the other two if-then statements. We can define multiple conditions and associate an action with each one of them. During the evaluation of this construct, the action corresponding to the true condition will be performed. The general syntax of this structure is:

```
if      condition1
then
        action1
elif    condition2
then
        action2
………….
………….
else
        action(n)
fi
```

The following script called *if_then_elif_fi.sh* is an enhanced version of the *if_then_else_fi.sh* script. It will accept an integer value as an argument and tell if it is positive, negative, or zero. If a non-integer value or no command line argument is supplied, the script will print a complaint.

nl if_then_elif_fi.sh

```
1    #!/bin/bash
2    if       [ $1 −gt 0 ]
3    then
4                 echo  "$1 is a positive integer value".
5                 exit  1
6    elif     [ $1 −eq 0 ]
7    then
8                 echo  "$1 is a zero integer value".
9                 exit  2
10   elif     [ $1 −lt 0 ]
11   then
12                echo  "$1 is a negative integer value".
13                exit  3
14   else
15                echo  "$1 is not an integer value. Please supply an integer".
16                exit  4
17   fi
```

Run this script four times: the first time with a positive integer, the second time with 0, the third time with a negative integer, and the fourth time with a non-integer value. Check the exit code after each execution to determine where the script exited.

 # if_then_elif_fi.sh 10
10 is a positive integer value.
 # echo $?
1

 # if_then_elif_fi.sh 0
0 is a zero integer value.
 # echo $?
2

 # if_then_elif_fi.sh –10
-10 is a negative integer value.
 # echo $?
3

 # if_then_elif_fi.sh abcd
abcd is not an integer value. Please supply an integer.
 # echo $?
4

Another example for the if-then-elif-fi statement is provided below. This script is called *ex200_ex300.sh*, and it will display the name of the Red Hat exam RHCSA or RHCE for the entered exam code ex200 or ex300. If a random or no argument is provided, it will print "Usage: Acceptable values are ex200 and ex300".

 # nl ex200_ex300.sh
```
1    #!/bin/bash
2    if        [ "$1" = ex200 ]
3    then
4            echo "RHCSA"
6    elif      [ "$1" = ex300 ]
7    then
8            echo "RHCE"
9    else
10           echo "Usage: Acceptable values are ex200 and ex300".
11   fi
```

Run this script three times: the first time with argument ex200, the second time with argument ex300, and the third time with something random as an argument:

 # ex200_ex300.sh ex200
RHCSA
 # ex200_ex300.sh ex300
RHCE

 # ex200_ex300.sh

Usage: Acceptable values are ex200 and ex300.

> **EXAM TIP:** A good understanding of the usage of logical statements is important.

Looping Statements

While working as a RHEL administrator, you will often need to perform a task on a number of given elements or repeatedly until the specified condition becomes true or false. For instance, if several disks need to be initialized for use in LVM, you can either run the *pvcreate* command on each disk one at a time or employ a loop to do it for you. Likewise, based on a condition, you may want a program to continue to run until the condition becomes either true or false.

There are three statements you can use to implement looping. They are called *for-do-done, while-do-done,* and *until-do-done.*

The for-do-done construct performs an operation on a list of given values until the list is exhausted. The while-do-done statement performs an operation repeatedly until the specified condition becomes false. The until-do-done structure does the opposite of what while-do-done does. It performs an operation repeatedly until the specified condition becomes true.

Test Conditions

The *let* command is used in looping constructs to evaluate the condition at each iteration. It compares the value stored in a variable against a pre-defined value. Each time the loop does an iteration, the variable value is altered. You can enclose the test condition for arithmetic evaluation within double parentheses (()) or double quotes instead of using the *let* command explicitly.

Table 14-3 lists operators that can be used with the *let* command.

Operator	Description
−	Unary minus.
!	Unary negation.
+	Addition.
−	Subtraction.
*	Multiplication.
/	Division.
%	Remainder.
<	Less than.
<=	Less than or equal to.
>	Greater than.
>=	Greater than or equal to.
=	Assignment.
==	Comparison for equality.
!=	Comparison for non-equality.

Table 14-3 let Operators

Having described various test condition operators, let's look at a few example scripts and see how some of these can be utilized.

The for-do-done Loop

The for-do-done loop is executed on an array of elements until all the elements in the list are used up. Each element is assigned to a variable one after the other for being processed within the loop. The syntax of the for-do-done loop is:

```
for  VAR  in  list
do
     command block
done
```

The *for_do_done.sh* script below initializes the variable COUNT to 0. The for-do-done loop will read each letter sequentially from the range placed within curly brackets (no spaces before the letter A and after the letter Z), assign it to the variable LETTER, and display the value on the screen. The *expr* command is an arithmetic processor and it is used to increment the COUNT by 1 at each loop iteration.

```
# nl for_do_done.sh
1   #!/bin/bash
2   COUNT=0
3   for  LETTER  in  {A..Z}
4   do
5           COUNT=`/usr/bin/expr $COUNT + 1`
6           echo "Letter $COUNT is [$LETTER]"
7   done
```

The output of the script will be:

```
# for_do_done.sh
Letter 1 is [A]
Letter 2 is [B]
Letter 3 is [C]
. . . . . . . .
Letter 24 is [X]
Letter 25 is [Y]
Letter 26 is [Z]
```

Another example is provided below. This script called *create_user.sh* can be used to create several user accounts. As each account is created, the value of variable ? is checked. If the value is 0, a message saying the account is created successfully will be displayed, otherwise the script will terminate. In case of a successful account creation, the *passwd* command will be invoked to assign the user the same password as their username.

```
# nl create_user.sh
1   #!/bin/bash
2   for  USER  in  user{10..14}
3   do
4           echo "Creating account for user $USER".
5           /usr/sbin/useradd –m –d /home/$USER –s /bin/bash $USER
```

```
6            if [ $? = 0 ]
7                 then
8                        echo $USER | /usr/bin/passwd --stdin $USER
9                        echo "$USER is created successfully."
10                else
11                       echo "Failed to create account $USER".
12                       exit
13           fi
14   done
```

The result of the script execution below confirms the addition of four new user accounts:

create_user.sh
Creating account for user user10.
Changing password for user user10.
passwd: all authentication tokens updated successfully.
user10 is created successfully.
Creating account for user user11.
Changing password for user user11.
passwd: all authentication tokens updated successfully.
user11 is created successfully.
Creating account for user user12.
Changing password for user user12.
passwd: all authentication tokens updated successfully.
user12 is created successfully.
Creating account for user user13.
Changing password for user user13.
passwd: all authentication tokens updated successfully.
user13 is created successfully.
Creating account for user user14.
Changing password for user user14.
passwd: all authentication tokens updated successfully.
user14 is created successfully.

If this script is re-executed without modifying the list of elements, the following will appear:

create_user.sh
Creating account for user user10.
useradd: user 'user10' already exists
Failed to create account user10.
Creating account for user user11.
useradd: user 'user11' already exists
Failed to create account user11.
Creating account for user user12.
useradd: user 'user12' already exists
Failed to create account user12.
Creating account for user user13.
useradd: user 'user13' already exists
Failed to create account user13.

Creating account for user user14.
useradd: user 'user14' already exists
Failed to create account user14.

EXAM TIP: A good understanding of the looping constructs is important.

The while-do-done Loop

The while-do-done loop checks for a condition and goes on executing a block of commands until the specified condition becomes false. The general syntax of this looping construct is:

```
while        condition
do
     command block
done
```

The condition specified is usually an arithmetic expression containing the *test* or the *let* command in either an implicit or an explicit mode, but they are normally used implicitly.

Let's look at the following *while_do_done.sh* menu-driven program. The entire case statement (logical construct) is defined as a block of commands within the while-do-done loop. When you choose one of the listed options, the command associated with that option will run. Once the command execution is finished, you will be prompted to press Enter to go back to the menu. The loop will continue until you choose to exit the program by selecting option 5.

```
# nl while_do_done.sh
1    #!/bin/bash
2    while  true
3    do
4            /usr/bin/clear
5            echo "                    Menu "
6            echo "    ---------------------------------------------------"
7            echo "    [1] Display Date and Time Information".
8            echo "    [2] Display Basic System Information".
9            echo "    [3] Display Local Information".
10           echo "    [4] Display Mounted File Systems".
11           echo "    [5] Exit".
12           echo "    ===================================="
13           echo
14           echo -e "Enter Your Choice [1-5]: \c "
15           read  VAR
16           case $VAR  in
17                   1) echo  "Current System Date and Time is `/usr/bin/timedatectl`"
18                   echo
19                   echo  "Press Enter to go back to the Menu......"
20                   read
21                   ;;
22                   2) /usr/bin/hostnamectl
23                   echo
```

```
24                    echo  "Press Enter to go back to the Menu......"
25                    read
26                    ;;
27                    3) /usr/bin/localectl
28                    echo  "Press Enter to go back to the Menu......"
29                    read
30                    ;;
31                    4) /usr/bin/df –h
32                    echo  "Press Enter to go back to the Menu......"
33                    read
34                    ;;
35                    5) echo  "Exiting .........   Bye Bye"
36                    exit  0
37                    ;;
38                    *) echo  "You have selected an invalid option".
39                    echo  "Please choose a valid option".
40                    echo  "Press Enter to go back to the Menu......"
41                    read
42                    ;;
43          esac
44    done
```

When you execute this script, the menu will appear as follows and it will wait for your input:

 # while_do_done.sh
                          Menu
----
    [1] Display Date and Time Information.
    [2] Display Basic System Information.
    [3] Display Local Information.
    [4] Display Mounted File Systems.
    [5] Exit.
===================================
Enter Your Choice [1-5]:

Now, for instance, if we enter option 4, the program will display all mounted file systems:

Enter Your Choice [1-5]: **4**

Filesystem	Size	Used	Avail	Use%	Mounted on
/dev/mapper/vg00-root	8.8G	3.3G	5.5G	38%	/
devtmpfs	488M	0	488M	0%	/dev
tmpfs	498M	92K	497M	1%	/dev/shm
tmpfs	498M	20M	478M	4%	/run
tmpfs	498M	0	498M	0%	/sys/fs/cgroup
/dev/vde1	381M	0	381M	0%	/mntvfat
/dev/vdb1	181M	1.6M	167M	1%	/mntext3
/dev/mapper/vg00-home	297M	21M	277M	7%	/home
/dev/vda1	497M	119M	379M	24%	/boot

Press Enter to go back to the Menu......

Pressing the Enter key will take you back to the menu. To terminate program execution, input option number 5.

Another example of a while-do-done construct is presented below. This script called *cuser.sh* is a variant of *create_user.sh*. It reads usernames from a file called *userlist.txt* and creates the accounts as listed in the file. The script assigns a matching password upon successful creation of a user. Most of the code here is from the *create_user.sh* script.

```
# nl cuser.sh
 1    #!/bin/bash
 2    FILE=/root/userlist.txt
 3    cat $FILE | while read USER
 4    do
 5            echo "Creating account for user $USER".
 6            /usr/sbin/useradd –m –d /home/$USER –s /bin/bash $USER
 7    if [ $? = 0 ]
 8            then
 9                    echo $USER | /usr/bin/passwd --stdin $USER
10                    echo "$USER successfully created."
11            else
12                    echo "Failed to create user account $USER".
13            exit
14    fi
15    done
```

And here is what is in the */root/userlist.txt* file:

```
# cat /root/userlist.txt
user4000
user5000
user6000
```

You can change the usernames in the .txt file and re-run the script for creating additional accounts.

Chapter Summary

In this chapter, we learned the basics of bash shell scripting. This chapter started with an overview of scripting, then jumped directly into writing and analyzing example scripts. We wrote and inspected simple code and gradually advanced to more complicated scripts. We learned a technique to pinpoint problem lines in our scripts. After understanding and practicing the scripts presented in this chapter, you should be able to write your own scripts, debug them, and examine scripts written by others.

Chapter Review Questions

1. What are the three major components in a shell scripts?
2. Which looping construct can be used to perform an action on listed items?
3. What is the function of the *shift* command?
4. You can script the startup and shutdown of a database. True or False?
5. What does the *echo* command do without any arguments?

6. The until-do-done loop continues to run until the specified condition becomes true. True or False?
7. What would the command *echo $?* do?
8. When would you want to use an exit code in a script?
9. What would you modify in a shell script to run it in the debug mode?
10. What are the two fundamental types of logical constructs outlined in this chapter?
11. Which command is used to write interactive scripts?
12. What would != imply in a looping condition?
13. What comments may you want to include in a shell script? Write any six.
14. What is one benefit of writing shell scripts?
15. What would the command *bash –x /usr/local/bin/script1.sh* do?

Answers to Chapter Review Questions
1. The three major components in a shell script are commands, control structures, and comments.
2. The for-do-done loop.
3. The *shift* command moves an argument to the left.
4. True.
5. The *echo* command inserts an empty line in the output when used without arguments.
6. True.
7. This command will display the exit code of the last command executed.
8. The purpose of using an exit code is to determine exactly where the script quits.
9. We would specify –x as an argument to the shell path.
10. The if-then-fi and case constructs.
11. The *read* command is used to write interactive scripts.
12. != would check the value for non-equality.
13. The author name, creation date, last modification date, location, purpose, and usage.
14. One major benefit of writing shell scripts is to automate lengthy and repetitive tasks.
15. This command will execute *script1.sh* in debug mode.

DIY Challenge Labs
The following labs are useful to strengthen most of the concepts and topics learned in this chapter. It is expected that you perform these labs without any additional help. A step-by-step guide is not provided, as the implementation of these labs requires the knowledge that has been presented in this chapter. Use defaults or your own thinking for missing information.

Lab 14-1: Write a Script to Create Logical Volumes
For this lab, present 2x1GB virtual disks to your system. Write a single bash shell script to create 2x800MB partitions on each disk using *parted* and then bring both partitions into LVM control with the *pvcreate* command. Create a volume group called *vgscript* and add both PVs to it. Create three logical volumes each of size 500MB and name them *lvscript1*, *lvscript2*, and *lvscript3*.

Lab 14-2: Write a Script to Create File Systems
This lab is a continuation of Lab 14-1. Write another bash shell script to create xfs, ext4, and vfat file system structures in each logical volume. Create mount points */mnt/xfs*, */mnt/ext4*, and */mnt/vfat*, and mount the file systems. Include the *df* command with –h to list the mounted file systems.

Chapter 15

Configuring Bonding, Teaming, IPv6, and Routing

This chapter describes the following major topics:

➤ Overview of link aggregation, and interface bonding and teaming

➤ Configure interface bonding manually and via NetworkManager CLI

➤ Configure interface teaming manually and via NetworkManager CLI

➤ Use graphical tools for bonding and teaming setup

➤ Understand IPv6 and how to view its assignments

➤ Configure and test IPv6 addresses

➤ Introduction to routing and routing table

➤ Add static routes manually and by editing appropriate files

RHCE Objectives:

31. Configure networking and hostname resolution statically or dynamically
55. Use network teaming or bonding to configure aggregate network links between two Red Hat Enterprise Linux systems
56. Configure IPv6 addresses and perform basic IPv6 troubleshooting
57. Route IP traffic and create static routes

L

Link aggregation is a technique by which two or more network interfaces are logically configured to provide higher performance using their combined bandwidth and fault tolerance should all but one of them fail. Two common methods for link aggregation are bonding and teaming, and both are supported natively in RHEL7.

The continuous expansion of the Internet and a mushrooming demand for IP addresses has opened doors for the use of IPv6 addresses. The current deployment of IPv6 is limited; however, it will not be uncommon in the near future to see computing devices using these addresses.

Routing selects network paths for the transmission of IP traffic between two computing devices that may be located thousands of kilometers apart on distinct networks. Routers are specialized hardware devices that are employed for data routing purposes, and they are deployed in abundance to route Internet, business, and personal traffic. A RHEL system can also be configured to provide routing, but with limited capability.

Link Aggregation

Link aggregation is a term used in corporate networks to combine the capabilities of two or more physical or virtual Ethernet network interfaces to function as a single logical network pipe. The resultant aggregate offers three major advantages: better throughput, load balancing across all interfaces, and fault tolerance in the event all but one interface in the aggregate fail. RHEL7 supports two link aggregation methods that are referred to as *bonding* and *teaming*. Support for bonding has been around in RHEL for years; however, with the release of RHEL7, we now also have the ability to form interface teaming. If we compare the features presented by both methods, we will observe that teaming is a better option. In fact, RHEL7 offers a tool called *bond2team* for those who wish to migrate from their existing bonding setups to teaming.

Bonding and teaming can be configured with IPv4 and IPv6 assignments by editing files, and using tools such as the NetworkManager CLI or TUI, or the GNOME Network Connections GUI. Additional tasks such as activating and deactivating logical channels can also be performed with these and other OS tools as well. Chapter 12 "Administering Network Interfaces and Network Clients" discussed these tools in detail. A repeat of them will be evident in upcoming exercises.

Interface Bonding

Interface bonding provides the ability to bind two or more network interfaces together into a single, logical bonded channel that acts as the master for all slave interfaces that are added to it. An IP address is applied to the bond rather than to individual slaves within the bond. Users and applications will see the bond device as the connection to use rather than the individual interfaces within it.

The support for bonding is integrated entirely into the kernel as a loadable module. This module is called *bonding*. A bonded channel is configured to use one of several modes of operation that dictate its overall behavior. Some of the modes are described in Table 15-1.

Mode of Operation	Description
Round-robin	This mode moves network traffic serially starting with the first slave and going to the last, and then back to the first. This mode supports both load balancing and fault tolerance. It is specified as balance-rr.

Active-backup	Only one slave is active at a time, and all others are available but in passive mode. In the event that the active slave fails, one of the passive slaves takes over and becomes active. This mode of operation does not provide load balancing; however, it does support fault tolerance. It is specified as active-backup.
XOR	This mode uses the source and destination Ethernet addresses to transfer network traffic. This mode provides both load balancing and fault tolerance. It is specified as balance-xor.
Broadcast	This mode transmits network traffic on all slaves. This mode provides fault tolerance only. It is specified as broadcast.

Table 15-1 Modes of Operation for Bonding Channel

Exercise 15-1: Configure Interface Bonding by Editing Files

This exercise should be done on *server1*. However, the new interface allocation will be done on *host1*.

The allocation of a pair of virtual network interfaces to *server1* and the formation of a bonding channel with IP 192.168.1.110 was mentioned in Chapter 01 "Installing RHEL7 on Physical Computer Using Local DVD".

In this exercise, you will add two new interfaces on 192.168.1.0/24 network to *server1* and call them *eth2* and *eth3*. You will form a bond by creating configuration files and executing appropriate commands to activate it. You will reboot the system to verify bond activation. You will assign hostname *server1bond.example.org* with alias *server1bond*. You will add IP and hostname mapping to the *hosts* table.

1. Open the virtual console for *server1* on *host1*. Click "Show virtual hardware details" | Add Hardware | Network. Select Source device "Virtual network 'rhnet_virt' : NAT" from the drop-down list and Device model virtio. We created this network in Chapter 06 "Configuring Server Virtualization and Network Installing RHEL7". Leave the MAC address to the default. Click Finish to complete the new interface assignment.
2. Repeat step 1 and add another interface.
3. Log on to *server1* and run the *ip* command to check the new interfaces:

    # **ip addr**
    . . . .
    4: eth2: <BROADCAST,MULTICAST,UP,LOWER_UP> mtu 1500 qdisc pfifo_fast state UP qlen 1000
        link/ether 52:54:00:0c:ec:ff brd ff:ff:ff:ff:ff:ff
    5: eth3: <BROADCAST,MULTICAST,UP,LOWER_UP> mtu 1500 qdisc pfifo_fast state UP qlen 1000
        link/ether 52:54:00:28:91:f0 brd ff:ff:ff:ff:ff:ff

    The output indicates the presence of two new interfaces by the name *eth2* and *eth3*.

4. Load the bonding driver called "bonding" in the kernel with the *modprobe* command if it is not already loaded, and verify with the *modinfo* command:

    # **modprobe bonding**

modinfo bonding

filename:	/lib/modules/3.10.0-123.el7.x86_64/kernel/drivers/net/bonding/bonding.ko
alias:	rtnl-link-bond
author:	Thomas Davis, tadavis@lbl.gov and many others
description:	Ethernet Channel Bonding Driver, v3.7.1
version:	3.7.1
license:	GPL
srcversion:	E52AE00A79EA6FEFB5BF718
depends:	
intree:	Y
vermagic:	3.10.0-123.el7.x86_64 SMP mod_unload modversions
signer:	Red Hat Enterprise Linux kernel signing key
sig_key:	00:AA:5F:56:C5:87:BD:82:F2:F9:9D:64:BA:83:DD:1E:9E:0D:33:4A
sig_hashalgo:	sha256
parm:	max_bonds:Max number of bonded devices (int)

. . . .

5. Generate UUIDs for both new interfaces using the *uuidgen* command:

    # **uuidgen eth2**
    15d44a70-554d-49c6-9ea0-c1ba3200f797
    # **uuidgen eth3**
    2f9aec97-d5d1-4fe1-81b0-60e6080c0352

6. Use the *vi* editor to create a file called *ifcfg-bond0* in the */etc/sysconfig/network-scripts*
    directory for *bond0* with the following settings. Use the interface type Bond. This virtual
    device will serve as the bonding master with round-robin as the load balancing technique. The
    rest of the settings are self-explanatory.

    # **cd /etc/sysconfig/network-scripts**
    # **vi ifcfg-bond0**
    DEVICE=bond0
    NAME=bond0
    TYPE=Bond
    BONDING_MASTER=yes
    BONDING_OPTS="mode=balance-rr"
    ONBOOT=yes
    BOOTPROTO=none
    IPADDR=192.168.1.110
    NETMASK=255.255.255.0
    GATEWAY=192.168.1.1
    IPV4_FAILURE_FATAL=no
    IPV6INIT=no

7. Use the *vi* editor to create *ifcfg-eth2* and *ifcfg-eth3* files in the */etc/sysconfig/network-scripts*
    directory for *eth2* and *eth3* interfaces with the following settings. Set the MASTER directive
    to *bond0*. Both interfaces will act as slaves with no IP addresses assigned to them.

# vi ifcfg-eth2
DEVICE=eth2
NAME=eth2
UUID=15d44a70-554d-49c6-9ea0-c1ba3200f797
TYPE=Ethernet
ONBOOT=yes
MASTER=bond0
SLAVE=yes
# vi ifcfg-eth3
DEVICE=eth3
NAME=eth3
UUID=2f9aec97-d5d1-4fe1-81b0-60e6080c0352
TYPE=Ethernet
ONBOOT=yes
MASTER=bond0
SLAVE=yes

8. Deactivate and reactivate *bond0* with the *ifdown* and *ifup* commands:

ifdown bond0 ; ifup bond0
Connection successfully activated (D-Bus active path:
/org/freedesktop/NetworkManager/ActiveConnection/3)

9. Check the status of *bond0* and the slaves with the *ip* command. It should also show the assigned IP.

ip addr
. . . .
4: eth2: <BROADCAST,MULTICAST,UP,LOWER_UP> mtu 1500 qdisc pfifo_fast state UP qlen 1000
   link/ether 52:54:00:0c:ec:ff brd ff:ff:ff:ff:ff:ff
5: eth3: <BROADCAST,MULTICAST,UP,LOWER_UP> mtu 1500 qdisc pfifo_fast state UP qlen 1000
   link/ether 52:54:00:28:91:f0 brd ff:ff:ff:ff:ff:ff
6: bond0: <NO-CARRIER,BROADCAST,MULTICAST,MASTER,UP> mtu 1500 qdisc noqueue state UP
   link/ether ba:73:ec:58:d5:c1 brd ff:ff:ff:ff:ff:ff
   inet **192.168.1.110**/24 brd 192.168.1.255 scope global bond0
     valid_lft forever preferred_lft forever

10. Restart the system to ensure the configuration survives system reboots:

reboot

11. Repeat step 9 to verify the bond and IP assignments.
12. Open the *hosts* file and append the following entry to it:

vi /etc/hosts
192.168.1.110   server1bond.example.org   server1bond

Using the nmcli Command to Configure Bonding and Teaming

The *nmcli* command is a NetworkManager service tool that allows you to add, show, alter, delete, start, and stop bonding and teaming interfaces, and control and report their status. This tool operates on network connections and devices in addition to a few other object types. For additional information, see Chapter 12 "Administering Network Interfaces and Network Clients".

Exercise 15-2: Configure Interface Bonding with NetworkManager CLI

This exercise is intended to be done on *server2*; however, the new interface allocation will be done on *host1*.

The allocation of a pair of virtual network interfaces to *server2* and the formation of a bonded channel with IP 192.168.1.120 was mentioned in Chapter 01 "Installing RHEL7 on Physical Computer Using Local DVD".

In this exercise, you will add two new interfaces on 192.168.1.0/24 network to *server2* and call them *eth2* and *eth3*. You will configure a bond and activate it using the NetworkManager commands. You will reboot the system to verify bond activation. You will assign hostname *server2bond.example.org* with alias *server2bond*. You will add IP and hostname mapping to the *hosts* table. Finally, you will run a *ping* test from *server2bond* to *server1bond* to confirm connectivity.

1. Open the virtual console for *server2* on *host1*. Click "Show virtual hardware details" | Add Hardware | Network. Select Source device "Virtual network 'rhnet_virt' : NAT" from the drop-down list and Device model virtio. We created this network in Chapter 06. Leave the MAC address to the default. Click Finish to complete the new interface assignment.
2. Repeat step 1 and add another interface.
3. Check the operational status of the NetworkManager service:

    # **systemctl status NetworkManager**
    NetworkManager.service - Network Manager
      Loaded: loaded (/usr/lib/systemd/system/NetworkManager.service; enabled)
      Active: active (running) since Sun 2014-12-14 00:13:36 EST; 3min 32s ago
    Main PID: 909 (NetworkManager)
      CGroup: /system.slice/NetworkManager.service
          └─909 /usr/sbin/NetworkManager --no-daemon
    . . . .

4. List all available network interfaces including the ones just added:

    # **nmcli dev status**

DEVICE	TYPE	STATE	CONNECTION
eth0	ethernet	connected	eth0
eth1	ethernet	connected	eth1
eth2	ethernet	disconnected	--
eth3	ethernet	disconnected	--
lo	loopback	unmanaged	--

    The output indicates the presence of two new interfaces by the name *eth2* and *eth3*.

---

5. Load the bonding driver in the kernel with the *modprobe* command if it is not already loaded, and verify with the *modinfo* command:

 # modprobe bonding
 # modinfo bonding
filename:	/lib/modules/3.10.0-123.el7.x86_64/kernel/drivers/net/bonding/bonding.ko
alias:	rtnl-link-bond
author:	Thomas Davis, tadavis@lbl.gov and many others
description:	Ethernet Channel Bonding Driver, v3.7.1
version:	3.7.1
license:	GPL
srcversion:	E52AE00A79EA6FEFB5BF718
depends:	
intree:	Y
vermagic:	3.10.0-123.el7.x86_64 SMP mod_unload modversions
signer:	Red Hat Enterprise Linux kernel signing key
sig_key:	00:AA:5F:56:C5:87:BD:82:F2:F9:9D:64:BA:83:DD:1E:9E:0D:33:4A
sig_hashalgo:	sha256
parm:	max_bonds:Max number of bonded devices (int)

. . . .

6. Add a logical interface called *bond0* of type bond with connection name bond0, load balancing policy round-robin, IP address 192.168.1.120/24, and gateway 192.168.1.1:

**# nmcli con add type bond con-name bond0 ifname bond0 mode balance-rr **
ip4 192.168.1.120/24 gw4 192.168.1.1
Connection 'bond0' (88b9e708-8dee-4fe8-8b8f-1c989a0bab4a) successfully added.

This command has added a bond device and created an *ifcfg-bond0* file in the */etc/sysconfig/network-scripts* directory with all necessary directives.

7. Show the contents of the *ifcfg-bond0* file:

 # cat /etc/sysconfig/network-scripts/ifcfg-bond0
DEVICE=bond0
BONDING_OPTS=mode=balance-rr
TYPE=Bond
BONDING_MASTER=yes
BOOTPROTO=none
IPADDR0=192.168.1.120
PREFIX0=24
GATEWAY0=192.168.1.1
DEFROUTE=yes
IPV4_FAILURE_FATAL=no
IPV6INIT=yes
IPV6_AUTOCONF=yes
IPV6_DEFROUTE=yes
IPV6_PEERDNS=yes
IPV6_PEERROUTES=yes

IPV6_FAILURE_FATAL=no
NAME=bond0
UUID=88b9e708-8dee-4fe8-8b8f-1c989a0bab4a
ONBOOT=yes

8. Add *eth2* and *eth3* interfaces as slaves to the master bond device *bond0*:

    # **nmcli con add type bond-slave ifname eth2 master bond0**
    Connection 'bond-slave-eth2' (210b1f1e-3e3b-42af-937b-c42088cabf7d) successfully added.
    # **nmcli con add type bond-slave ifname eth3 master bond0**
    Connection 'bond-slave-eth3' (d5c1c635-2971-43a7-b0ce-efe7c5dd44c7) successfully added.

    This command has added *eth2* and *eth3* interfaces as slaves to *bond0*, and has created *ifcfg-bond-slave-eth2* and *ifcfg-bond-slave-eth3* files in the */etc/sysconfig/network-scripts* directory with all necessary directives.

9. Show the contents of the *ifcfg-bond-slave-eth2* and *ifcfg-bond-slave-eth3* files:

    # **cat /etc/sysconfig/network-scripts/ifcfg-bond-slave-eth2**
    TYPE=Ethernet
    NAME=bond-slave-eth2
    UUID=210b1f1e-3e3b-42af-937b-c42088cabf7d
    DEVICE=eth2
    ONBOOT=yes
    MASTER=bond0
    SLAVE=yes
    # **cat /etc/sysconfig/network-scripts/ifcfg-bond-slave-eth3**
    TYPE=Ethernet
    NAME=bond-slave-eth3
    UUID=d5c1c635-2971-43a7-b0ce-efe7c5dd44c7
    DEVICE=eth3
    ONBOOT=yes
    MASTER=bond0
    SLAVE=yes

10. Activate *bond0*. By default, the slave devices are already up and operational. If not, you will have to activate them prior to starting the bond.

    # **nmcli con up bond0**
    Connection successfully activated (D-Bus active path:
    /org/freedesktop/NetworkManager/ActiveConnection/5)

11. Check the new connection and IP assignments:

    # **ip addr | grep bond0**
    4: eth2: <BROADCAST,MULTICAST,SLAVE,UP,LOWER_UP> mtu 1500 qdisc pfifo_fast master
    bond0 state UP qlen 1000
    5: eth3: <BROADCAST,MULTICAST,SLAVE,UP,LOWER_UP> mtu 1500 qdisc pfifo_fast master
    bond0 state UP qlen 1000

6: bond0: <BROADCAST,MULTICAST,MASTER,UP,LOWER_UP> mtu 1500 qdisc noqueue state UP

    inet **192.168.1.120**/24 brd 192.168.1.255 scope global bond0

The output confirms the IP address assignment to the bond and the operational status of the interface devices.

12. Show the connection information for the bond and slaves:

    # **nmcli con show | egrep 'bond0|eth2|eth3'**
    bond0   88b9e708-8dee-4fe8-8b8f-1c989a0bab4a   bond   bond0
    bond-slave-eth3   d5c1c635-2971-43a7-b0ce-efe7c5dd44c7   802-3-ethernet   eth3
    bond-slave-eth2   210b1f1e-3e3b-42af-937b-c42088cabf7d   802-3-ethernet   eth2

13. Restart the system to confirm that the configuration remains persistent across reboots:

    # **reboot**

14. Run steps 11 and 12 again to verify the bond and IP assignments.
15. Open the *hosts* file and append entries for both *server1bond* and *server2bond* to it:

    # **vi /etc/hosts**
    192.168.1.110   server1bond.example.org   server1bond
    192.168.1.120   server2bond.example.org   server2bond

16. Copy this *hosts* file to *server1* so that both systems have the same entries:

    # **scp /etc/hosts server1:/etc**

17. Test network connectivity by transmitting ping traffic (use –c 3 to send three packets) from *server2bond* to *server1bond*:

    # **ping –c 3 server1bond**
    PING server1bond.example.com (192.168.1.110) 56(84) bytes of data.
    64 bytes from server1bond.example.com (192.168.1.110): icmp_seq=1 ttl=64 time=0.235 ms
    64 bytes from server1bond.example.com (192.168.1.110): icmp_seq=2 ttl=64 time=0.247 ms
    64 bytes from server1bond.example.com (192.168.1.110): icmp_seq=3 ttl=64 time=0.306 ms
    --- server1bond.example.com ping statistics ---
    3 packets transmitted, 3 received, 0% packet loss, time 2000ms
    rtt min/avg/max/mdev = 0.235/0.262/0.306/0.036 ms

Interface Teaming

Interface teaming is introduced in RHEL7 as an additional choice to implement enhance throughput and fault tolerance at the network interface level. While bonding is still supported in RHEL7, it is not in conflict with teaming in any way. There are certain differences between the two though. Bonding has been in RHEL for a long period, and it is matured and robust. Teaming, in comparison, is a new implementation. Teaming handles the flow of network packets faster than bonding does. And unlike bonding, which is accomplished purely in the kernel space and provides no user control over its operation, teaming only requires the integration of the essential code into the kernel and the rest is implemented via the *teamd* daemon, which gives users the ability to control it with the *teamdctl* command.

EXAM TIP: Teaming is preferred over bonding as a method of establishing link aggregation.

Like bonding, teaming can be configured by either editing the files directly or using the NetworkManager CLI, TUI, or GNOME Network Connection GUI.

Exercise 15-3: Configure Interface Teaming by Editing Files

This exercise should be done on *server1*. However, the new interface allocation will be done on *host1*.

The allocation of a pair of virtual network interfaces to *server1* and the formation of a teamed channel with IP 192.168.2.110 was mentioned in Chapter 01 "Installing RHEL7 on Physical Computer Using Local DVD".

In this exercise, you will add two new interfaces on 192.168.2.0/24 network to *server1*, and will call them *eth4* and *eth5*. You will generate UUIDs for the new interfaces. You will form a team of the two interfaces by creating configuration files and executing appropriate commands to activate and confirm it. You will reboot the system to verify team activation. You will assign the hostname *server1team.example.net* with alias *server1team*. You will add IP and hostname mapping to the *hosts* table.

1. Open the virtual console for *server1* on *host1*. Click "Show virtual hardware details" | Add Hardware | Network. Select Source device "Virtual network 'rhnet_virsh' : NAT" from the drop-down list and Device model virtio. We created this network in Chapter 06. Leave the MAC address to the default. Click Finish to complete the new interface assignment.
2. Repeat step 1 and add another interface.
3. Log on to *server1* and run the *ip* command to check the new interfaces:

   # **ip addr**
   . . . .
   6: eth4: <BROADCAST,MULTICAST,UP,LOWER_UP> mtu 1500 qdisc pfifo_fast state UP qlen 1000
       link/ether 52:54:00:47:30:d7 brd ff:ff:ff:ff:ff:ff
   7: eth5: <BROADCAST,MULTICAST,UP,LOWER_UP> mtu 1500 qdisc pfifo_fast state UP qlen 1000
       link/ether 52:54:00:47:30:d7 brd ff:ff:ff:ff:ff:ff

   The output indicates the presence of two new interfaces by the name *eth4* and *eth5*.

4. Install the team software:

   # **yum –y install teamd**

5. Load the team driver in the kernel with the *modprobe* command if it is not already loaded, and verify with the *modinfo* command:

   # **modprobe team**

```
# modinfo team
filename:        /lib/modules/3.10.0-123.el7.x86_64/kernel/drivers/net/team/team.ko
alias:           rtnl-link-team
description:     Ethernet team device driver
author:          Jiri Pirko <jpirko@redhat.com>
license:         GPL v2
srcversion:      39F7B52A85A880B5099D411
depends:
intree:          Y
vermagic:        3.10.0-123.el7.x86_64 SMP mod_unload modversions
signer:          Red Hat Enterprise Linux kernel signing key
sig_key:         00:AA:5F:56:C5:87:BD:82:F2:F9:9D:64:BA:83:DD:1E:9E:0D:33:4A
sig_hashalgo:    sha256
```

6. Generate UUIDs for both new interfaces and a logical team device called *team0* using the *uuidgen* command:

```
# uuidgen eth4
bc85731f-8f4e-4ccd-9af7-deb0da7d37e7
# uuidgen eth5
f2823a4f-8933-408d-8969-ec20c0ee4b91
```

7. Use the *vi* editor and create a file called *ifcfg-team0* in the */etc/sysconfig/network-scripts* directory for *team0* with the following settings. Use the interface type Team. This virtual device will serve as the teaming master with round-robin as the load balancing technique. The rest of the settings are self-explanatory.

```
# cd /etc/sysconfig/network-scripts
# vi ifcfg-team0
DEVICE=team0
NAME=team0
DEVICETYPE=Team
TEAM_CONFIG='{"runner": {"name": "activebackup"}, "link_watch": {"name":"ethtool"}}'
ONBOOT=yes
PREFIX=24
BOOTPROTO=none
IPADDR0=192.168.2.110
NETMASK0=255.255.255.0
GATEWAY0=192.168.2.1
```

8. Use the *vi* editor and create *ifcfg-eth4* and *ifcfg-eth5* files in the */etc/sysconfig/network-scripts* directory for *eth4* and *eth5* interfaces with the following settings. Use the UUIDs generated in step 5 for the interfaces and set the TEAM_MASTER directive to *team0*. Both interfaces will act as slaves with no IP addresses assigned to them.

```
# vi ifcfg-eth4
DEVICE=eth4
NAME=eth4
UUID=bc85731f-8f4e-4ccd-9af7-deb0da7d37e7
DEVICETYPE=TeamPort
ONBOOT=yes
TEAM_MASTER=team0
TEAM_PORT_CONFIG='{"prio": 9}'
# vi ifcfg-eth5
DEVICE=eth5
NAME=eth5
UUID=f2823a4f-8933-408d-8969-ec20c0ee4b91
DEVICETYPE=TeamPort
ONBOOT=yes
TEAM_MASTER=team0
TEAM_PORT_CONFIG='{"prio": 10}'
```

9. Activate *team0* with the *ifup* command:

    ```
    # ifup team0
    Connection successfully activated (D-Bus active path:
    /org/freedesktop/NetworkManager/ActiveConnection/10)
    ```

10. Check the status of *team0* and the slaves with the *ip* command. It should also show the assigned IP.

    ```
    # ip addr
    . . . . . . . .
    6: eth4: <BROADCAST,MULTICAST,UP,LOWER_UP> mtu 1500 qdisc pfifo_fast master team0
    state UP qlen 1000
        link/ether 52:54:00:47:30:d7 brd ff:ff:ff:ff:ff:ff
    7: eth5: <BROADCAST,MULTICAST,UP,LOWER_UP> mtu 1500 qdisc pfifo_fast master team0
    state UP qlen 1000
        link/ether 52:54:00:47:30:d7 brd ff:ff:ff:ff:ff:ff
    11: team0: <BROADCAST,MULTICAST,UP,LOWER_UP> mtu 1500 qdisc noqueue state UP
        link/ether 52:54:00:47:30:d7 brd ff:ff:ff:ff:ff:ff
        inet 192.168.2.110/24 brd 192.168.2.255 scope global team0
         valid_lft forever preferred_lft forever
    ```

11. Get the details of the team devices:

    ```
    # teamnl team0 ports
    7: eth5: up 0Mbit HD
     6: eth4: up 0Mbit HD
    ```

12. Check the status of the team and the included interfaces:

---

teamdctl team0 state
```
setup:
  runner: activebackup
ports:
  eth5
    link watches:
      link summary: up
      instance[link_watch_0]:
        name: ethtool
        link: up
  eth4
    link watches:
      link summary: up
      instance[link_watch_0]:
        name: ethtool
        link: up
```

13. Restart the system to ensure the configuration survives system reboots:

    # reboot

14. Repeat steps 10 and 11 to verify the team, interfaces, and IP assignments.
15. Open the *hosts* file and append the following entry to it:

    # vi /etc/hosts
    192.168.2.110   server1team.example.net   server1team

Exercise 15-4: Configure Interface Teaming with NetworkManager CLI

This exercise presents an alternative way for configuring a teamed channel. This exercise is intended to be done on *server2*; however, the new interface allocation will be done on *host1*.

The allocation of a pair of virtual network interfaces to *server2* and the formation of a teamed channel with IP 192.168.2.120 was mentioned in Chapter 01 "Installing RHEL7 on Physical Computer Using Local DVD".

In this exercise, you will add two new interfaces on 192.168.2.0/24 network to *server2* and call them *eth4* and *eth5*. You will configure a team using NetworkManager CLI. You will reboot the system to verify team activation. You will assign the hostname *server2team.example.net* with alias *server2team*. You will add IP and hostname mapping to the *hosts* table. Finally, you will run a *ping* test from *server2team* to *server1team* to confirm connectivity.

1. Open the virtual console for *server1* on *host1*. Click "Show virtual hardware details" | Add Hardware | Network. Select Source device "Virtual network 'rhnet_virsh' : NAT" from the drop-down list and Device model virtio. We created this network in Chapter 06. Leave the MAC address to the default. Click Finish to complete the new interface assignment.
2. Repeat step 1 and add another interface.
3. Check the operational status of the NetworkManager service:

```
# systemctl status NetworkManager
NetworkManager.service - Network Manager
   Loaded: loaded (/usr/lib/systemd/system/NetworkManager.service; enabled)
   Active: active (running) since Mon 2014-12-15 09:28:56 EST; 3min 58s ago
 Main PID: 917 (NetworkManager)
   CGroup: /system.slice/NetworkManager.service
           └─ 917 /usr/sbin/NetworkManager --no-daemon
. . . . . . . .
```

4. List all available network interfaces including the ones just added:

```
# nmcli dev status
DEVICE      TYPE        STATE          CONNECTION
bond0       bond        connected      bond0
eth0        ethernet    connected      eth0
eth1        ethernet    connected      eth1
eth2        ethernet    connected      bond-slave-eth2
eth3        ethernet    connected      bond-slave-eth3
eth4        ethernet    disconnected   --
eth5        ethernet    disconnected   --
lo          loopback    unmanaged      --
```

The output indicates the presence of two new interfaces by the name *eth4* and *eth5*.

5. Load the team driver in the kernel with the *modprobe* command if it is not already loaded, and verify with the *modinfo* command:

```
# modprobe team
# modinfo team
filename:       /lib/modules/3.10.0-123.el7.x86_64/kernel/drivers/net/team/team.ko
alias:          rtnl-link-team
description:    Ethernet team device driver
author:         Jiri Pirko <jpirko@redhat.com>
license:        GPL v2
srcversion:     39F7B52A85A880B5099D411
depends:
intree:         Y
vermagic:       3.10.0-123.el7.x86_64 SMP mod_unload modversions
signer:         Red Hat Enterprise Linux kernel signing key
sig_key:        00:AA:5F:56:C5:87:BD:82:F2:F9:9D:64:BA:83:DD:1E:9E:0D:33:4A
sig_hashalgo:   sha256
. . . . . . . .
```

6. Add a logical interface called *team0* of type team with connection name team0, IP address 192.168.2.120/24, and gateway 192.168.2.1:

```
# nmcli con add type team con-name team0 ifname team0 ip4 192.168.2.120/24 \
gw4 192.168.2.1
Connection 'team0' (9d3e2053-e83f-49fb-98fb-1ec0ac57c260) successfully added.
```

This command has added a bond device and created *ifcfg-team0* file in the */etc/sysconfig/network-scripts* directory with all necessary directives.

7. Show the contents of the *ifcfg-team0* file:

> # **cat /etc/sysconfig/network-scripts/ifcfg-team0**
> DEVICE=team0
> DEVICETYPE=Team
> BOOTPROTO=none
> IPADDR0=192.168.2.120
> PREFIX0=32
> GATEWAY0=192.168.2.1
> DEFROUTE=yes
> IPV4_FAILURE_FATAL=no
> IPV6INIT=yes
> IPV6_AUTOCONF=yes
> IPV6_DEFROUTE=yes
> IPV6_PEERDNS=yes
> IPV6_PEERROUTES=yes
> IPV6_FAILURE_FATAL=no
> NAME=team0
> UUID=9d3e2053-e83f-49fb-98fb-1ec0ac57c260
> ONBOOT=yes

8. Add *eth4* and *eth5* interfaces as slaves to the team:

> # **nmcli con add type team-slave con-name eth4 ifname eth4 master team0**
> Connection 'eth4' (22c69e0e-e185-464d-b1c0-784119490fd1) successfully added.
> # **nmcli con add type team-slave con-name eth5 ifname eth5 master team0**
> Connection 'eth5' (30557806-c821-4002-87d2-03df6483f675) successfully added.

This command has added *eth4* and *eth5* interfaces as slaves to *team0*, and has created *ifcfg-eth4* and *ifcfg-eth5* files in the */etc/sysconfig/network-scripts* directory with all necessary directives.

9. Show the contents of the *ifcfg-eth4* and *ifcfg-eth5* files:

> # **cat /etc/sysconfig/network-scripts/ifcfg-eth4**
> BOOTPROTO=dhcp
> DEFROUTE=yes
> PEERDNS=yes
> PEERROUTES=yes
> IPV4_FAILURE_FATAL=no
> IPV6INIT=yes
> IPV6_AUTOCONF=yes
> IPV6_DEFROUTE=yes
> IPV6_PEERDNS=yes
> IPV6_PEERROUTES=yes
> IPV6_FAILURE_FATAL=no
> NAME=eth4
> UUID=22c69e0e-e185-464d-b1c0-784119490fd1

```
DEVICE=eth4
ONBOOT=yes
TEAM_MASTER=team0
DEVICETYPE=TeamPort
```
cat /etc/sysconfig/network-scripts/ifcfg-eth5
```
BOOTPROTO=dhcp
DEFROUTE=yes
PEERDNS=yes
PEERROUTES=yes
IPV4_FAILURE_FATAL=no
IPV6INIT=yes
IPV6_AUTOCONF=yes
IPV6_DEFROUTE=yes
IPV6_PEERDNS=yes
IPV6_PEERROUTES=yes
IPV6_FAILURE_FATAL=no
NAME=eth5
UUID=30557806-c821-4002-87d2-03df6483f675
DEVICE=eth5
ONBOOT=yes
TEAM_MASTER=team0
DEVICETYPE=TeamPort
```

10. Activate *team0*:

    # **nmcli con up team0**
    Connection successfully activated (D-Bus active path:
    /org/freedesktop/NetworkManager/ActiveConnection/8)

11. Check the new connection and IP assignments:

    # **ip addr | grep team0**
    6: eth4: <BROADCAST,MULTICAST,UP,LOWER_UP> mtu 1500 qdisc pfifo_fast master team0
      state UP qlen 1000
    7: eth5: <BROADCAST,MULTICAST,UP,LOWER_UP> mtu 1500 qdisc pfifo_fast master team0
      state UP qlen 1000
    12: team0: <BROADCAST,MULTICAST,UP,LOWER_UP> mtu 1500 qdisc noqueue state UP
      inet **192.168.2.120**/24 brd 192.168.2.255 scope global team0

  The output indicates the IP assigned to the team interface with all the interface devices up.

12. Show the connection information for the team and slaves:

    # **nmcli con show | egrep 'team0|eth4|eth5'**

NAME	UUID	TYPE	DEVICE
Team team0	702de3eb-2e80-897c-fd52-cd0494dd8123	team	team0
eth5	d9ced338-a402-60eb-c131-0fd3ab4b5ab7	802-3-ethernet	eth5
eth4	ec71fbbd-fc4d-4d04-b8de-dfe6afa31635	802-3-ethernet	eth4

13. Get the details of the team devices:

teamnl team0 ports
7: eth5: up 0Mbit HD
6: eth4: up 0Mbit HD

14. Check the status of the team and the included interfaces:

teamdctl team0 state
setup:
  runner: activebackup
ports:
  eth4
    link watches:
      link summary: up
      instance[link_watch_0]:
        name: ethtool
        link: up
  eth5
    link watches:
      link summary: up
      instance[link_watch_0]:
        name: ethtool
        link: up
  runner:
    active port: eth5

15. Restart the system to confirm configuration persistence across reboots:

reboot

16. Run steps 11 to 14 again to verify the team and IP assignments.
17. Open the *hosts* file and append the following entries to it:

vi /etc/hosts
192.168.2.110   server1team.example.net   server1team
192.168.2.120   server2team.example.net   server2team

18. Copy this hosts file to *server2* so that there are the same entries on both servers:

scp /etc/hosts server2:/etc

19. Once the setup is complete, issue the *ping* command (with –c option to send three packets) to test connectivity with *server1team*:

ping –c 3 server1team
PING server1team.example.com (192.168.2.110) 56(84) bytes of data.
64 bytes from server1team.example.com (192.168.2.110): icmp_seq=1 ttl=64 time=0.254 ms
64 bytes from server1team.example.com (192.168.2.110): icmp_seq=2 ttl=64 time=0.408 ms
64 bytes from server1team.example.com (192.168.2.110): icmp_seq=3 ttl=64 time=0.411 ms
--- server1team.example.com ping statistics ---

3 packets transmitted, 3 received, 0% packet loss, time 1999ms
rtt min/avg/max/mdev = 0.254/0.357/0.411/0.076 ms

Graphical Network Administration Tools for Configuring Bonding and Teaming

RHEL7 offers Network Settings and Network Connections tools for graphical management of network interfaces including the administration of bonding and teaming. The Network Settings (or Control Network) is located in the Control Center and it may be accessed by clicking the network icon at the top right-hand corner in the GNOME desktop or by clicking Applications | System Tools | Settings | Network. Figure 15-1 shows the window that appears when this tool is invoked on *server1*.

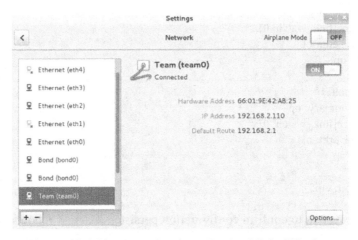

Figure 15-1 Network Settings Tool – Main Window

The Network Connections tool can be invoked by running the *nm-connection-editor* command in an X terminal window or by choosing Application | Sundry | Network Connections. Figure 15-2 shows the window that appears when this tool is brought up on *server1*.

Figure 15-2 Network Connections Tool – Main Window

Both tools allow us to create new bonding and teaming connections, as well as modify the existing ones in addition to other interface management functions. To create a new connection, simply click the + sign in the bottom left corner on the Network Settings tool or the Add button in the Network Connections tool and select the type of connection to create. Once this is completed, both tools provide a common interface for configuration. Figure 15-3 shows the window that appears when "team" is selected as a connection type. It will be very similar for the bond connection type.

Figure 15-3 Add a Teaming Channel

We can assign a name of our choice to the connection in the space provided at the top. The four tabs—General, Team/Bond, IPv4 Settings, IPv6 Settings—allow us to configure a new channel. The tab Team (or Bond) lets us enter type-specific data; the rest of the tabs are associated with IP assignments, DNS, routing, and other general configuration items.

We can also use these tools to modify the settings of an existing team/bond connection. This can be done by highlighting a configured team/bond interface and then clicking Options (Network Settings) or Edit (Network Connections) on the main window of either tool.

IPv6

With the explosive growth of the Internet, the presence of an extremely large number of systems requiring an IP, and an ever-increasing demand for additional addresses, the conventional IPv4 address space, which provides approximately 4.3 billion addresses, has almost been exhausted. To meet the future demand, a new version of IP is now available and its use is on the rise. This new version is referred to as *IPv6* (IP version 6). By default, IPv6 is enabled in RHEL7 for all configured standalone and logical interfaces, unless it is disabled manually.

IPv6 is a 128-bit software address providing access to 2^{128} addresses, which is approximately 340 undecillion (340 followed by 36 zeros) addresses. This is an extremely large space, and it is expected to fulfill the IP requirements for several decades to come.

Unlike IPv4 addresses, which are represented as four dot-separated octets, IPv6 addresses contain eight colon-separated groups of four hexadecimal numbers. A sample v6 IP would be 1204:bab1:21d1:bb43:23a1:9bde:87df:bac9. It looks a bit daunting at first sight; however, methods to simplify their representation do exist.

Below, the *ip addr* command output from *server1* shows IPv6 addresses for configured interfaces:

ip addr | grep inet6
    inet6 ::1/128 scope host
    inet6 fe80::5054:ff:fe17:918d/64 scope link
    inet6 fe80::5054:ff:fe39:169a/64 scope link
    inet6 fe80::5054:ff:fe47:30d7/64 scope link
    inet6 fe80::5054:ff:fe6d:d236/64 scope link

It shows five IPv6 addresses. The first one belongs to the loopback interface, and the following IPv6 addresses are assigned to *eth0, eth1, team0,* and *bond0* interfaces, respectively.

Managing IPv6

IPv6 can be assigned to interfaces using any of the network management tools available to us. The *ip* command, the NetworkManager tools, the Network Settings tool, and the Network Connections tool all have the ability to configure interfaces with IPv6 assignments. Entries added with the *ip* command do not survive system reboots; however, those added with the other mentioned tools stay persistent, as they are stored in interface configuration files in the */etc/sysconfig/network-scripts* directory. Alternatively, we can directly add or modify entries in these files as required. The next exercise will demonstrate how to add IPv6 addresses manually by directly editing interface configuration files.

EXAM TIP: Both IPv4 and IPv6 addresses can be assigned to a single network interface port and they should work without any conflicts.

For using the GUI tools for IPv6 assignments, refer to Figure 15-3 (tab IPv6 Settings) in the previous section. For using the NetworkManager CLI for this purpose, refer to Chapter 12 "Administering Network Interfaces and Network Clients".

Exercise 15-5: Configure and Test IPv6 Addresses

This exercise should be done on *server1* and *server2*.

In Chapter 12, "Administering Network Interfaces and Network Clients", we configured *eth1* interface on both *server1* and *server2* with IPv4 addresses 192.168.0.111 and 192.168.0.121, respectively. In this exercise, you will edit their interface configuration files on both systems and assign static IPv6 addresses. You will assign them hostnames *server1ipv6.example.com* and *server2ipv6.example.com* with aliases *server1ipv6* and *server2ipv6*, respectively. You will add IPv6 and hostname mapping to the *hosts* table. You will reboot the systems to verify configuration persistence. Finally, you will run a *ping* test from *server1ipv4* to *server2ipv4* and another from *server2ipv6* to *server1ipv6* to confirm IPv4 and IPv6 connectivity. You will also attempt to *ssh* into *server2ipv6* from *server1ipv6*.

   1.   Log on to *server1* and *server2* in separate windows and run the following command to determine IPv6 status:

[server1]# **ip addr show eth1**
3: eth1: <BROADCAST,MULTICAST,UP,LOWER_UP> mtu 1500 qdisc pfifo_fast state UP qlen 1000
    link/ether 52:54:00:39:16:9a brd ff:ff:ff:ff:ff:ff
    inet **192.168.0.111**/24 brd 192.168.0.255 scope global eth1
      valid_lft forever preferred_lft forever
    inet6 **fe80::5054:ff:fe39:169a**/64 scope link
      valid_lft forever preferred_lft forever
[server2]# **ip addr show eth1**
3: eth1: <BROADCAST,MULTICAST,UP,LOWER_UP> mtu 1500 qdisc pfifo_fast state UP qlen 1000
    link/ether 52:54:00:96:13:58 brd ff:ff:ff:ff:ff:ff
    inet **192.168.0.121**/24 brd 192.168.0.255 scope global eth1
      valid_lft forever preferred_lft forever
    inet6 **fe80::5054:ff:fe96:1358**/64 scope link
      valid_lft forever preferred_lft forever

The output indicates the assignment of static IPv4 addresses and DHCP-generated IPv6 addresses.

2. Open the interface configuration file *ifcfg-eth1* in the */etc/sysconfig/network-scripts* directory on both servers and ensure they contain the following lines:

[server1]
IPV6INIT=yes
IPV6ADDR=2602:306:cc2d:f591::A/64
IPV6_DEFAULTGW=2602:306:cc2d:f591::1
[server2]
IPV6INIT=yes
IPV6ADDR=2602:306:cc2d:f591::B/64
IPV6_DEFAULTGW=2602:306:cc2d:f591::1

The IPV6INIT directive enables the IPv6 support for the (*eth1*) interface and the IPV6ADDR and IPV6_DEFAULTGW directives set the specified IPv6 address and default gateway.

3. Open the *hosts* table on both servers and append the following:

2602:306:cc2d:f591::A server1ipv6.example.com server1ipv6
2602:306:cc2d:f591::B server2ipv6.example.com server2ipv6

4. Deactivate and reactivate *eth1* interface on both servers so that the new IPv6 assignments take effect along with the existing IPv4 addresses:

[server1]# **ifdown eth1 ; ifup eth1**
Connection successfully activated (D-Bus active path:
/org/freedesktop/NetworkManager/ActiveConnection/12)
[server2]# **ifdown eth1 ; ifup eth1**
Connection successfully activated (D-Bus active path:
/org/freedesktop/NetworkManager/ActiveConnection/12)

5. Reboot both systems:

   # **reboot**

6. Check that IPv4 and IPv6 assignments are there on both servers:

   [server1]# **ip addr show eth1**
   3: eth1: <BROADCAST,MULTICAST,UP,LOWER_UP> mtu 1500 qdisc pfifo_fast state UP qlen 1000
       link/ether 52:54:00:39:16:9a brd ff:ff:ff:ff:ff:ff
       inet **192.168.0.111**/24 brd 192.168.0.255 scope global eth1
         valid_lft forever preferred_lft forever
       inet6 **2602:306:cc2d:f591::a**/64 scope global
         valid_lft forever preferred_lft forever
       inet6 fe80::5054:ff:fe39:169a/64 scope link
         valid_lft forever preferred_lft forever
   [server2]# **ip addr show eth1**
   3: eth1: <BROADCAST,MULTICAST,UP,LOWER_UP> mtu 1500 qdisc pfifo_fast state UP qlen 1000
       link/ether 52:54:00:96:13:58 brd ff:ff:ff:ff:ff:ff
       inet **192.168.0.121**/24 brd 192.168.0.255 scope global eth1
         valid_lft forever preferred_lft forever
       inet6 **2602:306:cc2d:f591::b**/64 scope global
         valid_lft forever preferred_lft forever
       inet6 fe80::5054:ff:fe96:1358/64 scope link
         valid_lft forever preferred_lft forever

7. Perform two connectivity tests—one for IPv4 from *server1ipv4* to *server2ipv4* and the second for IPv6 from *server1ipv6* to *server2ipv6*:

   [server1]# **ping –c 2 server2ipv4**
   PING server2ipv4.example.com (192.168.0.121) 56(84) bytes of data.
   64 bytes from server2ipv4.example.com (192.168.0.121): icmp_seq=1 ttl=64 time=0.402 ms
   64 bytes from server2ipv4.example.com (192.168.0.121): icmp_seq=2 ttl=64 time=0.394 ms
   --- server2ipv4.example.com ping statistics ---
   2 packets transmitted, 2 received, 0% packet loss, time 1000ms
   rtt min/avg/max/mdev = 0.394/0.398/0.402/0.004 ms
   [server1]# **ping6 –c 2 server2ipv6**
   PING server2ipv6(server2ipv6.example.com) 56 data bytes
   64 bytes from server2ipv6.example.com: icmp_seq=1 ttl=64 time=0.084 ms
   64 bytes from server2ipv6.example.com: icmp_seq=2 ttl=64 time=0.072 ms
   --- server2ipv6 ping statistics ---
   2 packets transmitted, 2 received, 0% packet loss, time 1000ms
   rtt min/avg/max/mdev = 0.072/0.078/0.084/0.006 ms

   The above tests show that the two servers have both IPv4 as well as IPv6 assignments configured on one of their Ethernet interfaces, and that both are functioning without any issues.

8. Test *ssh* access from *server2ipv6* to *server1ipv6*:

```
[server1]# ssh server1ipv6
The authenticity of host 'server1ipv6 (2602:306:cc2d:f591::a)' can't be established.
ECDSA key fingerprint is 9b:c6:eb:6e:46:ee:17:4d:71:3d:0f:93:1c:19:a8:5b.
Are you sure you want to continue connecting (yes/no)? yes
Warning: Permanently added 'server1ipv6,2602:306:cc2d:f591::a' (ECDSA) to the list of known
hosts.
root@server1ipv6's password:
Last login: Tue Dec 16 14:53:14 2014 from 192.168.0.13
[root@server1 ~]#
```

Both successful testings validate the IPv4 and IPv6 assignments.

Though the use of IPv6 is growing fast and its support is available in RHEL7 by default, our focus will still be on IPv4 in this book. We will continue to use the term IP to represent IPv4 protocol, unless stated otherwise.

Routing

Routing is the process of choosing paths on the network along which to send network traffic. This process is implemented with the deployment of specialized and sophisticated hardware devices called *routers*. Routers are widely used on the Internet and in corporate networks for this purpose. A RHEL system may also be configured to route traffic to other networks; however, that capability will be not as sophisticated.

When systems on two distinct networks communicate with each other, proper routes must be in place for them to be able to talk. For instance, if a system on network A sends a data packet to a system on network B, one or more routing devices is involved to route the packet to the correct destination network. The two networks can be located in a close proximity or across continents. Once the data packet reaches a router, the router selects the next router along the path toward the destination node. The packet passes from one router to another until it reaches the router that is able to deliver the packet directly to the destination system. Each router along the path is referred to as a *hop*. Most advanced routers have the ability to construct their routing tables automatically and intelligently to bypass network failures and congestions. There are many protocols used for routing purposes. However, the *Routing Information Protocol* (RIP) and the *Open Shortest Path First* (OSPF) are more common and widely employed.

One of three rules is applied in the routing mechanism to determine the correct route:

- ✓ If the source and destination systems are on the same network, the packet is sent directly to the destination system.
- ✓ If the source and destination systems are on two different networks, all defined (static or dynamic) routes are tried one after the other. If a proper route is determined, the packet is forwarded to it, which then forwards the packet to the correct destination.
- ✓ If the source and destination systems are on two different networks but no routes are defined between them, the packet is forwarded to the *default router* (or the *default gateway*), which attempts to search for an appropriate route to the destination. If found, the packet is delivered to the destination system.

Routing Table

A *routing table* preserves information about available routes and their status. It may be built and updated dynamically or manually by adding or removing routes. The *ip* command can be used to view entries in the routing table on our RHEL7 system:

```
# ip route
default via 192.168.0.1 dev eth0  proto static  metric 1024
192.168.0.0/24 dev eth0     proto kernel  scope link  src 192.168.0.110
192.168.0.0/24 dev eth1     proto kernel  scope link  src 192.168.0.111
192.168.1.0/24 dev bond0 proto kernel  scope link  src 192.168.1.110
192.168.2.0/24 dev team0 proto kernel  scope link  src 192.168.2.110
```

The output is organized in multiple columns that are explained in Table 15-2:

Column	Description
Network destination	Displays the address and netmask of the destination network. The keyword default identifies the IP address of the default gateway for sending out traffic to other networks in the absence of a proper route.
dev	Name of the physical or virtual network interface to be used to send out traffic.
proto	Identifies the routing protocol as defined in the /etc/iproute2/rt_protos file. The proto kernel implies that the route was installed by the kernel during auto-configuration. The proto static means that the route was installed by you to override dynamic routing.
scope	Determines the scope of the destination as defined in the /etc/iproute2/rt_scopes file. Values may be global, nowhere, host, or link.
src	Shows the source address associated with the interface for sending data out to the destination.
metric	Displays the cost of using a route, which is usually the number of hops to the destination system. Systems on the local network are one hop, and each subsequent router thereafter is an additional hop.

Table 15-2 Routing Table

Some other commands, such as *route*, will display additional columns of information that include flags, references, use, and iface. Common flag values are U (route is up), H (destination is a host), G (route is a gateway); references are not used in Linux; use indicates the count of lookups for the route; and iface shows the network interface to be used for sending data packets out.

Managing Routes

Managing routes involves adding, modifying, or deleting routes, and setting the default route. The *ip* command, the NetworkManager TUI and CLI tools, the Network Settings GUI, or the Network Connections GUI can be used for route administration. Entries added with the *ip* command do not survive system reboots; however, those added with the other mentioned tools stay persistent, as they are saved in interface specific *route-** files (*route-eth1, route-bond0, route-team0*, and so on) in the */etc/sysconfig/network-scripts* directory. Alternatively, we can directly create or modify these files as desired. The next exercise will demonstrate how to add static routes manually with the *ip* command first and then add the entries to appropriate route configuration files for persistence. The GUI tools have the Routes option available when IPv4 or IPv6 Settings is selected as illustrated in Figure 15-3 earlier in this chapter.

Exercise 15-6: Add Static Routes Manually

This exercise should be done on *server1*.

In this exercise, you will temporarily add a static route to network 192.168.3.0/24 via *eth1* with gateway 192.168.0.1 and another one to network 192.168.4.0/24 via *team0* with gateway 192.168.2.1 using the *ip* command. You will reboot the system and check for their availability. You will permanently re-add the routes by creating files in the */etc/sysconfig/network-scripts* directory and adding entries. You will reboot the system to confirm their persistence. Finally, you will delete both routes.

1. Add a static route to 192.168.3.0/24 via *eth1* with gateway 192.168.0.1:

    # **ip route add 192.168.3.0/24 via 192.168.0.1 dev eth1**

2. Add a static route to 192.168.4.0/24 via *team0* with gateway 192.168.2.1:

    # **ip route add 192.168.4.0/24 via 192.168.2.1 dev team0**

3. Show the routing table to validate the addition of the new routes:

    # **ip route**
    . . . .
    192.168.3.0/24 via 192.168.0.1 dev eth1
    192.168.4.0/24 via 192.168.2.1 dev team0

4. Reboot the system and run *ip route* again to confirm the removal of the new routes.
5. Create files *route-eth1* and *route-team0* in */etc/sysconfig/network-scripts* and insert the following entries:

    # **cd /etc/sysconfig/network-scripts**
    # **vi route-eth1**
    ADDRESS0=192.168.3.0
    NETMASK0=255.255.255.0
    GATEWAY0=192.168.0.1
    # **vi route-team0**
    ADDRESS0=192.168.4.0
    NETMASK0=255.255.255.0
    GATEWAY0=192.168.2.1

6. Restart *eth1* and *team0* interfaces for the routes to take effect:

    # **ifdown eth1   ; ifup eth1**
    # **ifdown team0 ; ifup team0**

7. Run the *ip route* command again to validate the presence of the new routes.

8. Delete both routes by removing their entries from the routing table and deleting the route configuration files:

   # **ip route del 192.168.3.0/24**
   # **ip route del 192.168.4.0/24**
   # **rm –f route-eth1 route-team0**

9. Confirm the deletion:

   # **ip route**

You should not see the routes.

Chapter Summary

This chapter began with an overview of the concept of link aggregation, and continued with presenting its benefits and various implementation methods. We looked at interface bonding and teaming, and performed several exercises to demonstrate how to set them up by hand-editing configuration files and using the NetworkManager CLI. We also provided an overview of the graphical network management tools for configuring bonding and teaming. We tested the connections between the two RHEL7 servers to validate their functionality.

We then looked at Internet Protocol version 6, the use of which is on the rise. We reviewed the basics of IPv6 and configured it on both servers. This configuration was performed to demonstrate how both IPv4 and IPv6 addresses could co-exist on the same interface. We tested successful configuration by sending test packets.

The last topic of this chapter discussed routing. Routing is vital in the sense that it provides the backbone for transferring IP traffic among networks over public and private networks. We looked at the function of a routing table and saw how to view table entries. Lastly, we added new routes using commands and by editing interface-specific route configuration files.

Chapter Review Questions

1. Bonding supports IPv4 as well as IPv6, while teaming does not. True or False?
2. What is the function of the default gateway?
3. Which command is used to display the hardware address of a network interface?
4. Which directory is used to store the interface configuration files?
5. What is the purpose of the ONBOOT directive in the interface configuration file?
6. Name two implementations of link aggregation in RHEL7.
7. The */etc/hosts* file maintains the hostname to hardware address mappings. True or False?
8. What does the *ip addr* command produce?
9. Which link aggregation method is implemented in both kernel space and userland?
10. It is not possible to configure an IPv6 address on an interface that is already using an IPv4 address. True or False?
11. Which command can be run at the command prompt in an X terminal window to bring up the graphical Network Connections tool?

Answers to Chapter Review Questions

1. False. Both bonding and teaming support IPv4 as well as IPv6.

2. The default gateway is used in the absence of usable routes to a destination.
3. The *ip* command.
4. The */etc/sysconfig/network-scripts* directory.
5. The value of this directive determines whether to activate this interface at system boot.
6. The two implementations for link aggregation in RHEL7 are teaming and bonding.
7. False. This file maintains IP to hostname mappings.
8. This command displays IP assignments, hardware address, and other data for network interfaces.
9. Teaming is implemented in both user and kernel spaces.
10. False. An interface can have both IPv4 and IPv6 addresses assigned, and working.
11. The command to bring up the graphical Network Connections tool is *nm-connection-editor*.

DIY Challenge Labs

The following labs are useful to strengthen most of the concepts and topics learned in this chapter. It is expected that you perform these labs without any additional help. A step-by-step guide is not provided, as the implementation of these labs requires the knowledge that has been presented in this chapter. Use defaults or your own thinking for missing information.

Lab 15-1: Set Up Teaming between Two Systems Using NetworkManager TUI

Present a pair of network interfaces to each server and configure them as a team on both servers. Assign them IPv4 addresses on 192.168.1.0/24 network and use any hostnames. Execute ping tests to confirm operational health. Ensure the configuration survives system reboots. Use configuration at will where missing.

Lab 15-2: Set Up Bonding between Two Systems Using NetworkManager TUI

Present a pair of network interfaces to each server and configure them as a bond on both servers. Assign them any IPv6 addresses and hostnames. Execute ping6 tests to confirm operational health. Ensure the configuration survives system reboots. Use configuration at will where missing.

Lab 15-3: Configure Static Routes

Configure a persistent static route to 192.168.5.0/24 network on one system and attach it to the team interface created in Lab 15-1. Configure another persistent static route to 192.168.5.0/24 network on the other system and attach it to the bond interface created in Lab 15-2. Ensure the configuration survives system reboots. Use configuration at will where missing.

Chapter 16

Synchronizing Time with NTP

This chapter describes the following major topics:

➤ Introduction to the Network Time Protocol service
➤ Overview of time sources, NTP roles, and stratum levels
➤ Understand NTP packages and tools
➤ Analysis of the configuration file
➤ Use and configure NTP client, server, and peer
➤ Overview of the graphical configuration tool
➤ Update system clock and query NTP servers

RHCE Objectives:

40. Configure a system to use time services
82. Synchronize time using other NTP peers

T he Network Time Protocol service maintains the clock on the system and keeps it synchronized with a more accurate and reliable source of time. Providing accurate and uniform time for systems on the network allows time-sensitive applications, such as monitoring software, backup tools, scheduling utilities, billing systems, file sharing protocols, and authentication programs, to perform correctly and precisely. It also aids logging and auditing services to capture messages and alerts in log files with accurate timestamps.

Understanding Network Time Protocol

Network Time Protocol (NTP) is a networking protocol for synchronizing the system clock with timeservers that are physically closer and redundant for high accuracy and reliability. This protocol was developed over three decades ago and it is still widely in use, with tens of millions of computing devices employing it to obtain time from tens of thousands of configured NTP servers spread across the globe. NTP supports both client-server as well as peer-to-peer configurations with an option to use either public-key or symmetric-key cryptography for authentication. When using this protocol, time accuracies are typically within a millisecond. Having precise time on networked systems allows time-sensitive applications, such as logging and monitoring software, backup and scheduling tools, financial and billing systems, authentication and email applications, and file and storage sharing protocols, to function with precision.

The NTP daemon, called *ntpd*, uses the UDP protocol over well-known port 123, and it runs on all participating servers, peers, and clients. This daemon typically starts at system boot and continuously operates to keep the operating system clock in sync with a more accurate source of time. In order to understand NTP, a discussion of its components and roles is imperative.

Time Source

A *time source* is any device that acts as a provider of time to other devices. The most accurate source of time is provided by atomic clocks that are deployed around the globe. Atomic clocks use *Universal Time, Coordinated* (UTC) for time accuracy. They produce radio signals that radio clocks use for time propagation to computer servers and other devices that require accuracy in time. When choosing a time source for a network, preference should be given to the one that is physically close and takes the least amount of time to send and receive NTP packets.

The most common sources of time employed on computer networks are the local system clock, an Internet-based public timeserver, a radio clock, and a satellite receiver.

Local System Clock

You can arrange for one of the RHEL systems to function as a provider of time using its own clock. This requires the maintenance of correct time on this server either manually or automatically via the *cron* daemon. Keep in mind, however, that this server has no way of synchronizing itself with a more reliable and precise external time source. Therefore, using a local system clock as a timeserver with reliance on its own clock is the least recommended option.

Internet-Based Public Timeserver

Several public timeservers (visit *www.ntp.org* for a list) are available via the Internet for the provision of time on the network. One of the systems on the local network is identified and configured to obtain time from one or more of the public timeservers. To use a time source, you may need to open a port in the firewall to allow NTP traffic to pass through. Internet-based timeservers are spread around the world and are typically operated by government agencies, research organizations, and universities. This option is preferred over the use of the local system clock.

Radio/Atomic Clock

A radio clock is regarded as the most accurate provider of time. A radio clock receives time updates from one or more atomic clocks. *Global Positioning System* (GPS), *National Institute of Science and Technology* (NIST) radio station WWVB broadcasts in the Americas, and DCF77 radio broadcasts in Europe are some popular radio clock methods. Of these, GPS-based sources are perfect. A direct use of signals from any of these devices requires connectivity of some hardware to a computer system that is intended to be used as an organizational or site-wide timeserver.

NTP Roles

A role is a function that a system performs from an NTP standpoint. A system can be configured to assume one or more of the following roles:

Primary NTP Server

A *primary* NTP server gets time from one of the time sources mentioned above, and provides time to one or more secondary servers or clients, or both. It can also be configured to broadcast time to secondary servers and clients.

Secondary NTP Server

A *secondary* NTP server receives time from a primary server or directly from one of the time sources mentioned above. It can be used to provide time to a set of clients to offload the primary, or for redundancy. The presence of a secondary server on the network is optional, although highly recommended. A secondary NTP server can also be configured to broadcast time to clients and peers.

NTP Peer

An NTP *peer* provides time to an NTP server and receives time from it. All peers work at the same stratum level, and all of them are considered equally reliable. Both primary and secondary servers can be peers of each other.

NTP Client

An NTP *client* receives time from either a primary or a secondary server. A client can be configured in one of the following ways:

✓ As a *polling* client that contacts a defined NTP server directly for time synchronization.
✓ As a *broadcast* client that listens to time broadcasts by an NTP server. A broadcast client binds itself with the NTP server that responds to its requests and synchronizes its clock with it. The NTP server must be configured in the broadcast mode in order for a broadcast client to be able to bind to it. A broadcast NTP configuration cannot span the local subnet.
✓ A *multicast* client operates in a similar fashion as a broadcast client; however, it is able to span the local subnet. The NTP server must be configured in the multicast mode in order for a multicast client to work with it.
✓ A *manycast* client automatically discovers manycast NTP servers and uses the ones with the best performance. The NTP server must be configured in the manycast mode in order for a manycast client to work with it.

Stratum Levels

As you are aware, there are different types of time sources available to synchronize the system time. These time sources are categorized hierarchically into multiple levels, which are referred to as *stratum levels* based on their distance from the reference clocks (atomic, radio, and GPS). The reference clocks operate at stratum level 0 and are assumed to be the most accurate provider of time with little to no delay.

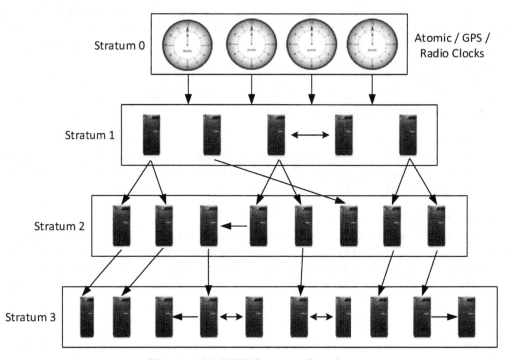

Figure 16-1 NTP Stratum Levels

Besides stratum 0, there are fifteen additional stratum levels that range between 1 and 15. Of these, servers operating at stratum 1 are considered the most accurate, as they get time directly from a stratum 0 device. See Figure 16-1. A stratum 0 device cannot be used on the network directly. It is attached to one of the computers on the network via an RS-232 connection, for example, and then that computer is configured to operate at stratum 1. Servers functioning at stratum 1 are called *timeservers* (or *primary timeservers*) and they can be set up to provide time to stratum 2 servers over a network path via NTP packets. Similarly, a stratum 3 server can be configured to synchronize its time with a stratum 2 server, and so on. Servers sharing the same stratum can be configured as peers to exchange time updates with each other.

If a secondary server is also configured to get time from a stratum 1 server directly, it will act as a peer to the primary server.

There are a number of public NTP servers available for free to synchronize with the system time. You do not have to connect your system directly to a stratum 0 device.

Managing Network Time Protocol

This section discusses the management tasks including installing the NTP software, configuring an NTP server, peer, and client, configuring a broadcast NTP server and client using a combination of manual file editing and commands, and testing the configurations. This section also introduces the graphical tool for NTP administration.

Before we get into the setup tasks, let's look at the software packages, utilities, and the main NTP configuration file.

NTP Packages and Utilities

There is only one required software package that needs to be installed on the system for NTP. This package is called "ntp" and it includes all the necessary support to configure the system as an NTP server, peer, or client. RHEL7 includes version 4.2.6 of this package. Additionally, a package called "ntpdate" may also be installed to get access to a command that is used to update the system with an NTP server without the involvement of the *ntpd* daemon. You can use the *yum* command on *server1* to list whether these two packages are installed:

yum list installed | grep ^ntp
ntp.x86_64   4.2.6p5-18.el7   @ftprepo
ntpdate.x86_64   4.2.6p5-18.el7   @anaconda/7.0

The above output confirms the presence of both packages on the system.

These packages bring several administration commands, some of which are described in Table 16-1.

Command	Description
ntpdate	Updates the system date and time immediately. This command is deprecated and will be removed from a future RHEL release. Use ntpd –q instead.
ntpq	Queries the NTP daemon.
ntpd	NTP daemon program that must run on a system to use it as a server, peer, or client.
ntpstat	Shows time synchronization status.

Table 16-1 NTP Administration Commands

We will use these tools later in this chapter.

NTP Configuration File

The key configuration file for NTP is called *ntp.conf*, and it is located in the */etc* directory. This file can be modified by hand, and the directives in it can be set based on the role the system is intended to play. Some key directives from this file are:

driftfile   /var/lib/ntp/drift
logfile   /var/log/ntp.log
restrict   default nomodify notrap nopeer noquery
restrict   192.168.1.0 mask 255.255.255.0 nomodify notrap
server   0.rhel.pool.ntp.org iburst
server   1.rhel.pool.ntp.org iburst

server	2.rhel.pool.ntp.org iburst	
server	3.rhel.pool.ntp.org iburst	
server	127.127.1.0	# local clock
peer		
broadcast	192.168.1.255 autokey	# broadcast server
broadcastclient		# broadcast client
broadcast	224.0.1.1 autokey	# multicast server
multicastclient	224.0.1.1	# multicast client
manycastserver	239.255.254.254	# manycast server
manycastclient	239.255.254.254 autokey	# manycast client
crypto		
includefile	/etc/ntp/crypto/pw	
keys	/etc/ntp/keys	

> **EXAM TIP:** The /etc/ntp.conf is the only configuration file that is modified for NTP server, peer, and client. Understanding of how entries are defined for these roles is important.

Table 16-2 describes these directives.

Directive	Description
driftfile	Specifies the location of the driftfile (default is /var/lib/ntp/drift). This file is used by the ntpd daemon to keep track of local system clock accuracy.
logfile	Specifies the location of the log file.
restrict	Sets access control restrictions on inbound NTP queries. Several defaults are defined with this directive including nomodify, notrap, nopeer, and noquery. The nomodify option disallows any modification attempts by other NTP servers; the notrap option disables control messages from being captured; the nopeer option prevents remote servers from establishing peer relationship; and the noquery option disallows remote ntpq queries but answers time queries. The second restrict directive allows time requests from systems on the 192.168.1.0/24 network; however, it disallows modification attempts and does not capture control messages.
server	Specifies the hostname or IP address of the timeserver. By default, the file contains four public timeserver entries. The iburst option helps improve the time taken for initial synchronization. The server directive with IP 127.127.1.0 specifies to use the local system clock as the provider of time.
peer	Specifies the hostname or IP address of the peer.
broadcast	Specifies the hostname or IP address of the broadcasting timeserver. The autokey option describes the type of authentication to use. This option is preferred in an environment with a large number of NTP clients.
broadcastclient	The presence of this directive sets the system as a broadcastclient.
multicastclient	Enables reception of multicast server messages to the specified multicast group address.
manycastserver	Specifies the hostname or IP address of the manycast timeserver.

Directive	Description
manycastclient	Sets the system as a manycast client. The autokey option describes the type of authentication to use.
crypto	Enables public-key or symmetric-key authentication.
includefile	This file stores the password to be used to decrypt encrypted files that contain private keys.
keys	This file stores authentication keys.

Table 16-2 Description of /etc/ntp.conf Directives

There are several additional directives and options that may be defined in this file.

Exercise 16-1: Use Pre-Defined NTP Polling Client

This exercise should be done on *server2*.

By default, the NTP software comes pre-configured for use as an NTP client. The configuration file, */etc/ntp.conf*, already has four public NTP server entries.

In this exercise, you will activate the NTP service and check to ensure that it is functional.

1. Install the NTP software (if it is not already installed):

   # **yum –y install ntp**

2. Ensure that the following public NTP server entries are defined in the */etc/ntp.conf* file:

   # **grep ^server /etc/ntp.conf**
   server 0.rhel.pool.ntp.org iburst
   server 1.rhel.pool.ntp.org iburst
   server 2.rhel.pool.ntp.org iburst
   server 3.rhel.pool.ntp.org iburst

3. Enable the *ntpd* daemon to autostart at reboots:

   # **systemctl enable ntpd**
   ln -s '/usr/lib/systemd/system/ntpd.service' '/etc/systemd/system/multi-user.target.wants/ntpd.service'

4. Start the NTP service and check its status:

   # **systemctl start ntpd**
   # **systemctl status ntpd**
   ntpd.service - Network Time Service
     Loaded: loaded (/usr/lib/systemd/system/ntpd.service; enabled)
     Active: active (running) since Thu 2015-01-08 09:08:17 EST; 19min ago
    Main PID: 21475 (ntpd)
     CGroup: /system.slice/ntpd.service
           └─21475 /usr/sbin/ntpd -u ntp:ntp -g
   Jan 08 09:08:17 server2.example.com ntpd[21475]: Listen normally on 12 team0...3
   Jan 08 09:08:17 server2.example.com ntpd[21475]: Listening on routing socket...s
   Jan 08 09:08:17 server2.example.com systemd[1]: Started Network Time Service.

```
Jan 08 09:08:17 server2.example.com ntpd[21475]: 0.0.0.0 c016 06 restart
Jan 08 09:08:17 server2.example.com ntpd[21475]: 0.0.0.0 c012 02 freq_set ke...M
Jan 08 09:08:17 server2.example.com ntpd[21475]: 0.0.0.0 c011 01 freq_not_set
Jan 08 09:08:18 server2.example.com ntpd[21475]: 0.0.0.0 c614 04 freq_mode
Jan 08 09:25:09 server2.example.com ntpd[21475]: 0.0.0.0 0612 02 freq_set ke...M
Jan 08 09:25:09 server2.example.com ntpd[21475]: 0.0.0.0 0615 05 clock_sync
```

5. Check whether the system is bound to the NTP servers:

 # ntpq −p

remote	refid	st	t	when	poll	reach	delay	offset	jitter
+mail.stygium.ne	209.51.161.238	2	u	50	64	377	14.221	-29.571	8.492
+bitdonut.co	128.105.39.11	3	u	51	64	377	16.036	-20.181	15.913
ellen.linuxgene	142.3.100.2	2	u	2	64	1	16.452	0.881	4.770
*ntp3.torix.ca	.PPS.	1	u	47	64	377	18.853	-26.535	10.077

The above output indicates that the *ntpd* daemon on *server2* is currently bound to an NTP server *ntp3.torix.ca*. Details for each column in this output are provided later in this chapter.

6. Check the status of NTP client:

 # ntpstat
```
synchronised to NTP server (67.215.197.149) at stratum 3
   time correct to within 61 ms
   polling server every 128 s
```

Exercise 16-2: Configure NTP Server and Polling Client

This exercise should be done on *server1* (NTP server) and *server2* (NTP client).

In this exercise, you will set up *server1* as an NTP server and sync time to its local clock and provide time to clients on the network. You will use the IP 127.127.1.0 which is reserved for this purpose. You will disable existing public timeserver entries from the configuration file. You will open UDP port 123 in the firewall to allow NTP traffic to pass through. You will configure *server2* as a polling client to obtain time from *server1* and disable other default server entries from its configuration file as well.

1. Install the NTP software on *server1* (if it is not already installed):

 # yum −y install ntp

2. Comment out all server directives from the */etc/ntp.conf* file and add a new one with IP 127.127.1.0:

```
#server  0.rhel.pool.ntp.org  iburst
#server  1.rhel.pool.ntp.org  iburst
#server  2.rhel.pool.ntp.org  iburst
#server  3.rhel.pool.ntp.org  iburst
server  127.127.1.0
```

3. Enable the NTP service to autostart at reboots:

 # systemctl enable ntpd
ln -s '/usr/lib/systemd/system/ntpd.service' '/etc/systemd/system/multi-user.target.wants/ntpd.service'

4. Open UDP port 123 in the firewall persistently and load the new rule:

 # firewall-cmd --permanent --add-service ntp
 # firewall-cmd --reload

5. Start the *ntpd* service and check its status:

 # systemctl start ntpd
 # ntpq −p

remote	refid	st	t	when	poll	reach	delay	offset	jitter
*LOCAL(0)	.LOCL.	5	l	1	64	1	0.000	0.000	0.000

The above output indicates that the *ntpd* daemon on *server1* is using its own clock as the timeserver.

6. Disable the server directives in the */etc/ntp.conf* file on *server2* and add the following to use *server1* as the timeserver:

```
#server  0.rhel.pool.ntp.org  iburst
#server  1.rhel.pool.ntp.org  iburst
#server  2.rhel.pool.ntp.org  iburst
#server  3.rhel.pool.ntp.org  iburst
server  server1.example.com
```

7. Restart *ntpd* on *server2* and check the status of binding with the *ntpq* command:

 # systemctl restart ntpd
 # ntpq −p

remote	refid	st	t	when	poll	reach	delay	offset	jitter
*server1.example	LOCAL(0)		6	u	1	64	1	0.195	5.215	0.000

The above output confirms the NTP association of *server2* with *server1*.

Exercise 16-3: Configure an NTP Peer

This exercise should be done on *host1*.

In this exercise, you will configure *host1* as a peer of NTP server *server1* and test the configuration.

1. Install the NTP software on *host1* (if it is not already installed):

 # yum −y install ntp

2. Comment out all server directives from the *etc/ntp.conf* file and add the following with either the hostname or IP address of *server1*:

    #server 0.rhel.pool.ntp.org iburst
    #server 1.rhel.pool.ntp.org iburst
    #server 2.rhel.pool.ntp.org iburst
    #server 3.rhel.pool.ntp.org iburst
    peer server1.example.com

3. Enable the NTP service to autostart at reboots:

    # **systemctl enable ntpd**
    ln -s '/usr/lib/systemd/system/ntpd.service' '/etc/systemd/system/multi-user.target.wants/ntpd.service'

4. Open UDP port 123 in the firewall persistently and load the new rule:

    # **firewall-cmd --permanent --add-service ntp**
    # **firewall-cmd --reload**

5. Restart the *ntpd* service and check its status:

    # **systemctl restart ntpd**
    # **ntpq –p**

remote	refid	st	t	when	poll	reach	delay	offset	jitter
*server1.example	LOCAL(0)	6	u	42	64	17	0.108	7.000	1.340

The above output indicates that the *ntpd* daemon on *host1* has an association with *server1*.

Exercise 16-4: Configure a Broadcast Server and Client

This exercise should be done on *server2* (NTP server) and *host1* (NTP client).

In this exercise, you will set up *server2* as an NTP client to obtain time from the original four NTP servers and broadcast time to devices on the local network (192.168.0.0/24). You will open UDP port 123 in the firewall to allow NTP traffic to pass through. You will configure *host1* as a broadcast client to get time from the broadcast. This exercise assumes that the NTP software is already loaded on both *server2* and *host1*.

1. Ensure that the following entries are defined in the *etc/ntp.conf* file on *server2* as shown below:

    server 0.rhel.pool.ntp.org iburst
    server 1.rhel.pool.ntp.org iburst
    server 2.rhel.pool.ntp.org iburst
    server 3.rhel.pool.ntp.org iburst
    broadcast 192.168.0.255

2. Enable the NTP service to autostart at reboots:

   # systemctl enable ntpd

3. Open UDP port 123 in the firewall persistently and load the new rule:

   # firewall-cmd --permanent --add-service ntp
   # firewall-cmd --reload

4. Restart the *ntpd* service and check its status:

   # systemctl restart ntpd
   # ntpq −p

remote	refid	st	t	when	poll	reach	delay	offset	jitter
*kirdu.smartacti	213.251.128.249	2	u	12	64	1	27.098	-2.381	0.467
ntp2.tranzeo.co	206.108.0.132	2	u	11	64	1	23.936	0.802	0.372
2607:4100:2:ff:	.INIT.	16	u	-	64	0	0.000	0.000	0.000
mail.stygium.ne	209.51.161.238	2	u	10	64	1	14.107	3.081	0.549
192.168.0.255	.BCST.	16	u	-	64	0	0.000	0.000	0.000

   The above output indicates that the *ntpd* daemon on *server2* is using the public NTP servers as the provider of time. It also shows that this server is broadcasting time to devices on the 192.168.0.0 network.

5. Disable the server directives in the */etc/ntp.conf* file on *host1* and add broadcastclient and disable directives as shown. Disable secret-key authentication as well.

   #server 0.rhel.pool.ntp.org iburst
   #server 1.rhel.pool.ntp.org iburst
   #server 2.rhel.pool.ntp.org iburst
   #server 3.rhel.pool.ntp.org iburst
   broadcastlient
   disable auth

6. Restart *ntpd* on *host1* and check the status of binding with the *ntpq* command:

   # systemctl restart ntpd
   # ntpq −p

remote	refid	st	t	when	poll	reach	delay	offset	jitter
*server2.example	LOCAL(0)	6	u	42	64	17	0.111	6.500	1.260

   The above output confirms the NTP association of *host1* with broadcast server *server2*.

Overview of System-Config-Date Tool

The NTP client service can be set up using the graphical System-Config-Date tool. This tool is not installed by default. Run the following to install it:

yum –y install system-config-date

In order to run this tool, execute *system-config-date* in an X terminal window or choose Applications | Sundry | System-Config-Date in the GNOME desktop. The System-Config-Date tool will open up as shown in Figure 16-2.

Figure 16-2 System-Config-Date Tool for NTP Client Configuration

Select "Synchronize date and time over the network" and add the IP address(es) of time servers under NTP Servers. Select "Speed up initial synchronization" to instruct the tool to run the *ntpdate* command and immediately bring the local system clock close to the first NTP server listed. Choose "Use Local Time Source" if you wish to use the local system clock as the provider of time. Click OK when done.

> **EXAM TIP:** The GUI tool is simple to use. It updates the /etc/ntp.conf file for you.

Updating System Clock Manually

You can run the *ntpdate* command anytime to instantly bring the system clock close to the time on an NTP server. The NTP service must not be running in order for this command to work. Run *ntpdate* manually and specify either the hostname or the IP address of the remote timeserver to immediately sync your system time. For example, to bring the clock on *server1* at par with the clock on *server2*, run the following set of commands on *server1*:

systemctl stop ntpd
ntpdate server2
8 Jan 21:31:59 ntpdate[32502]: step time server 192.168.0.120 offset 1.125541 sec
systemctl start ntpd

Restart the *ntpd* service after executing the *ntpdate* command so that the local clock continues to poll configured timeservers for updates.

Querying NTP Servers

We used the NTP query tool called *ntpq* earlier in this chapter to query the status of server association and time synchronization. This command sends out requests to and receives responses from NTP servers, as well as reports the outcome on the screen. The *ntpq* command may also be run in an interactive mode.

Run this tool with the –p option to print a list of NTP servers known to the system along with a summary of their status:

```
# ntpq –p
     remote          refid        st t  when  poll  reach  delay   offset   jitter
==========================================================================
+ntp-1.asininete  128.252.19.1    2  u  681   1024   377  49.962   0.396    1.125
c1110364-13198.   206.108.0.133   2  u  603   1024   377  17.652  -7419.5  5606.63
ns2.dargalsolut   .INIT.         16  u   -    1024    0    0.000   0.000    0.000
*ks4001083.ip-19  192.93.2.20     2  u  774   1024   377  27.667   2.601    1.366
192.168.0.255     .BCST.         16  u   -     64     0    0.000   0.000    0.000
```

The *ntpq* command produces the output in ten columns, which are explained in Table 16-3.

Column	Description
remote	Shows IP addresses or hostnames of NTP servers and peers. Each IP/hostname may be preceded by one of the following characters: * Indicates the current source of synchronization. # Indicates the server selected for synchronization, but distance exceeds the maximum. o Displays the server selected for synchronization. + Indicates the system considered for synchronization. x Designated false ticker by the intersection algorithm. . Indicates the systems picked up from the end of the candidate list. - Indicates the system not considered for synchronization. Blank Indicates the server rejected because of high stratum level or failed sanity checks.
refid	Shows a reference ID for each timeserver.
st	Displays a stratum level. Stratum level 16 indicates an invalid level.
t	Shows available types: l = local (such as a GPS clock), u = unicast, m = multicast, b = broadcast, and - = netaddr (usually 0).
when	Displays time, in seconds, when a response was last received from the server.
poll	Shows a polling interval. Default is 64 seconds.
reach	Expresses the number of successful attempts to reach the server. The value 001 indicates that the most recent probe was answered, 357 indicates that one probe was unanswered, and the value 377 indicates that all recent probes were answered.
delay	Indicates a length of time, in milliseconds, it took for the reply packet to return in response to a query sent to the server.

Column	Description
offset	Shows a time difference, in milliseconds, between server and client clocks.
jitter	Displays a variation of offset measurement between samples. This is an error-bound estimate.

Table 16-3 ntpq Command Output Description

Chapter Summary

This chapter discussed the Network Time Protocol service. It described various sources of obtaining time, different roles that systems could play from an NTP standpoint, and elaborated on the strata paradigm. We looked at NTP packages and utilities available for performing various NTP management tasks, and continued with a discussion of a primary NTP configuration file and several directives that could be set in that file.

We performed a variety of exercises to strengthen the concepts learned. Finally, we reviewed the graphical NTP client configuration tool, and saw how to update system clock instantly and query NTP servers.

Chapter Review Questions

1. Which graphical tool may be used to configure an NTP client?
2. What is the default polling interval set on an NTP client?
3. Write the command that would list the current source of time synchronization.
4. What protocol and port does NTP use?
5. Can an NTP server be configured to broadcast time on the network? True or False?
6. Name two common sources for obtaining time.
7. What is the purpose of the drift file?
8. Define stratum levels.
9. What would happen if you run the *ntpdate* command for instant time update while the *ntpd* daemon is running on the system?
10. Write a difference between an NTP peer and an NTP client.
11. What would the command *ntpdate server.ntp.org* do?

Answers to Chapter Review Questions

1. The System-Config-Date tool.
2. The default polling interval is sixty-four seconds.
3. The *ntpq* command with the –p switch.
4. NTP uses the UDP protocol and port 123.
5. True.
6. The two common sources for getting time are public timeservers and radio clocks.
7. The *ntpd* daemon uses the drift file to keep track of local system clock accuracy.
8. Stratum levels determine the proximity of a time source.
9. The *ntpdate* command will display a message that the NTP socket is busy.
10. An NTP peer provides time while an NTP client may obtain time from it.
11. This command will instantly synchronize the system's time with the specified server's time.

DIY Challenge Labs

The following labs are useful to strengthen the concepts and topics learned in this chapter. It is expected that you perform these labs without any additional help. A step-by-step guide is not provided, as the implementation of these labs requires the knowledge that has been presented in this chapter. Use defaults or your own thinking for missing information.

Lab 16-1: Configure the Network Time Protocol Service

Obtain a list of public timeservers from *www.ntp.org* and configure *server2* as a peer of one of them. Configure polling client on *server1* using the GUI program to sync its clock with *server2*. Run appropriate commands on *server2* to validate its peer association and on *server1* to verify its binding with *server2*.

## Chapter 17

Working with Firewalld and Kerberos

This chapter describes the following major topics:

➢ Overview of firewalld

➢ Zones, services, ports, direct language, rich language, and port forwarding

➢ Basics of Network Address Translation and IP masquerading

➢ Manage firewalld, zones, services, ports, rich language rules, masquerading, and port forwarding

➢ Understand Kerberos and associated terms

➢ How does the Kerberos authentication system function?

➢ Kerberos packages and common administration commands

➢ Configure a system to function as a Kerberos client

➢ Overview of the graphical Authentication Configuration tool

RHCE Objectives:

58. Use firewallD and associated mechanisms such as rich rules, zones and custom rules, to implement packet filtering and configure network address translation (NAT)

60. Configure a system to authenticate using Kerberos

Firewalld

Firewalld is a new way of interacting with iptables rules. It allows the administrator to enter new security rules and activate them during runtime without disconnecting existing connections. It places network interfaces in different zones based on the level of trust for the traffic transmitted through them, thereby providing the administrator the flexibility to activate specific zones only. Network Address Translation is a feature that enables a system on the internal network to access the Internet via an intermediary device. IP masquerading, in contrast, enables more than one system on the internal network to access the Internet via an intermediary device. In either case, the systems' IP addresses on the internal network are concealed from the outside world, and only one IP address is seen. That one IP address is of the intermediary device.

Kerberos is a client/server authentication protocol that works on the basis of digital tickets to allow systems communicating over non-secure networks to prove their identity to one another before being able to use kerberized network services. Kerberos uses a combination of Kerberos services and encrypted keys for the implementation of secure authentication mechanism on the network.

Understanding Firewalld

RHEL7 has introduced an improved mechanism for security rules management called *Firewalld* (*dynamic firewall*). One of the primary reasons for adding the support for firewalld in RHEL7 is its ability to activate changes dynamically without disconnecting established connections. Firewalld is managed by a daemon process called *firewalld* that is responsible for the configuration and monitoring of system firewall rules. The old method of using the *iptables* command requires the reload of all defined rules, including those that are already in an active and established state, whenever there is a change. Firewalld supports the D-BUS implementation and it brings the concept of network zones to manage the security rules. Everything in firewalld relates to one or more zones. Iptables does not have a daemon process, as it is implemented purely in the kernel space. We can activate either of the two at a time.

Firewalld configuration is stored in the */etc/firewalld* directory and can be customized as desired. Its essential code runs in the kernel space interfacing with netfilter to implement the firewall rules. The rest of the code including the daemon is implemented in userland providing full user control over its operations. The userland management tools are the command *firewall-cmd* and the graphical tool called *firewall-config*. In addition, it allows us to create and modify zone and service configuration files by hand, and activate them as desired.

In this chapter, we use the *firewall-cmd* command for demonstration purposes. For details on how to use the graphical *firewall-config* tool, see Chapter 11 "Controlling Access through Firewall and SELinux".

Network Zones

Firewalld zones classify incoming network traffic for simplified firewall management. Zones define the level of trust for network connections based on principles such as a source IP or network interface for incoming network traffic. The inbound traffic is checked against zone settings and it is handled appropriately as per configured rules in the zone. Each zone can have its own list of services and ports that are opened or closed. We can create zones with different rulesets. For instance, on a RHEL7 system with multiple network interfaces, we can group interfaces based on pre-defined trust levels and place them into one or more zones that may be activated or deactivated independently as one entity.

Firewalld provides nine zones by default that are illustrated in Figure 17-1. These system-defined zone files are XML-formatted and are located in the */usr/lib/firewalld/zones* directory. In contrast, all user-defined zone configuration is stored in separate XML files in the */etc/firewalld/zones* directory.

```
[root@host1 zones]# pwd
/usr/lib/firewalld/zones
[root@host1 zones]# ll
total 36
-rw-r-----.  1 root root 299 Feb 28 06:53 block.xml
-rw-r-----.  1 root root 293 Feb 28 06:53 dmz.xml
-rw-r-----.  1 root root 291 Feb 28 06:53 drop.xml
-rw-r-----.  1 root root 304 Feb 28 06:53 external.xml
-rw-r-----.  1 root root 400 Feb 28 06:53 home.xml
-rw-r-----.  1 root root 415 Feb 28 06:53 internal.xml
-rw-r-----.  1 root root 315 Feb 28 06:53 public.xml
-rw-r-----.  1 root root 162 Feb 28 06:53 trusted.xml
-rw-r-----.  1 root root 342 Feb 28 06:53 work.xml
```

Figure 17-1 Firewalld Default Zone Files

These zones are listed in Table 17-1 are sorted by trust level from untrusted to trusted. We need to select the zone that best suits our network requirements, and then we can tailor it further to meet our specific needs.

Trust Level	Description
Drop	Drops all inbound connection requests without sending a message back.
Block	Blocks all inbound connection requests with icmp-host-prohibited message for IPv4 or icmp6-adm-prohibited message for IPv6 sent.
Public	Allows selected inbound connection requests and disallows the rest. This is the default zone and all network interfaces are assigned to it by default. This zone is suited for use in public places.
External	Allows selected inbound connection requests with masquerading active.
Dmz	Allows selected inbound connection requests. This is suited for systems with limited access to their internal network.
Work	Allows selected inbound connection requests from other corporate systems.
Home	Allows selected inbound connection requests from other home systems.
Internal	Allows selected inbound connection requests on internal networks where most systems are trusted.
Trusted	Allows all inbound connection requests; used on a highly trusted network.

Table 17-1 Pre-Defined Zones

By default, the public zone is the default zone; however, this designation can be assigned to one of the other eight zones or to a new custom zone. Here are the default contents of the */usr/lib/firewalld/zones/public.xml* public zone file:

```
<?xml version="1.0" encoding="utf-8"?>
<zone>
 <short>Public</short>
```

```
<description>For use in public areas. You do not trust the other computers on networks to not harm your
computer. Only selected incoming connections are accepted.</description>
<service name="ssh"/>
<service name="dhcpv6-client"/>
</zone>
```

As you can see, the file contains straightforward and self-explanatory information. It indicates that
only ssh and DHCPv6 inbound connections are allowed by default.

We can use one of these zone files as a template to create our own custom zone and place it in the
/etc/firewalld/zones directory. This custom zone can then be altered with the *firewall-cmd* command
or the graphical *firewall-config* tool to suit our specific needs.

EXAM TIP: You need to ensure the rules you add are for the right zone.

Each zone on the system may have one or more interfaces assigned to it. When a service request
arrives, firewalld checks whether it is already defined in a zone by the IP it is originated from (the
source network) or the network interface it is coming through. If yes, it binds the request with that
zone; otherwise, it binds the request with the default zone. This allows us to define and activate
several zones at a time even if there is only one network interface on the system.

Services

Services are an essential component of firewalld zones. In fact, using services in zones is the
preferred method for firewalld configuration and management. A service typically contains a port
number, protocol, and an IP address. Service configuration is stored in separate XML files located
in the */usr/lib/firewalld/services* and */etc/firewalld/services* directories for system- and user-defined
services, respectively. The configuration files located in the user-defined service directory
(*/etc/firewalld/services*) take precedence over the ones located in the other directory. It is
recommended to copy one of the files from */usr/lib/firewalld/services* to */etc/firewalld/services*,
rename it, and use the *firewall-cmd* command or the graphical *firewall-config* tool to alter the
contents to suit specific needs. Figure 16-2 shows a listing of the files for some of the pre-defined
services. These service definitions can be used to permit connections and traffic for particular
network services for a zone.

```
[root@host1 services]# pwd
/usr/lib/firewalld/services
[root@host1 services]# ll
total 188
-rw-r-----. 1 root root 412 Feb 28 06:53 amanda-client.xml
-rw-r-----. 1 root root 320 Feb 28 06:53 bacula-client.xml
-rw-r-----. 1 root root 346 Feb 28 06:53 bacula.xml
-rw-r-----. 1 root root 305 Feb 28 06:53 dhcpv6-client.xml
-rw-r-----. 1 root root 234 Feb 28 06:53 dhcpv6.xml
-rw-r-----. 1 root root 227 Feb 28 06:53 dhcp.xml
-rw-r-----. 1 root root 346 Feb 28 06:53 dns.xml
-rw-r-----. 1 root root 374 Feb 28 06:53 ftp.xml
```

Figure 17-2 Firewalld Services Files

All user-defined and system-defined service configuration is stored in XML files in the
/etc/firewalld/services and */usr/lib/firewalld/services* directories, respectively.

Ports

Network ports in firewalld may also be defined directly without using the service configuration technique, as mentioned in the previous sub-section. In essence, defining network ports does not require the presence of a service or a service configuration file. The same two tools, *firewall-cmd* and *firewall-config*, used for zone and service configuration are also used for port configuration.

Direct Interface and Rich Language

Firewalld gives us the ability to pass security rules directly to iptables using the direct interface mode; however, these rules are not persistent. They remain in place only until the firewalld service is restarted or configuration is reloaded. This may cause serious issues in a production environment. To address this problem, firewalld provides the support for a high-level language, called the *rich language*, that allows us to build complex rules without the knowledge of iptables syntax, and activate them either persistently or for a specified period of time after which they are deleted automatically. The rich language rules are also built and managed with the same two management tools, *firewall-cmd* and *firewall-config*.

Rich language uses several elements to set rules and name them. These elements include a source address or range with an appropriate netmask; destination address or range with an appropriate netmask; service name; port number or range; protocol; masquerade (enable or disable); forward-port (destination port number or range to divert traffic to); log and log level; and an action (accept: to grant new connection requests, reject: to disallow requests with a reason returned, or drop: to discard requests without informing the sender).

Network Address Translation and IP Masquerading

Network Address Translation (NAT) refers to the process of altering the IP address of a source or destination network that is enclosed in a datagram packet header while it passes through a device that supports this type of modification. In other words, NAT allows a system on the internal network (home or corporate network) to access external networks (the Internet) using a single, registered IP address configured on an intermediary device (a router or firewall). IP *masquerading* is a variant of NAT and it allows several systems on the internal network (192.168.0.0) to access the Internet using that single IP (52.29.71.18) of the intermediary device. See Figure 17-3.

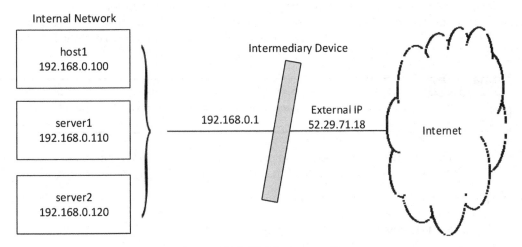

Figure 17-3 IP Masquerading

With masquerading, requests originated from any of the internal systems appear to the outside world as being originated from the intermediary device with IP 52.29.71.18. The intermediary device stores the IP addresses of the source systems in its cache, along with randomly generated port numbers assigned to them, to keep traffic segregated for each system. The masquerading technique saves us from purchasing official IPs for each system on the internal network.

In order for a RHEL system with the netfilter module loaded in the kernel space, we need at least two configured network interfaces to be able to use masquerading. Masquerading can be activated either persistently or for a specified period of time after which it is deleted automatically. Masquerading is also managed with the same two management tools.

Port Forwarding

We may have to redirect inbound traffic to a port to access an application servicing on that port on our internal system. This port is defined on the intermediary device (router or the netfilter module on RHEL). For example, to allow external access to the HTTP service listening on port 8080 on an internal system, both internal system IP and port number are defined on the intermediary device to ensure inbound requests are forwarded to the desired destination. This feature is referred to as *port forwarding* or *port mapping*.

Managing Firewalld

Firewalld offers a single command called *firewall-cmd* to view and manage firewall rulesets including those for masquerading and port forwarding. It gives us the ability to enter rules either on a persistent or temporary basis. The persistent rules are recorded in appropriate files and are not activated unless the *firewalld* service is restarted or instructed to reload the rules from the files. On the contrary, the temporary rules take effect as soon as they are entered; however, they do not survive a service restart or reload, because they are stored in memory. The difference between restarting the service and reloading the rules is that restarting interrupts all established connections, removes all temporary rules in place, and re-activates all persistent rules. On the other hand, reloading does not disturb existing persistent connections, but it discards all temporary rules in place. It also loads new and modified persistent rules that have been defined since the last restart or reload.

The *firewall-cmd* command has many options to view and manage its own operation, as well as view and administer zones, services, ports, masquerading, port forwarding, and so on. It also provides the ability to use the direct interface and rich language options to enter rules. We will discuss options specific to each of these management tasks in this section.

> **EXAM TIP:** Check /var/log/messages, /var/log/secure, and service-specific log files to identify any issues with a non-functional service. You may want to turn off the firewall during troubleshooting. Do not forget to turn it back on.

To view and manage its own operation, you can use the *firewall-cmd* command to check the operational state of the service, and reload or restart it. The following demonstrates a few examples.

To display whether the service is running:

```
# firewall-cmd --state
running
```

The *systemctl* command may also be used for this purpose, but it provides more details:

systemctl status firewalld
firewalld.service - firewalld - dynamic firewall daemon
  Loaded: loaded (/usr/lib/systemd/system/firewalld.service; enabled)
  Active: active (running) since Wed 2014-12-17 11:59:42 EST; 4 days ago
 Main PID: 724 (firewalld)
  CGroup: /system.slice/firewalld.service
        └─724 /usr/bin/python -Es /usr/sbin/firewalld --nofork –nopid

To restart the service:

systemctl restart firewalld

To reload the permanent rules without interrupting existing persistent connections:

firewall-cmd --reload
success

firewalld Command Options for Zone Management
Viewing and managing firewalld zones involves several tasks that can be performed with the *firewall-cmd* command. There are several options available with the command and are described in Table 17-2.

Option	Description
--get-default-zone --set-default-zone	Displays/sets the default zone for both runtime and persistent configurations.
--get-active-zones	Displays all active zones.
--get-zones	Lists all available zones.
--list-all	Lists details for the default zone.
--list-all-zones	Lists details for all zones.
--new-zone	Adds a new zone.
--delete-zone	Removes a zone.
--permanent	Used to make a permanent change. Creates or updates appropriate zone files in the /etc/firewalld/zones directory.
--zone	Used for operations on a non-default zone.

Table 17-2 Zone Management Options

For each permanent change, the corresponding zone file is updated in the */etc/firewalld/zones* directory.

EXAM TIP: Always add firewall rules persistently using the --permanent option with the command.

Exercise 17-1: View and Manage Zones
This exercise should be done on *server1*.

In this exercise, we will demonstrate the use of various zone management options described in Table 17-2. You will display the default, and summary and details for all active and available zones.

You will display details for a specific zone. You will add a new zone called testzone, confirm its creation, and then delete it. You will change the default zone to external and show the directive that is modified with this new setting. Finally, you will set the default zone back to its original value.

1. Display the current default zone setting:

    # **firewall-cmd --get-default-zone**
    public

2. Display a list of all active zones along with the interfaces assigned to them:

    # **firewall-cmd --get-active-zones**
    public
      interfaces: bond0 eth0 eth1 eth2 eth3 eth4 eth5 team0

3. Display details for all active zones:

    # **firewall-cmd --list-all**
    public (default, active)
      interfaces: bond0 eth0 eth1 eth2 eth3 eth4 eth5 team0
      sources:
      services: dhcpv6-client ssh
      ports: 5901-5902/tcp
      masquerade: no
      forward-ports:
      icmp-blocks:
      rich rules:

4. Display a list of all available zones:

    # **firewall-cmd --get-zones**
    block dmz drop external home internal public trusted work

5. Display details for all available zones:

    # **firewall-cmd --list-all-zones**
    < a long output is generated listing details for all the nine zones currently exist on server1 >

6. Display details for a specific zone:

    # **firewall-cmd --list-all --zone external**
    external
      interfaces:
      sources:
      services: ssh
      ports:
      masquerade: yes
      forward-ports:
      icmp-blocks:

rich rules:

7. Add a new zone called testzone and show its file contents:

    # firewall-cmd --new-zone testzone --permanent
    success
    # cat /etc/firewalld/zones/testzone.xml
    <?xml version="1.0" encoding="utf-8"?>
    <zone>
    </zone>

8. Remove testzone and confirm the deletion of corresponding file:

    # firewall-cmd --delete-zone testzone --permanent
    # ll /etc/firewalld/zones
    -rw-r--r--. 1 root root 444 Dec 22 12:24 public.xml
    -rw-r--r--. 1 root root 409 Dec 22 12:10 public.xml.old

9. Change the default zone to external, and verify:

    # firewall-cmd --set-default-zone external
    # firewall-cmd --get-default
    external

10. The default zone information is recorded in the *etc/firewalld/firewalld.conf* file. *grep* for the DefaultZone directive to confirm the new setting:

    # grep –i defaultzone /etc/firewalld/firewalld.conf
    DefaultZone=external

11. Reset the default zone value to the public zone and confirm:

    # firewall-cmd --set-default-zone public
    # firewall-cmd --get-default
    public

firewalld Command Options for Service Management

Viewing and managing firewalld services involves several tasks that can be performed with the *firewall-cmd* command. There are several options available with the command and are described in Table 17-3.

Option	Description
--get-services	Displays available services.
--list-services	Lists services for a zone.
--query-service	Tells whether a service is added.
--add-service	Adds a service to a zone.
--remove-service	Removes a service from a zone.
--new-service	Adds a new service.
--delete-service	Deletes an existing service.

Option	Description
--permanent	Used with the add and remove options for persistence.
--zone	Used for operations on a non-default zone.

Table 17-3 Service Management Options

For each permanent change, the corresponding zone file is updated in the */etc/firewalld/zones* directory. For a new service addition or removal, a file is created or removed from the */etc/firewalld/services* directory.

Exercise 17-2: View and Manage Services

This exercise should be done on *server1*.

In this exercise, we will demonstrate the use of various service management options described in Table 16-3. You will display all available services, list all services for the default and internal zones, and query whether the tftp service is available in the default and work zones. You will add a new service called testservice and add it to the work zone. Finally, you will remove this service from the zone and from the system.

1. List all available services:

    # **firewall-cmd --get-services**
    amanda-client bacula bacula-client dhcp dhcpv6 dhcpv6-client dns ftp high-availability http https imaps ipp ipp-client ipsec kerberos kpasswd ldap ldaps libvirt libvirt-tls mdns mountd ms-wbt mysql nfs ntp openvpn pmcd pmproxy pmwebapi pmwebapis pop3s postgresql proxy-dhcp radius rpc-bind samba samba-client smtp ssh telnet tftp tftp-client transmission-client vnc-server wbem-https

2. List all services defined in the default (public) and internal zones:

    # **firewall-cmd --list-services**
    dhcpv6-client ssh
    # **firewall-cmd --list-services --zone internal**
    dhcpv6-client ipp-client mdns samba-client ssh

3. Query whether the tftp service is available in public and work zones:

    # **firewall-cmd --query-service tftp**
    no
    # **firewall-cmd --query-service tftp --zone work**
    no

4. Create a service template for a new service called testservice and check the file in the */etc/firewalld/services* directory:

    # **firewall-cmd --permanent --new-service testservice**
    # **ll /etc/firewalld/services/testservice***
    -rw-r--r--. 1 root root 60 Dec 22 12:49 testservice.xml

5. Modify the *testservice.xml* file and include the following information:

```
# vi /etc/firewalld/services/testservice.xml
<?xml version="1.0" encoding="utf-8"?>
<service>
<short>testservice</short>
<description>Custom testservice</description>
<port protocol="tcp" port="11111"/>
</service>
```

6. Add the testservice to the work zone and activate it:

    # firewall-cmd --permanent --add-service testservice --zone work
    # firewall-cmd --reload

7. List all services for the work zone to confirm the presence and activation of the new service:

    # firewall-cmd --list-services --zone work
    dhcpv6-client ipp-client ssh testservice

8. Remove the testservice service from the work zone and then delete it from the system:

    # firewall-cmd --permanent --remove-service testservice --zone work
    # firewall-cmd --permanent --delete-service testservice

9. Reload the rules and list all services for the work zone to verify the deletion:

    # firewall-cmd --reload
    # firewall-cmd --list-services --zone work
    dhcpv6-client ipp-client ssh

firewalld Command Options for Port Management

Viewing and managing firewalld ports involves several tasks that can be performed with the
firewall-cmd command. There are several options available with the command and are described in
Table 17-4.

Option	Description
--list-ports	Lists ports added to a zone.
--add-port	Adds a port to a zone.
--remove-port	Removes a port from a zone.
--query-port	Checks whether a port is added to a zone.
--permanent	Used with the add and remove options for persistence.
--zone	Used for operations on a non-default zone.

Table 17-4 Port Management Options

For each permanent change, the corresponding zone file is updated in the */etc/firewalld/zones*
directory.

Exercise 17-3: View and Manage Ports

This exercise should be done on *server1*.

In this exercise, we will demonstrate the use of various port management options described in Table 16-4. You will display all ports for the default zone and query whether TCP port 53 is added to the dmz zone. You will add TCP port 53 to the default zone persistently and UDP port range 1000 to 1010 to the work zone temporarily. Finally, you will remove port 53 and port range 1000 to 1010 from respective zones.

1. Display ports defined for the default zone:

    # **firewall-cmd --list-ports**
    5901-5902/tcp

2. Query whether TCP port 53 is added to the dmz zone:

    # **firewall-cmd --query-port 53/tcp --zone dmz**
    no

3. Add TCP port 53 to the default (public) zone permanently and activate it:

    # **firewall-cmd --permanent --add-port 53/tcp**
    # **firewall-cmd --reload**

4. Add UDP port range 1000 to 1010 to the work zone temporarily:

    # **firewall-cmd --add-port 1000-1010/udp --zone work**

5. Confirm the addition for both of the above:

    # **firewall-cmd --list-ports**
    5901-5902/tcp 53/tcp
    # **firewall-cmd --list-ports --zone work**
    1000-1010/tcp

6. Remove temporary port range 1000-1010 from the work zone and confirm:

    # **firewall-cmd --reload**
    # **firewall-cmd --list-ports --zone work**

7. Remove port 53 from the default zone permanently and activate the change:

    # **firewall-cmd --permanent --remove-port 53/tcp ; firewall-cmd --reload**

8. Validate the removal:

    # **firewall-cmd --list-ports**
    5901-5902/tcp

firewalld Command Options for Using Rich Language Rules

Viewing and managing firewalld rich rules involves several tasks that can be performed with the *firewall-cmd* command. There are several options available with the command and are described in Table 17-5.

Option	Description
--list-rich-rules	Lists rich rules added to a zone.
--add-rich-rule	Adds a rich rule to a zone.
--remove-rich-rule	Removes a rich rule from a zone.
--query-rich-rule	Checks whether a rich rule is added to a zone.
--permanent	Used with the add and remove options.
--zone	Used for operations on a non-default zone.

Table 17-5 Rich Language Options

For each permanent change, the corresponding zone file is updated in the */etc/firewalld/zones* directory.

Exercise 17-4: Manage Rules Using Rich Language

This exercise should be done on *server1*.

In this exercise, we will demonstrate the use of various rule management options using the rich language as described in Table 16-4. You will add a persistent rich rule to the default zone and a temporary rich rule to the dmz zone with a twenty-four hour validity. You will list the added rules. Lastly, you will remove both rich rules and confirm.

1. Add a persistent rich rule to the default zone to allow inbound HTTP access from network 192.168.3.0/24. This rule should log messages with a prefix "HTTP Allow Rule" at the info level. Load the new rule.

    ```
    # firewall-cmd --add-rich-rule 'rule family="ipv4" source address="192.168.3.0/24" \
    service name="http" log prefix="HTTP Allow Rule" level="info" accept' \
    --permanent
    # firewall-cmd --reload
    ```

2. Display the code added to the default zone file for this permanent rich rule:

    ```
    # cat /etc/firewalld/zones/public.xml
    . . . . . . . .
      <rule family="ipv4">
       <source address="192.168.3.0/24"/>
       <service name="http"/>
       <log prefix="HTTP Allow Rule" level="info"/>
       <accept/>
      </rule>
    . . . . . . . .
    ```

3. Add a temporary rich rule to the dmz zone to reject inbound telnet access from network 192.168.4.0/24. This rule should log messages with a prefix "telnet Access Denied" at the info level and should automatically expire after remain in place for twenty-four hours.

    # **firewall-cmd --add-rich-rule 'rule family="ipv4" source address="192.168.4.0/24" \
    service name="telnet" log prefix="telnet Access Denied" level="info" reject' \
    --timeout="86400" --zone dmz**

4. Display both rich rules:

    # **firewall-cmd --list-rich-rules**
    rule family="ipv4" source address="192.168.3.0/24" service name="http" log prefix="HTTP Allow Rule" level="info" accept
    # **firewall-cmd --list-rich-rules --zone dmz**
    rule family="ipv4" source address="192.168.4.0/24" service name="telnet" log prefix="telnet Access Denied" level="info" reject

5. Remove both rules:

    # **firewall-cmd --remove-rich-rule 'rule family="ipv4" service name="http" \
    source address="192.168.3.0/24" log prefix="HTTP Allow Rule" level="info" accept'\
    --permanent**
    # **firewall-cmd --reload**

6. Confirm the deletion of both rules:

    # **firewall-cmd --list-rich-rules**
    # **firewall-cmd --list-rich-rules --zone dmz**

firewalld Command Options for Masquerade Management

Viewing and managing firewalld masquerading involves several tasks that can be performed with the *firewall-cmd* command. There are several options available with the command and are described in Table 17-6.

Option	Description
--add-masquerade	Adds a masquerade to a zone.
--remove-masquerade	Removes a masquerade from a zone.
--query-masquerade	Checks whether a masquerade is added to a zone.
--permanent	Used with the add and remove options for persistence.
--zone	Used for operations on a non-default zone.

Table 17-6 Masquerading Management Options

For each permanent change, the corresponding zone file is updated in the */etc/firewalld/zones* directory.

Exercise 17-5: Add and Remove Masquerading

This exercise should be done on *server1*.

In this exercise, we will use internal and external zones. We assume that the internal zone has *eth1* (192.168.0.111) and the external zone has *team0* (192.168.2.110) interfaces added. We also assume that the IP of *team0* is official and that it acts as the gateway for outgoing requests.

1. Ensure *eth1* and *team0* are configured correctly, and are already part of internal and external zones, respectively.
2. Add masquerading support to the external zone:

   # **firewall-cmd --zone external --add-masquerade**

3. Query on the external zone to confirm the setting:

   # **firewall-cmd --query-masquerade --zone external**
   yes

4. Remove masquerading support from the external zone:

   # **firewall-cmd --remove-masquerade --zone external**

firewalld Command Options for Port Forwarding

Viewing and managing firewalld port forwarding involves several tasks that can be performed with the *firewall-cmd* command. There are several options available with the command and are described in Table 17-7.

Option	Description
--list-forward-ports	Lists all forwarded ports for a zone.
--add-forward-port	Adds a port to a zone to forward traffic to.
--remove-forward-port	Removes a forwarded port from a zone.
--query-forward-port	Checks whether a port is set for forwarding in a zone.
--permanent	Used with the add and remove options for persistence.
--zone	Used for operations on a non-default zone.

Table 17-7 Port Forwarding Management Options

For each permanent change, the corresponding zone file is updated in the */etc/firewalld/zones* directory.

Exercise 17-6: Add and Remove Port Forwarding

This exercise should be done on *server1*.

In this exercise, we will enable masquerading on the external zone first and then demonstrate the use of various port forwarding options described in Table 17-7. You will forward inbound telnet traffic to a local port, ftp traffic to a range of ports, smtp traffic to a different IP, and tftp traffic to a port on a different IP permanently. You will activate all the rules and display them. Finally, you will remove all port forwarding rules configured in this exercise.

1. Enable masquerading on the external zone:

   # **firewall-cmd --zone external --add-masquerade**

2. Forward inbound telnet traffic to port 1000 on the same system:

    **# firewall-cmd --zone external --add-forward-port port=23:proto=tcp:toport=1000 \
    --permanent**

3. Forward inbound ftp traffic to port range 1001 to 1005 on the same system:

    **# firewall-cmd --zone external --permanent \
    --add-forward-port port=21:proto=tcp:toport=1001-1005**

4. Forward inbound smtp traffic to the same port number but to IP 192.168.0.121:

    **# firewall-cmd --zone external --permanent \
    --add-forward-port port=25:proto=tcp:toaddr=192.168.0.121**

5. Forward inbound tftp traffic to 192.168.0.121:1010:

    **# firewall-cmd --zone external --permanent \
    --add-forward-port port=69:proto=tcp:toport=1010:toaddr=192.168.0.121**

6. Activate the above persistent rules:

    # firewall-cmd --reload

7. Display the above rules:

    # firewall-cmd --list-forward-port --zone external
    port=25:proto=tcp:toport=:toaddr=192.168.0.121
    port=21:proto=tcp:toport=1001-1005:toaddr=
    port=69:proto=tcp:toport=1010:toaddr=192.168.0.121
    port=23:proto=tcp:toport=1000:toaddr=

8. Remove all port forwarding rules added to the external zone:

    **# for i in `firewall-cmd --zone external --list-forward-port` ; do firewall-cmd \
    --zone external --permanent --remove-forward-port $i ; done**

9. Reload the firewall rules and confirm deletion:

    # firewall-cmd --reload ; firewall-cmd --zone external --list-forward-port

Understanding and Managing Kerberos

The default user authentication scheme employed in RHEL and most other operating systems requires a user to enter their password at each login attempt and at each use of a remote service, such as rlogin, rcp, rsh, telnet, ftp, ssh, NFS, and Samba. This scheme involves the transmission of unencrypted user passwords across unsecure networks, posing a serious security threat.

Kerberos is a network authentication protocol that presents a secure mechanism using a blend of secret-key cryptography and a trusted third party to authenticate users to services running on remote servers. It employs strong encryption and a complex identification algorithm for authentication.

The Kerberos authentication mechanism surrounds a central administration server that generates, issues, and validates digital identities for users and systems within its administrative domain. A user is initially granted a master ticket that is used to identify the user to that central server. When the user needs to access a service that runs on a remote server within the administrative domain, the user's master ticket is presented to the central server as proof of identity, along with a request to allow access to the remote service. Upon validation of the user's identity, the central server provides the user with another ticket that is used as an authorization to access that particular remote service. The user forwards this new ticket to the remote service to gain access. Both master and additional tickets are stored locally on the client system. For each subsequent access attempt to this service, the stored service ticket is used for identification and authentication, eliminating the need for user password transmission over the network. All exchange of information between the client and central server, and the client and remote server is transparent from a user perspective.

The Kerberos protocol was developed at the Massachusetts Institute of Technology (MIT). RHEL7 includes the support for version 5 of this protocol, which is the latest. Kerberos uses port 88 for general communication, and port 749 for the administration of Kerberos database via commands such as *kadmin* and *kpasswd*. Kerberos may be configured to use either TCP or UDP protocol. The */etc/services* file shows the port and protocol information for various services including Kerberos. The following is an excerpt from this file:

```
# grep –i kerberos /etc/services
```

kerberos	88/tcp	kerberos5 krb5	# Kerberos v5
kerberos	88/udp	kerberos5 krb5	# Kerberos v5
kpasswd	464/tcp	kpwd	# Kerberos "passwd"
kpasswd	464/udp	kpwd	# Kerberos "passwd"
kerberos-adm	749/tcp		# Kerberos `kadmin' (v5)
kerberos-adm	749/udp		# kerberos administration
kftp-data	6620/tcp		# Kerberos V5 FTP Data
kftp-data	6620/udp		# Kerberos V5 FTP Data
kftp	6621/tcp		# Kerberos V5 FTP Control
kftp	6621/udp		# Kerberos V5 FTP Control
ktelnet	6623/tcp		# Kerberos V5 Telnet
ktelnet	6623/udp		# Kerberos V5 Telnet

The Kerberos ticketing system relies heavily on resolving hostnames and on accurate timestamps to issue and expire tickets. Therefore, it requires adequate clock synchronization and a working DNS server (or an accurate */etc/hosts* file) to function correctly.

Terminology

Several key Kerberos terms need to be comprehended before we go into further detail. They are described below.

Authentication: The process of verifying the identity of a user (or service).

Authentication Service (AS): A service that runs on the Key Distribution Center (KDC) server to authenticate clients and issue initial tickets.

Client: A user or service (such as NFS or Samba) that requests for the issuance of tickets to use network services.

Credentials: A ticket along with relevant encryption keys.

Key Distribution Center (KDC) Database: A database of principals and their corresponding encryption keys.

Key Distribution Center (KDC) Server: A central server, also called a Kerberos server, that runs the Authentication Service (AS) and the Ticket Granting Service (TGS). It stores and maintains the KDC database.

Principal: A verified client (user or service) that is recorded in the KDC database and to which the KDC can assign tickets.

Realm: The administrative territory of a KDC, with one or more KDCs and several principals.

Service Host: A system that runs a kerberized service that clients can use.

Session Key: An encrypted key that is used to secure communication among clients, KDCs, and service hosts.

Service Ticket: An encrypted digital certificate used to authenticate a user to a specific network service. It is issued by the Ticket Granting Service (TGS) after validating a user's Ticket Granting Ticket (TGT), and it contains a session key, the principal name, an expiration time, etc. A service ticket can be thought of as a visa stamped on a passport (TGT) by the issuing country (TGS) to be allowed to enter a foreign country (network service on a service host).

Ticket Granting Service (TGS): A service that runs on the KDC to generate and issue service tickets to clients.

Ticket Granting Ticket (TGT): An initial encrypted digital certificate that is used to identify a client to TGS at the time of requesting service tickets. It is issued by the AS after validating the client's presence in the KDC database, and comprises of the client's hostname and IP, the time of ticket generation, an expiration time, an encrypted session key, etc. A TGT is encrypted using a user's password, and it is valid for a few hours only, after which it may be renewed transparently and automatically. A TGT can be thought of as a passport that authenticates the holder's identity and authorizes them to travel to foreign countries.

How Kerberos Authenticates Clients

The Kerberos authentication process can be separated into three parts: an initial stage of getting a TGT (passport), a service stage to obtain a service ticket (visa), and access the service (travel to the visa issuing country). Here is how it works.

A user contacts the AS for initial authentication via the *kinit* command. The AS asks for the user's password, validates it, and generates a TGT for the user. The AS also produces a session key using the user's password. The AS returns the credentials (TGT plus the session key) to the user, which the user decrypts by entering their password. The credentials are saved in the client's credential cache. The TGT has a limited validity and it is set to expire after a few hours.

Later, when the user needs to access a service running on a remote service host, they send the TGT and the session key to the TGS asking to grant the desired access. The TGS verifies the user's credentials by decrypting the TGT, and assembles a service ticket for the desired service and encrypts it with the service host's secret key. It transmits the service ticket to the user along with a session key. The user stores the service ticket in their credential cache. The user presents these credentials to the service host, which decrypts the service ticket with its secret key and validates the user's identity and the authorization to access the service. The user is then allowed access to the service. During this entire communication process, the user's password is not transmitted over the network. All communication is encrypted and clients properly authenticated.

Figure 17-4 presents a simple illustration of how the Kerberos authentication mechanism works. It shows how initial communication takes place (1 and 2) between a client (user1 on server1) and the KDC (AS on server2), how a service ticket is requested (3) and issued (4), and finally how the client (user1 on server1) establishes a link with the service (telnetd) on the service host (host1). The Figure shows that all three systems are located within a Kerberos realm called EXAMPLE.COM.

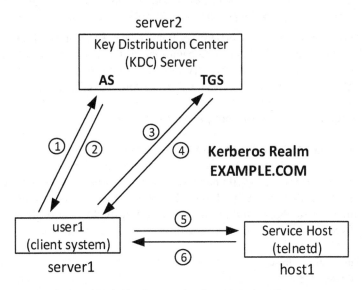

Figure 17-4 Kerberos Authentication Process

Kerberos Packages and Utilities

There are two software packages that provide Kerberos server and client functionality. These packages are krb5-server and krb5-workstation. Additional packages may be auto-selected and auto-loaded during installation to satisfy dependency requirements.

Several tools become available after the Kerberos software is installed. Some of the key client commands are described in Table 17-8.

Command	Description
kinit	Obtains and caches TGT.
kdestroy	Destroys tickets stored in credential cache.
klist	Lists cached tickets.
kpasswd	Changes a principal's password.
kadmin	Administers Kerberos database via the kadmind daemon.
kadmin.local	Same as kadmin, but performs operations directly on the KDC database.

Table 17-8 Kerberos Commands

We will use some of these commands in this chapter. Check man pages for the others if needed.

Exercise 17-7: Configure a Client to Authenticate Using Kerberos

This exercise should be done on *server1*.

This exercise assumes that *server2* is running Kerberos services (both KDC and admin services) for realm EXAMPLE.COM, the *root* user is added as an admin principal, DNS is disabled, and the *hosts* file is updated with appropriate mappings for both servers. It is also presumed that the */etc/ssh/sshd_config* file on the Kerberos server has KerberosAuthentication, GSSAPIAuthentication, and GSSAPIDelegateCredentials directives set to yes, and the *sshd* service restarted. We will use *server2* as the service host as well.

In this exercise, you will configure Kerberos client on *server1* to authenticate via Kerberos server *server2.example.com*. You will add *server1* principal to the KDC database, and create and store the key file locally on the client. You will modify the ssh client configuration file and activate the use of Kerberos. Finally, you will obtain a TGT for *user1* and log in as them to test the configuration.

1. Install the required Kerberos client packages:

   # **yum –y install krb5-workstation**

2. Ensure that the */etc/krb5.conf* file has the following directives set. The first three directives disable DNS lookups and set the default Kerberos realm. The next set of directives defines the hostnames for the KDC and admin servers, and the last set of directives sets the mappings between DNS domains and Kerberos realms.

   ```
   dns_lookup_realm = false
   dns_lookup_kdc = false
   default_realm = EXAMPLE.COM
   [realms]
    EXAMPLE.COM = {
     kdc = server2.example.com
     admin_server = server2.example.com
    }
   [domain_realm]
    example.com = EXAMPLE.COM
    .example.com = EXAMPLE.COM
   ```

3. Log in as the *root* principal (assumed to be added as part of Kerberos server setup) and add *server1* as a host principal to the KDC database:

   # **kadmin –p root/admin**
   Authenticating as principal root/admin with password.
   Password for root/admin@EXAMPLE.COM:
   kadmin: **addprinc –randkey host/server1.example.com**
   WARNING: no policy specified for host/server1.example.com@EXAMPLE.COM; defaulting to no policy
   Principal "host/server1.example.com@EXAMPLE.COM" created.

4. While logged in, extract the principal's key and store it locally in a keytab file called *krb5.keytab* in the */etc* directory:

   kadmin: **ktadd –k /etc/krb5.keytab host/server1.example.com**
   Entry for principal host/server1.example.com with kvno 2, encryption type aes256-cts-hmac-sha1-96 added to keytab WRFILE:/etc/krb5.keytab.
   Entry for principal host/server1.example.com with kvno 2, encryption type aes128-cts-hmac-sha1-96 added to keytab WRFILE:/etc/krb5.keytab.
   Entry for principal host/server1.example.com with kvno 2, encryption type des3-cbc-sha1 added to keytab WRFILE:/etc/krb5.keytab.
   Entry for principal host/server1.example.com with kvno 2, encryption type arcfour-hmac added to keytab WRFILE:/etc/krb5.keytab.
   Entry for principal host/server1.example.com with kvno 2, encryption type camellia256-cts-cmac added to keytab WRFILE:/etc/krb5.keytab.
   Entry for principal host/server1.example.com with kvno 2, encryption type camellia128-cts-cmac added to keytab WRFILE:/etc/krb5.keytab.
   Entry for principal host/server1.example.com with kvno 2, encryption type des-hmac-sha1 added to keytab WRFILE:/etc/krb5.keytab.
   Entry for principal host/server1.example.com with kvno 2, encryption type des-cbc-md5 added to keytab WRFILE:/etc/krb5.keytab.

5. Activate the use of Kerberos for authentication:

   # **authconfig --enablekrb5 --update**

6. Edit the */etc/ssh/ssh_config* client configuration file and ensure the following two lines are set as shown:

   GSSAPIAuthentication yes
   GSSAPIDelegateCredentials yes

7. Log in as *user1* and execute the *kinit* command to obtain a TGT from the KDC. Enter the password for *user1* when prompted.

   $ **kinit**
   Password for user1@EXAMPLE.COM:

8. List the TGT details received in the previous step:

   $ **klist**
   Default principal: user1@EXAMPLE.COM
   Valid starting   Expires   Service principal
   11/01/15 20:58:23   12/01/15 20:58:23   krbtgt/EXAMPLE.COM@EXAMPLE.COM
        renew until 11/01/15 20:58:23

The configuration is complete and you should now be able to log back in to *server2* as *user1* without being prompted for a password.

Overview of Authentication Configuration Tool for Kerberos Client Setup

The graphical Authentication Configuration tool allows you to configure the Kerberos client service on the system. This tool was previously used in Chapter 12 "Administering Network Interfaces and Network Clients" to configure an LDAP client. This tool may be invoked by running the *authconfig-gtk* or the *system-config-authentication* command in an X terminal window or choosing Applications | Sundry | Authentication in the GNOME desktop.

Figure 17-5 Authentication Configuration Tool – Kerberos Authentication Config

Figure 17-5 shows the tool's interface. It shows the LDAP data in the User Account Configuration section that you entered at the time of setting up an LDAP client in Chapter 12. Choose "Kerberos password" as the Authentication Method for systems in the EXAMPLE.COM realm. Both KDC and Admin services are assumed to be running on *server2.example.com*. Leave the other two options unchecked unless you have a functional DNS server available and want to resolve hostnames to realms and locate KDCs for realms using the DNS. Click Apply when done.

EXAM TIP: Use the GUI tool to set up a client and check its configurtaion if you experience issues with using commands or modifying files directly.

Chapter Summary

This chapter covered two important advanced system administration topics: firewalld and Kerberos. We learned the basics of firewalld and its components, and saw how network interfaces are defined in various zones based upon the level of trust. We also looked at how services could be set up and used. The usages of direct and rich languages were discussed. We studied network address translation and IP masquerading, and performed several exercises to strengthen the firewalld concepts learned.

We looked at Kerberos and its benefits, learned its terminology, and saw software packages and various client-side utilities. We studied how this method of authentication worked. We also performed an exercise to demonstrate the setting up of a Kerberos client.

Chapter Review Questions

1. Why is Kerberos authentication preferred over password-based authentication?
2. What is the name of the graphical firewalld configuration tool?
3. What is the name of the kernel module that implements iptables firewall?
4. What is the initial Kerberos ticket referred to as?
5. Define Network Address Translation.
6. Network interfaces are added based on the trust level of traffic that passes through them. What is the component name where interfaces are added?
7. What are the names of the two key services that run on a KDC server?
8. Firewalld is a replacement for iptables. True or False?
9. What is a Kerberos credential?
10. Which option syntax is correct: --add-port=53 or --add-port 53?
11. What does the --new-zone option do?
12. What is a major difference between rules set up using the direct interface and rich language?
13. How many registered IP addresses are needed to obtain if all of the systems on the network are behind an intermediary device?
14. By convention, a Kerberos realm is defined in lowercase letters. True or False?
15. Name two differences between firewalld and iptables.
16. Which utility is used to obtain a TGT?
17. What is the difference between a ticket-granting ticket and a service ticket?
18. What is the userland component of firewalld called?
19. What is the use of the --permanent option with the firewall-cmd command?
20. What happens if a rule is set without specifying the --permanent option?
21. What is the difference between --add-service and --new-service options?
22. What is the primary command line tool to manage firewalld rules?

Answers to Chapter Review Questions

1. Kerberos-based authentication eliminates the frequent use of unencrypted user passwords over the network.
2. The name of the graphical firewalld management tool is *firewall-config*.
3. The name of the kernel module is netfilter.
4. The initial digital ticket is referred to as a ticket-granting ticket.
5. NAT hides private IP addresses used on the internal network from the outside world.
6. The name of the firewalld component where interfaces are defined is zone.

7. The two key services that run on a KDC server are called Authentication Service and Ticket Granting Service.
8. False.
9. A Kerberos credential is a ticket along with relevant encryption key.
10. Both are correct.
11. This option lets you add a new zone to the firewalld configuration.
12. Rules set up using the direct interface are not persistent, and they are lost if firewalld service is restarted or rules reloaded. On the other hand, rich language rules are persistent across service restarts and rules reloads.
13. Only one.
14. False.
15. Firewalld activates new rules without disconnecting existing connections and it is implemented in both kernel and user spaces.
16. The *kinit* utility is used to obtain a TGT for user.
17. A ticket-granting ticket identifies a principal to the Kerberos server, while a service ticket authorizes a principal to access a kerberized network service.
18. The userland component of firewalld is referred to as the *firewall-cmd* command.
19. This option stores the rule in a configuration file.
20. The rule is activated temporarily right away.
21. The first option adds an existing service to a zone and the second option creates a new service.
22. The primary command line tool for firewalld management is called *firewall-cmd*.

DIY Challenge Labs

The following labs are useful to strengthen the concepts and topics learned in this chapter. It is expected that you perform these labs without any additional help. A step-by-step guide is not provided, as the implementation of these labs requires the knowledge that has been presented in this chapter. Use defaults or your own thinking for missing information.

Lab 17-1: Create a Persistent firewalld Service

Create a firewalld service called labserv on *server2* and add it to the internal zone. This service should allow traffic on port range 1546-1549 for both UDP and TCP protocols. Start this service and display details for verification. Make sure that this service is auto-activated at firewalld restarts.

Lab 17-2: Create a Persistent Rich Rule

Create a rich rule in the external zone to allow FTP access from network 192.168.4.0/24. This rule should prefix "FTP Allow Rule" with each logged messages at the warning level. Check appropriate files to confirm the rule addition. Load the new rule and verify with commands.

Lab 17-3: Configure a Kerberos Client

Configure *user3* on *host1* to authenticate using Kerberos on *server2*. Create *user3* if they do not already exist. Run appropriate commands to test the configuration.

Chapter 18

Tuning Kernel Parameters, Reporting System Usage, and Logging Remotely

This chapter describes the following major topics:

➤ Understand kernel parameters

➤ Overview of run-time and boot-time parameters

➤ Modify run-time and boot-time parameters

➤ Report system resource usage with sysstat and dstat toolsets

➤ Overview of remote system logging

➤ Set up a system as a loghost server

➤ Set up a system as a loghost client

RHCE Objectives:

59. Use /proc/sys and sysctl to modify and set kernel runtime parameters
62. Produce and deliver reports on system utilization (processor, memory, disk, and network)
64. Configure a system to log to a remote system
65. Configure a system to accept logging from a remote system

The behavior of the default kernel installed during the installation process may be changed by modifying the values of one or more of its parameters. There are several kernel parameters that may be tuned for a smooth installation and proper operation of certain applications and database software during runtime. Moreover, a system may be booted with specific boot-time parameters supplied to the kernel.

Monitoring and reporting utilization of processors, memory, disks, and network interface resources is a key in determining bottlenecks in the system. Monitoring helps identify any potential performance issues and the monitored data can be stored for auditing or analysis.

Logs generated on one system may be forwarded to and stored on a remote system. This makes the remote system a central repository for all messages generated on that system. The remote system may be configured to receive forwarded messages from several clients.

Understanding and Tuning Kernel Parameters

We discussed the Linux kernel in Chapter 07 "Booting RHEL7, Updating Kernel, and Logging Messages" at length. We also looked at modules that added support for software and hardware components to the kernel. There is another element that controls the behavior of the kernel, and it is called a kernel *parameter*. We will discuss kernel parameters and look at how to tune and use them to alter the kernel conduct both during the normal system operational state and at boot.

Run-Time Parameters

Run-time parameters control the kernel behavior while the system is operational. The default parameter values are typically acceptable for normal system operation; however, one or more of them must be modified in order to meet the requirements for smooth installation and proper operation of certain applications, such as database or ERP software.

RHEL7 has over a thousand runtime kernel parameters with more added as new modules and applications are installed on the system. These parameters are set automatically during kernel loading. The current list of active runtime parameters may be viewed with the *sysctl* command as follows:

```
# sysctl –a
abi.vsyscall32 = 1
crypto.fips_enabled = 0
debug.exception-trace = 1
debug.kprobes-optimization = 1
dev.hpet.max-user-freq = 64
dev.mac_hid.mouse_button2_keycode = 97
dev.mac_hid.mouse_button3_keycode = 100
dev.mac_hid.mouse_button_emulation = 0
. . . . . . . .
vm.scan_unevictable_pages = 0
vm.stat_interval = 1
vm.swappiness = 30
vm.user_reserve_kbytes = 29940
vm.vfs_cache_pressure = 100
vm.zone_reclaim_mode = 0
```

Runtime values for these parameters are stored in various files located under sub-directories in the *proc/sys* directory and can be altered on the fly by changing associated files. This change remains in effect until either the value is re-adjusted or the system is rebooted. This temporary change can be accomplished with the *sysctl* or the *echo* command. To make the change survive across system reboots, the value must be defined either directly in the */etc/sysctl.conf* file or in a file under the */etc/sysctl.d* directory.

By default, *sysctl.conf* contains only a few comments. There is another file, */usr/lib/sysctl.d/00-system.conf*, that stores system default settings. The contents of this file are captured from *server1* and displayed below:

cat /usr/lib/sysctl.d/00-system.conf
Disable netfilter on bridges.
net.bridge.bridge-nf-call-ip6tables = 0
net.bridge.bridge-nf-call-iptables = 0
net.bridge.bridge-nf-call-arptables = 0
# Controls the maximum shared segment size, in bytes
kernel.shmmax = 4294967295
# Controls the maximum number of shared memory segments, in pages
kernel.shmall = 268435456

The five uncommented lines in the above output indicate the setting of five parameters through this file, and this can be verified with the *sysctl* command. The following *grep*s for the kernel.shmmax parameter for confirmation:

# **sysctl –a | grep kernel.shmmax**
kernel.shmmax = 4294967295

The output confirms that the value for the parameter in the runtime kernel as well as in the */usr/lib/sysctl.d/00-system.conf* file is identical.

Exercise 18-1: Tune Run-Time Kernel Parameters

This exercise should be done on *server1*.

In this exercise, you will set the value of sunrpc.tcp_fin_timeout parameter to 18 and ensure that this change takes effect right away. Reboot the system and observe the value of this parameter. You will change this parameter value again to 16 and making sure that it is persistent. Reboot the system again and observe the result.

1. Display the current value of sunrpc.tcp_fin_timeout parameter using either of the following:

   # **sysctl sunrpc.tcp_fin_timeout**
   sunrpc.tcp_fin_timeout = 15
   # **cat /proc/sys/sunrpc/tcp_fin_timeout**
   15

2. Change the value from 15 to 18 instantly with either of the following:

```
# sysctl –w sunrpc.tcp_fin_timeout=18
sunrpc.tcp_fin_timeout = 18
# echo 18 > /proc/sys/sunrpc/tcp_fin_timeout
```

3. Reboot the system and check the value of the parameter again. You will observe that the value is reset to 15.

```
# sysctl sunrpc.tcp_fin_timeout
sunrpc.tcp_fin_timeout = 15
```

4. Change the value to 16 persistently by appending an entry to the *etc/sysctl.conf* file:

```
sunrpc.tcp_fin_timeout=18
```

5. Load the new value from the *etc/sysctl.conf* file:

```
# sysctl –p
sunrpc.tcp_fin_timeout = 16
```

EXAM TIP: To store kernel parameter values persistently, add them to the /etc/sysctl.conf file.

At this point, you can reboot the system and then check to ensure that the new value has survived the reboot.

Boot-Time Parameters

Boot-time parameters, also referred to as command-line options, affect the boot behavior of the kernel. Their purpose is to pass any hardware-specific information that the kernel would otherwise not be able to determine automatically, or to override random values that the kernel would detect by itself. Boot-time parameters are supplied to the kernel via the GRUB2 interface.

The entire boot string along with the command-line options can be viewed after the system has booted up and it is in operational state. This information is gathered and stored in the */proc/cmdline* file, and can be viewed with the *cat* command as follows:

```
# cat /proc/cmdline
BOOT_IMAGE=/vmlinuz-3.10.0-123.el7.x86_64 root=UUID=04801120-a151-46c2-90b7-437770c61af2
ro rd.lvm.lv=vg00/swap vconsole.font=latarcyrheb-sun16 crashkernel=auto vconsole.keymap=us
rd.lvm.lv=vg00/root rhgb quiet LANG=en_CA.UTF-8
```

The output shows the kernel name, version, UUID of the root file system, and several other boot-time parameters that were passed to the kernel by default at the last system boot. This information is stored in the */boot/grub2/grub.cfg* file on x86 systems.

EXAM TIP: Make a copy of the grub.cfg file before attempting to modify it manually. If the original file becomes inconsistent, you can boot the system into single user and put the copy back on the original file.

There are two options to supply boot-time parameters to the kernel. We can either modify the *grub.cfg* file and add the required parameters to the default kernel boot string or specify them at boot-time by interacting with GRUB2. With the first option, the change will be permanent and it will be applied each time the system is rebooted. The second option is effective for one particular boot only.

Exercise 18-2: Tune Boot-Time Kernel Parameters

This exercise should be done on *server1*.

In this exercise, you will modify the default kernel boot entry and append a kernel parameter called kernstack with value 1 to it. You will ensure that this change is persistent. You will reboot the system and display the file contents of */proc/cmdline* to verify the presence of the parameter.

1. Check the kernel boot string that was used at the last system boot:

   # **cat /proc/cmdline**
   BOOT_IMAGE=/vmlinuz-3.10.0-123.el7.x86_64 root=UUID=04801120-a151-46c2-90b7-437770c61af2 ro rd.lvm.lv=vg00/swap vconsole.font=latarcyrheb-sun16 crashkernel=auto vconsole.keymap=us rd.lvm.lv=vg00/root rhgb quiet LANG=en_CA.UTF-8

2. Open the */boot/grub2/grub.cfg* file and navigate to the "BEGIN /etc/grub.d/10_linux" section. Add "kernstack=1" to the linux16 directive under the first menuentry item as highlighted in bolded text below:

   ### BEGIN /etc/grub.d/10_linux ###
   menuentry 'Red Hat Enterprise Linux Server, with Linux 3.10.0-123.el7.x86_64' --class red --class gnu-linux --class gnu --class os --unrestricted $menuentry_id_option 'gnulinux-3.10.0-123.el7.x86_64-advanced-04801120-a151-46c2-90b7-437770c61af2' {
           load_video
           set gfxpayload=keep
           insmod gzio
           insmod part_msdos
           insmod xfs
           set root='hd0,msdos1'
           if [x$feature_platform_search_hint = xy]; then
             search --no-floppy --fs-uuid --set=root --hint='hd0,msdos1' 2d9d642b-fe71-4afe-ad39-90c73c4aabb1
           else
             search --no-floppy --fs-uuid --set=root 2d9d642b-fe71-4afe-ad39-90c73c4aabb1
           fi
           linux16 /vmlinuz-3.10.0-123.el7.x86_64 root=UUID=04801120-a151-46c2-90b7-437770c61af2 ro rd.lvm.lv=vg00/swap vconsole.font=latarcyrheb-sun16 crashkernel=auto vconsole.keymap=us rd.lvm.lv=vg00/root rhgb quiet LANG=en_CA.UTF-8 **kernstack=1**
           initrd16 /initramfs-3.10.0-123.el7.x86_64.img
   }

3. Reboot the system for testing.
4. Display the file contents of */proc/cmdline* again, and check to confirm that the kernel did boot with the kernstack option:

```
# cat /proc/cmdline
BOOT_IMAGE=/vmlinuz-3.10.0-123.el7.x86_64 root=UUID=04801120-a151-46c2-90b7-
437770c61af2 ro rd.lvm.lv=vg00/swap vconsole.font=latarcyrheb-sun16 crashkernel=auto
vconsole.keymap=us rd.lvm.lv=vg00/root rhgb quiet LANG=en_CA.UTF-8 kernstack = 1
```

Generating System Usage Reports

Monitoring system resources and reporting their utilization are important system administration tasks. System resources include CPU, memory, disk, and network. There are several tools available and their use is dependent on what report you wish to generate. RHEL comprises of sysstat and dstat software packages that include tools to monitor the performance and usage of these resources, and generate reports. Moreover, numerous native tools in RHEL are available for monitoring and reporting resource utilization to ascertain where, if any, bottlenecks exist. These tools include *df* for viewing disk and file system utilization, *vmstat* for viewing virtual memory statistics, *top* for realtime viewing of CPU, memory, swap, and processes, and so on. See chapters in the RHCSA section for details on these tools.

The sysstat Toolset

The sysstat toolset includes several additional monitoring and performance reporting commands such as *cifsiostat, iostat, mpstat, nfsiostat, pidstat, sadf,* and *sar*. These commands are described in Table 18-1.

Command	Description
cifsiostat	Reports read and write operations on CIFS file systems.
iostat	Reports CPU, device, and partition statistics.
mpstat	Reports activities for each available CPU.
nfsiostat	Reports read and write operations on NFS file systems.
pidstat	Reports statistics for running processes.
sa1	Captures and stores binary data in sadd (system activity daily data) files located in the /var/log/sa directory.
sa2	Captures and stores daily reports in sardd (system activity reporter daily data) files located in the /var/log/sa directory.
sadc	System activity data reporter. Samples and writes binary data in sadd files located in the /var/log/sa directory at a specified number of times with a specified interval.
sadf	Displays data gathered by the sar command in various formats.
sar	System activity reporter. Gathers and reports system activities, and stores the data in binary format.
dstat	Reports CPU, disk, network, paging, and system statistics. More powerful and versatile than the vmstat and iostat commands combined.

Table 18-1 sysstat Performance and Reporting Commands

You may need to install the sysstat package on the system. Run the following to install it:

```
# yum –y install sysstat
```

The sysstat service references two configuration files, *sysstat* and *sysstat.ioconf*, which are located in the */etc/sysconfig* directory. The *sysstat* file defines three directives: HISTORY, COMPRESSAFTER, and SADC_OPTIONS, by default, as shown below:

# **grep –v ^# /etc/sysconfig/sysstat | grep –v ^$**
HISTORY=28
COMPRESSAFTER=31
SADC_OPTIONS="–S DISK"

The first directive sets a limit on the number of days (default is 28) to keep the log files, the second directive determines the age (default is 31) of the log files after which they are compressed, and the third directive defines the arguments to be passed to the *sadc* command when it is executed. The *sysstat.ioconf* file directs how to gather disk I/O information, and this file is normally left intact.

In addition to the two configuration files, a cron job file */etc/cron.d/sysstat* is available with two default entries as shown below:

*/10 * * * * root /usr/lib64/sa/sa1 1 1
53 23 * * * root /usr/lib64/sa/sa2 –A

The first entry executes the *sa1* command at every ten-minute interval and collects and stores data in sadd files. This command is a front-end to the *sadc* command, and it is intended to run via cron.

The second cron entry executes the *sa2* command every day at 11:53 p.m., and captures statistical data and writes it in the */var/log/sa/sardd* files. This command is the front-end to the *sar* command, and it is intended to run via cron as well.

The raw data collected with the *sa1*, *sa2*, and *sar* commands can be read and extracted with the *sadf* command. Let's first review some of the key options available with *sadf*. Table 18-2 describes them.

Option	Description
–d	Generates a report in a database-friendly format.
–D	Generates a report in a database-friendly format with the time expressed in seconds since the epoch time.
–e	Expresses the end time in the twenty-four hour format.
–p	Generates a report in the awk-friendly format.
–s	Expresses the start time in the twenty-four hour format.
–x	Generates a report in the XML-friendly format.

Table 18-2 sadf Command Options

Let's use some of these options in the following example to generate a report with data extracted between 9:00 a.m. and 5:00 p.m. on the fifteenth of the month:

sadf –s 09:00:00 –e 17:00:00 /var/log/sa/sa15
server1.example.com   599   2014-12-15 05:10:01 UTC all %user   0.31
server1.example.com   599   2014-12-15 05:10:01 UTC all %nice   0.00
server1.example.com   599   2014-12-15 05:10:01 UTC all %system 0.05
server1.example.com   599   2014-12-15 05:10:01 UTC all %iowait 0.08

```
. . . . . . . .
    server1.example.com   599   2014-12-16 04:50:01 UTC all   %iowait   0.00
    server1.example.com   599   2014-12-16 04:50:01 UTC all   %steal    0.00
    server1.example.com   599   2014-12-16 04:50:01 UTC all   %idle    99.67
```

You may redirect the above output to a file for future review.

The following example produces a database-friendly report on CPU (–u), memory (–r), disk (–d), and network interfaces (–n) by running the *sar* command using data from the twentieth of the month:

```
# sadf –d /var/log/sa/sa20 -- –urd –n DEV
# hostname;interval;timestamp;CPU;%user;%nice;%system;%iowait;%steal;%idle
server1.example.com;599;2014-12-20 05:10:01 UTC;-1;0.35;0.00;0.06;0.00;0.00;99.59
server1.example.com;599;2014-12-20 05:20:01 UTC;-1;0.36;0.00;0.05;0.00;0.00;99.59
server1.example.com;599;2014-12-20 05:30:01 UTC;-1;0.33;0.00;0.04;0.00;0.00;99.63
. . . . . . . .
```

In the above example, the options specified after the two hyphen characters are actually the *sar* command options. Table 18-3 lists and describes some of the key *sar* switches.

Option	Description
–d	Reports block devices.
–n	Reports network devices.
–P	Reports the specified number of CPU.
–r	Reports memory usage.
–S	Reports swap space utilization statistics.
–u	Reports CPU usage.

Table 18-3 sar Command Options

There are more options available to the *sar* command. Check the man pages for details.

The dstat Tool

The dstat package includes a single monitoring and reporting tool, which is called *dstat*. This tool is versatile and it is a replacement for the *vmstat*, *iostat*, and *ifstat* commands with enhanced features and extra counters. It displays real-time system resource utilization. This tool may be used during system performance testings and for troubleshooting. You may need to install the dstat package on the system using the following:

```
# yum –y install dstat
```

Run the *dstat* command with the –cdmn options to view the utilization for CPU (–c), disk (–d), memory (–m), and network (–n):

 # dstat –cdmn

	99		15	1895	342	1132	287	365		
	100				342	1132	287	365	60	118
10	90				342	1132	287	365	596	822
	100				342	1132	287	365	60	358
1	99				342	1132	287	365	1086	1022
	100				342	1132	287	365	60	102
	100				342	1132	287	365	306	358
	100				342	1132	287	365	60	358
1	99				342	1132	287	365	3940	920

For each resource, *dstat* reports statistics in multiple columns. This report can be written to a CSV file and imported in Excel to view the statistics in graphs.

In addition to the cdmn options used in the above example, Table 18-4 describes a few more switches that can be used for additional statistics in the output.

Option	Description
–g	Reports paging.
–y	Reports system statistics.
–p	Reports process statistics.
–r	Reports read and write request statistics.
–s	Reports swap space statistics.

Table 18-4 dstat Command Options

For instance, run *dstat* with all the options listed in Table 18-4.

 # dstat –gyprs

		33	48	0.0		0.3	0.45	0.19		500
		22	36							500
		23	44							500
		23	37							500
		20	39							500
		23	37							500
		16	32							500
		22	29							500
		19	37							500
		83	29							500
		18	35							500
		31	51							500

As mentioned earlier, the *dstat* command is versatile. It has more options available. Check the man pages for details.

Logging System Messages Remotely

We discussed local system logging in detail via the *rsyslogd* service in Chapter 07 "Booting RHEL7, Updating Kernel, and Logging Messages". Capturing and logging local messages on the system is the default behavior of this service. However, there may be circumstances that demand for consolidation of all local logs on to a central system for reasons such as audit or ease of system management.

> **EXAM TIP:** Remote logging has recently been removed from the official exam objectives list for RHCE. I have left this topic here just in case Red Hat decides to re-add it.

The same *rsyslogd* service supports network logging as well. We set up a central system (*server1*), called *loghost*, to receive and log messages generated on remote clients. We then configure the remote clients (*server2* and *host1*) to forward their messages to the loghost for storage. See Figure 18-1.

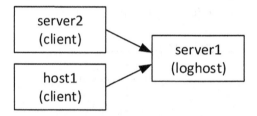

Figure 18-1 Remote System Logging

For both server and client configurations, we need to modify the same configuration file—*/etc/rsyslog.conf*—that was analyzed in Chapter 07 for local logging. Only a few changes are needed in this file on the server and the clients to establish the setup for storing and forwarding all client messages. We can configure the clients to forward logs for one or more specific rules, or just about every rule that exists in the *rsyslog.conf* file. The *rsyslogd* service supports both TCP and UDP protocols; however, we prefer to use TCP, as it is more reliable and connection-oriented. If you prefer to use UDP, simply add one @ sign as a prefix to the loghost name in the *rsyslog.conf* file. See the usage below:

```
*.*    @@remote-host:514
*.*    @remote-host:514
```

The first entry above identifies the use of TCP and the second entry implies the use of UDP. These entries also show the default well-known port (514) used by the network logging service.

Exercise 18-3: Configure a System as a Loghost

This exercise should be done on *server2*.

In this exercise, you will configure this system as a loghost to receive forwarded messages from *server1* and store them locally. You will use the TCP protocol and allow traffic to pass through port 514 unhindered.

1. Open the */etc/rsyslog.conf* file in a text editor and uncomment the following two directives located in the MODULES section:

   $ModLoad imtcp
   $InputTCPServerRun 514

2. Add TCP port 514 to the default firewalld zone, and load the new rule:

   # **firewall-cmd --permanent --add-port 514/tcp**
   success
   # **firewall-cmd --reload**
   success

3. Set the correct SELinux port type on TCP port 514:

   # **semanage port –a –t syslogd_port_t –p tcp 514**

4. Set the *rsyslog* service to autostart at each system reboot:

   # **systemctl enable rsyslog**

5. Restart the *rsyslog* service and check its operating state:

   # **systemctl restart rsyslog**
   # **systemctl status rsyslog**
   rsyslog.service - System Logging Service
     Loaded: loaded (/usr/lib/systemd/system/rsyslog.service; enabled)
     Active: active (running) since Thu 2015-01-15 07:45:01 MIST; 5s ago
    Main PID: 20166 (rsyslogd)
     CGroup: /system.slice/rsyslog.service
           └─20166 /usr/sbin/rsyslogd -n

This completes the setup for loghost and it is ready to receive remote forwarded messages.

Exercise 18-4: Configure a System as a Loghost Client
This exercise should be done on *server1*.

In this exercise, you will configure this system to forward all log messages to the loghost configured in the previous exercise. You will generate a custom message on *server1* and check for its presence in the */var/log/messages* file on the loghost to validate the setup.

1. Open the */etc/rsyslog.conf* file in a text editor and add the following to the bottom of the file:

   . @@192.168.0.120:514

2. Set the *rsyslog* service to autostart at each system reboot:

   # **systemctl enable rsyslog**

---

3. Restart the *rsyslog* service and check its operating state:

systemctl restart rsyslog
systemctl status rsyslog
rsyslog.service - System Logging Service
   Loaded: loaded (/usr/lib/systemd/system/rsyslog.service; enabled)
   Active: active (running) since Wed 2015-01-14 15:56:54 EST; 5s ago
  Main PID: 2001 (rsyslogd)
   CGroup: /system.slice/rsyslog.service
        └─2001 /usr/sbin/rsyslogd -n

4. Generate a custom log message:

logger –i "This is a test message from root on server1"

5. Log on to the loghost and tail the */var/log/messages* file:

tail /var/log/messages
Jan 14 16:18:13 server1 root[3907]: This is a test message from root on server1

The alert generated on the loghost client is logged to the *messages* file on the loghost. This completes the setup for a loghost client and confirms the operation of the service as configured.

Chapter Summary

This chapter presented three topics: kernel parameter tuning, system resource usage reporting, and remote system logging.

We discussed run-time and boot-time kernel parameters and demonstrated how to modify their values temporarily and permanently.

Next, we looked at monitoring and reporting system resource utilization. We discussed several tools and saw how to generate and display reports using them. We learned the *sa1*, *sa2*, and *sar* commands for capturing performance data and storing it in files and a different tool to display the stored data.

Finally, we covered the setup of a central logging environment with one loghost and one client after briefly discussing the benefits associated with central logging. We tested the client/server setup by generating and capturing log messages.

Chapter Review Questions

1. What is the default port used by the *rsyslog* service?
2. Which command is used to display the performance data captured with the *sar* command?
3. Which temporary file stores the boot string that is used to boot the system?
4. The *sar* command may be used to display data for a specified time range. True or False?
5. Which command in the dstat package displays real-time performance data for CPU, memory, disk, and network?
6. Why would you need to modify a runtime kernel parameter?
7. Which software package includes the *dstat* command?
8. What would the command *sysctl* do with the –p switch?

9. Kernel parameters cannot be modified in multi-user target. True or False?
10. What is the name of the primary file for defining kernel parameters?
11. What two commands can you use to alter a runtime kernel parameter?
12. Where do you store the boot-time parameters persistently?
13. What would the command *sysctl –w net.ipv4.tcp_abc=3* do?
14. How would you verify the boot-time parameter supplied to boot the current system?

Answers to Chapter Review Questions

1. The *rsyslog* service uses port 514 by default.
2. The *sadf* command is used to display the performance data collected with *sar*.
3. The */proc/cmdline* temporary file stores the boot string used to boot the system.
4. False.
5. The *dstat* command.
6. We modify a runtime parameter to support the installation and operation of a software driver or application.
7. The dstat software package includes the *dstat* command.
8. This command will load the kernel parameters defined in the */etc/sysctl.conf* file.
9. False.
10. The */etc/sysctl.conf* file.
11. You can use either the *sysctl* or the *echo* command.
12. Boot-time kernel parameters are stored in the */boot/grub2/grub.cfg* file.
13. This command will write the specified kernel parameter and its value to the */etc/sysctl.conf* file.
14. By looking at the contents of the */proc/cmdline* file.

DIY Challenge Labs

The following labs are useful to strengthen the concepts and topics learned in this chapter. It is expected that you perform these labs without any additional help. A step-by-step guide is not provided, as the implementation of these labs requires the knowledge that has been presented in this chapter. Use defaults or your own thinking for missing information.

Lab 18-1: Modify a Run-Time Kernel Parameter

Modify the value of a kernel parameter kernel.msgmax to 131072 and ensure that the value survives system reboots. Check the value after rebooting the system.

Lab 18-2: Modify a Boot-Time Kernel Parameter

Modify the default kernel and add a boot-time parameter abcd=2. Reboot the system and verify the entry in the */proc/cmdline* file.

Lab 18-3: Set Up a Central Loghost System

Set up *host1* as a central loghost to receive and store messages from *server1*. Configure the service to use UDP on port 1050. Test the functionality by generating an alert on *server1* and confirming its reception in the */var/log/message* file on *host1*.

## Chapter 19

Sharing Block Storage with iSCSI

This chapter describes the following major topics:

➢ Introduction to the iSCSI protocol
➢ Description of various iSCSI terms
➢ iSCSI target and initiator software packages
➢ Tools to administer iSCSI target and initiator
➢ Initiator configuration and database files
➢ Configure a system as an iSCSI target and share disk-based storage
➢ Configure a system as an iSCSI initiator and mount the discovered storage persistently
➢ Configure an iSCSI target to share file-based storage and mount it on an iSCSI initiator persistently

RHCE Objectives:

61. Configure a system as either an iSCSI target or initiator that persistently mounts an iSCSI target

iSCSI is a storage networking protocol used to share a computer's local storage with remote clients using the SCSI commandset over an existing IP network infrastructure. The clients see the shared storage as a locally attached hard disk and can use any available disk and file system management tools to partition, format, and mount it. This way, unused storage on one system can be utilized by other systems without the need of physically relocating it or re-organizing cables.

Understanding the iSCSI Protocol

The *Internet Small Computer System Interface* (iSCSI) is a storage networking transport protocol that carries SCSI commands over IP networks, including the Internet. This protocol enables data transfer between iSCSI clients and iSCSI storage servers instituting a *Storage Area Network* (SAN) of disparate storage. As this protocol is designed to work on IP networks, the distance between clients and storage servers is irrelevant as long as the link between them is fast and stable. Once a proper configuration is in place and a connection is established, any storage shared by a storage server appears as a locally attached hard disk to the client.

An iSCSI SAN is a low-cost alternative to the expensive Fibre Channel-based SAN (FC SAN). It does not require special or dedicated cabling, switches, and host controller adapters as does the FC SAN; rather, it uses the existing network infrastructure for storage sharing. In environments, however, where superior performance is sought, deployment of dedicated network infrastructure is recommended to evade potential bandwidth issues. Furthermore, an iSCSI SAN can be scaled without an outage or additional investment. This protocol communicates over port 3260 and uses TCP by default.

Unlike the NFS and CIFS protocols (discussed in subsequent chapters) that are used for network file sharing, iSCSI presents the network storage to clients as a local raw block disk drive. The clients can carve the disk up using any disk partitioning software, such as parted or LVM. The shared network storage does not have to be an entire physical or virtual disk; rather, it could be a simple file, an LVM logical volume, a disk partition, a RAID partition, or a ramdisk. In all cases, it appears to clients as just another regular local disk.

Figure 19-1 Basic iSCSI Target and Initiator Arrangement

Figure 19-1 shows a basic iSCSI SAN with *server2* acting as a storage server and *server1* as its client. In iSCSI nomenclature, a storage server is referred to as a target and a client is referred to as an initiator. We will use this basic arrangement to build our small iSCSI SAN in the following exercises.

Terminology

The iSCSI technology has several terms that need to be grasped in order to fully understand how it works and is configured. This knowledge will also benefit you in performing the exercises offered later in this chapter. The key iSCSI terms are described below.

ACL: An ACL (*access control list*) controls an iSCSI client access to target LUNs.

Addressing: iSCSI assigns a unique address to each target server. It supports multiple addressing formats; however, the IQN (*iSCSI qualified name*) is most common. A sample IQN is shown below:

iqn.2015-01.com.example:testiscsilun0

In the above sample, iqn identifies the iSCSI address format, 2015-01 represents the year and month when your organization (example.com in this example) registered this domain, com.example represents the reversed domain name of your organization, and :testiscsilun0 represents a string of your choice to uniquely identify this address among hundreds of other targets that may exist on the system.

Alias: An *alias* is an optional string of up to 255 characters that may be defined to give a description to an iSCSI LUN. For instance, "Oracle ABC DB Archive Log Files, LUN 001" might be an alias assigned to a LUN that is used explicitly to store archive log files for an Oracle DB instance named ABC. An alias helps identify a LUN quickly.

Authentication: *Authentication* allows initiators and targets to prove their identity at the time of discovery and normal access. The iSCSI protocol supports CHAP-based authentication (*challenge-handshake authentication protocol*) methods that use usernames and passwords, but hide the network transmission of passwords. These methods are referred to as *CHAP initiator authentication* and *mutual CHAP authentication*. The former requires the initiators to prove their identity to the target by entering valid credentials (one-way authentication), and the latter requires both the initiator and the target to supply their credentials to each other to confirm their identities (two-way authentication). The third option, the *demo mode*, is the default option, and it is used to disable the authentication feature and open full access for all initiators to all exported target LUNs.

Backstore: A *backstore* is a local storage resource that serves as the backend for the LUN presented to the initiator. A backstore may be an entire physical or virtual disk (block), a standard partition (block), a RAID partition (block), an LVM logical volume (block), a plain file (fileio), or a ramdisk image (ramdisk). The first four represents disk-based block devices, the fileio identifies the backstore as a plain file that is treated as a disk image, and the ramdisk image represents the kernel memory that is treated as a block device. There is another backstore type called pscsi, however, it is recommended to use the block backstore type instead of pscsi.

Initiator: An *initiator* is a client system that accesses LUNs presented by a target server. Initiators are either software- or hardware-driven. A software initiator is a kernel module that uses the iSCSI protocol to emulate a discovered LUN as a block SCSI disk. A hardware initiator, on the other hand, uses a dedicated piece of hardware called an HBA (*host bus adapter*) to perform the same function. An HBA offloads system processors by processing SCSI commands on onboard processors, resulting in improved system performance.

iSNS: An iSNS (*internet Storage Name Service*) is a protocol that is used by an initiator to discover shared LUNs.

LUN: A LUN (*logical unit number*) represents a single addressable logical SCSI disk that is exported on the target server. From an initiator perspective, a LUN is just like any other hard disk attached to it. Disk management software, such as parted and LVM, treat both LUN and hard disk identically.

Node: A *node* is a single discoverable object on the iSCSI SAN. It may represent a target server or an initiator. A node is identified by its IP address or a unique iSCSI address (see Addressing).

Portal: A *portal* is a combination of an IP address and TCP port that a target server listens on and initiators connect to. iSCSI uses TCP port 3260 by default.

Target: A *target* is a server that emulates a backstore as a LUN for use by an initiator over an iSCSI SAN. A target may be a dedicated hardware RAID array or a RHEL server with appropriate software support loaded in the kernel. The term "target" also represents an object with one or more LUNs enclosed within it. To avoid confusion, where applicable, we will use the term "target server" to represent a storage server, and the term "target LUN" for a LUN exported by the target server.

TPG: A TPG (*target portal group*) represents one or more network portals assigned to a target LUN for running iSCSI sessions for that LUN.

iSCSI Software Packages

A single software package, *targetcli*, needs to be installed on the target server in order to provide the iSCSI target functionality. This package has a number of dependencies that are also installed with it. *targetcli* implements the open source *Linux IO* (LIO) iSCSI target subsystem in the kernel to support the configuration and sharing of storage resources and their presentation as block storage to clients over IP networks. This utility is used to manage the LIO subsystem and it runs as a shell interface.

On the client side, the iSCSI initiator functionality becomes available when the iscsi-initiator-utils package is installed. This package brings the *iscsiadm* management command, the */etc/iscsi/iscsid.conf* configuration file, and other relevant commands and files.

Managing iSCSI Target Server and Initiator

Managing iSCSI on the target server involves setting up a backstore, building an iSCSI target on the backstore, assigning a network portal, creating a LUN, exporting the LUN, establishing an ACL, and saving the configuration. Managing iSCSI on the initiator involves discovering a target server for LUNs, logging on to discovered target LUNs, and using disk management tools to partition, format, and mount the LUNs. These tasks are covered in exercises presented in this section.

Understanding the targetcli Command for Target Administration

The *targetcli* command is an administration shell that allows you to display, create, modify, and delete target LUNs. It is a complete iSCSI target configuration tool in RHEL7 that acts as an interface between you and the LIO subsystem in the kernel. It gives you the ability to present local storage resources backed by a file, whole disk, logical volume, RAID partition, standard partition, or ramdisk to iSCSI clients as block storage. This tool provides a hierarchical view (similar to the Linux directory tree) of all target LUNs configured on the target server.

Several kernel modules load in the memory to support the setup and operation of iSCSI LUNs on the target server. You can view the modules that are currently loaded by running the *lsmod* command:

```
# lsmod | grep target
iscsi_target_mod    278732  1
target_core_mod     299412  2 iscsi_target_mod
```

There are additional modules that are loaded when specific target types are configured. These modules include target_core_iblock for a disk type target, target_core_file for a plain file type target, and so on.

Here is the shell interface that is invoked when you run *targetcli* at the Linux command prompt:

targetcli
targetcli shell version 2.1.fb34
Copyright 2011-2013 by Datera, Inc and others.
For help on commands, type 'help'.
/>

Run *help* at the tool's prompt to view available subcommands:

/> **help**

. . . .
AVAILABLE COMMANDS
=======================

The following commands are available in the current path:
 - bookmarks action [bookmark]
 - cd [path]
 - clearconfig [confirm]
 - exit
 - get [group] [parameter...]
 - help [topic]
 - ls [path] [depth]
 - pwd
 - refresh
 - restoreconfig [savefile] [clear_existing]
 - saveconfig [savefile]
 - sessions [action] [sid]
 - set [group] [parameter=value...]
 - status
 - version

The output lists numerous subcommands of which some are described in Table 19-1.

Subcommand	Description
ls	Shows the downward view of the tree from the current location.
pwd	Displays the current location in the tree.
cd	Navigates in the tree.
exit	Quits the targetcli shell interface.
saveconfig	Saves the modifications.
get / set	Gets (or sets) configuration attributes.
sessions	Displays details for open sessions.

Table 19-1 targetcli Subcommands

While in the *targetcli* shell, there are different paths that point to a single target, and each one of them includes a different set of subcommands. The shell prompt changes to reflect the current path as you navigate in the tree. You can use the *pwd* subcommand to view your current location in the tree. The *cd* subcommand helps you navigate in the tree, and without any options, it displays the full object tree view from where you can highlight and select a desired path and get there directly.

Run the *ls* subcommand to list the entire object hierarchy from the root of the tree:

```
/> ls
o- / ............................................................. [...]
  o- backstores ………................................. [...]
  | o- block ........................... [Storage Objects: 0]
  | o- fileio ........................... [Storage Objects: 0]
  | o- pscsi ........................... [Storage Objects: 0]
  | o- ramdisk ....................... [Storage Objects: 0]
  o- iscsi ............................................ [Targets: 0]
  o- loopback ..................................... [Targets: 0]
```

The tree currently shows an empty view.

If you want to move to the block target path under backstores, run the following:

```
/> cd /backstores/block
```

And run the following to go to the iscsi directory:

```
/> cd /iscsi
```

While in any of the object directories, running the *ls* command shows information specific to that object only. For instance, run *ls* while in the /iscsi directory:

```
/iscsi> ls
o- iscsi ............................................ [Targets: 0]
```

The *targetcli* command may alternatively be run directly from the command prompt. Exercise 19-3 demonstrates this use.

Adding 1x2GB Virtual Disk to Target Server

As indicated in Chapter 01 "Installing RHEL7 on Physical Computer Using Local DVD", *server2* will have 1x2GB virtual disk for iSCSI exercises. We will create it on *host1* and attach it to *server2* using a combination of *qemu-img* and *virsh* commands. To that end, execute *qemu-img* while in the */var/lib/libvirt/images* directory on *host1* and create a 2GB image file for the new disk using raw format:

```
# cd /var/lib/libvirt/images
# qemu-img create –f raw server2.example.com-virsh.img 2G
Formatting 'server2.example.com-virsh.img', fmt=raw size=2147483648
```

The next step is to attach this image file to *server2* using the *virsh* command so that the server sees it. Specify the image file name with the --source option and a disk name (*vdb*) with the --target option to appear on *server2* as. Ensure that this assignment is stored persistently.

**virsh attach-disk server2.example.com --source **
/var/lib/libvirt/images/server2.example.com-virsh.img --target vdb --persistent
Disk attached successfully

Verify the attachment of the new storage device *vdb* on *host1*:

virsh domblklist server2.example.com --details | grep vdb
file   disk   vdb   /var/lib/libvirt/images/server2.example.com-virsh.img

Now, log on to *server2* and issue the *lsblk* command. You should be able to see the new device there.

lsblk | grep vdb
vdb   252:16   0   2G   0   disk

The above output confirms the appearance of a new disk on the system. For more details on creating and presenting virtual storage, refer to Chapter 06 "Configuring Server Virtualization and Network Installing RHEL7".

We will configure this new disk on *server2* as an iSCSI target LUN and access it as a block disk on *server1* (iSCSI initiator).

Exercise 19-1: Configure a Disk-Based iSCSI Target LUN
This exercise should be done on *server2*.

In this exercise, you will install the targetcli software on *server2* (target server), set the *target* service to autostart at system reboots, define the entire *vdb* disk as a backstore, build a target using this backstore, assign a network portal to the target, create a LUN in the target, disable authentication, and create and activate a firewalld service for iSCSI port 3260.

1. Run the *yum* command to install the targetcli package:

    # **yum –y install targetcli**
    . . . .
    Installed:
      targetcli.noarch 0:2.1.fb34-1.el7
    Dependency Installed:
      pyparsing.noarch 0:1.5.6-9.el7
      python-configshell.noarch 1:1.1.fb11-3.el7
      python-kmod.x86_64 0:0.9-4.el7
      python-rtslib.noarch 0:2.1.fb46-1.el7
      python-urwid.x86_64 0:1.1.1-3.el7
    Complete!

2. Set the *target* service to autostart at system reboots:

   # systemctl enable target
   ln -s '/usr/lib/systemd/system/target.service' '/etc/systemd/system/multi-user.target.wants/target.service'

3. Launch the *targetcli* shell and change into /backstores/block to build a backstore called iscsidisk1 using the *vdb* disk:

   /> cd /backstores/block
   /backstores/block> **create iscsidisk1 dev=/dev/vdb**
   Created block storage object iscsidisk1 using /dev/vdb.

4. Display the backstore construction:

   /backstores/block> **ls**
   o- block .... [Storage Objects: 1]
     o- iscsidisk1 .... [/dev/vdb (2.0GiB) write-thru deactivated]

5. Build an iSCSI target with address iqn.2015-01.com.example.server2:iscsidisk1 on the iscsidisk1 backstore in the default TPG after changing into the /iscsi directory:

   /backstores/block> **cd /iscsi**
   /iscsi> **create iqn.2015-01.com.example.server2:iscsidisk1**
   Created target iqn.2015-01.com.example.server2:iscsidisk1.
   Created TPG 1.

6. Display the target construction:

   /iscsi> **ls**
   o- iscsi .... [Targets: 1]
     o- iqn.2015-01.com.example.server2:iscsidisk1 .... [TPGs: 1]
       o- tpg1 .... [no-gen-acls, no-auth]
         o- acls .... [ACLs: 0]
         o- luns .... [LUNs: 0]
         o- portals .... [Portals: 0]

7. Create a network portal for the target using the IP (192.168.0.120) to be used for iSCSI traffic and the default port by changing into the *iqn.2015-01.com.example.server2:iscsidisk1/tpg1* directory. This will make the target discoverable and accessible on the network.

   /iscsi> **cd iqn.2015-01.com.example.server2:iscsidisk1/tpg1**
   /iscsi/iqn.20...sidisk1/tpg1> **portals/ create 192.168.0.120**
   Using default IP port 3260
   Created network portal 192.168.0.120:3260.

8. Display the network portal construction:

```
/iscsi/iqn.20…sidisk1/tpg1> ls
o- tpg1 ............................................................ [no-gen-acls, no-auth]
  o- acls .................................................................... [ACLs: 0]
  o- luns .................................................................... [LUNs: 0]
  o- portals ............................................................... [Portals: 1]
    o- 192.168.0.120:3260 ........................................... [OK]
```

9. Create a LUN called lun0 in the target and export it to the network:

```
/iscsi/iqn.20…sidisk1/tpg1> luns/ create /backstores/block/iscsidisk1
iscsidisk1
Created LUN 0
```

10. Display the LUN construction:

```
/iscsi/iqn.20…sidisk1/tpg1> ls
o- tpg1 ............................................................ [no-gen-acls, no-auth]
  o- acls .................................................................... [ACLs: 0]
  o- luns .................................................................... [LUNs: 1]
  | o- lun0 ............................................ [block/iscsidisk1 (/dev/vdb)]
  o- portals ............................................................... [Portals: 1]
    o- 192.168.0.120:3260 ........................................... [OK]
```

11. Disable authentication so that any initiator can access this LUN. The
    demo_mode_write_protect=0 attribute makes the LUN write-enabled and the
    generate_node_acls=1 attribute enables the use of TPG-wide authentication settings (this
    disables any user-defined ACLs):

```
/iscsi/iqn.20…sidisk1/tpg1> set attribute authentication=0 \
demo_mode_write_protect=0 generate_node_acls=1
Parameter demo_mode_write_protect is now '0'.
Parameter authentication is now '0'.
Parameter generate_node_acls is now '1'.
```

12. Return to the root of the tree and display the entire configuration for this target LUN:

```
/iscsi/iqn.20…sidisk1/tpg1> cd /
/> ls
o- / ......................................................................... [...]
  o- backstores ........................................................... [...]
  | o- block ................................................. [Storage Objects: 1]
  | | o- iscsidisk1 ................ [/dev/vdb (2.0GiB) write-thru activated]
  | o- fileio ............................................... [Storage Objects: 0]
  | o- pscsi ................................................ [Storage Objects: 0]
  | o- ramdisk ............................................. [Storage Objects: 0]
  o- iscsi ...................................................... [Targets: 1]
  | o- iqn.2015-01.com.example.server2:iscsidisk1 ............. [TPGs: 1]
```

```
|   o- tpg1 .............................................. [gen-acls, no-auth]
|     o- acls .......................................................... [ACLs: 0]
|     o- luns .......................................................... [LUNs: 1]
|     | o- lun0 ........................................ [block/iscsidisk1 (/dev/vdb)]
|     o- portals ................................................... [Portals: 1]
|       o- 192.168.0.120:3260 ..................................... [OK]
o- loopback ................................................. [Targets: 0]
```

13. Exit out of the shell interface. By default, the auto_save_on_exit directive is set to true, which instructs the *exit* subcommand to save the configuration before exiting.

    /> exit
    Global pref auto_save_on_exit=true
    Last 10 configs saved in /etc/target/backup.
    Configuration saved to /etc/target/saveconfig.json

    The configuration is stored in the */etc/target/saveconfig.json* file as indicated in the *exit* subcommand output above. You can use the *cat* or *more* command to view the file contents if you wish to. It also backs up and stores the previous ten configuration files in the */etc/target/backup* directory just in case you want to revert to one of them.

14. Add a service called iscsitarget by creating a file called *iscsitarget.xml* in the */etc/firewalld/services* directory to permit iSCSI traffic on port 3260. Add the following contents to the file:

    # vi /etc/firewalld/services/iscsitarget.xml
    <?xml version="1.0" encoding="utf-8"?>
    <service>
     <short>iSCSI</short>
     <description>This is to permit the iSCSI traffic to pass through the firewall</description>
     <port protocol="tcp" port="3260"/>
    </service>

15. Add the new iscsitarget service to firewalld and activate it:

    # firewall-cmd --permanent --add-service iscsitarget ; firewall-cmd --reload
    success
    success

This completes the configuration of an iSCSI target LUN on *server2* and it is now ready to be discovered and used on the iSCSI initiator *server1*.

Understanding the iscsiadm Command for Initiator Administration

The primary tool to discover iSCSI targets, to log in to them, and to manage the iSCSI discovery database is the *iscsiadm* command. This command interacts with the *iscsid* daemon and reads the */etc/iscsi/iscsid.conf* file for configuration directives at the time of discovering and logging in to new targets.

The *iscsiadm* command has four modes of operation that are described in Table 19-2.

Mode	Description
Discovery	Queries the specified portal for available targets based on the configuration defined in the /etc/iscsi/iscsi.conf file. The records found are stored in discovery database files located in the /var/lib/iscsi directory.
Node	Establishes a session with the target and creates a corresponding device file for each discovered LUN in the target.
Session	Displays current session information.
Iface	Defines network portals.

Table 19-2 iscsiadm Command Operating Modes

There are several options available with the *iscsiadm* command, some of which are described in Table 19-3.

Option	Description
–D (--discover)	Discovers targets using discovery records. If no matching record is found, a new record is created based on settings defined in the /etc/iscsi/iscsi.conf file.
–l (--login)	Logs in to the specified target.
–L (--loginall)	Logs in to all discovered targets.
–m (--mode)	Specifies one of the supported modes of operation: discovery, node, fw, iface, and session.
–p (--portal)	Specifies a target server portal.
–o (--op)	Specifies one of the supported database operators: new, delete, update, show, or non-persistent.
–T (--targetname)	Specifies a target name.
–t (--type)	Specifies a type of discovery. Sendtargets (st) is usually used. iSNS is another available type.
–u (--logout)	Logs out from a target.
–U (--logoutall)	Logs out from all targets.

Table 19-3 iscsiadm Command Options

We will use most of these options shortly.

The /etc/iscsi/iscsid.conf File

The */etc/iscsi/iscsid.conf* file is the iSCSI initiator configuration file that defines several options for the *iscsid* daemon that dictate how to handle an iSCSI initiator via the *iscsiadm* command. During an iSCSI target discovery, the *iscsiadm* command references this file and creates discovery and node records, and stores them in *send_targets* (or other supported discovery type) and *nodes* sub-directories under the */var/lib/iscsi* directory. The records saved in *send_targets* are used when you attempt to perform discovery on the same target server again, and the records saved in *nodes* are used when you attempt to log in to the discovered targets.

The following shows the default uncommented entries from the *iscsid.conf* file. The *grep* command is used to remove commented and empty lines from the output.

```
# grep –v '^#|^$' /etc/iscsi/iscsid.conf
iscsid.startup = /bin/systemctl start iscsid.socket iscsiuio.socket
node.startup = automatic
node.leading_login = No
node.session.timeo.replacement_timeout = 120
node.conn[0].timeo.login_timeout = 15
node.conn[0].timeo.logout_timeout = 15
node.conn[0].timeo.noop_out_interval = 5
node.conn[0].timeo.noop_out_timeout = 5
node.session.err_timeo.abort_timeout = 15
node.session.err_timeo.lu_reset_timeout = 30
node.session.err_timeo.tgt_reset_timeout = 30
node.session.initial_login_retry_max = 8
node.session.cmds_max = 128
node.session.queue_depth = 32
node.session.xmit_thread_priority = -20
node.session.iscsi.InitialR2T = No
node.session.iscsi.ImmediateData = Yes
node.session.iscsi.FirstBurstLength = 262144
node.session.iscsi.MaxBurstLength = 16776192
node.conn[0].iscsi.MaxRecvDataSegmentLength = 262144
node.conn[0].iscsi.MaxXmitDataSegmentLength = 0
discovery.sendtargets.iscsi.MaxRecvDataSegmentLength = 32768
node.conn[0].iscsi.HeaderDigest = None
node.session.nr_sessions = 1
node.session.iscsi.FastAbort = Yes
```

The /etc/iscsi/initiatorname.iscsi File

The */etc/iscsi/initiatorname.iscsi* file stores the discovered node names along with optional aliases using the InitiatorName and InitiatorAlias directives, respectively. This file is read by the *iscsid* daemon on startup, and it is used by the *iscsiadm* command to determine node names and aliases. A sample entry from this file is shown below:

```
InitiatorName=iqn.2014-09.net.example.server5:mdblun01
InitiatorAlias="LUN01 for MariaDB Database Files"
```

This file is updated manually with discovered node names that exist in the */var/lib/iscsi/nodes* directory.

Exercise 19-2: Mount the iSCSI Target on Initiator

This exercise should be done on *server1*.

In this exercise, you will install the iscsi-initiator-utils software package on *server1*, set the *iscsid* service to autostart at system reboots, discover available targets, log in to a discovered target, and create a file system using LVM. You will add an entry for the file system to the */etc/fstab* file and mount it manually. You will reboot the system to ensure the file system is automatically remounted.

1. Run the *yum* command to install the iscsi-initiator-utils package:

   # yum –y install iscsi-initiator-utils

   . . . .
   Installed:
     iscsi-initiator-utils.x86_64 0:6.2.0.873-21.el7
   Dependency Installed:
     iscsi-initiator-utils-iscsiuio.x86_64 0:6.2.0.873-21.el7
   Complete!

2. Set the *iscsid* service to autostart at system reboots:

   # systemctl enable iscsid

   ln -s '/usr/lib/systemd/system/iscsid.service' '/etc/systemd/system/multi-user.target.wants/iscsid.service'

3. Execute the *iscsiadm* command in sendtargets type (–t) discovery mode (–m) to locate available iSCSI targets from the specified portal (–p):

   # iscsiadm –m discovery –t st –p 192.168.0.120

   192.168.0.120:3260,1 iqn.2015-01.com.example.server2:iscsidisk1

   The above command also adds the new record to appropriate discovery database files located in the */var/lib/iscsi* directory, and starts the *iscsid* daemon. This information remains persistent unless you delete it.

4. Log in (–l) to the target (–T) in node mode (–m) at the specified portal (–p) to establish a target/initiator session:

   **# iscsiadm –m node –T iqn.2015-01.com.example.server2:iscsidisk1 \
   –p 192.168.0.120 –l**

   Logging in to [iface: default, target: iqn.2015-01.com.example.server2:iscsidisk1, portal: 192.168.0.120,3260] (multiple)
   Login to [iface: default, target: iqn.2015-01.com.example.server2:iscsidisk1, portal: 192.168.0.120,3260] successful.

5. View information for the established iSCSI session (–m) and specify printlevel (–P) 3 for verbosity:

   # iscsiadm –m session –P3

   iSCSI Transport Class version 2.0-870
   version 6.2.0.873-21
   Target: iqn.2015-01.com.example.server2:iscsidisk1 (non-flash)
       Current Portal: 192.168.0.120:3260,1
       Persistent Portal: 192.168.0.120:3260,1
           ****
           Interface:
           ****
           Iface Name: default

```
Iface Transport: tcp
Iface Initiatorname: iqn.1994-05.com.redhat:df707aba1117
Iface IPaddress: 192.168.0.110
Iface HWaddress: <empty>
Iface Netdev: <empty>
SID: 1
iSCSI Connection State: LOGGED IN
iSCSI Session State: LOGGED_IN
Internal iscsid Session State: NO CHANGE
*********
Timeouts:
*********
Recovery Timeout: 120
Target Reset Timeout: 30
LUN Reset Timeout: 30
Abort Timeout: 15
*****
CHAP:
*****
username: <empty>
password: ********
username_in: <empty>
password_in: ********
***********************
Negotiated iSCSI params:
***********************

. . . . . . . .
Attached SCSI devices:
***********************
Host Number: 2  State: running
scsi2 Channel 00 Id 0 Lun: 0
        Attached scsi disk sda        State: running
```

The output shows details for the target and the established session. It also shows the name of the LUN (*sda*) as identified on the initiator at the very bottom of the output.

6. Edit the */etc/iscsi/initiatorname.iscsi* file and add the target information:

    InitiatorName=iqn.2015-01.com.example.server2:iscsidisk1

7. Execute the *lsblk* and *fdisk* commands and *grep* for sda to see the new LUN:

    ```
    # lsblk | grep sda
    sda          8:0  0  2G  0  disk
    # fdisk –l | grep sda
    Disk /dev/sda: 2147 MB, 2147483648 bytes, 4194304 sectors
    ```

8. The */var/log/messages* file has captured several messages for the new LUN. *grep* for sda to view them.

> # **grep sda /var/log/messages**
> Jan 16 11:53:25 server1 kernel: sd 2:0:0:0: [sda] 4194304 512-byte logical blocks: (2.14 GB/2.00 GiB)
> Jan 16 11:53:25 server1 kernel: sd 2:0:0:0: [sda] Write Protect is off
> Jan 16 11:53:25 server1 kernel: sd 2:0:0:0: [sda] Write cache: enabled, read cache: enabled, supports DPO and FUA
> Jan 16 11:53:25 server1 kernel: sda: unknown partition table
> Jan 16 11:53:25 server1 kernel: sd 2:0:0:0: [sda] Attached SCSI disk

9. Use LVM to initialize (*pvcreate*) this LUN (*/dev/sda*), create (*vgcreate*) a volume group (*vgiscsi*) and add the physical volume to it, create (*lvcreate*) a logical volume (*lviscsi1*) of size 1GB, format (*mkfs.xfs*) the logical volume (*/dev/vgiscsi/lviscsi1*) with xfs structures, create (*mkdir*) a mount point (*/iscsidisk1*), add (*vi*) an entry to the */etc/fstab* file making sure to use the _netdev option, mount (*mount*) the new file system, and execute the *df* command for mount confirmation:

> # **pvcreate –v /dev/sda**
> # **vgcreate –v vgiscsi /dev/sda**
> # **lvcreate –L 1G vgiscsi –n lviscsi1 –v**
> # **mkfs.xfs /dev/vgiscsi/lviscsi1**
> # **mkdir /iscsidisk1**
> # **vi /etc/fstab**
> /dev/vgiscsi/lviscsi1   /iscsidisk1   xfs   _netdev   0   0
> # **mount /iscsidisk1**
> # **df –h | grep iscsidisk1**
> /dev/mapper/vgiscsi-lviscsi1   1014M   33M   982M   4%   /iscsidisk1

10. Reboot *server1* to ensure that the client configuration survives. Run the *df* command after the system is back up. You should be able to see the iSCSI file system mounted.

Exercise 19-3: Configure a File-Based iSCSI Target and Mount it on Initiator

This exercise should be done on *server2* (target server) and *server1* (initiator).

For this exercise, presume that targetcli and iscsi-initiator-utils software packages are already installed on *server2* and *server1*, respectively.

In this exercise, you will configure a 50MB plain file as a backstore, build a target using this backstore, assign a network portal to the target, create a LUN in the target, export the LUN, disable authentication, and create and activate a firewalld service for iSCSI port 3260. You will discover this target on the initiator, log in to it, and create a file system using *parted*. You will add an entry for the file system to the */etc/fstab* file using the file system's UUID and mount the file system manually. You will reboot *server1* to ensure the file system is automatically remounted.

On *server2* (iSCSI target server):

1. Create a file called *iscsifile1.img* of 50MB in the */usr* directory as a fileio type backstore called iscsifile1:

   # **targetcli /backstores/fileio create iscsifile1 /usr/iscsifile1.img 50M**
   Created fileio iscsifile1 with size 52428800

2. Display the backstore construction:

   # **targetcli ls /backstores/fileio**
   o- fileio .... [Storage Objects: 1]
     o- iscsifile1 .. [/usr/iscsifile1.img (50.0MiB) write-back deactivated]

3. Build an iSCSI target with address iqn.2015-01.com.example.server2:iscsifile1 on the iscsifile1 backstore in the default TPG:

   # **targetcli /iscsi create iqn.2015-01.com.example.server2:iscsifile1**
   Created target iqn.2015-01.com.example.server2:iscsifile1.
   Created TPG 1.

4. Display the target construction:

   # **targetcli ls /iscsi**
   o- iscsi .... [Targets: 2]
     o- iqn.2015-01.com.example.server2:iscsifile1 .... [TPGs: 1]
     | o- tpg1 .... [no-gen-acls, no-auth]
     | o- acls .... [ACLs: 0]
     | o- luns .... [LUNs: 0]
     | o- portals .... [Portals: 0]
   . . . .

5. Create a network portal for the target using the IP (192.168.0.120) to be used for iSCSI traffic and the default port. This will make the target discoverable and accessible on the network.

   # **targetcli /iscsi/iqn.2015-01.com.example.server2:iscsifile1/tpg1/portals/ create **
   192.168.0.120
   Using default IP port 3260
   Created network portal 192.168.0.120:3260.

6. Display the network portal construction:

   # **targetcli ls /iscsi/iqn.2015-01.com.example.server2:iscsifile1/tpg1**
   o- tpg1 .... [no-gen-acls, no-auth]
     o- acls .... [ACLs: 0]
     o- luns .... [LUNs: 0]
     o- portals .... [Portals: 1]
       o- 192.168.0.120:3260 .... [OK]

---

7. Create a LUN called lun0 in the target and export it to the network:

    **# targetcli /iscsi/iqn.2015-01.com.example.server2:iscsifile1/tpg1/luns/ create \
    /backstores/fileio/iscsifile1**
    Created LUN 0.

8. Display the LUN construction:

    # targetcli ls /iscsi/iqn.2015-01.com.example.server2:iscsifile1/tpg1
    o- tpg1 .... [no-gen-acls, no-auth]
      o- acls .... [ACLs: 0]
      o- luns .... [LUNs: 1]
      | o- lun0 .... [fileio/iscsifile1 (/usr/iscsifile1.img)]
      o- portals .... [Portals: 1]
        o- 192.168.0.120:3260 .... [OK]

9. Disable authentication so that any initiator can access this LUN. The
    demo_mode_write_protect=0 attribute makes the LUN write-enabled and the
    generate_node_acls=1 attribute enables the use of TPG-wide authentication settings (this
    disables any user-defined ACLs):

    **# targetcli /iscsi/iqn.2015-01.com.example.server2:iscsifile1/tpg1 set attribute \
    authentication=0 demo_mode_write_protect=0 generate_node_acls=1**
    Parameter demo_mode_write_protect is now '0'.
    Parameter authentication is now '0'.
    Parameter generate_node_acls is now '1'.

10. Display the entire tree view for this target from the root of the hierarchy:

    # targetcli ls /
    o- / .... [...]
      o- backstores .... [...]
      | o- block .... [Storage Objects: 1]
      | | o- iscsidisk1 .... [/dev/vdb (2.0GiB) write-thru activated]
      | o- fileio .... [Storage Objects: 1]
      | | o- iscsifile1 ... [/usr/iscsifile1.img (50.0MiB) write-back activated]
      | o- pscsi .... [Storage Objects: 0]
      | o- ramdisk .... [Storage Objects: 0]
      o- iscsi .... [Targets: 2]
      | o- iqn.2015-01.com.example.server2:iscsifile1 .... [TPGs: 1]
      | | o- tpg1 .... [gen-acls, no-auth]
      | | o- acls .... [ACLs: 0]
      | | o- luns .... [LUNs: 1]
      | | | o- lun0 .... [fileio/iscsifile1 (/usr/iscsifile1.img)]
      | | o- portals .... [Portals: 1]
      | | o- 192.168.0.120:3260 .... [OK]
      . . . .
      o- loopback .... [Targets: 0]

11. Save the configuration to the *etc/target/saveconfig.json*:

 # targetcli saveconfig
Last 10 configs saved in /etc/target/backup.
Configuration saved to /etc/target/saveconfig.json

The configuration is stored in the *etc/target/saveconfig.json* file as indicated in the *exit* subcommand output above. You can use the *cat* or *more* command to view the file contents if you want to. It also backs up and stores the previous ten configuration files in the */etc/target/backup* directory just in case you want to revert to one of them.

12. (Do this step and step 13 only if they were not done previously). Add a service called iscsitarget by creating a file called *iscsitarget.xml* in the */etc/firewalld/services* directory to permit iSCSI traffic on port 3260. Add the following contents to the file:

 # vi /etc/firewalld/services/iscsitarget.xml
<?xml version="1.0" encoding="utf-8"?>
<service>
 <short>iSCSI</short>
 <description>This is for allowing the iSCSI traffic to pass through the firewall</description>
 <port protocol="tcp" port="3260"/>
</service>

13. Add the new iscsitarget service to firewalld and activate it:

 # firewall-cmd --permanent --add-service iscsitarget ; firewall-cmd --reload
success
success

On *server1* (iSCSI initiator):

14. (Do this step if it was not previously done). Set the *iscsid* service to autostart at system reboots:

 # systemctl enable iscsid
ln -s '/usr/lib/systemd/system/iscsid.service' '/etc/systemd/system/multi-user.target.wants/iscsid.service'

15. Execute the *iscsiadm* command in the sendtargets (–t) discovery mode (–m) to locate available iSCSI targets from the specified portal (–p):

 # iscsiadm –m discovery –t st –p 192.168.0.120
192.168.0.120:3260,1 iqn.2015-01.com.example.server2:iscsidisk1
192.168.0.120:3260,1 iqn.2015-01.com.example.server2:iscsifile1

The above command also adds the new record to appropriate discovery database files located in the */var/lib/iscsi* directory, and starts the *iscsid* daemon. This information remains persistent unless you delete it.

16. Log in (–l) to the target (–T) in node mode (–m) at the specified portal (–p) to establish a target/initiator session:

 # iscsiadm –m node –T iqn.2015-01.com.example.server2:iscsifile1 –p 192.168.0.120 –l
Logging in to [iface: default, target: iqn.2015-01.com.example.server2:iscsifile1, portal: 192.168.0.120,3260] (multiple)
Login to [iface: default, target: iqn.2015-01.com.example.server2:iscsifile1, portal: 192.168.0.120,3260] successful.

17. View information for the established iSCSI session (–m) and specify printlevel (–P) 3 for verbosity:

 # iscsiadm –m session –P3
. . . .
Target: iqn.2015-01.com.example.server2:iscsifile1 (non-flash)
    Current Portal: 192.168.0.120:3260,1
    Persistent Portal: 192.168.0.120:3260,1
        ****
        Interface:
        ****
        Iface Name: default
        Iface Transport: tcp
        Iface Initiatorname: iqn.1994-05.com.redhat:df707aba1117
        Iface IPaddress: 192.168.0.110
        Iface HWaddress: <empty>
        Iface Netdev: <empty>
        SID: 2
        iSCSI Connection State: LOGGED IN
        iSCSI Session State: LOGGED_IN
        Internal iscsid Session State: NO CHANGE
        ****
        Timeouts:
        ****
        Recovery Timeout: 120
        Target Reset Timeout: 30
        LUN Reset Timeout: 30
        Abort Timeout: 15
        *****
        CHAP:
        *****
        username: <empty>
        password: ********
        username_in: <empty>
        password_in: ********
        ****
        Negotiated iSCSI params:
        ****
        . . . .
        Attached SCSI devices:

```
**********************
```
Host Number: 3 State: running
scsi3 Channel 00 Id 0 Lun: 0
    Attached scsi disk sdb   State: running

The output shows details for the target and the established session. It also shows the name of the LUN (*sdb*) as identified on the initiator at the very bottom of the output.

18. Edit the */etc/iscsi/initiatorname.iscsi* file and add the target information:

    InitiatorName=iqn.2015-01.com.example.server2:iscsifile1

19. Execute the *lsblk* and *fdisk* commands and *grep* for sdb to see the new LUN:

    # **lsblk | grep sdb**
    sdb   8:16 0   50M 0 disk
    # **fdisk –l | grep sdb**
    Disk /dev/sdb: 52 MB, 52428800 bytes, 102400 sectors

20. The */var/log/messages* file has captured several messages for the new LUN. *grep* for sdb to view them.

    # **grep sdb /var/log/messages**
    Jan 16 16:33:38 server1 kernel: sd 3:0:0:0: [sdb] 102400 512-byte logical blocks: (52.4 MB/50.0 MiB)
    Jan 16 16:33:38 server1 kernel: sd 3:0:0:0: [sdb] Write Protect is off
    Jan 16 16:33:38 server1 kernel: sd 3:0:0:0: [sdb] Write cache: enabled, read cache: enabled, supports DPO and FUA
    Jan 16 16:33:38 server1 kernel: sdb: unknown partition table
    Jan 16 16:33:38 server1 kernel: sd 3:0:0:0: [sdb] Attached SCSI disk

21. Use *parted* to label this disk (*/dev/sdb*), create a 50MB primary partition, display the disk's partition table, format (*mkfs.ext4*) the partition (*/dev/sdb1*) with ext4 structures, create (*mkdir*) a mount point (*/iscsifile1*), determine the file system's UUID (*blkid*), add (*vi*) an entry to the */etc/fstab* file using the UUID and making sure to use the _netdev option, mount (*mount*) the new file system, and execute the *df* command for mount confirmation:

    # **parted /dev/sdb mklabel msdos**
    # **parted /dev/sdb mkpart primary 1 50m**
    # **parted /dev/sdb print**
    Model: LIO-ORG iscsifile1 (scsi)
    Disk /dev/sdc: 52.4MB
    Sector size (logical/physical): 512B/512B
    Partition Table: msdos
    Disk Flags:

Number	Start	End	Size	Type	File system	Flags
1	1000kB	50.0MB	49.0MB	primary	ext4	

mkfs.ext4 /dev/sdb1
mke2fs 1.42.9 (28-Dec-2013)
Filesystem label=
OS type: Linux
Block size=1024 (log=0)
Fragment size=1024 (log=0)
Stride=0 blocks, Stripe width=4096 blocks
12000 inodes, 47852 blocks
2392 blocks (5.00%) reserved for the super user
First data block=1
Maximum filesystem blocks=33685504
6 block groups
8192 blocks per group, 8192 fragments per group
2000 inodes per group
Superblock backups stored on blocks:
	8193, 24577, 40961
Allocating group tables: done
Writing inode tables: done
Creating journal (4096 blocks): done
Writing superblocks and filesystem accounting information: done
mkdir /iscsifile1
blkid | grep sdb
/dev/sdb1: UUID="342e8148-95b3-4324-8e19-668aef950c2c" TYPE="ext4"
# vi /etc/fstab
UUID="342e8148-95b3-4324-8e19-668aef950c2c"   /iscsifile1   ext4   _netdev 0 0
# mount /iscsifile1
# df –h | grep iscsifile1
/dev/sdb1   42M   1.1M   37M   3%   /iscsifile1

22. Reboot *server1* to ensure that the client configuration survives for both exercises. Run the *df* command after the system is back up for confirmation.

Chapter Summary

This chapter presented the basics of iSCSI and demonstrated its implementation in a client/server setting. We started with an overview of the iSCSI protocol and described various terms. The iSCSI implementation on the server offers a single utility to set up and view storage targets and another tool on the client side to discover and manage the discovered storage targets. There are several administration tasks involved in setting up a LUN on the target server and presenting it to an initiator. Likewise, there are several administration tasks involved on the initiator side to discover, format, and mount the discovered LUN just like any other local disk drive. We looked at these tools and used them in the implementation of the exercises.

Chapter Review Questions

1. Once an iSCSI LUN is discovered and logged on, it is used just like any other locally attached hard disk. True or False?
2. What is the use of the *targetcli* command?
3. Name the file on the initiator where you store node names.
4. What is the directory location for iSCSI database files?

5. Which protocol may be used to authenticate iSCSI discovery and logging?
6. Can a plain file be used as an iSCSI backing store?
7. Discovered LUNs on the initiator cannot be partitioned using LVM. True or False?
8. Which file stores the settings that are used during a discovery?
9. What is the default port used by the iSCSI protocol?
10. Which two files are updated in the */var/lib/iscsi* directory if sendtargets discovery type is used for discovering targets?
11. What is the use of the *iscsiadm* command?
12. Name the target and initiator packages.

Answers to Chapter Review Questions

1. True.
2. The *targetcli* command is used to configure a storage resource into an exported LUN.
3. The name of the file on the initiator that stores node names is */etc/iscsi/initiatorname.iscsi*.
4. The iSCSI database files are located in the */var/lib/iscsi* directory.
5. The CHAP protocol may be used for iSCSI discovery and logging authentication.
6. Yes, a plain file can be configured as a backing store.
7. False.
8. The */etc/iscsi/iscsid.conf* file stores the settings that are used during target discovery.
9. The default port used by iSCSI is 3260.
10. The two files updated in the */var/lib/iscsi* directory are *send_targets* and *nodes*.
11. The *iscsiadm* command is used for discovering, logging in, and administering iSCSI targets and LUNs.
12. The name of the target package is targetcli and that of the initiator package is iscsi-initiator-utils.

DIY Challenge Labs

The following labs are useful to strengthen the concepts and topics learned in this chapter. It is expected that you perform these labs without any additional help. A step-by-step guide is not provided, as the implementation of these labs requires the knowledge that has been presented in this chapter. Use defaults or your own thinking for missing information.

Lab 19-1: Build an iSCSI LUN on an LVM Logical Volume and Mount it on Initiator

Build an iSCSI target using a 300MB logical volume as a backstore and export the LUN to an initiator. Use a non-default port 2020 and ensure both firewalld and SELinux are aware of this setting. Initialize a portion (200MB) of the LUN on initiator and format it with xfs file system structures. Make appropriate modifications on the initiator so that the new file system is automatically mounted after system reboots.

## Chapter 20

Sharing File Storage with NFS

This chapter describes the following major topics:

➤ Understand NFS concepts and benefits
➤ Overview of NFS versions, security, daemons, commands, and files
➤ Understand the exports file and various NFS server options
➤ Understand SELinux requirements for NFS
➤ Export a share on NFS server and mount it on NFS client
➤ Export a share to NFS client for group collaboration on NFS client
➤ Understand various NFS mount options
➤ Export and mount a share with Kerberos security enabled
➤ View NFS I/O statistics

RHCE Objectives:

26. Mount and unmount NFS network file systems
73. Provide network shares to specific clients
74. Provide network shares suitable for group collaboration
75. Use Kerberos to control access to NFS network shares

T he Network File System protocol allows the sharing of files between systems over the network. It lets a directory or file system on one system to be mounted and used remotely on another system as if it exists locally on that system. Users will not see a difference between the Network File System and another local file system.

Shares may be used for collaboration among group members on a remote system, and can be secured using the Kerberos authentication system to prevent unauthorized access and ensure data integrity.

There are read and write activities that occur between the server and client while shares are accessed and files modified. These I/O activities can be monitored and used to troubleshoot performance issues.

Understanding Network File System

Network File System (NFS) is a networking protocol that allows file sharing over the network. The Network File System service is based upon the client/server architecture whereby users on one system access files, directories, and file systems (we're going to call them "shares") residing on a remote system as if they are mounted locally on their system. The remote system that makes its shares available for network access is referred to as an NFS server, and the process of making the shares accessible is referred to as *exporting*. The shares the NFS server exports may be accessed by one or more systems. These systems are called NFS clients, and the process of making the shares accessible on clients is referred to as *mounting*. See Figure 20-1 for a simple NFS client/server arrangement that shows two shares */export1* and */export2* exported on the network to a remote system, which has them mounted there.

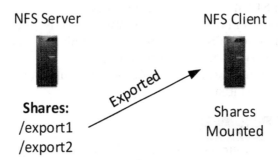

Figure 20-1 NFS Server/Client

A system can provide both server and client functionality concurrently. When a directory or file system share is exported, the entire directory structure beneath it becomes available for mounting on the client. A sub-directory or the parent directory of a share cannot be re-exported if it exists in the same file system. Similarly, a mounted share cannot be exported further. A single exported file share is mounted on a directory mount point.

NFS uses the *Remote Procedure Call* (RPC) and *eXternal Data Representation* (XDR) mechanisms that allow a server and client to communicate with each other using a common language that they both understand. This allows the NFS server and client to run on two different operating systems with different hardware platforms.

Benefits of Using NFS

The use of NFS provides several benefits, some of which are highlighted below:

- ✓ Supports a variety of operating system platforms including Linux, UNIX, and Microsoft Windows.
- ✓ Multiple NFS clients can access a single share simultaneously.
- ✓ Enables the sharing of common application binaries and other read-only information, resulting in reduced administration overhead and storage cost.
- ✓ Gives users access to uniform data.
- ✓ Allows the consolidation of scattered user home directories on the NFS server and then exporting them to the clients. This way users will have only one home directory to maintain.

NFS Versions

RHEL7 provides the support for NFS versions 3, 4.0, and 4.1, with NFSv4 being the default. NFSv3 supports both TCP and UDP transport protocols, asynchronous writes, and 64-bit file sizes that gives clients the ability to access files of sizes larger than 2GB.

NFSv4 and NFSv4.1 are *Internet Engineering Task Force* (IETF) standard protocols that provide all the features of NFSv3 protocol, plus the ability to transit firewalls and work on the Internet, enhanced security, encrypted transfers, support for ACLs, greater scalability, better cross-platform interoperability, and better handling of system crashes. They use the TCP protocol by default, but can work with UDP for backward compatibility. They use usernames and groupnames rather than UIDs and GIDs for files located on network shares.

> NFSv4.1 is the latest NFS protocol version, and one of its attractive features is the support of pNFS (parallel NFS). This new feature greatly improves the I/O performance by allowing NFS clients parallel and direct access to the share that sits on a remote physical storage system, and limiting the NFS server role to regulate metadata and manage access.

In this chapter, we will focus on the NFSv4 protocol, as it is the default protocol version used in RHEL7. A mix of both v4.0 and v4.1 clients and servers work as well. Then we will focus on NFSv4.0 protocol, which applies to v4.1 as well unless mentioned otherwise.

NFS Security

NFS security is paramount in NFSv4, which guarantees secure operation on WANs. When an NFS client attempts to access a remote share, an exchange of information takes place with the server to identify the client and the user on the server, authenticate them to the server, and authorize their access to the share. In-transit data between the two entities is encrypted to prevent eavesdropping and unauthorized access. NFS may be configured to use an existing Kerberos server for authentication, integrity, and data encryption. The NFS protocol uses TCP port 2049 for all communications between the server and client; hence, this port must be opened in the firewall for the NFS traffic to pass through.

NFS Daemons

NFS is a client/server protocol that employs several daemon programs to work collaboratively in order to export and mount shares, and manage I/O between them. One of these daemons need to run

---

on the NFS server, and the rest run on both the server and the client. These daemon processes are described in Table 20-1.

Daemon	Description
nfsd	NFS server process that responds to client requests on TCP port 2049 for file access and operations. It also provides the file locking and recovery mechanism. If the client sees an issue with the state of a file on the share, it notifies this server process for an action.
rpcbind	Runs on both the server and client. It converts RPC program numbers into universal addresses to facilitate communication for other RPC-based services. Access to this service can be controlled via TCP Wrappers.
rpc.rquotad	Runs on both the server and client. It displays user quota information for a remotely mounted share on the server, and it allows the setup of user quotas on a mounted share on the client.
rpc.idmapd	Runs on both the server and client to control the mappings of UIDs and GIDs with their corresponding usernames and groupnames based on the configuration defined in the /etc/idmapd.conf file.

Table 20-1 NFS Daemons

NFS Commands

There are numerous commands available to establish and manage NFS shares and to monitor their I/O. A proper understanding of the usage of these commands is necessary for smooth administration of NFS. Refer to Table 20-2 for an explanation.

Command	Description
exportfs	Server command that exports shares listed in the /etc/exports file and the files in the /etc/exports.d directory with .exports extension. It is also used to display the exported shares as listed in the /var/lib/nfs/etab and /proc/fs/nfs/exports files. Some of the key switches available with this command are: –r to re-export entries listed in the /etc/exports file, –a to perform an action on all configured shares listed in the /etc/exports file or exported shares listed in the /var/lib/nfs/etab file, –u to unexport the specified share, and –v to enable verbosity. This command displays the list of shares when executed without any options.
mount	Client command that mounts a share specified at the command line or listed in the /etc/fstab file, and adds an entry to the /etc/mtab file. Without any options, this command can also be used to display mounted shares as listed in the /etc/mtab file.
nfsiostat	Client command that provides NFS I/O statistics on mounted shares by consulting the /proc/self/mountstats file.
nfsstat	Displays NFS and RPC statistics by consulting the /proc/net/rpc/nfsd (server) and /proc/net/rpc/nfs (client) files, respectively.
mountstats	Client command that displays per-mount statistics by consulting the /proc/self/mountstats file.

Table 20-2 NFS Commands

Commands such as *rpcinfo* and *showmount* are also available; however, they are not needed in an NFSv4 environment. If you still want to use them, you might have to disable the firewall in order for them to work as desired. For details, view the man pages for these commands if needed.

NFS Configuration and Functional Files

NFS reads configuration data from various files at startup and during its operation. Table 20-3 describes key configuration and functional files.

File	Description
/etc/exports	Server file that contains share definitions for export.
/var/lib/nfs/etab	Server file that records entries for exported shares whether or not they are remotely mounted. This file is updated each time a share is exported or unexported.
/etc/nfsmount.conf	Client file that defines settings used at mounting shares.
/etc/fstab	Client file system table that contains a list of shares to be mounted at system reboots or manually with the mount command. This file also maintains a list of local file systems.
/etc/mtab	Client file that keeps track of mounted shares, as well as the local file systems. The mount and umount commands update this file.
/etc/sysconfig/nfs	A server- and client-side NFS startup configuration file.

Table 20-3 NFS Configuration and Functional Files

Of these, the *exports* and *fstab* files are manually updated, the *nfsmount.conf* and */etc/sysconfig/nfs* files do not need any modifications if NFSv4 is used with default settings, and the *etab* and *mtab* files are automatically updated when the *exportfs* and *mount/umount* commands are executed.

The /etc/exports File and NFS Server Options

The */etc/exports* file defines the configuration for NFS shares. It contains one-line entry per share to be exported. For each share, a pathname, client information, and options are included. These options govern the share access on the clients. Options must be enclosed within parentheses and there must not be any space following the hostname. If an option is specified, it will override its default setting; the other defaults will remain effective. Some of the common options are described in Table 20-4, with their default values shown in square brackets.

Option	Description
*	Represents all possible matches for hostnames, IP addresses, domain names, or network addresses.
all_squash (no_all_squash) [no_all_squash]	Treats all users, including the root user, on the client as anonymous users.
anongid=GID [65534]	Assigns this GID explicitly to anonymous groups on the client.
anonuid=UID [65534]	Assigns this UID explicitly to anonymous users on the client.
async (sync) [sync]	Replies to client requests before changes made by previous requests are written to disk.
fsid	Identifies the type of share being exported. Options are device number, root, or UUID. This option applies to file system shares only.

Option	Description
mp	Exports only if the specified share is a file system.
root_squash (no_root_squash) [root_squash]	Prevents the root user on the client from gaining superuser access on mounted shares by mapping root to an unprivileged user account called nfsnobody with UID 65534.
rw (ro) [ro]	Allows file modifications on the client.
sec [sec=sys]	Limits the share export to clients using one of these security methods: sys, krb5, krb5i, or krb5p. The sys option uses local UIDs and GIDs, and the rest use Kerberos for user authentication, krb5 plus integrity check, and krb5i plus data encryption, respectively.
secure / (insecure) [secure]	Allows access only on clients using ports lower than 1024.
subtree_check (no_subtree_check) [no_subtree_check]	Enables permission checks on higher-level directories of a share.
wdelay (no_wdelay) [wdelay]	Delays data writes to a share if it expects the arrival of another write request to the same share soon, thereby reducing the number of times the actual writes to the share must be made.

Table 20-4 exportfs Command Options

The following shows a few sample entries to understand the syntax of the *exports* file:

```
/export1     client1  client2  client3.example.com(rw,insecure)
/export2     client4.example.com(rw)  192.168.1.20(no_root_squash)  192.168.0.0/24
```

The first example above will export */export1* to *client1* and *client2* using all the defaults and to *client3.example.com* with read/write and insecure options. The second example will export */export2* to *client4.example.com* with read/write option to a client with IP 192.168.1.20 with no_root_squash option, and to the 192.168.0.0/24 network with all the default options. Check the manual pages of the *exports* file for additional examples.

Configuring NFS Server and Client

This section presents several exercises on how to set up the NFS service and export a share; mount the share on the client by making updates to appropriate files and start the NFS client processes; export and mount another share for group collaboration; and export and mount a different share and use Kerberos authentication for controlling access to it on the client. These exercises will solidify the knowledge you have gained in this chapter.

SELinux Requirements for NFS Operation

SELinux protects systems by setting appropriate controls using contexts and booleans. Before you proceed to the exercises, let's look at the NFS-specific SELinux contexts on processes and files, and also see the booleans that may need to be modified for NFS to function properly. By default, the SELinux policy allows NFS to export shares on the network without making any changes to either file contexts or booleans. All NFS daemons are confined by default, and are labeled with appropriate domain types. For instance, the *nfsd* process is labeled with the kernel_t type, *rpcbind* is labeled with the rpcbind_t type, *rpc.mountd* is labeled with the nfsd_t type, and so on. This information can be verified with the following:

 # ps -eZ | egrep 'nfs|rpc'

```
system_u:system_r:rpcbind_t:s0      28209 ?        00:00:00 rpcbind
system_u:system_r:nfsd_t:s0         28210 ?        00:00:00 rpc.mountd
system_u:system_r:kernel_t:s0       28216 ?        00:00:00 nfsd4
system_u:system_r:kernel_t:s0       28217 ?        00:00:00 nfsd4_callbacks
system_u:system_r:kernel_t:s0       28221 ?        00:00:00 nfsd
system_u:system_r:kernel_t:s0       28222 ?        00:00:00 nfsd
system_u:system_r:kernel_t:s0       28223 ?        00:00:00 nfsd
system_u:system_r:kernel_t:s0       28224 ?        00:00:00 nfsd
system_u:system_r:kernel_t:s0       28225 ?        00:00:00 nfsd
system_u:system_r:kernel_t:s0       28226 ?        00:00:00 nfsd
system_u:system_r:kernel_t:s0       28227 ?        00:00:00 nfsd
system_u:system_r:kernel_t:s0       28228 ?        00:00:00 nfsd
system_u:system_r:rpcd_t:s0         28232 ?        00:00:00 rpc.idmapd
system_u:system_r:rpcd_t:s0         28233 ?        00:00:00 rpc.rquotad
system_u:system_r:rpcd_t:s0         28419 ?        00:00:00 rpc.statd
```

Similarly, NFS configuration and functional files already have proper SELinux contexts in place and, therefore, they need no modifications. For instance, the context on the */etc/exports* file is:

 # ll –Z /etc/exports

-rw-r--r--. root root system_u:object_r:exports_t:s0 /etc/exports

However, any directory or file system that you want to export on the network for sharing purposes will need to have either public_content_ro_t or public_content_rw_t SELinux type applied. This is only required if more than one file-sharing service, such as any combination of NFS and CIFS, NFS and FTP, or CIFS and FTP, are used. For the use of NFS alone, there is no need to make this change on the directory or file system being shared.

The SELinux policy includes numerous booleans that may be of interest from an NFS operation standpoint. These booleans need a careful review to see which ones might require a toggle for NFS to operate well. Most of these booleans relate to services, such as HTTP, KVM, and FTP, that want to use mounted NFS shares to store their files. There is one boolean called samba_share_nfs, which is enabled in case the same directory or file system is shared via both NFS and CIFS. We will look at this boolean in Chapter 21 "Sharing File Storage with Samba".

To list the booleans other than the ones mentioned above, run the *getsebool* command as follows:

 # getsebool –a | egrep '^nfs|^use_nfs'

nfs_export_all_ro --> on
nfs_export_all_rw --> on
nfsd_anon_write --> off
use_nfs_home_dirs --> off

The output lists four booleans, and they are described in Table 20-5.

Boolean	Purpose
nfs_export_all_ro	Allows/disallows share exports in read-only mode.
nfs_export_all_rw	Allows/disallows share exports in read/write mode.

Boolean	Purpose
nfsd_anon_write	Allows/disallows the nfsd daemon to write anonymously to public directories on clients.
use_nfs_home_dirs	Allows/disallows NFS clients to mount user home directories.

Table 20-5 NFS SELinux Booleans

Some of these booleans will be used in our exercises.

Exercise 20-1: Export Shares to NFS Client

This exercise should be done on *server1*.

In this exercise, you will create a directory called */common* and export it with the NFSv4 protocol to *server2* in read/write mode with root squash disabled. You will create another directory called */nfsrhcsa* and export it with the NFSv4 protocol to *server2* in read-only mode. You will ensure that appropriate SELinux controls are enabled for the NFS service and it is allowed through the firewall. You will confirm the exports using a command and file.

1. Install the NFS package called nfs-utils:

    # **yum –y install nfs-utils**
    Package 1:nfs-utils-1.3.0-0.el7.x86_64 already installed and latest version
    Nothing to do

2. Create */common* and */nfsrhcsa* directories for use as mount points:

    # **mkdir /common /nfsrhcsa**

3. Activate the SELinux booleans persistently to allow NFS exports in both read-only and read/write modes, and verify the activation:

    # **setsebool –P nfs_export_all_ro=1 nfs_export_all_rw=1**
    # **getsebool –a | grep nfs_export**
    nfs_export_all_ro --> on
    nfs_export_all_rw --> on

4. Add the NFS service persistently to the firewalld configuration to allow the NFS traffic on TCP port 2049 to pass through, and load the rule:

    # **firewall-cmd --permanent --add-service nfs ; firewall-cmd --reload**
    success
    success

5. Set the *rpcbind* and NFS services to autostart at system reboots:

    # **systemctl enable rpcbind nfs-server**
    ln -s '/usr/lib/systemd/system/rpcbind.service' '/etc/systemd/system/multi-user.target.wants/rpcbind.service'

ln -s '/usr/lib/systemd/system/nfs-server.service' '/etc/systemd/system/nfs.target.wants/nfs-server.service'

ln -s '/usr/lib/systemd/system/rpcbind.socket' '/etc/systemd/system/sockets.target.wants/rpcbind.socket'

ln -s '/usr/lib/systemd/system/nfs.target' '/etc/systemd/system/multi-user.target.wants/nfs.target'

6. Start the *rpcbind* and NFS services, and confirm their status:

    # **systemctl start rpcbind nfs**
    # **systemctl status rpcbind nfs**
    rpcbind.service - RPC bind service
       Loaded: loaded (/usr/lib/systemd/system/rpcbind.service; enabled)
       Active: active (running) since Tue 2015-01-27 07:45:10 EST; 1h 48min ago
     Main PID: 1844 (rpcbind)
       CGroup: /system.slice/rpcbind.service
            └─1844 /sbin/rpcbind -w

    nfs-server.service - NFS Server
       Loaded: loaded (/usr/lib/systemd/system/nfs-server.service; enabled)
       Active: active (exited) since Tue 2015-01-27 08:41:17 EST; 51min ago
     Main PID: 4369 (code=exited, status=0/SUCCESS)
       CGroup: /system.slice/nfs-server.service

7. Open the */etc/exports* file in a text editor and add an entry for */common* to export it to *server2* with read/write and no_root_squash options, and another entry for */nfsrhcsa* to export it to *server2* using the sync option:

    /common   server2.example.com(rw,no_root_squash)
    /nfsrhcsa   server2.example.com(sync)

    ┌───┐
    │ **EXAM TIP:** Use at least one option when adding an entry to the /etc/exports file. │
    └───┘

8. Export the entries defined in the */etc/exports* file:

    # **exportfs –avr**
    exporting server2.example.com:/common
    exporting server2.example.com:/nfsrhcsa

9. Show the contents of the */var/lib/nfs/etab* file:

    # **cat /var/lib/nfs/etab**
    /common
    server2.example.com(rw,sync,wdelay,hide,nocrossmnt,secure,no_root_squash,no_all_squash,no_subt
    ree_check,secure_locks,acl,anonuid=65534,anongid=65534,sec=sys)
    /nfsrhcsa
    server2.example.com(ro,sync,wdelay,hide,nocrossmnt,secure,no_root_squash,no_all_squash,no_subtr
    ee_check,secure_locks,acl,anonuid=65534,anongid=65534,sec=sys)

The NFS service is now set up on *server1* with both */common* and */nfsrhcsa* shares available for mounting on the client. The */nfsrhcsa* share is created for use in two exercises in Chapter 10 "Constructing and Using File Systems and Swap".

For practice, if you want to unexport one of these shares, you can do so with the *exportfs* command by specifying the –u option with it. The following unexports */common*:

> # **exportfs –u server2.example.com:/common**

Confirm the unexport:

> # **exportfs –v | grep common**

Before proceeding, re-export the share using the following:

> # **exportfs –avr**

NFS Client Options

You have just shared a directory as an NFS share on the network with several default, read/write, and no_root_squash options. On the client, the *mount* command is used to connect the NFS share to the file system hierarchy. This command supports several options as well, and some common options are described in Table 20-6 with their default values shown in square brackets.

Option	Description
ac (noac) [ac]	Specifies whether to cache file attributes for better performance.
async (sync) [async]	Causes the I/O to happen asynchronously.
defaults	Selects the following default options automatically: rw, suid, dev, exec, auto, nouser, and async.
exec / noexec [exec]	Allows the execution of binaries.
fg / bg [fg]	Use fg (foreground) for shares that must be available to the client to boot successfully or operate properly. If a foreground mount fails, it is retried for retry minutes in the foreground until it either succeeds or times out. With bg (background), mount attempts are tried repeatedly for retry minutes in the background without hampering the system boot process or hanging the client.
hard / soft [hard]	With the hard option, the client tries repeatedly to mount a share until either it succeeds or times out. With the soft option, if a client attempts to mount a share for retrans times unsuccessfully, an error message is displayed.
_netdev	Mounts a share only after the networking has been started.
nfsvers	Specifies the NFS version to be used.
remount	Attempts to remount an already mounted share with, perhaps, different options.
retrans=n [3]	The client retransmits a read or write request for n times after the first transmission times out. If the request does not succeed after the n retransmissions have completed, a soft mount displays an error message and a hard mount continues to retry.

Option	Description
retry=n [2 minutes for fg and 10,000 minutes for bg]	Tries to mount a share for the specified amount of time before giving up.
rsize=n [negotiated]	Specifies the size of each read request.
rw / ro [rw]	rw allows file modifications, and ro prevents file modifications.
sec=mode [sys]	Specifies the type of security to be used. The default uses local UIDs and GIDs. Additional choices are krb5, krb5i, and krb5p, and they use Kerberos for user authentication, krb5 plus integrity check, and krb5i plus data encryption, respectively.
suid / nosuid [suid]	Allows users to run setuid and setgid programs.
timeo=n [600]	Sets a wait timeout, in tenths of a second, for NFS read and write requests to be responded before it retries again for retrans times. When the number of retrans attempts have been made, a soft mount displays an error message while a hard mount continues to retry.
wsize=n [negotiated]	Specifies the size of each write request.

Table 20-6 mount Command Options

You will see the usage of some of these options in the following exercises.

Exercise 20-2: Mount a Share on NFS Client

This exercise should be done on *server2*.

In this exercise, you will access and mount the */common* share exported in the previous exercise. You will create a mount point for it called */nfsrhcemnt*, and add an entry to the file system table so that this share is automatically mounted at system reboots. You will confirm the share mount using commands, and test access by creating a file in the mount point and viewing it on the NFS server.

1. Install the NFS package called nfs-utils:

    # **yum –y install nfs-utils**
    Package 1:nfs-utils-1.3.0-0.el7.x86_64 already installed and latest version
    Nothing to do

2. Create */nfsrhcemnt* mount point:

    # **mkdir /nfsrhcemnt**

3. Set the *rpcbind* service to autostart at system reboots:

    # **systemctl enable rpcbind**
    ln -s '/usr/lib/systemd/system/rpcbind.service' '/etc/systemd/system/multi-user.target.wants/rpcbind.service'
    ln -s '/usr/lib/systemd/system/rpcbind.socket' '/etc/systemd/system/sockets.target.wants/rpcbind.socket'

4. Start the *rpcbind* service, and confirm its status:

systemctl start rpcbind
systemctl status rpcbind
rpcbind.service - RPC bind service
   Loaded: loaded (/usr/lib/systemd/system/rpcbind.service; enabled)
   Active: active (running) since Mon 2015-01-26 13:08:21 MIST; 1 day 17h ago
  Main PID: 32466 (rpcbind)
   CGroup: /system.slice/rpcbind.service
       └─32466 /sbin/rpcbind -w

5. Open the */etc/fstab* file and add the following entry to automatically mount the share at system reboots:

server1.example.com:/common   /nfsrhcemnt   nfs   _netdev,rw   0   0

6. Mount the new share using either of the following:

mount /nfsrhcemnt
mount −t nfs −o rw server1:/common /nfsrhcemnt

7. Confirm the mount using either of the following:

mount | grep nfsrhcemnt
server1:/common on /nfsrhcemnt type nfs4
(rw,relatime,vers=4.0,rsize=131072,wsize=131072,namlen=255,hard,proto=tcp,port=0,timeo=600,retr
ans=2,sec=sys,clientaddr=192.168.0.120,local_lock=none,addr=192.168.0.110)
# **df −h | grep nfsrhcemnt**
server1:/common   8.8G 3.4G 5.4G 39% /nfsrhcemnt

A mount point should be empty when an attempt is made to mount a share on it, otherwise, the contents of the mount point will hide. As well, the mount point must not be in use or the mount attempt will fail.

8. Create a file called *nfsrhcetest* under */nfsrhcemnt* on the client and confirm its creation by running *ll* on */common* on the NFS server:

[server2] # **touch /nfsrhcemnt/nfsrhcetest**
[server1] # **ll /common**
-rw-r--r--. 1 root root 0 Jan 27 14:22 nfsrhcetest

The remote share is successfully mounted on *server2*, and it can be accessed as any other local file system. Access to it is also tested by creating a file on the NFS client and validating its presence on the NFS server.

EXAM TIP: Do not forget to update the /etc/fstab file on the client.

Exercise 20-3: Export a Share for Group Collaboration on NFS Client

This exercise should be done on *server1* (NFS server) and *server2* (NFS client).

On *server1*, you will create a group called *nfssdatagrp*, add members *user3* and *user4* to it, create a directory called */nfssdata* with ownership and owning group belonging to user *nfsnobody* and group *nfssdatagrp*, enable the setgid bit on the directory, and export it to *server2* for group collaboration on that system. On *server2*, you will create *user3* and *user4*, and group *nfssdatagrp*. Add both users to this group, create */nfssdatamnt* mount point, add an entry to the *fstab* file, and mount the share on */nfssdatamnt*. You will confirm the mount, and the permissions and owning group. You will log in as *user3* and *user4*, and create files for group collaboration.

On *server1* (NFS server):

1. Add group *nfssdatagrp* with GID 7777:

   # **groupadd –g 7777 nfssdatagrp**

2. Add *user3* and *user4* to this group:

   # **usermod –G nfssdatagrp user3**
   # **usermod –G nfssdatagrp user4**

3. Create */nfssdata* directory:

   # **mkdir /nfssdata**

4. Set ownership and owning group on this directory to user *nfsnobody* and group *sdatagrp*, respectively:

   # **chown nfsnobody:nfssdatagrp /nfssdata**

5. Enable the setgid bit on */nfssdata*:

   # **chmod 2770 /nfssdata**

6. Verify the new permissions on */nfssdata*:

   # **ll –d /nfssdata**
   drwxrws---. 2 nfsnobody nfssdatagrp 6 Jan 27 14:54 /nfssdata

7. Complete steps 1, 3, 4, 5, and 6 from Exercise 20-1 if they were not previously run.

8. Open the */etc/exports* file in a text editor and add the following entry to export */nfssdata* to *server2* with read/write and no_root_squash options:

   /nfssdata   server2.example.com(rw,no_root_squash)

9. Export the entry defined in the */etc/exports* file:

 # exportfs –avr
exporting server2.example.com:/nfssdata
exporting server2.example.com:/common

10. Show the contents of the */var/lib/nfs/etab* file:

 # cat /var/lib/nfs/etab | grep nfssdata
/nfssdata
server2.example.com(rw,sync,wdelay,hide,nocrossmnt,secure,no_root_squash,no_all_squash,no_subt
ree_check,secure_locks,acl,anonuid=65534,anongid=65534,sec=sys,rw,secure,no_root_squash,no_all
_squash)

On *server2* (NFS client):

11. Add group *nfssdatagrp* with GID 7777:

 # groupadd –g 7777 nfssdatagrp

12. Create user accounts *user3* and *user4* (use the matching UIDs/GIDs as on *server1*):

 # useradd user3 ; useradd user4

13. Assign password *user123* to *user3* and *user4* (passwords assigned this way is not
recommended; however, it is okay in a lab environment):

 # echo user123 | passwd --stdin user3
Changing password for user user3.
passwd: all authentication tokens updated successfully.
 # echo user123 | passwd --stdin user4
Changing password for user user4.
passwd: all authentication tokens updated successfully.

14. Add *user3* and *user4* to the *nfssdatagrp* group:

 # usermod –G nfssdatagrp user3
 # usermod –G nfssdatagrp user4

15. Open the */etc/fstab* file and add the following entry to automatically mount the share at
system reboots:

server1.example.com:/nfssdata   /nfssdatamnt   nfs   _netdev,rw   0   0

16. Create */nfssdatamnt* mount point:

 # mkdir /nfssdatamnt

17. Mount the new share using either of the following:

```
# mount /nfssdatamnt
# mount −t nfs −o rw server1:/nfssdata /nfssdatamnt
```

18. Confirm the mount using either of the following:

```
# mount | grep nfssdata
server1.example.com:/nfssdata on /nfssdatamnt type nfs4
(rw,relatime,vers=4.0,rsize=131072,wsize=131072,namlen=255,hard,proto=tcp,port=0,timeo=600,retr
ans=2,sec=sys,clientaddr=192.168.0.120,local_lock=none,addr=192.168.0.110)
# df −h | grep nfssdata
server1.example.com:/nfssdata  8.8G  3.4G  5.4G  39% /nfssdatamnt
```

19. Confirm that */nfssdatamnt* has proper permissions and owning group:

```
# ll −d /nfssdatamnt
drwxrws---.  2 nfsnobody nfssdatagrp 6 Jan 28 06:54 /nfssdatamnt
```

20. Log on as *user3* and create *nfssdatatest3* file, then log in as *user4* and create *nfssdatatest4* file:

```
# su − user3
$ touch /nfssdatamnt/nfssdatatest3 ; exit
# su − user4
$ touch /nfssdatamnt/nfssdatatest4 ; exit
```

21. Confirm the creation of the two files with ownership belonging to *user3* and *user4*, respectively, and owning group to *nfssdatagrp*:

```
# ll /nfssdatamnt
-rw-rw-r--.  1 user3 nfssdatagrp 0 Jan 28 08:38 nfssdatatest3
-rw-rw-r--.  1 user4 nfssdatagrp 0 Jan 28 08:38 nfssdatatest4
```

The remote share is successfully mounted on *server2* for group collaboration. Both group members can share files created under this mount point.

Exercise 20-4: Provide Secure Access to NFS Share with Kerberos

This exercise should be done on *server1* (NFS server) and *server2* (Kerberos server and NFS client).

This exercise assumes that *server2* is running Kerberos services (both KDC and admin services) for realm EXAMPLE.COM, the *root* user is added as an admin principal, DNS is disabled, the *hosts* file is updated with appropriate mappings for both *server1* and *server2*, and these servers are already added as host principals (host/server1 and host/server2) to the KDC database with their keytab files stored in the */etc* directory by the name *krb5.keytab*. It is also assumed that the NFS service is running on *server1*, which will also be used as the service host.

> **EXAM TIP:** You may have to copy an existing keytab file from a specified location to the /etc directory.
> **EXAM TIP:** You do not have to worry about updating the /etc/hosts file. DNS will be in place with all hostnames resolvable.

In this exercise, you will create and store the key file locally on the client, obtain a TGT for *user1*, and log in as this user to test the configuration.

On *server1* (NFS server):

1. Follow the steps provided in Exercise 20-1 to create and export */nfskrb5* directory with the following entry in the */etc/exports* file:

   /nfskrb5   server2.example.com(sec=krb5p,rw,no_root_squash)

2. Activate the nfs-secure-server service at system reboots:

   # systemctl enable nfs-secure-server
   ln -s '/usr/lib/systemd/system/nfs-secure-server.service' '/etc/systemd/system/nfs.target.wants/nfs-secure-server.service'

3. Start the nfs-secure-server service and confirm its status:

   # systemctl start nfs-secure-server
   # systemctl status nfs-secure-server
   nfs-secure.service - Secure NFS
     Loaded: loaded (/usr/lib/systemd/system/nfs-secure.service; disabled)
     Active: active (running) since Wed 2015-01-28 09:05:13 MIST; 844ms ago
     Process: 28910 ExecStart=/usr/sbin/rpc.gssd $RPCGSSDARGS (code=exited, status=0/SUCCESS)
    Main PID: 28911 (rpc.gssd)
     CGroup: /system.slice/nfs-secure.service
          └─28911 /usr/sbin/rpc.gssd

On *server2* (NFS client):

4. Activate the nfs-secure service at system reboots:

   # systemctl enable nfs-secure
   ln -s '/usr/lib/systemd/system/nfs-secure.service' '/etc/systemd/system/nfs.target.wants/nfs-secure.service'

5. Start the nfs-secure service and confirm its status:

   # systemctl start nfs-secure
   # systemctl status nfs-secure
   nfs-secure.service - Secure NFS
     Loaded: loaded (/usr/lib/systemd/system/nfs-secure.service; disabled)
     Active: active (running) since Wed 2015-01-28 09:05:13 MIST; 844ms ago
     Process: 28910 ExecStart=/usr/sbin/rpc.gssd $RPCGSSDARGS (code=exited, status=0/SUCCESS)

Main PID: 28911 (rpc.gssd)
    CGroup: /system.slice/nfs-secure.service
        └─28911 /usr/sbin/rpc.gssd

6. Open the */etc/fstab* file and add the following entry for the share so that it is mounted automatically at system reboots:

server1.example.com:/nfskrb5   /nfskrb5mnt   nfs   sec=krb5p   0   0

7. Create the required mount point with the *mkdir* command:

    # **mkdir /nfskrb5mnt**

8. Mount the new share using either of the following:

    # **mount /nfskrb5mnt**
    # **mount –t nfs –o rw,sec=krb5p server1:/nfskrb5 /nfskrb5mnt**

The secure remote share is successfully mounted on *server2*. Now, a user with TGT should be able to access the NFS mount.

You might have to install the ipa-client application on the NFS client and execute the *ipa-client-setup* utility to prepare the groundwork for this secure mount.

Monitoring NFS Activities

Monitoring NFS activities typically involves capturing and displaying read and write statistics on the NFS server and client. Tools such as *nfsstat*, *nfsiostat*, and *mountstats* are available and may be used for this purpose. The details that these tools provide require an in-depth understanding of various fields and parameters that are depicted in the output. The following presents only a high-level introduction of these tools. See the man pages for details.

The *nfsstat* command can be run on both the NFS server and client to produce NFS and RPC I/O statistics. It can be used to display server (–s), client (–c), NFS (–n), and RPC (–r) statistics. With the –m option, it shows all activities on mounted shares, and without any options, it exhibits both NFS and RPC statistics.

Here is a sample output of this command when it is executed without any options on the NFS server (*server1*):

```
# nfsstat
Server rpc stats:
calls        badcalls     badclnt      badauth      xdrcall
533          0            0            0            0

Server nfs v4:
null         compound
3        0%  530      99%

Server nfs v4 operations:
op0-unused   op1-unused   op2-future   access       close        commit
0        0%  0        0%  0        0%  20       2%  5        0%  0        0%
create       delegpurge   delegreturn  getattr      getfh        link
0        0%  0        0%  0        0%  178     22%  26       3%  0        0%
lock         lockt        locku        lookup       lookup_root  nverify
0        0%  0        0%  0        0%  14       1%  0        0%  0        0%
open         openattr     open_conf    open_dgrd    putfh        putpubfh
5        0%  0        0%  5        0%  0        0%  188     23%  0        0%
putrootfh    read         readdir      readlink     remove       rename
7        0%  0        0%  5        0%  0        0%  0        0%  0        0%
renew        restorefh    savefh       secinfo      setattr      setcltid
325     40%  0        0%  0        0%  7        0%  5        0%  5        0%
setcltidconf verify       write        rellockowner bc_ctl       bind_conn
5        0%  0        0%  0        0%  0        0%  0        0%  0        0%
exchange_id  create_ses   destroy_ses  free_stateid getdirdeleg  getdevinfo
0        0%  0        0%  0        0%  0        0%  0        0%  0        0%
getdevlist   layoutcommit layoutget    layoutreturn secinfononam sequence
0        0%  0        0%  0        0%  0        0%  0        0%  0        0%
set_ssv      test_stateid want_deleg   destroy_clid reclaim_comp
0        0%  0        0%  0        0%  0        0%  0        0%
```

This command also includes the client-side activities if run on the NFS client. Here is a sample from *server2*:

```
# nfsstat
Server rpc stats:
calls        badcalls     badclnt      badauth      xdrcall
0            0            0            0            0

Client rpc stats:
calls        retrans      authrefrsh
51015        0            51015

Client nfs v4:
null         read         write        commit       open         open_conf
0        0%  0        0%  0        0%  0        0%  10       0%  0        0%
open_noat    open_dgrd    close        setattr      fsinfo       renew
0        0%  0        0%  0        0%  0        0%  39       0%  50585   99%
setclntid    confirm      lock         lockt        locku        access
7        0%  5        0%  0        0%  0        0%  0        0%  27       0%
getattr      lookup       lookup_root  remove       rename       link
144      0%  30       0%  52       0%  0        0%  0        0%  0        0%
symlink      create       pathconf     statfs       readlink     readdir
0        0%  0        0%  26       0%  10       0%  0        0%  1        0%
server_caps  delegreturn  getacl       setacl       fs_locations rel_lkowner
65       0%  0        0%  0        0%  0        0%  0        0%  0        0%
secinfo      exchange_id  create_ses   destroy_ses  sequence     get_lease_t
13       0%  0        0%  0        0%  0        0%  0        0%  0        0%
reclaim_comp layoutget    getdevinfo   layoutcommit layoutreturn getdevlist
0        0%  0        0%  0        0%  0        0%  0        0%  0        0%
(null)
0        0%
```

The *nfsiostat* command is an NFS client-side utility that produces read and write statistics for each mounted share by consulting the */proc/self/mountstats* file. You can specify a time interval and a count of iterations for the execution of this command.

Here is a sample output of this command when it is executed without any options on *server2*:

```
# nfsiostat
server1.example.com:/common mounted on /nfsrhcemnt:

   op/s         rpc bklog
   0.04         0.00
read:               ops/s           kB/s           kB/op              retrans        avg RTT (ms)   avg exe (ms)
                    0.000   0.000   0.000          0 (0.0%)   0.000   0.000
write:              ops/s           kB/s           kB/op              retrans        avg RTT (ms)   avg exe (ms)
                    0.000   0.000   0.000          0 (0.0%)   0.000   0.000

server1.example.com:/nfssdata mounted on /nfssdatamnt:

   op/s         rpc bklog
   0.04         0.00
read:               ops/s           kB/s           kB/op              retrans        avg RTT (ms)   avg exe (ms)
                    0.000   0.000   0.000          0 (0.0%)   0.000   0.000
write:              ops/s           kB/s           kB/op              retrans        avg RTT (ms)   avg exe (ms)
                    0.000   0.000   0.000          0 (0.0%)   0.000   0.000
```

The *mountstats* command also consults the */proc/self/mountstats* file and displays the NFS read and write statistics for the specified mounted share. You can specify the --nfs or --rpc option with the command to restrict it to display NFS or RPC statistics only.

Here is a sample output of the *mountstats* command when it is executed on the */nfsrhcemnt* mount point on *server2*:

```
# mountstats /nfsrhcemnt
Stats for server1.example.com:/common mounted on /nfsrhcemnt:
  NFS mount options: rw,vers=4.0,rsize=131072,wsize=131072,namlen=255,acregmin=3,acregmax=60,acdirmin=30,
60,hard,proto=tcp,port=0,timeo=600,retrans=2,sec=sys,clientaddr=192.168.0.120,local_lock=none
  NFS server capabilities: caps=0xffff,wtmult=512,dtsize=32768,bsize=0,namlen=255
  NFSv4 capability flags: bm0=0xfdffbfff,bm1=0xf9be3e,bm2=0x0,acl=0x3,pnfs=notconfigured
  NFS security flavor: 1  pseudoflavor: 0

NFS byte counts:
  applications read 0 bytes via read(2)
  applications wrote 0 bytes via write(2)
  applications read 0 bytes via O_DIRECT read(2)
  applications wrote 0 bytes via O_DIRECT write(2)
  client read 0 bytes via NFS READ
  client wrote 0 bytes via NFS WRITE

RPC statistics:
  58 RPC requests sent, 58 RPC replies received (0 XIDs not found)
  average backlog queue length: 0
```

Chapter Summary

This chapter introduced one of the most common Linux system administration tasks, the administration of shares using the NFS protocol. It explained the concepts, benefits, versions, and security associated with NFS, and described various daemons, commands, and files involved in NFS management on the server and the client. The chapter demonstrated several exercises to strengthen the concepts learned by setting up NFS services to export and mount shares to be used for various purposes, and they included the configuration of a Kerberized NFS service. Finally, the chapter presented tools to display and monitor NFS usage statistics.

Chapter Review Questions

1. Which port must be enabled in the firewall to allow NFS traffic to pass through?
2. Which command can be used to export a share?
3. What is the role of the nfsnobody user account?
4. Is this command syntax correct? *mount –t nfs –o rw <hostname>:<share> /mnt_point*
5. Which option would you use with the *exportfs* command to unexport a share?
6. Write the names of at least three SELinux booleans that are related to NFS.
7. What kind of information does the */var/lib/nfs/etab* file store?
8. Name the three commands to get NFS read and write statistics.
9. Which file is updated when the *exportfs* command is executed successfully?
10. What is the default NFS version used in RHEL7?
11. Which daemon is no longer needed if NFSv4 is used on both server and client?
12. What is the purpose of the all_squash option used with a share?
13. What is the difference between the Kerberos krb5i and krb5p security levels?
14. Which daemon is responsible for mapping UIDs and GIDs with their corresponding usernames and groupnames?
15. Which file is referenced by the *nfsiostat* and *mountstats* commands to produce reports?
16. What is the name of the NFS configuration file?
17. What does this line entry in the */etc/exports* file mean? */dir1   *(rw)*
18. Which file needs to be modified to completely disable the support for older NFS versions?

Answers to Chapter Review Questions

1. The port 2049.
2. The *exportfs* command.
3. The nfsnobody user account provides unprivileged access to files.
4. Yes, it is correct.
5. The –u option.
6. The nfs_export_all_ro, nfs_export_all_rw, and nfsd_anon_write booleans.
7. It stores information about all exported shares.
8. The *nfsstat*, *nfsiostat*, and *mountstats* commands.
9. The */var/lib/nfs/etab* file.
10. The default NFS version used in RHEL7 is version NFSv4.
11. The *rpcbind* daemon.
12. The all_squash option treats all users on the NFS client as anonymous users.
13. krb5i provides data integrity while krb5p provides data integrity as well as encryption.
14. The *rpc.idmapd* daemon.
15. The */proc/self/mountstats* file.
16. The */etc/sysconfig/nfs* file.
17. This would export */dir1* in read/write mode to all systems.
18. The */etc/sysconfig/nfs* configuration file.

DIY Challenge Labs

The following labs are useful to strengthen the concepts and topics learned in this chapter. It is expected that you perform these labs without any additional help. A step-by-step guide is not provided, as the implementation of these labs requires the knowledge that has been presented in this chapter. Use defaults or your own thinking for missing information.

Lab 20-1: Share a Directory with NFS

Configure the NFS services and export */var/log* to systems on the local network in read-only mode. Ensure that the NFS server supports all NFS versions. Mount the share on another RHEL7 system persistently using all the default mount options.

Lab 20-2: Share a Directory for Group Collaboration

Create a group and add users to it as members. Create a directory and assign it to the group. Set appropriate bits on the directory to prepare it for group collaboration. Use NFS and share the directory in read/write mode to a specific client. Create a mount point on the client and a group with the same name as that created on the server. Ensure that the same group members exist on the client as well. Mount the share persistently and test to ensure the group members are able to share files.

Lab 20-3: Access NFS Shares via Kerberos

Create a directory and share it with NFS using Kerberos krb5i security level. Create a mount point on the client and mount it persistently. Set up Kerberos services if needed.

Chapter 21

Sharing File Storage with Samba

This chapter describes the following major topics:

➢ Describe Samba and its features and benefits
➢ Samba daemons, commands, and configuration files
➢ Analyze the Samba configuration file and understand software packages
➢ Describe SELinux requirements for Samba
➢ Configure Samba to provide network shares to clients
➢ Configure Samba client to access and mount the share
➢ Configure Samba to provide network share for group collaboration on Samba clients
➢ Configure Samba client to access a share using Kerberos authentication

RHCE Objectives:

26. Mount and unmount CIFS network file systems
76. Provide network shares to specific clients
77. Provide network shares suitable for group collaboration
78. Use Kerberos to authenticate access to shared directories

Samba

Samba is a networking protocol that allows Linux and UNIX systems to share file and print resources with Windows and other Linux and UNIX systems. It is the standard Windows interoperability suite of programs for Linux and UNIX. Samba offers numerous benefits, including a seamless interaction with Microsoft Windows systems. RHEL7 includes the support for Samba software v4.1, which uses the SMB3 protocol that allows encrypted transport connections to Windows and other Linux-based Samba servers. The Samba service is configured with the help of a single configuration file and a few commands.

Understanding Samba

Server Message Block (SMB), now widely known as the *Common Internet File System* (CIFS), is a networking protocol developed by Microsoft, IBM, and Intel in the late 1980s to enable Windows-based PCs to share file and print resources with one another. This protocol has been used in Windows operating systems as the primary native protocol for file and printer sharing. Samba was developed in the Linux world to share file and print resources with Microsoft Windows systems using the SMB format. This allowed Linux systems to participate in Windows workgroups and domains, as well as share Windows resources with other Linux systems and UNIX.

In Samba terminology, the system that shares its file and print resources is referred to as a *Samba server*, and the system that accesses those shared resources is referred to as a *Samba client*. The network file shares may be used for collaboration among group members with accounts on different systems running a mix of Linux and Windows operating systems. Moreover, user home directories that exist on Windows may be shared with Linux systems, and vice versa. This would eliminate the need of having a separate home directory on each system for each user to log on. A single system can be configured to provide both Samba server and client functionality concurrently.

Benefits of Using Samba

The use of Samba provides several benefits, some of which are listed below:

- ✓ Samba shares can be accessed on Windows, as well as UNIX and other Linux systems.
- ✓ Windows shares can be accessed and mounted on Linux.
- ✓ Linux and Windows domain user credentials can be used interchangeably on either platform for authentication and authorization.
- ✓ A Samba server can:
    - ✓ Act as a print server for Windows systems.
    - ✓ Be configured as a *Primary Domain Controller* (PDC) and as a *Backup Domain Controller* (BDC) for a Samba-based PDC.
    - ✓ Be set up as an Active Directory member server on a Windows network.
    - ✓ Provide *Windows Internet Name Service* (WINS) name resolution.

Samba Daemon

Samba and CIFS are client/server protocols that employ the *smbd* daemon on the server to share and manage directories and file systems. This daemon process uses TCP port 445 for operation, and it is also responsible for share locking and user authentication.

Samba Commands

There are numerous commands available to establish and manage Samba functionality on the server and client. A proper understanding of the usage of these commands is essential for smooth administration. Refer to Table 21-1 for an explanation.

Command	Description
mount	Mounts a Samba share specified at the command line or listed in the /etc/fstab file. It adds an entry for the mounted share to the client's /etc/mtab file and can be used to display mounted shares listed in this file.
mount.cifs	Mounts a Samba share on the client.
pdbedit	Maintains a local user database in the /var/lib/samba/private/smbpasswd file on the server.
smbclient	Connects to a Samba share to perform FTP-like operations.
smbpasswd	Changes Samba user passwords.
testparm	Tests the syntax of the smb.conf file.
umount	Functions opposite to that of the mount command.

Table 21-1 Samba Commands

There are additional commands available; however, their discussion is beyond the scope of this book.

Samba Configuration and Functional Files

Samba references several files at startup and during its operation. These files include those that store configuration data and logs. Table 21-2 describes key configuration and functional files.

File	Description
/etc/samba/smb.conf	Samba server configuration file.
/etc/samba/smbusers	Maintains Samba and Linux user mappings.
/etc/sysconfig/samba	Contains directives used at Samba startup. Stores Samba startup configuration.
/var/lib/samba/private/smbpasswd	Maintains Samba user passwords. This file is used for authentication purposes. Samba user passwords may be different from their Linux user passwords.
/var/log/samba	Directory location for Samba logs.

Table 21-2 Samba Configuration and Functional Files

Some of these files are present on the system, while others are created during a server setup.

Understanding Samba Configuration File

The *smb.conf* file is the primary configuration file for setting up a Samba server. You specify share definitions and set parameter values to modify their behavior. This file has two major sections: Global Settings and Share Definitions. Global Settings defines the directives that affect the overall Samba server behavior and includes options for networking, logging, standalone server, domain members, domain controller, browser control, name resolution, printing, and file systems. Share Definitions sets share-specific directives for home and custom shares. Most settings in the global section are applied to all other sections in the file provided the other sections do not have them defined explicitly.

The following shows an excerpt from the *smb.conf* file with directives of our interest:

```
#============== Global Settings =======================
[global]
# ---------------------- Network Related Options --------------------
        workgroup        = MYGROUP
        server string    = Samba Server Version %v
;       netbios name     = MYSERVER
;       interfaces       = lo eth0 192.168.12.2/24 192.168.13.2/24
;       hosts allow      = 127. 192.168.12. 192.168.13.
# ----------------------- Logging Options ---------------------------
        log file         = /var/log/samba/log.%m
        max log size     = 50
# ---------------------- Standalone Server Options --------------------
        security         = user
        passdb backend   = tdbsam
#================ Share Definitions ====================
[homes]
        comment          = Home Directories
        browseable       = no
        writable         = yes
;       valid users      = %S
;       valid users      = MYDOMAIN\%S
; [Profiles]
;       path             = /var/lib/samba/profiles
;       browseable       = no
;       guest ok         = yes
; [public]
;       comment          = Public Stuff
;       path             = /home/samba
;       public           = yes
;       writable         = yes
;       write list       = +staff
```

The directive names used in this file are case insensitive, the white space before and after an equal sign is ignored, and any text that follows the # or ; sign is treated as a comment.

Description of directives located in the Network Related Options, Logging Options, Standalone Server Options, and Share Definitions from the preceding output is provided in Table 21-3. The rest of the options are beyond the scope.

Directive	Global Settings
Network-Related Options	
workgroup	The name of the workgroup that the server is (or appears to be) a part of.
server string	Any description that identifies this system as a Samba server.

Directive	Global Settings
netbios name	The name of the Samba server by which it is known.
interfaces	Specifies the network interface name, or host or network IP to be served. This directive is useful when there are multiple configured network interfaces on the system.
hosts allow / hosts deny	Allows/disallows the specified networks or domain names to access the shares. May also be set at the individual share level.
	Logging Options
log file	Defines separate log file names in the /var/log/samba directory for every client that connects to this Samba server.
max log size	Specifies the size in KBs for the log file to grow to before it is rotated. A 0 sets it to grow to an unlimited size. The default size is 50KB.
	Standalone Server Options
security	Defines one of the following authentication options: • ads = performs authentication on an Active Directory server. • domain = performs authentication on a domain controller. • server = performs authentication on a server. • user = matches usernames/passwords with those on clients. This is the default.
passdb backend	Specifies the backend to be used for storing user and group information. This directive supports three options: • smbpasswd = uses the /var/lib/samba/private/smbpasswd file. • tdbsam (Trivial Database Security Accounts Manager) = sets up a trivial local account database in the /var/lib/samba directory. This is the default. • ldapsam (LDAP Security Accounts Manager) = uses a remote LDAP account database.
Directive	**Share Definitions**
comment	A short description of the share displayed with a client query response.
browsable	Allows/disallows clients to see the share.
writable	Allows/disallows read/write access to the share. This directive is opposite to the "read only" directive.
valid users	Specifies a comma-separated list of users or groups, or a combination, that are allowed to log in to the share (group names are prefixed with the @ sign). If this directive is empty or not defined, all users will be able to log in.
path	Sets the absolute path to the share.
guest ok	Allows/disallows users to access the share as a guest without having to enter a password. This is same as the public directive.
public	Allows/disallows everyone read-only access to the share. This directive is same as "guest ok".
write list	Specifies a comma-separated list of users or groups, or a combination, that can write to the share (group names are prefixed with the @ sign). The value of this directive applies even if the "read only" directive is set to yes.
guest only	Allows/disallows only the guest users to access the share.

Directive	Global Settings
force group	Specifies a Linux group that is assigned as the default group to files created for group collaboration.
create mask	Specifies a umask value assigned to files at the time of their creation.

Table 21-3 Directives in the smb.conf File

There are numerous other directives available to be set in this file. Check the man pages for *smb.conf* for details.

EXAM TIP: Make sure that you understand various directives and how to define their values in the smb.conf file.

The *smb.conf* configuration file is automatically reloaded if *smbd* detects a change in it, or you can reload the updated configuration using the *systemctl* command with the --reload option. Reloading the configuration does not affect established connections.

Samba Software Packages

There are several software packages that need to be installed on the system to configure it as a Samba server or client. The *rpm* command below produces a list of the Samba packages that are currently installed on *server1*:

```
# yum list installed | grep ^samba
samba.x86_64              4.1.1-31.el7        @ftprepo
samba-common.x86_64       4.1.1-31.el7        @ftprepo
samba-libs.x86_64         4.1.1-31.el7        @anaconda/7.0
```

Table 21-4 describes these packages, as well as the packages that will be installed later for our exercises.

Package	Description
samba	Provides the Samba server support.
samba-client	Includes utilities for performing various operations on server and client.
samba-common	Provides Samba man pages, commands, and configuration files.
samba-libs	Contains library routines used by Samba server and client.
cifs-utils	Client-side utilities for mounting and managing CIFS shares.

Table 21-4 Samba Software Packages

A Samba server needs all packages except for the cifs-utils package to be able to provide network shares. On the client side, however, only cifs-utils and samba-client packages are needed, along with any dependent packages.

Configuring Samba Server and Client

This section presents several exercises to set up the Samba service and share a directory or file system; mount the share on the client; share and mount another share for group collaboration; and share and mount a different share and use Kerberos authentication for controlling access to it on the client. These exercises will solidify the knowledge you have gained in this chapter.

SELinux Requirements for Samba Operation

SELinux protects systems by setting appropriate controls using contexts and booleans. Before you proceed to the exercises, let's look at the Samba-specific SELinux contexts on processes and files, and also see the booleans that may need to be modified for Samba to function properly. The Samba daemon is confined by default and is labeled appropriately with smbd_t domain type. This information can be verified with the following:

ps –eZ | grep smbd
system_u:system_r:smbd_t:s0   28046 ?   00:00:00 smbd

Similarly, Samba configuration and functional files already have proper SELinux contexts in place; therefore, they need no modifications. For instance, the context on the */etc/samba/smb.conf* file is:

ll –Z /etc/samba/smb.conf
-rw-r--r--. root root system_u:object_r:samba_etc_t:s0 /etc/samba/smb.conf

However, any directory or file system that you want to share on the network with Samba alone needs to have samba_share_t type applied to it. In case of multiple file-sharing services, such as any combination of CIFS and NFS, CIFS and FTP, or NFS and FTP, sharing the same directory or file system, you will need to use either the public_content_ro_t or public_content_rw_t type instead.

The SELinux policy includes numerous booleans that may be of interest from a Samba operation standpoint. These booleans need a careful review to see which ones might require a toggle for Samba to operate well. Most of these booleans relate to services, such as HTTP, KVM, and FTP, that want to use mounted Samba shares to store their files. There is one boolean called samba_share_nfs, which is enabled in case the same directory or file system is shared via both NFS and CIFS.

To list Samba-related booleans, run the *getsebool* command as follows:

getsebool –a | egrep 'samba|smb|cifs'
cobbler_use_cifs --> off
ftpd_use_cifs --> off
git_cgi_use_cifs --> off
git_system_use_cifs --> off
httpd_use_cifs --> off
ksmtuned_use_cifs --> off
mpd_use_cifs --> off
polipo_use_cifs --> off
samba_create_home_dirs --> off
samba_domain_controller --> off
samba_enable_home_dirs --> off
samba_export_all_ro --> off
samba_export_all_rw --> off
samba_portmapper --> off
samba_run_unconfined --> off
samba_share_fusefs --> off
samba_share_nfs --> off
sanlock_use_samba --> off

---

smbd_anon_write --> off
use_samba_home_dirs --> off
virt_sandbox_use_samba --> off
virt_use_samba --> off

The above output shows twenty-two booleans that should be reviewed and modified as required. Table 21-5 describes the purpose of some key booleans.

Boolean	Purpose
ftpd_use_cifs	Allows/disallows a mounted Samba share to be used as a public file transfer location by the FTP service.
httpd_use_cifs	Allows/disallows a mounted Samba share to be used by the Apache service.
samba_create_home_dirs	Allows/disallows Samba to create home directories.
samba_enable_home_dirs	Allows/disallows Samba to share user home directories.
samba_export_all_ro	Allows/disallows Samba to share in read-only mode.
samba_export_all_rw	Allows/disallows Samba to share in read/write mode.
smbd_anon_write	Allows/disallows Samba to write to public directories with public_content_rw_t type.
use_samba_home_dirs	Allows/disallows Samba clients to mount user home directories.

Table 21-5 Samba-Related SELinux Booleans

We will use some of these booleans in our exercises.

Exercise 21-1: Provide Network Shares to Samba Client

This exercise should be done on *server1*.

Part 1: In this exercise, you will share the */common* directory (path), which you also shared via NFS in the previous chapter. You will make this share browsable (browsable) with login (valid users) and write (writable) access given to only (write list) *user10* from systems in the *example.com* domain (hosts allow). This share should have read-only (public) access given to *user3*, and it should not be accessible (hosts deny) from 192.168.2.0/24 network.

Part 2: In this exercise, you will create a directory called */smbrhcsa* (path) in browsable mode (browsable) with login (valid users) and write (writable) access allocated to only (write list) *user1*, and read-only (public) access to *user3*. This share is being created for an exercise in Chapter 10 "Constructing and Using File Systems and Swap".

For both parts of this exercise, you will ensure that appropriate SELinux controls are enabled for the Samba service and it is allowed through the firewall.

1. Install Samba server packages samba and samba-client:

    # **yum –y install samba samba-client**
    Package samba-4.1.1-31.el7.x86_64 already installed and latest version
    Package samba-client-4.1.1-31.el7.x86_64 already installed and latest version
    Nothing to do

2. Create */smbrhcsa* directory:

    # **mkdir /smbrhcsa**

3. Activate the SELinux booleans persistently to allow Samba shares in both read-only and read/write modes, and allow Samba and NFS to share */common*. Verify the activation.

    # **setsebool –P samba_export_all_ro=1 samba_export_all_rw=1 samba_share_nfs=1**
    # **getsebool –a | egrep 'samba_export|samba_share_nfs'**
    samba_export_all_ro --> on
    samba_export_all_rw --> on
    samba_share_nfs --> on

4. Add SELinux file types public_content_rw_t on */common* and samba_share_t on */smbrhcsa* directories to the SELinux policy rules:

    # **semanage fcontext –at public_content_rw_t "/common(/.*)?"**
    # **semanage fcontext –at samba_share_t "/smbrhcsa(/.*)?"**

5. Apply the new contexts on both directories and confirm:

    # **restorecon /common /smbrhcsa**
    # **ll –Zd /common /smbrhcsa**
    drwxr-xr-x. root root unconfined_u:object_r:public_content_rw_t:s0 /common
    drwxr-xr-x. root root unconfined_u:object_r:samba_share_t:s0 /smbrhcsa

6. Add the Samba service persistently to the firewalld configuration to allow Samba traffic on TCP port 445 to pass through, and load the rule:

    # **firewall-cmd --permanent --add-service=samba; firewall-cmd --reload**
    success
    success

7. Rename the *smb.conf* file to *smb.conf.old*, and create a new file called *smb.conf* with the following entries only:

    ```
    [global]
        workgroup       = EXAMPLE
        server string   = server1 is the Samba Server Sharing /common and /smbrhcsa
        hosts allow     = 127. 192.168.0. .example.com
        interfaces      = lo eth0 192.168.0.
        passdb backend  = smbpasswd
        security        = user
        log file        = /var/log/samba/%m.log
        max log size    = 5000
    [common]
        comment         = /common directory available to user10
        hosts deny      = 192.168.2.0/24
        browsable       = yes
    ```

```
path            = /common
public          = yes
valid users     = user10
write list      = user10
writable        = yes
[smbrhcsa]
comment         = /smbrhcsa directory available to user1
browsable       = yes
path            = /smbrhcsa
public          = yes
valid users     = user1
write list      = user1
writable        = yes
```

8. Execute the *testparm* command to check for any syntax errors in the file. Use the –v switch to display other defaults that are not defined in the file.

    # **testparm**
    Load smb config files from /etc/samba/smb.conf
    rlimit_max: increasing rlimit_max (1024) to minimum Windows limit (16384)
    Processing section "[common]"
    Processing section "[smbrhcsa]"
    Loaded services file OK.
    Server role: ROLE_STANDALONE
    Press enter to see a dump of your service definitions
    [global]
          workgroup = EXAMPLE
          server string = server1 is the Samba Server Sharing /common and /smbrhcsa
          interfaces = lo, eth0, 192.168.0.
          passdb backend = smbpasswd
          log file = /var/log/samba/%m.log
          idmap config * : backend = tdb
          hosts allow = 127., 192.168.0., .example.com
    [common]
          comment = /common directory available to user10
          path = /common
          valid users = user10
          write list = user10
          read only = No
          guest ok = Yes
          hosts deny = 192.168.2.0/24
    [smbrhcsa]
          comment = /smbrhcsa directory available to user1
          path = /smbrhcsa
          valid users = user1
          write list = user1
          read only = Yes
          guest ok = Yes

9. Create Linux user *user10* with password user123:

    # **useradd user10**
    # **echo user123 | passwd --stdin user10**

10. Add (–a) *user10* to Samba user database */var/lib/samba/private/smbpasswd*, and assign them password user123. Show the contents of the *smbpasswd* file.

    # **smbpasswd –a user10**
    New SMB password:
    Retype new SMB password:
    startsmbfilepwent_internal: file /var/lib/samba/private/smbpasswd did not exist. File successfully created.
    Added user user10.
    # **cat /var/lib/samba/private/smbpasswd**
    user10:2003:XXXXXXXXXXXXXXXXXXXXXXXXXXXXXXXXXXX:EACB2C6A3AAA4ED476ED2741BE8C7A4E:[U   ]:LCT-54CAD791:

11. Display (–L) the user information verbosely using the *pdbedit* command:

    # **pdbedit –Lv**

    Unix username: user10
    NT username:
    Account Flags: [U   ]
    User SID: S-1-5-21-638622928-855739789-1126480426-5006
    Primary Group SID: S-1-5-21-638622928-855739789-1126480426-513
    Full Name:
    Home Directory: \\server1\user10
    HomeDir Drive:
    Logon Script:
    Profile Path: \\server1\user10\profile
    Domain: SERVER1
    Account desc:
    Workstations:
    Munged dial:
    Logon time: 0
    Logoff time: never
    Kickoff time: never
    Password last set: Thu, 29 Jan 2015 20:00:01 EST
    Password can change: Thu, 29 Jan 2015 20:00:01 EST
    Password must change: never
    Last bad password: 0
    Bad password count: 0
    Logon hours: FFFFFFFFFFFFFFFFFFFFFFFFFFFFFFFFFFFFFFFFFFFF

12. Set the Samba service to autostart at system reboots:

systemctl enable smb
ln -s '/usr/lib/systemd/system/smb.service' '/etc/systemd/system/multi-user.target.wants/smb.service'

13. Start the Samba service, and confirm its status:

systemctl start smb
systemctl status smb
smb.service - Samba SMB Daemon
   Loaded: loaded (/usr/lib/systemd/system/smb.service; enabled)
   Active: active (running) since Wed 2015-01-28 21:30:51 EST; 22h ago
  Main PID: 28046 (smbd)
   Status: "smbd: ready to serve connections..."
   CGroup: /system.slice/smb.service
       ├─28046 /usr/sbin/smbd
       └─28047 /usr/sbin/smbd

14. List (–L) the shares available on the server as *user10* (–U) using the *smbclient* command:

smbclient –L //localhost –U user10
Enter user10's password:
Domain=[EXAMPLE] OS=[Unix] Server=[Samba 4.1.1]
   Sharename   Type   Comment
   -------------   ------   ------------
   common   Disk   /common directory available to user10
   smbrhcsa   Disk   /smbrhcsa directory available to user1
   IPC$ IPC   IPC Service (server1 is the Samba Server Sharing /common and /smbrhcsa)
Domain=[EXAMPLE] OS=[Unix] Server=[Samba 4.1.1]
   Server   Comment
   ---------   ------------
   Workgroup   Master
   --------------   ---------

The Samba service is now set up on *server1* with */common* and */smbrhcsa* shared over the network, and are available for accessing and mounting on the client.

Exercise 21-2: Access and Mount a Share on Samba Client
This exercise should be done on *server2*.

In this exercise, you will access and mount the */common* share exported in the previous exercise. You will create *user10* using the same UID that is used on *server1*. You will create a mount point called */smbrhcemnt*, and add an entry to the file system table so that this share is automatically mounted at system reboots. You will confirm the share access and mount using commands, and test access by creating a file in the mount point and viewing it on the Samba server. You will store the username and password for *user10* in a file owned by *root* with 0400 permissions.

1. Install the Samba client packages samba-client and cifs-utils:

 # yum –y install samba-client cifs-utils
Package samba-client-4.1.1-31.el7.x86_64 already installed and latest version
Package cifs-utils-6.2-6.el7.x86_64 already installed and latest version
Nothing to do

2. Create Linux users *user10* with password user123 (use matching UID/GID as on *server1*):

   # useradd user10
   # echo user123 | passwd --stdin user10

3. List (–L) what shares are available from *server1* using the *smbclient* command:

   # smbclient –L //server1/common –U user10
   Enter user10's password:
   Domain=[EXAMPLE] OS=[Unix] Server=[Samba 4.1.1]
       Sharename   Type   Comment
       -------------   ------   ------------
       common   Disk   /common directory available to user10
       smbrhcsa   Disk   /smbrhcsa directory available to user1
       IPC$ IPC   IPC Service (server1 is the Samba Server Sharing /common and /smbrhcsa)
   Domain=[EXAMPLE] OS=[Unix] Server=[Samba 4.1.1]
   . . . .

4. Log on to the */common* share as *user10* using the *smbclient* command:

   # smbclient //server1/common –U user10
   Enter user10's password:
   Domain=[EXAMPLE] OS=[Unix] Server=[Samba 4.1.1]
   smb: \>

The connection is successfully established with the */common* share. You can run the *help*
subcommand to list available commands, use *ls* to list files in the share, use *get*/*mget* and *put*/*mput*
to transfer one or more files, and so on. Issue *exit* when done to disconnect.

5. Create */smbrhcemnt* mount point:

   # mkdir /smbrhcemnt

6. Mount */common* on the */smbrhcemnt* mount point as *user10*:

   # mount //server1/common /smbrhcemnt –o username=user10
   Password for user10@//server1/common: *******

7. Execute the *df* and *mount* commands to check the mount status of the share:

   # df –h | grep smbrhcemnt
   //server1/common   8.8G 3.4G 5.4G 39% /smbrhcemnt

mount | grep smbrhcemnt

//server1/common on /smbrhcemnt type cifs
(rw,relatime,vers=1.0,cache=strict,username=user10,domain=SERVER1,uid=0,noforceuid,gid=0,nof
orcegid,addr=192.168.0.110,unix,posixpaths,serverino,acl,rsize=1048576,wsize=65536,actimeo=1)

8. Create a file called */etc/samba/smbrhcecred* and add the credentials for *user10* to it:

# vi /etc/samba/smbrhcecred
username=user10
password=user123

9. Set ownership on the file to *root* and permissions to 0400:

chown root /etc/samba/smbrhcecred && chmod 0400 /etc/samba/smbrhcecred

10. Open the */etc/fstab* file and add the following entry to automatically mount the share at system reboots:

//server1/common /smbrhcemnt cifs rw,credentials=/etc/samba/smbrhcecred 0 0

You can add the _netdev option to instruct the system to wait for networking to establish before attempting to mount this file system.

EXAM TIP: Do not forget to update the /etc/fstab file on the client.

---

11. Create a file called *smbrhcetest* as *user10* under */smbrhcemnt* and confirm its creation by running *ll* on */common* on the Samba server:

[server2] $ touch /smbrhcemnt/smbrhcetest
[server1] # ll /common
-rw-r--r--. 1 root   root   0 Jan 27 14:22 nfsrhcetest
-rw-r--r--. 1 user10 user10 0 Jan 29 21:15 smbrhcetest

The remote share is successfully mounted on *server2*, and it can be accessed as any other local file system. Access to it is also tested by creating a file on the Samba client and validating its presence on the Samba server.

Exercise 21-3: Provide a Share for Group Collaboration on Samba Client

This exercise should be done on *server1* (Samba server) and *server2* (Samba client).

In this exercise, (on *server1*) you will create users *user11* and *user12* and a group called *smbgrp*. You will add the two users to group *smbgrp*, create a directory called */smbsdata*, set owning group on the directory to group *smbgrp*, permissions to 0770, and share */smbsdata* for group collaboration. (on *server2*) You will create *user11* and *user12* and group *smbgrp*, and add both users to this group as members. You will create */smbsdatamnt* mount point for this share and add an entry to the *fstab*

---

file. You will mount the share on *smbsdatamnt* and confirm the mount. You will log in as *user3* and then as *user4* and create files for group collaboration.

On *server1* (Samba server):

1. Install samba and samba-client software packages (if they are not already there).
2. Create Linux users *user11* and *user12* with password user123 (this way of setting a user password is done for ease; it is not recommended):

   # useradd user11 ; useradd user12
   # echo user123 | passwd --stdin user11
   # echo user123 | passwd --stdin user12

3. Add group *smbgrp* with GID 8888:

   # groupadd –g 8888 smbgrp

4. Add *user11* and *user12* as members to *smbgrp*:

   # usermod –G smbgrp user11
   # usermod –G smbgrp user12

5. Create */smbsdata* directory:

   # mkdir /smbsdata

6. Set owning group on */smbsdata* to *smbgrp*:

   # chgrp smbgrp /smbsdata

7. Set permissions to 0770 on the directory:

   # chmod 0770 /smbsdata

8. Activate the SELinux booleans persistently to allow the share in both read-only and read/write modes, and verify the activation:

   # setsebool –P samba_export_all_ro=1 samba_export_all_rw=1
   # getsebool –a | grep samba_export
   samba_export_all_ro --> on
   samba_export_all_rw --> on

9. Add SELinux file context with type samba_share_t on */smbsdata* directory to the SELinux policy rules:

   # semanage fcontext –at samba_share_t "/smbsdata(/.*)?"

10. Apply the new context on the directory, and confirm:

restorecon /smbsdata
ll –Zd /smbsdata
drw-rw----. root smbgrp unconfined_u:object_r:samba_share_t:s0 /smbsdata

11. Add the Samba service persistently to the firewalld configuration to allow Samba traffic on TCP port 445 to pass through, and load the rule:

    # **firewall-cmd --permanent --add-service=samba; firewall-cmd --reload**

12. Append the following to the */etc/samba/smb.conf* file. Leave */common* and */smbrhcsa* entries intact if they were previously added.

    [smbsdata]
comment	= /smbsdata directory for group collaboration
browsable	= yes
path	= /smbsdata
public	= no
valid users	= @smbgrp
write list	= @smbgrp
writable	= yes
force group	= +smbgrp
create mask	= 0770

13. Check for any syntax errors in the file using the *testparm* command:

    # **testparm**

14. Add *user11* and *user12* to the Samba user database */var/lib/samba/private/smbpasswd* (this file will be created) and assign them password user123:

    # **smbpasswd –a user11**
    # **smbpasswd –a user12**

15. Display the user information using the *pdbedit* command:

    # **pdbedit –Lv**

16. Set the Samba service to autostart at system reboots:

    # **systemctl enable smb**

17. Start the Samba service and confirm its status:

    # **systemctl start smb**
    # **systemctl status smb**

18. List (–L) the shares available on the server as *user11* (–U) using the *smbclient* command:

```
# smbclient –L //localhost –U user11
Enter user11's password:
Domain=[EXAMPLE] OS=[Unix] Server=[Samba 4.1.1]
    Sharename      Type      Comment
    -------------  ------    ------------
    smbsdata       Disk     /smbsdata directory for group collaboration
    smbrhcsa       Disk     /smbrhcsa directory available to user1
    common         Disk     /common directory available to user10
    IPC$           IPC      IPC Service (server1 is the Samba Server Sharing /common and /smbrhcsa)
Domain=[EXAMPLE] OS=[Unix] Server=[Samba 4.1.1]
    . . . . . . . .
```

On *server2* (Samba client):

19. Install samba, samba-client, and cifs-utils software packages (if they are not already there).
20. Create Linux users *user11* and *user12* with password user123 (use matching UIDs/GIDs as on *server1*):

    ```
    # useradd user11 ; useradd user12
    # echo user123 | passwd --stdin user11
    # echo user123 | passwd --stdin user12
    ```

21. Add group *smbgrp* with GID 8888:

    ```
    # groupadd –g 8888 smbgrp
    ```

22. Add *user11* and *user12* as members to *smbgrp*:

    ```
    # usermod –G smbgrp user11
    # usermod –G smbgrp user12
    ```

23. List (–L) what shares are available from *server1* using the *smbclient* command:

    ```
    # smbclient –L //server1 –U user11
    Enter user11's password:
    Domain=[EXAMPLE] OS=[Unix] Server=[Samba 4.1.1]
        Sharename    Type    Comment
        -----------  ------  ------------
        smbsdata     Disk    /smbsdata directory for group collaboration
        smbrhcsa     Disk    /smbrhcsa directory available to user1
        common       Disk    /common directory available to user10
        IPC$         IPC     IPC Service (server1 is the Samba Server Sharing /common and /smbrhcsa)
    Domain=[EXAMPLE] OS=[Unix] Server=[Samba 4.1.1]
        . . . . . . . .
    ```

24. Log on to the */smbsdata* share as *user11* using the *smbclient* command:

    ```
    # smbclient //server1/smbsdata –U user11
    Enter user11's password:
    ```

Domain=[EXAMPLE] OS=[Unix] Server=[Samba 4.1.1]
smb: \\>

25. Create */smbsdatamnt* mount point:

    # **mkdir /smbsdatamnt**

26. Mount */smbsdata* on to the */smbsdatamnt* mount point as *user11*:

    # **mount //server1/smbsdata /smbsdatamnt –o username=user11**
    Password for user11@//server1/smbsdata: *******

27. Execute the *df* and *mount* commands to check the mount status of the share:

    # **df –h | grep smbsdata**
    //server1/smbsdata   8.8G 3.4G 5.4G 39% /smbsdatamnt
    # **mount | grep smbsdata**
    //server1/smbsdata on /smbsdatamnt type cifs
    (rw,relatime,vers=1.0,cache=strict,username=user11,domain=SERVER1,uid=0,noforceuid,gid=0,nof
    orcegid,addr=192.168.0.110,unix,posixpaths,serverino,acl,rsize=1048576,wsize=65536,actimeo=1)

28. Create */etc/samba/smbsdatacred* file and add the credentials for *user11* to it so that this user is
    able to mount this share:

    # **vi /etc/samba/smbsdatacred**
    username=user11
    password=user123

29. Set ownership on the file to *root* and permissions to 0400:

    # **chown root /etc/samba/smbsdatacred && chmod 0400 /etc/samba/smbsdatacred**

30. Open the */etc/fstab* file and add the following entry to automatically mount the share at
    system reboots:

    //server1/smbsdata /smbsdatamnt cifs rw,credentials=/etc/samba/smbsdatacred 0   0

    You can add the _netdev option to instruct the system to wait for networking to establish before attempting to
    mount this file system.

31. Unmount and remount this file system to test the entry placed in the *fstab* file works:

    # **umount /smbsdatamnt**
    # **mount /smbsdatamnt**
    # **mount | grep smbsdatamnt**
    //server1/smbsdata on /smbsdatamnt type cifs
    (rw,relatime,vers=1.0,cache=strict,username=user11,domain=SERVER1,uid=0,noforceuid,gid=0,nof
    orcegid,addr=192.168.0.110,unix,posixpaths,serverino,acl,rsize=1048576,wsize=65536,actimeo=1)

32. Create a file called *smbsdatatest11* as *user11* and another file called *smbsdatatest12* as *user12* under */smbsdatamnt*. List the directory contents to ensure both files have the owning group *smbgrp*.

```
# su – user11
$ touch /smbsdatamnt/smbsdatatest11 ; exit
# su – user12
$ touch /smbsdatamnt/smbsdatatest12 ; exit
# ll /smbsdatamnt
-rw-rw----. 1 user11  smbgrp 0 Jan 31 07:47 smbsdatatest11
-rw-rw----. 1 user12  smbgrp 0 Jan 31 07:47 smbsdatatest12
```

The remote share is successfully mounted on *server2* for group collaboration. Both group members can share files created under this mount point.

Exercise 21-4: Provide Secure Access to Samba Share with Kerberos

This exercise should be done on *server1* (Samba server) and *server2* (Kerberos server and Samba client).

This exercise assumes that *server2* is running Kerberos services (both KDC and admin services) for realm EXAMPLE.COM, the *root* user is added as an admin principal, DNS is disabled, and the *hosts* file is updated with appropriate mappings for both *server1* and *server2*. It is also assumed that the Samba service is running on *server1*, which will also be used as the service host.

> **EXAM TIP:** You do not have to worry about updating the /etc/hosts file. DNS will be in place with all hostnames resolvable.

In this exercise, you will add the Samba server as a cifs principal and produce a keytab for it and store it locally. You will add appropriate entries to the Samba server for a share and test access on the client.

On *server2* (Kerberos server):

1. Log in as the *root* principal and add *server1* as a cifs principal to the KDC database:

   ```
   # kadmin –p root/admin
   Authenticating as principal root/admin with password.
   Password for root/admin@EXAMPLE.COM:
   kadmin: addprinc –randkey cifs/server1.example.com
   WARNING: no policy specified for cifs/server1.example.com@EXAMPLE.COM; defaulting to no policy
   Principal "cifs/server1.example.com@EXAMPLE.COM" created.
   ```

2. Generate a keytab for the new principal and store it in the */etc/krb5.keytab* file:

   ```
   kadmin: ktadd –k /etc/krb5.keytab cifs/server1.example.com
   ```

3. Ensure that the file has the ownership and owning group set to *root*, and permissions to 0600.

> **EXAM TIP:** You may have to copy an existing keytab file from a specified location to the /etc directory.

4. Copy the keytab file to the Samba server *server1*:

   # **scp /etc/krb5.keytab server1:/etc**

On *server1* (Samba server):

5. Follow the steps provided in Exercise 21-1 to create and share */smbkrb5* directory for *user7* access with security set to ADS and Kerberos realm set to EXAMPLE.COM. Create the user if they do not exist.

On *server2* (Samba client):

6. Confirm access to the share by logging in to it using Kerberos (–k) credentials:

   # **smbclient –k //server1/smbkrb5 –U user7**

7. Create */smbkrb5mnt* mount point:

   # **mkdir /smbkrb5mnt**

8. Mount */smbkrb5* on to the */smbkrb5mnt* mount point as *user7*:

   # **mount //server1/smbkrb5 /smbkrb5mnt –o username=user7,sec=krb5,rw**

9. Verify the mount with the *df* and *mount* commands.
10. Open the */etc/fstab* file and add the following entry to automatically mount the share at system reboots:

    //server1/smbkrb5   /smbkrb5mnt   cifs   username=user7,rw,sec=krb5   0   0

11. Create a file called *smbkrb5test7* as *user7* under */smbkrb5mnt*, and check its existence on the Samba server.

You can reboot the Samba client at this point to test if the share is automatically remounted after the system is back up. A user with TGT should now be able to access the mount.

Chapter Summary

This chapter discussed the Samba service, another file-sharing service. The chapter began with an introduction of Samba, the SMB and CIFS protocols, and Samba features. The chapter described Samba daemons and commands, and analyzed the main Samba configuration file with an explanation of some of the key directives that are commonly used. It then presented basic information on Samba software packages. The SELinux requirements were discussed, and then the chapter presented four exercises on configuring Samba server and client for network sharing directories for simple and group uses, and with Kerberos authentication.

Chapter Review Questions

1. What is the use of the *pdbedit* command?
2. Samba is used for file and printer sharing on the network. True or False?
3. What is the use of the "valid users" directive?
4. What is the name of the main Samba server configuration file and where is it located?
5. What is the new name for the SMB protocol?
6. The *smbclient* command is used to mount Samba shares on a Linux system. True or False?
7. Can "force group" directive be used for group collaboration?
8. What does the directive browsable mean in Samba?
9. What is the purpose of the *mount.cifs* command?
10. What would the Samba directive *write list = @dba* do?
11. What is the purpose of the *testparm* command?
12. What would the directive *hosts allow = 192.168.23* in the global section of the Samba configuration file imply?
13. What is the difference between the "public" and "guest ok = yes" directives?
14. What SELinux file context would you set on a directory to be shared only by Samba?
15. What SELinux file context would you set on a directory to be shared in read/write mode by Samba and NFS?
16. What is the name of the Samba daemon?
17. What is the default location where Samba stores user passwords?
18. Where does the Samba server log its activities?
19. Provide two benefits of using Samba on Linux.
20. User home directories on a Samba server can be used by Windows clients and vice versa. True or False?
21. When would you activate the Samba boolean samba_export_all_rw?
22. Samba can be configured as a DNS server. True or False?

Answers to Chapter Review Questions

1. The *pdbedit* command is used to administer the Samba user database.
2. True.
3. The "valid users" directive limits the login access to a Samba share to the specified users or groups.
4. The main Samba server configuration file is called *smb.conf* and it is located in the */etc/samba* directory.
5. Common Internet File System (CIFS).
6. False. The *smbclient* command is used to list available shares and it provides an FTP-like interface to a share.
7. Yes, this directive can be used to set up a share for group collaboration.
8. The browsable directive gives users the ability to browse the contents of a Samba share.
9. The *mount.cifs* command is used to mount a CIFS share.
10. This directive would give write access to the members of the *dba* group.
11. The *testparm* command is used to validate the settings in the *smb.conf* file.
12. This directive would allow systems on the 192.168.23 network to access the Samba service.
13. There is no difference between the two directives.
14. The samba_share_t file context.
15. The public_content_rw_t file context.
16. The Samba daemon is called *smbd*.

17. Samba stores user passwords in the */var/lib/samba/private* directory.
18. The Samba server logs its activities in the */var/log/samba* directory.
19. Samba shares can be accessed on Windows and vice versa, and a Samba server can be configured to function as a PDC in a Windows environment.
20. True.
21. This boolean needs to be activated when you want to export a share in read/write mode.
22. False.

DIY Challenge Labs

The following labs are useful to strengthen the concepts and topics learned in this chapter. It is expected that you perform these labs without any additional help. A step-by-step guide is not provided, as the implementation of these labs requires the knowledge that has been presented in this chapter. Use defaults or your own thinking for missing information.

Lab 21-1: Share a Directory with Samba

Share a directory for read-only access by guest accounts and give them the ability to browse this share. Restrict access to the share to systems in the example.com domain only. Configure the share on the client for automatic remount after system reboots. Implement necessary firewalld and SELinux rules.

Lab 21-2: Share a Directory with Samba for Group Collaboration

Share a directory for group collaboration. Create a group account, create three users, and add the three users to the group. Configure access for this share on the client in read/write mode and ensure that it is automatically remounted after system reboots. Implement necessary firewalld and SELinux rules.

## Chapter 22

Hosting Websites with Apache

This chapter describes the following major topics:

- Overview of HTTP protocol and Apache web service
- Apache features, daemon, commands, configuration file, log files, and software packages
- Examine Apache configuration file
- Describe Apache access control
- Configure and test Apache web servers with varying configuration
- Overview of Apache virtual host and use benefits
- Configure and test Apache virtual hosts
- Understand Apache web servers over SSL/TLS layers
- Configure and test Apache secure virtual hosts
- Overview of CGI scripts
- Add CGI scripts to web servers

RHCE Objectives:

66. Configure a virtual host
67. Configure private directories
68. Deploy a basic CGI application
69. Configure group-managed content
70. Configure TLS security

Web servers are computer systems that run special programs to host websites for business, government, and personal use. These special programs use the HTTP protocol, or its secure cousin, HTTPS, to transfer and exchange information with remote clients. There are millions of web servers in use today that run a variety of these programs to serve clients. Apache is one such program, and it is more popular and widely deployed than its counterparts.

HTTP and the Apache Web Server

The *HyperText Transfer Protocol* (HTTP) is a networking protocol that provides clients with access to web content over the Internet and the corporate network. The term *hypertext* refers to structured text that uses *hyperlinks* to allow non-sequential access to information hosted on a *web server* via the HTTP protocol. A web server is also referred to as an *HTTP server*. A web client is usually a web browser, such as Firefox, Internet Explorer, and Google Chrome, that fully understands the HTTP protocol to be able to talk to the web server. This client/server arrangement built on the HTTP protocol forms the basis for the World Wide Web.

Apache is the most popular program that provides web services to clients using the HTTP and HTTPS protocols. It is more secure, scalable, and modular than most of its counterparts. Apache is supported on virtually every computer operating system. Since its inception in 1995, Apache has grown to be the world's most widely used web server software. Apache is an open-source program that is developed and maintained under the supervision of the Apache Software Foundation, a not-for-profit organization enacted to coordinate Apache software project activities.

RHEL7 includes the support for version 2.4.6 of the Apache HTTP Server software.

Apache Features

Apache is a feature-rich web server software. Some of its common features are:

- ✓ Support for hosting multiple websites with different names on a single system.
- ✓ Access control at the host, user, and group levels.
- ✓ Dynamic loading of modules when needed.
- ✓ Integration of common configuration settings as the default in the source code for easier management.
- ✓ Support for various authentication methods, including password authentication and digital certificate authentication.
- ✓ Support for compression methods for faster transfers and lower bandwidth utilization.
- ✓ Support for intrusion detection and prevention.
- ✓ Works over SSL (Secure Sockets Layer) and TLS (Transport Layer Security) protocols to provide secure web service.
- ✓ Support for separate configuration files for separate services stored in separate locations.
- ✓ Support for proxy load balancing.

Apache Daemon

The Apache HTTP server is a client/server application that relies on the *httpd* daemon running on the server to allow the transfer of web content. This daemon process uses TCP port 80 for non-secure and TCP port 443 for secure operations, by default. The software can be configured to listen on any other port number as long as it is available and appropriate permissions are enabled in firewalld and SELinux.

Apache Commands

There are a few commands available to control the Apache daemon and perform certain configuration tasks on the web server. A proper understanding of the usage of these commands is essential for smooth administration. Table 22-1 lists and explains them.

Command	Description
apachectl	Starts, stops, restarts, and checks the status of, the httpd process (the systemctl command may be used instead). Tests the syntax of Apache configuration files (the httpd command may also be used instead).
htpasswd	Creates and updates files to store usernames and passwords for basic authentication of Apache users. Specify the –c option to create a file and –m to use MD5 encryption for passwords.
httpd	Server program for the Apache web service. With the –t option, it checks for any syntax errors in the Apache configuration files.

Table 22-1 Apache Commands

There are additional commands available; however, their discussion is beyond the scope.

Apache Configuration Files

By default, all Apache web server configuration and supporting files are stored under the */etc/httpd* directory. The primary configuration file, *httpd.conf*, is under the *conf* sub-directory. Additional configuration files are under *conf.d*, and the configuration files that load modules are placed under the *conf.modules.d* sub-directory. An *ll* on the */etc/httpd* directory produces the following output:

```
# ll /etc/httpd
drwxr-xr-x.  2  root  root    35  Feb  3 10:15  conf
drwxr-xr-x.  2  root  root    93  Feb  3 14:42  conf.d
drwxr-xr-x.  2  root  root  4096  Feb  3 14:42  conf.modules.d
lrwxrwxrwx. 1  root  root    19  Feb  3 10:15  logs -> ../../var/log/httpd
lrwxrwxrwx. 1  root  root    29  Feb  3 10:15  modules -> ../../usr/lib64/httpd/modules
lrwxrwxrwx. 1  root  root    10  Feb  3 10:15  run -> /run/httpd
```

The output also indicates the presence of three directories: */var/log/httpd*, */usr/lib64/httpd/modules*, and */run/httpd*. These directories store Apache log files, additional modules, and runtime information for Apache, respectively.

At Apache server startup, the module files are processed first to load necessary modules, followed by the *httpd.conf* file and then any additional configuration files from the */etc/httpd/conf.d* directory.

> **EXAM TIP:** Understanding of the directives in httpd.conf and ssl.conf files is important. Refer to log files when attempting to test a web page.

Analysis of the httpd.conf File

The *httpd.conf* file contains numerous directives that can be set as per requirements. Table 22-2 describes general directives that affect the overall operation of the Apache web server.

Directive	Description
Group	Default is apache. Specifies the owning group for the httpd daemon.
Include	Default is conf.modules.d/*.conf with respect to ServerRoot. Specifies the location of module configuration files to be loaded at Apache startup.
Listen	Default is 80. Specifies a port number to listen for client requests. Specify an IP address and a port if you wish to limit the web server access to a specific address.
ServerRoot	Default is /etc/httpd. Directory location to store configuration, error, and log files.
User	Default is apache. Specifies the owner for the httpd daemon.

Table 22-2 General Directives

There are several directives defined under "Main server configuration" in the file. These directives set up the default web server, which responds to client requests that are not handled by virtual hosts. The values of these directives are also valid for any configured virtual hosts, unless they are overridden. Some key directives are explained in Table 22-3.

Directive	Description
AddHandler	Maps a file extension to the specified handler.
AccessFileName	Default is .htaccess. Specifies the file to be used for access control information. See AllowOverride and Require directives, and Table 22-6 and 22-7.
Alias	Defines a directory location to store files outside of DocumentRoot.
AllowOverride	Default is None. Defines types of directives that can be defined in AccessFileName files. These directives are used to control user or group access to private directories, as well as to control host access. Some other common options are: All: Allows the use of all AccessFileName-supported directives. AuthConfig: Allows the use of authorization directives, such as AuthName, AuthType, AuthUserFile, AuthGroupFile, and Require, in AccessFileName.
CustomLog	Default is combined and stored in logs/httpd/access_log with respect to ServerRoot. Specifies the custom log file and identifies its format.
DirectoryIndex	Default is index.html. Specifies the web page to be served when a client requests an index of a directory.
DocumentRoot	Default is /var/www/html. Specifies the directory location for website files.
ErrorLog	Default is logs/error_log with respect to ServerRoot. Specifies the location to log error messages.
IncludeOptional	Default is conf.d/*.conf with respect to ServerRoot. Specifies the location of additional configuration files to be processed at Apache startup.

Directive	Description
LogFormat	Sets the format for logging messages.
LogLevel	Default is warn. Specifies the level of verbosity at which messages are logged. Other options are debug, info, notice, error, crit, alert, and emerg.
Options	Default is FollowSymLinks. Sets features associated with web directories. Some common features are: ExecCGI: Allows the execution of CGI scripts. FollowSymLinks: Allows directories external to DocumentRoot to have symlinks. Indexes: Displays a list of files on the web server if no *index.html* file is available in the stated directory. Includes: Allows server-side includes. MultiViews: Allows substitution of file extensions. All: Allows all options besides MultiViews. None: Disables all extra features.
Require	Allows or denies access to the specified user, group, host, network, or domain. See Table 22-6 for details and usage examples.
ScriptAlias	Specifies a directory location to store CGI (Common Gateway Interface) scripts.
ServerAdmin	Default is root@localhost. Specifies the email address of the webmaster.
ServerName	Default is www.example.com:80. Specifies the web server name (or IP address) and port number.

Table 22-3 Main Server Directives

A lot of information is defined within containers in the *httpd.conf* file. There are four types of containers: Directory, IfModule, Files, and VirtualHost, and each of them marks its beginning and ending as listed in Table 22-4.

Container Begins	Container Ends
<Directory .... >	</Directory>
<Files .... >	</Files>
<IfModule .... >	</IfModule>
<VirtualHost .... >	</VirtualHost>

Table 22-4 Container Beginning and Ending

The default *httpd.conf* file does not include examples for virtual host containers; however, an exercise later in this chapter will show you how to define it.

Apache Log Files

Apache log files are located in the */var/log/httpd* directory, which is symbolically linked from the */etc/httpd/logs* directory. An *ll* on this directory is shown below. The *access_log* and *error_log* files log access to the web server and error messages, respectively.

```
# ll /var/log/httpd
-rw-r--r--. 1 root root  224 Feb 3 10:31 access_log
-rw-r--r--. 1 root root 1249 Feb 3 10:31 error_log
```

It is recommended that separate log files be used for each website.

Apache Software Packages

There are several software packages that need to be installed on the system to set up standard and secure HTTP web servers. The *yum* command below produces a list of these packages:

```
# yum list installed | grep httpd
httpd.x86_64          2.4.6-17.el7      @ftprepo
httpd-tools.x86_64    2.4.6-17.el7      @ftprepo
```

Table 22-5 describes these packages:

Package	Description
httpd	Provides Apache HTTP server software for building non-secure websites.
httpd-tools	Contains tools for use with the Apache web server.

Table 22-5 HTTP Software Packages

Access Control

There are several directives available that can be used to control access to the web server for specific users, groups, or hosts. We will cover the directives that are of our interest.

Controlling Access for Users and Groups

Limiting access to private directories to specific users and groups is managed through a set of directives that are defined in a *.htaccess* file or directly in the directory container in the *httpd.conf* file. These users are assigned passwords that may be different from their RHEL passwords. The key directives to control access at user and group levels are described in Table 22-6.

Directive	Description
AuthType	Sets basic authentication.
AuthName	Adds general comments.
AuthBasicProvider	Default is file. Specifies the type of authentication to be used.
AuthUserFile	Specifies the file that contains authorized user passwords.
AuthGroupFile	Specifies the file that contains authorized group passwords.
Require	See Table 22-7 for details and usage examples.

Table 22-6 Directives for Access Control to Private Directories

Controlling Access at the Host Level

The Apache web server can be configured to limit access from a specific host, network, or domain. This level of control lets you permit or deny access requests based on the settings of the Require directive. Table 22-7 provides examples to describe the usage of this directive for host-level, as well as user- and group-level access controls.

Require Directive	Effect
Require user <username or UID>	Access is granted to the specified user only (used to grant access to private directories).
Require not user <username or UID>	Access is denied to the specified user.
Require group <group name or GID>	Access is granted to the specified group members only (used to grant access to group-managed contents).
Require not group <group name or GID>	Access is denied to members of the specified group.
Require valid-user	Access is granted to all valid users.
Require ip 192.168.0 15.2	Access is granted from 192.168.0 and 15.2 networks only.
Require not ip 192.168.0 15.2	Access is denied from 192.168.0 and 15.2 networks.
Require host server2	Access is granted from server2.
Require not host server2	Access is denied from server2.
Require host example.com	Access is granted from example.com domain.
Require not host .example.com	Access is denied from example.com domain.
Require all granted	Access is granted from everywhere.
Require all denied	Access is denied from everywhere.

Table 22-7 Access Control with Require Directive

A few examples are presented below with different combinations of user, group, and host level access control.

Example 1: To allow *user1*, *user2*, and *dba* group members to access the contents of */var/www/example* with no password authentication required:

```
<Directory /var/www/example>
    AllowOverride None
    Require user user1 user2
    Require group dba
</Directory>
```

Example 2: To allow *user1*, *user2*, and *dba* group members to access the contents of */var/www/example* from domain *example.net*, network 192.168.0, and host *server2.example.com*, and disallow access from domain *example.org*. No password authentication is required.

```
<Directory /var/www/example>
    AllowOverride None
    Require user user1 user2
    Require group dba
    Require host example.net server2.example.com
    Require ip 192.168.0
    Require not host example.org
</Directory>
```

Example 3: To allow *user1*, *user2*, and *dba* group members to access the contents of */var/www/example* from domain *example.net*, network 192.168.0, and host *server2.example.com*, and disallow access from domain *example.org*. Both users and group members must enter their passwords to access the following directory contents:

```
<Directory /var/www/example>
    AllowOverride AuthConfig
    AccessFileName conf/.htaccess
</Directory>
```

The *.htaccess* file will have the following:

AuthType	Basic
AuthName	"This site is password-protected."
AuthBasicProvider	file
AuthUserFile	/etc/httpd/conf/.userdb
AuthGroupFile	/etc/httpd/conf/.groupdb
Require	user user1 user2
Require	group dba
Require	host example.net server2.example.com
Require	ip 192.168.0
Require	not host example.org

Configuring Apache Web Servers

Having gone through the material provided in this chapter so far and the knowledge and understanding developed based on that, you should now be able to perform the exercises provided in this section. You might need to adjust settings presented in these exercises to make them work on your systems.

SELinux Requirements for Apache Operation

There are a number of booleans associated with the Apache service. Run the SELinux Configuration tool *system-config-selinux*, go to Boolean, and then filter out "httpd". This will list all associated booleans. Some of the common booleans that affect Apache are described in Table 22-8.

Boolean	Description
httpd_anon_write	Allows/disallows Apache to write to directories labeled with the public_content_rw_t type, such as public directories.
httpd_sys_script_anon_write	Allows/disallows Apache scripts to write to directories labeled with the public_content_rw_t type, such as public directories.
httpd_enable_cgi	Enables/disables execution of CGI scripts labeled with the httpd_sys_script_exec_t type.
httpd_enable_ftp_server	Allows/disallows Apache to act as a FTP server and listen on port 21.
httpd_enable_homedirs	Enables/disables Apache's access to user home directories.
httpd_use_cifs	Allows/disallows Apache to use mounted Samba shares with cifs_t type.
httpd_use_nfs	Allows/disallows Apache to use mounted NFS shares with nfs_t type.

Table 22-8 Common SELinux Booleans for Apache

In addition to the booleans, having proper SELinux file context on Apache files and directories is mandatory for Apache to operate smoothly. There are three key directories where the Apache information is typically stored: */etc/httpd*, */var/www*, and */var/log/httpd*. Run the *ll* command with the –Zd options on these directories to check the current SELinux context:

 # ll –Zd /etc/httpd
drwxr-xr-x. root root system_u:object_r:httpd_config_t:s0 /etc/httpd
 # ll –Zd /var/www
drwxr-xr-x. root root system_u:object_r:httpd_sys_content_t:s0 /var/www
 # ll –Zd /var/log/httpd
drwx------. root root system_u:object_r:httpd_log_t:s0 /var/log/httpd

The output indicates that SELinux labels httpd_config_t, httpd_sys_content_t, and httpd_log_t are set on directories containing Apache configuration, web content, and log files, respectively. Files beneath these directories inherit their parent directory's context. If you wish to store this information at different directory locations, ensure that appropriate SELinux file contexts are applied to the directories to ensure a smooth operation.

Exercise 22-1: Configure the Default Apache Web Server

This exercise should be done on *server1* and *server2*.

In this exercise, you will set up an Apache web server for basic operation using the default settings in the *httpd.conf* file. You will install the Apache web server software and the elinks text browser. You will ensure that appropriate firewall rules are in place to allow the HTTP traffic to pass through. You will enable the HTTP service to autostart at system reboots and start the service. You will test the web server's functionality by accessing the default page from the elinks web browser. You will install the elinks web browser on *server2* and access the default web server from there.

On *server1* (web server):

1. Install the software packages for Apache and elinks (browser):

    # yum –y install httpd elinks
    . . . .
    Installed:
      elinks.x86_64 0:0.12-0.36.pre6.el7
      httpd.x86_64 0:2.4.6-17.el7
    Complete!

2. Add the http service to firewalld persistently and reload the rules to allow traffic on HTTP port 80:

    # firewall-cmd --permanent --add-service=http ; firewall-cmd --reload
    success
    success

3. Set the Apache service to autostart at system reboots:

systemctl enable httpd
ln -s '/usr/lib/systemd/system/httpd.service' '/etc/systemd/system/multi-user.target.wants/httpd.service'

4. Start the Apache service and check the running status:

systemctl start httpd
systemctl status httpd
httpd.service - The Apache HTTP Server
  Loaded: loaded (/usr/lib/systemd/system/httpd.service; enabled)
  Active: active (running) since Tue 2015-02-03 10:26:00 EST; 3s ago
 Main PID: 26836 (httpd)
  Status: "Processing requests..."
  CGroup: /system.slice/httpd.service
       ├─26836 /usr/sbin/httpd -DFOREGROUND
       ├─26837 /usr/sbin/httpd -DFOREGROUND
       ├─26838 /usr/sbin/httpd -DFOREGROUND
       ├─26839 /usr/sbin/httpd -DFOREGROUND
       ├─26840 /usr/sbin/httpd -DFOREGROUND
       └─26841 /usr/sbin/httpd -DFOREGROUND

5. Verify access to the default web page using the following:

elinks http://localhost

```
Test Page for the Apache HTTP Server on Red Hat En... (1/2)
            Red Hat Enterprise Linux Test Page

    This page is used to test the proper operation of the
    Apache HTTP server after it has been installed. If you
    can read this page, it means that the Apache HTTP
    server installed at this site is working properly.

    _____

If you are a member of the general public:

    The fact that you are seeing this page indicates that
    the website you just visited is either experiencing
    problems, or is undergoing routine maintenance.

    If you would like to let the administrators of this
    website know that you've seen this page instead of the
    page you expected, you should send them e-mail. In
    general, mail sent to the name "webmaster" and
    directed to the website's domain should reach the
    appropriate person.
```

To exit out of the elinks browser window, press the ESC key and then Enter to view the File menu. Press x and then Enter again to quit.

Run the *tail* command on the *error_log* and *access_log* files located in the */var/log/httpd* directory to view any error and access messages generated.

On *server2* (web client):

6. Install the elinks browser software:

    # **yum –y install elinks**

7. Access the web server using the elinks browser:

    # **elinks http://server1.example.com**

You should be able to see the default web page.

Exercise 22-2: Modify the Default Web Server to Use a Different Home Page and Hostname

This exercise should be done on *server1* and *server2*.

In this exercise, you will modify the web server configured in the previous exercise and use *webserver1.example.com* as its hostname with alias *webserver1*. You will create a new home page in the default DocumentRoot directory. You will test the web server's functionality by accessing it using the new hostname from both systems.

1. Create a web page in the default DocumentRoot directory */var/www/html*:

    # **cd /var/www/html ; vi index.html**
    This is webserver1 (exercise 22-2).

2. Modify the entry for *server1* in the */etc/hosts* file to look like the following:

    192.168.0.110 server1.example.com server1 webserver1.example.com webserver1

    EXAM TIP: You do not have to worry about updating the /etc/hosts file. DNS will be in place with all hostnames resolvable.

    ---

3. Open the */etc/httpd/conf/httpd.conf* file and modify the following directives:

    ServerAdmin root@webserver1.example.com
    ServerName webserver1.example.com

4. Check the syntax of the *httpd.conf* file for any errors:

    # **httpd –t**
    Syntax OK

5. Verify access to the new web page using the following:

    # **elinks http://webserver1.example.com**
    http://webserver1.example.com/
    This is webserver1 (exercise 22-2).

To exit out of the elinks browser window, press the ESC key and then Enter to view the File menu. Press x and then Enter again to quit.

Run the *tail* command on the *error_log* and *access_log* files located in the */var/log/httpd* directory to view any error and access messages generated.

Log on to *server2* and update the entry for *server1* in the */etc/hosts* file as it was done on *server1*. Now execute the following to access the new web page:

> # **elinks http://webserver1.example.com**

You should be able to see the default web page.

Exercise 22-3: Extend the Web Server to Provide Access to a Private Directory

This exercise should be done on *server1*.

In this exercise, you will extend the functionality of the web server configured and updated in the previous two exercises to provide access to a private directory called *privusr* located under a different DocumentRoot called */var*. You will restrict access to this private directory for *user1* only.

1. Create the private directory in DocumentRoot:

   > # **mkdir /var/privusr**

2. Change the ownership and owning group to *user1*, and permissions to 0711 on the directory:

   > # **chown user1:user1 /var/privusr ; chmod 0711 /var/privusr**

3. Create an *index.html* file in the private directory:

   > # **vi /var/privusr/index.html**
   > This is webserver1 (exercise 22-3) providing user1 access to a private directory.

4. Add SELinux file context with type httpd_sys_content_t on the */var/privusr* directory to the SELinux policy:

   > # **semanage fcontext –at httpd_sys_content_t "/var/privusr(/.*)?"**

5. Apply the new rule to the directory:

   > # **restorecon –Rv /var/privusr**
   > restorecon reset /var/privusr context unconfined_u:object_r:var_t:s0->unconfined_u:object_r:httpd_sys_content_t:s0

EXAM TIP: Add a new file context to the SELinux policy first, and then apply it. This will prevent the context to reset to the original value should SELinux relabeling happens.

---

6. Open the *httpd.conf* file and modify the following directives:

    ServerAdmin root@webserver1.example.com
    ServerName webserver1.example.com
    DocumentRoot "/var"
    <Directory /var/privusr>
        AllowOverride AuthConfig
    </Directory>

7. Check the syntax of the *httpd.conf* file for any errors:

    # **httpd –t**
    Syntax OK

8. Create the *.htaccess* file in the */var/privusr* directory and add the following to it:

    # **cd /var/privusr ; vi .htaccess**
    AuthType Basic
    AuthName "Password-protected User Contents. Enter your credentials to log in:"
    AuthUserFile "/etc/httpd/conf/.userdb"
    Require user user1

9. Set password for *user1* and store it in the AuthUserFile (*/etc/httpd/conf/.userdb*) using the *htpasswd* command. This password can be different from the user's Linux password. Display the contents of the AuthUserFile.

    # **cd /etc/httpd/conf ; htpasswd –c .userdb user1**
    New password:
    Re-type new password:
    Adding password for user user1
    # **cat .userdb**
    user1:$apr1$CMmJ4ru9$yMiBitQNS5hjOQDJPSIrx.

10. Change owning group on the AuthUserFile file to apache, and permissions to 0640:

    # **chgrp apache .userdb ; chmod 0640 .userdb**

11. Restart the Apache web service:

    # **systemctl restart httpd**

12. Test the configuration for *user1* from local and remote systems using the Firefox browser:

    http://webserver1.example.com/privusr

Run the *tail* command on the *error_log* and *access_log* files located in the */var/log/httpd* directory to view error and access logs.

At this point, check the access to the web page set up in the previous exercises.

Exercise 22-4: Modify the Web Server to Provide Access to Group-Managed Contents

This exercise should be done on *server1*.

In this exercise, you will modify the functionality of the web server configured and updated in the previous exercises to provide access to a directory called *privgrp* for group collaboration. You will restrict access to this directory for *dba* group members only. Do not change what was done in the previous three exercises.

1. Create the directory for group-managed contents in DocumentRoot:

    # **mkdir /var/privgrp**

2. Create group *dba* (if it does not exist) and add *user10* and *user11* as its members:

    # **groupadd dba ; usermod –G dba user10 ; usermod –G dba user11**

3. Change the owning group to *dba* and permissions to 0771 on the directory:

    # **chgrp dba /var/privgrp ; chmod 0771 /var/privgrp**

4. Create an *index.html* file in the directory:

    # **vi /var/privgrp/index.html**
    This is webserver1 (exercise 22-4) providing dba group members access to a directory.

5. Add SELinux file context with type httpd_sys_content_t on the */var/privgrp* directory to the SELinux policy:

    # **semanage fcontext –at httpd_sys_content_t "/var/privgrp(/.*)?"**

6. Apply the new rule to the directory:

    # **restorecon –Rv /var/privgrp**
    restorecon reset /var/privgrp context unconfined_u:object_r:var_t:s0->unconfined_u:object_r:httpd_sys_content_t:s0

7. Open the */etc/httpd/conf/httpd.conf* file and modify the following directives:

    ```
    ServerAdmin root@webserver1.example.com
    ServerName webserver1.example.com
    DocumentRoot "/var"
    <Directory /var/privusr>
        AllowOverride AuthConfig
    </Directory>
    <Directory /var/privgrp>
        AllowOverride AuthConfig
    </Directory>
    ```

8. Check the syntax of the *httpd.conf* file for any errors:

    # httpd –t
    Syntax OK

9. Create the *.htaccess* file in the */var/privgrp* directory and add the following to it:

    # cd /var/privgrp ; vi .htaccess
    AuthType Basic
    AuthName "Password-protected Group Contents. Enter your credentials to log in:"
    AuthUserFile "/etc/httpd/conf/.grouppassworddb"
    AuthGroupFile "/etc/httpd/conf/.groupdb"
    Require group dba

10. Create AuthGroupFile (*/etc/httpd/conf/.userdb*) and add group information:

    # cd /etc/httpd/conf ; vi .groupdb
    dba: user10 user11

11. Change the owning group on the AuthGroupFile file to apache, and permissions to 0640:

    # chgrp apache .groupdb ; chmod 0640 .groupdb

12. Set passwords for group members *user10* and *user11*, and store them in the AuthUserFile (*/etc/httpd/conf/.grouppassworddb*) using the *htpasswd* command:

    # htpasswd –c .grouppassworddb user10
    New password:
    Re-type new password:
    Adding password for user user10
    # htpasswd .grouppassworddb user11
    New password:
    Re-type new password:
    Adding password for user user11

13. Restart the Apache web service:

    # systemctl restart httpd

14. Test the configuration for *user10* and *user11* from local and remote systems using the Firefox browser:

    http://webserver1.example.com/privgrp

Run the *tail* command on the *error_log* and *access_log* files located in the */var/log/httpd* directory to view error and access logs.

At this point, check the access to the web pages set up in the previous exercises.

Exercise 22-5: Modify the Web Server to Limit Access to Select Hosts on a Non-Default Port

This exercise should be done on *server1*.

In this exercise, you will modify the functionality of the web server configured and updated in the previous exercises to allow access from systems in the *example.com* domain and 192.168.1 network only, and via port 8989. Do not make any other changes.

1. Modify the previous */etc/httpd/conf/httpd.conf* file contents as follows:

    ```
    ServerAdmin root@webserver1.example.com
    ServerName webserver1.example.com:8989
    DocumentRoot "/var"
    <Directory /var/privusr>
       AllowOverride AuthConfig
       Require host example.com
       Require ip 192.168.1.0/24
    </Directory>
    <Directory /var/privgrp>
       AllowOverride AuthConfig
       Require host example.com
       Require ip 192.168.1.0/24
    </Directory>
    ```

    You can add the .htaccess file contents set up in the previous exercises for user and group access to private contents directly to the *httpd.conf* file in their respective directory containers. This method is preferred.

2. Check the syntax of the *httpd.conf* file for any errors:

    # **httpd –t**

3. Restart the Apache web service.
4. Add TCP port 8989 to the default firewalld zone:

    # **firewall-cmd --permanent --add-port 8989/tcp ; firewall-cmd --reload**

5. Add TCP port 8989 with SELinux type http_port_t to the SELinux policy, and confirm:

    # **semanage port –at http_port_t –p tcp 8989**
    # **semanage port –l | grep ^http_port_t**
    http_port_t   tcp   8989, 80, 81, 443, 488, 8008, 8009, 8443, 9000

6. Test the configuration from systems in the *example.com* domain and on 192.168.1.0/24 network by typing the following URLs in the Firefox browser:

    http://webserver1.example.com:8989/privusr
    http://webserver1.example.com:8989/privgrp

You can run the *tail* command on the *error_log* and *access_log* files located in the */var/log/httpd* directory to view error and access logs.

Understanding and Configuring Apache Virtual Hosts

Apache allows us to run multiple virtual hosts on a single system for shared hosting of several distinct websites. This technique offers a low-cost hosting solution for customers. Each hosted website can either share a common IP address or be configured with a unique IP. Both mechanisms direct the inbound web traffic to an appropriate virtual host.

Virtual Host Configuration File

The primary configuration file for defining virtual hosts is *httpd.conf*; however, a preferred approach is to have a separate file for each virtual host stored in the */etc/httpd/conf.d* directory to avoid cluttering *httpd.conf*. Common directives used within a virtual host container are ServerAdmin, ServerName, DocumentRoot, ErrorLog, CustomLog, and are explained in Table 22-3 earlier in this chapter. In addition, the Require directive may also be used for access control.

A sample container for a virtual host is provided below to understand its syntax:

```
<VirtualHost *:80>
DocumentRoot /var/www/html/vh1.example.com
ServerAdmin admin@vh1.example.com
ServerName vh1.example.com
ErrorLog logs/vh1.example.com-error_log
CustomLog logs/vh1.example.com-access_log common
</VirtualHost>
```

As you can visualize, the syntax of a virtual host container is identical to that of the Apache web servers that were configured in the previous section with the exception of the enclosure name. If you store this container in a file, such as *vh1.example.com.conf*, and place it in the */etc/httpd/conf.d* directory, you should be able to use it as an additional web server running on your system after making some necessary changes on the system.

Virtual host configuration files are checked for syntax errors with the *httpd* command as follows:

 # httpd –D DUMP_VHOSTS
AH00112: Warning: DocumentRoot [/var/www/html/vh1.example.com] does not exist
VirtualHost configuration:
*:80   is a NameVirtualHost
     default server vh1.example.com (/etc/httpd/conf.d/vh1.example.com.conf:1)
     port 80 namevhost vh1.example.com (/etc/httpd/conf.d/vh1.example.com.conf:1)
     port 80 namevhost vh1.example.com (/etc/httpd/conf.d/vh1.example.com.conf:1)

Exercise 22-6: Configure a Simple Virtual Host

This exercise should be done on *server1*.

For this exercise, it is assumed that httpd and elinks software packages are already installed, the http service is enabled in the firewall, and it is configured to autostart at system reboots.

In this exercise, you will configure a virtual host called *vhost1.example.com* with alias *vhost1*. You will test the virtual host's functionality by accessing it from the elinks web browser.

1. Create a file in the */etc/httpd/conf.d* directory called *vhost1.conf* containing the following text:

   # vi /etc/httpd/conf.d/vhost1.conf
   <VirtualHost *:80>
        ServerAdmin admin@vhost1.example.com
        DocumentRoot /var/www/html/vhost1
        ServerName vhost1.example.com
        ErrorLog logs/vhost1-error_log
        CustomLog logs/vhost1-access_log combined
   </VirtualHost>

2. Create DocumentRoot for storing web contents:

   # mkdir /var/www/html/vhost1

3. Create an *index.html* file in DocumentRoot with some text:

   # vi /var/www/html/vhost1/index.html
   This web page is to test virtual host for Exercise 22-6.

4. Check the syntax of the virtual host configuration for any errors:

   # httpd –D DUMP_VHOSTS
   VirtualHost configuration:
   *:80   is a NameVirtualHost
          default server vhost1.example.com (/etc/httpd/conf.d/vhost1.conf:1)
          port 80 namevhost vhost1.example.com (/etc/httpd/conf.d/vhost1.conf:1)
          port 80 namevhost vhost1.example.com (/etc/httpd/conf.d/vhost1.conf:1)

5. Open the */etc/hosts* file and modify the *server1* entry to look like:

   192.168.0.110 server1.example.com server1 webserver1.example.com webserver1 \
   vhost1.example.com vhost1

   Make the above change to the *hosts* file on *server2* and *host1* as well, so that you can test access to this virtual host from there.

6. Restart the Apache server process:

   # systemctl restart httpd

7. Test access from both local and remote systems using *elinks*:

   # elinks http://vhost1.example.com

Run the *tail* command on *vhost1-access_log* file in the */var/log/httpd* directory to view messages.

Exercise 22-7: Configure a More Complex Virtual Host

This exercise should be done on *server1*.

For this exercise, it is assumed that httpd and elinks software packages are already installed, and the http service is configured to autostart at system reboots.

In this exercise, you will configure a virtual host called *vhost2.example.com* with alias *vhost2*, DocumentRoot */var/vhost2*, and port 8900. You will make necessary adjustments in firewalld and SELinux configuration. You will test the virtual host's functionality by accessing it from the elinks web browser.

1. Create a file in the */etc/httpd/conf.d* directory called *vhost2.conf* containing the following text:

    # vi /etc/httpd/conf.d/vhost2.conf
    <VirtualHost *:8900>
        ServerAdmin admin@vhost2.example.com
        DocumentRoot /var/vhost2
        ServerName vhost2.example.com
        ErrorLog logs/vhost2-error_log
        CustomLog logs/vhost2-access_log combined
    </VirtualHost>

2. Create DocumentRoot for storing web contents:

    # mkdir /var/vhost2

3. Create an *index.html* file in DocumentRoot with some text:

    # vi /var/vhost2/index.html
    This web page is to test a more complex virtual host setup for Exercise 22-7.

4. Check the syntax of the virtual host configuration for any errors:

    # httpd –D DUMP_VHOSTS
    VirtualHost configuration:
    *:8900   is a NameVirtualHost
        default server vhost2.example.com (/etc/httpd/conf.d/vhost2.conf:1)
        port 8900 namevhost vhost2.example.com (/etc/httpd/conf.d/vhost2.conf:1)
        port 8900 namevhost vhost2.example.com (/etc/httpd/conf.d/vhost2.conf:1)

5. Open the */etc/hosts* file and modify the *server1ipv4* entry to look like:

    192.168.0.111 server1ipv4.example.com server1ipv4 vhost2.example.com vhost2

    Make the above change to the *hosts* file on *server2* and *host1* as well, so that you can test access to this virtual host from there.

---

6. Add SELinux file context with type httpd_sys_content_t on the */var/vhost2* directory to the SELinux policy:

   # **semanage fcontext –at httpd_sys_content_t "/var/vhost2(/.*)?"**

7. Apply the new rule to DocumentRoot recursively:

   # **restorecon –Rv /var/vhost2**
   restorecon reset /var/vhost2 context unconfined_u:object_r:var_t:s0-
   >unconfined_u:object_r:httpd_sys_content_t:s0
   restorecon reset /var/vhost2/index.html context unconfined_u:object_r:var_t:s0-
   >unconfined_u:object_r:httpd_sys_content_t:s0

8. Add TCP port 8900 with SELinux type http_port_t to the SELinux policy and confirm:

   # **semanage port –at http_port_t 8900 –p tcp**
   # **semanage port –l | grep 8900**
   http_port_t   tcp   8900, 8989, 80, 81, 443, 488, 8008, 8009, 8443, 9000

9. Add TCP port 8900 to the default firewalld zone:

   # **firewall-cmd --permanent --add-port 8900/tcp ; firewall-cmd --reload**

10. Restart the Apache server process:

    # **systemctl restart httpd**

11. Test access from both local and remote systems using *elinks*:

    # **elinks http://vhost2.example.com**

Run the *tail* command on *vhost2-access_log* file in the */var/log/httpd* directory to view messages.

> **EXAM TIP:** The standard web server as well as all standard and secure virtual hosts that you will configure during the exam, must be operational and accessible via a web browser.

Understanding and Configuring Apache Web Servers over SSL/TLS

Secure Sockets Layer (SSL) is a cryptographic protocol that allows networked systems to communicate securely. SSL can be used with the *Transport Layer Security* (TLS) protocol to add data integrity, privacy, and secure authentication. With a combination of both protocols, in-transit data is safeguarded against eavesdropping, unauthorized access, and data tampering. Apache web servers that operate on top of SSL and TLS layers may be referred to as HTTPS (*HyperText Transfer Protocol Secure*) or SSL web servers. An HTTPS server uses a digital identity certificate in order to prove its authenticity to clients when they attempt to form a connection, and to establish a two-way encrypted communication channel for exchange of data with them. A trusted digital identity certificate is signed and issued by a *Certificate Authority* (CA). To obtain one, the applicant generates a private/public encryption key pair and a *Certificate Signing Request* (CSR) on the server for which the certificate is desired. The CSR contains applicant identity, such as company details and contact information, as well as the public key and the hostname of the system. The CSR is encoded before it is transmitted to the CA. The CA reviews the CSR and issues a signed certificate after validating the data provided in the CSR.

Another type of digital certificates is referred to as a *self-signed certificate*. A self-signed certificate is produced locally on the system, and it is primarily used for testing purposes. During its creation, you can skip answering most identity questions.

HTTPS/SSL Software Packages

There are two software packages that need to be installed on the system to set up an HTTPS web server. These packages add necessary support to the kernel, and bring the tools and configuration files that are used for setting up secure web services. These packages are described in Table 22-9.

Package	Description
mod_ssl	Provides configuration files necessary to configure a secure web server over SSL and TLS layers.
openssl	Manages certificates, and supports secure communication between systems.

Table 22-9 HTTPS/SSL Software Packages

The installation of mod_ssl installs the *ssl.conf* file in the */etc/httpd/conf.d* directory, which is the configuration file for setting up a secure web server. This file is equivalent to the *httpd.conf* file that is used for non-secure Apache web servers. The openssl package loads the *openssl* command and a directory tree with some templates under */etc/pki*. You may use the *yum* command as demonstrated below to check the install status of these packages:

```
# yum list installed | egrep '^mod|openssl'
mod_ssl.x86_64          1:2.4.6-17.el7      @ftprepo
openssl.x86_64          1:1.0.1e-34.el7     @anaconda/7.0
openssl-libs.x86_64     1:1.0.1e-34.el7     @anaconda/7.0
```

The OpenSSL Toolkit

The openssl toolkit offers a variety of subcommands to create and manage encryption keys, CSRs, and digital certificates, test HTTPS server and client connections, and so on. If called without any arguments, *openssl* enters the interactive mode with an OpenSSL> prompt, allowing us to run the subcommands directly from this prompt. There are some 110 subcommands and are divided into three sets: standard, cipher (encoding and encryption), and message-digest (detection of and protection against data corruption). You can list subcommands for each set by running the *openssl* command as follows:

```
# openssl list-standard-commands
# openssl list-cipher-commands
# openssl list-message-digest-comands
```

The OpenSSL Configuration File and its Analysis

By default, the SSL configuration file, *ssl.conf*, is stored in the */etc/httpd/conf.d* directory. An *ll* on the file produces the following output:

> # **ll /etc/httpd/conf.d/ssl.conf**
> -rw-r--r--. 1 root root 9426 Mar 20 2014 ssl.conf

This file is processed after the *httpd.conf* file completes its processing at Apache service startup or reload. This file sets directives necessary to run secure web servers. It is divided into two sections: SSL Global Context and SSL Virtual Host Context. One directive, "Listen 443 https", that is defined at the beginning of the file is not part of either section. It indicates the default port that the secure web server listens on.

The SSL Global Context section includes directives that apply to the default secure server and to all secure virtual hosts. These directives are not typically modified, as their default values are sufficient for most implementations.

The SSL Virtual Host Context section contains plenty of directives. Some of them are presented below with their default values:

```
## SSL Virtual Host Context
<VirtualHost _default_:443>
#DocumentRoot "/var/www/html"
#ServerName www.example.com:443
ErrorLog logs/ssl_error_log
TransferLog logs/ssl_access_log
LogLevel warn
SSLEngine on
SSLProtocol all -SSLv2
SSLCertificateFile /etc/pki/tls/certs/host1.crt
SSLCertificateKeyFile /etc/pki/tls/private/host1.key
<Files ~ "\.(cgi|shtml|phtml|php3?)$">
    SSLOptions +StdEnvVars
</Files>
<Directory "/var/www/cgi-bin">
    SSLOptions +StdEnvVars
</Directory>
CustomLog logs/ssl_request_log \
      "%t %h %{SSL_PROTOCOL}x %{SSL_CIPHER}x \"%r\" %b"
</VirtualHost>
```

The <VirtualHost _default_:443> directive identifies the port number with an IP address or *. The next five directives—DocumentRoot, ServerName, ErrorLog, TransferLog, and LogLevel—and the CustomLog directive before the end of the file, have the same meaning that was provided under the *httpd.conf* file analysis earlier in this chapter. The SSLEngine directive must be set to on if you intend to use SSL. The next three directives—SSLProtocol, SSLCertificateFile, and SSLCertificateKeyFile—specify the SSL version to use, the location of the SSL certificate, and the location of the SSL key. The <Files> and <Directory> sub-containers specify the file types containing dynamic contents and their location.

OpenSSL Log Files

OpenSSL log files are located in the */var/log/httpd* directory, which is symbolically linked from the */etc/httpd/logs* directory. An *ll* on this directory for ssl logs is shown below. The *ssl_access_log*, *ssl_error_log*, and *ssl_request_log* files capture access to the web server, error messages, and request messages, respectively.

 # ll /var/log/httpd
```
-rw-r--r--. 1  root  root       0  Feb  8 03:39  ssl_access_log
-rw-r--r--. 1  root  root       0  Feb  8 03:39  ssl_error_log
-rw-r--r--. 1  root  root       0  Feb  8 03:39  ssl_request_log
```

It is recommended to use separate log files for each website.

Exercise 22-8: Generate a Key Pair and Self-Signed Certificate

This exercise should be done on *server1*.

In this exercise, you will generate encryption keys and a self-signed certificate for use in the next exercise using the *openssl* command. You will move the key file to the default location.

1. Install mod_ssl and openssl software packages:

   # yum –y install mod_ssl openssl
   ```
   . . . . . . . .
   Installed:
     mod_ssl.x86_64 1:2.4.6-17.el7
     openssl.x86_64 1:1.0.1e-34.el7
   Complete!
   ```

2. Change into the */etc/pki/tls/certs* directory and generate a private key of size 2048 bits using the RSA algorithm. Save the key in a file called *server1.example.com.key*.

   # cd /etc/pki/tls/certs
   **# openssl genpkey –algorithm rsa –pkeyopt rsa_keygen_bits:2048 **
   –out server1.example.com.key
   ```
   ...........................+++
   ................................................................+++
   ```

   You can view the man pages of the *openssl* command for details, and run "openssl genpkey" to obtain help on the options used.

3. Create a certificate signing request using the private key generated in the previous step and store it in a file called *server1.example.com.csr*. Enter data as indicated in the output below:

   # openssl req –new –key server1.example.com.key –out server1.example.com.csr
   You are about to be asked to enter information that will be incorporated into your certificate request.
   What you are about to enter is what is called a Distinguished Name or a DN.
   There are quite a few fields but you can leave some blank
   For some fields there will be a default value, If you enter '.', the field will be left blank.

Country Name (2 letter code) [XX]:**CA**
State or Province Name (full name) []:**Ontario**
Locality Name (eg, city) [Default City]:**Toronto**
Organization Name (eg, company) [Default Company Ltd]:**example**
Organizational Unit Name (eg, section) []:**example**
Common Name (eg, your name or your server's hostname) []:**server1.example.com**
Email Address []:**info@server1.example.com**
Please enter the following 'extra' attributes
to be sent with your certificate request
A challenge password []:
An optional company name []:

4. Generate a self-signed certificate (*server1.example.com.crt*) with a validity of 120 days (–days) using the private key (*server1.example.com.key*) and certificate signing request (*server1.example.com.csr*) created in previous steps:

    # **openssl x509 –req –days 120 –signkey server1.example.com.key **
    –in server1.example.com.csr –out server1.example.com.crt
    Signature ok
    subject=/C=CA/ST=Ontario/L=Toronto/O=example/OU=example/CN=server1.example.com/emailAddress=info@server1.example.com
    Getting Private key

5. List the three files generated as a result:

    # **ll server1.***
    -rw-r--r--. 1 root root 1346 Feb 6 11:04 server1.example.com.crt
    -rw-r--r--. 1 root root 1078 Feb 6 11:02 server1.example.com.csr
    -rw-r--r--. 1 root root 1704 Feb 6 11:01 server1.example.com.key

6. Protect the private key with permissions 0600 and store it in the */etc/pki/tls/private* directory:

    # **chmod 0600 server1.example.com.key ; mv server1.example.com.key ../private**

7. Check the validity and status of the certificate using the *openssl* command:

    # **openssl s_client –connect localhost:443 –state**
    CONNECTED(00000003)
    SSL_connect:before/connect initialization
    SSL_connect:SSLv2/v3 write client hello A
    SSL_connect:SSLv3 read server hello A
    depth=0 C = --, ST = SomeState, L = SomeCity, O = SomeOrganization, OU =
    SomeOrganizationalUnit, CN = server1.example.com, emailAddress = root@server1.example.com
    . . . .
    Certificate chain
    0 s:/C=--
    /ST=SomeState/L=SomeCity/O=SomeOrganization/OU=SomeOrganizationalUnit/CN=server1.example.com/emailAddress=root@server1.example.com

i:/C=--
/ST=SomeState/L=SomeCity/O=SomeOrganization/OU=SomeOrganizationalUnit/CN=server1.exam
ple.com/emailAddress=root@server1.example.com
Server certificate
-----BEGIN CERTIFICATE-----
MIIEBjCCAu6gAwIBAgICGeIwDQYJKoZIhvcNAQELBQAwgbcxCzAJBgNVBAYTAi0t
MRIwEAYDVQQIDAITb21lU3RhdGUxETAPBgNVBAcMCFNvbWVDaXR5MRkwFwYDVQQK
. . . .

This key and the certificate will be used in our next exercise.

Exercise 22-9: Configure a Secure Virtual Host
This exercise should be done on *server1*.

In this exercise, you will configure a secure virtual host on default port 443 using the encryption key and certificate generated in the previous exercise. You will make necessary adjustments in firewalld and SELinux configurations. You will test the web server's functionality by accessing it from the elinks web browser.

1. Create DocumentRoot:

   # **mkdir /var/www/html/secure**

2. Open the */etc/httpd/conf.d/ssl.conf* file and modify the directives as per below. Leave other settings intact.

   ```
   <VirtualHost *:443>
   DocumentRoot "/var/www/html/secure"
   ServerName server1.example.com:443
   SSLCertificateFile /etc/pki/tls/certs/server1.example.com.crt
   SSLCertificateKeyFile /etc/pki/tls/private/server1.example.com.key
   </VirtualHost>
   ```

3. Check the syntax of the virtual host configuration for any errors:

   # **httpd –D DUMP_VHOSTS**
   ```
   VirtualHost configuration:
   *:443          is a NameVirtualHost
           default server server1.example.com (/etc/httpd/conf.d/ssl.conf:8)
           port 443 namevhost server1.example.com (/etc/httpd/conf.d/ssl.conf:8)
           port 443 namevhost server1.example.com (/etc/httpd/conf.d/ssl.conf:8)
   ```

4. Create *index.html* in DocumentRoot with some text:

   # **vi /var/www/html/secure/index.html**
   This web page is to test a more complex virtual host setup for Exercise 22-9.

5. Apply the default SELinux file context on the */var/www/html* directory:

---

restorecon –Rv /var/www/html

6. Add the https service to firewalld persistently and reload the rules to allow traffic on HTTP port 443:

    # firewall-cmd --permanent --add-service=https ; firewall-cmd --reload

7. Restart the Apache service:

    # systemctl restart httpd

8. Test access from both local and remote systems using *elinks*:

    # elinks https://server1.example.com

Run the *tail* command on the *server1-ssl_access_log* file in */var/log/httpd* to view what is going on.

Overview of CGI and CGI Scripts

So far, we have talked about web servers that show static web content in a browser window. These web servers read *index.html* files (and other data files with static information), and simply display that information as-is on the screen.

Apache allows us to add dynamic content to our websites. With this functionality added to a website, a program is executed in the background and its output is displayed on the screen when the website is accessed, rather than showing the program content itself. This interfacing between a program and web server can be implemented using the *Common Gateway Interface* (CGI) method. CGI presents a standard technique of generating dynamic content on websites using these programs, which are referred to as *CGI Scripts*. CGI scripts may be written in Perl, Ruby, Python, C, shell, or some other programing language. In fact, any program can be used as a CGI script. Some of the common uses of CGI scripts are to obtain user input, query or update backend databases, email input data, monitor web traffic, etc.

A very basic CGI script sets the type of content to process, such as text or text/html, followed by what to execute.

This section briefly describes the setup of a non-secure web server that executes a CGI script and display the output on the screen. The ScriptAlias directive in the *httpd.conf* file defines the location of storing CGI files.

Exercise 22-10: Deploy a Basic CGI Script

This exercise should be done on *server1*.

For this exercise, it is assumed that httpd and elinks software packages are already installed, the http service is enabled in the firewall, and it is configured to autostart at system reboots.

In this exercise, you will configure a web server to execute a CGI script and display its output in a browser window. You will configure appropriate SELinux settings.

1. Create a script called *systime.sh* in the */var/www/cgi-bin* directory and add the following text to it:

```
# vi /var/www/cgi-bin/systime.sh
#!/bin/bash
echo "Content-type: text"
echo
echo "The current system time is `date`"
```

2. Add the execute permission to this script for everyone:

   # chmod +x /var/www/cgi-bin/systime.sh

3. Activate the SELinux boolean httpd_enable_cgi:

   # setsebool –P httpd_enable_cgi 1

4. Restart the Apache service:

   # systemctl restart httpd

5. Test access from both local and remote systems using *elinks*:

   # elinks http://server1/cgi-bin/systime.sh

Run the *tail* command on the *server1-ssl_access_log* file in */var/log/httpd* to view what is going on. You can use the –lrt options with the *ll* command on the */var/log/httpd* directory to see which log files have been recently updated.

Exercise 22-11: Run a Basic CGI Script from a non-default location

This exercise should be done on *server1*.

For this exercise, it is assumed that httpd and elinks software packages are already installed, the http service is enabled in the firewall, and it is configured to autostart at system reboots.

In this exercise, you will configure a web server to execute a CGI script and display its output in a browser window. You will store the CGI script in */var/dynpage* directory. You will configure appropriate SELinux settings.

1. Create */var/dynpage* directory to store CGI scripts:

   # mkdir /var/dynpage

2. Create a script called *sysmem.sh* in the */var/dynpage* directory with some text:

   ```
   # vi /var/dynpage/sysmem.sh
   #!/bin/bash
   echo –e "Content-type: text\n"
   echo
   echo "The system memory usage is $(free –m) "
   ```

3. Add the execute permission to this script for everyone:

   # **chmod +x /var/dynpage/sysmem.sh**

4. Activate the SELinux boolean httpd_enable_cgi:

   # **setsebool –P httpd_enable_cgi 1**

5. Add SELinux file context with type httpd_sys_script_exec_t on the */var/dynpage* directory to the SELinux policy:

   # **semanage fcontext –at httpd_sys_script_exec_t "/var/dynpage(/.*)?"**

6. Apply the new rule to the directory recursively:

   # **restorecon –Rv /var/dynpage**

7. Open the *httpd.conf* file and modify the ScriptAlias directive and the location of the CGI scripts as follows:

   ```
   ScriptAlias /cgi-bin/ "/var/dynpage/"
   <Directory "/var/dynpage">
       AllowOverride None
       Options None
       Require all granted
   </Directory>
   ```

8. Restart the Apache service:

   # **systemctl restart httpd**

9. Test access from both local and remote systems using *elinks*:

   # **elinks http://server1/cgi-bin/sysmem.sh**

Run the *tail* command on the *server1-ssl_access_log* file in */var/log/httpd* to view what is going on.

Chapter Summary

This chapter discussed Apache standard and secure web servers. It started with an overview of the HTTP protocol and standard Apache web service. The chapter presented Apache features, its daemon, commands, configuration files, log files, software packages, and access control, and provided an examination of the configuration file. After grasping the basics, the chapter presented a series of exercises with varying requirements to configure standard web services on the system to strengthen the concepts learned. The chapter's focus shifted to virtual web hosting, an Apache feature that supports the hosting of multiple secure and non-secure websites on a single system, and presented a demonstration of setting up two virtual hosts.

The following topic covered another Apache feature that allows the configuration of secure websites. Under this topic, a discussion of the SSL toolkit and secure web server configuration file was provided, followed by an exercise on how to generate a self-signed certificate and another one on how to configure a secure website using that certificate were offered.

Finally, the chapter explained the role of CGI scripts in building dynamic web pages and demonstrated their use.

Chapter Review Questions

1. What would the directive setting "Require user user2 user3" do?
2. Why do we run the *httpd* command with the –t switch?
3. Where would you define the user-level security for Apache?
4. What is the significance of the ScriptAlias directive?
5. What are the ServerAdmin and ServerName directives used for?
6. What would the directive setting "Require not host host1" do?
7. How does a virtual host container begin and end? Provide the syntax.
8. List three features of the Apache web server.
9. What would the SELinux boolean httpd_enable_cgi imply?
10. Can the *apachectl* command be used to start, restart, or stop the Apache web server daemon? Yes or no.
11. What is the use of the *htpasswd* command?
12. What is the use of the AuthUserFile directive?
13. What is the name and location of the standard web server configuration file?
14. What kind of a programming language is CGI?
15. What are the default ports used for standard and secure web servers?
16. What is a CSR?
17. What should be the SELinux type set on web content files?
18. Describe the use of ServerRoot and DocumentRoot directives.
19. What is the primary command in openssl software package?
20. Write the difference between a regular web server and a virtual host.
21. What is the default location for Apache log files?
22. What is the name and location of the secure web server's configuration file?
23. What is the command "httpd –D DUMP_VHOSTS" used for?
24. What is the default name for the directive AccessFileName?

Answers to Chapter Review Questions

1. This directive setting would restrict the access to *user2* and *user3*.
2. The httpd command with –t checks the syntax of the Apache configuration file, and reports errors if found.
3. The user-level security can be defined in the *httpd.conf* or *.htaccess* file.
4. The ScriptAlias directive defines the directory location for CGI scripts.
5. The ServerAdmin directive defines the administrator's email address and the ServerName directive specifies the hostname of the web server.
6. This directive setting would disallow *host1* from accessing the website.
7. <VirtualHost> marks the beginning and </VirtualHost> marks the ending of a virtual host container.
8. Three features of Apache include its ability to share a single IP address amongst multiple virtual hosts, support for LDAP authentication, and support to run on virtually every hardware platform and operating system software.
9. The httpd_enable_cgi directive enables or disables the use of CGI scripts.

---

10. Yes, the *apachectl* command can be used to perform these operations.
11. The *htpasswd* command creates and manages the files that store credentials for authorized users.
12. The AuthUserFile directive points to the file that stores authorized user passwords.
13. The standard configuration file is called *httpd.conf* and it is located in the */etc/httpd/conf* directory.
14. CGI is not a programming language; it is an interface between the web server and a program.
15. The default ports used for standard and secure web servers are 80 and 443, respectively.
16. A CSR is a certificate signing request that is submitted to a CA to obtain a signed digital certificate.
17. The SELinux type httpd_sys_content_t should be set on web content files.
18. The ServerRoot directive specifies the directory location to store configuration, error, and log files, and the DocumentRoot directive defines the location to store website files.
19. The main tool provided in the openssl software package is called *openssl*.
20. A regular web server runs a single website, whereas, you can run as many virtual hosts on a single system as the hardware capacity of the system supports.
21. The Apache log files are located in the */var/log/httpd* directory.
22. The secure web server's configuration file is called *ssl.conf* and it is located in the */etc/httpd/conf.d* directory.
23. The *httpd* command with –D DUMP_VHOSTS checks virtual host configuration information for errors.
24. The AccessFileName sets the file name where access control information is stored.

DIY Challenge Labs

The following labs are useful to strengthen the concepts and topics learned in this chapter. It is expected that you perform these labs without any additional help. A step-by-step guide is not provided, as the implementation of these labs requires the knowledge that has been presented in this chapter. Use defaults or your own thinking for missing information.

Lab 22-1: Configure a Web Server with User-Based and Host-Based Security

Establish the web service on port 80 to provide both user-based and host-based security. Create DocumentRoot */usr/local/webcnts* and store *index.html* in it. Disallow *user1* and members of *dba* group from *example.com*.

Lab 22-2: Configure a Web Server to Host Two Websites

Configure the web service to host two virtual hosts *www.website1.com* and *www.website2.com* to listen on ports 1001 and 1002, respectively.

Lab 22-3: Configure a Secure Virtual Host

Configure a secure virtual host on port 10101.

Lab 22-4: Deploy a CGI Script

Configure the web service to execute the *for_do_done.sh* script created in Chapter 14 "Writing Shell Script".

## Chapter 23

Sending and Receiving Electronic Mail

This chapter describes the following major topics:

➤ Introduction to SMTP and electronic mail
➤ Overview of common terms and protocols
➤ How the mail system works
➤ Understand Postfix, its daemons, commands, configuration files, and log files
➤ Describe the use of various Postfix configuration files
➤ Review of SELinux requirements for Postfix operation
➤ Configure Postfix as a central mail server and test operation
➤ Set up Postfix as a relay host for local users and network users

RHCE Objectives:

79. Configure a system to forward all email to a central mail server

E mail

E mail is the most widely used service on the Internet, and it is an effective, convenient, and easy-to-use communication tool that allows people to stay in touch with one another and share their thoughts and files electronically. Moreover, it is a productive messaging tool that every business relies on for instant, simultaneous communication with several people. The email system works similar to the way the traditional postal service operates. The primary protocol on which the entire email system stands is SMTP. There are numerous email server and client programs available, and several of them are supported in RHEL7 that can be configured on corporate networks for email exchange.

SMTP and the Email System

Simple Mail Transport Protocol (SMTP) is a networking protocol that is responsible for transporting email messages from one email server to another. It establishes a reliable connection between the source and the destination email server for message handover. This protocol runs on top of the IP protocol and uses well-known TCP port 25 for its operation. Using a combination of these protocols, a message is transported on the network or the Internet, passing through one or several routing devices to reach its ultimate identified destination.

An email message (just like an addressed envelope) typically has four parts: the sender's ID and domain name, the receiver's email address, a subject line, and a message body. The SMTP protocol uses the first two items to determine the sender and receiver's domains, based on which it decides whether the message is destined for the local network. If the message is destined for the local network, the SMTP protocol delivers the message to the receiving user's mailbox. If not, it sends the message across the Internet to the correct target system.

Common Terms

An operational email system typically performs four key functions: *Mail User Agent* (MUA), *Mail Submission Agent* (MUA), *Mail Transport Agent* (MTA), and *Mail Delivery Agent* (MDA). Some programs are designed to perform one of these functions only; however, most programs have the ability to do more than one. These four functions and other key components of the email system are described below.

Mail User Agent (MUA)

A *Mail User Agent* is an email client program used to compose messages, and to submit them to an outgoing MTA. On the receiving side, an MUA pulls the message into the inbox of the user and allows them to read. An MUA uses either the POP or IMAP protocol for mail retrieval. Some common MUAs are *mail, mailx, mutt, evolution, pine, elm, thunderbird,* and *Outlook.*

Mail Submission Agent (MSA)

A *Mail Submission Agent* is responsible for accepting new mail messages from an MUA. The MSA function may be integrated within an MUA or MTA, or it may be a separate program. It uses TCP port 587; however, it normally works on the SMTP port.

Mail Transport Agent (MTA)

A *Mail Transport Agent* is responsible for transporting a message from a sending mail server, and another MTA is responsible for accepting the message at a receiving mail server, and they both use SMTP. There may be more than one MTA involved before the message actually gets to the final destination. The most widely used MTA is *sendmail*; however, *Postfix* is a more popular alternative due to its simplicity and better performance. In RHEL7, sendmail is deprecated in favor of Postfix.

Mail Delivery Agent (MDA)

A *Mail Delivery Agent* is responsible for delivering an incoming message to a local mail spool location for storage. The MDA may be a separate program or its functionality may be integrated within an MTA. Examples of MDA are *procmail* and *maildrop*.

Post Office Protocol (POP)

The *Post Office Protocol* is used by an MUA and it is responsible for downloading user mail messages from the mail server to their local inboxes, and optionally, delete them on the server to free up space. This protocol proves to be more useful for users who use a single system to check their mail, or for those with intermittent Internet connections. The latest POP version is referred to as POP3, and it uses TCP port 110 for its operation. A secure cousin of POP3 is referred to as POP3s, which works on top of the SSL layer to provide secure authentication and data privacy. POP3s listens on TCP port 995.

Internet Message Access Protocol (IMAP)

The *Internet Message Access Protocol* is used by an MUA and it is responsible for downloading user mail messages from the mail server to their local inboxes. Unlike POP3, IMAP is more useful for users who use multiple systems to access their mail, and for those with slow Internet connections. The latest IMAP version is referred to as IMAP4, and it uses TCP port 143 for its operation. A secure cousin of IMAP4 is referred to as IMAPs, which works on top of the SSL layer to provide secure authentication and data privacy. IMAPs listens on TCP port 993.

Smart Host (Relay)

A *smart host* is an MTA that is configured with the intent to deliver email messages on behalf of other systems. The other systems may have non-persistent connection to the Internet or lack the capacity to perform this function efficiently.

Mail Queue

A *mail queue* is a directory location where submitted email messages are stored temporarily for further processing. The default mail queue for Postfix is located in the */var/spool/postfix* directory.

Mailbox

A *mailbox* is a location for storing user email messages. By default, a mailbox file is created under the */var/spool/mail* directory for each user account created on the system with a matching name.

How the Email System Works

A fully functional email system from a sender standpoint requires an email client (MUA) to compose an email message with all the relevant information, a program (MSA) that takes this email message and submits it to a temporary location (mail queue) for further processing, and another program (MTA) for transporting that email message over the network or the Internet to the destination system (another MTA) using the SMTP protocol. On the receiving side, the MTA receives that message and invokes an MDA, which forwards the message to a temporary mail spool location and holds it there until an MUA picks it up and saves it in the mailbox of the user via either POP3 or IMAP protocol. The mail server authenticates the user before allowing the MUA to access their email. See Figure 23-1 for a high-level process flow.

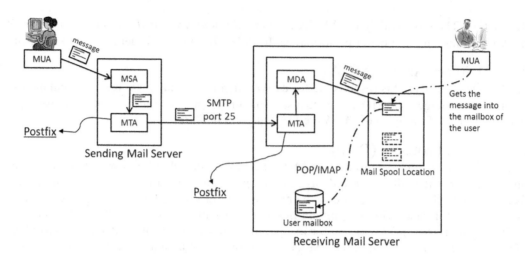

Figure 23-1 Email – From Sender to Receiver

The flow of the email system from a sender to a receiver can be summarized as depicted in Figure 23-2.

MUA → MSA → MTA → Network / Internet → MTA → MDA → MUA

Figure 23-2 Email System Process

We can analogize the entire process of an email system to the traditional postal system for delivery of a letter (email message). From a sender perspective, a person (MUA) writes a letter and puts it in an envelope with a receiver's name, destination address, and appropriate postage, and drops it at a mail facility. A postal worker (MSA) picks up the letter and takes it to a postal facility (mail queue) for culling, postmarking, scanning, barcoding, sorting, etc. After the processing is complete, the letter is transported (MTA) via a carrier (SMTP) to the delivery post office (another MTA) close to the destination address. A postal worker (MDA) gets the letter and delivers it to the mailbox of the receiver. The receiver (MUA) uses their mailbox key (authentication) to access the letter.

Depending on the location of the sending and receiving MUAs, the message may be transported across a large corporate network or over the Internet using several routing devices. In either case, DNS is employed for name resolution. For local delivery, the MTA simply places the message into the mailbox of the user for pickup by an MUA.

The remainder of this chapter covers Postfix at length; other tools mentioned earlier are beyond the scope.

Understanding Postfix

Postfix is sendmail compatible; however, it is easier to configure and administer, and it is more modular, more secure, and offers better performance. It includes features such as pattern matching for filtering unwanted mail, and support for setting up several virtual mail domains on a single system. Postfix is the default MTA used in RHEL7. It uses the SMTP protocol over port 25 for mail transfers. By default, Postfix, out of the box, is ready to accept mail from local system users.

Postfix Daemons

The primary service daemon for Postfix is the *master* daemon located in the */usr/libexec/postfix* directory. This daemon process starts several agent processes, such as *nqmgr*, *pickup*, and *smtpd*, on demand to carry out tasks on its behalf. Each agent has a small, well-defined function and operates with the minimal privilege required for a successful execution of that function. The network queue manager agent, *nqmgr*, is responsible for mail transmission, relay, and local delivery, and the *pickup* agent transfers mail messages from the */var/spool/postfix* directory to the */var/spool/mail* directory in collaboration with the *smtpd* agent. These agent processes terminate after servicing clients or being inactive for a pre-determined period of time. The *master* and all agent processes work collaboratively to manage the entire Postfix email system.

Postfix Commands

Postfix offers several commands to administer the email system. These commands include Postfix-specific utilities, as well as general operating system tools, that are described in Table 23-1.

Command	Description
alternatives	Displays and sets the default MTA.
mail/mailx	Sends and receives email.
postalias/newaliases	Processes the aliases database, which is /etc/aliases by default.
postconf	Displays and modifies the Postfix configuration stored in the main.cf file.
postfix	Controls the operation of the Postfix service, including starting, stopping, health checking, and reloading the configuration.
postmap	Processes and converts some configuration files into Postfix-compatible databases.
postqueue/mailq	Lists and controls Postfix queue.

Table 23-1 Postfix and Other Mail Commands

Some of these commands are used later in this chapter. View the man pages for the rest for details and usage.

Postfix Configuration Files

Postfix configuration files are located in the */etc/postfix* directory, with the exception of the *aliases* file, which is stored in */etc*. A list of the configuration files can be viewed with the *ll* command:

```
# ll /etc/postfix
-rw-r--r--. 1 root root 20876  Jan 26 2014  access
-rw-r--r--. 1 root root 11681  Jan 26 2014  canonical
-rw-r--r--. 1 root root  9904  Jan 26 2014  generic
-rw-r--r--. 1 root root 21545  Jan 26 2014  header_checks
-rw-r--r--. 1 root root 27176  Jan 26 2014  main.cf
-rw-r--r--. 1 root root  6105  Jan 26 2014  master.cf
-rw-r--r--. 1 root root  6816  Jan 26 2014  relocated
-rw-r--r--. 1 root root 12549  Jan 26 2014  transport
-rw-r--r--. 1 root root 12494  Jan 26 2014  virtual
```

Some essential configuration files are explained below.

The access File

The *access* file may be used to establish access control based on email addresses, or hosts, domains, or network addresses for Postfix use. The controls are placed in the form "pattern action". Each pattern has an associated action, such as OK or REJECT. The following shows some examples.

To allow access to the specified IP address:

    192.168.122.20 OK

To allow access to systems in the *example.org* domain:

    example.com OK

To reject access to systems on the 192.168.3 network:

    192.168.3 REJECT

The contents of this file are converted into an indexed database called *access.db* for Postfix use. After making changes to the *access* file, run the *postmap* command on the file to create or update the database:

> **# postmap /etc/postfix/access**
> **# ll /etc/postfix/access***
> -rw-r--r--. 1 root root 20876 Jan 26 2014 /etc/postfix/access
> -rw-r--r--. 1 root root 12288 Feb 12 07:47 /etc/postfix/access.db

You can use firewalld as an alternative to using this database for host, domain, or network access control.

The canonical File

This optional file is used to establish mapping for local and non-local mail addresses. The mapping can be done on incoming mail from other users, domains, and networks, and it is configured in the form "pattern result". The following shows some examples.

To forward mail sent to a local user *user1* to *user1@yahoo.com*:

    user1 user1@yahoo.com

To forward all mail destined for *example.org* domain to another domain *example.com*:

    @example.org   @example.com

The contents of this file are converted into an indexed database called *canonical.db* for Postfix use. After making changes to the *canonical* file, run the *postmap* command on the file to create or update the database:

> **# postmap /etc/postfix/canonical**
> **# ll /etc/postfix/canonical***
> -rw-r--r--. 1 root root 11681 Jan 26 2014 /etc/postfix/canonical
> -rw-r--r--. 1 root root 12288 Feb 12 08:10 /etc/postfix/canonical.db

The generic File

This optional file is used to establish mapping for local and non-local mail addresses throught outgoing mail. The syntax of this file is identical to that of the *canonical* file.

The contents of this file are converted into an indexed database called *generic.db* for Postfix use. After making changes to the *generic* file, run the *postmap* command on the file to create or update the database:

 # postmap /etc/postfix/generic
 # ll /etc/postfix/generic*
-rw-r--r--. 1 root root   9904 Jan 26 2014   /etc/postfix/generic
-rw-r--r--. 1 root root 12288 Feb 12 08:21 /etc/postfix/generic.db

The main.cf File

The *main.cf* file is the primary Postfix configuration file, which defines global settings for its operation. These settings include the identification of the host, domain, origin, and destination to be served, the mail owner, the network interfaces to listen on, the name and location of the aliases database, the queue and user mailbox directory locations, and so on. Some key directives from this file are shown below in the order in which they appear in the *main.cf* file, and this order is important.

```
queue_directory        = /var/spool/postfix
command_directory      = /usr/sbin
daemon_directory       = /usr/libexec/postfix
mail_owner             = postfix
myhostname             = host2.example.com
mydomain               = example.com
myorigin               = $myhostname
inet_interfaces        = localhost
mydestination          = $myhostname, localhost.$mydomain, localhost
mynetworks             = 192.168.2.0/24, 127.0.0.0/8
relayhost              = $mydomain
alias_maps             = hash:/etc/aliases
alias_database         = hash:/etc/aliases
mail_spool_directory   = /var/spool/mail
```

These directives are explained in Table 23-2.

Directive	Description
queue_directory	Location of Postfix queue.
command_directory	Location of the Postfix commands.
daemon_directory	Location of the Postfix daemons.
mail_owner	Owner name for Postfix queue and daemons.
myhostname	FQDN of the Postfix server.
mydomain	Domain name of the Postfix server.
myorigin	Host or domain name the outgoing mail appears to have originated from.
inet_interfaces	Network interfaces to be used for incoming mail.
mydestination	Domains the Postfix server accepts mail from.

Directive	Description
mynetworks	IP addresses of trusted networks.
relayhost	Hostname of another mail server (smart host) to forward mail to. This mail server will act as an outgoing mail gateway.
alias_maps	Aliases database used by local delivery agent.
aliases_database	Aliases database generated with the newaliases command.
mail_spool_directory	Location for storing user mailboxes.

Table 23-2 main.cf Directives

You can use the *postconf* command to display the default (–d) settings that are not defined in the file:

 # postconf –d
bounce_notice_recipient = postmaster
access_map_defer_code = 450
access_map_reject_code = 554
address_verify_cache_cleanup_interval = 12h
address_verify_default_transport = $default_transport
address_verify_local_transport = $local_transport
address_verify_map = btree:$data_directory/verify_cache
address_verify_negative_cache = yes
. . . .

You can view the settings that are defined explicitly in the file using the *postconf* command with the –n switch:

 # postconf –n
alias_database = hash:/etc/aliases
alias_maps = hash:/etc/aliases
command_directory = /usr/sbin
config_directory = /etc/postfix
daemon_directory = /usr/libexec/postfix
data_directory = /var/lib/postfix
debug_peer_level = 2
debugger_command = PATH=/bin:/usr/bin:/usr/local/bin:/usr/X11R6/bin ddd
$daemon_directory/$process_name $process_id & sleep 5
html_directory = no
inet_interfaces = localhost
inet_protocols = all
mail_owner = postfix
mailq_path = /usr/bin/mailq.postfix
manpage_directory = /usr/share/man
mydestination = $myhostname, localhost.$mydomain, localhost
newaliases_path = /usr/bin/newaliases.postfix
queue_directory = /var/spool/postfix
readme_directory = /usr/share/doc/postfix-2.10.1/README_FILES
sample_directory = /usr/share/doc/postfix-2.10.1/samples

```
sendmail_path = /usr/sbin/sendmail.postfix
setgid_group = postdrop
unknown_local_recipient_reject_code = 550
```

Rather than editing the *main.cf* file manually for modifications, you can alter a directive value directly from the command prompt using the *postconf* command. For instance, the following sets the inet_interfaces directive to all:

postconf –e inet_interfaces=all

Verify the change by *grep*ing for this directive in the file:

# **grep ^inet_interfaces /etc/postfix/main.cf**
Inet_interfaces = all

There is no need for the conversion of this file into a database as you did for the files discussed previously. Postfix reads this configuration file to obtain settings.

> **EXAM TIP:** Understanding and use of mydomain, mydestination, myhostname, mynetworks, myorigin, inet_interfaces, and relayhost directives is important.

The master.cf File

The *master.cf* file defines configuration settings for the *master* daemon and the way it should interact with other service agents to achieve mail delivery. An excerpt from the file is provided below:

cat /etc/postfix/master.cf

```
. . . . . . . .
# service    type     private  unpriv   chroot    wakeup  maxproc  command + args
#            (yes)    (yes)    (yes)    (never)   (100)
# ==============================================================================
smtp         inet     n        -        n         -       -        smtpd
pickup       unix     n        -        n         60      1        pickup
cleanup      unix     n        -        n         -       0        cleanup
qmgr         unix     n        -        n         300     1        qmgr
. . . . . . . .
```

For each service listed in the first column, there are seven columns that define how the service is to be used. These columns are explained in Table 23-3.

Column	Description
service	Name of the service.
type	Transport mechanism to be used.
private	Whether the service is for Postfix use only.
unpriv	Whether the service is to be run by non-*root* users.
chroot	Whether the service is to be chrooted for the mail queue.
wakeup	Wake up interval for the service.
maxproc	Maximum number of threads the service can spawn.

Column	Description
command + args	Command associated with the service plus any arguments.

Table 23-3 master.cf File Description

There is no need to convert this file into a database. Postfix references this file for service agent settings.

The relocated File

This optional file contains information of users that have moved. This file is syntactically identical to the *canonical* and *generic* files. The following shows an example.

Assuming *user1* has moved from *example.com* domain to *example.net*, you can forward all email received on their old address to a new one by adding the following line to the *relocated* file:

    user1@example.com user1@example.net

The contents of this file are converted into an indexed database called *relocated.db* for Postfix use. After making changes to the *relocated* file, run the *postmap* command on the file to create or update the database:

```
# postmap /etc/postfix/relocated
# ll /etc/postfix/relocated*
-rw-r--r--. 1 root root  6816 Jan 26 2014  /etc/postfix/relocated
-rw-r--r--. 1 root root 12288 Feb 12 10:15 /etc/postfix/relocated.db
```

The transport File

This optional file is used to establish mappings between email addresses and message delivery transports and next-hop destinations in the transport:nexthop format. An example of transport is local or smtp and that for nexthop a hostname or a domain name. For instance, the following entry sets up a mapping between a user email address and a host:

    user1@example.com smtp:host1.example.com

The contents of this file are converted into an indexed database called *transport.db* for Postfix use. After making changes to the *transport* file, run the *postmap* command on the file to create or update the database:

```
# postmap /etc/postfix/transport
# ll /etc/postfix/transport*
-rw-r--r--. 1 root root 12549 Jan 26 2014  /etc/postfix/transport
-rw-r--r--. 1 root root 12288 Feb 12 10:20 /etc/postfix/transport.db
```

The virtual File

This optional file may be used to redirect mail intended for one user to one or more other email addresses, or to implement a virtual alias domain with all email addresses aliased to addresses in other domains. The first example below redirects email for *user1* to users *root* and *user3*, and the second example redirects email for *user1* in the *example.com* domain to user *root*:

```
user1  root, user3
user1@example.com  root
```

The contents of this file are converted into an indexed database called *virtual.db* for Postfix use. After making changes to the *virtual* file, run the *postmap* command on the file to create or update the database:

postmap /etc/postfix/virtual
ll /etc/postfix/virtual*
```
-rw-r--r--.  1  root  root  12494  Jan 26  2014   /etc/postfix/virtual
-rw-r--r--.  1  root  root  12288  Feb 12  10:25  /etc/postfix/virtual.db
```

The /etc/aliases File

The */etc/aliases* file delivers a mechanism to forward mail destined for local recipients to other local or remote addresses. Postfix references this file to determine alias settings. Some default contents from this file are displayed below:

cat /etc/aliases
```
. . . . . . . .
# General redirections for pseudo accounts.
bin:         root
daemon:      root
adm:         root
lp:          root
sync:        root
shutdown:    root
. . . . . . . .
# Person who should get root's mail
#root:       marc
```

The preceding output indicates that the *root* user receives messages generated by system users. You can set up something similar for other users too. For instance, if you wish to forward email for a deleted user account, *user50*, to a local user, *user1*, and a remote user, *user2@host1.example.com*, open the *aliases* file and add the following entry:

```
user50:      user1, user2@host1.example.com
```

This file also allows you to create a mailing group with all members receiving the mail sent to the group. Here is how you would define a mailing group *lnxadmteam* with members *user1*, *user2*, and *user3*. Add the following line to the *aliases* file:

```
lnxadmteam:          user1, user2, user3
```

After any modifications have been made to the *aliases* file, the Postfix service needs to be apprised. To this end, the contents of this file are converted into an indexed database called *aliases.db* by executing the *newaliases* command:

```
# newaliases
# ll /etc/aliases*
-rw-r--r--.  1  root  root   1518  Jun  7 2013   aliases
-rw-r--r--.  1  root  root  12288  Feb 12 10:45  aliases.db
```

Postfix Logging

All mail messages and alerts are logged to the */var/log/maillog* file, and are related to starting and stopping the Postfix service, successful and unsuccessful user connection attempts, mail sent and disallowed, warning messages, and so on. The *maillog* is a plain text file and may be viewed with any file viewing utility, such as *head*, *tail*, *cat*, *more*, or *view*. The following shows an excerpt from the file:

```
# tail /var/log/maillog
Feb 12 13:36:30  server1  postfix/postfix-script[11571]: starting the Postfix mail system
Feb 12 13:36:30  server1  postfix/master[11573]: daemon started -- version 2.10.1, configuration
/etc/postfix
```

This log file grows over time depending on how busy the mail system is. The syslog service rotates this file once a week to prevent it from getting too large, and it saves previous four weeks of backup in the same directory.

EXAM TIP: You can open another terminal session on the system to run 'tail –f' on a log file.

Managing Postfix

Managing Postfix involves several configuration and administration tasks, including setting up Postfix as a network mail server and as a smart host, applying appropriate access controls, mapping email addresses, and creating aliases. These tasks are covered in exercises presented in this section.

SELinux Requirements for Postfix Operation

SELinux protects systems by setting appropriate controls using contexts and booleans. Before you proceed with the exercises, let's look at the Postfix-specific SELinux contexts on processes, files, and port, and discuss the booleans that may need to be modified for Postfix to function properly. By default, all Postfix daemons, including *master*, *pickup*, and *qmgr*, run confined in their own domains and are labeled appropriately. For instance, the domain type associated with the *master* process is postfix_master_t, and that for *pickup* and *qmgr* are postfix_pickup_t and postfix_qmgr_t, respectively. This can be confirmed with the *ps* command as follows:

```
# ps –eZ | grep postf
system_u:system_r:postfix_master_t:s0 12017 ?   00:00:00 master
system_u:system_r:postfix_pickup_t:s0 12018 ?   00:00:00 pickup
system_u:system_r:postfix_qmgr_t:s0   12019 ?   00:00:00 qmgr
```

The SELinux file types associated with Postfix are postfix_exec_t on the */etc/postfix* configuration directory, postfix_data_t on the */var/lib/postfix* data directory, and postfix_spool_t on the */var/spool/postfix* incoming and outgoing mail directory. Here is an *ll* command output that verifies this information:

```
# ll –Zd /etc/postfix /var/lib/postfix /var/spool/postfix
drwxr-xr-x. root    root system_u:object_r:postfix_etc_t:s0    /etc/postfix
drwx------. postfix root system_u:object_r:postfix_data_t:s0   /var/lib/postfix
drwxr-xr-x. root    root system_u:object_r:postfix_spool_t:s0  /var/spool/postfix
```

The SELinux type associated with the SMTP port is smtp_port_t, and it is in place by default. Here is the *semanage* command output that validates this information:

```
# semanage port –l | grep smtp
smtp_port_t    tcp    25, 465, 587
```

From a SELinux boolean perspective, there is a solo boolean that is associated with Postfix, and we can see this with the *getsebool* command:

```
# getsebool –a | grep postfix
postfix_local_write_mail_spool --> on
```

This boolean allows or disallows Postfix to write to the local mail spool on the system, and, by default, it is turned on.

By looking at the above SELinux settings for Postfix, we can establish that there are no changes required to make Postfix function smoothly in the SELinux enforcing mode.

Exercise 23-1: Configure a Central Mail Server

This exercise should be done on *server1*.

In this exercise, you will configure Postfix to serve systems on the local network (192.168.0.0/24). You will add *server1* as the MTA in the *example.com* domain, listening on all network interfaces with DNS lookups disabled (disable_dns_lookups directive). You will check the Postfix configuration for any syntax errors, configure appropriate host-based access rules in firewalld, set Postfix to autostart at system reboots, start the Postfix service, and ensure that it is set as the default MTA. You will send an email to a local user *user3* to ensure that the mail service is working for local users.

1. Install the Postfix software package:

   ```
   # yum –y install postfix
   Package 2:postfix-2.10.1-6.el7.x86_64 already installed and latest version
   Nothing to do
   ```

2. Open the *main.cf* file in a text editor and set or modify the following directives. Leave other settings intact.

   ```
   myhostname        = server1.example.com
   mydomain          = example.com
   myorigin          = $myhostname
   inet_interfaces   = all
   mydestination     = $myhostname, localhost.$mydomain, localhost, $mydomain
   mynetworks        = 192.168.0.0/24, 127.0.0.0/8
   ```

```
disable_dns_lookups        = yes
```

The default method for the mail system to resolve hostnames is DNS; however, in the absence of DNS service, you can instruct the mail system to use the *hosts* file instead by defining the disable_dns_lookups directive in the *main.cf* file and setting its value to yes.

3. Check for any syntax errors in the *main.cf* file using the *postfix* command:

    # postfix check

4. Review the changes made in the *main.cf* file with the *postconf* command:

    # postconf –n
```
alias_database            = hash:/etc/aliases
alias_maps                = hash:/etc/aliases
command_directory         = /usr/sbin
config_directory          = /etc/postfix
daemon_directory          = /usr/libexec/postfix
data_directory            = /var/lib/postfix
disable_dns_lookups       = yes
inet_interfaces           = all
inet_protocols            = all
mail_owner                = postfix
mail_spool_directory      = /var/spool/mail
mydestination             = $myhostname, localhost.$mydomain, localhost, $mydomain
mydomain                  = example.com
myhostname                = server1.example.com
mynetworks                = 192.168.0.0/24, 127.0.0.0/8
myorigin                  = $myhostname
queue_directory           = /var/spool/postfix
```

You may get additional lines in the output based on what was modified in the file.

5. Add the smtp service to firewalld persistently and reload the rules to allow traffic on SMTP port 25:

    # firewall-cmd --permanent --add-service smtp; firewall-cmd --reload

6. Set Postfix to autostart at system reboots:

    # systemctl enable postfix
```
ln -s '/usr/lib/systemd/system/postfix.service' '/etc/systemd/system/multi-
user.target.wants/postfix.service'
```

7. Start the Postfix service and check its operational status:

```
# systemctl start postfix
# systemctl status postfix
postfix.service - Postfix Mail Transport Agent
   Loaded: loaded (/usr/lib/systemd/system/postfix.service; enabled)
   Active: active (running) since Thu 2015-02-12 17:44:13 EST; 3s ago
  Process: 14879 ExecStop=/usr/sbin/postfix stop (code=exited, status=0/SUCCESS)
  Process: 14893 ExecStart=/usr/sbin/postfix start (code=exited, status=0/SUCCESS)
  Process: 14891 ExecStartPre=/usr/libexec/postfix/chroot-update (code=exited, status=0/SUCCESS)
  Process: 14888 ExecStartPre=/usr/libexec/postfix/aliasesdb (code=exited, status=0/SUCCESS)
 Main PID: 14965 (master)
   CGroup: /system.slice/postfix.service
           ├─14965 /usr/libexec/postfix/master -w
           ├─14966 pickup -l -t unix -u
           └─14967 qmgr -l -t unix -u
```

8. Configure Postfix as the default MTA using the *alternatives* command and verify:

    # alternatives --set mta /usr/sbin/sendmail.postfix
    # alternatives --display mta | grep current
    link currently points to /usr/sbin/sendmail.postfix

9. Mail a message to *user3* with the subject (–s) "Local Delivery Test" to test local mail delivery (the *mail* command is part of the mailx package, which needs to be installed if it is not already there):

    # date | mail –s "Local Delivery Test" user3

10. Switch to *user3* account and run the *mail* command to check whether this user has received the email. Press Enter at the & prompt to view the message and type *q* at the next & prompt to quit.

    ```
    # su – user3
    $ mail
    Heirloom Mail version 12.5 7/5/10.  Type ? for help.
    "/var/spool/mail/user3": 1 message 1 new
    >N  1 root      Fri Feb 13 11:42  18/626   "Local Delivery Test"
    &
    Message  1:
    From root@server1.example.com  Fri Feb 13 11:42:50 2015
    Return-Path: <root@server1.example.com>
    X-Original-To: user3
    Delivered-To: user3@server1.example.com
    Date: Fri, 13 Feb 2015 11:42:50 -0500
    To: user3@server1.example.com
    Subject: Local Deliver Test
    User-Agent: Heirloom mailx 12.5 7/5/10
    Content-Type: text/plain; charset=us-ascii
    From: root@server1.example.com (root)
    Status: R
    ```

Fri Feb 13 11:42:50 EST 2015
& **q**
Held 1 message in /var/spool/mail/user3

You can *tail* the */var/log/maillog* file to view messages generated during the implementation of this exercise.

This completes the procedure to set up a central mail server with Postfix.

EXAM TIP: By default, your email appears to have originated from server1.example.com. However, if you would like to change it to your domain name example.com, for instance, open main.cf and set myorigin directive to $mydomain. Save and quit the file, and restart Postfix. Try sending another test email and check the "From" line in the email.

Exercise 23-2: Test Central Mail Server from Remote Client

This exercise should be done on *server2* (mail client) and *server1* (mail server).

In this exercise, you will install the Postfix software package, modify it to avoid DNS lookups, enable Postfix, and start it. You will send an email to *root* on the mail server for verification. You will log on to *server1* as user *root* and verify the receipt.

On *server2* (mail client):

1. Install the Postfix software package:

    # **yum –y install postfix**

2. Open the *main.cf* file in a text editor and add the following directive at the beginning of the file:

    disable_dns_lookups   = yes

3. Set Postfix to autostart at system reboots:

    # **systemctl enable postfix**

4. Start the Postfix service:

    # **systemctl start postfix**

5. Mail a message to *root@server1.example.com* with the subject "Remote Delivery Test" to test network mail delivery:

    # **date | mail –s "Remote Delivery Test" root@server1.example.com**

On *server1* (mail server):

---

6. Run the *mail* command to check whether the email has been received. Press Enter at the & prompt to view the message and type *q* at the next & prompt to quit. Install the mailx package to access the *mail* command if it is not already there.

> # **mail**
> Heirloom Mail version 12.5 7/5/10. Type ? for help.
> "/var/spool/mail/root": 1 message 1 new
> >N 1 root   Fri Feb 13 11:46 21/854   "Remote Delivery Test"
> &
> Message 1:
> From root@server2.example.com Fri Feb 13 11:46:00 2015
> Return-Path: <root@server2.example.com>
> X-Original-To: root@server1.example.com
> Delivered-To: root@server1.example.com
> Date: Sat, 14 Feb 2015 03:46:00 +1100
> To: root@server1.example.com
> Subject: Remote Delivery Test
> User-Agent: Heirloom mailx 12.5 7/5/10
> Content-Type: text/plain; charset=us-ascii
> From: root@server2.example.com (root)
> Status: R
> Sat Feb 14 03:46:00 MIST 2015
> & **q**
> Held 1 message in /var/spool/mail/root

You can *tail* the */var/log/maillog* file on both servers to view messages generated during the implementation of this exercise. Also, you can find the incoming mail for each user in the */var/spool/mail* directory.

This completes the procedure for sending email from a remote system and receiving it on the mail server.

> **EXAM TIP:** By default, your email appears to have originated from server2.example.com. However, if you would like to change it to your domain name example.com, for instance, open main.cf and set mydomain directive to example.com and myorigin directive to $mydomain. Save and quit the file, and restart Postfix. Try sending another test email and check the "From" line in the email.

Exercise 23-3: Configure Postfix to Forward Local Mail to a Central Mail Server and Reject Incoming Mail

This exercise should be done on *host1* (mail client) and *server1* (mail server).

In this exercise, you will install and configure Postfix on *host1* to deny all incoming email (access control) and forward (relayhost) localhost mail to the central mail server (*server1*). You will disable the use of DNS for lookups. You will ensure that any mail received on the central mail server appears to have originated from *example.com* and not *host1.example.com*. You will check the Postfix configuration for any syntax errors, configure appropriate host-based access rules in firewalld, set Postfix to autostart at system reboots, start the Postfix service, and ensure that it is set as the default MTA. You will send an email to a local user *user1* on *host1* and confirm its receipt on the mail server.

On *host1* (mail client):

1. Install the postfix software package:

    # **yum –y install postfix**
    Package 2:postfix-2.10.1-6.el7.x86_64 already installed and latest version
    Nothing to do

2. Open the *main.cf* file in a text editor and set or modify the following directives. Leave other settings intact.

myhostname	= host1.example.com
mydomain	= example.com
myorigin	= $mydomain
inet_interfaces	= localhost
mydestination	= localhost
relayhost	= server1.example.com
disable_dns_lookups	= yes

3. Check for any syntax errors in the *main.cf* file using the *postfix* command:

    # **postfix check**

4. Review the changes made in the *main.cf* file with the *postconf* command:

    # **postconf –n**
command_directory	= /usr/sbin
config_directory	= /etc/postfix
daemon_directory	= /usr/libexec/postfix
data_directory	= /var/lib/postfix
disable_dns_lookups	= yes
inet_interfaces	= localhost
mail_owner	= postfix
mydestination	= localhost
mydomain	= example.com
myhostname	= host1.example.com
myorigin	= $mydomain
queue_directory	= /var/spool/postfix
relayhost	= server1.example.com

    You may get additional lines in the output based on what was modified in the file.

5. Add the smtp service to firewalld persistently and reload the rules to allow traffic on SMTP port 25:

    # **firewall-cmd --permanent --add-service smtp; firewall-cmd --reload**

6. Set Postfix to autostart at system reboots:

 # systemctl enable postfix
ln -s '/usr/lib/systemd/system/postfix.service' '/etc/systemd/system/multi-user.target.wants/postfix.service'

7. Start the Postfix service and check its operational status:

   # systemctl start postfix

8. Configure Postfix as the default MTA using the *alternatives* command, and verify:

   # alternatives --set mta /usr/sbin/sendmail.postfix
   # alternatives --display mta | grep current
   link currently points to /usr/sbin/sendmail.postfix

9. Mail a message to *user1* (this account should exist on both *host1* and *server1*) with the subject (–s) "Relay Host Delivery Test" to test the relay host functionality:

   # date | mail –s "Relay Host Delivery Test" user1

On *server1* (mail server):

10. Log on to *server1* as user *user1*, and run the *mail* command to check whether this user has received the email. Press Enter at the & prompt to view the message and type *q* at the next & prompt to quit.

    $ mail
    Heirloom Mail version 12.5 7/5/10. Type ? for help.
    "/var/spool/mail/user1": 1 message 1 new
    >N 1 root   Thu Feb 12 19:11 20/781   "Relay Host Delivery Test"
    &
    Message 1:
    From root@example.com Thu Feb 12 19:11:12 2015
    Return-Path: <root@example.com>
    X-Original-To: user1
    Delivered-To: user1@server1.example.com
    Date: Thu, 12 Feb 2015 19:11:12 -0500
    To: user1@server1.example.com
    Subject: Relay Host Delivery Test
    User-Agent: Heirloom mailx 12.5 7/5/10
    Content-Type: text/plain; charset=us-ascii
    From: root@example.com (root)
    Status: R
    Thu Feb 12 19:11:12 EST 2015
    & q
    Held 1 message in /var/spool/mail/user1

You can *tail* the */var/log/maillog* file on both servers to view messages generated during the implementation of this exercise. In addition, you can find the incoming mail for each user in the */var/spool/mail* directory.

This completes the procedure to set up and test a relay host for localhost only.

Exercise 23-4: Configure Postfix to Receive Local Network Mail and Forward All Mail to a Central Mail Server

This exercise involves *host1* (relay host), *server1* (mail server), and *server2* (mail client).

In this exercise, you will extend the ability of the mail client configured on *host1* to accept all incoming email and forward both local and incoming mail to the central mail server (*server1*). The rest of the configuration will stay the same. You will submit an email on *server2* to *user1@host1.example.com* and it should be received by *user1* on the mail server.

On *host1* (relay host):

1. Open the *main.cf* file in a text editor and set or modify the following directives. Leave other settings intact.

myhostname	= host1.example.com
mydomain	= example.com
myorigin	= $mydomain
inet_interfaces	= all
mydestination	= $myhostname, localhost.$mydomain, localhost, $mydomain
mynetworks	= 192.168.0.0/24, 127.0.0.0/8
relayhost	= server1.example.com
disable_dns_lookups	= yes

2. Restart the Postfix service:

   # **systemctl restart postfix**

On *server2* (mail client):

3. Mail a message to *user1@host1.example.com* with the subject (–s) "Relay Host Delivery Test Exercise 23-4" to test the relay host functionality from a network system:

   # **date | mail –s "Relay Host Delivery Test Exercise 23-4" user1@host1.example.com**

On *server1* (mail server):

4. Log on to *server1* as *user1* and run the *mail* command to check whether this user has received the email. Press Enter at the & prompt to view the message and type *q* at the next & prompt to quit.

   $ **mail**
   "/var/spool/mail/user1": 1 message 1 new
   >N 1 root   Thu Feb 13 20:23 23/878   "Relay Host Delivery Test Exercise 23-4"
   & **q**
   Held 1 message in /var/spool/mail/user1

You can *tail* the */var/log/maillog* file on *host1* and *server1* to view messages generated during the testing.

This completes the procedure to set up and test a relay host for network systems.

Chapter Summary

This chapter presented an introduction to email service and provided several exercises to practice the implementation. The chapter examined the SMTP protocol and described common terms and protocols that are part of the email system. It described how the email system works and analogized it to the traditional postal system. It discussed Postfix daemons and commands, analyzed various required and optional configuration files, and discussed SELinux file, process, and port contexts, as well as booleans. The chapter demonstrated the configuration of a central mail server for the network, relayhosts for local and network use, and how to test them.

Chapter Review Questions

1. What is the use of the mydestination directive?
2. What is the name of the Postfix access control file?
3. Evolution is an example of an MTA. True or False?
4. What functionality does an MTA provide?
5. What is the default myorigin directive setting?
6. The *mail* command may be used to verify the functionality of a mail server. True or False?
7. Directives in the *main.cf* file can be modified directly from the command line. What command is used for this purpose?
8. Which file does Postfix use to log mail alerts?
9. Which Postfix command is used to convert text configuration files into indexed databases?
10. Which file controls the behavior of Postfix daemons and agents?
11. Where are the Postfix configuration files located?
12. An MUA is responsible to transport email messages over the network. True or False?
13. What is the equivalent Postfix command for *mailq*?
14. What command would you use to display or alter the current MTA?
15. Why do we use the disable_dns_lookups directive?
16. What protocol and port does the mail system use?
17. What would the command *postconf –n* do?
18. What is the purpose of the relayhost directive?
19. What two protocols are used to pull user mail in to their inboxes?
20. What would the entry "example.com REJECT" in the *access* file imply?
21. How do you notify Postfix service of a change in the */etc/aliases* file?
22. When should you run the *postfix check* command?
23. Which file defines mapping for email addresses?
24. The *access* file can be used to allow or disallow a host, domain, or network from accessing the Postfix service. True or False?
25. Which command would you run to update the aliases database?
26. What would the command *postconf –e setgid_group=postdrop* do?
27. What is the name of the main daemon for the Postfix service?
28. By default, all Postfix daemons and agents run in their own SELinux domains. True or False?

Answers to Chapter Review Questions

1. The mydestination directive defines the hosts and domains that the mail server is configured to serve.
2. The name of the Postfix access control file is *access*.

3. False. Evolution is an MUA program.
4. An MTA is responsible for transporting email messages between mail servers.
5. The default myorigin directive is set to $myhostname.
6. False. The *mail* command is used to read and compose email messages.
7. The *postconf* command can be used to modify directives in the *main.cf* file directly from the command prompt.
8. Postfix uses the */var/log/maillog* file for logging.
9. The *postmap* command is used to convert configuration files into indexed databases.
10. The *master.cf* file controls the behavior of Postfix daemons and agents.
11. The Postfix configuration files are located in the */etc/postfix* directory.
12. False. An MUA is used to read and compose email messages.
13. The equivalent command is *postqueue* with the –p switch.
14. The *alternatives* command is used to display and alter the current MTA setting.
15. The disable_dns_lookups is used to enable or disable the use of DNS lookups.
16. The mail system uses the SMTP protocol on well-known port 25.
17. This command displays non-default Postfix settings.
18. The relayhost directive specifies the mail server to forward mail to.
19. POP3 and IMAP protocols are used to pull user mail messages into their inboxes.
20. This entry would reject incoming mail from systems in the *example.com* domain.
21. By executing the *newaliases* command.
22. After making changes to the *main.cf* file for syntax errors.
23. In the */etc/aliases* file.
24. True.
25. The *newaliases* command is run after making edits in the *aliases* file.
26. This command will modify the directive's value in the *main.cf* file without having to open the file in a text editor.
27. The main daemon for the Postfix service is called *master*.
28. True.

DIY Challenge Labs

The following labs are useful to strengthen the concepts and topics learned in this chapter. It is expected that you perform these labs without any additional help. A step-by-step guide is not provided, as the implementation of these labs requires the knowledge that has been presented in this chapter. Use defaults or your own thinking for missing information.

Lab 23-1: Establish a Network Mail Server and Test It

Establish a RHEL7 system as a network mail server for network 192.168.1.0/24. This server should reject inbound mail from 192.168.0.0/24 and *example.org*. Create a mapping in the appropriate file to forward mail destined for *user1* and group *dba* to *user3*. On the client, ensure that outbound mail appears to originate from *example.com* domain.

Lab 23-2: Establish a Forwarding Mail Server and Test It

Configure a RHEL7 system to relay localhost as well as all inbound mail to the central mail server set up in the previous lab. On the client, ensure that outbound mail appears to originate from *example.net* domain.

## Chapter 24

Configuring DNS

This chapter describes the following major topics:

- ➤ Understand domain name system and name resolution
- ➤ Overview of BIND
- ➤ Recognize DNS components: name space, domains, root servers, roles, types, zones, and software packages
- ➤ Analyze configuration and zone files
- ➤ Review SELinux requirements
- ➤ Configure a caching-only nameserver
- ➤ Describe DNS client configuration files and lookup tools
- ➤ Configure DNS client and test server configuration
- ➤ Troubleshoot DNS client issues

RHCE Objectives:

71. Configure a caching-only name server
72. Troubleshoot DNS client issues

D omain Name System is an OS- and hardware-independent network service

used for determining the IP address of a system by providing its hostname and vice versa. This mechanism is employed to map human-friendly hostnames to their assigned numerical IP addresses by consulting one or more servers offering this popular service. This service has been used on the Internet and corporate networks as the de facto standard for this purpose. It works based on the client/server architecture where one central server provides name resolution service to many remote clients. Configuration of domain name system setup requires a good comprehension of the concepts, components, configuration files, and tools involved. Moreover, this knowledge helps troubleshoot issues should they arise.

Domain Name System and Name Resolution

Domain Name System (DNS) is a tree-like distributed structure that is employed on the Internet and corporate networks as the de facto standard for resolving hostnames to their numerical IP addresses for computer systems, mobile devices, networking gear, storage arrays, imaging equipment, and any other device with a unique IP address. *Name resolution* is the technique that employs DNS for this purpose. Determining the IP address of a hostname is referred to as *forward name resolution* (or simply *name resolution*) and determining the hostname associated with an IP address is referred to as *reverse name resolution*. DNS is platform-independent and it is supported on virtually every operating system, including UNIX, Linux, Windows, and MAC.

What is BIND?

BIND, *Berkeley Internet Name Domain*, is an open source implementation of DNS on UNIX and Linux operating system platforms. BIND was developed at the University of California, Berkeley, a little over three decades ago, and it has since been the most popular DNS application in use on the Internet and private networks. RHEL7, like its precursor versions, supports BIND and offers it as the standard DNS software.

DNS Name Space and Domains

The DNS *name space* is a hierarchical organization of all the domains on the Internet. The root of the name space is represented by a dot. The hierarchy right below the root represents *top-level domains* (TLDs) that are either generic, such as .com, .net, .edu, .org, and .gov, and referred to as *gTLDs*, or specific to two-letter country-code, such as .ca and .uk, and referred to as *ccTLDs*. A DNS *domain* is a collection of one or more systems. Sub-domains fall under domains and are separated by a dot. For example, the .com domain consists of second-level domains, such as .redhat and .ibm, with further division into multiple, smaller third-level domains, such as .*bugzilla.redhat.com* under .*redhat.com.*

Figure 24-1 exhibits a sample hierarchy of the name space, showing the top three domain levels.

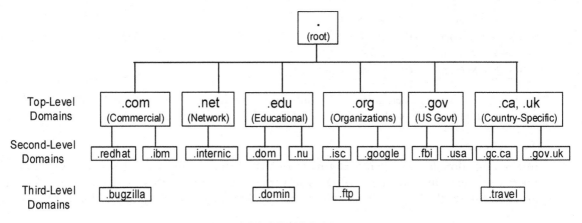

Figure 24-1 DNS Hierarchy

At the deepest level of the hierarchy are the *leaves* (systems, nodes, or any device with an IP address) of the name space. For example, a network switch *net01* in *.travel.gc.ca* sub-domain will be known as *net01.travel.gc.ca*. If a dot is added to the end of this name to look like *net01.travel.gc.ca.*, it will be referred to as the *Fully Qualified Domain Name* (FQDN) for *net01*.

The division of a domain into multiple sub-domains allows the delegation of management responsibility for each sub-domain to different groups of administrators by adding a dedicated DNS server to each sub-domain with full authority on the information that the sub-domain possesses. This distributed management approach simplifies the overall DNS administration in large and complex environments, as well as make it fault tolerant.

In order to run an Internet-facing server, a unique domain name needs to be chosen and registered. There are accredited domain registrars in every region of the world that are licensed by the *Internet Corporation for Assigned Names and Numbers* (ICANN). A list of all authorized registrars is available at *www.internic.net*. You may, alternatively, search the Internet for a registrar in your region, or simply contact your *Internet Service Provider* (ISP).

DNS Root Servers

The *root servers* sit at the top of the DNS hierarchy in the root zone (See Figure 24-1) and are managed and maintained by different organizations authorized by ICANN. At present, there are thirteen operational root servers, with a number of mirrors for each one and are placed across the globe to offload the main servers. Information about the root servers is supplied as part of bind software, and it is stored in the *named.ca* file in the */var/named* directory. A list of these servers with their IP addresses is provided below:

a.root-servers.net.	198.41.0.4
b.root-servers.net.	192.228.79.201
c.root-servers.net.	192.33.4.12
d.root-servers.net.	199.7.91.13
e.root-servers.net.	192.203.230.10
f.root-servers.net.	192.5.5.241
g.root-servers.net.	192.112.36.4
h.root-servers.net.	128.63.2.53
i.root-servers.net.	192.36.148.17

j.root-servers.net.	192.58.128.30
k.root-servers.net.	193.0.14.129
l.root-servers.net.	199.7.83.42
m.root-servers.net.	202.12.27.33

The root servers handle queries for TLDs only and provide the client with the IP address of the name server that is responsible for the requested TLD.

DNS Roles

A role is a function that a system performs from a DNS standpoint. A system is typically configured to operate as one of the three types of DNS server or as a client. A DNS server, also referred to as a *nameserver*, stores the DNS records for a domain and responds to client queries for name resolution.

Primary DNS Server: A *primary* (a.k.a. *master*) *DNS server* has the authority over its domain (or sub-domain) and maintains that domain's original (or master) data. Each domain must have one primary server with one or more other optional DNS servers, referred to as secondary and caching servers. Zone data files are maintained on the primary server and they can be propagated to secondary servers.

Secondary DNS Server: A *secondary* (a.k.a. *slave*) *DNS server* also has the authority for its domain and stores that domain's zone data files; however, these files are copied over from the primary server. When updates are made to the zone files on the primary server, the secondary server gets a copy of the updated files automatically. This type of DNS server is set up for redundancy or offloading the primary. It is recommended to have at least one secondary server per domain to supplement the primary.

Caching DNS Server: A *caching DNS server* has no authority for any domains. It gets data from a primary or secondary server and caches it locally in the memory. Like a secondary server, a caching server is used for redundancy and load sharing, but its more common use is due to its ability to provide faster responses to queries as it stores data in the memory rather than on the disk. This type of DNS server is typically employed at ISP locations to respond to hundreds of thousands of queries every minute.

Forwarding DNS Server: A *forwarding DNS server* has no authority for any domains. It simply forwards an incoming query to a specified DNS server.

DNS Client: A *DNS client* is used for initiating and sequencing hostname queries by referencing nameserver information defined in resolver configuration files.

Types of Nameserver Configurations

There are two fundamental types of DNS server configurations referred to as *authoritative* and *recursive*. An authoritative DNS server is usually a primary or secondary server that provides authoritative responses to name resolution queries from its own zone data files. In contrast, a recursive DNS server, which is usually a caching server, is able to query the next available DNS server in order to get a response if it does not have one. This type of server configuration does not store authoritative records; rather the server polls other authoritative servers for that information. Upon receiving a reply, the caching server caches it locally for a preset time period.

DNS Zones and Zone Files

Every DNS server maintains complete information about the portion of the DNS name space it is responsible for. This information includes a complete set of authoritative data files. The portion of the name space for which a DNS server has a complete set of authoritative data files is known as the server's *zone*, and the set of authoritative data files is known as *zone files* or *zone databases*. The zone files contain directives and resource records. Directives control the behavior of a DNS server and instruct how to undertake tasks or apply special settings to the zone; resource records describe zone limits and assign each individual host an identity. In order to provide the name resolution service to a zone, resource records must be defined; directives are optional. Directives in a zone file are prepended by the $ sign. Some of the common directives are $INCLUDE, $ORIGIN, and $TTL that let you include additional zone files, append the domain name to simple hostnames, and define the default validity (*time to live*) setting, in seconds, for the zone, respectively. Common resource records are A, CNAME, MX, NS, PTR, and SOA, and are described in Table 24-1.

Record	Description
A or AAAA	Address record. Specifies an IPv4 or IPv6 address to be mapped to a hostname.
CNAME	Canonical Name record. Maps an alias to a real name.
MX	Mail Exchanger record. Points to a weighted list of mail servers configured to receive mail for a domain.
NS	Nameserver record. Specifies the name of an authoritative nameserver.
PTR	Pointer record. Points to a different location in the namespace. It is usually used for reverse lookups.
SOA	Start Of Authority record. Defines key authoritative data for a namespace that includes primary DNS server, email address of the administrator, and the following: Serial: indicates the number of times this zone file has been updated. Refresh: identifies the amount of time secondary servers wait before requesting zone updates. Retry: determines the amount of time secondary servers wait before they re-issue a request for zone updates. Expiry: sets the amount of time for secondary servers to be marked non-authoritative for this zone if they are unable to contact the primary. Minimum: denotes the amount of time nameservers cache the zone's data. Values may be specified in seconds (default), minutes (M), hours (H), days (D), or weeks (W). Comments are followed by the ; character. A domain name at the very beginning identifies the owning domain for this zone file. If there is a @, it will point to the value of the $ORIGIN variable. The IN before the SOA identifies it as an Internet record.

Table 24-1 Resource Records

A sample zone file is presented below, along with explanation in brackets:

```
$TTL  86400                                              [24 hours; time to hold data in cache]
$ORIGIN example.com                                     [name of the domain]
@ IN  SOA  server1.example.com.  root.example.com.  (   [@ sign is a placeholder for domain name]
    0 ; serial                                          [0 updates of this file]
   1D ; refresh                                         [refresh wait time]
   1H ; retry                                           [retry wait time]
   1W ; expire                                          [time after which data is considered outdated]
   3H) ; minimum                                        [minimum time data remain in cache]
           IN   NS      server1.example.com.            [name of the DNS server]
server1   IN   A       192.168.0.110                    [IP of the DNS server]
           IN   MX  8   server1.example.com.            [hostname of an mail server; the lower the MX
                                                         number, the higher the priority]
server1   IN   A       192.168.0.110                    [IP of the mail server]
           IN   MX  9   server2.example.com.            [hostname of another mail server]
server2   IN   A       192.168.0.120                    [IP of the mail server]
```

All zone database files are maintained on the primary DNS server.

BIND Software Packages and Service Daemon

In order to provide the BIND service, several software packages need to be installed on the system. These packages add necessary support to the operating system, and bring the tools and configuration and zone files that are used for setting up and testing a DNS server. Table 24-2 describes these packages.

Package	Description
bind	Provides software to configure a DNS server.
bind-libs	Contains library files for bind and bind-utils packages.
bind-utils	Comprises of resolver tools, such as dig, host, and nslookup.

Table 24-2 BIND Software Packages

We may use the *yum* command as shown below to check the install status of these packages:

```
# yum list installed | grep ^bind
bind.x86_64                 32:9.9.4-14.el7    @ftprepo
bind-libs.x86_64            32:9.9.4-14.el7    @ftprepo
bind-libs-lite.x86_64       32:9.9.4-14.el7    @ftprepo
bind-license.noarch         32:9.9.4-14.el7    @ftprepo
bind-utils.x86_64           32:9.9.4-14.el7    @ftprepo
```

The above output indicates two additional packages, bind-libs-lite and bind-license, that deliver additional library routines and copyright information, respectively.

The BIND server package also loads the *named* daemon binary file in addition to commands and configuration files. This daemon process listens on well-known port 53 and supports both TCP and UDP protocols for operation. It must run on the system to provide DNS services.

Analysis of the Default Nameserver Configuration File

The */etc/named.conf* is the main DNS configuration file and it is read each time the DNS server daemon is started or restarted. It provides the DNS server with the names and locations of zone databases for all the domains the server is responsible for. This file typically contains options, zone, and include statements. Each statement begins with a { and ends in };. The default version of this file is pre-configured for use as a caching-only name server. A sample *named.conf* file is shown below:

```
// See /usr/share/doc/bind*/sample/ for example named configuration files.
options {
        listen-on              port 53 { 127.0.0.1; 192.168.0.111; };
        listen-on-v6           port 53 { ::1; };
        directory              "/var/named";
        dump-file              "/var/named/data/cache_dump.db";
        statistics-file        "/var/named/data/named_stats.txt";
        memstatistics-file     "/var/named/data/named_mem_stats.txt";
        pid-file               "/run/named/named.pid";
        allow-query            { localhost; };
. . . . . . . .
        recursion              yes;
        dnssec-enable          yes;
        dnssec-validation      yes;
        dnssec-lookaside       auto;
};
logging {
        channel default_debug {
                file "data/named.run";
                severity dynamic;
        };
};
zone "." IN {
        type hint;
        file "named.ca";
};
include "/etc/named.rfc1912.zones";
```

In this file, comments begin with the // characters or can be enclosed within /* and */ tags. Options can be defined at the global level within the options statement or at an individual level within a zone statement, as required. Individual options override the global options. The listen-on directive defines port 53, which the DNS server uses to listen to queries on the localhost interface and the interface configured with the 192.168.0.111 address. The systems (or networks or domains), defined within curly brackets and separated by the semicolon character, are called *match-list*. The directory directive identifies the working directory location for the *named* service. The dump-file and statistics-file directives specify the location for the DNS dump and statistics files. The memstatistics-file specifies the location for the memory usage statistics file. The pid-file directive provides the file name and location to store the *named* daemon's PID. The allow-query directive defines a match-list, which enables the specified systems to query the DNS server. You can restrict queries to one or more networks by specifying IP addresses of the networks. The recursion directive instructs the DNS server to act as a recursive server. The next three directives—dnssec-enable, dnssec-validation, and dnssec-lookaside—are related to DNS security. The logging function instructs the DNS server to log debug messages of dynamic severity to the */var/named/data/named.run* file.

There is one zone statement defined in this file. The . zone defines the root servers to query as defined in the *named.ca* file whose location is with respect to the directory directive setting. The type hint for this zone implies that one of the root servers will point hostname queries to a nameserver that will fulfill them.

The include directive at the bottom of the file instructs *named* to process the specified file. The default entry is for the *named.rfc1912.zones* file.

The *named.conf* file must have *named* as the owning group and read permission at the group level.

Analysis of the Default Zone Configuration File

The */etc/named.rfc1912.zones* is the default DNS zone configuration file that points to the zone databases located in the */var/named* directory. This file is defined with the include directive in the *named.conf* file, and is processed each time the DNS server daemon is started or restarted. The default version of this file provides the DNS server with zone information for localhost only. For each zone statement, it specifies a zone name, its type (master for primary, slave for secondary, or forward for forwarding DNS server), its file name that stores zone data, and the hostnames that are allowed to submit dynamic updates to the zone with the allow-update directive. Each statement begins with a { and ends in };. There are many other directives that can be defined in this file to customize the behavior. The default version of this file is ready for use as a localhost caching nameserver. The following shows a few statements from this file:

```
zone "localhost" IN {
    type master;
    file "named.localhost";
    allow-update { none; };
};
zone "1.0.0.127.in-addr.arpa" IN {
    type master;
    file "named.loopback";
    allow-update { none; };
};
zone "0.in-addr.arpa" IN {
    type master;
    file "named.empty";
    allow-update { none; };
};
```

Each statement in this file points to a relevant zone file in the */var/named* directory. You can use the *ll* command to view a list. Here are the *named.empty, named.localhost,* and *named.loopback* files that correspond to zone entries above:

```
-rw-r-----. 1  root  named  152  Dec 15  2009  named.empty
-rw-r-----. 1  root  named  152  Jun 21  2007  named.localhost
-rw-r-----. 1  root  named  168  Dec 15  2009  named.loopback
```

The default contents of the *named.localhost* zone file are shown below:

```
$TTL 1D
@   IN  SOA  @  rname.invalid. (
           0      ; serial
           1D     ; refresh
           1H     ; retry
           1W     ; expire
           3H )   ; minimum
    NS     @
    A      127.0.0.1
    AAAA   ::1
```

For an explanation of zone data, see the sub-section "DNS Zones and Zone Files" earlier in this chapter.

DNS Message Logging

All DNS messages and alerts are logged to the */var/log/messages* log file and are related to starting and stopping the *named* process, zone loading and unloading, general information, warning messages, and so on. This information may be viewed with any file viewing utility, such as *head, tail, cat, more,* or *view*. The following shows a *grep* on *named* PID 26989:

 # grep 26989 /var/log/messages
Feb 17 08:11:23 server1 named[26989]: starting BIND 9.9.4-RedHat-9.9.4-14.el7 -u named
Feb 17 08:11:23 server1 named[26989]: ---
Feb 17 08:11:23 server1 named[26989]: BIND 9 is maintained by Internet Systems Consortium,
Feb 17 08:11:23 server1 named[26989]: Inc. (ISC), a non-profit 501(c)(3) public-benefit
Feb 17 08:11:23 server1 named[26989]: corporation. Support and training for BIND 9 are
Feb 17 08:11:23 server1 named[26989]: available at https://www.isc.org/support
Feb 17 08:11:23 server1 named[26989]: ---
. . . .
Feb 17 08:11:23 server1 named[26989]: adjusted limit on open files from 4096 to 1048576
Feb 17 08:11:23 server1 named[26989]: zone 0.in-addr.arpa/IN: loaded serial 0
Feb 17 08:11:23 server1 named[26989]: zone 1.0.0.127.in-addr.arpa/IN: loaded serial 0
Feb 17 08:11:23 server1 named[26989]: zone
1.0.0.0.0.0.0.0.0.0.0.0.0.0.0.0.0.0.0.0.0.0.0.0.0.0.0.0.0.0.0.0.ip6.arpa/IN: loaded serial 0
Feb 17 08:11:23 server1 named[26989]: zone localhost.localdomain/IN: loaded serial 0
Feb 17 08:11:23 server1 named[26989]: zone localhost/IN: loaded serial 0
Feb 17 08:11:23 server1 named[26989]: all zones loaded
Feb 17 08:11:23 server1 named[26989]: running

EXAM TIP: You can open another terminal session on the system to run 'tail –f' on this log file.

This log file grows over time depending on how busy the system is. The syslog service rotates this file once a week to prevent it from getting too large, and saves previous four weeks of backup in the same directory.

Configuring BIND Server

Managing BIND involves several configuration and administration tasks, including setting up a primary, secondary, or caching name server, and client. These tasks are covered in exercises presented in this section.

SELinux Requirements for BIND Operation

SELinux protects systems by setting appropriate controls using contexts and booleans. Before you proceed with implementing the exercises, let's look at the BIND-specific SELinux contexts on processes, files, and port, and also see the booleans that may require a toggle for BIND to function properly. By default, the *named* daemon runs confined in its own domain, and it is labeled appropriately with domain type named_t. This can be confirmed with the *ps* command as follows:

> # **ps –eZ | grep named**
> system_u:system_r:named_t:s0   26989   ?   00:00:00 named

The SELinux file type associated with the */etc/named.conf* and */etc/named.rfc1912.zones* files is named_conf_t and that for the zone directory */var/named* is named_zone_t. Here is an *ll* command output that verifies this information:

> # **ll –Zd /etc/named.conf /etc/named.rfc1912.zones /var/named**
> -rw-r-----. root named system_u:object_r:named_conf_t:s0 /etc/named.conf
> -rw-r-----. root named system_u:object_r:named_conf_t:s0 /etc/named.rfc1912.zones
> drwxr-x---. root named system_u:object_r:named_zone_t:s0 /var/named

The SELinux type associated with the DNS port is dns_port_t, and it is in place by default. Here is the *semanage* command output that validates this information:

> # **semanage port –l | grep dns_**
> dns_port_t   tcp   53
> dns_port_t   udp   53

From a SELinux boolean standpoint, there are two booleans that are associated with BIND, and we can see this with the *getsebool* command:

> # **getsebool –a | grep ^named**
> named_tcp_bind_http_port --> off
> named_write_master_zones --> off

These booleans determine whether the BIND service can bind a TCP socket to HTTP ports and write to master zone files, respectively. Both booleans are turned off by default and do not need to be toggled for our exercises in this chapter.

By looking at the above SELinux settings for BIND, we can establish that there are no changes required to make it function smoothly in the SELinux enforcing mode.

Exercise 24-1: Configure a Caching-Only DNS Server

This exercise should be done on *server1*.

In this exercise, you will configure *server1* as a primary DNS server. You will install the BIND software, modify the *named.conf* file, set the BIND service to autostart at system reboots, start the BIND service, and open port 53 in the firewall.

1. Install the BIND software packages:

    # **yum –y install bind bind-utils**

    . . . .
    Installed:
      bind.x86_64 32:9.9.4-14.el7
      bind-utils.x86_64 32:9.9.4-14.el7
    Dependency Installed:
      bind-libs.x86_64 32:9.9.4-14.el7
    Complete!

2. Open the *named.conf* file in a text editor and set or modify the following directives. Leave other settings intact.

    options {
        listen-on   port 53 {any; };
        allow-query   { any; };
        recursion   yes;
        dnssec-enable   no;
        dnssec-validation no;
    };

3. Check the configuration file using the *named-checkconf* command:

    # **named-checkconf**

4. Set *named* to autostart at system reboots:

    # **systemctl enable named**
    ln -s '/usr/lib/systemd/system/named.service' '/etc/systemd/system/multi-user.target.wants/named.service'

5. Start the BIND service and check its operational status:

    # **systemctl start named**
    # **systemctl status named**
    named.service - Berkeley Internet Name Domain (DNS)
       Loaded: loaded (/usr/lib/systemd/system/named.service; enabled)
       Active: active (running) since Tue 2015-02-17 10:12:11 EST; 3s ago
      Process: 28250 ExecStop=/bin/sh -c /usr/sbin/rndc stop > /dev/null 2>&1 || /bin/kill -TERM
    $MAINPID (code=exited, status=0/SUCCESS)
      Process: 28812 ExecStart=/usr/sbin/named -u named $OPTIONS (code=exited, status=0/SUCCESS)
      Process: 28810 ExecStartPre=/usr/sbin/named-checkconf -z /etc/named.conf (code=exited,
    status=0/SUCCESS)
     Main PID: 28814 (named)

CGroup: /system.slice/named.service
└─28814 /usr/sbin/named -u named

6. Add the named service to firewalld persistently and reload the rules to allow traffic on DNS port 53:

 # firewall-cmd --permanent --add-service dns; firewall-cmd --reload

This completes the configuration of a caching-only DNS server. At this point, if you wish to view log entries for this instance of the BIND daemon, execute the *pidof named* command, and *grep* for the PID in the */var/log/messages* file, as explained in the previous section.

Understanding, Configuring, and Troubleshooting DNS Client

Now that a DNS server is in place and ready for use, we need to look at the client-side configuration files that are consulted when hostname queries are made. Moreover, there are several tools available in RHEL that we need to look at to see how they can be used to query hostnames via the DNS server we configured in the previous exercise. We can use the same tools and a few others to troubleshoot DNS client issues. This section discusses the files and tools, and then presents a simple exercise to configure a DNS client and test the DNS server. Finally, it provides some information on how to troubleshoot a non-functioning client.

Overview of DNS Client Configuration Files

Primarily, there are two files of interest, a resolver configuration file called *resolv.conf* and a name service switch configuration file called *nsswitch.conf*. Both files are located in the */etc* directory and are installed at the time of OS installation.

The Resolver Configuration File

The *resolv.conf* file is the DNS resolver configuration file where we define information to support hostname lookups. This file may be updated manually using a text editor. It is referenced by resolver utilities, such as *dig*, *host*, and *nslookup*, to obtain necessary information for query purposes. There are three key directives set in this file: domain, nameserver, and search. Table 24-3 describes these directives.

Directive	Description
domain	Specifies the default domain name to be searched for queries. In the absence of this directive, the domain associated with the hostname is assumed, and if the hostname is without a domain name, then the root domain is considered. This directive is useful in a multi-domain environment.
nameserver	Specifies up to three DNS server IP addresses to be queried one at a time in the order in which they are listed for name resolution. If none specified, the DNS server on the localhost is assumed.
search	Specifies up to six domain names, of which the first must be the local domain. The resolver appends these names one at a time in the order in which they are listed to the hostname being looked up. In the absence of this directive, the local domain is assumed.

Table 24-3 The Resolver Configuration File

A sample entry is provided below, depicting the syntax of the three directives:

```
domain       example.com
search       example.com
nameserver  191.11.11.22
```

On a system with this file absent, the resolver utilities only query the name server configured on the localhost, determine domain name from the hostname of the system, and construct the search path from the domain name.

The Name Service Switch Configuration File

The *nsswitch.conf* file is referenced by many system and network tools to determine the source, such as NIS, NIS+, LDAP, DNS, or local files, for obtaining information about users, user aging, groups, mail aliases, hostnames, networks, protocols, and so on. In the presence of multiple sources, this file also identifies the order in which to consult them and what to do next based on the status result we receive from the preceding source. There are four keywords—success, notfound, unavail, and tryagain—that affect this behavior. The keywords are described in Table 24-4.

Keyword	Meaning	Default Action
success	Information found in the source and returned to the requester.	return (do not try the next source).
notfound	Information not found in the source.	continue (try the next source).
unavail	Source down, not responding, or service is disabled or not configured.	continue (try the next source).
tryagain	Source or service is busy temporarily. Try again later.	continue (try the next source).

Table 24-4 Name Service Source Status

The following example entry shows the syntax for defining entries in the *nsswitch.conf* file. It shows two sources for name resolution: DNS (the */etc/resolv.conf* file) and the */etc/hosts* file:

```
hosts:       dns       files
```

Based on the default behavior, the search will terminate if the requested information is found in DNS. However, we can alter this behavior and instruct the lookup program to return if the requested information is not found in DNS. The modified entry will look like:

```
hosts:       dns [NOTFOUND=return]   files
```

This altered entry will ignore the *hosts* file.

Overview of DNS Lookup Utilities

Once a DNS server is set up and available, we can use one of the client tools provided by the bind-utils package to perform queries for hostname lookups. These tools include *dig*, *host*, and *nslookup*, and are elaborated below.

The dig Utility

dig (*domain information groper*) is a DNS lookup utility. It queries the nameserver specified at the command line or consults the *resolv.conf* file to determine the nameservers to be used for lookups if no nameserver is supplied with the command. In case the nameservers are unable to fulfill the query, the *dig* command contacts one of the root DNS servers listed in the */etc/named.ca* file for directions. This tool may be used for DNS troubleshooting because of its flexibility and verbosity. The following shows a few examples on the usage.

To perform a lookup to get the IP address of *redhat.com* using the nameservers listed in the *resolv.conf* file:

```
# dig redhat.com
; <<>> DiG 9.9.4-RedHat-9.9.4-14.el7 <<>> redhat.com
;; global options: +cmd
;; Got answer:
;; ->>HEADER<<- opcode: QUERY, status: NOERROR, id: 38080
;; flags: qr rd ra; QUERY: 1, ANSWER: 1, AUTHORITY: 0, ADDITIONAL: 1
;; OPT PSEUDOSECTION:
; EDNS: version: 0, flags:; udp: 4096
;; QUESTION SECTION:
;redhat.com.                IN    A
;; ANSWER SECTION:
redhat.com.        60    IN    A    209.132.183.105
;; Query time: 85 msec
;; SERVER: 24.226.1.93#53(24.226.1.93)
;; WHEN: Thu Feb 19 18:29:41 EST 2015
;; MSG SIZE  rcvd: 55
```

To perform a reverse lookup on the IP address of *redhat.com* using the nameservers listed in the *resolv.conf* file, use the −x option and specify the IP address:

```
# dig −x 209.132.183.105
; <<>> DiG 9.9.4-RedHat-9.9.4-14.el7 <<>> -x 209.132.183.105
;; global options: +cmd
;; Got answer:
;; ->>HEADER<<- opcode: QUERY, status: NOERROR, id: 53034
;; flags: qr rd ra; QUERY: 1, ANSWER: 1, AUTHORITY: 8, ADDITIONAL: 12
;; OPT PSEUDOSECTION:
; EDNS: version: 0, flags:; udp: 4096
;; QUESTION SECTION:
;105.183.132.209.in-addr.arpa.  IN    PTR
;; ANSWER SECTION:
105.183.132.209.in-addr.arpa. 600 IN   PTR    redirect.redhat.com.
;; AUTHORITY SECTION:
209.in-addr.arpa.    1553  IN    NS    z.arin.net.
209.in-addr.arpa.    1553  IN    NS    w.arin.net.
209.in-addr.arpa.    1553  IN    NS    t.arin.net.
209.in-addr.arpa.    1553  IN    NS    r.arin.net.
209.in-addr.arpa.    1553  IN    NS    v.arin.net.
```

```
209.in-addr.arpa.    1553   IN     NS     y.arin.net.
209.in-addr.arpa.    1553   IN     NS     x.arin.net.
209.in-addr.arpa.    1553   IN     NS     u.arin.net.
;; ADDITIONAL SECTION:
u.arin.net.          16297  IN     A      204.61.216.50
u.arin.net.          13476  IN     AAAA   2001:500:14:6050:ad::1
t.arin.net.          42829  IN     A      199.253.249.63
t.arin.net.          2777   IN     AAAA   2001:500:98::63
w.arin.net.          16061  IN     A      72.52.71.2
w.arin.net.          16061  IN     AAAA   2001:470:1a::2
v.arin.net.          42218  IN     A      63.243.194.2
v.arin.net.          13476  IN     AAAA   2001:5a0:10::2
z.arin.net.          1035   IN     A      199.212.0.63
z.arin.net.          11003  IN     AAAA   2001:500:13::63
y.arin.net.          3111   IN     A      192.42.93.32
;; Query time: 110 msec
;; SERVER: 24.226.1.93#53(24.226.1.93)
;; WHEN: Thu Feb 19 18:31:01 EST 2015
;; MSG SIZE rcvd: 462
```

The host Utility

host is a simple DNS lookup utility that works on the same principles as the *dig* command in terms of nameserver determination. This tool produces much less data in the output. Here are a few examples on its usage.

To perform a lookup to get the IP address of *redhat.com* using the nameservers listed in the *resolv.conf* file:

> # **host redhat.com**
> redhat.com has address **209.132.183.105**
> redhat.com mail is handled by 10 mx2.redhat.com.
> redhat.com mail is handled by 5 mx1.redhat.com.

To perform a reverse lookup on the IP address of *redhat.com* using the nameservers listed in the *resolv.conf* file:

> # **host 209.132.183.105**
> 105.183.132.209.in-addr.arpa domain name pointer redirect.redhat.com.

You can use the –a option for detailed output.

The nslookup Utility

nslookup is another DNS lookup utility. It queries the nameservers listed in the *resolv.conf* file or specified at the command line. The following shows a few examples of its usage.

To perform a lookup to get the IP address of *redhat.com* using the nameservers listed in the *resolv.conf* file:

```
# nslookup redhat.com
Server:      24.226.1.93
Address:   24.226.1.93#53
Non-authoritative answer:
Name:   redhat.com
Address:   209.132.183.105
```

To perform a reverse lookup on the IP address of *redhat.com* using the nameservers listed in the *resolv.conf* file:

```
# nslookup 209.132.183.105
Server:          24.226.1.93
Address:         24.226.1.93#53
Non-authoritative answer:
105.183.132.209.in-addr.arpa    name = redirect.redhat.com.
Authoritative answers can be found from:
209.in-addr.arpa        nameserver = t.arin.net.
209.in-addr.arpa        nameserver = u.arin.net.
209.in-addr.arpa        nameserver = v.arin.net.
209.in-addr.arpa        nameserver = r.arin.net.
209.in-addr.arpa        nameserver = x.arin.net.
209.in-addr.arpa        nameserver = y.arin.net.
209.in-addr.arpa        nameserver = z.arin.net.
209.in-addr.arpa        nameserver = w.arin.net.
u.arin.net      internet address = 204.61.216.50
u.arin.net      has AAAA address 2001:500:14:6050:ad::1
t.arin.net      internet address = 199.253.249.63
t.arin.net      has AAAA address 2001:500:98::63
w.arin.net       internet address = 72.52.71.2
w.arin.net       has AAAA address 2001:470:1a::2
v.arin.net      internet address = 63.243.194.2
v.arin.net      has AAAA address 2001:5a0:10::2
z.arin.net      internet address = 199.212.0.63
z.arin.net      has AAAA address 2001:500:13::63
y.arin.net      internet address = 192.42.93.32
```

The *nslookup* utility can be invoked in interactive mode without supplying an argument to it:

```
# nslookup
>
```

At the prompt, you can specify a nameserver to use for queries. For instance typing "server server1" at the nslookup prompt will instruct it to use *server1* as the nameserver for queries.

```
> server server1
Default server: server1
Address: 192.168.0.110#53
```

Now you can perform a simple query by typing a hostname, such as:

> **ibm.com**
Server: server1
Address: 192.168.0.110#53
Non-authoritative answer:
Name: ibm.com
Address: 129.42.38.1
> **exit**

Type *exit* at the nslookup prompt to quit.

Exercise 24-2: Configure DNS Client and Test Server Configuration

This exercise should be done on *server2*.

In this exercise, you will install the bind-utils package and test the caching-only nameserver you set up in the previous exercise. You will then modify the resolver configuration file and add an entry for the new nameserver. You will ensure that the name service switch file contains proper hosts entry. You will test the nameserver again.

1. Install the DNS client software package bind-utils:

    # **yum –y install bind-utils**
    Package 32:bind-utils-9.9.4-14.el7.x86_64 already installed and latest version
    Nothing to do

2. Test the functionality of the caching-only nameserver with the *dig* and *host* commands:

    # **dig @server1 linux.org**
    ; <<>> DiG 9.9.4-RedHat-9.9.4-14.el7 <<>> @server1 linux.org
    ; (1 server found)
    ;; global options: +cmd
    ;; Got answer:
    ;; ->>HEADER<<- opcode: QUERY, status: NOERROR, id: 8605
    ;; flags: qr rd ra; QUERY: 1, ANSWER: 1, AUTHORITY: 2, ADDITIONAL: 3
    ;; OPT PSEUDOSECTION:
    ; EDNS: version: 0, flags:; udp: 4096
    ;; QUESTION SECTION:
    ;linux.org.   IN   A
    ;; ANSWER SECTION:
    linux.org.   3600   IN   A   107.170.40.56
    ;; AUTHORITY SECTION:
    linux.org.   86400 IN   NS   ns2.iqnection.com.
    linux.org.   86400 IN   NS   ns1.iqnection.com.
    ;; ADDITIONAL SECTION:
    ns1.iqnection.com.   3600   IN   A   209.92.37.10
    ns2.iqnection.com.   3600   IN   A   192.241.130.43
    ;; Query time: 207 msec

```
;; SERVER: 192.168.0.110#53(192.168.0.110)
;; WHEN: Thu Feb 19 04:44:21 EST 2015
;; MSG SIZE  rcvd: 135
```
host linux.org 192.168.0.110
```
Using domain server:
Name: 192.168.0.110
Address: 192.168.0.110#53
Aliases:
linux.org has address 107.170.40.56
linux.org mail is handled by 20 mx.iqemail.net.
```

The above demonstrated the use of hostname and IP address of the caching-only nameserver at the command line.

3. Open the resolver configuration file and add the following entry:

    nameserver   192.168.0.110

4. Open the name service switch configuration file and ensure the hosts entry looks like the following:

    hosts: files   dns

5. Test the functionality of the caching-only nameserver again with the *dig* and *nslookup* commands without specifying the nameserver at the command line:

    # **dig linux.org**
    ```
    . . . . . . . .
    ;; ANSWER SECTION:
    linux.org.        3473   IN    A     107.170.40.56
    . . . . . . . .
    ;; SERVER: 192.168.0.110#53(192.168.0.110)
    ;; WHEN: Thu Feb 19 04:45:10 EST 2015
    ;; MSG SIZE  rcvd: 153
    ```
    # **nslookup linux.org**
    ```
    Server:      192.168.0.110
    Address:     192.168.0.110#53
    Non-authoritative answer:
    Name:  linux.org
    Address: 107.170.40.56
    ```

The above outputs indicate that both commands now use the caching nameserver for lookups without being explicitly supplied at the command line.

If the client is configured to receive IP assignments from a DHCP server, edit the associated network interface file in the */etc/sysconfig/network-scripts* directory and set the PEERDNS directive to no to prevent the client from receiving nameserver information.

Troubleshooting DNS Client Issues

Once a nameserver is configured properly on a system and tested locally, the next step is to test it from a remote client. If the testing works out satisfactory, proceed with making persistent changes to client configuration files and mirror the changes across all clients that are intended to use this nameserver for name resolution. During the testing, knowledge of simple tools, such as *ping*, *ip*, *dig*, *nslookup*, and *host*, is essential to help resolve problems quickly if encountered. Since DNS is a network service, a stable and robust network infrastructure is key for its successful operation.

The first step toward setting up DNS client or troubleshooting is to verify the persistent addition and loading of the dns service to firewalld on the nameserver. To do this, log on to *server1* (nameserver) and run the following:

firewall-cmd --list-services
dhcpv6-client **dns** ftp http https kerberos nfs ntp samba smtp ssh tftp

In case of its absence, run the following to add and load it:

firewall-cmd --permanent --add-service dns ; firewall-cmd --reload

On a configured and functional local nameserver, the above is the only step to verify from a remote client.

Now, on *server2* (client), verify connectivity with the nameserver using the *ping* command. Send just two packets to its hostname or IP address.

ping 192.168.0.110 –c2
PING 192.168.0.110 (192.168.0.110) 56(84) bytes of data.
64 bytes from 192.168.0.110: icmp_seq=1 ttl=64 time=0.299 ms
64 bytes from 192.168.0.110: icmp_seq=2 ttl=64 time=0.389 ms
--- 192.168.0.110 ping statistics ---
2 packets transmitted, 2 received, 0% packet loss, time 1000ms
rtt min/avg/max/mdev = 0.299/0.344/0.389/0.045 ms

The connectivity is fully operational as indicated by the above output. Based on the successful outcome, proceed to the next step.

If, however, *ping* reports errors, you need to check whether the physical or virtual network interface on the 192.168.0 network is configured properly and is active:

ip addr show eth0
2: eth0: <BROADCAST,MULTICAST,UP,LOWER_UP> mtu 1500 qdisc pfifo_fast state UP qlen 1000
    link/ether 52:54:00:81:ca:82 brd ff:ff:ff:ff:ff:ff
    inet 192.168.0.120/24 brd 192.168.0.255 scope global eth0
      valid_lft forever preferred_lft forever
    inet6 fe80::5054:ff:fe81:ca82/64 scope link
      valid_lft forever preferred_lft forever

The above report shows that *eth0* is up and it has the IP address on the correct subnet. You may want to re-run the *ping* test if it reported an issue. It is possible that the server was over-busy at that time.

Assuming the network connectivity is okay, the next step is to use one of the lookup tools, such as *dig*, to see whether you are able to resolve a hostname. Specify the IP of the nameserver with the command.

 # dig @192.168.0.110 getitcertify.com

. . . .
;; ANSWER SECTION:
getitcertify.com.   561   IN   A   184.168.53.1
. . . .
;; SERVER: 192.168.0.110#53(192.168.0.110)
;; WHEN: Fri Feb 20 07:56:59 EST 2015
;; MSG SIZE rcvd: 163

Based on the successful outcome of this command, proceed to the next step.

If, however, *dig* reports an error, you will need to re-visit the nameserver configuration.

Assuming *dig* reported as expected, you will then open the *resolv.conf* and *nsswitch.conf* files and add or modify the following entries to look like:

nameserver 192.168.0.110   # this entry should go in /etc/resolv.conf file
hosts: files   dns   # this entry should go in /etc/nsswitch.conf file

The above changes are persistently stored.

Re-run *dig* but do not specify the nameserver at the command line. Let it refer to the *resolv.conf* file for the nameserver. The output will report the nameserver (highlighted) used for the query.

 # dig www.getitcertify.com

. . . .
;; ANSWER SECTION:
www.getitcertify.com. 2310 IN   CNAME getitcertify.com.
getitcertify.com.   600   IN   A   184.168.53.1
. . . .
;; SERVER: 192.168.0.110#53(192.168.0.110)
;; WHEN: Fri Feb 20 08:18:29 EST 2015
;; MSG SIZE rcvd: 163

Now you can go ahead and update the *nsswitch.conf* and *resolv.conf* files on other clients.

Chapter Summary

This chapter described DNS concepts and strengthened their study with implementation of exercises. The chapter introduced the domain name system and name resolution, and continued with the presentation of various terms, concepts, and components involved. It expounded what BIND was and described the name space, domains, root servers, kinds of nameservers, types of nameserver configurations, zones, software packages, service daemon, and log file. It presented an examination of default configuration and zone files.

The next part of the chapter demonstrated the configuration of a nameserver and client, and showed how to troubleshoot client-side issues using the knowledge gained in the first part of the chapter.

Chapter Review Questions

1. What is the main advantage of using a caching-only nameserver over the other types?
2. An MX record in the nameserver configuration file represents a mail server. True or False?
3. Name three utilities for hostname lookup.
4. What is the difference between DNS and BIND?
5. Given a hostname ca.redhat.com, what is the second level domain name?
6. Which two types of nameservers do not have authority for any domains?
7. Name the two types of nameserver configuration.
8. What would the entry "host: dns [TRYAGAIN=return] files" mean in the *nsswitch.conf* file?
9. What is the default location for storing zone files?
10. What would the command *host 10.22.112.22* do?
11. Provide the name of the software package that contains lookup utilities.
12. What type of nameserver is considered the most authoritative?
13. What is the name of the resolver configuration file?
14. Define reverse name resolution.
15. Name the four DNS server roles.
16. Which file lists details for the root name servers?
17. Which is the main configuration file for a DNS server?
18. Define name resolution in one sentence.
19. What is the term that represents the hierarchy of all domains on the Internet?
20. Provide a difference between zone file and zone database.
21. What is the name of the client file where you list DNS servers for query?
22. Is the DNS name space hierarchical or flat?
23. What is a fully qualified domain name?
24. What is the well-known port number used for DNS service?

Answers to Chapter Review Questions

1. The main advantage of using a caching nameserver than the other types is its ability to respond faster to queries.
2. True.
3. Three lookup utilities are *dig*, *host*, and *nslookup*.
4. DNS is a name resolution mechanism whereas BIND is a software that provides name resolution on UNIX and Linux platforms while conforming to DNS standards.
5. The second level of domain name in this construction is .redhat.
6. The forwarding and caching-only nameservers do not have authority for any domains.
7. The two types of nameserver configurations are referred to as authoritative and recursive.
8. This entry in the *nsswitch.conf* file would terminate a name lookup attempt if a nameserver were busy.
9. The zone files are located in the */var/named* directory by default.
10. This command would lookup for the host with the specified IP address.
11. The bind-utils package contains the lookup utilities.
12. The primary nameserver is considered the most authoritative.
13. The name of the resolver configuration file is *resolv.conf*.
14. Reverse name resolution is the ability to map the specified IP address with its hostname.
15. The four DNS server roles are master, secondary, caching, and forwarding.
16. The *named.ca* file contains root server information.
17. The main configuration file for DNS server is *named.conf*.

18. Name resolution resolves hostname to IP address and IP address to hostname.
19. The term used to represent the DNS hierarchy is called name space.
20. There is no difference between the two.
21. The */etc/resolv.conf* file.
22. The DNS name space is hierarchical.
23. A fully qualified domain name is a hostname with its domain name appended.
24. The DNS service uses the well-known port 53 for its operation.

DIY Challenge Labs

The following labs are useful to strengthen the concepts and topics learned in this chapter. It is expected that you perform these labs without any additional help. A step-by-step guide is not provided, as the implementation of these labs requires the knowledge that has been presented in this chapter. Use defaults or your own thinking for missing information.

Lab 24-1: Configure a Caching-Only Nameserver

Set up caching-only name service on *host1* and allow only *server1* to use this service as a client.

Chapter 25

Managing MariaDB

This chapter describes the following major topics:

➤ Introduction to databases and database management systems
➤ Understand relational database
➤ Overview of MariaDB
➤ Recognize MariaDB packages, daemon, commands, and configuration and log files
➤ Review SELinux requirements for MariaDB operation
➤ Identify MariaDB database and table operations
➤ Interact with MariaDB via its shell interface
➤ Create and manage database and tables, and query records
➤ Understand physical and logical backups
➤ Use tools to create and restore logical backups

RHCE Objectives:

83. Install and configure MariaDB
84. Backup and restore a database
85. Create a simple database schema
86. Perform simple SQL queries against a database

MariaDB is an open source database management system software that allows the creation and administration of databases. A database is a structured repository of data that is accessed and administered by a database management software, such as MariaDB. Databases created with MariaDB use the relational model to identify the database structure and data storage, organization, and handling. A relational database uses a table-based format.

Understanding Databases, DBMS, and MariaDB

A *database* is a structured collection of data, which is comprised of facts and figures of something, and can be processed to generate meaningful results. An example of "something" is a database that stores data about airlines, hotels, car rentals, and vacation packages. People access this database via a website to search and make bookings and reservations using a number of different combinations and options that are configured in the database. Moreover, the database also provides people with the ability to limit their searches to a specific service or expand to include two or more.

Databases are widely used in both public and private sectors, ranging from banking and financial services companies to manufacturing, telecommunication, airline, technology, education, research, libraries, hoteling, and government agencies. They are used for storage and retrieval of data to meet general and specific business requirements.

A database with a large amount of stored data accessed by a number of users concurrently using a variety of combinations and options requires a *database management system* (DBMS) that is able to store, manage, and manipulate that data. A DBMS is a software application, such as MariaDB, MySQL, Oracle, IBM DB2, Sybase, Ingress, Informix, PostgreSQL, and Microsoft SQL Server. Such management systems allow the definition, creation, configuration, administration, performance management, backup, and recovery of a database; storage, modification, and deletion of data in the database; and querying and retrieving of that data to produce desired reports for users or to feed to a requesting application. Furthermore, a DBMS also allows the administrator to place security controls on users in terms of what they can do.

Databases can be accessed by directly logging in to them. This type of access is typically granted to database architects and administrators who are responsible for their design, build, and management. Databases are accessed by end users or applications through other applications for data query and retrieval. This type of access does not require direct logging into the database.

What is a Relational Database?

A *relational database* is a type of database that is structured based on the relational model suggested by Edgar. F. Codd in 1970. It is a set of *tables* comprising *rows* (a.k.a. *tuples* or *records*) and *columns* (a.k.a. *fields* or *attributes*) for data storage and organization. Each row represents a single record, which is made up of column values. A column is made up of the same type of values. See Figure 25-1 for the three table components: row, column, and value.

Sno	First	Last	Born	Died	Age
1	Albert	Einstein	1879	1955	76
2	Isaac	Newton	1643	1727	84
3	Marie	Curie	1867	1934	67
4	Galileo	Galilei	1564	1642	78
5	Thomas	Edison	1847	1931	84
6	Alexander	Bell	1847	1922	75
7	Benjamin	Franklin	1706	1790	84
8	Louis	Pasteur	1822	1895	73

(Row points to record 4; Value points to 84 in row 7)

Figure 25-1 Table Components

In order to protect against entering duplicate records in a table, a column with unique values for each record is identified, and defined as a *primary key*. In Figure 25-1, column "Sno" can be chosen as a primary key, as it contains a distinct value for each record.

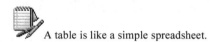 A table is like a simple spreadsheet.

For flexible data storage, organization, and retrieval, MariaDB allows the creation and use of multiple tables in a database to store distinct records about something, and then linking the tables together using a unique key. For instance, we can have a database with two tables, one consisting of the records shown in Figure 25-1, and the other with data about their inventions and a "Sno". We can then define the "Sno" column as a *foreign key* to establish a relationship between the two tables. A user querying record "1" will get information from both tables. This is an example of a one-to-one table relationship. MariaDB also supports one-to-many and many-to-many relationships.

Overview of MariaDB

MariaDB is a relatively new name in the RDBMS space. It is an enhanced binary replacement for the famous relational database management software MySQL, which was bought by Sun Microsystems (now Oracle) in 2008. Following the acquisition, the development of MySQL slowed down and there was less involvement from the community due to internal company policies. This led the original developers of MySQL to fork MariaDB with the intent to keep it free under GNU GPL and re-open the doors for its development to the community. The latest stable version of MariaDB is 10.0, which is equivalent to MySQL version 5.6 with several enhancements. MariaDB versions up to 5.5 followed MySQL version numbering; however, MariaDB developers later decided to change it to start at 10.0.

MariaDB Software Packages and Service Daemon

In order to configure the MariaDB service, several software packages need to be installed on the system. These packages add necessary support to the operating system, and bring the tools and configuration files that are used for setting it up. Table 25-1 describes these packages.

Package	Description
mariadb	Provides MariaDB client programs and a configuration file.
mariadb-server	Contains MariaDB server, tools, and configuration and log files.
Mariadb-libs	Comprises of essential library files for MariaDB client programs.

Table 25-1 MariaDB Software Packages

We may use the *yum* command as shown below to check the install status of these packages:

```
# yum list installed | grep ^mariadb
mariadb.x86_64              1:5.5.35-3.el7      @ftprepo
mariadb-libs.x86_64        1:5.5.35-3.el7      @anaconda/7.0
mariadb-server.x86_64     1:5.5.35-3.el7      @ftprepo
```

The MariaDB server package also loads the *mysqld* daemon binary file in addition to commands and configuration files. This daemon process listens on port 3306 and supports both TCP and UDP protocols for operation. It must run on the system to allow client access.

MariaDB Commands

MariaDB offers several commands for administration and query. However, only the commands we use in this chapter are described in Table 25-2.

Command	Description
mysql	Command line shell interface for administration and query.
mysql_secure_installation	Improves the security of MariaDB installation.
mysqldump	Backs up or restores one or more table or database.

Table 25-2 MariaDB Commands

The *mysql* shell interface is explained shortly, and the three tools listed in Table 25-2 are used in this chapter.

MariaDB Configuration Files

The primary configuration file for MariaDB is the */etc/my.cnf*, which sets global defaults for *mysql* shell program, *mysqld_safe* startup script, and the *mysqld* daemon process. The uncommented line entries from this file are presented below:

```
# grep –v ^# /etc/my.cnf
[mysqld]
datadir=/var/lib/mysql
socket=/var/lib/mysql/mysql.sock
symbolic-links=0
[mysqld_safe]
log-error=/var/log/mariadb/mariadb.log
pid-file=/var/run/mariadb/mariadb.pid
!includedir /etc/my.cnf.d
```

The *my.cnf* file contains two *configuration groups* by default. These groups are [mysqld] and [mysqld_safe] with some settings under each one of them. Their purpose is to separate the configuration needed by the *mysqld* daemon, *mysqld_safe* startup program, and *mysql* client program (client group not included in the default file) at startup. The directives in this file set several defaults, including the locations to store database files, log files, and the PID file. The includedir directive at the bottom of the file instructs the startup program to look for additional configuration files in the */etc/my.cnf.d* directory and process them if they exist. By default, there are three configuration files in this directory, which are listed below:

 # ll /etc/my.cnf.d
```
-rw-r--r--. 1 root root 295 Jan 28 2014 client.cnf
-rw-r--r--. 1 root root 232 Jan 28 2014 mysql-clients.cnf
-rw-r--r--. 1 root root 744 Jan 28 2014 server.cnf
```

These files set configurations for general clients, specific MariaDB client tools, and MariaDB server program *mysqld*, respectively. The default files have several configuration groups defined, but they all are empty.

For our purposes in this chapter, there is no need to modify any of these files.

Logging MariaDB Messages
The default file for storing MariaDB logs is *mariadb.log* located in the */var/log/mariadb* directory, as defined in the */etc/my.cnf* file. This log file captures all errors, alerts, warnings, informational, and other general messages related to MariaDB. Some sample entries from this file are shown below:

```
150220  7:39:15 mysqld_safe Starting mysqld daemon with databases from /var/lib/mysql
150220  7:39:15 InnoDB: The InnoDB memory heap is disabled
150220  7:39:15 InnoDB: Mutexes and rw_locks use GCC atomic builtins
150220  7:39:15 InnoDB: Compressed tables use zlib 1.2.7
150220  7:39:15 InnoDB: Using Linux native AIO
150220  7:39:15 InnoDB: Initializing buffer pool, size = 128.0M
150220  7:39:15 InnoDB: Completed initialization of buffer pool
InnoDB: The first specified data file ./ibdata1 did not exist:
InnoDB: a new database to be created!
150220  7:39:15  InnoDB: Setting file ./ibdata1 size to 10 MB
InnoDB: Database physically writes the file full: wait...
150220  7:39:15  InnoDB: Log file ./ib_logfile0 did not exist: new to be created
InnoDB: Setting log file ./ib_logfile0 size to 5 MB
InnoDB: Database physically writes the file full: wait...
150220  7:39:15  InnoDB: Log file ./ib_logfile1 did not exist: new to be created
InnoDB: Setting log file ./ib_logfile1 size to 5 MB
InnoDB: Database physically writes the file full: wait...
InnoDB: Doublewrite buffer not found: creating new
InnoDB: Doublewrite buffer created
InnoDB: 127 rollback segment(s) active.
InnoDB: Creating foreign key constraint system tables
InnoDB: Foreign key constraint system tables created
150220  7:39:16  InnoDB: Waiting for the background threads to start
```

150220 7:39:17 Percona XtraDB (http://www.percona.com) 5.5.35-MariaDB-33.0 started; log sequence number 0
150220 7:39:17 [Note] Plugin 'FEEDBACK' is disabled.
150220 7:39:17 [Note] Server socket created on IP: '0.0.0.0'.
150220 7:39:17 [Note] Event Scheduler: Loaded 0 events
150220 7:39:17 [Note] /usr/libexec/mysqld: ready for connections.
Version: '5.5.35-MariaDB' socket: '/var/lib/mysql/mysql.sock' port: 3306 MariaDB Server

This file may be referenced for troubleshooting, auditing, or other similar purposes.

Managing MariaDB

Managing MariaDB involves several database administration tasks, including various operations performed on databases and tables. These tasks include the installation of MariaDB software packages; listing, creating, switching into, and dropping databases; creating, describing, listing, renaming, and dropping tables; inserting, updating, querying, and deleting records in tables; and backing up and restoring databases and tables. These tasks are described in this section, along with demonstrations and hands-on exercises.

SELinux Requirements for MariaDB Operation

SELinux protects systems by setting appropriate controls using contexts and booleans. Before you proceed with the exercises, let's look at MariaDB-specific SELinux contexts on processes, files, and port, and also look at the booleans that may need to be modified for MariaDB to function properly. By default, the *mysqld* daemon process runs confined in its own domain, and it is labeled appropriately with domain type mysqld_t. This can be confirmed with the *ps* command:

ps –eZ | grep mysqld
system_u:system_r:mysqld_safe_t:s0   11224 ?   00:00:00 mysqld_safe
system_u:system_r:**mysqld_t**:s0   11382 ?   00:00:21 mysqld

The SELinux file type associated with the *mysqld* daemon file is mysql_exec_t, configuration files in the */etc/my.cnf.d* directory is etc_t, database files in the */var/lib/mysql* directory is *mysqld_db_t*, and log files located in the */var/log/mariadb* directory is *mysql_log_t*. Here is an *ll* command output that verifies this information:

ll –dZ /usr/libexec/mysqld /etc/my.cnf.d /var/lib/mysql /var/log/mariadb
drwxr-xr-x. root   root   system_u:object_r:etc_t:s0   /etc/my.cnf.d
-rwxr-xr-x. root   root   system_u:object_r:mysqld_exec_t:s0   /usr/libexec/mysqld
drwxr-xr-x. mysql mysql system_u:object_r:mysqld_db_t:s0   /var/lib/mysql
drwxr-x---. Mysql mysql system_u:object_r:mysqld_log_t:s0   /var/log/mariadb

The SELinux type associated with mysqld port is mysqld_port_t, and it is in place by default. Here is the *semanage* command output that validates this information:

semanage port –l | grep mysqld
mysqld_port_t   tcp   1186, 3306, 63132-63164

From a SELinux boolean perspective, there are two booleans that are associated with MariaDB, and we can see this with the *getsebool* command:

getsebool –a | grep mysql

mysql_connect_any → off
selinuxuser_mysql_connect_enabled → off

These booleans allow or disallow the *mysqld* daemon process to connect to any port and users to connect to the local MariaDB server, respectively. Both booleans are turned off by default and do not need to be toggled for the exercises in this chapter.

By looking at the above SELinux settings for MariaDB, we can establish that there are no changes required to make it function smoothly in the SELinux enforcing mode.

Exercise 25-1: Install and Configure MariaDB

This exercise should be done on *server1*.

In this exercise, you will install the MariaDB server software, including any dependent packages. You will secure its installation and set up a password for the *root* user account to access MariaDB.

1. Install the MariaDB server software package:

   # **yum –y install mariadb-server**

   . . . .
   Installed:
     mariadb-server.x86_64 1:5.5.35-3.el7
   Dependency Installed:
     mariadb.x86_64 1:5.5.35-3.el7
   Complete!

2. Set MariaDB service to autostart at system reboots:

   # **systemctl enable mariadb**
   ln –s '/usr/lib/systemd/system/mariadb.service' '/etc/systemd/system/multi-user.target.wants/mariadb.service'

3. Secure access to MariaDB installation using the *mysql_secure_installation* script and enter information as highlighted:

   # **mysql_secure_installation**
   NOTE: RUNNING ALL PARTS OF THIS SCRIPT IS RECOMMENDED FOR ALL MariaDB
       SERVERS IN PRODUCTION USE! PLEASE READ EACH STEP CAREFULLY!
   In order to log into MariaDB to secure it, we'll need the current password for the root user. If you've
   just installed MariaDB, and you haven't set the root password yet, the password will be blank,
   so you should just press enter here.
   Enter current password for root (enter for none): **[Press the Enter key here]**
   OK, successfully used password, moving on...
   Setting the root password ensures that nobody can log into the MariaDB root user without the proper
   authorisation.
   Set root password? [Y/n]   **[Press Enter to set the root database user password]**
   New password: **[Enter a password for the database user *root*]**
   Re-enter new password: **[Re-enter the password for the database user *root*]**

Password updated successfully!
Reloading privilege tables..
 ... Success!
By default, a MariaDB installation has an anonymous user, allowing anyone to log into MariaDB without having to have a user account created for them. This is intended only for testing, and to make the installation go a bit smoother. You should remove them before moving into a production environment.
Remove anonymous users? [Y/n]   **[Press Enter to remove all anonymous users]**
 ... Success!
Normally, root should only be allowed to connect from 'localhost'. This ensures that someone cannot guess at the root password from the network.
Disallow root login remotely? [Y/n] **n**   **[Do not disallow remote root user login]**
 ... skipping.
By default, MariaDB comes with a database named 'test' that anyone can access. This is also intended only for testing, and should be removed before moving into a production environment.
Remove test database and access to it? [Y/n] **n**   **[Do not remove the test database]**
 - Dropping test database...
 ... Success!
 - Removing privileges on test database...
 ... Success!
Reloading the privilege tables will ensure that all changes made so far will take effect immediately.
Reload privilege tables now? [Y/n] **[Press Enter for the changes to take effect right away]**
 ... Success!
Cleaning up...
All done! If you've completed all of the above steps, your MariaDB installation should now be secure.
Thanks for using MariaDB!

4. Add the MariaDB service to firewalld persistently and reload the rules to allow traffic on port 3306:

    # **firewall-cmd --permanent --add-service mysql ; firewall-cmd --reload**

5. Start the MariaDB service and check its operational status:

    # **systemctl start mariadb**
    # **systemctl status mariadb**
    mariadb.service – MariaDB database server
      Loaded: loaded (/usr/lib/systemd/system/mariadb.service; enabled)
      Active: active (running) since Fri 2015-02-20 07:39:18 EST; 5s ago
      Process: 11225 ExecStartPost=/usr/libexec/mariadb-wait-ready $MAINPID (code=exited, status=0/SUCCESS)
      Process: 11146 ExecStartPre=/usr/libexec/mariadb-prepare-db-dir %n (code=exited, status=0/SUCCESS)
     Main PID: 11224 (mysqld_safe)
      Cgroup: /system.slice/mariadb.service
              ├─11224 /bin/sh /usr/bin/mysqld_safe –basedir...
              └─11382 /usr/libexec/mysqld –basedir=/usr –d...
     . . . .

This completes the installation and initial configuration of MariaDB service.

Starting the MariaDB Shell and Understanding its Usage

Once you have the MariaDB server software installed and *root* user password setup, you can invoke its shell interface with the *mysql* command. Enter the user password when prompted.

mysql –u root –p
Enter password:
Welcome to the MariaDB monitor. Commands end with ; or \g.
Your MariaDB connection id is 26
Server version: 5.5.35-MariaDB MariaDB Server
Copyright © 2000, 2013, Oracle, Monty Program Ab and others.
Type 'help;' or '\h' for help. Type '\c' to clear the current input statement.
MariaDB [(none)]>

The MariaDB shell prompt appears, indicating that you have successfully logged in to it. The prompt indicates that there is no current connection to a database. There are several subcommands available here, so type *help* for a list:

MariaDB [(none)]> **help**
General information about MariaDB can be found at http://mariadb.org
List of all MySQL commands:
Note that all text commands must be first on line and end with ';'
?   (\?) Synonym for `help'.
Clear   (\c) Clear the current input statement.
Connect   (\r) Reconnect to the server. Optional arguments are db and host.
Delimiter   (\d) Set statement delimiter.
Edit   (\e) Edit command with $EDITOR.
Ego   (\G) Send command to mysql server, display result vertically.
Exit   (\q) Exit mysql. Same as quit.
Go   (\g) Send command to mysql server.
Help   (\h) Display this help.
Nopager   (\n) Disable pager, print to stdout.
Notee   (\t) Don't write into outfile.
Pager   (\P) Set PAGER [to_pager]. Print the query results via PAGER.
Print   (\p) Print current command.
prompt   (\R) Change your mysql prompt.
Quit   (\q) Quit mysql.
Rehash   (\#) Rebuild completion hash.
Source   (\.) Execute an SQL script file. Takes a file name as an argument.
Status   (\s) Get status information from the server.
System   (\!) Execute a system shell command.
tee   (\T) Set outfile [to_outfile]. Append everything into given outfile.
Use   (\u) Use another database. Takes database name as argument.
Charset   (\C) Switch to another charset. Might be needed for processing binlog with multi-byte
            charsets.
Warnings   (\W) Show warnings after every statement.
Nowarning   (\w) Don't show warnings after every statement.

For server side help, type 'help contents'

All subcommands have a short description indicating what they are used for. We will use the *status*, *use*, and *exit* subcommands in this chapter.

Displaying Connection Status

The *status* subcommand at the MariaDB prompt can be used to display the connection status:

MariaDB [(none)]> **status**
----
mysql Ver 15.1 Distrib 5.5.35-MariaDB, for Linux (x86_64) using readline 5.1
Connection id: 11
Current database:
Current user: root@localhost
SSL: Not in use
Current pager: stdout
Using outfile: "
Using delimiter: ;
Server: MariaDB
Server version: 5.5.35-MariaDB MariaDB Server
Protocol version: 10
Connection: Localhost via UNIX socket
Server characterset: latin1
Db   characterset: latin1
Client characterset: utf8
Conn. characterset: utf8
UNIX socket: /var/lib/mysql/mysql.sock
Uptime: 24 min 30 sec
Threads: 1 Questions: 63 Slow queries: 0 Opens: 15 Flush tables: 2 Open tables: 24 Queries per second avg: 0.042

The output provides general information about the connection, including an ID assigned to this session, the database it is connected to, the user name who invoked this session, and other miscellaneous information.

Subcommands for Database and Table Operations

The *mysql* MariaDB interface offers several subcommands for database management. Table 25-3 describes them.

Subcommand	Description
Database and Table Operations	
create	Creates a database or table.
drop	Drops a database or table.
show	Lists databases or tables.
Table Operations	
delete	Removes a record from a table.
describe (or desc)	Shows the structure of a table.

Subcommand	Description
insert	Inserts data into a table.
rename	Renames a table.
select	Retrieves data from a table.
update	Updates a record in a table.

Table 25-3 Database Administration Commands

Table 25-3 separates subcommands specific to both databases and tables, and tables only. Typical operations performed on both databases and tables include creating, dropping, and listing (or showing) them. Likewise, typical operations for table-only administration include the rename function, as well as inserting, updating, querying, and deleting records in tables.

Each subcommand executed at the MariaDB prompt expects a semicolon (:) at the end.

The usage of these subcommands is demonstrated in the following exercises.

Exercise 25-2: Create Database and Table, and Insert Records

This exercise should be done on *server1*.

In this exercise, you will create a database called *rhce*. You will create a table called *scientists* in this database using column names as shown in Table 25-4 below.

Sno	FirstName	LastName	City	Country	Age
1	Albert	Einstein	Ulm	Germany	76
2	Isaac	Newton	Woolsthorpe	UK	84
3	Marie	Curie	Warsaw	Poland	67
4	Galileo	Galilei	Pisa	Italy	78
5	Thomas	Edison	Milan	USA	84
6	Alexander	Bell	Edinburg	UK	75
7	Louis	Pasteur	Dole	France	73
8	Nicolaus	Copernicus	Toruri	Poland	70
9	James	Maxwell	Edinburg	UK	48
10	Pierre	Curie	Paris	France	47

Table 25-4 For use with Exercise 25-2

You will insert all the records as shown in Table 25-4 into the table and confirm their addition.

1. List what databases are available on the system using the *show* subcommand:

   MariaDB [none]> **show databases;**
   ```
   +------------------------+
   | Database               |
   +------------------------+
   | information_schema     |
   | mysql                  |
   +------------------------+
   ```
   2 rows in set (0.00 sec)

It shows the presence of two default databases.

2. Create a database called *rhce* using the *create* subcommand:

> MariaDB [none]> **create database rhce;**
> Query OK, 1 row affected (0.00 sec)

3. Verify the database creation using the *show* subcommand:

> MariaDB [none]> **show databases;**
> ```
> +--------------------+
> | Database           |
> +--------------------+
> | information_schema |
> | mysql              |
> | rhce               |
> +--------------------+
> ```
> 3 rows in set (0.00 sec)

The output shows a new database called *rhce* on the list.

4. Select the new database for further actions using the *use* subcommand:

> MariaDB [(none)]> **use rhce;**
> Database changed
> MariaDB [rhce]>

Observe that the prompt has changed to reflect the selected database.

5. Create a table called *scientists* in the *rhce* database using the *create* subcommand. For text columns, limit the number of characters to 20, and use integer type for Sno and Age columns.

> MariaDB [rhce]> **create table scientists (Sno int,FirstName varchar(20),LastName varchar(20),City varchar(20),Country varchar(20),Age int);**
> Query OK, 0 rows affected (0.10 sec)

6. Display the structure of the table with the *describe* (or *desc*) subcommand:

> MariaDB [rhce]> **desc scientists;**
> ```
> +-----------+-------------+------+-----+---------+-------+
> | Field     | Type        | Null | Key | Default | Extra |
> +-----------+-------------+------+-----+---------+-------+
> | Sno       | int(11)     | YES  |     | NULL    |       |
> | FirstName | varchar(20) | YES  |     | NULL    |       |
> | LastName  | varchar(20) | YES  |     | NULL    |       |
> | City      | varchar(20) | YES  |     | NULL    |       |
> | Country   | varchar(20) | YES  |     | NULL    |       |
> | Age       | int(11)     | YES  |     | NULL    |       |
> +-----------+-------------+------+-----+---------+-------+
> ```
> 6 rows in set (0.00 sec)

The output shows six columns. The first column indicates the field name, the second column specifies the type of data that can be stored in the field and any character limits that are set, the third column can be left to a null value, the fourth column denotes whether the field is a table key, the fifth column shows the default value for the field, and the last column displays any special properties associated with the field.

7. Insert all the records to the table using the *insert* subcommand and ensuring that values are enclosed within quotes:

MariaDB [rhce]> **insert into scientists values('1','Albert','Einstein','Ulm','Germany','76');**
MariaDB [rhce]> **insert into scientists values('2','Isaac','Newton','Woolsthorpe','UK','84');**
MariaDB [rhce]> **insert into scientists values('3','Marie','Curie','Warsaw','Poland','67');**
MariaDB [rhce]> **insert into scientists values('4','Galileo','Galilei','Pisa','Italy','78');**
MariaDB [rhce]> **insert into scientists values('5','Thomas','Edison','Milan','USA','84');**
MariaDB [rhce]> **insert into scientists values('6','Alexander','Bell','Edinburg','UK','75');**
MariaDB [rhce]> **insert into scientists values('7','Louis','Pasteur','Dole','France','73');**
MariaDB [rhce]> **insert into scientists values('8','Nicolaus','Copernicus','Toruri','Poland','70');**
MariaDB [rhce]> **insert into scientists values('9','James','Maxwell','Edinburg','UK','48');**
MariaDB [rhce]> **insert into scientists values('10','Pierre','Curie','Paris','France','47');**

8. Query all the records to confirm their addition to the table using the *select* subcommand:

MariaDB [rhce]> **select * from scientists;**

Sno	FirstName	LastName	City	Country	Age
1	Albert	Einstein	Ulm	Germany	76
2	Isaac	Newton	Woolsthorpe	UK	84
3	Marie	Curie	Warsaw	Poland	67
4	Galileo	Galilei	Pisa	Italy	78
5	Thomas	Edison	Milan	USA	84
6	Alexander	Bell	Edinburg	UK	75
7	Louis	Pasteur	Dole	France	73
8	Nicolaus	Copernicus	Toruri	Poland	70
9	James	Maxwell	Edinburg	UK	48
10	Pierre	Curie	Paris	France	47

10 rows in set (0.00 sec)

The above confirms the addition of all ten records to the *scientists* table in the *rhce* database.

Exercise 25-3: Perform SQL Queries against a Database

This exercise should be done on *server1*.

In this exercise, you will perform a number of queries against the database *rhce*.

1. Query all stored records:

   MariaDB [rhce]> **select * from scientists;**

Sno	FirstName	LastName	City	Country	Age
1	Albert	Einstein	Ulm	Germany	76
2	Isaac	Newton	Woolsthorpe	UK	84
3	Marie	Curie	Warsaw	Poland	67
4	Galileo	Galilei	Pisa	Italy	78
5	Thomas	Edison	Milan	USA	84
6	Alexander	Bell	Edinburg	UK	75
7	Louis	Pasteur	Dole	France	73
8	Nicolaus	Copernicus	Toruri	Poland	70
9	James	Maxwell	Edinburg	UK	48
10	Pierre	Curie	Paris	France	47

   10 rows in set (0.00 sec)

2. Query records for all scientists who died at the age of 84:

   MariaDB [rhce]> **select * from scientists where Age=84;**

Sno	FirstName	LastName	City	Country	Age
2	Isaac	Newton	Woolsthorpe	UK	84
5	Thomas	Edison	Milan	USA	84

   2 rows in set (0.00 sec)

3. Query records for all scientists who lived for 75 or more years:

   MariaDB [rhce]> **select * from scientists where Age > 75;**

   . . . .
1	Albert	Einstein	Ulm	Germany	76
2	Isaac	Newton	Woolsthorpe	UK	84
4	Galileo	Galilei	Pisa	Italy	78
5	Thomas	Edison	Milan	USA	84

   4 rows in set (0.00 sec)

4. Query records for all scientists with last name "Curie":

    MariaDB [rhce]> **select * from scientists where LastName='Curie';**

    ....
    | 3 | Marie | Curie | Warsaw | Poland | 67 |
    | 10 | Pierre | Curie | Paris | France | 47 |
    +------+-----------------+--------------+------------------+-----------+------+
    2 rows in set (0.00 sec)

5. Query records for all scientists who were born in Poland and Germany:

    MariaDB [rhce]> **select * from scientists where Country='Poland' or Country='Germany';**

    ....
    | 1 | Albert | Einstein | Ulm | Germany | 76 |
    | 3 | Marie | Curie | Warsaw | Poland | 67 |
    | 8 | Nicolaus | Copernicus | Toruri | Poland | 70 |
    +------+-----------------+--------------+------------------+-----------+------+
    3 rows in set (0.00 sec)

6. Query records for all scientists sorted by their first names:

    MariaDB [rhce]> **select * from scientists order by FirstName;**

    ....
    | 1 | Albert | Einstein | Ulm | Germany | 76 |
    | 6 | Alexander | Bell | Edinburg | UK | 75 |
    | 4 | Galileo | Galilei | Pisa | Italy | 78 |
    | 2 | Isaac | Newton | Woolsthorpe | UK | 84 |
    | 9 | James | Maxwell | Edinburg | UK | 48 |
    | 7 | Louis | Pasteur | Dole | France | 73 |
    | 3 | Marie | Curie | Warsaw | Poland | 67 |
    | 8 | Nicolaus | Copernicus | Toruri | Poland | 70 |
    | 10 | Pierre | Curie | Paris | France | 47 |
    | 5 | Thomas | Edison | Milan | USA | 84 |
    +------+-----------------+--------------+------------------+-----------+------+
    10 rows in set (0.00 sec)

7. Query records for all scientists sorted by their last names in descending (desc) order:

    MariaDB [rhce]> **select * from scientists order by LastName desc;**

    ....
    | 7 | Louis | Pasteur | Dole | France | 73 |
    | 2 | Isaac | Newton | Woolsthorpe | UK | 84 |
    | 9 | James | Maxwell | Edinburg | UK | 48 |
    | 4 | Galileo | Galilei | Pisa | Italy | 78 |
    | 1 | Albert | Einstein | Ulm | Germany | 76 |
    | 5 | Thomas | Edison | Milan | USA | 84 |
    | 10 | Pierre | Curie | Paris | France | 47 |
    | 3 | Marie | Curie | Warsaw | Poland | 67 |

```
| 8 | Nicolaus   | Copernicus | Toruri   | Poland | 70 |
| 6 | Alexander  | Bell       | Edinburg | UK     | 75 |
+------+-----------------+----------------+-----------------+-----------+------+
```
10 rows in set (0.00 sec)

8. Query records for all scientists who were born in countries starting with the letter U and followed by any letters (the % sign is used as a wildcard character):

MariaDB [rhce]> **select * from scientists where country like 'U%';**

. . . .
```
| 2 | Isaac   | Newton  | Woolsthorpe | UK  | 84 |
| 5 | Thomas  | Edison  | Milan       | USA | 84 |
| 6 | Alexander | Bell  | Edinburg    | UK  | 75 |
| 9 | James   | Maxwell | Edinburg    | UK  | 48 |
+------+-----------------+----------------+-----------------+-----------+------+
```
4 rows in set (0.00 sec)

9. Query records for all scientists who were born in France, Germany, and Italy, with output sorted in reverse on the first column:

MariaDB [rhce]> **select * from scientists where country='France' or country='Germany' or country='Italy' order by Sno desc;**

. . . .
```
| 10 | Pierre   | Curie    | Paris | France  | 47 |
| 7  | Louis    | Pasteur  | Dole  | France  | 73 |
| 4  | Galileo  | Galilei  | Pisa  | Italy   | 78 |
| 1  | Albert   | Einstein | Ulm   | Germany | 76 |
+------+-----------------+----------------+-----------------+-----------+------+
```
4 rows in set (0.00 sec)

10. Query records for all scientists who died in their 70s:

MariaDB [rhce]> **select * from scientists where age like '7%';**

. . . .
```
| 1 | Albert    | Einstein   | Ulm      | Germany | 76 |
| 4 | Galileo   | Galilei    | Pisa     | Italy   | 78 |
| 6 | Alexander | Bell       | Edinburg | UK      | 75 |
| 7 | Louis     | Pasteur    | Dole     | France  | 73 |
| 8 | Nicolaus  | Copernicus | Toruri   | Poland  | 70 |
+------+-----------------+----------------+-----------------+-------------+------+
```
5 rows in set (0.00 sec)

Exercise 25-4: Rename Table, and Update and Delete Records

This exercise should be done on *server1*.

In this exercise, you will rename the table *scientists* to *science* without affecting the data that it contains. You will update two records in the table and then delete them.

1. Rename the table *scientists* to *science* using the *rename* subcommand:

    MariaDB [rhce]> rename table scientists to science;
    Query OK, 0 rows affected (0.37 sec)

2. Confirm the above change:

    MariaDB [rhce]> show tables;
    ```
    +------------------+
    | Tables_in_rhce   |
    +------------------+
    | science          |
    +------------------+
    1 row in set (0.00 sec)
    ```

3. Verify that the records in the renamed table are unaffected:

    MariaDB [rhce]> select * from science;
    ```
    . . . . . . . .
    |  1  | Albert    | Einstein   | Ulm         | Germany | 76 |
    |  2  | Isaac     | Newton     | Woolsthorpe | UK      | 84 |
    |  3  | Marie     | Curie      | Warsaw      | Poland  | 67 |
    |  4  | Galileo   | Galilei    | Pisa        | Italy   | 78 |
    |  5  | Thomas    | Edison     | Milan       | USA     | 84 |
    |  6  | Alexander | Bell       | Edinburg    | UK      | 75 |
    |  7  | Louis     | Pasteur    | Dole        | France  | 73 |
    |  8  | Nicolaus  | Copernicus | Toruri      | Poland  | 70 |
    |  9  | James     | Maxwell    | Edinburg    | UK      | 48 |
    | 10  | Pierre    | Curie      | Paris       | France  | 47 |
    +------+----------------+--------------+----------------+----------+------+
    10 rows in set (0.00 sec)
    ```

4. Replace the fields Albert Einstein with Benjamin Franklin using the *update* subcommand:

    MariaDB [rhce]> update science set FirstName='Benjamin',LastName='Franklin' where Sno='1';
    Query OK, 1 row affected (0.06 sec)
    Rows matched: 1 Changed: 1 Warnings: 0

5. Confirm the above change by querying the table:

    MariaDB [rhce]> select * from science;
    ```
    . . . . . . . .
    |  1  | Benjamin | Franklin  | Ulm      | Germany | 76 |
    . . . . . . . .
    ```

6. Replace the fields Paris and 73 for Sno 7 with Cannes and 75 using the *update* subcommand:

    MariaDB [rhce]> **update science set City='Cannes',Age='75' where Sno='7';**
    Query OK, 1 row affected (0.04 sec)
    Rows matched: 1 Changed: 1 Warnings: 0

7. Confirm the above change:

    MariaDB [rhce]> **select * from science;**

    . . . .
    | 7 | Louis | Pasteur | Cannes | France | 75 |
    . . . .

8. Delete record numbers 1 and 7 from the table using the *delete* subcommand:

    MariaDB [rhce]> **delete from science where Sno='1' or Sno='7';**
    Query OK, 2 rows affected (0.36 sec)

9. Confirm the deletion:

    MariaDB [rhce]> **select * from science;**

    . . . .

2	Isaac	Newton	Woolsthorpe	UK	84
3	Marie	Curie	Warsaw	Poland	67
4	Galileo	Galilei	Pisa	Italy	78
5	Thomas	Edison	Milan	USA	84
6	Alexander	Bell	Edinburg	UK	75
8	Nicolaus	Copernicus	Toruri	Poland	70
9	James	Maxwell	Edinburg	UK	48
10	Pierre	Curie	Paris	France	47

    +------+-----------------+---------------+-----------------+-----------+------+
    8 rows in set (0.00 sec)

Backing Up and Restoring a Database or Table

Backup is a function of duplicating data to an alternative location for use in the event of a data loss. The alternative location is usually an external physical medium attached to the system locally or accessible via the network. A backup can also be redirected to a file for some specific use.

Restore is the opposite function of backup. It retrieves data from a backup location and puts it back to its original place.

There are two types of backups: *physical* backups and *logical* backups. A physical backup is a backup of actual files that may belong to an operating system, a database, or some other application. In contrast, a logical backup consists of SQL statements necessary to restore the data in case of data loss. This type of backup does not include database configuration or log files. A logical backup can be used for data migration from one server to another.

MariaDB offers a tool called *mysqldump* for creating logical backups of data. To restore logical backups, the *mysql* tool can be used. The syntax to employ these tools for backup and restore is provided below.

To backup all databases on the system, use the --all-databases option with the command and redirect the output to a file:

mysqldump –u root –p --all-databases > db_bkp_all.sql

To restore a specific database, such as DB1, from the above:

mysql –u root –p DB1 < db_bkp_all.sql

To backup specific databases, use the --databases option with the command and specify the database names to be backed up:

mysqldump –u root –p --databases DB1 DB2 DB3 > db_bkp_db123.sql

To restore all three databases from the above:

mysql –u root –p DB1 DB2 DB3 < db_bkp_db123.sql

To backup specific tables, such as tbl1 and tbl2, located in a database called DB1:

mysqldump –u root –p DB1 tbl1 tbl2 > tbl_bkp_tbl12.sql

To restore only tbl1 from the above:

mysql –u root –p DB1 tbl1 < tbl_bkp_tbl12.sql;

Exercise 25-5: Backup, Drop, Recreate, and Restore a Database
This exercise should be done on *server1*.

In this exercise, you will create a dump of the database *rhce* in a file in the */tmp* directory and then drop the entire database. You will recreate the database and restore the original structure from the dump.

1. Create a dump of the *rhce* database using the *mysqldump* command from the OS prompt and store it in *rhce_db.sql* file in the */tmp* directory:

    # **mysqldump –u root –p rhce > /tmp/rhce_db.sql**
    Enter password:

2. Drop the *rhce* database:

    # **mysql –u root –p**
    . . . .
    MariaDB [(none)]> **drop database rhce;**
    Query OK, 1 row affected (0.05 sec)

3. Confirm the removal of the database:

```
MariaDB [(none)]> show databases;
+--------------------+
| Database           |
+--------------------+
| information_schema |
| mysql              |
+--------------------+
2 rows in set (0.00 sec)
```

4. Recreate the *rhce* database and exit the MariaDB shell:

```
MariaDB [(none)]> create database rhce;
Query OK, 1 row affected (0.00 sec)
MariaDB [(none)]> quit
```

5. Restore the *rhce* database from the */tmp/rhce_db.sql* dump using the *mysql* command:

```
# mysql –u root –p rhce < /tmp/rhce_db.sql
Enter password:
```

6. Log back in with the *rhce* database selected and verify the presence of the *science* table:

```
# mysql –u root –p rhce
Enter password:
. . . . . . . .
MariaDB [(rhce)]> show tables;
+-----------------+
| Tables_in_rhce  |
+-----------------+
| science         |
+-----------------+
1 row in set (0.00 sec)
```

7. Query the *science* table; you should be able to see all the records before the database was deleted:

```
MariaDB [(rhce)]> select * from science;
+------+-----------+------------+------------+----------+------+
| Sno  | FirstName | LastName   | City       | Country  | Age  |
+------+-----------+------------+------------+----------+------+
|    2 | Isaac     | Newton     | Woolsthorpe| UK       |   84 |
|    3 | Marie     | Curie      | Warsaw     | Poland   |   67 |
|    4 | Galileo   | Galilei    | Pisa       | Italy    |   78 |
|    5 | Thomas    | Edison     | Milan      | USA      |   84 |
|    6 | Alexander | Bell       | Edinburg   | UK       |   75 |
|    8 | Nicolaus  | Copernicus | Toruri     | Poland   |   70 |
|    9 | James     | Maxwell    | Edinburg   | UK       |   48 |
```

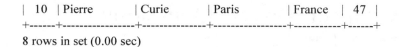

| 10 | Pierre | Curie | Paris | France | 47 |

8 rows in set (0.00 sec)

Now that you have completed all of the exercises, you may go ahead and drop the table or the database. To remove the table along with all the records that it contains, run the *drop* subcommand and verify with *show*:

MariaDB [(rhce)]> **drop table science;**
MariaDB [(rhce)]> **show tables;**

Similarly, you can drop the database along with all the tables that it contains:

MariaDB [(rhce)]> **drop database rhce;**
MariaDB [(rhce)]> **show databases;**

If you want to restore the database, the dump is in place in the */tmp* directory.

Chapter Summary

This chapter presented MariaDB database software and discussed its administration. The chapter introduced the concepts of databases, database management systems, and relational databases, and provided an overview of MariaDB and how it originated. Just like any other network service, MariaDB has its own service daemon, commands, configuration files, log file, service port, SELinux requirements, and so on. The various database administration operations that are executed on databases and enclosed objects were also discussed. A few exercises were presented to strengthen this learning. Finally, the chapter discussed backup and restore functions, and how to use the available tools to perform these tasks.

Chapter Review Questions

1. Define the term "database" in a simple sentence.
2. What does DBMS stand for?
3. What are the three major components in a table?
4. A relational database has two or more tables linked by a key. True or False?
5. What is the difference between a primary key and a foreign key?
6. MariaDB is a fork of MySQL database. True or False.
7. What is the name of the server daemon for MariaDB?
8. Which MariaDB software package contains the mysql shell interface program?
9. Which port is opened in the firewall to allow network access to MariaDB?
10. What are the six operations mentioned in this chapter that can be performed on a database?
11. What are the eleven operations mentioned in this chapter that can be performed on a table?
12. Write the mysql command to create a database called *rhcsa*.
13. Write a query to display all records in a table matching the name "Abraham".
14. What are the two major types of backups?
15. What is included in a logical backup?
16. Which command is used to create logical database backups?

Answers to Chapter Review Questions

1. A database is a collection of data.
2. DBMS is an acronym for Database Management System.
3. A table is composed of rows, columns, and values.
4. True.
5. A primary key is used within a table to uniquely identify a record, whereas a foreign key is used to relate two or more tables.
6. True.
7. The MariaDB daemon name is *mysqld*.
8. The mariadb software package includes this client program.
9. MariaDB server port number is 3306.
10. The five operations that can be performed on a database are create, list, use, drop, backup, and restore.
11. The eleven operations that can be performed on a table are create, describe, list, rename, drop, backup, restore, insert, update, query, and delete.
12. The command to create database called *rhcsa* will be "create database rhcsa;".
13. The query statement would be "select * from <table> where name='Abraham';".
14. The two major types of backups are physical and logical backups.
15. A logical backup includes the SQL statements necessary to rebuild a database.
16. The *mysqldump* command is used to create logical backups of databases.

DIY Challenge Labs

The following labs are useful to strengthen the concepts and topics learned in this chapter. It is expected that you perform these labs without any additional help. A step-by-step guide is not provided, as the implementation of these labs requires the knowledge that has been presented in this chapter. Use defaults or your own thinking for missing information.

Lab 25-1: Create a Database and Table, and Add Records

Install MariaDB software for both server and client. Create a database called *db1* and create a table called *tb1* in it. The table should include data about the five tallest skyscrapers in the world. It should have five columns: Height, Skyscraper Name, City, Country, and Continent. Perform SQL queries on the building records using different criteria.

Height	Skyscrapper Name	City	Country	Continent
828	Burj Khalifa	Dubai	UAE	Asia
632	Shanghai Tower	Shangai	China	Asia
601	Makkah Clock Royal Tower	Makkah	Saudi Arabia	Asia
541	One World Trade Center	New York	USA	North America
509	Taipei 101	Taipei	Taiwan	Asia

Lab 25-2: Update and Delete Records

Delete the first three records from *db1* and replace them with the three tallest concrete towers in the world (below table). Update the last two records in *db1* with the fourth and fifth tallest concrete structures (below table). Perform SQL queries using different criteria.

Height	Concrete Tower Name	City	Country	Continent
553	CN Tower	Toronto	Canada	North America
540	Ostankino Tower	Moscow	Russia	Europe
468	Oriental Pearl Tower	Shanghai	China	Asia
435	Milad Tower	Tehran	Iran	Asia
421	Kuala Lumpur Tower	Kuala Lumpur	Malaysia	Asia

Lab 25-3: Rebuild a Database

Take a logical backup of the *db1* database and then drop the database. Rebuild the database and confirm the table and all records in it.

Appendix A: Sample RHCSA Exam 1

Time Duration: 2.5 hours
Passing Score: 70% (210 out of 300)
Instructions: The RHCSA exam, EX200, is offered electronically on a desktop system running RHEL7. The exam presents a list of tasks that are to be completed within the stipulated time. Firewall and SELinux need to be taken into account. All settings performed on the systems must survive system reboots or you will not be given credits. Access to the Internet, printed material, and electronic devices is prohibited during the exam.

Setup for the Sample Exam:

Install RHEL7 (or its clone) on a physical system called hv1 with hypervisor and desktop/X Window support. Install a virtual machine called rhcsa1 and load minimal RHEL7 without GUI support. Do not configure a hostname and network interface duing rhcsa1 installation. Leave 2GB of disk space free in the system disk.

Instructions:

Instruction 01: Tasks furnished here are in addition to the exercises and labs presented in the RHCSA section of this book. No solutions are provided.

Instruction 02: Do not consult the material in this book or browse the Internet while taking this sample exam. However, you can refer to the online help and the documentation located in the /usr/share/doc directory.

Instruction 03: This exam should be done in a text console using commands or text tools.

Instruction 04: Perform all tasks on rhcsa1 unless otherwise indicated.

Instruction 05: You can reboot the system after completing each task or a few tasks, or wait until all tasks have been finished. Do not forget to retest the configuration after the reboot.

Instruction 06: Use your own judgement for making decisions where necessary.

Tasks:

Task 01: Assuming the root user password is lost for rhcsa1 and your system is running in multiuser target with no current root session open. Boot the system into an appropriate target and change the root user password to root1234.

Task 02: Configure the primary network interface with hostname rhcsa1.example.com (alias rhcsa1), IP address 192.168.0.251/24, gateway 192.168.0.1, and nameserver 192.168.0.1. You may use different IP assignments.

Task 03: Set the default boot target to multiuser.

Task 04: Set SELinux to enforcing mode.

Task 05: Perform a case-insensitive search for the pattern "then" in the /etc/profile file and save the result in the /var/tmp/pattern.txt. Make sure that empty lines are not included.

Task 06: Activate and start firewalld.

Task 07: Set the primary command prompt for user root to display the hostname, username, and current working directory information in that order.

Task 08: Create users barry, harry, larry, mary, and gary with home directories in /home. Set their passwords to Temp123$ and make accounts for mary and barry expire on December 31, 2017. Users larry and gary should have their secondary groups set to group dba (create this group if it does not exist).

Task 09: Create a directory called testdir2 as user mary in her home directory and set default ACLs on it for user barry for read and write access.

Task 10: Set up a FTP yum repository in the /var/ftp/pub/rhel7 directory on hv1, and configure a repo on rhcsa1.

Task 11: Create a logical volume called linuxadm of size equal to 10 LEs in vgtest volume group (create vgtest with PE size 32MB) with mount point /mnt/linuxadm and xfs file system structures. Create a file called linuxadmfile in the mount point. Set the file system to automatically mount at each system reboot.

Task 12: Add a group called linuxadmin and change group membership on /mnt/linuxadm to linuxadmin. Set read/write/execute permissions on /linuxadm for the owner and group members, and no permissions for others.

Task 13: Extend linuxadm file system in vgtest online by 35MB without losing any data.

Task 14: Create a swap partition of size 65MB on an available disk. Use its UUID and ensure it is activated after every system reboot.

Task 15: Create a standard partition of size 60MB on any available disk and format it with ext4 file system structures. Mount the file system on /mnt/stdext persistently using its UUID. Create a file called stdextfile in the mount point.

Task 16: Create a directory /direct01 and apply SELinux contexts for /root on it.

Task 17: Set up a cron job as the root user to search for core files in the /var directory and list them in /var/log/corefiles. This job should run every Monday at 1:20am system time.

Task 18: Use star and gzip to create a compressed archive of the /usr/local directory. Store the archive in /root using any name of your choice.

Task 19: Enable at access for user barry and deny for user gary.

Task 20: Modify the bootloader and set the default autoboot timer value to 2 seconds.

Reboot the system and validate the configuration.

Appendix B: Sample RHCSA Exam 2

===

Time Duration: 2.5 hours
Passing Score: 70% (210 out of 300)
Instructions: The RHCSA exam, EX200, is offered electronically on a desktop system running RHEL7. The exam presents a list of tasks that are to be completed within the stipulated time. Firewall and SELinux need to be taken into account. All settings performed on the systems must survive system reboots or you will not be given credits. Access to the Internet, printed material, and electronic devices is prohibited during the exam.

Setup for the Sample Exam:
Install RHEL7 (or its clone) on a physical system called hv1 with hypervisor and desktop/X Window support. Install a virtual machine called rhcsa2 and load minimal RHEL7 without GUI support. Configure hostname rhcsa2 and the primary network interface with IP 192.168.0.201/24, gateway 192.168.0.1, and DNS 192.168.0.1 during installation. Leave 2GB of disk space free in the system disk. You may want to build virtual machine for this sample exam on an existing hypervisor.

Instructions:
Instruction 01: Tasks furnished here are in addition to the exercises and labs presented in the RHCSA section of this book. No solutions are provided.

Instruction 02: Do not consult the material in this book or browse the Internet while taking this sample exam. However, you can refer to the online help and the documentation located in the /usr/share/doc directory.

Instruction 03: This exam should be done in a text console using commands or text tools.

Instruction 04: Perform all tasks on rhcsa2 unless otherwise indicated.

Instruction 05: You can reboot the system after completing each task or a few tasks, or wait until all tasks have been finished. Do not forget to retest the configuration after the reboot.

Instruction 06: Use your own judgement for making decisions where necessary.

Tasks:

Task 01: Create a user account called jerry with UID 2929 and shell /bin/tcsh. Create a user account called terry without login access. Create another user account called mary with all the default values. Set their passwords to Temp123$.

Task 02: Create a file called testfile as user jerry in his home directory and give user mary read and execute rights, and user terry no permissions at all. Make sure that existing rights on the file are unaltered.

Task 03: Create a directory called /testdir1 as root and configure it for collaboration among members of the admins group. Create the group with members jerry and terry.

Task 04: Set permissions on /linuxadm so that all files created underneath get the membership of the parent group.

Task 05: Create a logical volume lvol1 of size 100MB in vg02 volume group with mount point /mnt/lvol1 and ext4 file system structures. Create a file called lvolfile in the mount point.

Task 06: Create a swap logical volume called swapvol1 of size equal to 12 LEs in vg02 volume group, and activate it persistently.

Task 07: Create a standard partition of size 70MB on any available disk and format it with xfs file system structures. Assign a label called stdxfs1 to the file system. Mount the file system on /mnt/stdxfs persistently using its label. Create a file called stdxfsfile in the mount point.

Task 08: Search for all files in the entire directory structure that have been modified in the past 30 days and save their copies in /var/tmp/modfiles.txt.

Task 09: Configure /mnt/lvol1 so that users can delete their own files and not other users'.

Task 10: Change the default base home directory for new users to /usr.

Task 11: Enable cron access for user jerry and deny for user terry.

Task 12: Set up a cron job as user mary to display the output of the /usr/local directory at 15:35 every day.

Task 13: Use dc=example, dc=com, and LDAP server vm2.example.com with a certificate sitting in /etc/openldap/cacerts to allow ldapuser1 to be able to log on to rhcsa2.

Task 14: Upgrade the kernel to a higher version and set it as the default boot kernel. The existing kernel and its configuration must remain intact. Download a kernel from rpmfind.net for this task.

Task 15: Configure the system as an NTP client of server hv2 (configure NTP service on hv2; see RHCE section).

Task 16: Use tar and bzip2 to create a compressed archive of the /etc directory. Store the archive in /root using any name of your choice.

Task 17: Configure AutoFS to automatically mount the home directory for user victor under /dirnet when he logs on to the system (see the chapter on NFS in the RHCE section on how to configure the server side).

Task 18: Open port 100 in firewalld in the default zone.

Task 19: Perform a case-sensitive search for the pattern "file" in the /etc/profile file and save the output in the /var/tmp/pattern.txt file.

Task 20: Set up a FTP yum repository in the /var/ftp/pub/rhel7 directory on hv2, and configure a repo on rhcsa2.

Reboot the system and validate the configuration.

Appendix C: Sample RHCE Exam 1

Time Duration: 4 hours

Passing Score: 70% (210 out of 300)

Instructions: The RHCE exam, EX300, is offered electronically on a desktop system running RHEL7. The exam presents a list of tasks that are to be completed within the stipulated time. Firewall and SELinux are active and running, and they need to be taken into account. All settings performed on the systems must survive system reboots or you will not be given credits. Access to the Internet, printed material, and electronic devices is prohibited during the exam.

Setup for the Sample Exam:

Install RHEL7 (or its clone) on a physical system called hv3 with hypervisor and desktop/X Window support. Install two virtual machines (rhce1 and rhce2) and load minimal RHEL7 without GUI support. The virtual machines should have their primary interfaces configured with appropriate IP addresses on the same network.

Instructions for this Sample Exam:

Instruction 01: Tasks furnished here are in addition to the exercises and labs presented in the RHCSA section of this book. No solutions are provided.

Instruction 02: Do not consult the material in this book or browse the Internet while taking this sample exam. However, you can refer to the online help and the documentation located in the /usr/share/doc directory.

Instruction 03: This exam should be done in a text console using commands or text tools.

Instruction 04: You can reboot the system after completing each task or a few tasks, or wait until all tasks have been finished. Do not forget to retest the configuration after the reboot.

Instruction 05: Create user accounts harry, barry, and mary on both virtual machines and the hypervisor server, and set a password for them.

Instruction 06: Use your own judgement for making decisions where necessary.

Tasks:

Task 01: Set SELinux to enforcing mode on both virtual machines.

Task 02: Establish a caching DNS server on rhce1 to serve the local network.

Task 03: Configure the resolver on both virtual machines to use the caching DNS server.

Task 04: Configure LDAP client on rhce1 with search base dc=example, dc=com and self-signed certificate over SSL/TLS. This task presumes that LDAP service is running on rhce2 for domain example.com.

Task 05: Deny ssh access to user barry from example.net and all users from 192.168.0.200 on both virtual machines.

Task 06: Disable direct root login access via ssh on rhce2.

Task 07: Configure Apache on rhce1 to listen on port 22222 with DocumentRoot /var/www/client1 and password-protected access to user gary. Disallow access to this web server from systems in domain example.net.

Task 08: Configure a secure virtual host called svhostlab1.example.com on rhce1 accessible only from the local network. Create a self-signed certificate and use it.

Task 09: Configure Postfix on rhce2 so that mail destined for hv3 from localhost for user barry is received on rhce2. The mail should appear to have originated from the hostname. Log in as barry on rhce2 and verify the receipt.

Task 10: Modify Postfix on rhce2 so that mail destined for hv3 from local network for user harry is received on rhce2. The mail should appear to have originated from example.org domain. Log in as harry on rhce2 and verify the receipt.

Task 11: Add a route on rhce1 via an appropriate network interface to reach 192.168.10 network.

Task 12: Create a 1GB disk on hv3 and assign it to rhce1. Configure vg10 on the new disk on rhce1 and create a logical partition called lvoliscsi of 100 LEs. Configure iSCSI target on rhce1 using the logical volume and present it as a block disk to rhce2.

Task 13: Configure iSCSI initiator on rhce2 using the block device presented from rhce1. Create a volume group called iscsivg with 16MB PE size on rhce1 and then use 20 LEs to create a logical volume called initiatorlv in the volume group. Construct XFS file system structures in initiatorlv and mount it on /mnt/iscsilv on rhce2.

Task 14: Create a script on rhce1 so that it prints RHCSA when RHCE is entered, and vice versa. If no arguments are supplied, the script should print a usage message and exit.

Task 15: Configure IPv6 addresses on the primary interfaces on both rhce1 and rhce2. Assign hostnames rhce1ipv6 and rhce2ipv6. Add their entries to the hosts table. Run ping6 tests to verify the connectivity. Issue ping tests on the primary IPv4 addresses also to verify their operational state.

Task 16: Create four virtual interfaces on the hypervisor and assign two to rhce1 and the other two to rhce2. Configure bonding with IP assignments of your choice on both virtual machines. Run ping tests to verify the connection. Disable one of the interfaces while ping running. You should not notice a change. The bonding interfaces should be active after system reboots.

Task 17: Create two directories /smb1 and /smb2 on rhce1 and share them with Samba to rhce2 and example.com domain, respectively. Share /smb1 in read/write mode to admins group (create if it does not exist, and add harry and barry to it). Share /smb2 with read-only access to user mary only. Access and mount /smb1 on rhce2 on /mnt/smbshare1. Mount /smb2 on hv3 on /mnt/smbshare2. The user mary should not have write access to /mnt/smbshare2. Make sure the mounts survive system reboots.

Task 18: Create a MariaDB database called studentdb on rhce1 and add ten records each containing "student first name" (Allen, David, Mary, Dennis, Joseph, Dennis, Ritchie, Robert, David, and Mary), "student last name" (Brown, Brown, Green, Green, Black, Black, Salt, Salt, Suzuki, and Chen), program enrolled in (3 x mechanical, 3 x electrical, and 4 x computer science), expected graduation year (2 x 2017, 3 x 2018, 5 x 2020), and a student number (110-001 to 110-010).

Task 19: Query the studentdb database to find all students with their last names Green and graduating in 2017. Store the result in a file. Run another query to find all students with matching lastnames.

Task 20: Create a CGI script on rhce2 that displays the system hostname when accessed as www.rhce2.example.com.

Task 21: Create a directory called /both on rhce2 and share it with both Samba and NFS in read/write mode to users in the example.com domain. Access and mount the share on rhce1 using CIFS and NFS persistently on /mnt/bothshare.

Task 22: Set up a simple virtual host called vrhce2.example.com on rhce2 with index.html placed in DocumentRoot /var/vrhce2. Update the hosts table for name resolution. This virtual host should be accessible from everywhere.

Task 23: Create four virtual interfaces on the hypervisor and assign two to rhce1 and the other two to rhce2. Configure teaming with IP assignments of your choice on both virtual machines. Run ping tests to verify the connection. Disable one of the interfaces while ping running. You should not notice an issue. The team interfaces should be active after system reboots. The team setup should work and co-exist with IPv6 and bonding configurations in place.

Task 24: Configure NTP server on rhce2 and client on rhce1.

Reboot the system and validate the configuration.

Appendix D: Sample RHCE Exam 2

Time Duration: 4 hours
Passing Score: 70% (210 out of 300)
Instructions: The RHCE exam, EX300, is offered electronically on a desktop system running RHEL7. The exam presents a list of tasks that are to be completed within the stipulated time. Firewall and SELinux are active and running, and they need to be taken into account. All settings performed on the systems must survive system reboots or you will not be given credits. Access to the Internet, printed material, and electronic devices is prohibited during the exam.

Setup for the Sample Exam:
Install RHEL7 (or its clone) on a physical system called hv4 with hypervisor and desktop/X Window support. Install two virtual machines (rhce3 and rhce4) and load minimal RHEL7 without GUI support. The virtual machines should have their primary interfaces configured with appropriate IP addresses on the same network. You may want to build virtual machines for this sample exam on an existing hypervisor.

Instructions for this Sample Exam:
Instruction 01: Tasks furnished here are in addition to the exercises and labs presented in the RHCSA section of this book. No solutions are provided.

Instruction 02: Do not consult the material in this book or browse the Internet while taking this sample exam. However, you can refer to the online help and the documentation located in the /usr/share/doc directory.

Instruction 03: This exam should be done in a text console using commands or text tools.

Instruction 04: You can reboot the system after completing each task or a few tasks, or wait until all tasks have been finished. Do not forget to retest the configuration after the reboot.

Instruction 05: Create user accounts harry, barry, and mary on both virtual machines and the hypervisor server, and set a password for them.

Instruction 06: Use your own judgement for making decisions where necessary.

Tasks:
Task 01: Allow telnet access from host 192.168.2.20 and network 192.168.3 on both virtual machines.

Task 02: Configure IP forwarding on rhce4.

Task 03: Write a shell script on rhce3 to create three user accounts called user555, user666, and user777 with no login shell and passwords matching their usernames. Usernames should be listed in a file and the script should be able to get that information from that file.

Task 04: Share */shared* directory on rhce3 with Samba accessible to user larry and mary on the local network with write and browse capabilities. Access the share on rhce4 and set it for persistent mount on /mnt/cifsshare. Create a file in the mount point with some text identifying it, and verify the file creation on rhce3.

Task 05: Share */shared* directory on rhce3 in read/write mode with NFS to users on the local network. Mount it on rhce4 on /mnt/nfsshare. Create a file in the mount point with some text identifying it, and verify the file creation on rhce3.

Task 06: Configure Apache with "This is my web server" in index.html on rhce3. This web server should be accessible from rhce3, rhce4, and hv4 by typing webserver.rhce3.example.com.

Task 07: Configure a virtual host called vhostlab1.example.com on port 8000 on rhce3. Create an index.html file with some unique text in it for identification. Update DNS or the hosts table for resolution.

Task 08: Create a simple CGI script on rhce1 that displays the output of the lsblk command when accessed as www.rhce3.example.com.

Task 09: Configure user harry on rhce3 so that he is prompted for passphrase instead of a password from rhce4.

Task 10: Set up Postfix on rhce3 for the local network and have the mail for user mary forwarded to user larry, example.com to user barry, and any mail for group admins forwarded to user gary.

Task 11: Configure NTP server on hv4, peer on rhce3, and client on rhce4.

Task 12: Create four virtual interfaces on the hypervisor and assign two to rhce3 and the other two to rhce4. Configure teaming with IP assignments of your choice on both virtual machines. Run ping tests to verify the connection. Disable one of the interfaces while ping running. You should not notice a change. The team interfaces should be active after system reboots.

Task 13: Create a MariaDB database called rhcedb and add ten records containing firstname, lastname, city, country, and random social security/insurance numbers. The records should have some duplicate fields.

Task 14: Query the rhcedb database to find all people in a city with a specific social security/insurance number, and store the result in a file. Run another query to find all people with matching lastnames in a country.

Task 15: Create a backup of the rhcedb database and store it as a rhcedb.dump. Remove the rhcedb database, and restore it from the dump. Verify the records.

Task 16: Create two directories /nfs1 and /nfs2 on rhce3 and export them with NFS to rhce4 and example.com domain, respectively. Export /nfs1 in read/write mode and /nfs2 in read-only mode. Mount /nfs1 on rhce4 on /mnt/nfsshare1. Mount /nfs2 on hv4 on /mnt/nfsshare2. Touch a file in the mount points with some text for identification, and verify the file creation on rhce3. Make sure the mounts survive system reboots.

Task 17: Add port 9999 to SELinux and forward it to port 80 persistently.

Task 18: Create a 500MB disk on hv4 and assign it to rhce3. Configure iSCSI target on rhce3 using the disk and present it as a block disk to rhce4.

Task 19: Configure iSCSI initiator on rhce4 using the block device presented from rhce3. Create a standard partition and construct ext3 file system structures. Mount the file system on /mnt/iscsipar on rhce4 persistently using a label.

Task 20: Configure Apache on rhce4 with DocumentRoot /var/rhce4 and password-protected access to dba group members (create the group with two members).

Task 21: Configure rhce4 as a relayhost to forward mail from the localhost to rhce3. Send a test mail as the root user. The mail should appear to have originated from example.com domain. Log on to rhce3 as root and verify the receipt.

Task 22: Configure caching DNS service on rhce4 and test it.

Task 23: Configure a web server called srhce4.example.com on rhce4 that provides access to a private directory called /var/private to user barry.

Task 24: Create four virtual interfaces on the hypervisor and assign two to rhce3 and the other two to rhce4. Configure bonding with IP assignments of your choice on both virtual machines. Run ping tests to verify the connection. Disable one of the interfaces while ping running. You should not notice an issue. The bonding interfaces should be active after system reboots. The bond should work and co-exist with IPv6 and teaming setups.

Reboot the system and validate the configuration.

Bibliography

The following websites, forums, and guides were referenced in writing this book:

1. www.apache.org
2. www.centos.org
3. docs.redhat.com/docs/en-US
4. www.gnome.org
5. www.hp.com
6. www.ibm.com
7. www.ietf.org
8. www.isc.org
9. www.linux.org
10. www.linuxhq.com
11. www.netfilter.org
12. www.nsa.gov/research/selinux
13. www.ntp.org
14. www.opensource.org
15. www.openssh.org
16. www.oracle.com
17. www.pathname.com/fhs
18. www.postfix.org
19. www.redhat.com
20. www.samba.org
21. www.scientificlinux.org
22. www.sendmail.org
23. www.unix.org
24. www.wikipedia.org
25. RedHat installation guide for RHEL 7
26. RedHat deployment guide for RHEL 7
27. RedHat release notes for RHEL 7
28. RedHat security guide for RHEL 7
29. RedHat Security Enhanced Linux guide for RHEL 7
30. RedHat storage administration guide for RHEL 7
31. RedHat virtualization administration guide for RHEL 7
32. RedHat virtualization getting started guide for RHEL 7
33. RedHat virtualization host configuration and guest installation guide for RHEL 7
34. RedHat logical volume manager administration guide for RHEL 7
35. Red Hat Certified System Administrator & Engineer for RHEL 6 book by Asghar Ghori
36. HP-UX 11i v3 book by Asghar Ghori

Glossary

. (single dot)	Represents current directory.
.. (double dots)	Represents parent directory of the current directory.
Absolute mode	A method of giving permissions to a file or directory.
Absolute path	A pathname that begins with a /.
Access Control List	A method of allocating file permissions to a specific user or group.
Access mode	See File permissions.
Access rights	See File permissions.
ACL	See Access Control List.
Address Resolution Protocol	A protocol used to determine a system's Ethernet address when its IP address is known.
Address space	Memory location that a process can refer.
Anaconda	RHEL's installation program.
Apache	A famous HTTP web server software.
Archive	A file that contains one or more files.
Argument	A value passed to a command or program.
ARP	See Address Resolution Protocol.
ASCII	An acronym for American Standard Code for Information Interchange.
Auditing	System and user activity record and analysis.
Authentication	The process of identifying a user to a system.
AutoFS	The NFS client-side service that automatically mounts and unmounts an NFS share on an as-needed basis.
Automounter	See AutoFS.
Background process	A process that runs in the background.
Backup	Process of saving data on an alternative media such as a tape or another disk.
Bash shell	A feature-rich default shell available in Red Hat Enterprise Linux.
Berkeley Internet Name Domain	A UC Berkeley implementation of DNS for UNIX and UNIX-like platforms. See also DNS.
BIND	See Berkeley Internet Name Domain.
BIOS	Basic I/O System. Software code that sits in the computer's non-volatile memory and is executed when the system is booted.
Block	A collection of bytes of data transmitted as a single unit.
Block device file	A file associated with devices that transfer data randomly in blocks. Common examples are disk, CD, and DVD.
Bonding	A method of link aggregation.
Boolean	The on/off switch to permit or deny a particular SELinux rule for a service.
Boot	The process of starting up a system.
Bootloader	A program that loads the operating system.
Broadcast client	An NTP client that listens to time broadcasts over the network.
Broadcast server	An NTP server that broadcasts time over the network.

Bus	Data communication path among devices in a computer system.
Cache	A temporary storage area on the system where frequently accessed information is duplicated for quick future access.
Caching DNS	A system that obtains zone information from a primary or secondary DNS server and caches in its memory to respond quickly to client queries.
CentOS	A 100% unsponsored rebuild of Red Hat Enterprise Linux OS available for free.
CGI	See Common Gateway Interface.
Character special file	A file associated with devices that transfer data serially, one character at a time. Common examples are disk, tape, and mouse.
Child directory	A directory one level below the current directory.
Child process	A sub-process started by a process.
CIFS	Common Internet File System. Allows resources to be shared among Linux, UNIX and non-UNIX systems. Also may be referred to as Samba.
Common Gateway Interface	A method for web server software to delegate the generation of web content to executable files.
Command	An instruction given to the system to perform a task.
Command aliasing	Allows creating command shortcuts.
Command history	A feature that maintains a log of all commands executed at the command line.
Command interpreter	See Shell.
Command line editing	Allows editing at the command line.
Command prompt	The OS prompt where you type commands.
Compression	The process of compressing information.
Control group	A process management technique.
Core	A core is a processor that shares the chip with another core. Dual-core and quad-core processor chips are common.
Crash	An abnormal system shutdown caused by electrical outage or kernel malfunction, etc.
Current directory	The present working directory.
Daemon	A server process that runs in the background and responds to client requests.
Database	A collection of data.
Database Management System	A system that allows the storage, management, and manipulation of data in a database.
DBMS	See Database Management System.
De-encapsulation	The reverse of encapsulation. See Encapsulation.
Default	Pre-defined values or settings that are automatically accepted by commands or programs.
Default permissions	Permissions assigned to a file at the time of its creation.
Defunct process	See Zombie process.
Desktop manager	Software such as GNOME that provides graphical environment for users to interact with the system.
Device	A peripheral such as a printer, disk drive, or a CD/DVD device.
Device driver	The software that controls a device.
Device file	See Special file.

Direct Memory Access	Allows hardware devices to access system memory without processor intervention.
Directory structure	Inverted tree-like Linux/UNIX directory structure.
Disk-based file system	A file system created on a non-volatile storage device.
Disk partitioning	Creation of partitions on a given storage device so as to access them as separate logical containers for data storage.
Distinguished name	A fully qualified object path in LDAP DIT.
DIT	Directory Information Tree. An LDAP directory hierarchy.
DMA	See Direct Memory Access.
DNS	Domain Name System. A widely used name resolution method on the Internet.
Domain	A group of computers configured to use a service such as DNS or NIS.
Driver	See Device driver.
Encapsulation	The process of forming a packet through the seven OSI layers.
Encryption	A method of scrambling information for privacy and eavesdropping.
Encryption keys	A private and public key combination that is used to encrypt and decrypt data.
EOF	Marks the End OF File.
EOL	Marks the End Of Line.
Ethernet	A family of networking technologies designed for LANs.
Export	Making a file, directory or a file system available over the network as a share.
Extent	The smallest unit of space allocation in LVM. It is always contiguous. See Logical extent and Physical extent.
Fedora	Red Hat sponsored community project for collaborative enhancement of Red Hat Enterprise Linux OS.
Fibre channel	A family of networking technologies designed for storage networking.
File descriptor	A unique, per-process integer value used to refer to an open file.
File permissions	Read, write, execute or no permission assigned to a file or directory at the user, group or public level.
File system	A grouping of files stored in special data structures.
File Transfer Protocol	A widely used protocol for file exchange.
Filter	A command that performs data transformation on the given input.
Firewall	A software or a dedicated hardware device used for blocking unauthorized access into a computer or network.
Firewalld	A new way of managing iptables rules.
Firewalld zone	A method of segregating incoming network traffic.
FireWire	A bus interface standard designed for very fast communication.
Forwarding DNS	A system that forwards client requests to other DNS servers.
FTP	See File Transfer Protocol.
Full path	See Absolute path.
Gateway	A device that links two networks that run completely different protocols.
GID	See Group ID.
Globbing	See Regular expression.
GNOME	GNU Object Model Environment. An intuitive graphical user environment.
GNU	GNU Not Unix. A project initiated to develop a completely free Unix-like operating system.

GPL	General Public License that allows the use of software developed under GNU project to be available for free to the general public.
GPT	See GUID Partition Table.
Group	A collection of users that requires same permissions on a set of files.
Group collaboration	A collection of users belonging to more than one groups to share files.
Group ID	A numeric identifier assigned to a group.
GRUB	Grand Unified Bootloader is a GNU bootloader program that supports multiboot functionality.
Guest	An operating system instance that runs in a virtual machine.
GUI	Graphical User Interface.
GUID Partition Table	A small disk partition on a UEFI system that stores disk partition information.
Hardware Compatibility List	A list of computer devices that have been tested by Red Hat to support various versions of Red Hat Enterprise Linux.
Home directory	A directory where a user lands when he logs into the system.
Host-based security	Security controls put in place for allowing or disallowing hosts, networks, or domains into the system.
Hostname	A unique name assigned to a node on a network.
HTTP	See Hyper Text Transfer Protocol.
HTTPS	See Hyper Text Transfer Protocol Secure.
Hyper Text Transfer Protocol	Hyper Text Transfer Protocol. Allows access to web pages.
Hyper Text Transfer Protocol Secure	Secure cousin of HTTP. Allows access to secure web pages.
Hypervisor	Software loaded directly on the physical computer to virtualize its hardware.
IMAP	See Internet Message Access Protocol.
Init	An older method of system initialization.
Initial Setup	Program that starts at first system reboot after a system has been installed to customize authentication, firewall, network, timezone and other services.
Initiator	A client that access and mounts a remote storage device over an iSCSI SAN.
Inode	An index node number holds a file's properties including permissions, size and creation/modification time as well as contains a pointer to the data blocks that actually store the file data.
Interface card	A card that allows a system to communicate to external devices.
Internet	A complex network of computers and routers.
Internet Message Access Protocol	A networking protocol that is used to retrieve email messages.
Internet Small Computer System Interface	An IP-based storage networking protocol for sharing block storage.
Interrupt request	A signal sent by a device to the processor to request processing time.
I/O redirection	A shell feature that allows getting input from a non-default location and sending output and error messages to non-default locations.
IP address	A unique 32- or 128-bit software address assigned to a node on a network.
IPTables	A host-based packet-filtering firewall software to control the flow of data packets.
IRQ	See Interrupt request.

iSCSI	See Internet Small Computer System Interface.
Job scheduling	Execution of commands, programs, or scripts in future.
Journal	A new way of capturing, viewing, and managing log files in RHEL7.
KDC	See Key Distribution Centre.
Kerberos	A networking protocol used for user authentication over unsecure networks.
Kernel	Software piece that controls an entire system including all hardware and software.
Kernel-based Virtual Machine	Hypervisor software that supports virtualization of a physical computer.
Key Distribution Centre	A Kerberos server that provides tickets to clients, and stores and maintains the KDC database.
Kickstart	A technique to perform a hands-off, fully-customized, and automated network installation of RHEL.
KVM	See Kernel-based Virtual Machine.
LAN	See Local Area Network.
LDAP	See Lightweight Directory Access Protocol.
LDIF	LDAP Data Interchange Format. A special format used by LDAP for importing and exporting LDAP data among LDAP servers.
Lightweight Directory Access Protocol	A networking protocol that allows information retrieval from a directory server.
Link	An object that associates a file name to any type of file.
Link aggregation	A method of joining two or more network interfaces logically performance and redundancy.
Link count	Number of links that refers to a file.
Linux	An open source version of the UNIX operating system.
Load balancing	A technique whereby more than one servers serve client requests to share the load.
Local Area Network	A campus-wide network of computing devices.
Logical statement	A conditional statement used in shell scripting for logical decisions.
Logical extent	A unit of space allocation for logical volumes in LVM.
Logical volume	A logical container that holds a file system or swap.
Logging	A process of capturing desired alerts and forwarding them to preconfigured locations.
Logical Volume Manager	A common disk partitioning solution.
Login	A process that begins when a user enters a username and password at the login prompt.
Login directory	See Home directory.
Looping statement	A conditional statement used in shell scripting for repetitive execution.
LVM	See Logical Volume Manager.
MAC address	A unique 48-bit hardware address of a network interface. Also called physical address, Ethernet address and hardware address.
Machine	A computer, system, RHEL workstation, RHEL desktop or a RHEL server.
Mail Delivery Agent	A program that delivers email to recipient inboxes.
Mail Submission Agent	A program that submits email messages to a mail transfer agent.

Mail Transfer Agent	A program that transfers email messages from one system to another.
Mail User Agent	A mail client application that a user interacts with.
Major number	A number that points to a device driver.
MariaDB	A relational DBMS, which forked from MySQL.
Masquerading	A variant of NAT.
Master Boot Record	A small region on the disk that stores disk partition information.
MBR	See Master Boot Record.
MDA	See Mail Delivery Agent.
Metacharacters	Characters that have special meaning to the shell.
Minor number	A unique number that points to an individual device controlled by a specific device driver.
Module	Device drivers used to control hardware devices and software components.
Mounting	Attaching a device (a file system, a CD/DVD) to the directory structure.
MTA	See Mail Transfer Agent.
MUA	See Mail User Agent.
Name resolution	A technique to determine IP address by providing hostname.
Name space	A hierarchical organization of DNS domains on the Internet.
NAT	See Network Address Translation.
Netfilter	A framework that provides a set of hooks within the kernel to enable it to intercept and manipulate data packets.
Netmask	See Subnet mask.
Network	Two or more computers joined together to share resources.
Network Address Translation	Allows systems on an internal network to access external networks using a single IP address.
Network Time Protocol	A networking protocol used to synchronize system clocks.
NFS	Network File System. Allows Linux and UNIX systems to share files, directories and file systems.
NFS client	A system that mounts an exported Linux or UNIX resource.
NFS server	A system that exports a resource for mounting by an NFS client.
Niceness	It determines the priority of a process.
Node	A device connected directly to a network port and has a hostname and an IP address associated with it. A node could be a computer, an X terminal, a printer, a router, a hub, a switch, and so on.
Node name	A unique name assigned to a node.
NTP	See Network Time Protocol.
Octal mode	A method for setting permissions on a file or directory using octal numbering system.
Octal numbering system	A 3 digit numbering system that represents values from 0 to 7.
OpenLDAP	A free implementation of LDAP.
Open source	Any software whose source code is published and is accessible at no cost to the public under GNU GPL for copy, modification and redistribution.
OpenSSH	A free implementation of secure shell services and utilities.
Open Systems Interconnection	A layered networking model that provides guidelines to networking equipment manufacturers to develop their products for multi-vendor interoperability.
Orphan process	An alive child process of a terminated parent process.

OSI	See Open Systems Interconnection.
Owner	A user who creates a file or starts a process.
Package	A set of necessary files and metadata information that make up a software application.
Package database	A directory location that stores metadata for installed packages.
Package dependency	Additional required packages for a successful installation or functioning of another package.
Package group	A group of similar applications that can be managed as a single entity.
PackageKit	A group of graphical package management tools.
Paging	The process of transferring data between memory and swap space.
PAM	See Pluggable Authentication Module.
Parent directory	A directory one level above the current directory.
Parent process ID	The ID of a process that starts a child process.
Password aging	A mechanism that provides enhanced control on user passwords.
Pattern matching	See Regular expression.
Performance monitoring	The process of acquiring data from system components for analysis and decision-making purposes.
Permission	Right to read, write or execute.
Physical extent	A unit of space allocation on physical volumes in LVM.
Physical volume	A hard drive or a partition logically brought under LVM control.
PID	See Process ID.
Pipe	Sends output from one command as input to the second command.
Plug and play	Ability of the operating system to add a removable device to the system without user intervention.
Pluggable Authentication Module	A set of library routines that allows using any authentication service available on a system for user authentication, password modification and user account validation purposes.
POP	See Post Office Protocol.
Port	A number appended to an IP address. This number could be associated with a well-known service or is randomly generated.
Port forwarding	A method of directing incoming network traffic to an alternative network port.
POST	Power On Self Test runs at system boot to test hardware.
Post Office Protocol	A networking protocol that is used to retrieve email messages.
Postfix	A mail transfer agent used for sending and receiving mail.
PPID	See Parent process ID.
Primary DNS	A system that acts as the primary provider of DNS zones.
Primary prompt	The symbol where commands and programs are typed for execution.
Process	Any command, program, or daemon that runs on a system.
Process ID	A numeric identifier assigned by kernel to each process spawned.
Process state	One of multiple states in which a process is held during its lifecycle.
Processor	A CPU. It may contain more than one cores.
Prompt	See Primary prompt and Secondary prompt.
Protocol	A common language that communicating nodes understand.
Proxy	A system that acts on behalf of other systems to access network services.
Quoting	Treats the specified special character as a regular character.

RAID	Redundant Array of Independent Disks. A disk arrangement technique that allows for enhanced performance and fault tolerance.
RAID array	A disk storage subsystem that uses hardware RAID.
Realm	A term commonly used to identify a domain in LDAP.
Recovery	A function that recovers a crashed system to its previous normal state. It may require restoring lost data files.
Red Hat Subscription Management	A comprehensive management service provided by Red Hat to its clients.
Redirection	Getting input from and sending output to non-default destinations.
Referral	An entity defined on an LDAP server to forward a client request to some other LDAP server that contains the client requested information.
Regular expression	A string of characters commonly used for pattern matching and globbing.
Relational database	A type of database whose organization is based on the relational model of data.
Relative path	A path to a file relative to the current user location in the file system hierarchy.
Relay	A mail server configured to forward incoming mail to another mail server.
Remote logging	A configuration that allows one or several servers to send their alerts to a centralized remote loghost.
Replica	A secondary LDAP server that shares master LDAP server's load and provides high availability.
Repository	A directory location to store software packages for downloading and installing.
Rescue mode	A special boot mode for fixing and recovering an unbootable system.
Resolver	The client-side of DNS.
Rich language	The ability to pass firewall rules to iptables persistently.
RHEL	Red Hat Enterprise Linux.
RHSM	See Red Hat Management Subscription.
Root	See Superuser.
Router	A device that routes data packets from one network to another.
Routing	The process of choosing a path over which to send a data packet.
Root servers	The thirteen most accurate root DNS servers.
RPM	Red Hat Package Manager. A file format used for software packaging.
Run control levels	Different levels of RHEL operation.
Samba	A networking protocol for sharing file and print resources.
Samba client	A system that accesses a Samba share.
Samba server	A system that provides Samba shares.
SATA	Serial Advanced Technology Attachment. This disk technology is a successor to the PATA drives.
Schema	A set of attributes and object classes.
Scientific Linux	A 100% unsponsored rebuild of Red Hat Enterprise Linux OS available for free.
Script	A text program written to perform a series of tasks.
SCSI	Small Computer System Interface. A parallel interface used to connect peripheral devices to the system.
Search path	A list of directories where the system looks for the specified command.
Secondary DNS	A system that acts as an alternate provider of DNS zones.
Secondary prompt	A prompt indicating that the entered command needs more input.

Secure shell	A set of tools that gives secure access to a system.
Secure Socket Layer	A cryptographic protocol for secure communication.
Security context	SELinux security attributes set on files, processes, users, ports, etc.
Security Enhanced Linux	An implementation of Mandatory Access Control architecture for enhanced and granular control on files, processes, users, ports, etc.
SELinux	See Security Enhanced Linux.
Server (hardware)	Typically a larger and more powerful system that offers services to network users.
Server (software)	A process or daemon that runs on the system to serve client requests.
Set Group ID	Sets effective group ID.
Set User ID	Sets effective user ID.
Setgid	See Set group ID.
Setuid	See Set user ID.
Shadow password	A mechanism to store passwords and password aging data in a secure file.
Shared memory	A portion in physical memory created by a process to share it with other processes that communicate with that process.
Shell	The Linux/UNIX command interpreter that sits between a user and kernel.
Shell program	See Script.
Shell script	See Script.
Shell scripting	Programming in a Linux/UNIX shell to automate a given task.
Signal	A software interrupt sent to a process.
Single user mode	An operating system state in which the system cannot be accessed over the network.
Special characters	See Metacharacters.
Special file	A file that points to a specific device.
SSL	See Secure Socket Layer.
Standard error	A location to forward error messages to.
Standard input	A location to obtain input from.
Standard output	A location to forward output to.
Stderr	See Standard error.
Stdin	See Standard input.
Stdout	See Standard output.
Sticky bit	Disallows non-owners to delete files located in a directory.
Storage Area Network	A network of block storage.
Stratum level	The categorization of NTP time sources based on reliability and accuracy.
String	A series of characters.
Subnet	One of the smaller networks formed by dividing an IP address.
Subnet mask	Segregates the network bits from the node bits.
Subnetting	The process of dividing an IP address into several smaller subnetworks.
Sudo	A method of delegating a portion of superuser privileges to normal users.
Superblock	A small portion in a file system that holds the file system's critical information.
Superuser	A user with unlimited powers on a RHEL system.
Swap	Alternative disk or file system location for paging.
Switch	A network device that looks at the MAC address and switches the packet to the correct destination port based on the MAC address.

Symbolic link	A shortcut created to point to a file located somewhere in the file system tree.
Symbolic mode	A method of setting permissions on a file using non-decimal values.
Symlink	See Symbolic link.
System	A computer or partition in a computer that runs RHEL.
System Administrator	Person responsible for installing, configuring and managing a RHEL system.
System call	A mechanism that applications use to request service from the kernel.
System console	A display terminal that acts as the system console.
Systemd	A newer method of system initialization. It has replaced both SysVinit and Upstart in RHEL7.
System recovery	The process of recovering an unbootable system.
Tab completion	Allows completing a file or command name by typing a partial name at the command line and then hitting the Tab key twice.
Target	A logical collection of units, and may be viewed as equivalent to sysVinit run levels. All units within a target are treated as a single entity.
Target	A server sharing storage over an iSCSI network.
TCP/IP	Transmission Control Protocol / Internet Protocol. A stacked, standard suite of protocols for computer communication.
TCP Wrappers	A security software for limiting access into a system at user and host levels.
Teaming	A method of link aggregation.
Terminal	A window where commands are executed.
Test conditions	Conditions used in logical and looping constructs for decision-making.
Thin provisioning	An economical technique of storage allocation and utilization.
Thrashing	Excessive amount of paging.
Tilde substitution	Using tilde character as a shortcut to move around in the directory tree.
TLS	See Transport Layer Security.
Transport Layer Security	A protocol that works with SSL (or some other protocol) to add data integrity and privacy.
Tty	Refers to a terminal.
UID	See User ID.
Universally Unique IDentifier	A unique alphanumeric software identifier used to identify an object, such as a disk or disk partition.
Unmounting	Detaching a mounted file system or a CD/DVD from the directory structure.
Upstart	An event-based replacement for the legacy init program.
Unit	A systemd object used to organize service startups, socket creation, etc.
USB	Universal Serial Bus. A bus standard to connect peripheral devices.
User-based security	Security controls put in place for allowing or disallowing users from hosts, networks, or domains into the system.
User ID	A numeric identifier assigned to a user.
User mask	A value used in calculating default access rights on files.
User Private Group	Referred to the GID that matches with the user's UID for safeguarding the user's private data from other users on the system.
UUID	See Universally Unique IDentifier.
Variable	A temporary storage of data in memory.
Virtual console	One of several console screens available for system access.
Virtual file system	A file system that is created in memory at system boot and destroyed when the system is shut down.

Virtual host	An approach to host more than one websites on a single system using unique or shared IP addresses.
Virtualization	A technology that allows a single physical computer to run several independent logical computers (called virtual machines) with complete isolation from one another.
Virtual machine	A logical computer running on a physical computer.
Virtual Network Computing	A platform-independent client/server graphical desktop sharing application.
Volume group	A logical container that holds physical volumes, logical volumes, file systems and swap.
Web	A system of interlinked hypertext documents accessed over a network or the Internet via a web browser.
Web server	A system or service that provides web clients access to website pages.
Wide Area Network	A network with systems located geographically apart.
Wildcard characters	See Metacharacters.
X Window System	A protocol that provides users with a graphical interface for system interaction.
Zombie process	A child process that terminated abnormally and whose parent process still waits for it.
Zone	A delegated portion of a DNS name space.

Index

O

P

Q

R

CPSIA information can be obtained at www.ICGtesting.com
Printed in the USA
LVOW03s2003011015

456535LV00017B/608/P